For Reference

Not to be taken from this room

Salem
7 1,2
$150

MAGILL'S
LITERARY ANNUAL
2012

*Essay-Reviews of 200 Outstanding Books
Published in the United States During 2011*

With an Annotated List of Titles

Volume One
A-J

Edited by
JOHN D. WILSON
STEVEN G. KELLMAN

SALEM PRESS
A Division of EBSCO Publishing
Ipswich, Massachusetts   Hackensack, New Jersey

LIBRARY OF CONGRESS CATALOG CARD NO
ISBN (set): 978-1-58765-964-5
ISBN (vol. 1): 978-1-58765-965-2
ISBN (vol. 2): 978-1-58765-966-9

FIRST PRINTING

PRINTED IN THE UNITED STATES OF AMERICA

CONTENTS

CONTENTS

PUBLISHER'S NOTE

Magill's Literary Annual, 2012 follows a long tradition, beginning in 1954, of offering readers incisive reviews of the major literature published during the previous calendar year. The *Magill's Literary Annual* series seeks to evaluate critically 200 major examples of serious literature, both fiction and nonfiction, published in English, from writers in the United States and around the world. The philosophy behind our selection process is to cover works that are likely to be of interest to general readers that reflect publishing trends, that add to the careers of authors being taught and researched in literature programs, and that will stand the test of time. By filtering the thousands of books published every year down to 200 notable titles, the editors have provided librarians with an excellent reader's advisory tool and patrons with fodder for book discussion groups and a guide for choosing worthwhile reading material. The essay-reviews in the *Annual* provide a more academic "reference" review of a work than is typically found in newspapers and other periodical sources.

The reviews in the two-volume *Magill's Literary Annual, 2012* are arranged alphabetically by title. At the beginning of each volume is a complete alphabetical list of all covered books that provides readers with the title and author. In addition, readers will benefit from a brief description of each work in the volume. Every essay is approximately four pages in length. Each one begins with a block of reference information in a standard order:

- Full book title, including any subtitle
- *Author:* Name, with birth and death years when available
- *First published:* Original foreign-language title, with year and country, when pertinent
- Original language and translator name, when pertinent
- Introduction, Foreword, etc., with writer's name, when pertinent
- *Publisher:* Company name and city, number of pages, retail price
- *Type of work:* (chosen from standard categories)

Anthropology	Film
Archaeology	Fine arts
Autobiography	History
Biography	History of science
Current affairs	Language
Diary	Law
Drama	Letters
Economics	Literary biography
Education	Literary criticism
Environment	Literary history
Essays	Literary theory
Ethics	Media

Medicine	Poetry
Memoir	Psychology
Miscellaneous	Religion
Music	Science
Natural history	Short fiction
Nature	Sociology
Novel	Technology
Novella	Travel
Philosophy	Women's issues

- *Time*: Period represented, when pertinent
- *Locale*: Location represented, when pertinent
- Capsule description of the work
- *Principal characters* [for novels, short fiction] or *Principal personages* [for biographies, history]: List of people, with brief descriptions

The text of each essay-review analyzes and presents the focus, intent, and relative success of the author, as well as the makeup and point of view of the work under discussion. To assist readers further, essays are supplemented by a list of additional "Review Sources" for further study in a bibliographic format. Every essay includes a sidebar offering a brief biography of the author or authors. Thumbnail photographs of book covers and authors are included as available.

Three indexes can be found at the end of volume 2:

- Category Index: Groups all titles into subject areas such as current affairs and social issues, ethics and law, history, literary biography, philosophy and religion, psychology, and women's issues.
- Title Index: Lists all works reviewed in alphabetical order, with any relevant cross references.
- Author Index: Lists books covered in the annual by each author's name.

A searchable cumulative index, listing all books reviewed in *Magill's Literary Annual* between 1977 and 2012, as well as in *Magill's History Annual* (1983) and *Magill's Literary Annual, History and Biography* (1984 and 1985), can be found at our Web site, **www.salempress.com**, on the page for *Magill's Literary Annual, 2012*.

Our special thanks go to the editors for their expert and insightful selections: John D. Wilson is the editor of *Books and Culture* for *Christianity Today*, and Steven G. Kellman is a professor at the University of Texas at San Antonio and a member of the National Book Critics Circle. We also owe our gratitude to the outstanding writers who lend their time and knowledge to this project every year. The names of all contributing reviewers are listed in the front of volume 1, as well as at the end of their individual reviews.

COMPLETE ANNOTATED LIST OF TITLES

VOLUME 1

A satire set in the closing years of the Weimar Republic that exposes the brutalities and intolerance of the rising Nazi Party from the perspective of a teenage girl with little interest in politics.

A thorough examination of the life and career of the man who brought Lead Belly, Muddy Waters, and Woody Guthrie to the world's attention, this biography is at its finest when interweaving musical history with cultural history.

The collected journal entries of esteemed American critic and intellectual Alfred Kazin reveal his preoccupations and personal musings.

Chronicling the lives of four generations of the Hardelot family, this novel portrays bourgeois French society during the first half of the twentieth century and the struggle for individual happiness within this highly regulated social milieu.

John Darnton presents a compelling memoir about growing up in the shadow of a father killed in World War II. He reflects on his father's mythic presence in his life as he searches for the truth about his parents' marriage and his father's death.

Alone Together *presents a cautionary tale of how technology is changing human society by reducing the instances in which individuals interact with one another in person and with their full attention. Turkle proposes a need to scale back reliance on technology in order to prevent a crisis in human society.*

A history of American landscape design from the colonial era to the early twenty-first century, this book introduces key themes, personages, and problems in landscape design and demonstrates the consistent presence of gardening throughout the history and culture of the United States.

VOLUME 2

COMPLETE ANNOTATED LIST OF TITLES

A highly experimental, elaborate rendering of the dynamics of the imagination and the process of literary creation, The Seamstress and the Wind *presents a dream tale of a distraught mother, tracking down her missing child in the forbidding wastes of Argentina's Patagonia region.*

Representing over two decades of work by one of the most important Catalan authors, the stories in this collection focus on themes of obsessive love, personal loss, violence, and warfare.

Set in Germany during reunification, this novel breathes new life into the cliché of the seven-year itch.

A rainy day in Santiago, Chile, is the backdrop for the reunion of three aging leftists who survived the violent and oppressive Pinochet regime.

Castor examines how perceptions of gender affected the inheritance of royal titles and access to power by medieval women who were descended from kings or related to monarchs through marriage or motherhood, analyzing how their experiences influenced the acceptance of queens in later centuries.

The eventual meeting of two half sisters, daughters of a bigamist father, shapes their personal identities and feelings of self-worth.

Scott presents a meticulously researched account of the life of cultural anthropologist Ann Dunham, whose groundbreaking contributions had a profound impact on the lives of the poor in Indonesia and whose values shaped the life of her son, US president Barack Obama.

Bhattacharya's engaging debut novel chronicles the impressions, adventures, and realizations of a young man from India who spends a year in Guyana.

COMPLETE ANNOTATED LIST OF TITLES

Hollinghurst's fifth novel, The Stranger's Child, *is a complex study of English society, sexual mores, literary creation, and the reliability of memory and biography told through the history of the Valance and Sawle families from 1913 to 2008.*

Faced with a midlife crisis and turbulence in her marriage, a poet returns to her hometown and finds strength in forging connections with teenage girls, older women, and a young mother.

After the failure of their family's business, their mother's death, and their father's abandonment, Ava Bigtree and her siblings embark on very different journeys in strange and unfamiliar surroundings as they try to cope with their losses.

The author presents a comprehensive overview of the origins, rediscovery, and influence of a famous poem by Lucretius that foreshadowed the rise of modern thinking.

Packer's collection of stories about Northern California bring the reader into the heart of true-to-life experiences in which ordinary suburban characters navigate their way through loss and longing.

Hamill's tale about the end of a tabloid tells the story of how a man who has lived in the tabloid world far too long discovers life outside of his work. Hamill also explores the stories of a cross section of New Yorkers dealing with their own endings.

A thoughtful, mischievous, and masterful collection of poems by one of Australia's most accomplished living poets.

A young doctor's humanitarian mission to the Balkans also sends her on a quest to solve the mystery of her grandfather's death.

Adam Hochschild presents a brilliantly written account of Great Britain in World War I, focusing on individuals who opposed as well as supported the war

COMPLETE ANNOTATED LIST OF TITLES

CONTRIBUTING REVIEWERS

Richard Adler
University of Michigan, Dearborn

Michael Auerbach
Marblehead, Massachusetts

David Barratt
Montreat College

Melissa A. Barton
Westminster, Colorado

Elizabeth Bellucci
Independent Scholar

Margaret Boe Birns
New York University

Pegge Bochynski
Independent Scholar

Matthew J. Bolton
New York, New York

Jennifer L. Campbell
Lycoming College

Henry L. Carrigan Jr.
Northwestern University

C. L. Chua
California State University, Fresno

Joseph Dewey
University of Pittsburgh

Marcia B. Dinneen
Bridgewater State University

Sally S. Driscoll
State College, Pennsylvania

Robert C. Evans
Auburn University at Montgomery

Jack Ewing
Independent Scholar

Keith M. Finley
Southeastern Louisiana University

James Flaherty
Cambridge, Massachusetts

T. Fleischmann
Dowelltown, Tennessee

Amira Hanafi
Cairo, Egypt

Patricia King Hanson
Independent Scholar

Raymond Pierre Hylton
Virginia Union University

Micah L. Issitt
Independent Scholar

Robert Jacobs
Central Washington University

Jeffry Jensen
Glendale Community College

Grant Klarich Johnson
Kenyon College

Myra Junyk
Independent Scholar

Steven G. Kellman
University of Texas, San Antonio

Nicholas A. Kirk
Lincoln University

Kathryn Kulpa
Independent Scholar

Leon Lewis
Appalachian State University

Thomas Tandy Lewis
Appalachian State University

Barbara C. Lightner
Arlington Heights, Illinois

Victor Lindsey
Independent Scholar

R. C. Lutz
CII Group

David W. Madden
California State University, Sacramento

Cheryl Lawton Malone
Newton, Massachusetts

Charles E. May
*California State University,
Long Beach*

Laurence W. Mazzeno
Alvernia University

Daniel P. Murphy
Hanover College

Briana Nadeau
Los Angeles, California

William Nelles
*University of Massachusetts
Dartmouth*

David Peck
Laguna Beach, California

Marjorie Podolsky
*Penn State Erie, the Beh-
rend College*

Elizabeth D. Schafer
Loachapoka, Alabama

Lisa Scoggin
Boston, Massachusetts

Julia A. Sienkewicz
Duquesne University

Amy Sisson
*Houston Community
College*

Shawncey J. Webb
Taylor University

Batya Weinbaum
Empire State College

John Wilson
Editor, Christianity Today

After Midnight

Author: Irmgard Keun (1905–1982)
First published: *Nach Mitternacht*, 1937, in Germany
Translated from the German by Anthea Bell
Afterword by Geoff Wilkes
Publisher: Melville House (Brooklyn). 176 pp. $10.20
Type of work: Novel
Time: Late 1930s
Locale: Frankfurt, Germany

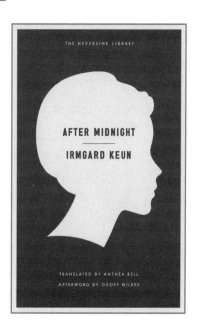

A satire set in the closing years of the Weimar Republic that exposes the brutalities and intolerance of the rising Nazi Party from the perspective of a teenage girl with little interest in politics.

Principal characters:

SUSANNE (SANNA) MODER, nineteen, a carefree girl who comes to Frankfurt to find adventure and love

GERTI, Sanna's stunningly attractive friend, in love with a man who is half Jewish

ALGIN MODER, Sanna's half brother, a successful writer whose works have been banned by the government

HEINI, Sanna's friend, a blacklisted journalist convinced that the rise of the Nazis means the end of German freedom and culture

LISKA MODER, Algin's wife, infatuated with Heini

ADELHEID, Sanna's aunt, a shopkeeper in Cologne, politically active and an enthusiastic advocate of the Nazis

FRANZ, Adelheid's troubled son, with whom Sanna falls in love

It is not difficult to see how readers coming to terms with the Jewish Holocaust via shelves of towering, often intimidating, works, both fiction and nonfiction, might have overlooked Irmgard Keun's *After Midnight*, a quirky romance set in Frankfurt during the insidious rise of Nazi Party leader Adolf Hitler. This satirical comedy of manners is a tale of mismatched lovers—one a pleasantly addled woman-child obsessed with parties and dresses, the other an introspective isolate who struggles with a dark past—finding their way to each other in a tumultuous world. But Keun is no fluffy romance writer, and *After Midnight* is no Weimar-era *Gone with the Wind*. Now, as part of the rediscovery of Keun by scholars of Nazi-era literature, Melville House has reissued *After Midnight*, first published in this translation in 1985; this is the first project in its ambitious Neversink Library series, dedicated to republishing landmark twentieth-century works that have gone unnoticed or been underappreciated.

As Hitler was emerging as a formidable political force in her native Germany, Keun challenged the Nazi policies of censorship and bigotry. When her first two novels, both popular and provocative feminist narratives, were banned in 1933, Keun audaciously sued the Third Reich for lost royalties. When the government then issued a warrant for her death, she went into exile. Writing *After Midnight* in the Netherlands, Keun utilized the breezy dynamics of a parlor comedy and that familiar narrative device of the modernist era, the unreliable narrator, to indict within her prose the National Socialist programs of institutionalized hatred, enforced conformity, and entrenched paranoia. She deftly satirizes her self-involved, vacuous narrator, who resolutely focuses on the superficial aspects of life in the city, including the etiquette of dating and flirting and questions of makeup, dress, and hairstyle. Keun juxtaposes this shallow sensibility with the darkening evidence of the political, social, and military changes redefining Germany, as well as the complicated (and desperate) strategies of adjustment being made by everyday Germans witnessing their nation's devolution into a nightmare police state.

With the deft strokes of portraiture, Keun creates vivid secondary characters whom the narrator observes without pondering the implications of their circumstances. For example, there is Berta, the precocious girl who is selected to present the visiting Führer with a bouquet and recite a poem in his honor. When Hitler's cavalcade does not have time to stop, the child is crestfallen. That evening, at her mother's prodding, Berta gets up on a table in a local café and dramatically performs the poem, whipping herself into such a frenzy that she collapses and dies. In another example, a nameless old man on a bicycle complains loudly about the street blockades set up in anticipation of the Führer's entourage; when the police haul him away, the crowd, incensed at the old man's disloyalty, actually attacks his bicycle. Keun's narrative strategy is a risky one, but the use of a character determined to remain unaware succeeds as a device for raising awareness in the reader.

The events of *After Midnight* take place during a single harrowing day and are told in the unsettling immediacy of present tense, supplemented by layers of backstory told through flashbacks. The narrative begins as Sanna Moder unexpectedly receives a letter from her cousin Franz, whom she has not seen since she moved from Cologne to Frankfurt a year earlier. Although they have been apart, Sanna has never forgotten her cousin, a pale, serious-minded young man with few friends.

Franz has struggled with the guilt of having deliberately set a fire years earlier when he was left alone with his newborn brother. The fire got out of hand and killed the baby. His inconsolable mother, Sanna's aunt Adelheid, never let Franz forget his carelessness, idolizing the dead child and tormenting Franz with recriminations. Sanna sympathized with Franz and found in him a soul mate, much to the chagrin of Adelheid, who perceived any relationship between the cousins as a potential threat to her financial security. When Sanna and Franz made plans to marry, Adelheid, who had enthusiastically embraced the new Nazi government, turned Sanna in to the local Gestapo, citing two harmless comments Sanna had made—that Hitler sweated when he spoke in public and that she would rather not listen to Hermann Göring's ranting radio addresses. Sanna was subsequently interrogated for three days, during which time she overheard the tormented cries of those being tortured by the Gestapo. She was released only after signing a confession admitting her subversive statements. Determined to distance herself from such terrifying realities, Sanna left the crestfallen Franz and headed for what she assumed would be the safer environs of a more cosmopolitan city to live with her older half brother, Algin, and his wife of four months, Liska.

In her twenties and already a writer of provocative novels about young women, Irmgard Keun consistently challenged the Nazi dictatorship, ultimately faking her own suicide in order to sneak back into Germany from exile. Keun fell into obscurity after the war, living in poverty in Berlin. A resurgence of interest shortly before her death established her as one the most important novelists of the Weimar Republic.

Keun makes the point that escape is, in the end, impossible, and flight from these problems is pointless. Once in Frankfurt, Sanna befriends Gerti, a strikingly beautiful girl in love with a man who is half Jewish. Even as the sassy and free-spirited Gerti makes uncomfortably critical remarks about the Nazis in café conversations, Sanna, while discomfited by her friend's boldness, will still not acknowledge the implications of Nazi bigotry. To Sanna, Hitler is still little more than an inconvenience, and she cannot see him as an encroaching threat.

Sanna has also learned that her half brother, a gifted and acclaimed writer, has fallen out of favor with the Nazi regime, which found his dense psychological novels depressing and un-German. Algin's income has dropped precipitously, and he ekes out a living as a journalist. Miserable, he ponders doing what the Nazi Party expects and penning an epic poem lionizing Hitler or celebrating the idealized Nature that figures so prominently in Nazi cultural propaganda. With characteristic insouciance, however, Sanna records her half brother's despair without outrage or concern. She is far too concerned with that evening's party being thrown by Algin's young wife.

That night, Sanna slowly leaves her state of obliviousness and begins to see the harsh reality of her surroundings. As Liska's party begins, Sanna is panicked when she cannot find Algin and is forced to consider the difficult possibility that he may have committed suicide. When she eventually finds him drunk in a nearby wine shop, he is making extravagant plans to run away after midnight and find refuge in the countryside; there, he believes, he can become the poet he once dreamed of being. It is a futile hope, as the spreading evil of the Nazis will reach the entire nation. Nazi Germany, as Keun cautions and Sanna begins to perceive, is not the place for happy endings.

After the party, Franz reappears in Sanna's life and the lovers reunite. Franz has fled Cologne after murdering a rival shopkeeper who caused Franz's business partner, Paul, to be imprisoned as a subversive. Now a fugitive, Franz is certain that an arrest will mean his execution. As Sanna struggles to comprehend her lover's actions, she encounters Gerti, who is now in tearful despair and fearful that her half-Jewish lover has been shipped to a Nazi labor camp.

But it is the grim death of Heini, a blacklisted journalist, that finally redeems Sanna. Heini emerges in the second half of the novel as Keun's political mouthpiece.

His gallows humor and witty repartee cannot disguise his deepening anxieties over the new face of Germany. For Keun, Heini embodies the despair of citizens whose love of country cannot brook the moral bankruptcy of the emerging government. Indeed, it is that charismatic despair, at once articulate and ironic, that compelled Algin's wife, Liska, to fantasize about having an affair with Heini. The evening's party was conceived as an elaborate strategy to attract Heini's attention; Liska is certain that if he can just see her in evening finery, he will be enchanted. It is, of course, a silly plot, typical of parlor comedies. Keun adroitly plays against those expectations and the too-clever plan turns frighteningly tragic. Far from being seduced, Heini, after declaiming to a scattering of bored guests about the dangers of the rising Nazi Party and the beginnings of Hitler's concentration camps, pulls out a small pistol and shoots himself in the temple.

Heini's death finally awakens Sanna to the threats surrounding her. She professes her love for the terrified Franz and they make plans to flee to the safe haven of Rotterdam, in the Netherlands. On the train, Sanna at last feels fear. She recalls her prior ignorance and tries to lapse once more into that state of unawareness but is unable to foresee the possibility of a happy ending. As Sanna closes her narrative, she prays to a seemingly inaccessible God for a bit of sunlight the next day. The meagerness of her prayer indicates the depth of her education and that she has now come of age. In the end, Keun offers love as the sole counterweight to a darkening universe surrendering to cataclysmic insanity. Critics have argued that this resolution is contrived and that a happy ending dulls Keun's satiric edge, but happiness is hardly what Keun offers. Sanna has been given the difficult gift of consciousness and only finds small consolation in another lost soul.

Joseph Dewey

Review Sources

Austin Chronicle, June 17, 2011 (Web).
Dialog International, August 8, 2007 (Web).
L Magazine, July 6, 2011 (Web) .
Millions, July 22, 2011 (Web).
NPR, May 31, 2011 (Web).
A Progressive on the Prairie, June 4, 2011 (Web).

Alan Lomax
The Man Who Recorded the World

Author: John Szwed (b. 1936)
Publisher: Viking (New York). 438 pp. $29.95
Type of work: Biography
Time: 1915–2002
Locale: United States

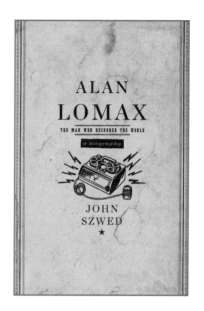

A thorough examination of the life and career of the man who brought Lead Belly, Muddy Waters, and Woody Guthrie to the world's attention, this biography is at its finest when interweaving musical history with cultural history.

Principal personages:
ALAN LOMAX (1915–2002), folklorist, folk song collector, folksinger, writer, filmmaker, and radio personality
JOHN LOMAX (1867–1948), his father, a folk song collector
BESS LOMAX (1921–2009), his sister
ANNA (ANNE) LOMAX WOOD, his daughter
ELIZABETH LYTTLETON HAROLD, his first wife
CARL SANDBURG (1878–1967), poet and folk song collector
HUDDIE LEDBETTER (LEAD BELLY) (1885–1949), blues singer
ZORA NEALE HURSTON (1891–1960), author, folklorist, and cultural anthropologist
WOODY GUTHRIE (1912–1967), folksinger and songwriter
CHARLES SEEGER (1886–1979), musicologist
PETE SEEGER (B. 1919), folksinger and songwriter
JELLY ROLL MORTON (1890–1941), jazz pianist, composer, and arranger
NICHOLAS (NICK) RAY (1911–1979), film director
PETER KENNEDY (1922–2006), folklorist
EWAN MACCOLL (1915–1989), folksinger and songwriter
MARGARET MEAD (1901–1978), anthropologist

Much of twentieth-century music can trace its roots to folk music. Blues singer Huddie "Lead Belly" Ledbetter influenced musicians from the Weavers and Pete Seeger to Lonnie Donegan (who inspired the entire British Invasion), while folksinger Woody Guthrie and his music held sway over Bob Dylan and countless others. It could be argued, though, that without the recordings and promotion of these and other artists by Alan Lomax, modern popular music would probably sound quite different.

Lomax was a man of many talents—a theorist, author, lecturer, promoter, film director, and radio producer, to name a few—but his primary focus was collecting folk music. He started by working with his father, John Lomax, driving around the southeastern United States with an old cylinder recorder in the back of the car and stopping anywhere they thought they could find authentic folk songs, including several prisons. It was at one of these prison stops that they discovered Lead Belly.

After Lead Belly was released from jail, he got a job working for the Lomaxes, who ended up promoting him around the country, especially in New York City. Eventually, many of Lead Belly's songs were covered by later artists, sometimes without proper attribution. His "Good Night Irene" became a number-one hit in 1950 for Pete Seeger's folk group, the Weavers. Elsewhere, in 1955, British skiffle artist Lonnie Donegan's appropriation of Lead Belly's "Rock Island Line" was extremely popular in both Britain and the United States, helping to convince future rock-and-roll stars to learn the guitar.

(WireImage)

Anthropologist and jazz scholar John Szwed has written several books, including Space Is the Place *(1998) and* So What: The Life of Miles Davis *(2002). He won a Grammy for* Doctor Jazz *(2005), a book packaged with* Jelly Roll Morton: The Complete Library of Congress Recordings with Alan Lomax *(2005).*

Alan Lomax left his work with his father for a job at the Library of Congress, where he continued to build up their collection of folk music by requesting recordings from others and collecting more music in the field. While working there, he promoted several important musicians, including Woody Guthrie, who wrote the lyrics to "This Land Is Your Land" and other well-known songs. Lomax continued to advocate for folk music in general, writing multiple books and songbooks as well as appearing in and writing for radio shows of the time. Lomax's collections included not only American music but also songs he had gathered in the field from the Caribbean and Europe. By the time of the Newport Folk Festivals in the mid-1960s, he was thought of as the "grandfather" of folk music. He even attempted to produce what he called "cantometrics," a grand unified theory of folk music that would help classify each folk song into one of several families, thereby connecting groups anthropologically in ways that might otherwise remain hidden. Whether one agreed or disagreed with him, one cannot deny that Lomax had a profound impact on both the music of the twentieth century and the study of it.

Musicologist and anthropologist John Szwed met Alan Lomax in 1961 and worked with him on and off for a number of years. Using this personal and professional knowledge, as well as the huge number of resources available at the Alan Lomax Archive at the Library of Congress, Szwed has created an in-depth look at Lomax's career and what drove him to do what he did. The author describes Lomax's numerous recording tours in great detail, noting the type of equipment he used (and its effect on the recording quality and length of performances), some of the specific recordings made, and his general approach to recording each singer, which the author notes was done with serious consideration for the individual performer in question. Szwed also examines some of the differences between John Lomax's attitudes toward his singer/subjects, which tended to be more objective, and Alan's attitudes, which tended to be more subjective and more typical of a young intellectual in the 1920s and 1930s. These attitudes were in part what continually pushed Alan to collect and promote folk music; he truly thought that folk music could lead to a better understanding of other cultures and a better society overall.

The ties between music, American culture, and the life of Alan Lomax form a substantial part of this book and are among its most interesting sections. In one instance, Szwed touches upon McCarthyism via the investigations by the House Un-American Activities Committee (HUAC) into (unfounded) allegations that Lomax was a Communist. Lomax lived in New York and worked with folklorist and anthropologist Zora Neale Hurston during the Harlem Renaissance, and so through his eyes, the reader gets a sense of that time and place as well. Szwed also uses Lomax's work with the Library of Congress during the Great Depression to discuss the programs of the New Deal, the Tennessee Valley Authority, and the Works Progress Administration, and delves into the concept of prison reform when writing about the prisons that Alan and his father visited during their recording trips. These events and concepts are described in such a way that, for most of the book, the reader sees Lomax in a cultural context. Much as Alan Lomax wanted to make folk music come alive for people rather than persist as an artifact of the past, John Szwed uses American culture to bring life to Lomax's exploits and career, which might otherwise sound somewhat dry and theoretical.

Szwed is perhaps less able to provide this sort of cultural context in his coverage of Lomax's work upon his return to the United States in 1958. After recording folk music in Europe for several years, many of Lomax's ideas were either behind or ahead of their time. Though the reader does get the occasional story about cultural events, such as his reaction when he heard Bob Dylan's amplified folk rock at the Newport Folk Festival in 1965, most of the material at this point covers Lomax's work on cantometrics, which was not mainstream. Although he received many grants for his studies, he was working in a relative vacuum, and so those cultural connections cannot be made as easily.

Szwed takes pains to cover the cultural and career aspects of Alan Lomax's life as comprehensively as can be expected in a book of this nature, though this comes at the expense of details regarding his personal life. While Szwed mentions Lomax's string of romances with various women, his friendships, his relationship with his father, and his personal difficulties, he does not dwell on them for any length of time, but rather focuses on how these relationships affected his work. Several of the letters that Szwed excerpts, for example, comment on Lomax's occasional ambivalence toward his work and his doubts about whether he should continue it. Considering the length of the book, this is perhaps not surprising, but if the reader is searching for an in-depth look at the psychological makeup of Alan Lomax, he or she might be advised to look elsewhere.

Janet Maslin, writing for the *New York Times*, laments that Szwed "stays within Lomax's perspective" and thinks that in so doing, he neglects the opportunity to explore more fully Lomax's sway on some of the numerous musicians who claim him as an influence. She illustrates her point with the example of Bob Dylan's *Chronicles: Volume One*, which includes much more information about Alan Lomax than Szwed includes about Bob Dylan.

The musical aspects of the book are also limited. When Szwed quotes individual songs, he does not include more than a few lines of lyrics. Again, this is to be expected, given that this is a biography meant for a general audience rather than an analytical text designed for the professional musicologist or musician. Still, a bit more coverage of the music itself could have both supported its connection to the cultural aspects of Lomax's work and added a little variety to the book overall, especially in the later chapters. Likewise, a discography of Lomax's published recordings and an annotated bibliography of his writings would be ideal features to include in future editions and could broaden the appeal of the text.

While the tone of Szwed's biography is sympathetic, he does not completely gloss over the negative aspects of his subject's life and personality. Szwed mentions that, especially later in life, many of Lomax's critics thought of him as "The People's Republic of Me," and that his work style could annoy those he worked with. Overall, however, the author paints a picture of a passionate, hardworking man who wanted to change the world by spreading folk music, and Szwed's Lomax is a man to be admired. Still, at least one reviewer wished that Szwed had addressed negative views such as those espoused by author Dave Marsh, who said that it was Lomax's "stupid 'folklorist' purism that ruined the folk music revival," or those expressed in the book *Lost Delta Found* (2005), which presents work by other researchers that Lomax allegedly used without giving proper credit.

Critically, the book has received generally positive reviews. In *JazzTimes*, Matt Lohr says that despite the incredibly active life Lomax led, "Szwed's book manages to cover it all with minimal difficulties," and that the book is "an engaging biography of a man who, as much as any twentieth-century figure, has shaped our contemporary understanding of music." Though most critics would have liked more details regarding Lomax's personal life, and some think that parts of it are a bit dry, they generally agree that the book is an important contribution to the literature.

Lisa Scoggin

Review Sources

Independent, January 7, 2011 (Web).
JazzTimes, March 27, 2011 (Web).
Los Angeles Times, January 16, 2011 (Web).
The New York Times, January 31, 2011, p. C4.
The Observer, April 12, 2011 (Web).
The Wall Street Journal, January 15, 2011 (Web).
The Washington Post, January 28, 2011 (Web).

Alfred Kazin's Journals

Editor: Richard M. Cook (b. 1941)
Publisher: Yale University Press (New Haven, CT). 632 pp. $45.00
Type of work: Diary
Time: Mid- to late-twentieth century
Locale: New York City

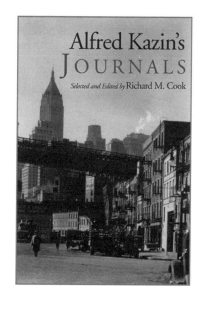

The collected journal entries of esteemed American critic and intellectual Alfred Kazin reveal his preoccupations and personal musings.

Principal personage:
ALFRED KAZIN (1915–1998), an influential post-World War II American literary critic and public intellectual

Born to Jewish immigrant parents in Brooklyn in 1915, Alfred Kazin rose to become one of the most prominent men of letters in American culture. When Kazin died in 1998, various writers recalled him—along with Lionel Trilling, Edmund Wilson, and Jacques Barzun—as one of the most influential public intellectuals of postwar America. Kazin wrote over a thousand reviews and essays, several books of literary criticism and history, and several volumes of autobiography. In the first of what was to become a trilogy of autobiographical volumes, *A Walker in the City* (1951), Kazin returns to his Brooklyn neighborhood of Brownsville, walking the streets and avenues of his childhood. He recalls the sights and sounds of his youth and those memories animate numerous questions regarding his identity, particularly his Jewishness. The loneliness and unhappiness of his youth, as well his struggles to understand the differences between religious Judaism and secular Judaism, stimulate much of Kazin's literary and cultural criticism and certainly loom large in his journals. By the time he was twenty-seven, Kazin had secured his reputation as a prominent literary historian and critic with the publication of the book *On Native Grounds: An Interpretation of Modern Prose Literature* (1942). Kazin spent day after day sitting in the New York Public Library, spinning out a series of evocative portraits of writer after writer, from William Dean Howells to Ernest Hemingway and Richard Wright. Kazin's stimulating prose and lucid insights into the evolution of American literature established him not as an academic critic but a professional man of letters. Kazin continued to probe the deep questions that flowed into the streams of modern American literature right up until his death. In 1997, just a year before he died, Kazin published *God and the American Writer*, in which he explored appreciatively and warmly the religious imagination of a number of American writers, from Herman Melville to William Faulkner. The themes that Kazin explored in his books—loneliness, religion,

Jewish identity, politics—he also explored in his journals. Cook's new edition marks a major literary and cultural event for followers of Kazin's work new and old.

Kazin's biographer, Richard M. Cook, performs a monumental service in selecting and gathering about one-sixth of Kazin's journals that are held in the Berg Collection of the New York Public Library. For over half a century, Kazin jotted his thoughts in a personal journal that is now over 7,000 pages long. He started keeping a journal during his school years as a way of assuaging loneliness and connecting to the world outside of Brownsville. As Cook points out, Kazin often looked back on this youthful practice as a sign of things to come—his lifelong passion for reading and writing and his compulsion to write to himself what he could not easily say to other people. Rather than thinking of his journals as a means of isolating himself from the rest of the world, Kazin viewed his journals as a way of bringing the self back into the world as its natural home. While no journals survive from his high school years, Kazin's first available journal entry dates from his sophomore year at City College in May 1933. Although no entries exist between 1935 and 1938, when he was studying for a master's degree at Columbia University, and only a few when he was writing *On Native Grounds* between 1938 and 1942, Kazin wrote almost obsessively from 1942 until his death in 1998. In fact, even though the last entry is from February 1998, Kazin's widow reports that he was even writing hours before he died. Kazin wrote whenever and wherever he could, on the subway or plane, during all times of day, three or four times a week. His need to record the passage of time from one day to the next provided the rhythm for his life. He thought of this practice as absolutely necessary to his spiritual well-being as well as an aid to his writing.

Because he was so assiduous about writing in his journals, he was able to work out and establish feelings and thoughts on the various topics he would later discuss in published books. Thus, in these selections, the reader will discover Kazin's thoughts on communism, anti-communism, liberalism, existentialism, Israel, modernism, New York City, the Vietnam War, the Kennedy administration, feminism, and neo-conservatism, as well as more personal matters, such as his identity as a writer and a Jew. Additionally, these journals offer Kazin's brutally honest reflections on his relationships with his wives and mistresses, and his musings on both his friends and enemies. In these journals, the reader comes across a fascinating assortment of names and figures, including Arthur Schlesinger Jr., Richard Hofstadter, Saul Bellow, Lionel Trilling, Hannah Arendt, Mary McCarthy, Edmund Wilson, Philip Roth, and Elie Wiesel.

While Kazin explores many topics in his journals, the subject of Jewishness and his own Jewish identity occupies him perhaps more than any other. In an entry dated January 1960, Kazin observes that his autobiography (he often called his journal his true biography) will always be most deeply the autobiography of a Jew. He often reflects on his own rise to power and influence, from his youth as a poor Jew to a respected judge of literature with the publication of *On Native Grounds*. In an entry from July 1963, he points out with some pride and not without a trace of ironic smugness that the beggarly Jewish radicals of the 1930s are now the ruling cultural pundits of American society. Although he felt like an outsider for some time, Kazin brags in this

Richard M. Cook is Chair of the English Department at the University of Missouri, St. Louis. He is the author of Alfred Kazin: A Biography *(2008) and has received fellowships from the John Simon Guggenheim Memorial Foundation and the National Endowment for the Humanities.*

same entry that he is now one of the standard bearers of American literary opinion, a real judge of young men. The deepening interest in the Holocaust in the 1960s strengthens Kazin's emphasis on Jewishness and his fascination with the ambiguities of Jewish history. In 1997, Kazin reflects on the ambiguities of Jewish history, as he observes the many incredible successes in the world of thought in contrast with so much ignominy, persecution, and murder. In the months before his death he would reflect on the Jew as victim and the Jew as conquistador, writing that he wanted to explore these aspects of Jewishness in a book he never wrote, "Jews: The Marriage of Heaven and Hell."

Kazin also used his journals to criticize all aspects of his life, including his writing life. He offers observations on his childhood in Brownsville, his early religious interests, his struggles with an overbearing mother and distant father, his constant bouts of loneliness, his dealings with publishers, and his often uncomfortable relationship with his children. He writes frankly about his sexual life, his affairs, and his tempestuous marital strife. He is astonishingly self-critical, reflecting on his irritable impatience with people, his tremendous need to be loved, and his weakness as a writer darting from one assignment to another, often leaving major projects unfinished. In an entry from September 1966, he proclaimed the deep importance of the journal to his life; Kazin thought of his journals as a private lie detector, his confession, his way of ascertaining authority and recovering it, making himself whole again.

Cook judiciously selects a significant array of entries from Kazin's journal and arranges them chronologically, dividing them helpfully into increments of five to seven years (1951–57, for example) to provide a thorough glimpse of Kazin's evolution as a thinker and writer. Kazin pulls no punches as he discusses his likes and dislikes. Cook provides superb introductions to each section of the journals, brilliantly setting Kazin's entries in their cultural, political, literary, and intellectual context. In addition, he amply annotates the entries, introducing readers to many now-forgotten figures who lived in Kazin's orbit as well as reminding readers of the significance of many other people and places. Cook's edition offers a very fitting companion piece to his previous publication *Alfred Kazin: A Biography* (2008).

Many critics have pointed out that the portrait of Kazin that emerges from these journals is very unflattering. Indeed, the journals reveal the psychological abuse he heaped on his wife, his unsparing condescension toward his enemies, and his sexual aggressiveness. Cook has provided an unflattering picture of a man whose literary criticism provided fresh insights into beloved and widely discussed works. Other critics have pointed out that the journals are mercilessly honest and swing between self-affirmation and self-loathing. To be sure, Kazin's journals reveal a complicated man who was often harsh in his judgments of others, but no less harsh in his judgment of himself.

Kazin hoped to publish an edition of his journals while he was still alive. In 1996, he published *A Lifetime Burning in Every Moment: From the Journals of Alfred Kazin.*

However, as Cook points out, the book contains a number of undated, edited, and re-written journal entries that present retrospective, often altered, reflections on events, people, and places in Kazin's life. Cook's edition of Kazin's journals offers a more complete picture of the life and work of one of America's most significant public intellectuals. While the journals of Kazin's contemporaries have long been available—most notably Edmund Wilson's journals and a selection of Lionel Trilling's journals—Kazin's have never been available until now. Reading these pages will give readers fresh insight into Kazin's books and encourage future generations to re-read his major works alongside the journals.

Henry L. Carrigan Jr.

Review Sources

The American Scholar 80, no. 1 (Winter 2011): 78–87.
Booklist 107, no. 17 (May 1, 2011): 61.
Library Journal 136, no. 11 (June 15, 2011): 90.
New York Review of Books 58, no. 13 (August 18, 2011): 51–53.
The New York Times, May 26, 2011, p. 6.
Publishers Weekly 258, no. 14 (April 4, 2011): 42.

All Our Worldly Goods

Author: Irène Némirovsky (1903–1942)
First Published: *Les Biens de ce monde*, 1947, in France
Translated from the French by Sandra Smith
Publisher: Viking Books (New York). 272 pp. $14.95
Type of work: Novel
Time: 1910–1940
Locale: Saint-Elme, France; Paris, France

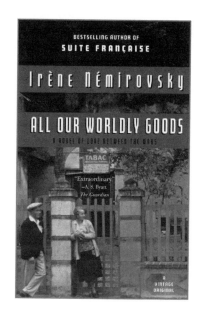

Chronicling the lives of four generations of the Hardelot family, this novel portrays bourgeois French society during the first half of the twentieth century and the struggle for individual happiness within this highly regulated social milieu.

Principal characters:
PIERRE HARDELOT, Charles and Marthe's son and Agnès's husband
AGNÈS (FLORENT) HARDELOT, Pierre's wife and a member of a lower social class
SIMONE (RENAUDIN) BURGÈRES, Pierre's rejected fiancée and the wife of Roland Burgères
GABRIELLE FLORENT, Agnès's widowed mother
MARTHE HARDELOT, Pierre's mother
CHARLES HARDELOT, Pierre's father
JULIEN HARDELOT, Pierre's grandfather and patriarch of the family
ROLAND BURGÈRES, Simone's husband, a shrewd businessman lacking proper bourgeois morality
GUY HARDELOT, Pierre and Agnès's rebellious son and Rose's husband
COLETTE HARDELOT, Pierre and Agnès's daughter
ROSE (BURGÈRES) HARDELOT, Simone and Roland's daughter and Guy's wife
NADINE LAURENT, Guy's mistress

In *All Our Worldly Goods*, Irène Némirovsky skillfully portrays French provincial upper-middle-class society between 1910 and 1940, a turbulent era marked by social change and two devastating world wars. Praised by critics for its realistic depiction of the French bourgeoisie, strong and sensitive exploration of the devastating effects of war, and unsentimental expression of the bonds of love, the novel examines the ways in which social pressures and periods of violence shape the lives of four generations of the Hardelot family.

The family resides in the provincial town of Saint-Elme, where patriarch Julien Hardelot owns a paper factory. In an attempt to bring additional wealth into the

Irène Némirovsky, a Russian Jew who immigrated to France after the Russian Revolution, was the author of numerous highly acclaimed novels and short stories published between the late 1920s and early 1940s. Following her death in Auschwitz in 1942, several of her works were published posthumously, including La vie de Tchekhov *(1946) and the Prix Renaudot–winning* Suite française *(2004).*

family, he arranges for his grandson Pierre to marry Simone Renaudin, a very wealthy young woman. Bound by his responsibility to his family and the strict code of behavior governing members of his social class, Pierre has no choice but to obey. However, he is deeply in love with Agnès Florent. Marriage with Agnès is unthinkable; from a family engaged in brewing, she is a member of the lower middle class, and she is already betrothed to a man more befitting her social standing. In defiance of all propriety, Pierre and Agnès meet secretly in the Coudre Woods. Agnès's betrothed learns of these meetings and ends their engagement, and her mother quarrels with Pierre's parents, Charles and Marthe Hardelot, insisting that Pierre marry Agnès. Taking advantage of the circumstances, Pierre asks Madame Florent for her daughter's hand in marriage.

Pierre's act of defiance and subsequent exile from Saint-Elme have dramatic effects on the family, which is further disrupted by the outbreak of World War I. Pierre goes to war, sending Agnès and their son, Guy, to Saint-Elme. War does not spare provincial France; as German forces approach the town, many of the residents flee, while Julien remains with the paper factory. Charles is killed during an air raid, and Saint-Elme is largely destroyed. Despite these tragedies, the war and its aftermath repair some of the damaged family relationships. With his son dead, Julien forgives Pierre and offers him a position in the factory, although he still refuses to accept Agnès. The family continues to heal, but life is once again disrupted when Guy, now an adult, returns to Saint-Elme after a suicide attempt. The events in the lives of the Hardelots seem to repeat, and another world war threatens the family and the nation.

Throughout *All Our Worldly Goods*, Némirovsky masterfully interweaves several disparate concepts to form a cohesive whole. The work is simultaneously a detailed portrayal of bourgeois life in provincial France, a poignant look at the devastation of war, and an affirming portrayal of the force and value of love and the possibility of achieving happiness. While the events of the novel are of great significance within the narrative, they truly play a secondary role, supporting the work's focus on the complexity of human relationships. The provincial bourgeois conflicts within the Hardelot family and the devastation of wartime and interwar France serve as catalysts for the human reactions and interactions that Némirovsky examines.

This examination extends at times to social critique, particularly in regard to the Hardelots and others of their socioeconomic class. While the objective third-person narration provides few opportunities for direct criticism, the author's choice of detail gives the work a subtle layer of critique. In keeping with her interest in relationships, Némirovsky focuses much of her social criticism on the rules governing human interaction. For her characters, every aspect of life is controlled by these rules; there is no spontaneity, no room for self-expression. Noting details such as the strictly controlled seating arrangements that are maintained even at the beach, a location associated with relaxation rather than restriction, the author calls attention to the ridiculous and arbitrary nature of such regulations.

Némirovsky further reinforces the strict social regulation of this society through her style of writing, aptly rendered in English by frequent Némirovsky translator Sandra Smith. Her descriptions of people, objects, and places are detailed but not embellished, and the novel itself displays a restrained, controlled style that surrounds the reader with the closed, ordered ambiance of the world in which the characters live. Often compared to the nineteenth-century French novelist Honoré de Balzac for her portrayal of this segment of French society, Némirovsky reveals the bourgeois obsession with money, possessions, success in business, and social correctness. Her work, like Balzac's, reflects a certain disdain for the bourgeoisie as a class. However, in contrast to Balzac, Némirovsky reveals her sympathy for the individual characters caught in this social milieu.

For Némirovsky, human emotion and attachment are significant and valuable forces, and her sympathetic treatment of individual members of the bourgeoisie grants their emotions and interactions significance for the reader. The characters are not caricatures, and the novel is not a farce. The author's social commentary is balanced by the multidimensionality of these sympathetic individuals. Thus, Némirovsky successfully depicts two meaningful love affairs while maintaining the novel's foundation in reality. Pierre and Agnès and Rose and Guy are portrayed as destined for and essential to each other, and their sympathetic depiction as young men and women struggling to overcome the social restrictions of the upper middle class supports the more traditionally romantic aspects of their respective love stories.

Likewise, Agnès's mother serves as the catalyst for these relationships, filling a role present in many romance narratives. However, her sympathetic portrayal lends a sense of realism to her actions in support of these socially unacceptable relationships. Orphaned early in life and forced to earn a living by giving singing lessons, she, unlike the tradition- and rule-bound upper bourgeoisie, believes in taking risks to achieve what one wants out of life. Given the backstory Némirovsky has provided for her, it seems reasonable that Madame Florent would seek to ensure the happiness of her daughter and grandson.

The German invasions and bombardments of France during World War I and the beginning of World War II occupy a considerable part of the novel, and Némirovsky aptly portrays the effects of these wars on families and individuals. Having lived through one world war and the beginning of another, Némirovsky showcases a variety of reactions to the threat. In the early moments of invasion, the characters attempt to deny what is happening or convince themselves that the war will last only a very short time. Then, as the German troops advance, the characters are faced with losing their homes, their possessions, and even their town. Némirovsky skillfully depicts their confusion and panic, emotions in sharp conflict with the bourgeois sense of order. Suddenly, life is no longer controlled and predictable.

The account of the war years provides Némirovsky with an additional opportunity to examine French provincial middle-class society, resulting in a powerful exploration of the actions taken by humans under great pressure. While the threat of subjugation or death heightens emotions and causes the characters to choose between fighting, fleeing, and remaining behind, their responses to the war are largely consistent with their previously established characteristics. Julien Hardelot's bourgeois concern with property and wealth is distilled by the pressures of World War I, and he refuses to leave the factory that symbolizes his socioeconomic standing. Pierre's sense of responsibility motivates him during both wars, leading him to the battlefield to protect his country and family in World War I. In World War II, he remains with the factory in Saint-Elme, but Némirovsky makes a distinction between Pierre's choice to stay behind and that of his grandfather. Pierre's concern is for the families of the workers who have gone to fight in the war, and he remains in Saint-Elme to ensure their safety, rather than that of his property. This consistency of character is effective in supporting the novel's overall realism.

Regardless of social standing or economic status, humans are resilient creatures, as Némirovsky makes readily apparent. Following the total devastation of World War I, the residents of Saint-Elme rebuild—albeit to the strict bourgeois standards of Julien. This resilience remains despite the onset of another war, and with an armistice signed by the end of the novel, the town's residents again prepare to rebuild. As the novel was completed several years before the end of World War II, this decidedly hopeful ending is pure conjecture. Némirovsky herself was unable to see France rebuild a second time. Having fled from Paris to the countryside early in the war, the author was arrested and deported in 1942, dying at the hands of the Nazis.

An artifact of wartime France and a complex exploration of love and family relationships in a time of social and national conflict, *All Our Worldly Goods* has been well received by both critics and readers. A number of critics have suggested that the novel is best viewed as a prequel to Némirovsky's *Suite française* (2004), a two-part novel that continues the chronicle of life in France during World War II.

Shawncey J. Webb

Review Sources

The Guardian, October 10, 2008 (Web).
Independent, October 17, 2008 (Web).
The New York Times Book Review, October 2, 2011, p. 12.
Richmond Times-Dispatch, October 23, 2011 (Web).
The Telegraph, October 4, 2008 (Web).

Almost a Family
A Memoir

Author: John Darnton (b. 1941)
Publisher: Alfred A. Knopf (New York).
Illustrated. 348 pp. $27.95
Type of work: Memoir, biography
Time: 1897 to the present
Locale: Michigan, Connecticut, New York City, New Guinea, and Washington, DC

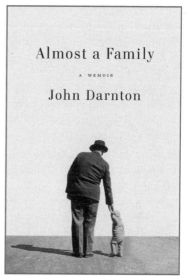

John Darnton presents a compelling memoir about growing up in the shadow of a father killed in World War II. He reflects on his father's mythic presence in his life as he searches for the truth about his parents' marriage and his father's death.

Principal personages:
JOHN DARNTON, author and Pulitzer Prize–winning reporter for the *New York Times*
BARNEY DARNTON, John's father, a *New York Times* war correspondent killed in World War II
ROBERT DARNTON, John's older brother, a celebrated historian
ELEANOR DARNTON, John's mother, nicknamed "Tootie"

John Darnton's personal and affecting book *Almost a Family: A Memoir* is many things. It is a meditation on growing up with only other people's memories of a lionized father. It is a searing account of a small family wracked by lies and deception. It is a detective story, following two brothers as they piece together the truth about their parents' marriage and the death of their father during World War II. Above all, it is a quest for meaning, as the author looks back on his life and reflects on the startling ways in which it was shaped by his youth and the father he never knew. Time folds in upon itself in the pages of this book as Darnton reminds readers of the power that an ever-present past can have in their lives and the fierce hold of the myths people create about themselves. The use of time and memory gives this memoir a universal resonance, as Darnton, a Pulitzer Prize–winning journalist and successful novelist, captures the messy complexity of life with clear and elegant prose. He writes with insightful retrospection about events in his life that he did not understand at the time. He does not shy away from describing youthful escapades that reflect no credit on him, but rather confronts painful realities about himself and his parents with the engaged objectivity of a good reporter. In doing so, Darnton has wrought an honest and moving tribute to the family he loves.

Darnton was born in the early hours of November 20, 1941, while his father, Byron "Barney" Darnton, sat in the waiting room just outside the maternity ward. Barney was reading Mark Twain's *Life on the Mississippi* (1883) at the time of the birth; when told he had another son, he made a note of it across the bottom of the pages he was on. This inscription is one of the few written references he ever made to his younger son, and Darnton scrutinizes every aspect of the words and writing to reconstruct the scene and envision the man he would never know. This absent father, lost in a great war, would nonetheless be a formative influence in the lives of his sons.

Admitting that he has no memories of his father, Darnton relies on his mother's stories and the facts that he has discovered on his own. He traces Barney's life from his birth in Michigan in 1897 through his service in the Michigan National Guard and the Thirty-Second Division in World War I. After serving in the war, Barney began a career in journalism, most notably as a reporter and correspondent for the *New York Times* newspaper. In addition to his career, Darnton describes his father's role in the Jazz Age, his reputation as a writer and a wit, and his great potential in the industry. Writing with the benefit of hindsight and history, Darnton knows that Barney's is a life that will be cut short.

When the United States entered World War II, Barney applied for a position as a war correspondent to continue working for the *New York Times*. Though he was in his forties and had a wife and two small children, Barney felt that it was his responsibility to leave them in order to fight for the kind of world in which he wanted them to live. Darnton shares a letter in which Barney wrote that he was certain his wife, Eleanor, would be able to manage without him, declaring, "She isn't the stuff that cracks under a bit of difficulty." Eleanor herself understood his need to leave for the front and knew that he was going even before he told her.

In February 1942, Barney joined the Allied forces in Australia, where he covered naval battles from a safe distance. When he was finally able to join troops on a combat mission against the Japanese in New Guinea, the two boats he was traveling with were bombed. While neither boat sustained a direct hit, a piece of shrapnel hit Barney in the back of the neck, killing him. Darnton meticulously reconstructs the events surrounding his father's death, compiling information from military records, letters, witnesses, and the notes that Barney himself was taking at the time of the attack. These passages are engrossing and uncluttered, revealing Darnton's distance from his subject while vividly describing the scene.

Although it marked a significant change in the lives of his family, Barney's death wasn't the only tragedy in young Darnton's life. Even as he relates information about condolences, funeral services, and a liberty ship named after his father, Darnton also begins to describe his mother's grief and her slow and devastating descent into alcoholism. The day her husband died, Eleanor sensed that something was wrong and soon learned that she was a widow. The void that Barney left in her life was a painful emptiness that wore through the strength Barney once saw in his wife. With that small piece of shrapnel, the Darntons' lives were changed forever.

Eleanor cherished the memory of her late husband and never remarried. She wrote a book, *The Children Grew* (1954), which paints a sentimental picture of her life alone with her children; in the book, she and the boys face the future with fortitude. In his own book, Darnton carefully traces her subsequent shift from fortitude to depression.

He describes his mother's newspaper work and how it led her to create the Women's National News Service organization. He also relates Eleanor's disappointment when the organization faltered and failed, noting that this was when her strong façade began to crumble. Growing more desperate and unable to take care of her children, she began to cope by drinking heavily.

John Darnton worked for the New York Times *for forty years as a reporter, editor, and foreign correspondent, during which time he won the George Polk Award twice and the Pulitzer Prize once. He has written several best-selling novels, including* Neanderthal *(1996),* The Experiment *(1999), and* The Darwin Conspiracy *(2005).*

Darnton's account of these years brilliantly captures a child's perspective on events that he only dimly comprehends. The early years of his boyhood were in many ways idyllic, and the transition from normalcy to dysfunction occurred so seamlessly that he scarcely noticed it happening. Gradually, however, he began to realize something was wrong, as friends began to make comments about his mother and her episodes of "grogginess" grew more frequent. Darnton and Robert increasingly had to fend for themselves, preparing their own meals and performing other daily tasks. Eleanor's inability to hold a job because of her alcoholism led to the deterioration of the family's financial circumstances; this was reflected in a series of moves, from their comfortable home in Connecticut to a rented flat in Washington, D.C., and then to a studio apartment in New York City. Finally, Eleanor hit bottom, was hospitalized, and joined Alcoholics Anonymous, after which time she never drank again.

Eventually, Robert and Darnton both received scholarships to attend the prestigious Phillips Academy in Andover, Massachusetts. There, the effects of their tumultuous childhoods manifested in different ways, with Darnton's rebellious behavior resulting in his expulsion from the school. From there, the author describes his education at the University of Wisconsin and his antiestablishmentarian behavior until he ultimately decides to marry and settle down. Through his mother and brother's contacts, he gets a job at the *New York Times*—unintentionally following in the footsteps of the father he never knew.

Through the years, Darnton advanced from copy boy to reporter to foreign correspondent before eventually becoming an editor. He describes his successes, which include several best-selling novels, two George Polk Awards, and the Pulitzer Prize, and how his ceaseless search for his father led him to write *Almost a Family*. The book deftly covers the passage of time, eventually finding Darnton ready to bring his father's story full circle.

Decades later, and still working at the same newspaper that led his father there in the first place, Darnton visits the Pongani sands where Barney died. While leaving the beach, Darnton is struck by the senselessness of Barney's death and the needlessness of the tragedy that ruined his family. He says of the experience, "It was not catharsis; it was revelation. I felt decades of illusion drop away and turn to anger." It is this illusion that permeates the entirety of the memoir. The notion of myth versus reality is central to *Almost a Family*, and with the precision of a journalist, Darnton explores the history—both real and imagined—of his father.

Almost a Family goes well beyond the story of a family. It is a moving piece about love and grief as well as an examination of the interconnectedness of the past and the present. It is also a tragic story of a son trying to separate the man his father truly was from the myth that he had always believed. Early in the book, Darnton notes, "Not having a father present didn't mean not having a father. There wasn't just an absence in my life. There was the presence of an absence . . ." It is this absence that eventually compelled Darnton to embark on the personal and literal journeys so masterfully described here.

Along the way, he makes surprising discoveries about his parents that explain some mysteries and raise even more. As the myths about his family fall away, they leave Darnton with a heightened appreciation of his parents as flawed but compelling individuals, doing their best in a complicated world. They are not heroes; they are simply brave and fallible people striving for the best for their family. The journey of exploration that Darnton undertakes is well worth following in this fascinating and evocative memoir.

Daniel P. Murphy

Review Sources

Booklist 107, no. 11 (February 1, 2011): 18.
Kirkus Reviews 78, no. 24 (December 15, 2010): 1248.
Library Journal 136, no. 2 (February 1, 2011): 71.
The New Yorker 87, no. 10 (April 25, 2011): 79.
The New York Review of Books 58, no. 8 (May 12, 2011): 22–23.
The New York Times Book Review, March 20, 2011, p. 13.
Publishers Weekly 258, no. 7 (February 14, 2011): 50.

Alone Together
Why We Expect More from Technology and Less from Each Other

Author: Sherry Turkle (b. 1948)
Publisher: Basic Books (New York). 360 pp.
$28.95
Type of work: Sociology, technology

Alone Together *presents a cautionary tale of how technology is changing human society by reducing the instances in which individuals interact with one another in person and with their full attention. Turkle proposes a need to scale back reliance on technology in order to prevent a crisis in human society.*

Principal personages:
RODNEY BROOKS, a roboticist employed by the Massachusetts Institute of Technology (MIT) who works in the Artificial Intelligence Laboratory
AARON EDSINGER, an MIT-educated roboticist and the designer of Domo, a talking robot
PIA LINDMAN, a performance artist who has experimented with creating communion between the human mind and artificial intelligence

In *Alone Together: Why We Expect More from Technology and Less from Each Other*, Sherry Turkle explores how human society is changing due to an inundation of technology and the proliferation of virtual worlds. Most importantly, she argues that it is necessary to reassess the directions in which we propose to adopt and champion technology, emphasizing that these decisions are not simply about entrepreneurship but also about ethics. The questions that she asks are probing, timely, and urgent, in large part because she demonstrates that the physical and the emotional well-being of many people are at stake. The most vulnerable figures in her narrative are children and the elderly, who are being increasingly "cared for" with technological assistance, often provided by mechanized toys that act as surrogates for human caretakers. While the expensive therapeutic robot Paro represents one end of this spectrum, Turkle also clearly shows that cell phones and computer technology often stand in for responsible and in-person parenting, leaving children increasingly detached from family structures and retreating into virtual worlds. She asks, "Are these psychologically, socially, and ethnically acceptable propositions? What are our responsibilities here?"

A fundamental strain of Turkle's book is the identification of a technology-triggered crisis in the family. She states that attachment to technology can form "postfamilial families" in which family members are isolated and alone within their own home as they spend more time with technology than with each other. Although the stresses from technology may most readily be traced in individual and family circumstances, the challenges are societal. Turkle asserts that the time has come to redirect the course of such troubling trends, arguing, "We make our technologies, and they, in turn, shape us. So, of every technology we must ask, Does it serve our human purposes?—a question that causes us to reconsider what these purposes are."

Alone Together is divided into two sections. Part 1 considers the history of the robotic movement as it relates to the development of social robotics, forms of artificial intelligence intended in some manner to play the role of companion or confidant to human users. Part 2 is dedicated to the exploration of networked technology, especially the phenomena of cell phone technology and social media. The two sections of the text are not entirely integrated, but for Turkle, the analysis of human interaction with robotic technology provides the psychological and behavioral evidence to support some of the concerns that she subsequently raises with regard to increasing human psychological dependence on technologies of various forms.

(Peter Urban)

Sherry Turkle is the Abby Rockefeller Mauzé Professor of the Social Studies of Science and Technology at the Massachusetts Institute of Technology. Her book Alone Together *completes a trilogy that began with* The Second Self: Computers and the Human Spirit *(1985) and continued with* Life on the Screen: Identity in the Age of the Internet *(1995).*

Unlike the discussion of networked technology in the second half of the book, the analysis of social robotics in part 1 may seem, at least for long stretches, comfortably removed from everyday concerns. Turkle presents her many years of research into the affectionate attachment of children to such toy creations as Tamagotchis, Furbies, and My Real Babies. These studies, as well as others on which Turkle depends, trace the attachment that children develop for social robots that seem "alive enough" to interact with their human users; these robots take the place of other, truly living companionship, be it with another child, a pet, or a parent. The stakes of the story rise, however, when Turkle begins to assess the impact of Paro, a therapeutic robot intended to provide physical and emotional companionship for the sick and elderly. The narrative that Turkle presents, in which individuals share their life stories and intimate personal histories with these machines because family and other human caretakers are lacking, is both poignant and frightening. The final chapters in this section, which consider the interaction of both children and adult visitors with Cog, Kismet, and Domo (all interactive robots that simulate emotions, conversation, and interaction with people), present a worrying pattern in which people willingly rely on these robots for feelings of affection and approval, even while knowing that the machines can offer no such emotional support. Such advanced technologies have become especially seductive to their audiences; Turkle concludes by noting that this technology is specifically designed to elicit an emotional attachment and create illusions of comfort and caring. She says, "We put robots on a terrain of meaning, but they don't know what we mean. And they don't mean anything at all." While Turkle acknowledges that people may feign caring about one another, fail to listen to another individual, or even act with deliberate cruelty, she argues that even such imperfectly human interactions are of greater inherent value than the fundamentally one-sided interactions between humans and machines.

The second half of Turkle's book engages with what she terms "the tethered self," meaning the individual constantly connected to networked technologies. She argues that the technological network offers people the ability to build a life based around "relationships with less," which are akin to those formed with robotic companions like Furbies and Paros. The danger of such rapports, she argues, is that they have the potential to "approach a new state of the self," fundamentally altering how individuals assess their own lives, relate to one another, and interact with their environments. Framed in this manner, Turkle clearly presents a high-stakes problem with which society must grapple, describing what she has observed to be individuals' "identity-building" through networked media. Second Life, Facebook, MySpace, and other social media websites all allow individuals to create virtual personae without working on developing their own abilities to interact in the real world with peers, family members, or colleagues. The result, as Turkle sees it, is the simultaneous habitation of real and virtual lives—what one of her subjects refers to as a "life mix," which Turkle describes as "the mash-up of what you have on- and offline." The new phenomenon is not insignificant, Turkle argues, because it has shifted people from "multitasking to multi-lifing."

Turkle analyzes the challenges and changes of the networked life from individual, familial, communal, and, to a lesser degree, global perspectives. The implications are varied and troubling. Some of them are familiar problems. Professionals, for example, are often expected to take the office with them, even on vacation, in the form of an omnipresent smartphone that must work even in remote corners of the globe. Parents eat dinner with their children while attending to business and pleasure on the ubiquitous smartphone, and children learn to act in the same manner. In her analysis of social networking communities, Turkle adroitly highlights the aspects of these interactions that deviate from normal human relationships. Indeed, she asserts that they cannot properly be called communities at all, because unlike real communities, virtual communities have no real shared place, conflicts, or responsibilities

Turkle's analysis suggests that individuals turn to networked communities as a means of escaping from the hurt, challenges, and complexities of real life, and that in so doing, they fail one another. Further, she convincingly explores how increased connectivity reduces the substance of communication. Conversations are limited to text messages and queries are confined to the types of questions that can be easily answered in a brief e-mail. Such interactions leave little room for emotions and intellectual growth. As Turkle laments, "The ties we form through the Internet are not, in the end, the ties that bind. But they are the ties that preoccupy. We text each other at family dinners, while we jog, while we drive, as we push our children on swings in the park."

The conclusions of Turkle's study are sobering, suggesting that significant changes in society already reflect the distancing influences of technology. One study that she cites, for example, found that college students in 2010 were "far less likely to say that it is valuable to try to put oneself in the place of others or to try to understand their feelings" than their peers in the 1980s or 1990s, demonstrating a drop of 40 percent in empathy. Ultimately, Turkle proposes that the present generations of adults have the opportunity to assess and reverse the damage that their own fascination with technology has caused. She concludes by saying, "We have invented inspiring and enhancing technologies, and yet we have allowed them to diminish us. The prospect of loving, or being loved by, a machine changes what love can be. We know that the young are tempted. They have been brought up to be. Those who have known lifetimes of love can surely offer them more." This is the closest to a solution that Turkle offers, and it seems that while her labor of fifteen years has enabled her to clearly articulate a troubling social trend, its solutions are far more nebulous.

Because of its polemical nature, and because Turkle here reverses her previously celebratory stance on technology, *Alone Together* will likely continue to receive a dramatic range of critical responses. Turkle's apparent nostalgia for a more "authentic" or "traditional" family or community structure should make the reader cautious, as no such single authenticity has ever existed. Still, her fundamental argument about the shifting stakes of deep personal interactions being challenged by all-consuming yet shallow digital or robotic relationships is undeniably relevant to an unprecedented condition in society. Given the sweeping breadth of her analysis and the troubling indicators of her data, Turkle's request for careful deliberation on the future of our dependence on technology seems both necessary and timely.

Julia A. Sienkewicz

Review Sources

Bloomberg Businessweek, March 3, 2011 (Web).
Booklist 107, no. 9/10 (January 1/15, 2011): 22.
ETC: A Review of General Semantics 68, no. 3 (July 2011): 365.
Kirkus Reviews 78, no. 21 (November 1, 2011): 1101.
The New York Times Book Review, January 23, 2011, p. 15.
The Washington Post, January 28, 2011 (Web).

American Eden
From Monticello to Central Park to Our Backyards:
What Our Gardens Tell Us about Who We Are

Author: Wade Graham (b. 1967)
Publisher: HarperCollins (New York). 480 pp. $35.00
Type of work: Fine arts, History

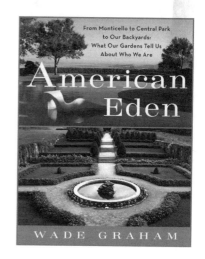

A history of American landscape design from the colonial era to the early twenty-first century, this book introduces key themes, personages, and problems in landscape design and demonstrates the consistent presence of gardening throughout the history and culture of the United States.

Principal personages:
ANDREW JACKSON DOWNING (1815–1852), a theorist and practitioner of landscape design

BEATRIX JONES FARRAND (1872–1959), a landscape architect known especially for her arts and crafts–style gardens

THOMAS JEFFERSON (1743–1826), the third president of the United States and an influential figure in garden and landscape design

CHARLES JENCKS (b. 1939), a landscape architect and postmodern theorist

RICHARD NEUTRA (1892–1970), an architect known for his role in shaping modern California landscape design

JACK NICKLAUS (b. 1940), a professional golfer and designer of golf courses

ISAMU NOGUCHI (1904–1988), a sculptor and designer of public projects

MARTHA SCHWARTZ (b. 1950), a landscape architect known for her urban landscapes

MARTHA STEWART (b. 1941), an author and media personality who has greatly influenced American gardens

EDITH WHARTON (1862–1937), an author of fiction instrumental in describing and shaping Gilded Age landscape design

FRANK LLOYD WRIGHT (1867–1959), a lead architect of the Prairie School

In *American Eden: From Monticello to Central Park to Our Backyards; What Our Gardens Tell Us About Who We Are*, Wade Graham offers a sweeping and fast-paced account of landscape history in the United States, from its origins in the gardening practices of seventeenth-century Europe to the trends of the early twenty-first century. As the title suggests, this account breathlessly juxtaposes designed gardens, both public and private, with their vernacular counterparts. Graham employs a conversational tone throughout the text and intersperses personal accounts, whether based on visits

(Courtesy of Wade Graham)

Wade Graham is a historian and garden designer and an adjunct professor of public policy at Pepperdine University. He has written for such publications as Garden Design *and* The New Yorker.

to the sites or on incidents from his own history, that allow the casual reader to become engaged in the history of landscape design in ways that would not be possible in more conventional academic texts.

In the introduction, he compels the reader to care about the history of landscapes, even when these are the mundane iterations of borders and lawns so common in the suburban yard. Graham asserts that by becoming familiar with the four-hundred-year scope of landscape history that he recounts, the reader will be able to make sense of the styles of landscape design that constitute quintessential gardening practices in the United States. Graham traces a pedigree of landscape design through diverse global trends and concludes that American gardens are the products of centuries of stylistic borrowing and reworking. This process of inspiration from multiple sources produces garden styles that he concludes have the potential to be "looser, freer, more idealistic, and more optimistic than the originals, and unapologetically ecumenical, unafraid to mix and match."

Graham's narrative of garden history in the United States features an interesting combination of expected protagonists of landscape design such as Thomas Jefferson and Andrew Jackson Downing and unexpected or even unknown gardeners such as the author's mother, whose California garden was featured in a 1976 issue of *Better Homes & Gardens*. Just as he is ecumenical in his selection of gardeners, so he is wide-ranging in his definition of what constitutes a garden. Thus, Graham considers major public parks such as New York City's Central Park and Chicago's Lurie Garden, site-specific land studies and land art such as Robert Smithson's 1967 *The Monuments of Passaic*, and works engaged with the artistic reframing of space such as the Bagel Garden created by Martha Schwartz in 1979. Other aspects of Graham's account are less diverse. With the exception of its discussion of Isamu Noguchi, the book does not include a treatment of minority landscapes or explore the ways in which public landscapes have either served or failed to serve a diverse urban clientele. Likewise, while he at times refers to the nineteenth-century trope of "Grandmother's garden," Graham focuses on landscape design that is oriented toward upper-class and corporate clients. One strength of the book, by contrast, is the attention that Graham pays to female landscape designers and gardeners, dedicating numerous pages to the work of Beatrix Jones Farrand, Ellen Biddle Shipman, and Kathryn Gustafson, among others.

American Eden is divided into chapters that flow chronologically. The first two chapters discuss gardening practices in the United States from the seventeenth to the mid-nineteenth century, while the third and fourth chapters engage with early modernity, beginning with the waning of the nineteenth century and extending as far as

1945. Chapters 5 and 6 push progressively through the twentieth century and place a strong emphasis on Graham's particular area of interest, the California garden. The final chapter engages with contemporary trends, beginning with an analysis of Martha Stewart and her iconic garden and ending with a discussion of the White House kitchen garden spearheaded by Michelle Obama.

Much of the book concerns American gardens after 1850, and Graham demonstrates greater subtlety in his accounts of modern, postmodern, and contemporary landscape practices. In these later sections, he deftly intertwines trends in studio art practices, architecture, gardening, and public landscapes in order to trace a rich history built on a complex network of influence and personalities. By contrast, although Graham traces significant European trends in landscape design and considers their influence on late eighteenth- and early nineteenth-century practices, his account of gardening until 1826 focuses almost exclusively on Thomas Jefferson without attending to the complex networks of gardeners, plant collectors, and landscape designers active in the United States during these years. Nevertheless, the lacuna of publications on this period in landscape design gives Graham's fifty-five-page first chapter a special significance, as it locates early American gardening practices within the larger history of landscape design in the United States.

The field of landscape history boasts few accessible texts that survey the gardens of the United States across such a broad historical period, and *American Eden* provides a significant, highly readable overview that may prove useful to students in both secondary and higher education. At the same time, it is a quirky, personal account filled with entertaining anecdotes; Graham reveals this aspect of the work early in the book, describing the personal effect of walking up a foggy path toward Jefferson's mansion house at Monticello. Suggesting a correlation between American gardens and American personalities, it focuses on the components of landscapes as well as the personalities of their designers and the effects of these personalities on the gardens themselves. Garden designers are approached as people, rather than as purveyors of traditional or nontraditional stylistic forms. This characteristic is common throughout the text but is especially evident in the final chapter, in which Graham analyzes the effects of Martha Stewart on personality, celebrity, and trends in landscape design.

Graham offers an account of American landscape history that does not always adhere to accepted narratives. Perhaps the most interesting aspect of his book for a reader versed in the history of landscape design is the way Graham navigates easily between concerns of art, interior decoration, aesthetics, and landscape architecture. In his account, landscape design movements such as Arts and Crafts and modernism are considered as vibrant aesthetic and cultural movements that transcend medium boundaries. This leads Graham to include discussion of figures not typically associated with gardens or landscapes, such as Richard Neutra; while Graham recognizes that the architect "didn't really make gardens per se," he notes that Neutra had a "controlling influence on how the modern garden would evolve." Graham likewise explores the frequent tensions that have occurred between architects and landscape architects, including the significant conflict that arose during the design of the Getty Museum in Los Angeles, California.

Just as he emphasizes the relationships between architects and landscape designers, Graham engages closely with the history of writing about gardens and the close relationships that have existed between authors and designers. Graham provides a lengthy and useful discussion of Andrew Jackson Downing and his pervasive influence on American garden design, connecting Downing closely with the European authors on whom his work depended. Perhaps most interesting in this regard is the section of the third chapter dedicated to Edith Wharton. In considering Wharton's novels alongside her travels, her study of European gardens, and her own landscape garden at her estate, the Mount, Graham provides an excellent case study of the close interconnection of design and literary practices.

A compelling overview of the history and significance of gardens in the United States, *American Eden* provides the reader with an understanding of the artistic, intellectual, and social networks within which such landscapes are formed and through which they are meant to resonate. While not an encyclopedic source, it offers a solid introduction to many of the key figures and themes of landscape history in the United States and allows beginning researchers to situate key figures within their chronological, stylistic, and conceptual contexts. Through his inclusion of both prominent and lesser-known figures and his interest in uniting national and international trends, Graham successfully expands the canon and scope of American landscape history, familiarizing readers with an exciting range of designers and their sources.

Julia A. Sienkewicz

Review Sources

Booklist 107, no. 8 (December 15, 2010): p. 14.
Kirkus Reviews 79, no. 1 (January 1, 2011): p. 34.
Publishers Weekly 258, no. 8 (February 21, 2011): pp. 128–29.
The Wall Street Journal, April 13, 2011, p. A15.

The Anatomy of Influence
Literature as a Way of Life

Author: Harold Bloom (b. 1930)
Publisher: Yale University Press (New Haven, CT). 368 pp. $32.50
Type of work: Literary nonfiction

The eminent critic's self-described "swan song" recapitulates the interpretive and critical principles that have informed his fifty-five years of teaching and writing about literature.

The Anatomy of Influence: Literature as a Way of Life, Harold Bloom's thirty-eighth book (not counting the hundreds of volumes he has edited and written introductions for), was published shortly before his eighty-first birthday and was intended as a "virtual swan song," a chance for the best-known literary critic in America to sum up his major concerns in one place. He explains in his brief preface, or "Praeludium," that the title alludes to Robert Burton's baroque *Anatomy of Melancholy* (1621), which Bloom had conceived as the model for this collection of essays. As reviewers were quick to note, however, the title also suggests two other crucial milestones in Bloom's career, Northrup Frye's groundbreaking *Anatomy of Criticism* (1957) and his own *The Anxiety of Influence: A Theory of Poetry* (1973). Having spent twenty years as a disciple of Frye, whom he considered "the foremost living student of Western literature," Bloom awoke from a nightmare in 1967 and began composing an essay. This essay would become *The Anxiety of Influence*, a work that freed Bloom from Frye's shadow (Frye himself would reject the book's approach and conclusions) and established the focus on literary influence that would direct most of Bloom's writing thereafter.

The overall contours of this book are loosely chronological, proceeding from the sixteenth to the twenty-first century. After three preliminary chapters on "The Point of View for My Work as a Critic," in which Bloom presents something of a critical self-portrait, he provides eight chapters on Shakespeare's influence, four essays on a range of poets from John Dryden to James Merrill, and seven essays on Walt Whitman's poetry and subsequent influence. Given that Bloom considers Shakespeare the most influential writer of all time and Walt Whitman the most original writer in the four centuries after Shakespeare, it will come as no surprise that about two-thirds of the book is devoted to close examination of the two. But for Bloom, "the structure of literary influence is labyrinthine, not linear," and he ranges freely back and forth between time periods and across national literatures to tease out the manifold and circuitous passages linking these writers with myriad others in complex patterns of "family romances."

Harold Bloom is a Sterling Professor of Humanities at Yale University, where he has taught literature since 1955. His numerous honors include a MacArthur Fellowship and the American Academy of Arts and Letters's Gold Medal for Belles Lettres and Criticism.

Bloom, who describes himself as a life-long student of influence in the life of the arts, considers that every great poet must first be inspired by previous great poetry, then find a way to creatively misread that poetry and escape from its influence to find his or her own distinctive voice. The anxiety of influence, Bloom argues, is not a matter of a poet's psychological state: "Temperament and circumstances determine whether a later poet *feels* anxiety at whatever level of consciousness." The important kind of influence anxiety "exists between poems and not between persons." While Bloom's concept of influence pays close attention to such traditional indices as allusions and verbal echoes as manifested in tropes, images, diction, syntax, and metrics, it runs much deeper, considering such factors as poetic stance and the struggle for poetic supremacy, in which the strongest poets engage with their precursors. Earlier notions of poetic influence saw this primarily as a matter of source study, of determining which works a given poet had read and studied and identifying their explicit allusions. By this model, literary history is a seamless and collegial process of cultural accumulation and collaboration. In Bloom's view, however, this model applies only to weak poets, those who accept and repeat the work of previous writers in diluted form. For strong poets, poetic influence is always a competitive struggle with quasi-Freudian undertones, as they must master and throw off the influence of their predecessors. Since the truly great writers can never be fully understood and transcended, and since a correct reading can only repeat the original texts, the strong writers must not only read but creatively *misread* the canon in order to find, or perhaps invent, the weaknesses of their predecessors.

Having previously made the case for this agonistic model of influence, Bloom now revises his stance. He recognizes that he overemphasized the antagonism between poets, taking the opportunity here "to revisit my previous account of influence. In this, my final statement on the subject, I define influence simply as *literary love, tempered by defense*. The defenses vary from poet to poet. But the overwhelming presence of love is vital to understanding how great literature works." A poet does not compete "simply to vanquish the rival, but to assert the integrity of his or her own writing self." While poets do struggle to assimilate and respond to the literature that came before them, that motivation is by no means simply, or even primarily, negative; rather, the predecessors who must be fought against are the authors of the work that the poets love the most.

Bloom identifies himself as an aesthetic critic of the sublime and rejects outright all feminist, Marxist, and ideology-driven critical theories that view poetry through the social context of its original publication. "I do not believe that poetry has anything to do with cultural politics," Bloom writes. "I ask of a poem three things: aesthetic splendor, cognitive power, and wisdom." This focus on aesthetics runs against the current of much contemporary criticism, which emphasizes social issues like gender, race, and sexuality. For Bloom, these factors are irrelevant, as they never help the reader differentiate between great and mediocre literature. Regarding sexual orientation, for example, he contends that

> All explanations based on sexual orientation seem useless to me in the context of imaginative literature. Many great and good poets have been bisexual or homoerotic or heterosexual or none of the above. Even more, many more weak poets, also were full of all possible orientations . . . Nothing in such namings can help us to estimate and appreciate the aesthetic value of Whitman, Crane, and Byron. There is no "homoerotic tradition" of authentic poetry, and it is useless to assume that there must be one.

While he does discuss dozens of scholarly studies of the authors he analyzes (though eschewing the standard critical apparatus of endnotes and bibliographies), he only cites critics whose work he admires, while those theorists whose work he disagrees with are dismissed with contempt as "the School of Resentment," a coterie of small-minded cynics who hate literature and desire only to cut greatness down to their own size.

Equally controversial has been Bloom's advocacy of the traditional concept of the literary canon, the conviction that some authors and some works of literature are more valuable than others and worthy of special consideration. Shakespeare is not just a socially constructed product of his time and place—dozens of inferior writers, such as Philip Massinger, occupied similar positions in social history—but a qualitatively superior artist who transcended the poetic rhetoric of his own precursor, Christopher Marlowe, and whose more capacious consciousness produced works genuinely superior to those of any other author. "I preach Bardolatry as the most benign of all religions," Bloom declares. ". . . For me, Shakespeare is God." Furthermore, Bloom argues that it is the critic's job to proclaim what is or is not literature of permanent value, to prevent readers from foundering "in tidal waves of sincere bad verse." He thus issues such sweeping pronouncements as "There are eight hundred pages of Whitman, and about one hundred or so remain the best work of any American writer ever." Noting that Joseph Conrad, for example, "has turned unfashionable and is excluded from the academy for his 'colonialist' sins," Bloom asserts, "He will return, as superior literature always does, burying its academic undertakers."

Bloom's unapologetic defense of the canon has irked many feminist and multicultural critics, who object that this approach privileges the white male heterosexual authors who, for historical reasons, have produced most of what Bloom would call literature. The claim that Bloom neglects women writers ignores many exceptions. In *The Book of J* (1990), for example, he argues that a woman authored much of the first five books of the Old Testament (he has since identified that woman as Bathsheba), and he includes Jane Austen, Emily Dickinson, George Eliot, and Virginia Woolf in the elite list of writers who make up *The Western Canon: The Books and Schools of the Ages* (1994).Here, he ranks Dickinson, Marianne Moore, and Elizabeth Bishop among "our central poets." But for Bloom, recent critical attempts to redress historical inequalities and even out the writers studied in the academy according to gender and race are misguided: "Robert Browning has been supplanted by his wife, Elizabeth

Barrett Browning, doubtless an estimable human being and now yet one more heroine of feminist literary critics, but except in snatches I find her scarcely readable." He challenges the standard notions of diversity by arguing that Shakespeare, who is read and admired in literally every corner of the globe, is the most genuinely multicultural of all authors.

Bloom does take the opportunity to modify and clarify some of his more sweeping statements about literature. In addition to the new emphasis on the role of love in the rivalries between strong poets, he also returns to the claim that was made famous as the subtitle of his bestseller *Shakespeare: The Invention of the Human* (1998): "We would have been here anyway, of course, but we would not have seen ourselves as what we are." Many readers will be pleased to find that *The Anatomy of Influence* also provides a preview of Bloom's long-overdue autobiographical memoir, detailing his personal involvement not just with literature but also with the many celebrated writers he has known. To a greater degree than in past writings, he weaves into his text a fascinating series of informal reminiscences and personal anecdotes about many of the foremost poets and critics of the past two generations, from John Ashbery, Alan Ginsberg, Mark Strand, and Tennessee Williams to M. H. Abrams, Kenneth Burke, F. O. Matthiessen, and Robert Penn Warren. Whereas some readers will delight in these passages, others might view them as mere name-dropping. The primary emphasis, however, as always for Bloom, is on his relationships with literary works. As he remarked in an interview about the book, it is "about what it is to fall in love with poems."

William Nelles

Review Sources

Boston Review, April 27, 2011 (Web).
Harper's Magazine, August 11, 2011 (Web).
The New York Times Book Review, May 22, 2011, p. 1.
Ugarte: A Literary Review, May 8, 2011 (Web).

And So It Goes
Kurt Vonnegut, A Life

Author: Charles J. Shields (b. 1951)
Publisher: Henry Holt (New York). 528 pp.
$30.00
Type of work: Literary biography
Time: 1922–2007
Locale: Indianapolis, Indiana; Schenectady and New York City, New York; West Barnstable, Massachusetts

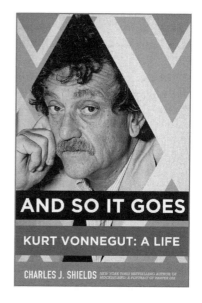

This biography of the popular late-twentieth-century American novelist paints Kurt Vonnegut's life and career in great detail but leaves large questions unanswered.

Principal personages:
KURT VONNEGUT JR., the novelist, short story writer, playwright, and essayist
BERNARD VONNEGUT, his older brother, in whose shadow Kurt spent much of his life
ALICE VONNEGUT, his older sister and ideal audience when he started writing
JANE MARIE COX VONNEGUT, Vonnegut's wife of more than thirty years
MARK VONNEGUT, their oldest son, and one of six children
JILL KREMENTZ, a photographer and writer, and Vonnegut's second wife
KNOX BURGER, Vonnegut's first editor and writing advisor
SEYMOUR "SAM" LAWRENCE, the Dell editor who first championed Vonnegut

Kurt Vonnegut Jr. was the Pied Piper of the 1960s. Young people so identified with the irreverent iconoclasm of novels like *God Bless You, Mr. Rosewater* (1965) and *Slaughterhouse-Five* (1969) that they would drive to his house on Cape Cod, seeking out warmth and wisdom. Instead, as Charles J. Shields shows in this first authoritative biography of the writer, they often found a cranky man who could be as cruel as he was funny. Shields provides windows into Vonnegut's troubled life and roller-coaster career but also leaves some parts of the writer's story in darkness.

Vonnegut was raised in Indianapolis, Indiana, in a German American family that fell from wealth and privilege to financial struggles after the stock market crash of 1929, when his father's architecture firm failed. Overshadowed by an older brother, Bernard, who was considered a scientific genius, Vonnegut early discovered humor and writing as keys to attention, especially from his supportive older sister Alice. Vonnegut dropped out of a failing college career at Cornell University in 1943, having spent most of his time working as a reporter and columnist for *The Cornell Daily Sun*, and he entered World War II as an infantryman. Sent as part of a replacement unit into the

Battle of the Bulge in 1944, Vonnegut was captured, and survived a hellish trip by foot and boxcar to a prisoner-of-war camp in Germany. The event that would define his life and his writing occurred when, as part of a unit sent to clear rubble from the city of Dresden—which its inhabitants believed was protected from further Allied attacks because it was an ancient city of no military value—he found shelter in a bunker beneath a slaughterhouse as bombers destroyed the city in raids intended to force Germany to its knees. Emerging to a moonscape where the beautiful city had once stood, Vonnegut was eventually freed (he had lost forty pounds) and shipped back to the United States. His horrific wartime experience would alter his life and, after a quarter century of trying to write it, the story would become the core narrative of his most famous novel, *Slaughterhouse-Five.*

Vonnegut married and moved to Chicago with his wife, Jane, to study anthropology at the University of Chicago, but he left without a degree again and went to work in the public relations department at General Electric's Schenectady, New York, plant, where his brother was a scientist. For some years, Vonnegut tried to break into the then-lucrative world of magazine fiction, and eventually he was helped by a friend from his days on the *Daily Sun*, Knox Burger, who had become the fiction editor at *Collier's* magazine at age twenty-six. After placing some dozens of stories, Vonnegut was able to leave General Electric and move to Cape Cod with his wife and growing family. Their three children would be joined by the three sons of Vonnegut's sister Alice, who died of cancer just after her husband was killed in a train wreck. Jane would control the chaos of this suddenly enlarged family while her husband holed away in a study, writing stories and novels and trying to make enough money to support them. His early novels (*Player Piano*, 1952, and *The Sirens of Titan*, 1959) sold poorly, but through *Mother Night* (1962), *Cat's Cradle* (1963), and *God Bless You, Mr. Rosewater*, Vonnegut gained a critical reputation and a growing fan base, even though his work was often marginalized as "science fiction" by reviewers and did not sell well. Shields begins the biography with a scene of Vonnegut driving his oldest son's Volkswagen to the University of Iowa Writers' Workshop for a teaching position in 1965. He was twenty years into his writing career and only his most recent novel, *God Bless You, Mr. Rosewater*, was still in print. Fewer than four years later, *Cat's Cradle* had sold over 150,000 copies and *Sirens of Titan* 200,000. Vonnegut's entrance onto the literary scene had been meteoric: *Slaughterhouse-Five* and *Breakfast of Champions* (1973) stayed on best-seller lists for months, and by the early1970s, Vonnegut had become a leading American novelist and a countercultural hero. Like Mark Twain a century before, Vonnegut became a noted speaker and celebrity, for he was a moralist who gave readers and listeners truth leavened with humor.

Over the next twenty years, Vonnegut wrote another seven novels, plays and screenplays, and a dozen collections of stories and talks, but none of his later works had the power of his first two bestsellers. Furthermore, and as Shields shows in some detail, the novelist had a troubled personal life that darkened his success. Jane had given up her own life plans to run the chaotic Vonnegut household, even as Kurt counted on her to be his editorial sounding board. His children loved him but were frightened of his mercurial personality, and friends witnessed his frequent outbursts. As Vonnegut's

(Michael Bailey)

Charles J. Shields has been a journalist and a reporter for public radio. He is the author of nonfiction books for young people, as well as the biography Mockingbird: A Portrait of Harper Lee *(2006).*

fame spread and he moved from struggling writer to literary celebrity, he entered a new world. He had extramarital affairs and was finally divorced from Jane after thirty-four years of marriage. He became lovers with Jill Krementz, a photographer and writer in New York City, and they married (later divorcing and remarrying) and adopted a young daughter, Lily. Vonnegut was clearly a difficult and complicated man, and Shields does not flinch from showing his lack of loyalty to agents and editors, his mistreatment of his first wife, and his rocky relationships with his children.

According to Shields's analysis, Vonnegut was always compensating, or trying to compensate, for a childhood of emotional and financial deprivation and an early life in the shadow of his favored brother. Even at his moments of greatest fame, he never escaped his insecurities and need for approval. The split between the private and public Vonnegut was greater than with most famous writers. The novelist who so appealed to the youth of the 1960s and 1970s was also conservative politically (see his famous short story "Harrison Bergeron"); his readers projected their liberal leanings onto his persona only to be disappointed to discover his more reactionary positions. Although he fought against censorship and the Vietnam War, his novels actually cry out not for revolution, but for an easier and simpler time, for an earlier America where tradition and free enterprise reigned, like the Indiana of his childhood.

As a novelist, however, Vonnegut helped to break down the boundaries of contemporary American fiction. *Slaughterhouse-Five* is an early example of metafiction, for on one level it is a novel about trying to write the novel, the struggling author appearing as a character in the first and last chapters. At its heart it is historical realism (except that Vonnegut never directly shows the bombing of Dresden) and an example of Vonnegut's peculiar brand of science fiction, as the central character Billy Pilgrim comes "unstuck in time" and moves easily from the war in 1944 to contemporary upstate New York (where he is a successful if apathetic optometrist), then to the planet Tralfamadore, where he lives with the voluptuous movie starlet Montana Wildhack in a zoo set up by Tralfamadorians to observe earthling behavior. At the same time, the novel's jerky, nonlinear structure is peppered with instances of Vonnegut's black humor. After the bombing of Dresden and in the moonscape of rubble and corpses, Billy is berated by an aged German couple for mistreating a horse, and his older comrade Edgar Derby is executed by their German guards for stealing a teapot. No American novel in the second half of the twentieth century so shattered realism's expectations and restrictions. *Breakfast of Champions* continued Vonnegut's success, with a novel set in the present in which Vonnegut is again a character and in which he rails against an America in which everyone acts like a robot.

Shields provides adequate analyses of novels like *Slaughterhouse-Five* and *Breakfast of Champions*, but he barely recognizes Vonnegut's overall importance to American fiction. Along with Richard Brautigan and Tom Robbins, Vonnegut revitalized contemporary fiction with his absurd, slapstick humor, and alongside novelists like E. L. Doctorow and Peter S. Beagle, he brought the popular subgenres of science fiction, the western, the fairy tale, and the detective novel into mainstream fiction, legitimizing their use in the name of postmodern anti-realism. These subgenres helped to break down the limitations of contemporary realist fiction. Shields downplays Vonnegut's development of black humor, calling it "comic-didactic" instead, but it is one of Vonnegut's distinctive traits and an element that he shared with writers like Terry Southern, William Kotzwinkle, and Hunter Thompson. Finally, Vonnegut joined novelists like Joseph Heller (*Catch 22*, 1961) and Ken Kesey (*One Flew Over the Cuckoo's Nest*, 1962) in producing ambitious fiction that took on the institutions of contemporary America, challenging the country to rethink its values.

A later critical biography will undoubtedly make up for the absences here and fill the gaps in the story. Shields had just started his interviews with the novelist when Vonnegut died from an accidental fall in 2007. Jill Krementz refused to talk with Shields after that, and he was denied access to Vonnegut's letters. While he has recorded hundreds of hours of interviews with other people from all stages of Vonnegut's life—and there are almost seventy pages of notes and bibliography to document the history—there is a hole where Krementz's voice should be. While Jane Vonnegut is portrayed as the saint who held Vonnegut's career and family together, Krementz comes across as a monster, a controlling woman who limited Vonnegut's access to friends and relations. She may have been terrible to him, but there is another story about their final years together that is not reported here.

David Peck

Review Sources

Los Angeles Times, November 13, 2011, p. E11.
The New York Times, November 20, 2011, p. C1.
Publishers Weekly 258, no. 31 (August 1, 2011): 34.
Seattle Times, November 20, 2011 (Web).

Apricot Jam
And Other Stories

Author: Aleksandr Solzhenitsyn (1918–2008)
First published: Individual short stories of the
collection, 1993–1998, in Russia
Translated from the Russian by Kenneth Lantz
and Stephan Solzhenitsyn
Publisher: Counterpoint (Berkeley, CA).
352 pp. $28.00
Type of work: Short fiction
Time: 1914–1994
Locale: Russia, East Prussia

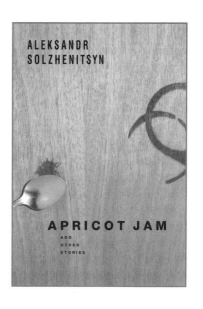

*In this posthumous collection, nine short sto-
ries expose Communist misrule in the Soviet
Union and the failures of post-Soviet Russia.*

Principal characters:

FEDYA, also known as Fyodor Ivanovich, a
young peasant
EGO, also known as Pavel Vasilyevich Ektov, an anti-Soviet rebel
ANATOLY PAVLOVICH VOZDVIZHENSKY, an engineering professor
NASTENKA, a member of the Communist youth organization
NASTENKA, a young teacher of literature
MAJOR BOYEV, an artillery officer in the waning days of World War II
YORKA ZHUKOV, a historical Soviet marshal
MITYA YEMTSOV, an idealistic factory manager
VALENTINA FILIPPOVNA, a young regional environmental official

The nine exquisite short stories collected in *Apricot Jam* represent a moving legacy of
Aleksandr Solzhenitsyn, one of the twentieth century's most significant Russian writers. Solzhenitsyn's groundbreaking 1962 novel, *Odin den' Ivana Denisovicha* (*One
Day in the Life of Ivan Denisovich*), powerfully exposed the horrors of Soviet leader
Joseph Stalin's gulag system of prison and forced labor camps for political dissidents,
and his further writings on similar topics led to his expulsion from the Soviet Union in
1974. His criticism of the inhumane aspects of Soviet Communism continues in many
of the stories in *Apricot Jam*.

Even though nearly all were written after Solzhenitsyn's return to democratic Russia in 1994, the first seven stories of *Apricot Jam* are set in the time of the Soviet
Union, ranging in period from the Communist coup to the end of World War II. The
last two stories depict in deliberately neutral language the pain of the transition from
the Soviet Union to post-Soviet Russia. A key, worrisome theme is the persistence of
Communist behavior patterns that continue to be followed by people in authority.

Aleksandr Solzhenitsyn was a Russian writer whose novel One Day in the Life of Ivan Denisovich *(1962) and three-volume work* The Gulag Archipelago *(1973–78) revealed the horrors of the politically motivated penal system of the Soviet Union. He was awarded the 1970 Nobel Prize in Literature.*

The title story, "Apricot Jam," brilliantly juxtaposes the fate of a victim of the Soviet regime with the life of a privileged writer in the early 1930s. The first part of the story is told in the form of a letter written by Fyodor Ivanovich, known as Fedya, and addressed to the Writer, a famous author of Soviet propaganda. In his letter, Fedya tells of how the Communists descended on his village and terrorized him and his family because they were kulaks, land-owning peasants considered by the Soviet government to be enemies of the poorer classes. Stalin unleashed a campaign of terror against the kulaks still living in their villages early in the 1930s; Solzhenitsyn personalizes this historical event through Fedya's letter.

Fedya's fondest memory from his untroubled past is of the apricot tree that grew in the garden of his family's home and the jam his mother made from its fruit. In an act symbolic of the brutality that Solzhenitsyn criticizes, the Communists chop down this apricot tree before sending Fedya and his family to labor camps. Fedya escapes deportation but is arrested by the secret service and later sent to a labor unit, where he experiences starvation, exhaustion, and illness. The story then shifts, becoming a third-person narrative set in the home of the Writer, who lives a life of privilege based on his favor with Stalin. Spreading fragrant apricot jam on his bread as he entertains guests, the Writer says that he received the letter from Fedya and considers its language a source of inspiration. Callously, he states that he will not reply to Fedya and will only use the writing style for himself.

This plot technique of juxtaposing two distinct but related narrative strands, which Solzhenitsyn called his "binary" system, occurs throughout *Apricot Jam*. The technique is related to the approach of dialectic criticism and philosophy, in which a thesis and its antithesis are juxtaposed and a synthesis is developed from the conflict. This final step is left by Solzhenitsyn to his readers. As the modern dialectical approach articulated by German philosopher Georg Wilhelm Friedrich Hegel was later modified and used by Karl Marx and his followers, Solzhenitsyn's use of his own term, binary storytelling, indicates his conscious attempt to distance his work from any Marxist tradition.

The other stories in *Apricot Jam* similarly feature Solzhenitsyn's binary technique and give personalized accounts of cruel events and actions, illustrating the many horrors of life in the early and Stalinist Soviet Union. "Ego" features a well-meaning, nonpolitical philanthropist named Pavel Vasilyevich Ektov who is swept up in the chaos of a rebellion against Communist rule. As the Communists oppress the peasants with never-ending food requisitions and many extrajudicial killings, Ektov joins a group of rebels and acquires the nickname Ego. He is successful at first but is betrayed, captured, and sent to Moscow's infamous Lubyanka Prison, a facility run by the Communist secret service, or Cheka. In the second part of the story, the Communists work to break his spirit. Solzhenitsyn's prose clearly evokes the psychological and physical terror meted out to Ego and his fellow political prisoners.

"The New Generation" is perhaps the most cheerful of the stories in *Apricot Jam*. After the Russian Revolution, engineering professor Anatoly Pavlovich Vozdvizhensky gives a passing grade to his academically hopeless worker-student Lyoshka Konoplyov, a tinsmith sent to the university by the new Communist authorities to prove the intelligence of the workers. When the professor is arrested and accused of sabotage in the second part of the story, his earlier act of kindness saves him from a terrible fate.

"Nastenka" tells the stories of two young Soviet women who share the same first name. The first Nastenka is an orphan raised by her grandfather, a Russian Orthodox priest, who joins the Communist youth organization, Komsomol, to avoid persecution. After she is raped by the chairman of a village soviet, she becomes sexually linked to a variety of cadres. The other Nastenka is an idealistic young woman who becomes a teacher of literature. However, she and her colleagues are consistently disturbed by the latest dictates from the government as to what literature should be taught and how it should be analyzed. While the Communist regime claims the body of one Nastenka, it claims the mind of the other.

The war story "Adlig Schwenkitten" tells of the sad fate of a Soviet artillery brigade toward the end of World War II. Drawing on his own experience as an artillery officer in the Red Army, Solzhenitsyn depicts the events that transpire as caused by a reckless disregard for security on the part of those in command. The story represents a kind of criticism of the Red Army that would have been almost impossible to publish in the Soviet Union. The same could be said for the social criticism of the story's companion piece, "Zhelyabuga Village," in which Solzhenitsyn showcases the silent wartime heroism of Russian villagers. The second part of the story shows that fifty-two years later, in democratic Russia, the courageous villagers have been forgotten and lead a poverty-stricken existence. Authorities continue to fail to support them, despite their valor during the war.

"Times of Crisis" is the fictionalized biography of the historical Soviet marshal Georgy Zhukov, the conqueror of Berlin. Called Yorka Zhukov in the story, Zhukov reflects as an old man on his life and his ill treatment by a jealous Stalin after the war. In order to get his autobiography published before his death, Zhukov compromises his material to honor the current Soviet leader, Leonid Brezhnev. In this story as in others, Solzhenitsyn uses facts and events from Soviet history to support his fictional writing; the historical Zhukov invented a flattering wartime meeting with young Brezhnev in the first edition of his autobiography.

The challenges related to the Soviet Union's transition to democratic Russia are the topic of the last two stories of *Apricot Jam*. In "Fracture Points," Mitya Yemtsov rises to become a decorated manager of a Soviet weapons factory. Determined to succeed,

Yemtsov ensures his factory's survival by beginning to manufacture consumer goods in the post-Soviet era. The second part of the story tells of the lawlessness gripping Russian society as organized crime begins to take root. A former student activist who has become a banker survives an assassination attempt, but the would-be assassin goes effectively unpunished. When the banker visits the elderly Yemtsov for advice, Yemtsov tells him to persist, just as he has done himself.

The last story, "No Matter What," was translated by Solzhenitsyn's son Stephan. In wartime, a straight-laced lieutenant discovers that some of his men have been stealing potatoes, yet when he reports this to his superior, he realizes that this man is abusing his food privileges himself. The second part of the story takes place in the post-Soviet era and concerns Valentina Filippovna, a regional environmental officer stationed in remote Siberia. During a visit by a minister's deputy, she realizes she is powerless to prevent environmental destruction fuelled by the greed of corrupt capitalists.

The nine stories of *Apricot Jam* serve as valuable reminders of the manifold horrors of life in the early decades of the Soviet Union. A master storyteller, Solzhenitsyn displays his clear eye for human behavior throughout the work, illuminating the things people are willing to do to save themselves and the many ways in which a cynical and callous leadership can cause suffering. As the final two stories illustrate, this ruthless exertion of power endures despite the changed system of government. As old Mitya Yemtsov tells the young banker in "Fracture Points," there remains only a faint light of hope for a better future. Yet, as Solzhenitsyn notes, this faint light persists. Despite the horrors and hardships chronicled in *Apricot Jam*, Solzhenitsyn's own hope for the future of his beloved Russia persists as well.

R. C. Lutz

Review Sources

Booklist 107, no. 22 (August 1, 2011): 18.
National Review 63, no. 17 (September 19, 2011): 47–49.
New Statesman 140, no. 5077 (October 31, 2011): 48–50.
Times Literary Supplement, no. 5666 (November 4, 2011): 19–20.

Art and Madness
A Memoir of Lust without Reason

Author: Anne Roiphe (b. 1935)
Foreword by Katie Roiphe
Publisher: Nan A. Talese (New York). 240 pp.
$24.95
Type of work: Memoir
Time: 1951–1966
Locale: New York City

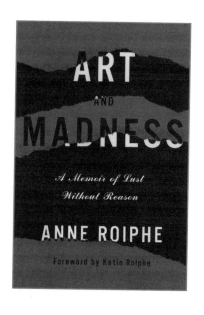

Roiphe's memoir discusses her search for love and identity in the sexist world of writers and artists in New York City during the late 1950s and early 1960s.

Principal personages:

ANNE ROIPHE, a young woman who lives through the two turbulent decades after World War II to become a successful writer

JACK RICHARDSON, Roiphe's first husband, an alcoholic playwright whom she supports

THE CHILD, Roiphe and Richardson's daughter Emily, who goes unnamed in the text

KATIE, Roiphe's daughter with her second husband

GEORGE PLIMPTON, the editor and cofounder of the prestigious literary journal *Paris Review*

HAROLD "DOC" HUMES, cofounder of the *Paris Review*

NORMAN MAILER, PETER MATTHIESSEN, LARRY RIVERS, SALVADOR DALI, and dozens of other writers and artists who cross paths with Roiphe in New York City

Anne Roiphe lived at the center of one of the most exciting places and periods in American cultural history: postwar Manhattan. Novelists like Bernard Malamud and J. D. Salinger were changing the landscape of American fiction, playwrights like Jack Gelber and Edward Albee were transforming theater, and artists like Jackson Pollack and Roy Lichtenstein were shattering the boundaries of the art world. It was a postwar artistic milieu marked by serial infidelity, rampant alcoholism, and premature death (poet Dylan Thomas, dead at forty-nine, in a Manhattan bar in 1953; painter Jackson Pollack at forty-four, in a car crash on a Long Island highway in 1956; poet Frank O'Hara at forty, run over by a dune buggy on a Fire Island beach in 1966—all alcohol-related deaths). To be part of this world in one's twenties was as exciting as life could get. To be married to an often-absent alcoholic playwright and care for a baby alone was a nightmare, however, one that Anne Roiphe's memoir captures powerfully. She describes this artistic scene from the inside, placing little blame on the social and cultural forces that took advantage of her sex, her youth, and her dreams; she had made the bed she wanted, and she chose to lie in it.

Art and Madness: A Memoir of Lust without Reason is Roiphe's story of the roughly ten years (1956–66) during which she married Jack Richardson, had a daughter, and tried to live as a single mother in a time when women received little support or encouragement to do so. The memoir comprises over fifty separate incidents or stories, ranging in length from one paragraph to twenty pages, all introduced by the year in which they took place and arranged in seemingly random order. The structure is slightly disorienting until the reader discovers that this choppy, staccato rhythm perfectly captures the jumpy, hallucinatory postwar world that the memoirist inhabited. The United States its citizens knew before World War II was gone, replaced by a culture in which the old values held little attraction, especially for the young artists and writers of New York's art scene. It was a world, as Roiphe writes, split between engineers and artists, between the conformist commuter families in the suburbs and the exhilarating parties of writers and artists in Manhattan, and she had picked sides.

Anne Roiphe grew up in a Manhattan family of privilege and went to Smith College in Northampton, Massachusetts, for a year (1953) before transferring to Sarah Lawrence College in Bronxville, New York. She spent time in Manhattan bars, where she met writers and artists, including playwright Jack Richardson. She and Richardson were married in Paris, then moved to Munich, Germany, where he had a year-long grant. They eventually returned to the Manhattan apartment that Roiphe's mother paid for. Roiphe got a secretarial job, but her husband spent most of their money on liquor and other women, even after his wife gave birth to their daughter.

There is pain in the pages describing the victimization of Roiphe and other wives and girlfriends at the time; there is an even worse betrayal of the children, whose fathers ignored and abandoned them, leaving them for other women and other families. The men here—Jack Richardson, Doc Humes, and many more—are portrayed as cruel, selfish, and unthinking. In one incident that took place after Roiphe and Richardson separated, she and her daughter ran into him on a Long Island beach, where he was playfully carrying the son of another woman on his shoulders. Another time, Humes missed his daughter's performance in *The Nutcracker* and promised her a horse in repayment—a cruel lie in horseless Manhattan. Later, Roiphe and the man who would become her second husband went to a summer party and found a baby, the child of painter Larry Rivers, screaming in a locked car. The neglect described in these scenes is senseless.

In her memoir, Roiphe realizes that she is a masochist and that she was sacrificing herself for men who were not worth it. Her self-delusions were fueled by the romantic myths of the period that she kept repeating to herself like broken mantras: that art is long and life is short, that alcohol is the fuel of genius, that it is better to sacrifice oneself for art and the artist than to die of thirst in the cultural deserts of suburban Westchester County. In the end, it was her daughter who saved her, making Roiphe realize that she had become a character in a story by John O'Hara or John Cheever and that she needed to find another life. In the final section of her book, Roiphe describes how she ultimately found the man with whom she would share happiness for forty years. Years after the events of *Art and Madness*, Roiphe met the ex-wife of writer Terry Southern and asked her if she regretted their life in the 1950s and 1960s. While Carol Southern declared that she would do it all again, Roiphe knew that she never would, and her memoir is a gripping testament to why not.

The 1950s, as she accurately paints the period, was a decade of restrictions and limitations. She could sneak into Jimmy Ryan's jazz club in Manhattan with a date as a seventeen-year-old, while her bright classmates at Smith spent their time knitting socks for their Ivy League boyfriends during lectures. The McCarthyism rampant in the period seemed aimed more often at the bohemian artists than at political radicals. Smith alumnae (including conservative columnist William F. Buckley's two sisters) started a campaign to withhold contributions to the college until two art professors were fired because they were Communists (and, as Roiphe imagines, likely gay). Roiphe's first job after college was at a New York public-relations firm hawking fallout shelters that would protect few in case of nuclear attack. It was a decade of fear— fear of Communists, of homosexuals, of atomic bombs, and of the unknown.

(© Mary Ellen Mark)

Anne Roiphe has written twenty books, both novels (including Up the Sandbox, *1970) and works of nonfiction (including* Fruitful: A Memoir of Modern Motherhood, *1996, a National Book Award finalist), as well as articles for the* New York Times, Vogue, *and* Elle. *She lives in New York City.*

The decade that followed, the 1960s, was in part a reaction to these fears. The promiscuity of the period—the orgies and attempts at open marriage Roiphe writes about—was the sexual dimension of a cultural revolution that revealed itself through the arts in happenings, stage nudity, and wildly experimental theater and film. It was a period, as Roiphe's title denotes, of lust and madness, two terms that characterize both art and love. The lust was sexual, certainly, as Roiphe's many affairs demonstrate, but it also refers to the artists' desire to live life to the fullest, to see and feel and experience everything. Madness has likewise been associated with art at least since the romantic poets, in the notion that artistic genius is somehow close to mental illness. Certainly a number of writers and artists who are mentioned in Roiphe's memoir experienced bouts of instability. Jack Richardson often acted physically as if he were an autistic child; Arthur Penn, who directed Jack's first play to negative reviews, had a house near the psychiatric hospital where playwrights Tennessee Williams and William Inge were both residents. At the same time, Roiphe tended to judge her own relationships in terms of their intensity, by their closeness to insanity. If love did not have a mad, dangerous, or exciting element, she rejected it. Both love and art in the late 1950s and early 1960s were thus defined by the same unhealthy qualities.

It was those toxic qualities that drove Roiphe to sacrifice herself for the writers and artists she gave herself to, certainly Jack Richardson, but also Doc Humes, George

Plimpton, novelist William Styron, and filmmaker Frank Perry. As Katie Roiphe, the daughter of Anne and her second husband, writes in her lovely foreword to this memoir, *Art and Madness* "tells the story of the girls who suffered for art, for the grandeur and silliness and exhilaration of the dream." Men abused Anne Roiphe, but the age ignored or even condoned the abuse. As a young woman, she had few female models; she had never known a woman doctor or a woman lawyer, she writes, and never knew any female playwrights, producers, directors, or agents. She had always wanted to be a writer, but was afraid that as a woman she had no subject. One of Roiphe's professors at Sarah Lawrence, poet Horace Gregory, taught his students that the personal is not a fit subject for art, and that the thoughts of women are hardly the stuff of literature. The feminist literary revolution that would so powerfully disprove these lies was just beginning at the time—Sylva Plath's *The Bell Jar* and Betty Friedan's *The Feminine Mystique* would both be published in 1963—and Anne Roiphe would become a vital part of it.

Roiphe's ability to capture so poignantly the chaos and absurdity of the period is proof of what a fine writer she has become. She recalls herself half a century ago, with her breathless energy and innocence, while also showing the limitations of her outlook at that time and pointing to the clues of what was wrong with her life and her dreams. There is, in short, a kind of double vision to *Art and Madness* that reveals the period in all its irrational movement and gives depth to the memoir. Roiphe knew that she wanted to be a writer, for example, and yet she sacrificed herself to male writers again and again, a conflict that creates a tension in herself and in her story. One illustration accompanies the text, a photograph taken of Roiphe in her twenties. It conveys not only her beauty but also her innocence and fragility. *Art and Madness* is a verbal portrait of beauty and sorrow and affirmation.

David Peck

Review Sources

Booklist 107, no. 9/10 (January 1, 2011): 36.
Kirkus Reviews 78, no. 22 (November 15, 2010): 20.
Library Journal 135, no. 20 (December 1, 2010): 117.
The New York Times Book Review, March 20, 2011, p. 15.
Publishers Weekly 258, no. 2 (January 10, 2010): 42–43.

The Art of Asking Your Boss for a Raise

Author: Georges Perec (1936–1982)
First published: *L'art et la manière d'aborder son chef de service pour lui demander une augmentation*, 2008, in France
Translated from the French by David Bellos
Introduction by David Bellos
Publisher: Verso Books (New York). 80 pp. $16.95
Type of work: Novella
Time: 1960s
Locale: A large corporation in Paris, France

Appearing for the first time in English translation, this short novella adapts the methodology of a computer program in an experimental text. With only occasional punctuation and capitalization, Perec describes the mind of an office employee summoning the courage to ask his boss for a raise.

Principal characters:

OFFICE EMPLOYEE, employee of large corporation who is attempting to ask his boss for a raise, addressed as "you"
MR. XAVIER (MR. X), head of office employee's department
MS. WYE, office employee's colleague

The Art of Asking Your Boss for a Raise follows the decision-making process of an office employee as he considers asking his boss for a raise. The text was the result of an invitation, as translator David Bellos recounts in his introduction, from Jacques Perriaud of the Computing Service of the Humanities Research Center in Paris in the 1960s. In the interest of applying relatively new computer technology to the creative arts, Perriaud challenged Perec to "use a computer's basic mode of operation as a writing device" by providing Perec with a computer-programming flowchart—the same one that is printed on the inside of the front and back covers of the 2011 edition of the novel, where it outlines the steps that an employee of a large corporation might take to solicit a raise—and asking him to turn it into literature. The text of *The Art of Asking Your Boss for a Raise* is the result: a literary extrapolation of the process that a computer program would follow to make a simple decision. Appropriately enough, the text first appeared in a journal about programmed learning. It was then adapted into a popular radio play and made into one of the final chapters of Perec's most famous novel, *La Vie mode d'emploi* (1978; *Life: A User's Manual*, 1987), before being published posthumously as the novella *L'art et la manière d'aborder son chef de service pour lui demander une augmentation* (2008).

In 1968, when he was writing *The Art of Asking Your Boss for a Raise*, Perec was not yet well known but had already begun composing experimental texts according to his own set of constraints. He was a member of Oulipo, a group of writers and mathematicians founded in 1960 by French writers Raymond Queneau and François Le Lionnais. Short for *Ouvroir de littérature potentielle*, the Workshop for Potential Literature, Oulipo is an organization dedicated to devising new structures and patterns for creating literature. Oulipians pursue constrained writing techniques, in which the writer composes a text while following a given rule or set of rules that limits what can and cannot be written. They believe that these constraints provide inspiration and stimulate the writer's imagination and view the resulting texts as embodiments of the constraints themselves.

Many of Perec's works stand today as extraordinary and frequently cited examples of Oulipian literature. His three-hundred-page novel *La disparition* (1969) is a lipogram, written entirely without the use of the letter *e*. One can only imagine the difficulty of translating such a work into English using the same constraint, and yet one of Perec's translators, Gilbert Adair, managed to do so, producing the novel *A Void* (1994). Perec's most famous work, *Life: A User's Manual*, draws from many of his earlier works, including *The Art of Asking Your Boss for a Raise*. In *Life*, Perec presents a complex series of interwoven stories about the inhabitants of a Parisian apartment building. Among the several underlying structures of the novel is the movement of a knight across a chessboard. The apartment building is a large, living chessboard, and the story follows the movement of the knight from room to room, through stairwells and hallways, telling the stories of the inhabitants. By using Perriaud's flowchart as inspiration, *The Art of Asking Your Boss for a Raise* also clearly follows Oulipian principles.

Perec wanted his writing to be fun and amusing, not just experimental. In keeping with his playful intent, *The Art of Asking Your Boss for a Raise* is a literary game in which the main player is an unnamed office employee who is merely addressed as "you" throughout the text. His first decision is to approach the boss to ask him for a raise. The boss, named "mr x," is rarely in his office to receive him, so the office employee repeatedly kills time by exchanging insubstantial chatter with a colleague named "ms wye." These character names suggest the *x* and *y* variables of a mathematical equation, while also pointing toward the cold anonymity of the corporate world.

The use of repetition allows the short and breathless text to simulate the uninterrupted flow of data being processed in real time. Perec weaves into the text a number of refrains that might remind any corporate employee of the cyclic nature of office work. On nearly every second page, the office employee is again wandering around the office area while waiting to see the boss:

> We advise you that in order to cope with the boredom that your monotonous pacing could easily prompt you should go have a chinwag with your colleague ms wye provided of course not only that ms wye is at her desk if she is not you would not have much of a choice save to circumperambulate the various departments which taken together constitute the whole or part of the organization of which you are an employee unless of course you were to go back to your own desk to wait for more auspicious times.

This perpetual movement—to and from the boss's office, to the office of Ms. Wye, back to his own desk, and out to feed the parking meter—is represented in the text by a serious dearth of punctuation and uppercase letters, resulting in what looks like one breathless sentence. The harried progression from thought to thought with only the rare pause blurs the time frame of the novella; it could be days, months, or even years before the employee even finds the chance to ask Mr. X for a raise, much less receives one. At times, reading the text feels just as exhausting as the employee's interminable quest.

One might expect such a text to be entirely unreadable, and at first approach it does appear that way. However, Perec manages, in the labyrinth of the computer algorithm, to abide by one of the novella's refrains: "our noble desire to keep things simple—for we must do our best to keep things simple." Despite the fact that without punctuation, there is no place for the reader to pause, the foundational logic of

Oulipo member Georges Perec is widely recognized as a master of experimental writing. His numerous works include novels, poetry, drama, radio plays, and short stories, many of which were composed using constrained writing techniques. He won the Prix Renaudot in 1965 for his first novel, Les Choses: Une histoire des années soixante *(1965;* Things: A Story of the Sixties, *1999), and the 1978 Prix Médicis for his most famous novel,* La Vie mode d'emploi *(1978;* Life: A User's Manual, *1987).*

the decision-making operation keeps the reader grounded in a process that is simple to follow. And, after all, at eighty pages, it does not take too much time to read.

This edition of *The Art of Asking Your Boss for a Raise* is a translation of the text from the original French. Fortunately, Perec has a loyal translator: Princeton University professor David Bellos, who, in addition to having translated six of Perec's books, is also the author of his biography, *Georges Perec: A Life in Words* (1993). In order to capture some of the idiosyncrasies of Perec's language, Bellos makes what turn out to be some disputable choices in the English text. For example, the name of the office employee's colleague in the French edition is Mlle. Yolande, which becomes Ms. Wye in the English manuscript. In another instance, Bellos translates "de deux choses l'une" to "it's one or t'other," a phrase with far less musicality in English. One detail mentioned in criticism of the translation is Bellos's choice of the word *circumperambulate* to describe the employee's repeated walks about the office; this word cannot be found in any English dictionary, and the translator claims to have learned it in his boyhood Latin class. Ultimately, however, Bellos preserves in translation the playfulness of Perec's original narrative.

The great success of Perec's text is that it transcends the sterility of program-planning methods, transforming the mundane inner workings of a computer into fresh, readable comedy. With characteristic joviality, Perec "give[s] a touch of human warmth to our schematic demonstration." In each attempt to meet with his boss, the office employee encounters an obstacle, and it is in these encounters that Perec injects imaginative life into corporate tedium. Mr. X turns out to have a number of daughters who may or may not have measles; he may or may not have swallowed a fishbone or eaten bad eggs at lunch; the employee's colleague Ms. Wye is alternately in a good or bad mood. As in the rest of his abundant work, Perec manages to bring a friendly humanity to even the dullest circumstances. In *The Art of Asking Your Boss for a Raise*, the reader is led through boredom and fun, from obsession to repose, guided by the ebb and flow of the office employee's frustrations.

The Art of Asking Your Boss for a Raise has immense relevance for twenty-first-century society. Written in 1968, it seems prescient for its time in its vision of a culture in which advanced technology is not only commonplace but fully integrated into daily life. While technology has a widely predicted potential for alienation, it is also commonly used as a tool for building communities and movements—in short, for drawing people closer together. Perec's life's project, like the work of his fellow Oulipians, was to join seemingly incompatible mathematics with literature to reveal the core humanity of technology. According to Oulipian principles, a text written according to a constraint describes the constraint; if *The Art of Asking Your Boss for a Raise* is a description of computer programming, then computer programming is stultifying and amusing, sometimes confusing and often monotonous, but always fundamentally alive.

Amira Hanafi

Review Sources

Barnes & Noble Review, March 24, 2011 (Web) .
The Guardian, June 11, 2011, p. 11.
Harvard Crimson, March 29, 2011 (Web).
Slant Magazine, March 17, 2011 (Web).
Words without Borders, May 15, 2011 (Web).

The Art of Fielding

Author: Chad Harbach (b. 1976)
Publisher: Little, Brown (New York). 528 pp.
$25.99
Type of work: Novel
Time: The present
Locale: Wisconsin and Georgia

A wise and winning debut novel about how baseball players at a small Wisconsin college learn to make life choices.

Principal characters:

HENRY "SKRIMMER" SKRIMSHANDER, star shortstop for the Westish College Harpooners

MIKE SCHWARTZ, Henry's mentor, catcher and captain of the Harpooners

OWEN "THE BUDDHA" DUNNE, Henry's gay roommate, right fielder for the Harpooners

GUERT AFFENLIGHT, a Melville scholar, the president of Westish College

PELLA AFFENLIGHT, Guert's rebellious daughter

DAVID, an architect, Pella's estranged husband

RON COX, the Westish College baseball coach

BRUCE GIBBS, chairperson of Westish College's board of trustees

ADAM STARBLIND, the ace pitcher for the Harpooners

SOPHIE SKRIMSHANDER, Henry's sister

IZZY AVILA, Henry's shortstop protégé

LEV TENNANT, cocaptain of the Harpooners and starting shortstop

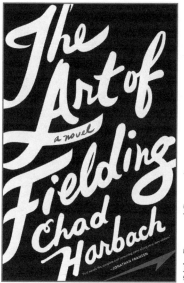

(Little, Brown and Company)

A near-perfect balance of individual and collective performance and the only major team sport not governed by the clock, baseball has been a special muse for many notable novels, including Bernard Malamud's *The Natural* (1952), Mark Harris's *Bang the Drum Slowly* (1956), Robert Coover's *The Universal Baseball Association, Inc., J. Henry Waugh, Prop.* (1968), and W. A. Kinsella's *Shoeless Joe* (1982). *The Art of Fielding* is a potent addition to that roster. Ten years in the making, Chad Harbach's debut novel attracted widespread attention before it even appeared in print. After publication, it became the subject of an October 2011 *Vanity Fair* article, "How a Book Is Born," that was expanded into an e-book by the same title. Penned by Harbach's *n+1* cofounder, Keith Gessen, *How a Book Is Born* uses *The Art of Fielding* to examine how books are created, acquired, edited, packaged, and promoted in the United States today. Gessen describes the long gestation of a novel that became the subject of a bidding war between major publishing houses. The winning bid from Little, Brown

(Little, Brown and Company)

Chad Harbach graduated from Harvard University and received his MFA from the University of Virginia. He is a cofounder and coeditor of the magazine n+1. The Art of Fielding, *which he worked on for ten years, is his first novel.*

was reportedly as high as $665,000—a hefty sum for a first novel, but one that was apparently justified when Harbach's book went on to enjoy one of the year's most remarkable critical and commercial successes.

Even readers who are bored by baseball can respond to an endearing novel by an author who recognizes the sport's affinities with literature itself. One character's reflections on his passion for baseball could easily apply to fiction in general and *The Art of Fielding* in particular: "You loved it because you considered it an art: an apparently pointless affair, undertaken by people with a special aptitude, which sidestepped attempts to paraphrase its value yet somehow seemed to communicate something true or even crucial about The Human Condition. The Human Condition being, basically, that we're alive and have access to beauty, can even erratically create it, but will someday be dead and will not." These are the sentiments of Mike Schwartz, the burly catcher and captain of the baseball team at Westish College, a small liberal arts college located in Wisconsin on the western shore of Lake Michigan.

Harbach establishes historic ties between the fictional Westish College and author Herman Melville that help him explore and revel in the correspondence between literature and baseball. In 1969, decades before the novel's present, Westish undergrad Guert Affenlight came across the long-lost text of a speech that Melville gave at the college in 1880. The discovery created a stir among Americanist scholars and inspired Affenlight to devote himself to Melville, seafaring, and literature. Affenlight went on to become an eminent professor of English at Harvard University until Westish lured him back to be its president. The college he returned to had since rebranded itself by exploiting its tenuous connection to the author of *Moby-Dick* (1851), erecting a statue of Melville in the middle of campus and changing the name of its sports teams from the Sugar Maples to the Harpooners. Similarly, a local bar is called Bartleby's in homage to the title character of Melville's short story *Bartleby, the Scrivener: A Story of Wall Street* (1853).

In such a setting, Harbach does not have to reach far to hint at parallels between Mike's maniacal quest for athletic perfection and Ahab's obsession with vanquishing the great white whale. While playing in a summer league, Mike gazes in awe at a scrawny seventeen-year-old shortstop named Henry Skrimshander: "The kid glided in front of the first grounder, accepted the ball into his glove with a lazy grace, pivoted, and threw to first. Though his motion was languid, the ball seemed to explode off his fingertips, to gather speed as it crossed the diamond. It smacked the pocket of the first baseman's glove with the sound of a gun going off. . . . He didn't seem to move faster than any other decent shortstop would, and yet he arrived instantly, impeccably, as if he had some foreknowledge of where the ball was headed. Or as if time slowed down for him alone." Skrimshander's hitting is adequate, but what is most notable about Henry is his consummate skill at fielding—a crucial, yet often slighted, part of the game. Convinced that Henry possesses "some single transcendent talent, some unique brilliance that the world would consent to call genius," Mike recruits him for Westish College. Though Henry, the son of the foreman at a metalworking shop, has no plans to attend college or to travel very far beyond his home town of Lankton, South Dakota, he follows Mike to Westish. Mike is determined to make Henry into the star of the Westish College Harpooners, and by demanding total submission to his rigorous regimen of daily workouts, he soon transforms his young recruit into a slugger and the starting shortstop for the team.

In its 104 years of competing in baseball, Westish College has never won a title, but Harbach follows the Harpooners throughout the season of Mike's senior year as they register victory after victory on their way to the national championship competition in Atlanta. They are sustained and inspired by Henry's flawless fielding. As he approaches the record for consecutive errorless games set by the storied shortstop Aparicio Rodriguez, Henry attracts the avid attention of major league agents and scouts. It is assumed by everyone, including Henry, that at the end of the season, he will be offered an enormous bonus and salary to leave college and turn pro. But during the game in which he is set to break the hallowed record, Henry throws a ball wildly over the head of his first baseman. It sails into the dugout, hitting his teammate and roommate, Owen Dunne, in the head and causing him to be hospitalized.

Henry becomes unable to execute the simplest infield throws. A victim of "Prufrockian paralysis. . . . a profound failure of confidence in the significance of individual action," the best shortstop in college baseball succumbs to "Steve Blass Disease," a mysterious condition named for an outstanding pitcher for the Pittsburgh Pirates who in 1973 suddenly lost the ability to throw strikes. Henry has thrown himself entirely into the task of becoming the consummate baseball player, but now finds himself bereft of purpose.

Harbach deftly interweaves the main story of Henry's breakdown with several subplots that offer piquant observations about life at a small, obscure college and the customs of its athletes. One such subplot is the May-December romance between Westish president Affenlight and Henry's roommate, Owen. A gifted young scholar who is proud of being both black and gay, Owen is nicknamed "the Buddha" for the serenity he projects amid the tumult of campus life. When the student delegation that he leads meets with the president to demand improvements in the college's environmental policies, Affenlight finds that he is smitten with a man for the first time in his life. Though sexual relationships between faculty and students are taboo, Affenlight conducts risky trysts with Owen in his presidential office. Meanwhile, Pella, Affenlight's estranged daughter, suddenly reappears. Pella dropped out of high school to run off with an older, married architect; now, after four years with David, she walks out on him and shows up at Westish, determined to show up her father and make something of herself. In the process, she becomes involved with Mike Schwartz.

The Art of Fielding is the title both of Harbach's novel and, within that novel, of a book by fictional baseball legend Aparicio Rodriguez. Treasured by Henry as his vade mecum, a scriptural authority that he has virtually memorized and keeps by his side to read and reread, Rodriguez's book is written as a series of numbered apothegms, brief Zen-like sayings. "*To field a ground ball must be considered a generous act and an act of comprehension,*" states number 59. "*One moves not against the ball but with it.*" Elsewhere, in maxim number 213, Rodriguez declares that "*Death is the sanction of all that the athlete does.*" Such philosophical reflections make it clear that the art of fielding is a subset of the art of living—and dying. Each character in Harbach's novel is tested against the wisdom of Rodriguez, the consummate fielder. Henry's eventual realization that "Maybe it wasn't even baseball that he loved but only this idea of perfection, a perfectly simple life in which every move had meaning, and baseball was just the medium through which he could make that happen" is also clearly a premise behind Harbach's literary effort. It justifies the use of baseball as the language of his novel. However, *The Art of Fielding* is not merely a baseball novel, and accounts of actual innings on the field are sparse. It is also a campus novel, in which the autonomous community of Westish College serves as both setting and character. And it is, above all, a coming-of-age novel, in which Henry, Mike, Owen, Pella, and even Affenlight learn valuable lessons about who they are and who they want to be.

For each of the characters, the Westish campus is a comfortable cocoon, a refuge from the terrors of the outside world, and each must learn to negotiate the balance between individual freedom and the alma mater that nurtures them all. The same delicate balance between player and team is necessary for success in baseball. A gentle meditation on the nature and price of success, *The Art of Fielding* asks whether the best is enemy of the good, whether monomaniacal pursuit of perfection is best scored as an error.

Steven G. Kellman

Review Sources

The Boston Globe, September 4, 2011, p. C7.
Minneapolis Star Tribune, September 14, 2011, p. E4.
Newsday, September 11, 2011, p. C24.
The New York Times, September 6, 2011, p. C1.
The New York Times Book Review, September 11, 2011, p. 16.
Pittsburgh Post-Gazette, September 18, 2011, p. F5.
San Francisco Chronicle, September 11, 2011, p. FE-1.
Toronto Star, October 9, 2011, p. IN6.
The Wall Street Journal, September 6, 2011, p. A19.
The Washington Post, September 6, 2011, p. C4.

An Atlas of Impossible Longing

Author: Anuradha Roy (b. 1967)
Publisher: Simon & Schuster (New York).
   319 pp. $14.00
Type of work: Novel
Time: 1907–1956
Locale: Bengal, India

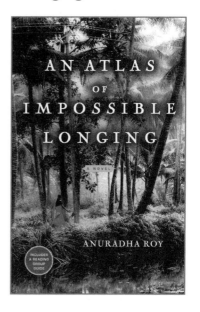

In this debut novel, three generations of a Bengali family struggle with personal, romantic, and economic challenges as India gains independence from Great Britain.

Principal characters:
MUKUNDA, an orphan boy adopted into the
   family of Amulya, his father's employer
BAKUL, daughter of Nirmal and Shanti
AMULYA, a patriarch; owner of an herbal potions and pills factory
KANANBALA, Amulya's wife
NIRMAL, second son of Amulya and Kananbala; father of Bakul
KAMAL, oldest son of Amulya and Kananbala
MANJULA, Kamal's wife
MEERA, a young widow who is related to Nirmal
LARISSA BARNUM, an English woman whose abusive husband, Digby, is murdered
SHANTI, Nirmal's wife; dies giving birth to Bakul
SULEIMAN CHACHA, a history teacher
FARHANA, also called Chachi, Suleiman Chacha's wife
AANGTI BABU, a real-estate developer
BARABABU, Mukunda's father-in-law

An Atlas of Impossible Longing takes its readers on an entrancing journey centered in northeastern India. There, Anuradha Roy's impressive debut novel follows the fate of an upper-middle-class Bengali family who faces the conflict between tradition and modernity. This conflict affects three generations of family members and spans the first half of the twentieth century.

Roy's novel was a great success upon its initial 2008 publication in the United Kingdom, and the 2011 American edition is poised to win an equally enthusiastic readership in the United States. Roy's novel fulfills its promise of a family romance told against the backdrop of exciting historical times, a promise realized through characters who struggle with one another against a richly rendered local environment that defines how the characters view themselves and what actions they allow themselves to take.

Critics have praised Roy's use of vivid sensory descriptions in her narrative. She has "a true gift for transporting the reader right into the heat, smells, and sights of India," writes *Library Journal* reviewer Lisa Rohrbaugh. The following passage is a vibrant description of the city of Calcutta, as observed by the novel's protagonist, Mukunda:

> I cooked some daal and rice, and having eaten it, sat alone on the terrace feeling the city throb below me while I looked up at the stars from my little oasis, drinking rum, feeling the familiar languor spread by degrees to my fingertips. If I went to the parapet of the terrace I could see the trams moving like lit caterpillars, pinging the wires above, and the squares of yellow lamplight in the houses around me.

Roy also helps situate the reader firmly in the novel's setting by including Bengali words for everyday items such as food or clothes, all of which are translated in a glossary at the book's end.

The novel begins at a festival of the tribal people who live in the forests around the rural Bengali city of Songarh. One of the guests of honor is a man named Amulya. Originally from the big city of Calcutta (also spelled Kolkata in contemporary usage), Amulya moved his family to Songarh in 1907 to open a factory manufacturing traditional Indian pharmaceuticals. At the festival, a young tribal woman offers Amulya a passion flower she has worn in her hair. Amulya accepts it, deeply moved. Returning home, he makes a show of identifying the flower with a botanical book in front of his wife, Kananbala, who becomes upset with him. Here, Roy depicts a traditional relationship, but with a modern sensitivity for the woman's point of view.

Amulya's encounter with the tribal woman influences him to perform an act of kindness that will have consequences for his family for generations to come. One of his employees has impregnated a tribal woman, who then gives birth to a son. However, there is no possibility for this relationship to flourish, so Amulya places the baby boy in an orphanage and sponsors his care.

By 1927, Amulya's pharmaceutical factory is prospering. Roy deftly characterizes the family members. Amulya is the aloof, ascetic, somewhat sentimental patriarch who is used to having things go his way. His first son, Kamal, is being groomed to take over his business, but Kamal's wife, Manjula, is infertile. Almost as in a fairy tale, it is the younger son, Nirmal, who is drawn most sympathetically. He is the pride of his mother, a young, handsome teacher who becomes an archaeologist. Where Kamal, born in the nineteenth century, represents business and acceptance of tradition, Nirmal is an idealist, a child of the young twentieth century. Roy portrays Kamal and other traditionalist characters as heartless and jealous, especially when compared to idealists like Nirmal.

Upon a visit of family relations, a suitable marriage for Nirmal is proposed. Shanti's mother has died, leaving her the only child of her father, a retired lawyer. Once the newlyweds arrive in the family home at Songarh, Kananbala's mental illness strikes and she suddenly obtains a fool's freedom. She surprises the household by insulting Shanti and Amulya; the next second, she reverts to her usual self. Stunned, the patriarch confines Kananbala to her room. This confinement touches on the novel's theme of home as both a sanctuary and a source of pain, a place of protection and punishment.

Kananbala's escape into temporary insanity drives a subsequent plot twist. From the confinement of her room, Kananbala witnesses the murder of Digby Barnum. Perhaps somewhat stereotypically, the British characters in Roy's novel are portrayed in a negative light. Digby Barnum is a wife-beater who is killed when he confronts his wife, Larissa, with her lover; the novel leaves open the question of whether the murderer is Larissa or her lover. The police inquiry leads nowhere, as Kananbala covers up for Larissa, exonerating her.

Tragedy strikes in 1929 when Shanti goes back to her father's palatial home by the river to give birth to her child. Ignoring all flood warnings, her father refuses to leave his home. When Shanti gives birth to her daughter, Bakul, no doctor can reach the flood-insulated home, and Shanti dies in childbirth. After taking home his infant daughter, Nirmal also leaves. Amulya dies of a heart attack. Once again, Roy shows that her characters' homes offer a refuge that is often illusory.

(MacLehose Press)

Anuradha Roy won the 2004 Outlook-Picador Non-Fiction Contest for her work as a journalist. Her first novel, An Atlas of Impossible Longing *(2008), has been translated into thirteen languages and was shortlisted for the Crossword Prize. Her second novel,* The Folded Earth, *was published in 2011.*

The second part of *An Atlas of Impossible Longing* opens eleven years later, in 1940. Bakul has grown into a mischievous eleven-year-old girl. She is good friends with Mukunda, the boy born of a tribal woman. After Amulya died, Nirmal took the boy from the orphanage into his own family home, where Mukunda has grown up on the margins of the family household as a member of indeterminate status. At age thirteen, he is the trusted friend of Bakul.

Roy develops a second plot line concerning Bakul's father, Nirmal. After over a decade of working at remote archeological digs and barely coming home, he is in charge of digging at Songarh's old fort. His sudden reappearance startles Bakul, and she reacts with teenage antagonism toward her father. At the same time, there is tender affection budding between Nirmal and Meera, a young widow in her mid-twenties. Nirmal and Meera are distant relatives. Six or seven years earlier, he asked her to live with him to look after Bakul.

Hostility on the part of Kamal and Manjula soon interferes, driven by class differences and traditionalism. First, Kamal begins to sexually harass Meera to show that she has lost respect in his eyes; in the traditional Bengali view, a widow was expected to throw herself on her husband's funeral pyre in an act of suttee, a practice outlawed by the British in 1829. That she is interested in Nirmal, a man who is not her late husband, is anathema to Kamal, even though—or perhaps especially since—Nirmal is his brother. To avoid shame and harassment, Meera leaves the household and returns to her own family. Kamal and Manjula then insist that Bakul and Mukunda must be separated because they have reached their teens. Reluctantly, Nirmal takes Mukunda away to a boarding school in Calcutta. At the end of the novel's second part, traditional forces have prevailed.

The third and final part of *An Atlas of Impossible Longing* is told from the perspective of Mukunda once he has graduated from school in Calcutta in 1945. As an outsider still hurting from being sent away, Mukunda cuts all ties with Nirmal after he graduates. At a time of deep religious antagonism between Hindus and Muslims in late colonial India, Hindu-raised Mukunda befriends Arif, a Muslim boy at school. Through Arif, Mukunda is taken into the home of a kindly elder couple, Suleiman and Farhana. Mukunda quickly takes to speaking of them as uncle and aunt, or Chacha and Chachi in the Bengali language.

Historical events shape the fates of Mukunda and the other characters. When sectarian violence worsens in Bengal, Chacha and Chachi leave predominantly Hindu Calcutta for the Muslim territory of their relatives, entrusting their home and their pet parrot, Noorie, to Mukunda's care. When colonial India splits up into Pakistan and the Union of India in 1947, Mukunda finds himself de facto owner of the abandoned house.

Roy's theme of home and family as both refuge and a source of angst, though present throughout the novel, appears frequently in the book's final part. Now in possession of Chacha and Chachi's house, Mukunda is introduced by an opportunistic clerk named Barababu to Aangti Babu, a shady real estate developer, and soon begins to work for him. As Mukunda rises in his job, Barababu gives him his middle daughter, Malini, as a wife. They have a son, Goutam. Mukunda also endeavors to complete a series of real estate transactions as part of his work for Aangti Babu, through which some surprising plot twists force him to face his past and his relationship with his adoptive family.

As a character, Aangti Babu is both an agent of change and a traditionalist. As a real-estate developer, he often advocates changes that uproot homes and other traditional structures in his community. At the same time, he is deeply superstitious, as evidenced by his belief in astrology and the reading of palms. When Mukunda consults Aangti's astrologer for a palm reading, the astrologer exclaims, "your palm is nothing but an atlas of impossible longings," making it clear that the title of Roy's novel refers to Mukunda's wild and untamed desires. In the end, Mukunda must decide if he will act on his desires or adhere to tradition, if he will forsake his young family for true love and his true home.

R. C. Lutz

Review Sources

Booklist 107, no. 13 (March 1, 2011): 24.
Library Journal 136, no. 3 (February 15, 2011): 101.
The New Yorker 87, no. 10 (April 25, 2011): 85.
The New York Times Book Review, June 26, 2011, p. 11.
Publishers Weekly 258, no. 3 (January 17, 2011): 24.

Attack of the Difficult Poems
Essays and Inventions

Author: Charles Bernstein (b. 1950)
Publisher: University of Chicago Press (Chicago). 296 pp. $95.00; paperback $26.00
Type of work: Essays, literary criticism, literary theory

Writing with a verve and edge uncommon in literary discourse, Bernstein presents a practical program for an active engagement with literature through a variety of essays.

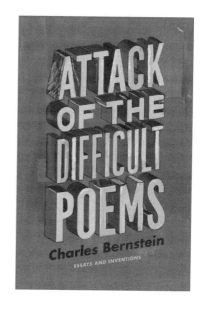

When writing about their craft, poets have traditionally been circumspect about their commitment to what is undoubtedly a central concern of their lives. In his *Defense of Poesie* (1585), Sir Philip Sidney declares that "of all writers under the Sunne, the Poet is the least lyer," claiming a kind of ultimate truth as the provenance of the poet. Another edition of the work was issued under the title *An Apology for Poetrie*, reinforcing the idea that the poet was an interloper among the more responsible practitioners of literary endeavor. Percy Shelley provides an ardent exposition of a similar argument in his *Defence of Poetry* (1840), while in the poem "Pardon, Old Fathers" (1914), W. B. Yeats seeks forgiveness and understanding for the fact that he has "nothing but a book" to prove worthy of his illustrious ancestors. Such reticence might have seemed obligatory for poets in the United Kingdom, but American poets beginning with Walt Whitman have expressed a much more self-confident sense of their mission. In *Attack of the Difficult Poems*, poet and critic Charles Bernstein collects nearly thirty "essays and inventions" that, as the back cover claims, defend "not just difficult poetry but poetry itself." As one of the initial members of a loose affiliation known as the L=A=N=G=U=A=G=E poets, Bernstein has been one of the most energetic advocates for a particular strain of or approach to American poetry. His opposition to and disparagement of what he regards as the standard methods for discussing poetry have made him a controversial figure and kept him outside of mainstream discourse, a position he clearly relishes and regards as necessary. Perhaps recalling the earlier defenses of poetry, Bernstein has taken an aggressive stance in naming the collection, with the clear implication that it is not only the poems but also the poets who have adopted the strategy encapsulated by the aphorism that offense, or attack, is the best defense.

The essays that begin the book set the terms and tone of the attack, preparing the ground for detailed explanations and demonstrations of the techniques Bernstein has used in his literature courses. The opening essay, "The Difficult Poem," is an appeal

(University of Chicago Press)

Charles Bernstein is the Donald T. Reagan Professor of English at the University of Pennsylvania and a fellow of the American Academy of Arts and Sciences. A coeditor of the groundbreaking poetry magazine L=A=N=G=U=A=G=E, *he has published numerous poetry collections, books of essays, and edited volumes.*

to the reader to reconsider the entire concept of difficulty with respect to poetry, as Bernstein is more concerned with the experience of reading poetry and the ways in which style and form affect that experience than with analysis. Bernstein's essays, then, go beyond but include his preferred kind of engagement with literature in an effort to examine and redefine the entire concept of education in the humanities, a discipline that he argues has been demeaned and distorted by a powerful push toward conformity that demonizes aesthetic invention and literary complexity. Because his opinions often run counter to common beliefs, even when supported by numerous examples, Bernstein begins the book with an address to the reader as an inducement to continue a conversation and introduces himself as a person concerned that the true pleasure of poetry has been ruined by a misconception of what "difficult" actually means. Rather than blaming or accusing anyone, Bernstein presents himself as a genial guide who can help the reader better read and understand such ostensibly difficult poetry.

If his introduction is successful, the reader will be excited by the possibility of what Bernstein promises as well as sufficiently sympathetic with his general take on the national cultural situation to be amused by Bernstein's sharp comments and ripostes. "Laughter is the necessary yeast of good class conversation," he declares in the essay "Wreading, Writing, Wresponding," and his wit and comic enunciations inform all of the essays. He is inclined to satirize critics and institutions with which he disagrees, and whether this satire is successful depends on the degree to which the reader agrees with him. The concluding essay, "Recantorium," is a striking example of this mode, and it is placed at the end of the volume both as a means of amusing and energizing the reader who has been caught up in the conversation and as a kind of catharsis for all the accumulated grievances that cannot be adequately addressed in any other fashion.

Attack of the Difficult Poems is imaginatively arranged to present Bernstein's ideas through a tightly argued and abundantly illustrated and supported series of essays, each one contributing to the thesis that an enriching experience with poetry can become available when all of the resources of language are open for exploration. Recognizing that almost everyone interested in poetry and poetics is likely to be involved to some degree with the academic aspects of the discipline, Bernstein has carefully constructed and tested a curriculum that can re-form the entire enterprise as he sees it. As Bernstein's own involvement with senior colleagues at a number of esteemed universities has resulted in clashes with standard practices of scholarship and publication, he sees as his primary readership untenured faculty members and, perhaps ideally, a public beyond the confines of the academy. A significant part of his plan is to debunk some of the strategies that have been formulated by people with a stake in the system, such as the fashioning of National Poetry Month and similar promotional occasions. Bernstein's targets in essays such as "Against National Poetry Month as Such" are the well-intentioned but clueless cohort that has confused marketing with artistic mastery, those who are convinced that poetry would be more popular if it were easy to understand, and those who want to celebrate the poet as a celebrity rather than as a person who "finds ways of doing things in a media-saturated environment that only poetry can do." Other essays, including "A Blow is Like an Instrument," criticize the rules and regulations formulated by organizations such as the Modern Language Association that, Bernstein argues, encourage conformity and place limits upon creative expression. Recalling an essay he submitted to *PMLA* that was rejected and described as "indulgent," Bernstein recasts the term as a compliment: "I *am* expressing eccentric opinions on literary matters, without *PMLA*'s brand of "clarity" and "evidence": eccentric, indulgent, disjointed, loose, inconsistent—and proud."

While Bernstein's caustic comments are either entertaining or infuriating depending on the reader's perspective, his argument would be less substantial without the presentation and explanation of the prototype course he has developed for what he calls the Writing Experiments seminar. In the essay "Wreading, Writing, Wresponding," Bernstein draws on the actual operation of the class itself, which is far from a closed model and more of an organic affair based on many concrete suggestions and directions. As a useful example of how such a course might be conducted, he offers questions and instructions to guide the teaching and learning experience. This sort of hard material reveals the philosophy of composition at the core of Bernstein's aesthetic principles and makes the book valuable even for a writer or teacher not fully in accord with Bernstein's ideas. Designed to guide students who are asked to record their responses to various poems, the essay includes prompt questions such as "What do you think of the poem?" and "What does the poem sound like, what does it remind you of?" These queries follow Bernstein's pattern of balancing unconventional and inventive insights with suppositions grounded in a tradition of inquiry familiar to people educated in the Western tradition of the Enlightenment. Thus, when he advocates "reading ambiently and associatively" in the essay "Creative Wreading & Aesthetic Judgment," the reader's suspicion that this is not really a practical method may be ameliorated by the evidence and information that Bernstein provides.

The second and third sections of the volume are titled "The Art of Immemorability" and "The Fate of the Aesthetic." Section 2 is devoted to the aurality that Bernstein regards as vital to literature, an element that he contends has been suppressed in favor of a print-oriented attitude. The essays here respond to the technology of the twenty-first century, covering what Bernstein calls analphabetic and postalphabetic language environments and noting the transformative effects of virtual textuality. The theoretical projections that Bernstein introduces are illuminated by examples such as the intertextual resonance between the words and illustrations in William Blake's prophetic books. Emphasizing the importance of performative poetry, Bernstein argues that "performance allows the poet to refocus attention to dynamics hidden within the scripted poem." He amply illustrates this concept with a range of references to the modernist poetry of such poets as T. S. Eliot, Ezra Pound, and Louis Zukofsky, as well as the popular songs of the Gershwin brothers, Cole Porter, Oscar Hammerstein, and others, which Bernstein insists are a part of a larger continuum of composition.

The third section includes shorter pieces revealing some of Bernstein's direct involvement in what could be called cultural controversies. He addresses the prevalence of the "fraudulent text" in the semiplayful, fascinating excursion "Fraud's Phantoms: A Brief Yet Unreliable Account of Fighting Fraud with Fraud" and satirizes attitudes toward modern poetry in "Poetry Bailout Will Restore Confidence of Readers," a pitch-perfect parodic evisceration of economic counsel. These high-spirited "inventions" lead to the book's concluding part, "Recantorium," a tour de force of sustained satire in which Bernstein confesses his faults. Beginning nearly every paragraph with some variation on the abject phrase, "I was wrong, I apologize, I recant," Bernstein seemingly renounces every ethical and aesthetic principle his entire collection has professed while actually deepening and reinforcing his argument. Ostensibly a reversal in which the author gratefully accepts as valid the denunciations he has received, "Recantorium" is a powerful statement of defiance, a call to continued resistance, and a superb signature statement by a compelling advocate for the arts.

Leon Lewis

Review Source

Times Higher Education, no. 2004 (June 23, 2011): 52.

Bad Intentions

Author: Karin Fossum (b. 1954)
First published: *Den onde viljen*, 2008, in Norway
Translated from the Norwegian by Charlotte Barslund
Publisher: Houghton Mifflin Harcourt (Boston). 224 pp. $24.00; paperback $13.95
Type of work: Novel
Time: The present
Locale: The woods around Dead Water Lake and Glitter Lake in rural southeastern Norway; an unnamed city in the same area

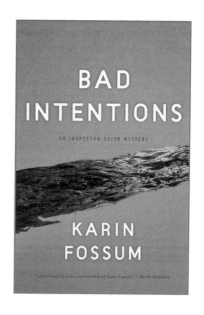

A veteran detective's investigation of two suspicious drownings evolves into a larger exploration of conscience, culpability, and the relationship between crime and peer pressure.

Principal characters:

JON MORENO, a depressed young man in his mid-twenties who mysteriously drowns
AXEL FRIMANN, Jon's friend, a successful advertising executive
PHILIP REILLY, also Jon's friend, a drug addict who works as a hospital porter
INGRERID MORENO, Jon's mother, a widow determined to discover the truth of her son's death
INSPECTOR KONRAD SEJER, a veteran homicide detective, a widower
MOLLY GRAM, a vibrant, eccentric young woman who befriended Jon in the hospital
KIM VAN CHAU, a socially awkward Vietnamese immigrant who disappeared under mysterious circumstances
YOO VAN CHAU, Kim's long-suffering mother, a widow

There is a forbidding Nordic chill at the heart of Karin Fossum's *Bad Intentions*, her ninth novel featuring the dogged and meticulous Norwegian detective Inspector Konrad Sejer. The bodies of two young men are found floating in the chilly waters of two remote lakes weeks apart, and Inspector Sejer suspects a connection. For new readers of the Sejer series, *Bad Intentions* is unlikely to be a conventionally satisfying procedural. The novel is a taut and tight construction, the prose clean and unadorned. There are no complicating subplots or clever twists, and no large cast of eccentric suspects, red herrings, elaborate clues, or forensic epiphanies. The detective himself is a relatively minor character. In the end, Fossum even denies her reader the tidy resolution that procedurals typically provide. The circumstances of both deaths and the difficulty of determining who is ultimately responsible give the novel the chilling morality of a Dostoevsky novel.

In the opening chapter, the reader witnesses an ambiguous event that ends in a death. It is mid-September. Three men, lifelong friends now in their twenties, head out to a remote cabin in rural southeastern Norway for a weekend. One, Axel Frimann, is a charismatic and successful advertising executive; another, Philip Reilly, is a lowly hospital porter addicted to prescription pharmaceuticals. Jon Moreno, frail and sickly, is currently a short-term patient in a mental institution, and the friends have gathered to help his recovery. On the first night, at Axel's suggestion, the men take a midnight boat ride. About a hundred yards offshore and without explanation, Jon Moreno falls over the side of the boat. Is it a suicide? An accident? All the reader knows is that Axel prevents Reilly from going after their friend, insisting they not contact the police until morning.

When Axel and Reilly return to the cabin, they concoct a believable story: their despondent friend got up in the middle of the night and did not return. As the reptilian Axel handles the police the following morning, Reilly is not so cool. Later, when the police begin to canvass the shore for the missing man, Reilly happens upon a litter of cats in the grass, all dead save for a runt that he immediately adopts. As he lavishes the stray kitten with care over the next several days, Fossum uses the relationship to suggest that this is Reilly's peculiar way of handling profound guilt, presumably the guilt of Jon's death. Only as the narrative unfolds does she reveal the darker motivation that has driven Reilly into a morass of guilt and drug addiction.

Inspector Sejer, a veteran of homicide investigations, suspects the men's story from the beginning. As in conventional police procedurals, Inspector Sejer methodically works the evidence of the apparent suicide. Police records indicate that the three men were part of a police investigation the previous December, a case involving the disappearance of a Vietnamese boy, Kim Van Chau. They gave the drunken boy a ride home from a housewarming party and claimed to have dropped him off near his home; no one has seen the boy since. Sejer visits the hospital where Jon was staying, where doctors tell him that antianxiety medications and therapy sessions had been helping him. Sejer wonders how a man unable to swim got one hundred yards away from shore, and why a man intending to commit suicide dressed so warmly and sent a text message to Molly Gram, his girlfriend and a fellow patient, saying that he was looking forward to seeing her after the weekend. When he talks to Jon's psychiatrist, Sejer is shown a rag doll that Jon made during therapy, a rag doll Jon had named (not coincidentally, he believes) Kim.

At Jon's funeral, where Axel delivers a pitch-perfect eulogy, the narrative shifts dramatically from the conventions of a police procedural. With the revelation that Jon kept a diary, Fossum focuses her attention on Jon's long-suffering mother, who, upon reading the diary, discovers a record of the young man's guilt, his shame, his hunger for absolution, and his sense of his own cowardice. The mother confronts Axel, certain that her son's friend knows what destroyed him, but Axel coolly tells her that Jon was simply ill and delusional. A representative of the twentysomething generation that the author presents as disconnected from moral responsibility, Axel begins to dominate Fossum's narrative. She describes his soulless professional career in advertising and his shallow love of the trappings of success, most notably his Mercedes. His father is shown to have lived an exemplary moral life, only to end up suffering a stroke and dying with little dignity, and Axel takes this as proof that the universe is ironic and amoral. Indeed, to underscore Axel's position as the narrative's moral abscess, his character is stricken with a fierce toothache. Not accidentally, the ache strikes a wisdom tooth.

The narrative then turns to the discovery of the missing Vietnamese boy, Kim Van Chau, in another nearby lake. The coincidence intrigues Inspector Sejer, who recalls Jon's therapy doll. When Sejer visits Kim's grieving mother, he learns the story of the boy's death. On a whim, the painfully shy boy had gone to a housewarming party in a nearby coastal town. He had hitchhiked and never returned. Sejer is moved by the woman's simple love for her son and rashly promises her an explanation. He reads in police reports that the party guests had gotten Kim drunk for their own amusement, and then, weary of their sport, had coaxed Axel Frimann, Jon Moreno, and Philip Reilly to take him home in the early hours of the morning.

As Fossum maneuvers the novel away from a conventional procedural, she creates

(© Bo-Aje Mellin)

Trained as a poet, Karin Fossum has emerged as one of the most intellectually probing practitioners of Scandinavian crime fiction, her work exploring the psyches of detectives, killers, and victims alike. Her award-winning, critically acclaimed Inspector Sejer titles, including Black Seconds *(2007) and* The Water's Edge *(2009), have been published in more than thirty countries.*

a moving counter-narrative of the emerging friendship between the grieving mothers, who struggle with questions and the shared certainty that somebody must bear the guilt for their sons' deaths. Answers seem unlikely, and even as the mystery thickens, Fossum moves Inspector Sejer off to the margins; he is subsequently featured only in brief, vulnerable moments, feeling his age as he stares at the mirror or meditating on death as he visits his wife's grave. The mothers, certain the investigation has hit a dead end, address an anonymous and accusatory letter to Axel, which sends him into a panic. He is determined to act.

By contrast, the weak Reilly tends to his guilt, slavishly ministering to his stray kitten and ingesting increasingly larger doses of painkillers. He punishes himself by reading passages about God's righteous judgment in the Qur'an. Anguished and distrustful of his friend, he prepares a cognac laced with enough medication to ensure his death. Axel arrives before Reilly can kill himself, and the two argue, Reilly weakly suggesting that perhaps they had not done enough for the Vietnamese boy, that perhaps they had unintentionally caused his death. In the novel's most disturbing moment, Axel shows Reilly the true nature of intentional evil, snatching his kitten and dispassionately throwing it out the upper-story apartment window. To underscore his indifference, Axel then calmly downs the cognac, and Reilly watches helplessly as his friend collapses dead in the bathroom. When the police come to arrest him, Sejer's examination of Axel's Mercedes having yielded a single Asian hair, Reilly commits the novel's single act of decency and confesses. Only then does Fossum reveal what truly happened on that December night.

For a traditional police procedural, *Bad Intentions* presents its audience with a most frustrating resolution. The reader may expect tidiness, but much as with the deaths of Jon Moreno and Axel Frimann, the reader instead becomes entangled in an ambiguous kind of murder story that is never quite as simple as mere murder. Each revelation obscures more than it reveals, and indeed raises irresolvable questions about the nature of responsibility itself, the blurred boundary between intention and accident, and the implications of circumstance and contingency. In the end, the most pressing questions may have to do with how human beings deal with guilt. The reader might experience a feeling of dissatisfaction upon reading the ending, in which Reilly, the least culpable of the three, is the only one left to answer for his crimes.

In the closing pages, Fossum describes Jon as he was before the novel began, waiting for his friends outside the hospital. He is reluctant to leave for the weekend getaway and only joins his friends after assuring himself that having a new girlfriend means his life is working out at last. In this moment, the reader may recall Inspector Sejer's confident promise to Kim's mother that he will find answers. Fossum ends her novel with a feeling of uncertainty and unease, leaving her audience adrift in chilling ambiguity.

Joseph Dewey

Review Sources

Independent, July 12, 2010 (Web).
Kirkus Reviews 79, no. 12 (June 16, 2011): 1005–6.
Newsweek 157, no. 21/22 (May 23/30, 2011): 82.
Times Literary Supplement, no. 5603/5604 (August 20/27, 2011): 22.

Baseball in the Garden of Eden
The Secret History of the Early Game

Author: John Thorn (b. 1947)
Publisher: Simon & Schuster (New York).
 384 pp. $26.00
Type of work: History
Time: 1830s–1909
Locale: New York City and New Jersey

The author addresses the myth that American baseball originated with Abner Doubleday, while examining the sport's likely origin and evolution during the 1800s.

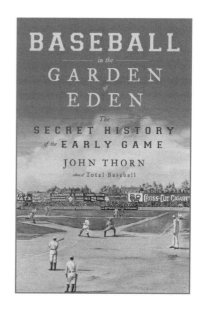

Principal personages:

ABNER DOUBLEDAY (1819–1893), Civil War general and alleged inventor of modern baseball

ALBERT SPALDING, early pitcher, owner, entrepreneur, and author

ALEXANDER JOY CARTWRIGHT (1820–1892), among the organizers of New York's Knickerbocker Base Ball Club (1845); credited by some with proposing the modern rules of baseball

ABRAHAM GILBERT MILLS, president of National League from 1883–1884, and head of the commission that was formed in 1905 and that credited Doubleday with the invention of baseball

LOUIS FENN WADSWORTH, attorney and member of the 1850s Knickerbockers who helped develop some of the modern rules of the sport

DANIEL LUCIUS ADAMS (DOC), early member of the Knickerbockers who helped draft and define the rules of the game

HENRY CHADWICK (1824–1908), sportswriter and statistician who developed many of the methods used in baseball statistics

Who invented the modern game of American baseball? If one subscribes to the long-believed story, the "Father of Baseball" was Abner Doubleday, a Civil War general who had conducted himself with honor at the Battle of Gettysburg. According to the report released in 1908 by the Special Base Ball Commission headed by A. G. Mills, Doubleday invented the game in 1839. Described as a young man living in Cooperstown, New York, Doubleday allegedly scratched out a diamond in a local field for other boys from the local Otsego Academy while establishing the rules of the game. The Cooperstown site would become the home of the National Baseball Hall of Fame one hundred years later, with Doubleday Field situated nearby. The Commission even located an alleged witness, one Abner Graves, who testified that he had watched

Doubleday invent the game. In 1934, eight years after Graves had died, a ball that became known as the "Doubleday Ball" was found in a trunk owned by Graves and was eventually put on display at the Baseball Hall of Fame. The museum's tongue-in-cheek description of the ball claimed that it was the actual one used by Doubleday in 1839, also hinting at the problematic nature of such a claim.

John Thorn is a sportswriter and baseball historian. He served as a consultant for Ken Burns's PBS series, Baseball. *In 2006, the Society for American Baseball Research honored Thorn with the Bob Davids Award for his achievements.*

In *Baseball in the Garden of Eden: The Secret History of the Early Game*, sportswriter and baseball historian John Thorn has both prefaced and completed his story with the Doubleday myth. As noted by the author, problems with the Mills Commission's findings began shortly after their publication. Critics reminded the Commission that Doubleday was not even in Cooperstown in 1839; he was a twenty-year-old plebe at the United States Military Academy. To his credit, Doubleday never claimed to have invented baseball, or even to have been associated with the game at all.

Other books or articles have addressed the reasons behind the Commission's findings in significant detail, but Thorn has provided a useful summary of the political background of the 1908 report, including the dispute between Albert Spalding and Henry Chadwick. Though born in England and an advocate of the British sport cricket, Chadwick was also a New York-based sportswriter and historian; he was credited with developing the baseball box score as well. Chadwick had long argued that baseball had derived from the British sport rounders, a game not much different from baseball. Chadwick had also been longtime editor of Spalding's Guide, an annual summary of baseball leagues and teams. Spalding argued for baseball being a completely American game, and it was this view, supported by Graves's dubious testimony, that was adopted by the Mills Commission.

The bulk of Thorn's research utilized a large number of letters and other primary sources in an attempt to answer the questions of who the actual originator of baseball was, and how the sport began and evolved. The answer to the first is clear—there was no single originator, but rather a number of key individuals whose ideas and suggestions led to the formation of a game recognizable even a century later. Thorn addresses the roles played by these individuals, principally Louis Wadsworth, Daniel "Doc" Adams, and Chadwick, but with a large supporting cast, in a chapter titled, "Four Fathers, Two Roads." The chapter title was derived from the Robert Frost poem, "The Road not Taken."

Thorn traces the earliest versions of the American game to the colonial period. Eighteenth-century children's games known as "Four Old Cat" and "Three Old Cat" involved activities with balls. Even George Washington during the winter at Valley Forge was reported to have played a game called wicket, in which a bowler aimed a ball at a stake while a batsman would attempt to hit the throw with a club. It was not until the1820s that something recognizable as baseball, or base ball, as it was then called, appeared. In 1823, a match was advertised for a lower Manhattan saloon called Jones' Retreat; nothing else is known, including whether such a game was even played. There was no sports section in newspapers of the time.

What is known is that by the 1840s local clubs began forming their own teams, usually playing only among themselves; sometimes matches were arranged with other organizations. The most famous of these clubs was the New York Knickerbockers, organized in 1845. On October 6, 1845, the first recorded intrasquad game was played, the date sometimes considered the official "birthday" of modern baseball. However, Thorn points out that at least five other clubs, less well known, had preceded the Knickerbockers in New York. Other cities were also known to have fielded squads. Among the original members and organizers of the Knickerbockers were Doc Adams, William Wheaton, William Tucker, and Wadsworth, the "four fathers" to whom Thorn alluded in the chapter title. Alexander Cartwright is often credited with establishing the boundaries of the game during his tenure with the team from 1845 to 1849; these boundaries include the distance between the pitcher and batter, the distance between bases, and even the number of men playing in the field. But Thorn writes that many of these dimensions were firmly established only after Cartwright had left New York in 1849, making his way eventually to Hawaii where he lived out the latter part of his life. More likely some of these dimensions were established by Adams during his tenure as president of the club and chair of its Committee to Revise the Constitution and By-Laws during the 1840s and 1850s, in which some of these rules were codified. Among the changes was establishment of nine innings as the length of a game rather than the winner defined as the team which first scored twenty-one runs. Thorn also credits Adams with introduction of the fielder called the shortstop.

It was not unusual during these times for clubs to travel across the river to New Jersey, where the game was played on the Elysian Fields in Hoboken. The site had a number of advantages. Not only was a field available away from the noise and smells of the city, but it was a place where viewers could comfortably watch the game. The Fields also lent themselves as a place of recreation for those wishing a rural setting with "pure air" and "delightful shades," as it was described by its proprietor, John Stevens. Thorn notes that during summer days as many as twenty thousand persons a day would travel the ferries across the river.

William Wheaton played a role similar to that of Doc Adams during the early years of the club. A lawyer by training and the club's first vice-president, Wheaton played a critical role in recruiting members for the team. It was Wheaton who drew up some of the rules that Adams later adopted. William Tucker, also a member of the Knickerbocker by-law committee, appeared to have played an important but lesser role in association with Wheaton.

Two forms of baseball, the "Two Roads" in the title, developed simultaneously during the first half of the nineteenth century: the New York game, which ultimately prevailed, and the Massachusetts game. The Massachusetts game, sometimes called round ball, was arguably the dominant form well into the 1850s. The game was played in a square, with the striker (batter) between the first and fourth bases (actually stakes). First base was only about thirty feet from home, and so the game was more open than that of the New York version. The ball could be hit in any direction, and runners could be put out by being hit or "soaked" with a ball thrown by a fielder.

Thorn does not directly address the question of why the New York game prevailed. He alludes to the possibility that greater publicity for the New York rules may have been a deciding factor. Thorn also suggests it was an easier form of play for the non-athlete, allowing for greater popularity among the masses. Regardless of the reasons, the Knickerbocker rules were adopted in a March 1857 meeting, considered by Chadwick to be the actual date in which the New York game was established.

By the mid-1850s, the popularity of the sport had spread to the extent that newspapers, the media of the times, were already referring to baseball as the "national pastime." The Civil War served to disseminate the sport even further, as men from all portions of the country learned the game and returned to their homes with it once the war had ended. Thorn has spent much of the remaining portion of the book describing the impact of several significant factors on the sport. First was the introduction of professionalism on teams. Major players, most notably Brooklyn pitcher Jim Creighton during the early 1860s, likely received some form of under-the-table compensation. However, the Cincinnati Base Ball Club, also known as the Red Stockings, was considered the first openly professional team during the years following the war. The success of the team served as a catalyst for squads in other cities to recruit and pay players. It was not long before these teams began to form more formal leagues, with the National Association of Professional Base Ball Players, formed in 1871, becoming the forerunner of such league play. A variety of problems plagued the league, resulting in its being disbanded in 1875 and replaced by the National League (NL) in 1876. Despite numerous problems during its early years, the NL has continued as the senior league for professional baseball into the twenty-first century.

While professionalism had a positive impact on baseball, gambling nearly destroyed the popularity of the sport. Thorn points out that the introduction of a box score in daily newspapers allowed the sport's supporters to follow a team and its players, but also provided a means for a statistical analysis of the player. Gamblers became a common feature at parks, betting not only on the outcome of a game, but on the actions of individual players. It was only a short time before gamblers attempted to influence the outcome of play, paying players for "hippodroming," or intentionally losing games. In an attempt to clean up the sport, a number of players were banned from the sport during the 1870s because of such play, but gamblers remained a significant problem well into the twentieth century. The problem reached its nadir in 1919, when eight members of the Chicago White Sox agreed to throw the World Series that year. Though those members were ultimately banned from professional baseball, it was arguably the advent of greater offense by teams, and most notably the impact of Babe Ruth, which allowed baseball to continue as the national game.

The strength of Thorn's work lies in his extensive use of primary sources, including letters written by those who were directly involved in baseball's early growth. Most followers of the sport's history are familiar with the major figures who appear in the book. What sets Thorn's writing apart from other books on the subject is his focus on individuals who, though largely forgotten, deeply influenced the sport's development.

Richard Adler

Review Sources

Booklist 107, no. 14 (March 15, 2011): 13.
Kirkus Reviews 79, no. 3 (February 1, 2011): 196.
Publishers Weekly 258, no. 6 (February 7, 2011): 48.
The New York Times Book Review, April 10, 2011 (Web).
USA Today, April 14, 2011, p. D3.

Battle Hymn of the Tiger Mother

Author: Amy Chua (b. 1962)
Publisher: Penguin (New York). 256 pp.
   $25.95; paperback $16.00
Type of work: Memoir
Time: 1993–2010
Locale: Mainly New Haven, Connecticut

A controversial account of how one parent deals with the successes and failures of attempting to raise her American-born daughters the Chinese way.

This is a story about a mother, two daughters, and two dogs.

This was *supposed* to be a story of how Chinese parents are better at raising kids than Western ones.

But instead, it's about a bitter clash of cultures, a fleeting taste of glory, and how I was humbled by a thirteen-year-old.

AMY CHUA

Principal personages:
AMY CHUA, a law professor born in America to
   ethnically Chinese immigrants
SOPHIA, Amy's older daughter
LOUISA, Amy's younger daughter
JED, Amy's husband and Sophia and Louisa's
   father, a Jewish American and law professor,
THE ELDER PROFESSOR CHUA, Amy's father, a
   computer scientist and engineer
MRS. CHUA, Amy's mother, a chemical engineer by education
FLORENCE, Jed's mother, a connoisseur of art
KATRIN CHUA, one of Amy's sisters, a medical researcher

In *Battle Hymn of the Tiger Mother*, Amy Chua chronicles her attempt to become a strict parent in the Chinese style, contrasting Eastern parenting methods with Western methods. Chua herself was born in America to ethnically Chinese parents. The oldest of four daughters, she was raised the Chinese way, with an emphasis on a strong work ethic, skill development, and academic success. Her father was a computer scientist and engineer, and her mother held a degree in chemical engineering. Teaching at schools like Purdue University and the University of California, Chua's father accepted positions and moved his family accordingly. Chua disobeyed her father, however, by attending Harvard University, where she earned a law degree and met Jed, her future husband (whose surname, Rubenfeld, never appears in the text). After law school, Chua taught at many schools before settling at Yale University, where she worked not only as a professor but, as she describes herself, as the mother of Sophia and of Louisa, who she calls "Lulu."

   As a parent, Chua was determined to avoid the decline of good parenting she observed in other ethnically Chinese families in America. The third generation, she claims, lives in prosperity because of the hard work of the immigrant and first American-born generations. In prosperity, the children of the third generation have become soft, disobedient, and generally Americanized, drawing too much value in their supposed individual rights. Conceding that some Chinese mothers are lax and some Western ones strict, Chua set herself to becoming specifically a "Chinese mother" to save her family from what she saw as Western decadence. Claiming to use a statistically valid stereotype, she discusses three big differences between Chinese and American parents: (1) Chinese parents consider their children to be strong enough psychologically to take harsh criticism, rather than so fragile as to need their self-esteem protected; (2) Chinese parents think their children are immensely indebted to them, whereas American parents think they owe a great debt to their children; (3) Chinese parents believe that they, not their children, are the ones to decide wisely what their children will or will not do.

So Chua labors at Chinese mothering, spending hour after hour tutoring, supervising, and risking the social ostracism of other mothers by refusing to allow Sophia and Lulu to indulge in such typical American childhood activities as playdates with other girls. Schoolwork is essential: no grade less than *A* is tolerated, and no rank other than first in the class earns a parent's praise. Then there is music, in the high cultural tradition of the West. Chua requires her daughters to learn Mandarin, but she thinks that European-style music in the broad sense of "classical" is essential to keeping her daughters from dragging the family down. At age three each girl starts piano lessons, and Chua quickly finds the highly structured Suzuki method to be just what she wants. Sophia becomes a fine pianist, winning contests and even playing in Carnegie Hall when she is fourteen. At her mother's direction, Lulu eventually takes up violin, first as an addition to piano and then as a substitute (her sister excels at piano, after all). The daily practice of the girls' fellow students is not nearly enough for the Tiger Mother, who remains close by during practices, ordering and threatening. The experience is not fun for the child or the mother, but Chua does not relent. When asked whether she is doing this for her children's sake or her own, Chua claims it is all for her children. Still, she recognizes that according to Chinese thinking a child is the parent's extension. Childhood is when a mother should strenuously train a daughter for the future and not let time be wasted in spontaneous discovery or other Western activities. Chua admits that having fun is not one of her talents.

Sophia may have little fun growing up, but she does not worry her mother. She is smart, industrious, cooperative, and musically gifted—a testimony to the Tiger Mother's methods. If Sophia were the only daughter, Chua could certainly maintain that Chinese parenting is better than Western parenting. According to the epigraph, this was the original intent for the book. But then Lulu spoils the plan.

By Chinese standards the younger sister is a rebel and seems to have an American spirit. As a three-year-old, she refuses to play gently on the piano, a rebellion that leads to Chua putting the thinly dressed little girl out the back door on a cold day and keeping her there until she decides to obey. When Lulu refuses, Chua has to give in for fear that her daughter will freeze. The conflicts continue as time goes by. Lulu, at age seven, angers her easily irritated mother by wanting to give up on a piece. Chua wins the encounter, making Lulu practice until, suddenly, her hands begin to work together and play the piece correctly. But at home music practice often turns into a shouting

*Amy Chua teaches law at Yale Universi-
ty. Her previous books are* World on Fire:
How Exporting Free Market Democracy
Breeds Ethnic Hatred and Global Instability *(2003) and* Day of Empire: How
Hyperpowers Rise to Global Dominance—and Why They Fall *(2007).*

battle between Chua and her younger daughter, who stalls and resents her mother's control. With the violin, Lulu shows feeling for
the music, but her resentment of her mother
grows stronger, so strong that she seriously
violates the Chinese code of conduct, rude-
ly acting out to a violin teacher. When her
mother refuses to drive her to get a haircut,
Lulu mutilates her hair as a gesture of spite.
She disobeys her mother further by refusing to propose a toast to her father on his
fiftieth birthday.

Finally, the war between Tiger Mother and rebellious daughter reaches its peak at
an outdoor café on Red Square in Moscow. For once, Chua does not made Lulu take
her violin on vacation with her. However, the tension rises anyway. When Chua tries
to get Lulu to eat caviar, the thirteen-year-old refuses, sending Chua into outrage at
Lulu's public disobedience, and sending Lulu into outrage at what she views as selfish,
maternal bullying. The scene ends with Lulu smashing a water glass on the ground and
Chua running across the square in tears, feeling inferior to Western mothers whose ill-
behaved children never act so outrageously in public. After this incident, the mother
admits defeat. She and Lulu quit violin practice, but Lulu keeps playing, albeit on a
less stressful schedule and without her mother's interference. Additionally, Lulu takes
up competitive tennis, playing on her own terms and losing with a smile.

Chua says that the Red Square outburst humbles her, but she seems too headstrong
for deep humiliation. Her parenting method has many admirable features: its emphasis
on work ethic, academic accomplishments, and respect for teachers and parents, as
well as its sense of family honor. There is also the aspect of compassion, which Chua
models for her daughters when she takes in Florence, her mother-in-law who suffers
from leukemia. She performs her duty lovingly in spite of the polite disagreement
between them, Florence favoring a parenting style of freedom over Chua's benevolent
control. Another model of compassion is her active concern for her sister Katrin, a
physician and researcher who is struggling with leukemia.

In January, 2011, *The Wall Street Journal* printed excerpts from the book under the
editorial title "Why Chinese Mothers Are Superior." Read outside of the context of
the Red Square outburst, the excerpts provoked a strong reaction, of which the majority was hostile, but the controversy also helped the book become a bestseller. Critics
drew attention to many of the aspects of parenting that Chua does not mention, such
as the merits of a child's social and emotional education. While Chua certainly points
out that the labels of "Western" and "Chinese" cannot speak to all kinds of parenting,
some critics still found her argument too generalized. For those critics who enjoy the
book as a whole, it provides a success story of one woman's relationship with her children, not to mention a humbling memoir of parenting's many difficulties. Chua's book
may still annoy those readers who subscribe to her views on the weakness of modern
American parenting and the superiority of Chinese methods. The book is helped by
the author's occasional humility and humor—most of it at the author's own expense.

For instance, Chua ends a serious meditation in the last chapter with the remark that she wants a third dog, one that presumably will achieve as little as the two Samoyeds she already has. In ways, however, the book is an extended boast, which may annoy readers who have not lived as privileged a life, for she makes little effort to hide her family's class status. Much of the book's audience will never host a dinner for distinguished foreign jurists, and few are likely to afford the private schools, private lessons, or the international traveling that characterizes this family's lifestyle. A parent need not overvalue the notion of self-esteem to refrain from calling his or her child trash.

Victor Lindsey

Review Sources

Atlantic Monthly 307, no. 3 (April 2011): 83–91.
Booklist 107, no. 8 (December 15, 2010): 5.
Commentary 131, no. 4 (April 2011): 53–55.
Educational Leadership 68, no. 8 (May 2011): 90–91.
Newsweek 157, no. 4 (January 24, 2011): 49.
The New Yorker 86, no. 46 (January 31, 2011): 70–73.
The New York Times, January 19, 2011, p. C1.
The New York Times Book Review, February 13, 2011, p. 7.
People 75, no. 3 (January 24, 2011): 50.
Publishers Weekly 257, no. 45 (November 15, 2010): 48–50.

Beautiful and Pointless
A Guide to Modern Poetry

Author: David Orr (b. 1974)
Publisher: HarperCollins (New York). 224 pp.
$25.99; paperback $14.99
Type of work: Literary criticism

Offers a fascinating, instructive, and provocative discussion of the place that modern poetry holds in the contemporary world.

As a poetry columnist for the *New York Times Book Review*, David Orr seeks to engage with the readers of his reviews and inspire them to read new books of poetry. He wishes to make a connection with his readership, but he is all too aware that much of the terminology and critical analysis he includes in his reviews comes across as a foreign language unintelligible to those not versed in poetry. While poetry was extremely popular in previous centuries, making poets such as the romantics celebrities within their contemporary cultures, the advent of modernism introduced poetry widely perceived as too difficult, demanding, and alienating for the common reader. In *Beautiful and Pointless*, Orr works to alleviate this difficulty, making it clear to casual readers that there are no hard-and-fast rules for reading a poem. Orr has not written this slim volume to teach readers the terminology of poetry or a foolproof system to crack the poetry "code." Rather, he attempts to pinpoint poetry's place on the spectrum of things to read, comprehend, and master.

In his introduction, Orr outlines the troubled relationship he has observed between casual readers and modern poetry, noting that as poetry has become more modern and complex, fewer people seem to want to read it. However, he argues that this disconnect is not necessarily due to a dislike of poetry; readers are usually confounded by poetry, not annoyed by it. These uninitiated readers, Orr is quick to point out, are not unintelligent. In fact, he notes that many of the readers confused and intimidated by poetry are capable people who excel in their individual fields but experience feelings of inadequacy when confronted with poetry. More often than not, such readers seem to be misled by their preconceptions of what poetry is supposed to be and do. Orr attributes this confusion to the widening divide between poet and audience and notes that many of the books that attempt to bridge this divide only succeed in making matters worse. Orr presents *Beautiful and Pointless* as an alternative to such works. Rather than attempt to explain the field of poetry in scholarly or theoretical terms or describe the various forms and techniques of the craft, he seeks to illuminate the ways in which modern poets think and express themselves and readers of modern poetry read and relate to poems. It is Orr's hope that with this knowledge, readers will be able to find a comfortable place in the world of poetry and engage in lively discussion about poems, rather than remain confused or give up on poetry entirely. This discussion may not be entirely positive, but it is a key part of the process. While poetry critics such as Orr can steer a reader toward poetry, the reader's response to each poem or poet is unique and deeply personal. To Orr, the fact that a response occurs is of more importance than the positive or negative nature of the response.

(Tom McGhee)

David Orr is as an award-winning reviewer and poetry critic. The poetry columnist for the New Times Book Review, *he has published additional reviews and essays in publications such as* Poetry.

The bulk of the book is divided into six chapters reminiscent of essays: "The Personal," "The Political," "Form," "Ambition," "The Fishbowl," and "Why Bother?" In "The Personal," Orr differentiates between the personal and the private in regard to poetry, and he further notes that the personal is not always what readers perceive it to be. While a poem may seem "personal," it may not in fact be literal; the poet may employ a first-person point of view simply to serve the greater intent of the poem. The reader, however, may misinterpret the identity of this poetic speaker and incorrectly assume that what the poet is saying is literally true. The necessity of this distinction becomes apparent as Orr recounts the reaction he received upon telling an acquaintance that he is a poetry critic—a person who, in the mind of the acquaintance, criticizes a vulnerable poet's heartfelt confessions. This anecdote aptly demonstrates another of the misconceptions about poetry that Orr seeks to correct. Novels and works of nonfiction, Orr points out, are frequently reviewed and analyzed by critics, and this practice has achieved mainstream acceptance. Yet, because poetry is considered by many to be a literary form that is personal, unapproachable, and ultimately different, the idea of critiquing it as one would critique any work is perceived to be inappropriate, as if the critic is critiquing the poet's soul.

Orr suggests that this frustrating disconnect would soon disappear if more people felt comfortable with poetry, and he further seems to suggest that this perception of the strangeness of poetry is due in part to the mythology that poets have created about their field. Many poets have invented catchphrases in order to justify poetry's vital importance to society, and Orr takes issue in particular with the American poet Rita Dove's statement that "poetry is language at its most distilled and most powerful." In addition to objecting to this statement for practical reasons—advertising slogans, for instance, can be even more distilled and powerful—Orr sees the statement and its ilk as representations of the "'Poetry as Super Language' school of thinking," which "inclines toward the not exactly modest." Orr aims to dispel the misguided air of mystery and the variety of platitudes and false pronouncements that represent poetry as something excessively great. Such representation confuses the reality of poetry, which in his view should be able to stand on its own and attract new believers in the art form without being sold on false pretenses.

Throughout the book, Orr reassures readers that reading poetry is a personal and individual experience, and there is no right or wrong way to read a poem. New or casual readers of poetry should not be intimidated or afraid of liking or disliking the wrong work. A well-read lover of poetry might be brought to tears by a particularly sentimental poem that most readers find trite; likewise, the same individual might read a critically acclaimed poem by an award-winning poet and find that it does not evoke an emotional response. Those who love or appreciate poetry are not necessarily better judges of what constitutes a good poem, and the power of a poem and its quality as a poem are not the same thing. "Your own response," Orr writes, is "the most vital and disturbing faculty you possess. . . . You want to become a reader of modern poetry, not a receiver of the verdicts of modern poetry critics."

In addition to demystifying poetry, Orr seeks to further explore the reality of poets themselves. Misconceptions in this area are, once again, based in part upon presentation. During the lifetime of a poet, he or she can be perceived as ambitious merely by presenting himself or herself as such. As Orr sees it, this willingness to be ambitious leads the public to view the poet as being great. Orr explains that such judgments often change over time, and the poet's contemporary reputation can be superseded by later analyses and critiques. He provides as an example the case of the poets Robert Lowell and Elizabeth Bishop, friends and contemporaries. Orr argues that Lowell was considered to meet the definition of a great poet during his lifetime, while Bishop, though successful, did not rise to that standard. In the decades following their deaths, however, Bishop increased in acclaim, possibly surpassing Lowell. The author comes to the conclusion that a poet's style is not a very accurate barometer of greatness. Orr additionally reminds readers that poets themselves are not a monolithic group and that they frequently disagree about subject matter, form, and language, among other topics. In the chapter "Form," he discusses some of the historical background behind such disagreements, noting that there are conservative poets who believe in employing fixed forms for writing, radical poets who express themselves in various free forms, and poets who employ a mixture of these techniques. This information further illuminates the inner workings of the poetry world, allowing casual readers of poetry to better understand the field and its products.

Orr's tone throughout *Beautiful and Pointless* is relaxed and witty, though at times he seems somewhat overly detached from his topic. The work itself is engaging and includes references to such aspects of popular culture as college football, Courtney Love, and *The Fellowship of the Ring*. Supporting his arguments with a variety of poetic quotations, Orr takes the opportunity to introduce readers to the works of poets with whom they may not be familiar. Some of Orr's provocative statements have garnered puzzlement from the poetry community and been questioned by a number of critics, but as he notes in his introduction, he does not expect his readers to agree with each of his points, nor does he want them to; the ability to disagree and form personal responses to poetry and poetry criticism is of paramount importance.

Mindful of his audience, Orr does not attempt to convert those who have no interest in poetry. He recognizes that his readership comprises those who are already somewhat familiar with poetry and those who want to be—interested outsiders, as he terms them. Orr serves this audience by removing some of the mystique of poetry, reminding readers that poets are human beings and that many of the apparent idiosyncrasies of poetry are not unique to the genre. The work is successful not in making poetry accessible to readers but in reminding interested readers that poetry *is* accessible. Ultimately, while Orr admits that poetry is at times less than beautiful, his work illustrates through humor, instructive perspective, and provocative analysis that it is rarely pointless.

Jeffry Jensen

Review Sources

Commonweal 138, no. 15 (September 9, 2011): 18–20.
Library Journal 136, no. 8 (May 1, 2011): 84.
The New York Times Book Review, April 10, 2011, p. 12.
Publishers Weekly 258, no. 13 (March 28, 2011): 2.

Believing Is Seeing
Observations on the Mysteries of Photography

Author: Errol Morris (b. 1948)
Publisher: Penguin (New York). Illustrated.
  336 pp. $40.00
Type of work: Essays
Time: Mid-twentieth century

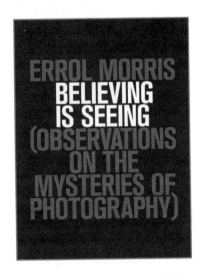

Filmmaker Errol Morris interrogates the relationship between image and reality, examining the stories behind several popular and controversial photographs.

As a boy, Errol Morris knew his father only through family stories and photographs. These pictures seemed to prove his existence, but at the same time they indicated his absence, to such an extent that Morris would never truly know him. This skepticism of vision, Morris suggests, has haunted him and his work, onscreen and in print, ever since.

Every essay in Morris's *Believing Is Seeing: Observations on the Mysteries of Photography* reads like a documentary film excursion. The study includes a five-page index, two pages of illustration credits, and twenty-six pages of notes. The text includes numerous photographs as well as transcripts of interviews conducted by the filmmaker, who presents the raw materials of his investigation as if inviting the reader to jump in and take part. Just as his documentaries, most popularly *The Thin Blue Line* (1988) and *The Fog of War* (2003), have questioned how the truth can be constructed and concealed, this collection of essays probes the ways in which observation follows belief. In Morris's own words, "What we see is often determined by our beliefs. Believing is seeing, not the other way around." Here, Morris focuses on a series of popular photographs, rooting each photo within a wider context with a conversational style and a rigorous search for truth.

Prompted by literary and cultural critic Susan Sontag, the first essay examines British photographer Roger Fenton's widely contested photographs of the Crimean War. As he travels to the Black Sea to discover for himself how Fenton might have posed these photographs (if in fact they were posed), Morris reveals the inherent ambiguity that results from any attempt to verify a photograph's supposed truth. The questions that emerge in this section pervade the essays that follow. What makes a posed photograph more truthful than an incidental photograph? If one is more ethical than the other, why is that the case? Can photography provide graphic evidence?

The second essay considers the ways in which photographs reveal and conceal, discussing specifically the *New York Times* photo of Ali Shalal Qaissi, the man incorrectly identified as the "Hooded Man" in a photo of the abuses at Abu Ghraib prison in Iraq.

In the photo, Qaissi holds the infamous picture of a prisoner wired for torture, standing on a box with his arms outstretched. Morris reflects that observers can make false inferences from a photograph "based on seeing nothing and imagining everything." Though he originally claimed to be the man in the photograph, Qaissi later admitted that was not the case. He was indeed a prisoner at Abu Ghraib, however, and has since become an advocate for former prisoners. Recognizing the image's power, he appropriated it for his business card.

Next, Morris approaches the photograph of US Army specialist Sabrina Harman leaning over a mutilated corpse, smiling at the camera as she gives a thumbs-up. Later, Harman was alarmed to learn that, contrary to what she had been told, Manadel al-Jamadi had died in interrogation. Morris includes pictures of the interrogation log book, supporting the actual story of his death. Further documents assert that al-Jamadi was put on ice in a body bag and thrown into a shower. In this case, the layers of manipulated truth are complicated by the overt fabrications that Harman's superiors provided to both prisoners and officers. Morris questions who really killed al-Jamadi, considering the CIA interrogator, his translator, and members of various military units. To date, no one from the CIA has been charged. According to Morris, some believe that CIA personnel involved with al-Jamadi's death were protected at the highest level of government. However, charges were ultimately brought against Sabrina Harman for taking photographs of his body. In an interview with Morris, Harman discloses that she was charged with "the destruction of government property . . . and then maltreatment, of taking the photo of the dead guy," and that military defense lawyers asked her to plead guilty to numerous charges, including altering evidence.

Focusing on the photo itself, which inspired the *New York Post* to label Harman as "The Ghoul Next Door," Morris unpacks the layers of story and truth that complicate the image. He consults a psychologist specializing in emotions and facial expressions, Paul Ekman, who claims that Harman's smile is a mere pose, lacking the movement of the eye-cover fold that indicates true enjoyment. Viewer responses to the photograph reveal that the initial reaction to seeing the body is horror, followed by the desire to smile back. Finally, viewers feel anger at the person smiling for having tricked them into enjoyment of viewing the dead body. However, as Morris argues, it is incorrect to assume that "the photographs tell it all," and similarly incorrect was the natural assumption that the girl smiling in the photograph was also the murderer. Morris writes,

> We see al-Jamadi's body, but we don't see the homicidal act that turned him from a human being into a corpse. We don't understand what the photograph means, nor what it is about. Instead of asking, Who is that man? Who killed him? the question becomes, Why is this woman smiling?

Harman claims that she was smiling because she wanted to expose murder, "to provide proof of what others were trying to deny" at Abu Ghraib. The photograph simply could not tell the complete story.

Chapter four pursues the subjects of captioning, propaganda, and fraud, as Morris considers newspaper accounts of the South Dakota drought of 1936 and *Time*

Academy Award–winning filmmaker Er-
rol Morris has produced and directed
such documentaries as The Thin Blue
Line *(1988),* Mr. Death: The Rise and
Fall of Fred A. Leuchter Jr. *(1999),* The
Fog of War: Eleven Lessons from the
Life of Robert S. McNamara *(2003), and*
Standard Operating Procedure *(2008).*
He has received awards from the Na-
tional Endowment for the Arts, the John
Simon Guggenheim Memorial Founda-
tion, and the John D. and Catherine T.
MacArthur Foundation.

magazine's coverage of Roosevelt's special train to the Dakotas in the same year. The pages are filled with reproductions of newspapers, reports from Farm Security Administration files, the photography of Arthur Rothstein, and interview transcripts. Morris's discussion of what these publishers wanted to convey is interspersed with his discussion of the ethics and aesthetics of cropping, as well as definitions of art. Morris reveals that Rothstein's famous photo *Fleeing a Dust Storm* (1944) was composed with Rothstein giving directions to his subjects as if to actors, a fact that offended many critics, who latched onto the notion that Rothstein's photos were really propaganda masquerading as art. Interviews with scholars James Curtis and William Stott, photographer Bill Ganzel, and the editors of *Film Forum* present radically different views of Rothstein's photos, leading Morris to conclude that a photograph can be interpreted in many different ways and can serve different functions simultaneously, such as "staged propaganda, documentary evidence, and fine art."

Continuing his discussion of propaganda and posing, Morris turns to Ben Curtis's Associated Press photo of a Mickey Mouse doll lying in a "bleak war zone landscape" in Tyre, Lebanon. The article that features the photo goes on to indict the Israeli military for flattening the apartment blocks in the background. Interviewing the photographer, Morris asks, "What is the viewer supposed to infer from such a scene? Is it disguised propaganda with a definite bias towards one side or another?" Curtis admits that the Israelis said that the place they bombed was housing for a Hezbollah operation, information that had not been in the caption. He claims that the toy was there as photographed, but Morris, demonstrating his background as a private investigator, wants to find the exact spot where the photo was taken. Drawing from satellite information of the wreckage of Tyre, he breaks down the area block by block and compares the satellite reconnaissance map with accounts of where the AP convoy would have been. But judging from the map, a number of buildings around the Mickey Mouse doll spot were destroyed. Morris asks, "So how did you stumble on Mickey Mouse?" Curtis explains the attraction of the image: "There were hardly any people at the scene. You can send pictures of the rubble, it tells you something, maybe, but you're looking for something that shows some humanity or shows some indication of what the place was like, who was living there." Ultimately, Morris finds that Curtis did not intend the photo to be taken as anti-Israeli propaganda. However, to emphasize the point of a simple image's capacity for misinterpretation, Morris reproduces the same photo attached to an article indicting Hezbollah for using civilians as human shields. He also adds a political cartoon that features Mickey Mouse strapped with dynamite and standing in front of a blackboard that reads, "How to Kill Jews and Go to Heaven."

The next chapter considers an ambrotype of three children that was found on the body of Amos Humiston, a Union soldier killed at the battle of Gettysburg during the Civil War. The photo fell into the hands of Dr. J. Francis Bourns, who at first used it to discover Humiston's identity but eventually used the photo for his own financial gain. In his typically thorough and detailed fashion, Morris supplements his text with Bourns's duplication, newspaper accounts, the transcript of his interview with Humiston's biographer, letters from Humiston to his wife, maps showing the regiment's course and where the letters to the wife were sent, a picture of the soldier with and without a beard, and a stereogram of the place where Humiston died. Also reproduced are the cards that were made out of both the picture of Humiston and the picture of his children. Bourns sold these cards to support an orphanage for the children of soldiers, but he was also guilty of taking advantage of Humiston's memory, to say nothing of the money he embezzled.

Combining the investigate style and epistemological complexity of Morris's documentary films, *Believing Is Seeing* is both a riveting, accessible read and a significant advance in the work of a popular thinker and artist. Morris's comments on the impossibility of certain kinds of knowledge have struck some reviewers as ironic, given his insistent and rigorous pursuit of the truth. Still, few recent writers or filmmakers have so enjoyably invited audiences to consider the tenability of knowledge.

Batya Weinbaum

Review Sources

The Christian Science Monitor, October 25, 2011 (Web).
Los Angeles Times, August 28, 2011 (Web).
Mother Jones 36, no. 5 (September/October 2011): 63.
The New York Times Book Review, September 1, 2011 (Web).

Binocular Vision
New and Selected Stories

Author: Edith Pearlman (b. 1936)
Publisher: Lookout Books (Wilmington, NC). 392 pp. $18.95
Type of work: Short stories

This collection of short fiction includes eighteen stories from Edith Pearlman's first three collections, plus sixteen new stories.

Principal characters:

CORNELIA FITCH, an elderly woman who decides to take her own life

JOE, a Southeast Asian who moves to Israel to care for an elderly man

LUCIENNE, a sixty-year-old retired high school teacher

MARTA PERERA DE LEFKOWITZ, a Polish Jewish doctor and Holocaust survivor, minister of health in a dictatorial Latin American country

ROBERT, a Jewish man who travels with his gay son to adopt a child on Yom Kippur

SONYA SOFRANKOVITCH, a woman who works in a displaced persons camp in Europe after World War II

SOPHIE, a seven-year-old girl who becomes separated from her parents in Boston

Edith Pearlman is among those rare fiction writers (such as Alice Munro, David Means, and Deborah Eisenberg) who, despite the entreaties of their publishers to write a novel, maintain their allegiance to the frequently ignored, often underrated short story form. Pearlman's first collection, *Vaquita and Other Stories* (1996), won the 1996 Drue Heinz Literature Prize and was subsequently published by the University of Pittsburg Press. However, since the prize is awarded only to short stories, *Vaquita* did not garner wide publicity or achieve impressive sales. Pearlman's second book, *Love among the Greats and Other Stories* (2002), published by Eastern Washington University Press, won the Spokane Prize for Short Fiction, but again reviewers did not give it much attention. Her third collection, *How to Fall* (2005), was published by Sarabande Books and won the Mary McCarthy Prize in Short Fiction. Still, her work remained relatively unknown.

In the introduction to Pearlman's fourth book, *Binocular Vision: New and Selected Stories*, Ann Patchett adds the following question to the list of great human mysteries: Why isn't Edith Pearlman famous? Patchett herself admits that until she served as guest editor for *Best American Short Stories* in 2006, she had never heard of Edith

Pearlman. Now, however, she is Pearlman's staunchest fan. In the *New York Times Book Review*, Roxanne Robinson begins her review of *Binocular Vision* with the lament, "Why in the world had I never heard of Edith Pearlman?" David Ulin, in the *Los Angeles Times*, confesses that he had never heard of Edith Pearlman before reading *Binocular Vision*, mitigating the admission by adding that had he known of Pearlman before now, he would have been deprived of the great joy of discovering her.

Binocular Vision is Pearlman's first book to receive significant attention. It is a generous collection, gathering eighteen stories from previous collections and sixteen "new," uncollected stories. Published by the creative writing department at the University of North Carolina in Wilmington, the collection has won the PEN/Malamud Award for "excellence in the art of the short story." The fact that it has taken reviewers over thirty years to "discover" and praise a writer in her mid-seventies says a great deal about how little respect the short story receives in the literary world, where the novel reigns supreme.

Pearlman's stories do not usually have the expansiveness of the stories of Alice Munro, which reviewers favor for being "novelistic." Rather, her work recalls the tightly woven stories of Bernard Malamud, Flannery O'Connor, and John Cheever, focusing on significant revelatory experiences of characters who suddenly understand something about themselves and the world in a metaphoric resolution. For example, the opening story, "Inbound," is about Sophie, a seven-year-old girl who becomes separated from her parents on the streets of Boston, and Lily, her little sister with Down's syndrome. Although Sophie feels alone and unknown, she also feels free in a way she has not felt since Lily's birth. Because her father has told her about the train tracks that run through the city—one outbound, one inbound— Sophie goes to the station, where she knows her parents will find her. Strikingly, she thinks those tracks are like her and Lily, running side by side but in different directions. Reunited with her family, Sophie sees the future unrolling before her as Lily calls out her name. It is a delicate, perfect story of a young girl's coming to terms with the difficulties she must face when she finds herself alone, but it is not the kind of story that reviewers would think of as complexly novelistic.

Although "Day of Awe" has more of the cultural context attractive to reviewers (an elderly man accompanies his gay son to a Central American country to adopt a young boy), it is a classic short story that moves toward a culminating metaphor of moral revelation. The story takes place on the evening of Yom Kippur. The man, conflicted about his son's sexual orientation, seeks some solace in the holy celebration even as he feels that he and his son are the only Jews in the entire cursed country. However, as he leaves a church with his son and the adopted boy, he comes to the kind of understanding that Bernard Malamud once wrote about: that we are all outcasts, all Jews. The young boy makes a gesture that looks at first as if he is waving the man off, but really the child is beckoning him. Seeing this, the man realizes the difference between what the gesture seems to say ("get lost") and what it actually means ("come here").

"Vaquita," the title story of Pearlman's first collection, is about Marta Perera de Lefkowitz, an elderly Polish Jewish doctor and Holocaust survivor who currently acts as the minister of health in a dictatorial Latin American country. She hopes to flee

(© Jonathan Sachs)

Edith Pearlman's short stories have been selected three times for Best American Short Stories. She has won three O. Henry Prizes and two Pushcart Prizes.

to Israel to escape persecution for her liberal views. Sixty years earlier, as a young woman in Czechoslovakia, she escaped the Nazis by hiding in a peasant's barn, where her only companion was a cow she called "my little cow," or *vaquita* in Spanish. The nurturing cow is metaphorically related to Marta's role as minister of health; when she tries, unsuccessfully, to start a breast-feeding campaign in the country, the milk formula companies scornfully call her "*la vaca*," the cow. During her subsequent escape through a rural part of the country, she encounters an eighteen-year-old girl with a nursing baby, a maternal image that stimulates her own nurturing nature. In a gesture of reconciliation typical of many of Pearlman's stories, she gives the girl a valuable diamond pin, even though she knows it means she will have to travel to Jerusalem penniless.

"Allog" centers on an immigrant community living in an apartment building in Israel. Joe, a Southeast Asian man, is brought to Israel to care for eighty-five-year-old Mr. Goldfanger, who is ill. Joe says the old man would be a kind of chieftain in his country, an *allog*, meaning a wise elder who is consulted on important questions. But the real wise man in the story is Joe himself, for he is something of a magician, able to repair anything and everything for the people in the building. Joe, Mrs. Goldfanger says, is descended from the angels. One of the occupants of the building is an opera singer referred to as "the soprano" (a friend of the central character in "Vaquita"). When the soprano has a heart attack, Joe is the one who gives her mouth-to-mouth resuscitation, but to no avail; when he gives up the effort, he is the one who cries. Because she has no family of her own, the soprano has left her belongings to Joe, who takes up residence in her apartment and becomes an *allog*. The term eventually loses its original meaning, "chieftain," and comes instead to mean "Resident Indispensable"—a title that some in Tel Aviv, the narration notes ironically, use for the janitor. Pearlman has said that the story, which was chosen for *Best American Short Stories* in 2000, came from her experience of living in Jerusalem and getting to know several East Asians who cared for the elderly. Admiring their tolerance and tact, qualities she felt were sometimes lacking in Israelis, she imagined the changes that might take place if these Asian caregivers had a wider influence.

The term "binocular vision" refers to vision in which both eyes fix on the same image at the same time, working together to create depth perception. In the title story, a young girl spies on the couple next door through her father's binoculars, assuming that this gives her access to their secrets; however, when one of the neighbors commits suicide, she realizes that this assumption is an illusion and that she knows nothing about them after all. Learning that the man had been living with his mother, the girl says, "I thought she was his wife," to which the mother replies, "So did she." One of the shortest stories in the collection, "Binocular Vision" is perhaps emblematic of the entire collection, for even though Pearlman's stories seem simple and straightforward on the surface, when looked at with the totality of vision, they take on hidden depth, exposing the secret lives of ordinary characters.

In "The Story," another short parable, sixty-year-old Lucienne, a retired high school teacher at a dinner party, tells the story of her father, who during World War II goes out with his twelve-year-old son and is stopped by the Nazis. When they try to take his son, the father denies that he knows the boy, calling him just some *goy*. In her comments in the 2003 *O. Henry Prize Stories*, Pearlman says someone told her this anecdote many years ago, but she always felt it was too tragic to repeat until she hit upon the idea of exploiting her own reluctance. Also emblematic is "Tess," a perfectly controlled, elegiac story about a two-year-old child on life support. The story moves inevitably toward the final moment, when the mother detaches the tube that supplies nutrients to the child's heart, so that the blood pools silently and invisibly like the monthly cycle the little girl will never have.

Some of Pearlman's stories offer such concise, compact tales that early reviewers may have thought they were formulaic and simplistic. For example, "Capers" is a relatively light story about an elderly couple who take up shoplifting to infuse their golden years with a little excitement. In "Girl in Blue with Brown Bag," a seventeen-year-old girl purloins a valuable painting for her sixty-seven-year-old tutor, only to find she must devise a clever way to give it to a museum without being caught. "Unravished Bride" is a delicate story about an abortive love affair that evokes the lovers on Keats's famous urn, a love that is frozen in time, never to be consummated. In "The Noncombatant," a forty-nine-year-old man dying of cancer and a woman who has lost her husband come together in a melancholic moment that replicates Alfred Eisenstaedt's famous photograph of a sailor kissing a nurse on V-J Day in Times Square.

The most highly praised stories in the collection are the ones that deal with the Jewish experience during and after World War II, especially those that create a kind of novelistic linkage and follow characters who reappear in other stories, . Three stories focus on Sonya Sofrankovitch, who works in a European displaced persons camp. "If Love Were All," the longest story in the collection, deals with Sonya's work for a relocation committee in London following the war.

Pearlman's most powerful stories are the brief, tightly written ones narrated with poetic language and culminating metaphor. One of her strongest and shortest is the concluding story of the collection, "Self-Reliance." In her contributor's notes to *Best American Short Stories* in 2006, Pearlman says the story came about after a young high school student asked her what she would write about if she were allowed to write just one more story. Pearlman immediately answered, "Death," and consequently she invented Cornelia Fitch, the elderly woman of "Self-Reliance," who suffers from cancer. In a highly controlled evocation of one woman's final transformative journey, Cornelia decides to take her own life. Now that reviewers have finally discovered the brilliant short stories of Edith Pearlman, readers should be very happy to learn that "Self-Reliance" will not, in fact, be her last.

Charles E. May

Review Sources

The Boston Globe, January 17, 2011 (Web).
Los Angeles Times, January 16, 2011 (Web).
The New York Times, January 16, 2011, p. 4.
Publishers Weekly 258, no. 3 (January 17, 2011): 8–9.
Writer 124, no. 9 (September 2011): 28–9.

Bismarck
A Life

Author: Jonathan Steinberg
Publisher: Oxford University Press (New York). Illustrated. 592 pp. $34.95
Type of work: Biography

Jonathan Steinberg presents a critical biography of Otto von Bismarck, the statesman who became a master of power politics and unified Germany by force.

Principal personages:
OTTO VON BISMARCK (1815–1898), statesman and German chancellor
WILHELM I (1797–1888), king of Prussia and first emperor of Germany
AUGUSTA (1811–1890), queen of Prussia and first empress of Germany

Otto von Bismarck engineered the unification of the modern German state on his own terms, overcoming seemingly insuperable obstacles. He was the chief minister of his monarch for twenty-eight years, during which period he dominated the diplomacy of Europe. So uncanny was his diplomatic genius that his successors in office frankly conceded that they were unequal to understanding, much less maintaining, the subtlety of his work. He became famous for his mastery of international power politics, which in the wake of his career became known as realpolitik. His devotion to a diplomacy of ruthless realism won him the admiration of later diplomats such as Henry Kissinger. These achievements easily make Bismarck a world historical figure; he reordered the political landscape of Europe in ways that altered the course of history in the tumultuous decades after his death.

Jonathan Steinberg, the author of *Bismarck: A Life*, holds his subject to be the most successful statesman of the nineteenth century, giving due credit to his diplomatic genius. However, Steinberg also considers the cost of Bismarck's triumphs. The state that Bismarck created, he points out, reflected his brutal methods and relentless quest for power, ensuring that only he could manage the unwieldy political structure of imperial Germany. After his forced retirement, he passed on a state that was domestically and diplomatically unstable. Within a quarter century, Germany had helped precipitate World War I, a conflict the imperial regime did not survive. Out of the postwar chaos, Adolf Hitler and his Nazi movement emerged and eventually seized power. Steinberg submits that there is a clear continuity between the Germany Bismarck created and the Germany that accepted Hitler as its leader. To blame Bismarck for Nazism is too great a stretch, to be sure, but it is undeniable, Steinberg argues, that Bismarck worked to undermine the success of genuine representative institutions in Germany, and his prolonged star turn as the head of government fostered a cult of the genius leader that Kaiser Wilhelm II would fail and Adolf Hitler would exploit. Consequently, the legacy of "the Iron Chancellor" is ultimately one of failure. Bismarck brought into being a German state that was fatally flawed, imbuing it with a militaristic spirit and paranoia that ultimately led to cataclysm. According to Steinberg, Bismarck did not believe in much, but his mistakes ensured that what he did believe in—the monarchy, the supremacy of the Junker aristocracy—survived for a mere generation after his death. Bismarck built grandly and brilliantly, but ultimately he built with sand.

Steinberg attributes both the successes and failures of Bismarck's statesmanship to failures of character. The picture that he paints of Bismarck is hardly complimentary, being that of a largely amoral egotist whose pettiness and vindictiveness confounded those around him. While diplomatic memoirs of his day record many instances of Bismarck's charm and scintillating conversation, his normal mode of interaction appears to have been cold and brusque. His social attachments were few and complicated, and during his career, he left behind a long string of associates whom he betrayed, discarded, or condemned at his convenience. Bismarck focused himself on attaining his goals, his own personal life and happiness subordinate to his insatiable need for mastery and victory. Without such grim determination, Steinberg suggests, Bismarck might not have orchestrated a succession of limited wars that swiftly and successfully unified Germany; however, a better man might have created a better Germany.

Steinberg traces Bismarck's tortured character back to an unhappy childhood among the Junkers, the Prussian landowning nobility, who fiercely protected their own aristocratic prerogatives and the Prussian monarchy. Junker families dominated the army and state offices in Prussia, and they would continue to be prominent in the new Germany until the Red Army finally overran their ancestral homelands in 1945. Bismarck's father was a bluff country squire, kindly and eccentric; he sought no distinction beyond influence in his own locality, and for this his son regarded him as weak. Bismarck's mother, well educated and demanding, sent her son to a boarding school, which he loathed. In later years, he claimed that he hated his mother even as a child and systematically lied to her in his letters.

Bismarck's anger toward his parents scarred his life and anticipated his own domestic issues, as he proved unable to build a healthy family life himself. He married a woman whose family and connections he thought would be useful to his political advancement, claiming to love her in spite of her intellectual inferiority and her refusal to act as a society hostess. She was known popularly for sharing and stoking his many hatreds. Bismarck's relations with his children were equally conflicted. When his eldest son fell in love with a relative of his political opponent, Bismarck prevented the marriage, heedless of the emotional consequences.

Bismarck's hatred of his mother led him to be vocally misogynistic throughout his life, despite his occasional platonic attachments to women in his social circle. The main focus of his misogynistic ire was the women of the royal family. Queen Augusta, the wife of King Wilhelm I, distrusted Bismarck's hold over her husband and disliked his reactionary politics. The crown princess Victoria, the eldest daughter

Jonathan Steinberg taught for thirty-three years at Cambridge University before becoming the Walter H. Annenberg Professor of Modern European History at the University of Pennsylvania. He is the author of Yesterday's Deterrent: Tirpitz and the Birth of the German Battle Fleet *(1993) and* All or Nothing: The Axis and the Holocaust, 1941–1943 *(2002).*

of Queen Victoria of Great Britain, encouraged her husband Frederick III's liberal beliefs and was appalled by Bismarck's methods and policies. Steinberg poses that one of the tragic ironies of Bismarck's life was that in his official relationship with the royal family, he recapitulated the drama of his early life, negotiating his way between "weak" men and "strong" women. The psychic strain on him was tremendous. One of the most startling aspects of Bismarck, the strong man who preached blood and iron, is that he was a hypochondriac, suffering from frequent nervous and physical breakdowns. He regularly retreated to his estates and was often away from his desk in Berlin for months at a time. However, if he was to exercise power, there could be no escape from contact with the royals and a perpetual guerrilla war with ladies who had their husbands' ears at the breakfast table.

Steinberg emphasizes that Bismarck's political career and his stunning achievements were entirely dependent upon the favor of his monarch and later the kaiser, Wilhelm I. Honorable, conscientious, and conservative, Wilhelm I was a very different man from Bismarck. Though frequently shocked and exasperated by the policies of his chancellor, he appreciated the advantages that his dynasty accrued and remained steadfastly loyal to his servant. Wilhelm I sustained Bismarck through crises and triumphs both. Bismarck never had a parliamentary party upon which he could rely, and he alienated most of his allies during his career's convoluted course, so his partnership with Wilhelm I was a matter of vital importance. By living to the ripe age of ninety-one years old, Wilhelm I ensured that Bismarck would enjoy decades in power and Germany would not evolve into a constitutional monarchy with firmly rooted liberal institutions. By another quirk of fate, Wilhelm I's son, Frederick III, who did want to develop a liberal constitution, ruled for only three months before dying of throat cancer. His son Wilhelm II inherited the autocracy Bismarck had created, and after ungratefully dismissing its architect, he led the now-faltering political machine to ruin with World War I.

Bismarck maintained his long hold on Wilhelm I by force of personality. Contemporary accounts often described him as "demonic." Steinberg writes of Bismarck's "sovereign self," a mysterious, personal magnetism with which he could bend people to his will, a quality that is all the more remarkable given that he was in no other way charismatic. He was not a compelling speaker or a leader in the conventional sense. Although he often wore a uniform, he was not a soldier, and in fact had avoided military service in his youth. In politics, he never managed to build a strong, reliable party; a virtuoso, he stood alone, focusing his intense passions on the pursuit and use of power. His fateful alliance with Wilhelm I gave him the opportunity to exercise gifts that might otherwise have been directed at the tenants of his Prussian estate.

The result was breathtaking. Bismarck forced the rapid unification of Germany under Prussian leadership, serially eliminating powers that might object: first Denmark, then Austria, and finally France. Steinberg submits that these wars established a tradition of German military efficiency and ruthlessness that would extend into the next century. Bismarck handled domestic opponents with the same brutal finesse that characterized his diplomacy, undercutting the local monarchs by instituting universal suffrage for the national legislature. Associating the nationalist cause with the monarchy, he was able to outmaneuver the liberals and, later, acquire a colonial empire. He launched the first welfare state in Europe, undermining any appeal that socialists might pose. What united Bismarck's diplomacy and politics was a taste for confrontation and conflict and a binary view of the world, clearly demarcated into black and white. What separated this view from others was that it was largely objective and drained of moral content, reflecting instead the calculus of power. His self-conscious decision to set aside moral and ideological scruples in his policy made it possible for him to see clearly through the fog of diplomacy better than his fellow statesmen and manipulate friends and adversaries when necessary.

Steinberg's compelling biography of Bismarck will remind readers of the importance of the individual in history and the capacity of a gifted person to bend events for good or ill. Whether Bismarck left the world a better or worse place is not immediately obvious. Steinberg's judgment of his subject is harsh, but the father of realpolitik has his defenders. Steinberg's book is impressive, but it will not likely be the last word on Otto von Bismarck.

Daniel P. Murphy

Review Sources

The American Spectator 44, no. 6 (July/August 2011): 81–4.
The Economist 398, no. 8727 (April 2, 2011): 80.
Library Journal 136, no. 5 (March 15, 2011): 122.
National Review 63, no. 9 (May 16, 2011): 47–50.
New Criterion 29, no. 10 (June 2011): 80–2.
The New York Times Book Review, April 3, 2011, p. 1.
Publishers Weekly 258, no. 3 (January 17, 2011): 37.
The Wall Street Journal, April 9, 2011, p. C8.

The Bitter Waters of Medicine Creek
A Tragic Clash Between White and Native America

Author: Richard Kluger (b. 1934)
Publisher: Alfred A. Knopf (New York). 352 pp.
$28.95
Type of work: History
Time: 1853–1857
Locale: Puget Sound area of Washington State

A historical account of the conflict between white settlers and the Nisqually nation of Washington State during and after the Puget Sound Indian War.

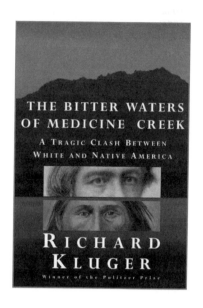

Principal personages:

LESCHI (1808–1858), chief of the Nisqually nation during the 1850s, tried and executed for murder after the Puget Sound Indian War

ISAAC STEVENS (1818–1862), the first governor of the Washington Territory

QUIEMUTH, Leschi's brother and a leading combatant in the Puget Sound War

CYNTHIA IYALL (b. 1961), descendant of Chief Leschi and chairman of the Nisqually tribal council since 2006, one of the chief architects of the effort to exonerate Leschi

WILLIAM FRASER TOLMIE (1833–1865), company manager of Fort Nisqually and an opponent of Stevens's policies regarding the Nisqually

ABRAM BENTON MOSES (?–1855), a member of the volunteer militia recruited to counter Native American aggression in the Puget Sound

SLUGGIA, a nephew of Leschi who gave military officers information that led to his arrest

In this work of revisionist history, Pulitzer Prize–winning author Richard Kluger distills the events surrounding the Puget Sound Indian War into a struggle between two ideologically charged leaders: Isaac Stevens, the military governor of the Washington Territory, and Leschi, the leader of the Nisqually nation, a small band of displaced Native Americans living at the edge of the Puget Sound. Drawing on numerous accounts from witnesses, legal officials, and historians, Kluger gives a detailed yet fast-paced account of the various military, legal, and bureaucratic forces that were brought to bear on the Nisqually in the effort to secure additional territory for colonization. While Kluger limits his scope to the Washington Territory, similar struggles between Native Americans and colonists occurred in many pioneer territories in the 1850s.

Kluger begins his investigation by briefly describing the political and social environment of the newly formed territories in the Pacific Northwest. Following the 1846

Richard Kluger won the Pulitzer Prize for his history of the American tobacco industry, Ashes to Ashes *(1996), while two of his other histories,* Simple Justice *(1976) and* The Paper *(1986), were National Book Award finalists. He has also published eight novels, beginning with* When the Bough Breaks *in 1964.*

Oregon treaty with the British government, traders and settlers began moving further into Washington, and the Puget Sound soon became an attractive area for potential colonization. Until 1853, settlement of the region amounted to a British trading outpost, Fort Nisqually, which was managed by the Hudson's Bay Company (HBC). The Nisqually nation maintained friendly relations with the white traders and trappers from the HBC. Leschi and his half brother Quiemuth traded with HBC representatives and were occasionally employed by the company to protect their goods and personnel. Company manager William Tolmie's records depict Leschi and the other Nisqually as friendly neighbors who were apparently willing to share their land and the abundant local resources with their British neighbors.

The problem arose from Washington, DC, where an expansionist policy was the dominant strain of political thought and where President Franklin Pierce and Congress were aggressively promoting local government officials who were able to secure new land for settlement. Fresh from the Mexican-American War, Pierce and Congress certainly wished to avoid Native American uprisings and other armed conflicts, but they made it clear that it was the duty of territorial leaders to secure binding treaties relocating Native American populations from more desirable territories and smoothing the way for further colonization. In addition, the 1850 gold rush in California meant that there were a plethora of settlers waiting to move further north, and the territories from Oregon to the edges of Washington were next in line for colonization.

General Isaac Stevens, a West Point graduate and Army-trained engineer, was appointed as the first governor of the newly settled Washington Territory. Having distinguished himself in the Mexican War, Stevens was an ambitious thirty-five-year-old politician who viewed his appointment as a chance to impress the upper echelons in the federal government. To this end, Stevens aimed to remove Native Americans from the territory by creating a treaty far more favorable to white interests than those secured by governors in other territories and states.

In his personal writings, Stevens's opinions of Native Americans range from admiration to disgust. Overall, he viewed Native Americans as inferior to whites in terms of morality and sophistication, but with a dignity and sincerity worthy of respect. After assuming the governorship, however, Stevens received direct orders from US secretary of state William Marcy to secure the removal of both HBC's Fort Nisqually trading post and the Native Americans living in the area. Stevens and Tolmie of the HBC became quick enemies, as Tolmie believed his company had rights under treaty to continue operations until an agreement had been reached between Great Britain and the US government. Tolmie, for his part, had the support of Leschi and other members of the Nisqually nation, a loose confederation of families who lived off the local land but had little in the way of formal government or leadership.

In 1854, Stevens appeared to have succeeded in his goal with the Treaty of Medicine Creek, a document allegedly signed by Leschi and other local tribal leaders that granted four thousand square miles to American settlers in return for the right to continue hunting on the land and the establishment of small reservation lands for each Native American family. Kluger's research indicates that Leschi never signed the Medicine Creek treaty and that his signature may have been forged. Whatever the truth was in this matter, is it clear that Leschi objected to the terms of the treaty and began organizing other Native Americans against Stevens. Leschi visited not only his own people but also other Native American groups in the region to gather support.

With tensions high, the event that touched off the Puget Sound Indian War was the 1855 White River Massacre, which resulted in eight casualties, including the death of volunteer militiaman Abraham Moses. An enraged Stevens declared martial law and openly called for the subjugation of all Native Americans in the area. "My plan is to make no treaty whatever with the tribes now in arms; to do away entirely with the reservations guaranteed to them; to make a summary example of all the leading spirits, and to place as a conquered people . . . the remains of those tribes on reservations," Stevens wrote in a letter to one of his colleagues.

Leschi's role in the massacre, like his part in signing the Medicine Creek treaty, is uncertain. Witnesses were unable to definitively place Leschi at the scene, and yet Leschi was formally accused of having murdered Moses. Some historians believe that the murder charge was a strategic move on Stevens's part, an effort to divide the Native Americans whom Leschi was attempting to unite. Stevens's tactics worked; although Leschi managed to evade authorities for some time, he was betrayed by his sister's son, Sluggia, who told military officers where to find his uncle.

Leschi's brother, Quiemuth, turned himself in to authorities soon after, but he was murdered before standing trial. The first jury charged with determining Leschi's guilt failed to reach a verdict due to a lack of evidence. The case was then brought before the territory's Supreme Court, where a spirited legal battle took place. In the end, Leschi was convicted and executed despite the apparent lack of strong evidence on the part of the prosecution. For a time, Stevens's brutal tactics ruined his credibility with federal officials, though he managed to revive his career and eventually served in the US Congress.

Kluger's historical account largely portrays Stevens as a villain, a position seemingly bolstered by most historical accounts of the conflict. The author's sympathy for the Native Americans whose culture was nearly destroyed in the Washington Territory is at no time hidden. His feelings are clear in his descriptions of their status before the arrival of white settlers, such as when he writes, "The Indians whom Isaac Stevens would soon encounter were truly blessed children of nature. It was their misfortune that history was about to catch up with paradise."

The bulk of *Bitter Waters* is a tensely written historical narrative of the events that occurred in and around the Puget Sound War, but Kluger diverges from his topic frequently to describe broader issues, such as the development of anti–Native American racism and the political pressures and promises that created the drive for western expansion. Additionally, Kluger's history examines the functions and failures of the American legal system in the mid-1800s and analyzes the way that the judicial branch was used and misused to address Native American displacement.

The 1857 Washington Supreme Court case of *Washington Territory v. Leschi, an Indian* was the first capital case tried before the newly formed supreme court of the territory. Questions about the legality and morality of the verdict and execution persisted, resulting finally in the decision to reexamine the case more than 150 years after Leschi's execution. In his epilogue, Kluger describes the efforts led by Nisqually tribal councilwoman Cynthia Iyall, a descendant of Leschi's, to bring his case back to the court after more than a century. Kluger ends his study on a more or less positive note, describing how Iyall and the Nisqually have strengthened their position in Washington State, moving toward prosperity with business interests in gambling and ecotourism.

With the publication of his Pulitzer Prize–winning examination of the tobacco industry, *Ashes to Ashes* (1996), Kluger demonstrated his capability for tackling controversial and complex topics and established himself as one of the nation's foremost historians. His history of segregation, *Simple Justice* (1976), which was nominated for a National Book Award, provides another example of his facility in navigating the labyrinthine landscape of social conflict.

His task in *Bitter Waters* is far more straightforward, as there is little if any effort made to defend or justify the actions of Stevens and his supporters. Kluger acknowledges, however, that Stevens was a product of his environment and that anti–Native American sentiment was rampant at the time, fueled by fear, greed, and prejudice. In the end, *Bitter Waters* is an exciting tale of a tragedy that, though largely unknown to most Americans, played out again and again during the long conflict between what he calls white and Native America. In his introductory preface, Kluger's aims are made clear as he asks why the plight of Native Americans has not been given the same attention as the struggles of other displaced populations around the globe. Kluger concludes that it may be a sense of shared guilt that makes it difficult for white Americans to examine the crimes of their own ancestors, perhaps coupled with the realization that Native American populations were left without sufficient numbers to rebound from the conflict. Kluger encourages his readers not to shy away from examining Native American history, if only for the lessons that history may provide to guide future actions. As Kluger concludes in the final sentence of his preface, "The cost of contemplating history is often an uneasy conscience."

Micah L. Issitt

Review Sources

Booklist 107, no. 7 (December 1, 2010): 12.
Library Journal 136, no. 1 (January 1, 2011): 111.
The New York Times Book Review, March 25, 2011 (Web).
Oregonian, March 26, 2011 (Web).
Publishers Weekly 257, no. 45 (November 15, 2010): 47.
San Francisco Chronicle, February 27, 2011 (Web).
Seattle Times, March 5, 2011 (Web).

Blake and the Bible

Author: Christopher Rowland (b. 1947)
Publisher: Yale University Press (New Haven, CT). 320 pp. $50.00
Type of work: History

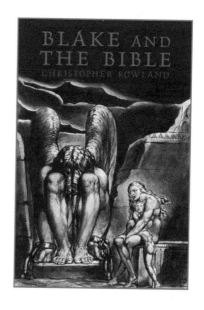

Christopher Rowland combines interpretations of William Blake's written and visual work to present an analysis of the artist as biblical theologian, self-styled prophet, and radical religious thinker.

Principal personages:

WILLIAM BLAKE (1757–1827), a British artist best known for his books in which he combined narratives with watercolor images

GERRARD WINSTANLEY (1609–1676), a radical Christian leader of the Digger movement, which emphasized the importance of communal land

ABIEZER COPPE (1619–1672), a radical Christian theorist whose ideas revolved around locating the divine within even the most humble members of humanity

RALPH CUDWORTH (1617–1688), a theologian who called for the integration of religious scholarship with a pious lifestyle

HANS DENCK (1495?–1527), an Anabaptist leader who conceived of Christian religion as originating in the inner heart of its followers rather than in rigid adherence to scripture

As an artist and a poet, William Blake produced imaginative works of nearly palpable passion. Perhaps because of the way his work inspires the imaginations, passions, and senses of his audience, Blake has long entranced both scholars and the general public. Although he struggled to gain an audience during his lifetime, Blake is now well respected as an intellectual and an artist, and in *Blake and the Bible*, Christopher Rowland argues that Blake used his work as a means to investigate the social, philosophical, and religious concerns of his historical moment.

Although Blake has long been studied for his contributions to both literature and the visual arts, the two schools of study have not always been in communication. Rowland begins a discussion between these two camps in order to engender a larger exploration of Blake's religious stance as it emerges in his artwork. He invites the reader to consider Blake as a religious thinker and skeptic, as a part of the tradition of radical religious thinkers that includes Gerrard Winstanley, Abiezer Coppe, Ralph Cudworth, and Hans Denck. In highlighting the artist's theological pedigree, Rowland engages the reader in a close reading of Blake as prophet and his work as an expression of prophecy.

A scholar of theology, Rowland crafts a masterful analysis of Blake's artistic and intellectual relationship with the Bible. In the introduction, he writes that studying Blake's work "reshapes the way in which one reads the Bible, views and experiences the world, and for that matter, God." This is an ambitious claim, implying Blake's ability to use art to change a viewer's mind about religion. Rowland's methodical analysis throughout sustains this bold assertion, as he uses textual and visual analysis and a close reading of relevant biblical passages to uncover Blake's intellectual and philosophical stance on religion. One of Blake's central concerns, Rowland reminds the reader, is the problem of blindly accepting the authority of a text. He takes this idea a bit further, suggesting that it was Blake's aim to encourage readers to question any single interpretation of the Bible and even submitting that Blake questioned the accuracy of the Bible itself as a means for reaching divine truth. Fittingly, Blake's suspicion of the authority of texts is reflected in his own work as well; Rowland argues that he produced multiple versions of his written and painted works in order to deliberately undermine any attempts at exclusive readings.

The prospective audience of a book such as this would include theologians, art historians, literary scholars, humanists, and anyone interested in any combination of these disciplines. Given Rowland's evident expertise in theology, it is not surprising that the book is directed predominantly toward readers with the same academic interests. In fact, for the general reader, the book's academic interpretations and vocabulary are likely to pose certain challenges. However, Rowland seems to wants to guide the reader toward some form of religious rediscovery, and in this way, the book may offer inspiration to those who, like Blake, seek a route to religious thought on independent, personal terms. For scholars with particular disciplinary stakes in Blake, it will come as good news that the chapters are topically divided in ways that allow for selective and strategic reading. The book is unified in its argument and well structured as a whole, with individual sections that offer largely isolated analyses of Blake. The analysis of key works merits the occasionally dense passage, and it is these individual chapters that allow the reader to dwell on particular manuscripts, images, or religious topics in isolation from the argument of the book as a whole.

Blake and the Bible begins with an introductory chapter that aims to persuade the reader of the Bible's importance to Blake's work. This chapter also provides a comprehensive and helpful overview of key concepts, such as Blake's critique of the authority of texts in religion, his interest in provoking a sensory response in his audience, and his interaction with a robust tradition of innovative religious thinkers. Alongside this introduction, Rowland provides a thorough and well-annotated chronology of Blake's life and work. This resource is useful for readers hoping to gain a sense of the scope of Blake's artistic and literary production. Likewise, the chronology is crucially important to Rowland's ultimate analysis, which seeks to weave an integrated interpretation of Blake's theology across the artist's career.

Chapters two and three, the most substantial sections in the book, offer close readings and interpretations of Blake's *Illustrations of the Book of Job* (1826), an artistic and literary project completed late in Blake's life (in three phases: the first in 1805–6, the second in 1821, and the final in 1825). Rowland presents his analysis in a straightforward manner, walking the reader through each plate of text and providing overviews of the contents of the images. Blake's engravings were a substantial project, featuring text from the book of Job alongside passages from other books of the Bible and images representing the scenes. The cumulative effect of these illustrations,

Christopher Rowland is the Dean Ireland Professor of the Exegesis of Holy Scripture at the University of Oxford. He has published extensively on theological topics ranging from radical Christian writers to the origins of Christianity.

Rowland asserts, is a kind of biblical interpretation, as the images provide visual, emotional, and sensory insights into the text itself. Later, Rowland reveals the reasoning behind his decision to begin the book with the analysis of *Illustrations of the Book of Job*, stating that the project represents "the acme of [Blake's] theological thinking." Indeed, through this analysis, the reader can piece together Rowland's three central themes regarding Blake's theology: "the critique of divine monarchy, the emphasis on the divine in the human, and the challenge to convention in the name of inspiration."

With his analysis of the Job engravings as a foundation, Rowland devotes the next six chapters to theological themes related to the question of Blake's approach to the Bible. Chapter four considers the idea of duality, or the opposing and seemingly contradictory aspects of religion, which Blake highlights by bringing together biblical lessons and imagery that appear at first to be at odds with one another. Chapter five focuses on three of Blake's other significant projects: *The Marriage of Heaven and Hell* (1790–93), *The First Book of Urizon* (1794), and his drawings for the *Book of Enoch* (1821). Here, in addition to the three central themes mentioned above, Rowland discusses Blake's "challenge to the religion of the book, divine transcendence, [and] divine punishment in judgment." Chapters six and seven respectively consider Blake's self-conscious understanding of himself as a religious prophet and his affinities and relationships with other religious thinkers, with the latter chapter divided into a series of discrete sections that explore the histories and perspectives of Gerrard Winstanley, Abiezer Coppe, Ralph Cudworth, and Hans Denck. In chapter eight, Rowland turns to Blake's analysis of Jesus as a radical religious figure, and in chapter ten, Rowland returns to art, considering the series of biblical illustrations that Blake completed between 1799 and 1805. Helpfully, he divides these illustrations into two categories: images that pertain to the life of Jesus and those that reflect on the book of Revelation. As in his treatment of Job, Blake illustrates his passages with a sensibility that is more abstract than literal, not always pairing a passage with an illustration of the literal event it describes. By borrowing passages from other parts of the Bible and making visual references to themes and anecdotes key to Blake but not necessarily directly related to the subject matter, the artist was able to maximize the potential of these passages with regard to his religious agenda.

In its concluding chapter, *Blake and the Bible* offers a rich summary of the key ideas laid out by Rowland's argument and provides suggestions for further reading about Blake that will surely inspire additional scholarship for casual readers and devoted scholars alike. Rowland surmises that Blake found the Bible to be primarily a stimulus for the imagination, and thus a stimulus for a passionate response—the response of a viewer to a piece of art. He identifies Blake's biblical approach as one that focuses mainly on the experience and reaction of the audience: "the creativity of the interpretative process is all-important, as the *affective* character of words and images is given its full weight in the impression made on the reader and/or viewer. So, immediacy of response is allowed its place, alongside the reasoned explanation of the effects that have been set in train by engagement which is intuitive and emotional as well as rational." Such an explanation of Blake's underlying ideas advances Rowland's overarching argument in several different ways and helps to explain how the imagery of Blake's illustrations can be both polemical and inspirational at once. In the end, Rowland brings full circle his analysis of the biblical text and its ultimate irrelevance to Blake's art, the implication being that the relationship between a religious text and its reader is not unlike the creative, interpretive relationship between an audience and a work of art. It is this very metaphor, Rowland hints, that Blake would have the audience consider in response to his own works, both written and illustrated.

By revealing the theological roots beneath William Blake's most widely known works, *Blake and the Bible* will significantly advance its audience's understanding of him as an intellectual artist. Through Rowland, the reader will learn to interpret the excitement of Blake's imagery and begin to make sense of the continuous intellectual project motivating his diverse body of work. By drawing attention to the religious consistency across the multiple versions of Blake's texts and images, Rowland succeeds in reshaping the reader's understanding of a complex artist.

Julia A. Sienkewicz

Review Sources

Romantic Circles Reviews, July 29, 2011 (Web).
Times Literary Supplement, no. 5641 (May 13, 2011): 26–27.

Blood, Bones, and Butter
The Inadvertent Education of a Reluctant Chef

Author: Gabrielle Hamilton (b. 1934)
Publisher: Random House (New York). 304 pp.
  $26.00; paperback $16.00
Type of work: Memoir
Time: 1970s to the present
Locale: Rural Pennsylvania; Europe; New York
  City; Ann Arbor, Michigan

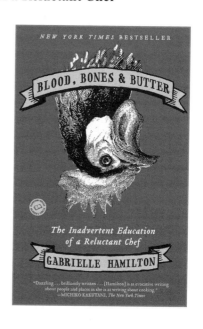

A candid, funny, and unsparing memoir of a life lived mainly in kitchens, Hamilton's story celebrates the pleasures of the table without concealing the dirty work of cooking.

Principal personages:

GABRIELLE HAMILTON, the author, chef and
  owner of a successful New York restaurant
MADELEINE HAMILTON, her mother, a skilled
  cook and native of France
JIM HAMILTON, her father, an artist and
  theatrical set designer
MELISSA HAMILTON, her sister, the only one of her four siblings Hamilton stayed close
  to as an adult
MISTY, a caterer and chef who becomes a mentor to Hamilton
THE MICHIGAN GIRLFRIEND, an unnamed young woman Hamilton meets during
  graduate school, who later moves to New York with her
MICHELE, Hamilton's husband, an Italian doctor and medical researcher
ALDA, Michele's mother, who lives in Puglia, Italy

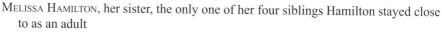

Blood, Bones, and Butter: The Inadvertent Education of a Reluctant Chef is neither a traditional memoir nor a typical "foodie" book. Though Hamilton is, in fact, a celebrated chef, she devotes little time to recipes, cooking techniques, or advice on how to run a restaurant. Rather, in a series of sharply detailed and gritty vignettes, she recreates some of her life's most vivid memories, all of them centered on food, cooking, and eating. From her father's legendary spring lamb roasts, with whole spit-roasted lambs dripping blood onto an open fire, to her Italian mother-in-law's simple lunch of zucchini, green beans, and chicory dressed in olive oil from her own trees, meals are the anchor of Hamilton's life, and she describes them so sensuously and intensely that the reader can see, smell, and all but taste that perfect omelet or crispy fried eggplant. As the title suggests, Hamilton does not shy away from describing in equally vivid terms the dirty, exhausting, and sometimes gruesome process of getting the food to the table.

Hamilton's memoir begins with her childhood, but it does not follow a straight chronological path. The author sometimes asks the reader's indulgence as she skips ten years ahead or detours to a flashback of an event previously left undisclosed. She focuses on a series of pivotal moments in her life that she is able to recreate with visceral clarity. The first memory Hamilton shares is

Gabrielle Hamilton is the chef and owner of Prune, a successful restaurant in New York City's East Village. She earned her MFA in fiction writing from the University of Michigan, and her work has appeared in the New Yorker, GQ, Bon Appétit, Saveur, *and* Food & Wine.

set in the 1970s, during her childhood in the midst of an artistic, unconventional family, where she was often unsupervised but never insecure. She describes her artist father, who hosted themed parties that were like elaborate set designs; her mother, a glamorous French ballet dancer in black eyeliner who managed to feed a family of five children while still wearing high heels; and her older brothers and sisters, with their teenage quirks and shared in-jokes. It was a comfortable, bohemian world, and it was about to end. Hamilton was eleven years old when her mother made the announcement that sundered and scattered her family.

When readers are next introduced to the author, it is after her parents' divorce, when she was a shoplifting, cocaine-snorting thirteen-year-old lying about her age to get jobs as a dishwasher or a busser in local restaurants. After graduating from an alternative high school at sixteen, Hamilton moved in with her sister in New York City and bluffed her way into a waitress job at the Lone Star Cafe, a popular "urban cowboy" bar and restaurant. There, Hamilton and some of the other waitstaff became involved in a fraud scheme; at one point, Hamilton writes, she was making more than ninety thousand dollars per year and spending most of it on drugs. When the scam was discovered by her employer, only Hamilton's age saved her from felony charges. Still a teenager, she enrolled in college, only to drop out two years later. Unemployed, depressed, and living with her father, Hamilton ends the first section of *Blood, Bones, and Butter*, titled "Blood," as a young woman without direction.

The second section, "Bones," finds Hamilton freelancing for several catering companies in New York and spending summers cooking at a children's camp. Bored with the kitchen, she had a moment of epiphany while catering a book awards dinner, and later applied to several graduate-level writing programs. She was accepted into the program at the University of Michigan, Ann Arbor, where she inevitably found herself in the kitchen again, working for a catering company in between attending poetry readings and grading student papers. She says little about her own writing process, but her hilarious description of a student party dominated by a singsong poet discoursing on the "tropes" of her work makes it clear that Hamilton did not fully embrace the graduate student ethos. She felt uncomfortable with academia, yet unfulfilled by preparing cheese platters for university functions.

An outsider in both worlds, Hamilton was inspired when Misty, the owner of the catering company, opened her own restaurant and began cooking daring, delicious food. Long familiar with the grunt work of kitchens, Hamilton saw something she perhaps had not considered: a place where cooking and creativity could meet. More than just a boss, Misty became Hamilton's mentor, a culinary guide who helped her find her way to the next phase of her life.

Hamilton writes that she never intended to open a restaurant; it seems to be something that just happened, something she drifted into as if by accident when a neighbor mentioned a vacant restaurant space closed down by bankruptcy. Hamilton's vividly described tour of the locked restaurant, then home to rotted meat, moldy fruit, rat droppings, and cockroaches, is enough to discourage almost any reader's appetite, but she could not stop dreaming of the restaurant that could be.

At this point in the narrative, Hamilton backtracks to a point in her youth when, to escape postcollege angst, she traveled through Europe on a Eurail pass. She lived for a time in France, staying with a friend of her mother's and working in her crêperie, and later found work as a dishwasher and prep cook at another restaurant in Greece. She remembers being hungry and how a salted potato and a wedge of cheese satisfied that hunger. Her memories of Europe, where most food was bought and prepared locally, made Hamilton think about the kind of restaurant she would like to have—one serving simple food prepared well, without themes or concepts or pretensions. Despite her lack of business experience, she decided to take the abandoned space and turn it into that kind of restaurant. She called it Prune, after her childhood nickname.

Readers who watch television's Food Network and dream of attaining celebrity status as a chef, or ogle the glossy pages of *Bon Appetit* and *Saveur* magazines and imagine the glamour of the white toque and apron, will probably be more horrified than delighted by the "Bones" section of *Blood, Bones, and Butter*, in which Hamilton addresses both the foodie culture and her daily routine in the restaurant. Working eighteen-hour days, cooking through the ninth month of her pregnancy, and disposing of dead rats did not faze her, but Hamilton felt deep discomfort when she was asked to speak at an academic conference about the status of women in the food industry. She resented being seen as a representative of her gender, a female chef instead of simply a chef. She also worried that aspiring chefs saw cooking as a stepping stone to fame rather than as a job to do well.

"Butter," the final section of Hamilton's memoir, focuses primarily on her marriage and family. She describes her somewhat unexpected marriage to an older Italian man, noting that she had previously identified as a lesbian and had little time to devote to a relationship. Hamilton recalls how Michele, her husband, was determined in his wooing. He made her ravioli, biking to different shops to get just the right ingredients, rolling and cutting the pasta by hand. In the end, it was not Michele's cooking that won Hamilton's heart but his mother, Alda, an eighty-year-old woman who still prepared daily meals using traditional cooking methods. Alda spoke almost no English and Hamilton knew little Italian, but the women spoke a shared language of food. The marriage began tentatively, with the couple keeping separate apartments even after they had children together. Hamilton even suggests that she married Michele in part to help him out of some immigration difficulties, yet she chose to have two children with him. She later writes of feeling deeply lonely within her marriage. It is clear that her marriage is complicated and difficult, and she writes frankly and matter-of-factly about the people in her life.

Food writer Anthony Bourdain called *Blood, Bones, and Butter* "the best memoir by a chef ever." Critics have praised the memoir, not only for its lusciously rendered descriptions of food and cooking, but also for its forthright, distinctive voice and writing style. One review compared Hamilton to legendary food writer M. F. K. Fisher, known for the quality of her prose as well as her luminous descriptions of memorable meals. While Hamilton is best known as a restaurant owner, her background and education as a writer shine through in her sharp and lyrical prose, as she skillfully describes both the pleasurable and the unsavory aspects of her life. Beyond her lush descriptions of food and her lively discussions of restaurants, Hamilton's book is also about family. Her honest, occasionally raw looks at her parents and her childhood push *Blood, Bones, and Butter* beyond a simple food memoir. Hamilton is a chef, but she is also a woman who plays many roles in building a home with her immediate and adopted families. Readers, regardless of whether or not they consider themselves foodies, will be engaged by this rich and captivating narrative.

Kathryn Kulpa

Review Sources

Booklist 107, no. 3 (October 1, 2010): 17.
Kirkus Reviews 78, no. 22 (November 15, 2010): 13.
Library Journal 136, no. 12 (July 1, 2011): 47.
Maclean's 124, no. 13 (April 11, 2011): 92.
The New York Times Book Review, March 13, 2011, p. L11.
Publishers Weekly 258, no. 6 (February 7, 2011): 47–48.

Blue Nights

Author: Joan Didion (b. 1934)
Publisher: Alfred A. Knopf (New York). 208 pp.
$25.00
Type of work: Memoir
Time: March 1966 through late 2010
Locale: New York City; in and around Los Angeles, California

Didion provides an intimate, unflinching look at her relationship with her adopted daughter, a promising photographer who died of natural causes at the age of thirty-nine.

Principal personages:

JOAN DIDION, an established and well-respected novelist and journalist

QUINTANA ROO DUNNE, Didion's precocious, intelligent daughter, who struggled with severe medical problems and profound emotional anxieties

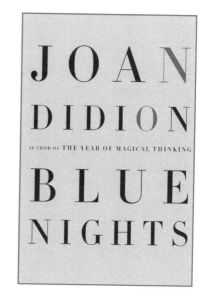

It is easy to want Joan Didion's *Blue Nights* to be something it does not aspire to be. Readers of Didion's previous memoir, *The Year of Magical Thinking* (2005)— a heartrending account of the sudden death of her husband, John Gregory Dunne— might approach *Blue Nights* expecting a sort of companion piece. Before the publication of *Magical Thinking*, Didion had been widely considered as a writer's writer, admired for her brittle, ironic pieces in which she positioned herself as an observer, set apart and coolly cerebral, assessing her cultural landscape and skewering sentimentality. An unguarded confession of her private struggle with grief, *Magical Thinking* evoked a profoundly emotional response from a wide range of readers who found a touching honesty in Didion's lyrical meditations on mortality. She was regarded as an inspiration for those of her contemporaries who were just beginning to adjust to the reality of death. An international best seller, the memoir was awarded the National Book Award in 2005, thrusting upon Didion the status of a celebrity.

Promotional materials have certainly linked the previous book with *Blue Nights*, another memoir, in which Didion confronts every parent's worst nightmare: the death of a child. *Magical Thinking* ends with the Didions' daughter, Quintana Roo, in an induced coma, battling pneumonia and septic shock. Quintana subsequently recovered and had just begun a promising life, newly married and preparing for a career in photography, when she endured a variety of medical catastrophes within just a handful of months, including a cerebral hemorrhage and pancreatitis. She would undergo five grueling surgeries and move in and out of ICU units, tethered to ventilators, until her death at age thirty-nine.

Such a harrowing experience would have made a powerful account had Didion been interested in such a memoir. But in *Blue Nights* the daughter remains, by Didion's own admission, elusive. Pieced together from fragments of recollection, Q, as her mother calls her, is a memory Didion cannot yet bring herself to confront. She draws a tantalizing but incomplete portrait of a mercurial, impulsive child, enigmatic to her own mother, whose very absence becomes for the reader what it has become for the grieving mother. As Didion sorts though mementos—faded photographs, graded schoolwork, old letters—a sense of Q's story emerges. Despite growing up with a privileged and wealthy lifestyle, an education in swanky schools, and early signs of a precocious and uninhibited sense of creativity, Q struggled with anxieties about abandonment and vulnerability even as a child. At age five, she phoned a nearby mental institution to verify symptoms of insanity. She soberly told her mother that a chickenpox blister was, in fact, cancer. At thirteen, she tried her hand at writing a novel about a confused teenage girl named Quintana who faces an abortion, while her parents remain coldly indifferent. Didion records her daughter's lifelong struggle with depression, her frequent escapes into alcohol, her wild mood swings (she was diagnosed with borderline personality disorder), and, in her final weeks, her longing to be done with medical procedures, to be allowed finally the release of death.

But the actual narrative of Quintana's death passes briefly. Like the grieving mother herself, this nonlinear memoir approaches the daughter only to retreat, unable to bear the pain of a direct encounter. Didion cuts quickly from events in Quintana's life to the narrative present, five years after her death. In doing so, the subject of *Blue Nights* increasingly becomes Didion herself. The dominant stylistic technique is the rhetorical question, which underscores the narrative as an act of self-interrogation, making it a narrative addressed to its own author. Appropriately, the memoir includes an account of Didion undergoing a full-body PET scan in the hope of pinpointing exactly why she loses her balance. This aspect of self-exposure, the almost clinical revelation of Didion herself, might serve as a metaphor for *Blue Nights*. With the same formidable eye for hypocrisy that long defined her analyses of American culture, Didion turns the occasion of her daughter's death into an often-excruciating self-analysis.

Most immediately, Didion probes what she sees as her many failures as a mother, admitting that she was not prepared for the responsibility when she decided to be a mother in her early twenties, with a career in journalism already under way. The baby was named impulsively after a remote Mexican state, the name of which Didion and her husband had chanced to see on a map and fallen in love with. Leaving the hospital with the baby, whom they adopted on the day of her birth, they realized they did not even have a bassinette. In retrospect, she admits to treating her daughter as both a doll that she could dress in elaborate accessories and a strong, independent, albeit highly strung adult. Didion faults herself for being unaware and unavailable, for ignoring now-obvious indications of her daughter's fragility and anxiety. She acknowledges how entangled she was in her career, how carefully she maintained the isolation that writers require, and how that environment of isolation was further complicated by the awkwardness of a child's relationship with her adoptive mother. For Didion, her relationship with her daughter was characterized by distance. She was unavailable to comfort her daughter even when, in her early thirties, Quintana flew to Dallas to meet her biological family.

Even more disquieting for Didion is her awareness that her gifts as a writer have begun to wane. Language, she says, has been an elegant and easy distraction, a way to contain and control, define and describe contradictory and elusive realities, and writing has long provided a shelter of prose and phrases. It has been her life's work to use language to construct artificial landscapes in which delight comes from the careful precision of her prose, the economy of her style, and the precision of details. Didion poignantly recalls coming across her daughter's journal in 1984, and how, despite the girl's painful revelations, she wanted only to correct the punctuation, adjust an inexact word or two, and redesign its gnarled syntax. With *Magical Thinking*, Didion frankly reconsidered her previous style, admitting that meaning may reside somewhere outside of prose. But after Quintana's death, Didion recalls busying herself with writing: selecting appropriate poems for the memorial service, throwing herself into a promotional tour for *Magical Thinking*, and ultimately immersing herself in the conversion of that book into a Broadway play, comforted by the artificial environment wherein her daughter was still alive.

(FilmMagic)

Joan Didion is the author of five novels, eight books of nonfiction, and several screenplays cowritten with her husband, John Gregory Dunne. Her noteworthy titles include Slouching toward Bethlehem *(1968),* Play It as It Lays *(1970), and* The Year of Magical Thinking *(2005). Known for her trenchant observations about American culture and her crystalline prose, Didion is among the most respected writers of her generation.*

It is a major moment in the narrative when an aging Didion confesses the difficulty with which she now composes sentences with the requisite care and precision; the right word has begun to elude her, and the environment she has so artfully constructed for decades has begun to usher her out. With dispassionate honesty, she acknowledges that she is increasingly wary of language's indirection, how it distracts and enables strategies for not confronting that which is most painful. Indeed, halfway through *Blue Nights*, as the reader is caught up in the spell of Didion's prose, the author abruptly acknowledges that even given her many elegant anecdotes and asides—Quintana's quirky childhood, the deaths of Didion's close friends and family members, her celebrity-rich life in Southern California—she has not yet actually addressed what is ostensibly the subject of the memoir.

At its most effective, *Blue Nights* speaks to the inevitability of aging and the need to acknowledge and surrender to that process. Didion compares the exotic blue light of late summer days, the gloaming that lingers just before the drop of night, to the moment when one has no choice but to contemplate his or her place in the passing of time. In what is in many ways the memoir's pivotal moment, Didion turns seventy-five. She records her increasing frailty, demonstrated in moments when she loses her balance, or when she cannot manipulate buttons or tie her shoes. She divulges evidence of failing eyesight, failing recollection, and times when she fears that she cannot even stand. In addition to the physical signs of aging—which include cases of shingles and neuritis, the latter a syndrome related to low body weight that requires physical therapy— Didion records the chance discovery in 2009 of an aneurysm at the base of her brain. Although the doctors assure her it is not imminently threatening, the discovery gives her the uneasy feeling that at any moment she might collapse. Didion mentions that what she fears worse than dying is a long-term coma, the suspended animation that might result from the implosion of the aneurysm. She recounts how, after a recent fainting spell, she was unable to drag herself to any of the twelve telephones in her townhouse. The memoir ends wistfully, as Didion studies a photo of Sophia Loren, born in the same year she was, and envies the Italian film star's stunning looks, undiminished by time.

With pitiless honesty, Didion offers an unsentimental record of her own transition into old age and the shame that attends her acceptance of her own vulnerability, helplessness, and mortality. As was the case for her husband, her daughter, and the many friends whose deaths she recalls here, death is something she must ultimately face alone. The memoir closes with Didion considering the vast implications of the question that is routinely asked on the hospital forms she finds herself filling out more and more often, the question of who to notify in case of an emergency. Didion can think of only her daughter, which leaves her with memory as her only consolation, as she prepares to step into her own blue night.

Joseph Dewey

Review Sources

The Boston Globe, November 6, 2011 (Web).
London Review of Books 33, no. 21 (November 3, 2011): 17–19.
Los Angeles Times, October 30, 2011 (Web).
Millions, November 1, 2011 (Web).
New York Magazine, October 16, 2011 (Web).
The New York Times, November 6, 2011, p. 15.
Obit Magazine, October 27, 2011 (Web).
The Observer, October 22, 2011 (Web).
San Francisco Chronicle, November 6, 2011 (Web). *USA Today*, October 31, 2011, p. D7.

A Book of Secrets
Illegitimate Daughters, Absent Fathers

Author: Michael Holroyd (b. 1935)
Publisher: Farrar, Straus and Giroux (New
York). 258 pp. $26.00
Type of work: Biography, memoir
Time: The nineteenth through the twenty-first
century
Locale: England, Italy

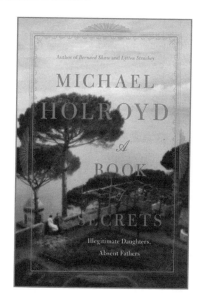

*An innovative British biographer explores the
lives of Eve Fairfax, Alice Keppel, Violet Trefusis, and other women who played important
roles in the life of Ernest Beckett, 2nd Baron
Grimthorpe.*

Principal personages:
ERNEST BECKETT (1856–1917), the second
  Baron Grimthorpe and owner of Villa
  Cimbrone
EVE FAIRFAX (1872–1978), Beckett's onetime
  fiancée, the model for a bust sculpted by Auguste Rodin
VIOLET TREFUSIS (1894–1972), Beckett's rumored illegitimate daughter, a novelist
ALICE KEPPEL (1868–1947), Beckett's rumored mistress, Trefusis's mother
VITA SACKVILLE-WEST (1892–1962), Trefusis's lover, a novelist and poet
CATHERINE TILL (b. 1935), a woman who believes that she is Beckett's descendant
AUGUSTE RODIN (1840–1917), a French sculptor commissioned by Beckett to create a
  bust of Fairfax
LUCY "LUIE" TRACY LEE (1865–1891), Beckett's first wife, mother of his legitimate
  son and daughters
JOSEPHINE "JOSÉ" CORNELIA BRINK (1869–1937), Beckett's mistress, mother of his
  illegitimate son

Michael Holroyd's unusual biography opens by describing the author's fascination
with a bust of Eve Fairfax that he originally saw in the Victoria and Albert Museum in
London. Eve Fairfax was the model for sculptor Auguste Rodin, and the pair engaged
in passionate correspondence as she continued to sit for the artist through the years.
Originally commissioned by her then-fiancé, Ernest Beckett, the bust captured Holroyd's imagination over a century after it was cast. The author traces how the young
woman had come to Paris with a letter of introduction seeking sittings. Using historical archives and fragments of letters, he pieces together the story of what must have
transpired between the famous artist and the young model.

Michael Holroyd is a London-based author and the recipient of numerous awards, among them the Heywood Hill Literary Prize and the David Cohen Prize for Literature. His many published works include two memoirs, nine books of nonfiction, and one novel. He was knighted in 2007 for his services to English literature.

Using his interest in Fairfax as a starting point, Holroyd discovers a number of women who existed on the fringes of Ernest Beckett's life. The lives of these women, variously fiancées, wives, mistresses, and daughters, make up the bulk of *A Book of Secrets,* united by their ties to Beckett and their peripheral roles in his history. Beckett is not the subject of this book, but his life and actions have a lasting effect on the marginalized women he encountered. Well crafted and meticulously researched, Holroyd's book is a rich, funny, and engaging work.

In the first section of the book, Holroyd discusses Eve Fairfax and her relationships with Beckett and Rodin. Beckett had been a banker and politician before inheriting the Grimthorpe peerage and becoming a baron. Shortly after gaining his title, Beckett cast off Fairfax as his fiancée. After six and a half years of sittings, Rodin presented the young woman with a bust he had made of her; her subsequent letters are full of anxieties that he would forget her. Holroyd carefully traces their affair, examining and interpreting their letters and visits. Their correspondence and meetings lasted for thirteen years, until World War I; Rodin died in 1917. Fairfax eventually sold the bust, thus ensuring its survival after her own death. She was also survived by a large book, the titular book of secrets, in which she kept her letters, autographs, sketches, and other keepsakes. Holroyd's deep interest in Fairfax's story is apparent in his book's early chapters. Her roles as a fiancée and an artist's muse were ultimately swept away, and she died impoverished and alone at the age of 107. Though her story is not, perhaps, immediately remarkable, the author constructs it with great care. Using her book, Holroyd creates a memorable history of a woman whose life and circumstances were dramatically altered by the more famous men she crossed paths with. Instead of relegating her to obscurity, the author has painstakingly reconstructed her life, ensuring that she will be remembered by more than just a statue.

Holroyd also describes Beckett's first wife, American heiress Lucy "Luie" Tracy Lee, and his affairs with his mistresses, including Josephine "José" Cornelia Brink and Alice Keppel. Although Lee gave birth to Beckett's legitimate son and two daughters and Brink bore him an illegitimate son, the author then shifts his narrative to Keppel and her daughter, Violet Trefusis. Despite being married, Keppel had multiple affairs, and her dalliance with Beckett led to the birth of Trefusis, another of the baron's illegitimate children. Trefusis was a novelist who, although married to a man, had a long-term lesbian relationship with writer Vita Sackville-West.

Trefusis's unconventional life is discussed frankly, as is her stormy and divisive personality. Holroyd provides commentary on her writing and her personal life, remaining sympathetic while also sharing her flaws. Trefusis and Sackville-West also interacted with author Virginia Woolf, and their affair, as well as Sackville-West and Woolf's own relationship, is allegedly featured in Woolf's novel *Orlando* (1928). Holroyd also discusses Trefusis's and Sackville-West's publications and their interactions with Woolf's Hogarth Press in their efforts to see their works in print. Trefusis's books include *Tandem* (1933), *Hunt the Slipper* (1937), *Pirates at Play* (1950), and the memoir *Don't Look Round* (1952). Holroyd examines these works as well as the writings of Sackville-West and Woolf in order to gain insight into the characters, lives, and interwoven affairs of these women. Here, he also meditates on the relationship between truth and imagination, as well as on feminine sexuality in the early twentieth century.

Another chapter covers the author's encounter with Catherine Till, who believes that she is Beckett's granddaughter, the illegitimate daughter of his son Ralph. Holroyd himself enters the narrative when he meets Till while they are both researching Beckett's lineage. He includes his dreams from before he meets with her as well as their actual encounters. One of the most memorable passages of the book describes a reckless drive the two embark on when traveling through Italy, an anecdote in which Holroyd demonstrates his skill as a comic writer. Both Till and Holroyd had visited Beckett's home of Villa Cimbrone, a palazzo above Ravello in Italy. The villa itself unites the stories of the women in *A Book of Secrets*.

Although it is history, this dizzying book about the significant women in the sixty-year lifespan of Ernest Beckett can at times read more like a novel, with many new plot turns and intrigue. It is a nonlinear story filled with tangents and shifts in time. Also evident is the exploration of the boundaries of biography as a literary form, as Holroyd does much to push the envelope of what is appropriate in the craft—often including his own part in the process of pursuit and inquisition of the people involved, who do in fact seem to behave like fictional characters.

To ground his peculiar stories in reality, Holroyd includes a family tree and a six-page select bibliography, including thirteen publications by Trefusis. A photographic section features a close-up of a bust of Eve Fairfax, pictures of Fairfax in both her twenties and her nineties, a picture of Ernest Beckett, a close-up of Fairfax's book, pictures of the villa and its contemporary visitors, the jackets of some of the books published by the individuals discussed, and a poem written on a Monte Carlo telegram form by Trefusis and Sackville-West in 1918–19. The author also references other biographies of the well-known personages about whom he writes, drawing upon this information throughout. He relates how his research uncovered an Italian woman who has read all of Trefusis's work and has arranged to get the copyrights so that she can translate everything into Italian. He also shares his discussions with people in the literary world, such as editors of Virago Press, about the likelihood of Trefusis's work making a comeback.

Despite all of the objective research that went into the writing of *A Book of Secrets*, the biography is still a personal and human story. Holroyd effectively conveys the passion of the women's affairs, both with Beckett and without. His use of love letters and other writings depicts the intensity of the relationships and the devastation caused when some of them ended. This is especially evident in the affair between Trefusis and Sackville-West. According to Holroyd, "Violet likened herself and Vita to two gamblers, both eager to win, each nervous to play a card." Their mothers, Alice Keppel and Lady Sackville respectively, were not in favor of the relationship between their daughters and wanted it to end, going so far as to destroy many of the letters between the pair. Trefusis, on the edge of a breakdown, went into a depression and began to loathe herself. She married her husband in 1919. Sackville-West sent her an alabaster head of a Medusa as a gift; Violet sent back a note proclaiming that her heart was broken. Despite the marriage, their affair continued.

Toward the end of *A Book of Secrets*, Holroyd's imagination returns to Villa Cimbrone and how it inspired his writing and his subjects. He compares the modern hotel that sits at the site with the home that Beckett once made there. The author imagines a scene in which Beckett and his extended family, whether legitimate or illegitimate, all come together in the same place and at the same time, learning about one another and their intertwined lives. He does this to complete what the purely historical narrative could not, imagining them discovering their connections and filling in the gaps in their stories.

Holroyd notes that, in writing the biography, he had "no settled agenda" and did not intend to pass judgment on the men and women in the text. Instead, he wanted to examine life and identity, as well as how they are affected by memory and the passage of time. While the book's narrative threads can, at times, feel loosely connected and even frayed, the diversions can be just as engrossing as the overarching stories. *A Book of Secrets* is not intended to be a straightforward family history; instead, it creates a web of characters as intricate and complicated as families often truly are.

Batya Weinbaum

Review Sources

The Guardian, October 28, 2010, p. 15.
Independent, December 2, 2011 (Web).
The New York Times, August 5, 2011 (Web).
The Washington Post, August 25, 2011 (Web).

Bowstring
On the Dissimilarity of the Similar

Author: Viktor Shklovsky (1893–1984)
First published: *Tetiva: o neskhodstve skhod-nogo*, 1970, in the Soviet Union
Translated from the Russian by Shushan Avagyan
Publisher: Dalkey Archive (Champaign, IL). 456 pp. $16.95
Type of work: Literary criticism

BOWSTRING: ON THE DISSIMILARITY OF THE SIMILAR VIKTOR SHKLOVSKY

The author's significant revision of his earlier theory of estrangement is translated into English for the first time.

Principal personages:

VIKTOR SHKLOVSKY (1893–1984), author, a key figure in the Russian formalist movement

DANTE ALIGHIERI (1265–1321), Italian Renaissance poet and prose writer, author of *The Divine Comedy* (1321)

MIKHAIL BAKHTIN (1895–1975), Russian philosopher, author, and literary theorist

MIGUEL DE CERVANTES (1547–1616), Spanish writer, author of *Don Quixote de la Mancha* (1605, 1615)

FYODOR DOSTOEVSKY (1821–1881), Russian novelist, author of *Crime and Punishment* (1866)

BORIS MIKHAILOVICH EICHENBAUM (1886–1959), Russian literary critic and key figure in the Russian formalist movement

VICTOR HUGO (1802–1885), French author

ALEXANDER PUSHKIN (1799–1837), Russian author and poet

FRANÇOIS RABELAIS (ca. 1494–1553), French author

LEO TOLSTOY (1828–1910), Russian novelist, author of *Anna Karenina* (1873–1877)

YURI NIKOLAEVICH TYNJANOV (1894–1943), Russian author, literary critic, and member of the Russian formalist movement

Bowstring is organized around the central concept of harmony in art through difference and tension that helps to heighten sensation or perception. The original literary image is one that author Viktor Shklovsky borrows from the ancient Greek philosopher Heraclitus in order to revise the concept of estrangement (*ostranenie*), which Shklovsky himself first coined in 1916. To describe the central visual and conceptual image of the bowstring, Shklovsky states, "The wooden stick is a single unity. The string made of sinew is another unity. The arched stick, bent by the string, becomes a bow. This is a new unity and it represents the first model of an artistic

(V. Slavinsky)

Viktor Shklovsky was a leading Russian literary critic who played a formative role in the Russian formalist movement during the first decades of the twentieth century. His work had a profound impact on Russian literature of his time, and his theoretical writings continue to be influential.

composition . . . The bow's harmony arises from the strained stick forced by the bowstring. Subsequently, harmony resides in unity and contradiction."

The original formulation of estrangement placed no value on the familiar, but rather on distancing the critic from the subject in order to heighten the critic's perception. Thus, form was of paramount importance, while content (encompassing history, environment, and other aspects of a literary work) was insignificant. In *Bowstring*, Shklovsky suggests instead that the tension between different elements of a work of art, acting in conjunction with the sensibilities of the reader, creates its power. The harmony of a work of art comes from the sum total of its unity and built-in contradictions.

In fleshing out this consideration of unity and tension in a work of art, Shklovsky wrote *Bowstring* as a system of literary montage that reflects the ideas at its core. The book combines elements of biography, memoir, literary criticism, and history in a series of loosely unified chapters. In choosing not to make a single argument readily apparent, Shklovsky seeks to guide the reader to new realizations through the juxtaposition of texts, thoughts, and analyses. He signals this technique obliquely in the prologue when, after introducing the concept of estrangement, he turns abruptly to the case of the *Drosophila* fruit fly. Though these flies appear to be "good for nothing," studying them can lead to significant new directions in scientific knowledge. Thus, insignificant or even nonsensical subjects can act as "detonators for triggering much larger explosions, entryways into knowledge, explorations of the new." This concept forms the organizing principle of the book, which juxtaposes narratives from Shklovsky's own life with epic tales, carnival revelries, and poignant stories about the lives and deaths of some of his closest friends and literary associates. Throughout *Bowstring,* truth cohabits with fiction, present with the past, and the living with the dead. The catholic borrowing of associations, sensations, and motifs allows *Bowstring* to resonate profoundly even as it puzzles, frustrates, and at times provokes the reader.

Ultimately, Shklovsky's work attempts to speak to the reader as a whole individual, a person who is made up of an accretion of life experiences. In seeking to understand myth and literary form, Shklovsky finds that each generation of art coexists with those that have preceded it, just as the mind of each individual constantly inhabits both the present and the past. Art, he argues, communicates through the recombination of familiar motifs that resonate because of their relationships with earlier works. The purpose of art, he suggests, lies precisely in its ability to combine, juxtapose, and reconfigure content in ways that resonate with the audience. As with the journeys of Odysseus and Gilgamesh, he concludes, the meaning is in the movement itself.

Shklovsky's text can be grouped into roughly three types of chapters, though it should be noted that these chapters are intermingled throughout the book. The first type consists of contemporary literary analysis and biography, featuring Shklovsky's interactions with the texts and biographies of his associates from within the Russian formalist movement. Of particular note are the lengthy chapters that he devotes to Boris Mikhailovich Eichenbaum and to Yuri Nikolaevich Tynjanov, respectively, in which he combines eulogy with biography and intellectual critique. Most significantly for the advancement of his central analysis, he reflects that his own past, present, and future work exists in an interconnected relationship with these deceased colleagues. In his chapter on Tynjanov, for example, he states, "I am walking along the wide steps of the past, having chosen Tynjanov as my Virgil. I go as a living man and as an echo of the past. But the echo is not only a sound from the past—sometimes it predicts the formation of the bottom, which we still cannot reach, and the years that are ahead of us." Existing simultaneously in the past, present, and future, Shklovsky's narrating voice utilizes the discussions of Eichenbaum, Tynjanov, and others to consider sweeping questions about the nature of art, intellectual pursuit, and the senseless frailty of the human condition. Notably, in this passage, Shklovsky also places himself in the footsteps of Dante, linking his *Bowstring* to Dante's *Divine Comedy*.

The second type of chapter in *Bowstring* consists of Shklovsky's literary analyses. Throughout the course of the book, he grapples with a wide range of texts that are diverse in terms of historical period, subject matter, and genre. In keeping with his interest in montage, he deliberately juxtaposes texts and passages that might not seem to fit naturally with one another and uses these charged comparisons to create greater meaning. Undoubtedly, the variety and stature of the texts that he considers will contribute to the ongoing interest in *Bowstring*, since readers can turn to Shklovsky for discussions of Dante Alighieri, Victor Hugo, François Rabelais, Alexander Pushkin, and Leo Tolstoy, among others. Equally significant are Shklovsky's thoughtful treatments of genre and of literary elements such as plot formation and the construction of time in novels. Of particular interest are the passages in which Shklovsky considers the nature of myth and mythic narratives.

The final type of chapter deals with the concept of art writ large. These will likely be the most influential sections of the book, as they explore concepts such as unity, perspective, and the image with an interdisciplinary approach that considers both literature and the visual arts, with occasional references to music as well. Shklovsky devotes several pages to laying out a definition of "image" that, perhaps unsurprisingly, is layered and self-referential. Qualities of the real world inspire "experiences and knowledge" in observers, thoughts that may take the form of images in their minds. Meanwhile, an image (in this case meaning a work of art) is created by an artist as a "model of reality." It is important that this artistic image is not reality, but rather "is unique. It's a reflection in which the features of the perceived thing are juxtaposed in their dissimilarity." The tension between the real and the artistic reconstruction of the real creates the space needed for perception. Similar discussions of comparison and perspective offer concrete examples of how Shklovsky's ideas about dissimilarity and unity might function in the sphere of visual arts, though for the most part he has gathered his evidence through literary analysis, offering only tantalizing metaphors, similes, and references to the other arts.

The most powerful moments of the book are those that speak universally about the concept of art, its creation, and—as much as it can be identified—its significance. In Shklovsky's analysis, art cannot exist without the real world, with which it exists in constant and tension. He writes, "I am convinced now that the very fact of perception of art depends upon a comparative juxtaposition of a work of art with the world. The artist, the poet orients himself in the world with the help of art and introduces into what we call the surrounding world his own artistic perception." Art is, thus, both shaped by the world and also an active agent in shaping its surroundings. The crucial intervention here is Shklovsky's own introduction of "the world" into his previous theory of estrangement. Now form and content must both be considered, since estrangement "simultaneously assumes the existence of a so-called content, supposing that content is the delayed, close examination of the world." Ultimately, for Shklovsky, the power of art lies in its ability to captivate the mind and emotions through its unexpected juxtapositions: "Science avoids the act of wondering, it tries to overcome the element of surprise. Art preserves it." For critics, then, Shklovsky backs away from proscriptive theory and analysis, advocating instead for a gentler montage of ideas and forms, one against another, since the "most important thing in the analysis of art is never to lose the sensation of art, never lose its palpability, because otherwise the very object of study becomes meaningless, nonexistent."

Shushan Avagyan's translation of *Bowstring* is a major contribution to both literary studies and the broader humanistic disciplines. Shklovsky conceived of the work as his own mature revision of the scholarship of his youth. With an English translation lacking for thirty years, however, many scholars have not had the benefit of Shklovsky's gentler, if less concrete, approach to literary analysis, which makes space for content as well as form in art. This shift may have a significant impact on how literary scholars regard the legacy of Russian formalism. Although Shklovsky's text is certainly most valuable when read in its entirety, the significance of the book also lies, in part, in the diverse audiences that may be attracted to particular segments of its narrative. Shklovsky's theorizations of art will be of great interest to scholars of the visual arts as well as of literature, while his considerations of myths from Gilgamesh to the *Iliad* will likewise be of interest to scholars of the classical world.

Julia A. Sienkewicz

Review Sources

Numéro Cinq, July 8, 2011 (Web).
Publishers Weekly 258, no. 22 (May 30, 2011): 60.

The Brilliant Disaster
JFK, Castro, and America's Doomed Invasion of Cuba's Bay of Pigs

Author: Jim Rasenberger (b. 1962)
Publisher: Scribner (New York). 480 pp.
$32.00; paperback $18.00
Type of work: History
Time: Mainly 1959–1961
Locale: Cuba; Washington, DC

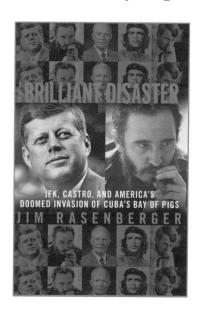

An account and analysis of the events leading up to the Bay of Pigs invasion, its preparation and execution, its outcome, its lingering aftermath, and the roles played by its major and minor protagonists.

Principal personages:

DWIGHT D. EISENHOWER (1890–1969), thirty-fourth president of the United States (1953–1961)

JOHN F. KENNEDY (1917–1963), thirty-fifth president of the United States (1961–1963)

FIDEL CASTRO (b. 1926?), head of state in Cuba (1959–2011)

ROBERT F. KENNEDY (1925–1968), attorney general of the United States (1961–1964)

ALLEN WELSH DULLES (1893–1969), director of the Central Intelligence Agency (CIA) (1953–1961)

RICHARD MELVIN BISSELL JR. (1909–1995), deputy director for plans at the CIA (1958–1962)

Jim Rasenberger, author of *The Brilliant Disaster: JFK, Castro, and America's Doomed Invasion of Cuba's Bay of Pigs*, has a personal, albeit secondhand, connection with the events surrounding the most embarrassing US foreign relations blunder of the early 1960s. His father, Washington attorney Raymond J. Rasenberger, was involved in team efforts to secure the release of the 1,183 Cuban anti-Castro insurgents of Brigade 2506 who had been left stranded by the ill-conceived and poorly executed Bay of Pigs invasion scheme, planned by the CIA and endorsed by two successive presidential administrations. His choice of title conveys a sense of irony; the term "brilliant" refers to the strategists and supporters of the plot to use a trained force of Cuban exiles to overturn a regime that was increasingly perceived as gravitating toward the Soviet Communist bloc. These planners, advisors, and strategists were indeed highly intelligent, including among their numbers such luminaries as Allen Dulles, Richard Bissell, McGeorge Bundy, Walt Rostow, Dean Rusk, Robert McNamara, Arthur Schlesinger Jr., and, of course, the Kennedy brothers. The mystery lies in the unfolding of events whereby such a gifted group of men, including two presidents, could have allowed such a tragic debacle to occur.

Rasenberger traces the chain of events back to the incrementally tense relationship between the United States and Cuba. After briefly summarizing the principal events prior to January 1, 1959, the date on which Fidel Castro's rebel forces overthrew the government of former strongman Fulgencio Batista, he then goes into greater detail, describing the incidents that gradually caused the Eisenhower administration to shift from seeing Castro as an admirable, revered freedom fighter to regarding him as a communist-leaning despot and therefore a Cold War adversary of the United States. The prospect of having such an antagonistic neighbor less than one hundred miles from shore, the threat he posed in offering the Soviet Union a foothold in the Western Hemisphere, and the possibility that his radical revolution might be exported to other Latin American nations were all factors that motivated President Dwight D. Eisenhower and his longtime CIA director, Allen Dulles, to begin planning for Castro's overthrow.

The covert operation, code-named Operation Zapata, was the latest in a series of semisecret CIA-sponsored initiatives to overturn anti-American regimes during the 1950s. These initiatives had thus far achieved their goals; the author cites the CIA-engineered coups in Iran (1953) and Guatemala (1954) as prime examples. Operation Zapata called for the training of anti-Castro Cuban exiles of varying backgrounds by CIA operatives at "Happy Valley," a base near Puerto Cabezas, Nicaragua. Air strikes (ostensibly carried out by Cuban pilots, but heavily augmented by US aircraft) were to damage and negate the Cuban Air Force, while the US Navy was to shadow a landing by some 1,300 to 1,500 Cuban exiles at Trinidad, a town on the southern coast of Cuba. The insurgents would go on to liberate the rest of the island, presumably assisted by uprisings and defections within Cuba itself, and a special provisional government friendly to American interests would be installed.

During the last months of the Eisenhower administration, Operation Zapata had gone so far forward with the president's total support and had assumed such momentum that it would have been difficult for any succeeding administration to completely derail it. To win the 1960 presidential election, John F. Kennedy had unmercifully lambasted his opponent, Vice President Richard M. Nixon, and the Eisenhower administration for being insufficiently vigorous in preventing Castro and communism from getting and keeping a foothold so close to the United States. Kennedy pledged to support Cuban rebels and destroy the Castro regime. This campaign tactic, Rasenberger argues, helped Kennedy win a close election but severely restricted his political choices in the months ahead.

Once in office, Kennedy found himself entangled in the covert operation. Throughout the final three months of planning, he continually seemed to be vacillating; in the end, he committed himself to the invasion, though with significant alterations that almost guaranteed disaster. In this context, Rasenberger rightfully singles out the belated change of the landing location from Trinidad to the Bahía de Cochinos (Bay of Pigs) and the refusal of the president to authorize the air support the exiles needed to avoid walking into a death trap. Those fighters not killed by the Cuban forces were taken as prisoners of war, and the United States government was exposed as a passel of bumbling, incompetent aggressors.

(Ellen Silverman)

Jim Rasenberger has written two previous books, High Steel: The Daring Men Who Built the World's Greatest Skyline, 1881 to the Present *(2004) and* America, 1908: The Dawn of Flight, the Race to the Pole, the Invention of the Model T, and the Making of a Modern America *(2007). He has also contributed to such publications as* Vanity Fair, Smithsonian, *and the* New York Times.

The new administration had suffered its biggest political setback. Both Castro and his sponsor, Soviet premier Nikita Khrushchev, were now wary of further CIA plots. The members of the stranded exile brigade, though released in 1962 amidst much fanfare and ceremony, were left with a bitter sense of betrayal. And, Rasenberger asserts, though the Kennedy administration seemed to rebound from this reversal, the incident actually had an enduring effect on it and on the succeeding presidential administrations of Lyndon B. Johnson and Richard M. Nixon.

Rasenberger is at his best when he unwinds the intricate series of conversations, misapprehensions, and lost opportunities leading up to the landings. He creates such suspense that some readers, despite already knowing the outcome of events, might vainly hope for them to transpire otherwise—as they might have, had Robert McNamara, McGeorge Bundy, or Dean Rusk spoken out more forcefully against the project at the time, or had Attorney General Robert Kennedy sensed that something was wrong, investigated, and alerted his brother. Demonstrating further his talent for putting together a compelling narrative, Rasenberger goes into a thrilling account of the actual military operations, the attempted subterfuges, and the fate of the exiles.

Rasenberger is slightly less persuasive when he puts forth his theories regarding the far-reaching impact of the "Bay of Pigs thing," as Richard Nixon called it in 1972. Rasenberger asserts that the Bay of Pigs affected such important subsequent events as the Cuban missile crisis, Kennedy's assassination in Dallas, the Vietnam War and the fall of Lyndon Johnson, and Watergate and Nixon's eventual resignation. Though Rasenberger makes a good case that the Bay of Pigs was a factor in all these events, it remains debatable whether it was as significant as the author indicates.

Rasenberger approaches and relates the invasion as though it were a Greek tragedy, a seemingly inexorable product of destiny replete with hubris and a foreordained sense of doom. For no individual, even John F. Kennedy, was this sense of hubris more evident and more devastating than it was for the genuinely brilliant CIA deputy director of plans Richard Melvin Bissell Jr. Bissell was born with significant advantages and had enjoyed a sensational career and rise to the top echelons of the CIA; in 1961, conventional wisdom regarded him as heir apparent to the aging Dulles. It was ironically one of his greatest strengths, his talent for being the "super salesman" or the "great persuader," that brought about his downfall. The author cites Bissell as the primary agent who was able to overcome or gloss over reservations and successfully pitch the Bay of Pigs scheme to a hesitant, and at times even skeptical, President Kennedy. Bissell's success proved to be his undoing; he was so closely identified with the plan that when it unraveled, so too did his career. He had to stoically endure being squeezed out of the CIA in February of 1962 and seeing the agency directorship that had once seemed to be his pass instead to Richard McCone, while he was reduced to the role of a historical footnote.

Kennedy himself is depicted rather ambivalently, as though Rasenberger, for all his research, obvious narrative skills, and erudition, remains uncertain about Kennedy's role and the extent of his culpability. It is difficult to determine which portrayal of Kennedy the author believes to be more accurate: that of the hesitant blunderer who sabotaged whatever slim chance the invasion had for success by limiting the intervention of US armed forces, or the political novice who naively placed excessive trust in the experts, only to suffer betrayal and the political consequences of open failure. Perhaps the author's dilemma merely reflects the challenges inherent in analyzing the larger legacy of the Kennedy administration, which is controversial in part because it was ended so abruptly by Kennedy's assassination, making what might have been as important as what actually occurred. Eisenhower's assessment in retirement that all would have been different had the Kennedy administration done all it could to insure Operation Zapata's success (as Eisenhower claimed he would have done) seems brutal, but may be close to the mark.

The Brilliant Disaster is a valuable contribution to the study of twentieth-century American history. While there have been many books written on the Bay of Pigs fiasco, none has told the story as effectively, in a fashion that is both popularized and academic, nor dealt as intensively with the larger implications of an invasion that most Americans would like to forget but cannot.

Raymond Pierre Hylton

Review Sources

Dallas Morning News, April 15, 2011 (Web).
Kirkus Reviews 79, no. 1 (January 1, 2011): 44.
Library Journal 136, no. 2 (February 1, 2011): 76.
Miami Herald, April 10, 2011 (Web).
Publishers Weekly, July 4, 2011 (Web).
Washingtonian, June 13, 2011 (Web).

The Buddha in the Attic

Author: Julie Otsuka (b. 1962)
Publisher: Alfred A. Knopf (New York). 144 pp.
$22.00; paperback $13.95
Type of work: Novel
Time: 1919–1924
Locale: Japanese American communities in the
San Joaquin Valley, California

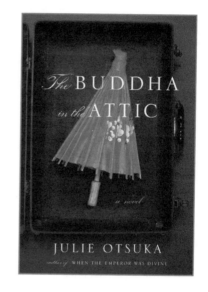

An experimental novel that recreates the expe-
riences of the generation of Japanese women
who immigrated to the United States shortly
after World War I, the so-called picture brides
sent to marry Japanese men already in Cali-
fornia.

It has long been the special task of historical
fiction to rescue from anonymity those groups
that a nation's history books have forgotten or
dismissed. There are, regrettably, many such groups in the United States, including
African slaves during the antebellum South, immigrants of the late nineteenth century,
suffragists who championed equal rights during the Gilded Age, and Native Americans who were displaced from their land and consigned to the indignities of reservation life. Writers of historical fiction have often sought to give voice to those groups
by creating compelling characters that will both embody a collective experience and
engage the reader's sympathy.

In *The Buddha in the Attic*, Julie Otsuka's spare and elegantly understated second
novel, the author quietly and audaciously upends that narrative premise, discarding
discrete characterizations in favor of a more unusual approach. From 1909 to the close
of World War I, in the wake of xenophobic legislation designed to prevent miscegena-
tion, an unknown number of Japanese women (estimates range from several hundred
to more than ten thousand) were brought to central California, having been bonded in
marriage to the Japanese men already living there. These women are known to cultural
historians collectively as the "picture brides." Many of them were initially brokered
into these arrangements by duplicitous professional matchmakers who used bogus photographs and counterfeit letters from the intended husbands as part of the negotiations.
The brides were, for the most part, poor and undereducated, and they entered into these
arranged marriages in the naive hope that life in the United States would fulfill their
dreams of a comfortable existence in a stable home. While they were keenly disappointed to find life in California difficult upon arrival, in a foreign land with unfamiliar customs and no common language, the women had no alternative. Some worked
as field hands and maids, while others clerked in shops and laundries. These brides
struggled to assimilate into life in a country where they were regarded with suspicion by

Julie Otsuka grew up in California as the daughter of second-generation Japanese Americans. She originally trained in the visual arts and first turned to fiction writing while in her thirties. Her first novel, When the Emperor Was Divine *(2003), drew lavish critical praise and earned her the prestigious Asian American Literary Award.*

locals who felt threatened by the prospect of unchecked tides of Asian immigration, a tension that only escalated as the United States moved toward war with Japan.

Rather than fashioning a single representative character, Otsuka allows the group to speak for itself; the novel is narrated in the first-person plural, "we," by a kind of choral narrator. Though unusual, this is a very flexible narrative strategy that allows Otsuka to give voice to immigrant women whom, ironically, their communities view as reticent and quiet. The "we" at once creates a profound empathy and maintains a careful, deliberate distance, underscoring Otsuka's larger objective of showing how entirely this story has disappeared from the wider cultural memory. Thus, the use of "we" works both to capture the scale of the situation and to record the women's experiences—their individual stories, hopes, fears, heartaches, and joys. Otsuka's is less a novel than a kind of social history, or, more precisely, a cultural autobiography.

Of course, Otsuka's narrative strategy of touching on literally hundreds of lives with a few spare sentences for each deliberately frustrates efforts at plot summary. There is no plot, no dialogue, and no interaction between or among characters. There are no scenes, as such, and no suspense. There is only the voice. Its consummate verisimilitude is the result of Otsuka's meticulous research, which she details in the book's acknowledgments. To recreate the experience of these mail-order brides, Otsuka divides her narrative into seven chapters that follow their evolution across two decades. "Come, Japanese!" recreates the arduous ocean crossing to San Francisco Harbor, as the women, many still in their early teens, struggle to adjust to homesickness and seasickness amid the heat and stench of steerage. "First Night" recounts the women's first meetings with their husbands and, most of them being virgins, their painful introduction into sexual services. "Whites," the longest chapter, relates the backbreaking work that is expected of them, from harvesting fruits and vegetables in the fields (six days a week in withering temperatures) to providing domestic help in homes and gardens. This chapter also follows them to the burgeoning cities of central California, to corner lunch counters and laundries, brothels and department stores, where they routinely endure the intolerance and bigotry of those who regard them as cheap labor and barely human. "Babies" records the women's difficult childbirth experiences: the pain, the lack of medical help, and the anxieties over their own survival and the survival of their newborns. "Children" traces the growing gap between the women and their American-born children, who abandon their culture's religious practices, speak only English, and dream of marrying Americans and securing their fortunes. "Traitors" covers the anxious months immediately after Pearl Harbor, when the women are faced with sudden hostility despite nearly two decades of residence in the United States. "Last Day" describes their heartbreaking relocation to massive government internment camps in Utah and Nevada as the federal government isolates them for reasons of national security.

In the closing chapter, "A Disappearance," the picture brides have disappeared and the narrative "we" is abruptly co-opted by the white Americans, the neighbors of the absent Japanese, whose homes are now locked up, their businesses closed. Although they have been told that the Japanese were taken to a safe place, this new narrative voice contemplates their failure to help their neighbors. Readers will notice that in contrast to the rich details and subtle emotional nuances of the previous chapters, this "we" comes across as shallow, insensitive, hypocritical, and xenophobic. As time passes, this "we" gradually loses their concern, as new neighbors move in and new businesses open. Rumors of trainloads of Japanese Americans being herded off like cattle to desert camps are ignored. The book closes with the new "we" deciding that they will never meet Japanese people again. It is a most haunting end.

The Buddha in the Attic can be profitably approached as a kind of prequel, or rather a prelude, to Otsuka's first novel, *When the Emperor Was Divine* (2003). This novel begins with an unnamed Japanese American family being uprooted from their home in Berkeley, California, and exiled to an inhospitable federal internment camp in Utah, where they will spend three brutal years in grim barracks enclosed by barbed wire and guarded by patrols. Working within a more familiar kind of historical fiction, Otsuka painstakingly recreates the family's routine in the camp in stark vignettes, and each individual family member in turn emerges in a clearly defined way.

As with that earlier book, and despite the volatile emotional issues involved (members of the author's immediate family having been subjected to government detainment and relocation), Otsuka maintains a scrupulously nonintrusive authorial presence in *The Buddha in the Attic*. As the women speak, Otsuka resists tempering the Greek choral recitation with her own contemporary anger. The style is thus deliberately understated, the sentences spare and precise, bringing to mind the austere, sculpted sentences of Ernest Hemingway. Whatever she records—the brutal rapes, the oppressive fourteen-hour days of labor, the racism of neighbors, the wrenching loneliness of children growing distant—Otsuka never indulges in pointed political commentary or bitter outrage. Nevertheless, the sentences accumulate and build, forming a text of witness testimony that compels without condemning. As Otsuka deftly manipulates basic patterns of syntax, the sentences invite reading aloud, even chanting. Her prose unfolds in a carefully measured rhythm of unadorned short sentences, then longer, terraced constructions. The cumulative effect is a verbal drama of emphasis and momentum that assumes the subtle music of a prose poem. Given the ugly subject matter—the harsh living conditions, the crushing cycle of anticipation and disappointment, the routine indignities, and finally the desert camps—Otsuka's sentences set the brutality to a difficult, distant music that creates a subtle bond between the reader and the characters.

To individuate the characters, Otsuka draws attention to telling objects, details that add nuance to the narrative "we." Aided by her early training in the visual arts (particularly in Matisse's studies of perspective), Otsuka paints her scenes with a striking physical clarity, emphasizing such details as the books the women treasure, the photos they carry, the clothes and jewelry they wear, the objects from the old country they could not give up, and the furnishings in their humble homes. Every scene in turn carries a vivid specificity, brought to life with carefully culled detail. With the scene-setting skill of Henry James, the modernist writer whose work first interested her in writing fiction, Otsuka invests each moment with striking immediacy that gives her narrative voice vitality and realism.

Otsuka draws her title from one such telling detail: a tiny brass Buddha left hanging and forgotten in the attic of the home of one of the women relocated to the government camps. Otsuka invites the reader to see the laughing Buddha as a kind of symbol, but because she is more poet than historian, the figurine suggests meaning rather than denoting it. The Buddha suggests, on one level, both the resilience of the picture brides in the inhospitable environment of central California and their betrayal by their adopted country; on another level, it is also suggestive of the women's religious identity, an identity that they tenaciously maintain even as their experience in the United States threatens to render it irrelevant. Perhaps the Buddha, as it hangs in the cobwebby attic, might also suggest the larger historical neglect that these brides endured, which Otsuka herself attempts to redress. Another possible reading might be found in the very material of the brass Buddha, brass being a material that endures. In this way, the figure might suggest, ultimately, the relevance of the picture brides' story in today's multicultural society. It might point to how their voices rightfully belong in any comprehensive record of American immigrant culture, even if their names have vanished in the passing of time.

Joseph Dewey

Review Sources

Booklist 107, no. 22 (August 2011): 22.
Daily Beast, September 16, 2011 (Web).
Kirkus Reviews 79, no. 10 (May 15, 2011): 814–15.
Milwaukee Journal Sentinel, August 19, 2011 (Web).
The New York Times, August 26, 2011, p. 12.
San Francisco Chronicle, August 28, 2011 (Web).

Bye-and-Bye
Selected Late Poems

Author: Charles Wright (b. 1935)
Publisher: Farrar, Straus and Giroux (New York). 384 pp. $30.00
Type of work: Poetry

Wright presents a collection of meditative and penetrating poems selected from five of his previous volumes.

An American poet who began to write poetry following an encounter with the works of Ezra Pound, Charles Wright achieved critical recognition with the publication of his 1970 collection *The Grave of the Right Hand*. A fascinating amalgam of humor, rural dialect, and unusual philosophical issues, Wright's poetry developed throughout the next four decades as he continued to challenge himself. With each successive collection, Wright mixed disjointed subjects and themes, creating a variety of innovative poems inspired by numerous sources. While Wright frequently looks to the future in his poetry, memories are fertile ground for his more inventive poems that often display strong connections to his rural Southern past. The richness of his work can be seen in the selection of poems included in *Bye-and-Bye: Selected Late Poems*, a volume that follows in the wake of Wright's earlier selected volumes *Country Music: Selected Early Poems* (1982), *The World of the Ten Thousand Things: Poems 1980–1990* (1990), and *Negative Blue: Selected Later Poems* (2000). *Bye-and-Bye* collects poems from *A Short History of the Shadow* (2002), *Buffalo Yoga* (2004), *Scar Tissue* (2006), *Littlefoot* (2007), and *Sestets* (2009).

The poems selected from *A Short History of the Shadow* introduce the reader to the extraordinary beauty of the Blue Ridge Mountains and explore the fleeting nature of time. Themes of impermanence, human suffering, and duality are prevalent; for every beautiful vision depicted in the poems, there is a darkness that blankets the horizon. The poet's words themselves become part of the landscape. Some of the poems Wright includes were written in tribute to the jazz musician Coleman Hawkins, and Wright fittingly composes the poems as if he were a jazz musician; he begins with a framework, but improvisation is a crucial part of the final product. Wright employs vivid language throughout the selected poems, fighting the onslaught of gloom and darkness. While there is never any certainty that all questions raised within the poems will be answered, the poet resolves not to give up the journey. Wright ends the poem "Polaroids" with the lines "We'll go, as Mandelstam tells us, into a growing numbness of time, / Insoluble, as long as landscape, as indistinct." As a poet for whom time, aging, and mortality are of great concern, Wright looks to the past and ponders what of value has been done, what the future will bring, and how much time remains to accomplish anything of consequence.

Fragments of memory and other monsters of the mind disturb the poet throughout his works, and the selected poems further explore these concepts. In "Nostalgia," Wright speaks of the feeling that "always comes when we least expect it, like a wave," leaving those experiencing it with memories and a sense of loss reminiscent of detritus and foam on a beach. He characterizes nostalgia as sand that weighs people down even as they claim to like the feeling. In a particularly frightening thought, he notes that one day, nostalgia may come to outweigh "whatever living existence we drop on the scales." All the poet can do at the end of the poem is plead to God to keep this day from arriving. In this poem and others, Wright establishes a link between imagery that is at once disjointed and whole and the counterbalance of language. Words seem to be always at the ready, serving as his protection against the elements in the world and in his head. The desire to discover some form of spirituality that can help to remedy the pain of the world is readily apparent.

From *Buffalo Yoga*, Wright selected shorter poems that concern the lives of several artists and writers that he admires, including Mark Rothko, Thomas Chatterton, Franz Kafka, and Ezra Pound, also including the title poem of that collection. "Buffalo Yoga" is an extended meditation on memory, landscape, and elegy. There is a meandering, Zen-like quality to the poem, and this Eastern influence is evident in such lines as "A poem is read by the poet who then becomes / That poem himself / For a little while" and "The world is a magic book, and we its sentences. / We read it and read ourselves." At the poem's end, Wright tells the reader that after closing this magic book, everyone returns "to what we once were before we became what we are. / This is the tale the world tells, this is the way it ends." The poem and its fellow selections are deliberately challenging, intriguing, circular, and darkly humorous. Themes of duality and opposition are again expressed, and these qualities are evident even in the title of the original collection. "Buffalo" is reminiscent of the American West, while "yoga" is an Eastern concept. The poet challenges not only himself but also the reader to experience opposing worlds at the same time.

The poems selected from *Scar Tissue* indicate that the poet is unsure whether imagination or reality can bring clarity of thought, yet he seems to understand his function in the process of exploring this concept. He raises the issue and presents a variety of images, but he cannot always provide a conclusion that the reader will find satisfying. Wright's poetic journey takes odd, meandering turns, and his poems reflect his maturation as a person and a poet and are characterized by frequent reflection on the passage of time. Throughout his career, Wright has made his search for confirmation that there is a spiritual realm evident in his poetry, and many of the poems selected from *Scar Tissue* build upon this theme. While the spiritual questions the poet raises may never be answered, he recognizes the need to ask. Some of the poems give rise to the idea that sacredness may exist in the natural world. In the poem "Last Supper," Wright introduces "dogwood blossoms like little crosses" and speaks to his interest in life after death, stating that "there is no end to the other world, / no matter where it is." He has reached an age at which the future is uncertain and the past haunted. Yet he describes himself as no more than a "God-fearing agnostic" in the poem "Confessions of a Song and Dance Man." Wright, or the poetic speaker, looks for proof of spiritual matters in "out-of-the-way places" but seemingly finds nothing: "Are you there, Lord, I whisper / knowing he's not around."

Charles Wright is an American poet whose collections include Hard Freight *(1973),* The Southern Cross *(1981),* Buffalo Yoga *(2004), and* Sestets *(2009). He received the National Book Award in 1983 and was awarded the 1998 Pulitzer Prize in poetry for* Black Zodiac *(1997).*

Wright reveals his personal history in "A Short History of My Life," beginning with his birth and continuing to chronicle his rebirths. He "was born for a second time" during his military years in Italy—a period coinciding with the beginning of his sustained interest in poetry. Wright springs ahead "some forty-five years" to his third birth. Commenting on his career as a poet, he notes that he has attempted to record his experiences and perception of the world. In this poem as well as several others, Wright wrestles with memories and the nostalgia that comes with the process of remembering. In "Scar Tissue," he admits that "it is impossible to say good-bye to the past." Whether directly or more subtly, these selected poems and the others in *Bye-and-Bye* make this fact readily apparent.

Bye-and-Bye includes the entirety of Wright's book-length poem *Littlefoot*, the title of which is also the name of one of his horses. The poem is divided into thirty-five parts that can each be read as a sketch that purposely adds to the whole. Chronicling Wright's seventieth year, these sketches paint landscapes and present the reader with intriguing slices of shadows and light. Individual sketches deal with many of Wright's recurring thematic concerns. In the eighth section, the poet reveals that "good luck is a locked door" and a key to the door is "around here somewhere," but whether it would be a good idea to give into the urge to find the key and make use of it is unclear. Memory is present, represented as a "thick staircase." Wright ends this particular sequence with the observation that "a lifetime isn't too much to pay / for such a reflection." Of course, there is a consequence for every life lesson. The poet learns that "things without shadows have shadows."

The remaining poems in the volume were selected from *Sestets*, Wright's collection of poems written in the six-line sestet form. These dazzling short poems serve as meditations on the natural world, mortality, and spirituality, illuminating episodes of great glory and great cruelty. In the poem "Tomorrow," Wright states that "if you don't shine you are darkness" and warns that "the future is merciless." The poet almost seems resigned to the fact that youthful exuberance, spirituality, and even poetry may not save the world from itself. Yet there is no desperation or immense grief in what the poet writes. For all the discontent in these poems, there still remains a sense of wonder that carries both the poet and the reader forward.

As a volume, *Bye-and-Bye* shows the mature Wright to be a poet of immense insight and provides a view into a world in which ecstasy and desperation inhabit the same landscape. As a poet, Wright seeks to penetrate the unknowable, to access the great mysteries of man through the linkage that only a poet can make between language and place and language and time. The spiritual quest is of great importance, and Wright carries the reader with him as he searches for meaning in the natural landscape and within himself. A poet of puzzles, he finds no easy philosophical answers in these poems; however, he carries out his journey with grace and purpose. Readers can revel in the many luminous images he has developed over time. With evocative language and thematic depth, *Bye-and-Bye* presents a selection of meditative poems by a significant and unmistakably American poet.

Jeffry Jensen

Review Source

Publishers Weekly 258, no. 8 (February 21, 2011): 114.

Caleb's Crossing

Author: Geraldine Brooks (b. 1955)
Publisher: Viking (New York). 306 pp. $26.95
Type of work: Novel
Time: 1660–1719, mostly between 1660 and 1665
Locale: Noepe (Martha's Vineyard) and Cambridge, Massachusetts

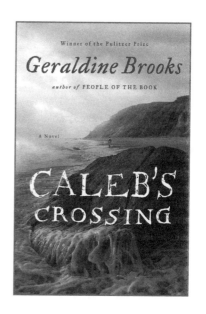

Brooks's historical novel about a Puritan girl in seventeenth-century Massachusetts who befriends a Wampanoag boy is based on the true story of Caleb Cheeshahteaumauk, the first Native American to graduate from Harvard University.

Principal characters:

BETHIA MAYFIELD, a Puritan girl from colonial Martha's Vineyard
CHEESHAHTEAUMAUK, a Wampanoag boy who takes the English name Caleb
MAKEPEACE MAYFIELD, Bethia's older brother
JOHN MAYFIELD, Bethia's father, a minister to the Christian people of Great Harbor (Edgartown) and Manitouwatootan
TEQUAMUCK, Caleb's uncle, a powerful Wampanoag pawaaw (priest-healer and wizard)

Australian Pulitzer Prize–winning novelist Geraldine Brooks has a knack for breathing warmth into cold historical fact. Fictional narrators give dimension to her stories, whether they are set in plague-ravaged seventeenth-century England, Virginia during the Civil War, Sarajevo in the 1940s, or Massachusetts in 1660. In *Caleb's Crossing*, the first-person narrator is Bethia Mayfield, an unassuming Puritan girl whose name literally means "servant of Jehovah." Bethia's thoughts and impressions bring life to Puritan New England.

Caleb's Crossing is loosely based on an actual event: the graduation of the first Native American, Caleb Cheeshahteaumauk, from Harvard University in 1665. Brooks's unmistakable skill as a researcher can be traced to the years she spent as a reporter for the *Sydney Morning Herald* and the *Wall Street Journal*. In the afterword to *Caleb's Crossing*, Brooks identifies the primary and secondary sources she used to provide context for this story, including the court testimony of Anne Hutchinson, the poems of Anne Bradstreet, and the writings of Daniel Gookin (ca. 1612–87), superintendent of the Indians of Massachusetts. She describes these few historical texts as "the slender scaffolding upon which I have rested my imaginative edifice."

At the start of the novel, the Massachusetts Bay Colony is only twenty-five years old. Bethia's grandfather, in a conflict with then-governor John Winthrop, had obtained the

Australian writer Geraldine Brooks is the author of several novels, including the Pulitzer Prize–winning March *(2005) and the international best sellers* Year of Wonders *(2001) and* People of the Book *(2008). She has also written the acclaimed nonfiction works* Nine Parts of Desire: The Hidden World of Islamic Women *(1994) and* Foreign Correspondence: A Pen Pal's Journey from Down Under to All Over *(1997).*

land patents for an island known as Martha's Vineyard, or Noepe, and brought Bethia's father there to start the settlement. Though life on the island is hard, the land is beautiful, lush, and uncultivated. Indigenous foods like clams, scallops, and berries are abundant. The Mayfields, along with a handful of other Puritan families, are the first white settlers in this New World paradise. But tensions on the island run high. Bethia's father, the liberal-minded minister John Mayfield, believes that he was called by God to convert the native inhabitants, the Wampanoag, to Christianity. The early Americans are unwilling to trust the Wampanoag, and many of the settlers, like the influential Alden family, are critical of the minister's efforts, preferring to steal from the Native Americans or slaughter them entirely.

The inevitable outcome of this conflict is foretold through the actions of Tequamuck, a powerful Wampanoag pawaaw, or priest; he foresees the subjugation of his land and people even as he struggles to maintain the Wampanoag way of life. His nephew Cheeshahteaumauk, however, is curious about the English settlers and their God. Young and willful, Cheeshahteaumauk ignores his uncle's warnings to avoid the strangers. The novel begins on the eve of John Mayfield's shocking invitation to this young man: to study and live in the Mayfield house.

The story unfolds through Bethia's perspective and the narration begins with her at age fifteen, having overheard her father's plans to bring the boy into their home. Three years earlier, she met and befriended Cheeshahteaumauk, an act forbidden by both the strict rules of her Puritan household and Tequamuck's powerful hold on the Native Americans. Bethia's father and her imperious older brother, ironically named Makepeace, constantly remind her of the boundaries of propriety and order. Bethia is a well-brought-up, thoughtful Puritan girl who knows that her secret meetings with Cheeshahteaumauk, whom she calls Caleb, are sins against God.

Bethia's youth and independence burst through the pages of what she calls her "spiritual diary." Her journal, written on stolen scraps of precious paper, describes the day she first met Caleb on a beach of "wide, white sand," when she was engaged in the "despised chore" of clamming for the family. At the time, twelve-year-old Bethia was angry with her father for deciding that Makepeace's preparation for attending Harvard was more important than her own education, despite her easy grasp of languages and study. When Bethia meets Caleb on that sensually described shore, she is surprised by his open and unguarded appearance. The diary invites the reader into her thoughts and fears as the two youths tentatively begin a friendship out of mutual curiosity and interest. Together, they transcend the boundaries of the era as they explore the island, learn each other's native languages, and share an intellectual intimacy forbidden by both cultures.

Though they revel in their closeness, they must keep the friendship a secret. Over the years, both children experience tragedy as well as joy. Bethia has lost her beloved twin brother, her dear mother, and the little sister entrusted to her care. Caleb's family has met with equal devastation; after spending the winter alone in the wilderness during a Wampanoag ritual of manhood, Caleb returns to discover that his band, including his mother, father, and brother, have all perished in a horrific outbreak of smallpox. It is obvious to Caleb and his people that Tequamuck was powerless to stop the spread of the devastating disease. Since only the white settlers remained immune to the sickness, Caleb decides that the English God is more powerful than those of the Wampanoag. Many Native Americans agree and begin converting to Christianity. Caleb accepts John Mayfield's invitation to join his household in order to study religion, Latin, Greek, and Hebrew and attend Harvard College like Makepeace, not because he accepts Christianity, but because he recognizes a force greater than his own gods. He hopes to find favor with the English God in order to save his people. Tequamuck, however, flees to the woods. Eventually, the priest openly curses Bethia's father as he leaves on a journey to England to recruit new settlers.

In *Caleb's Crossing*, the initial conflict created by the island setting is followed by a series of internal conflicts. How can Bethia exist and thrive in the narrow confines of her religious world? What hope has she for redemption when her nature is driven by independence and intelligence? Though thoughtful and religious, how can Bethia reconcile the evils of Christianity with the godlike benevolence of the Wampanoag beliefs? Caleb, too, faces his own internal conflicts that shine through Bethia's descriptions. Will he ever comprehend a wrathful God when his whole life has been surrounded by natural beauty? What can he do to make his uncle understand the path he has chosen? Does his drive to assimilate into English culture diminish the truth of his uncle's warnings?

One of Brooks's strengths is her facility with language. She imbues Bethia with the authentic voice of an early English immigrant in the New World. Archaic words like "misliked" and "alas" give color to her thoughts, while specific phrases such as "On the Lord's Day," "all of this was God's plan," and "Satan's voice" create a vivid portrait of this rich, historic period. While reflecting on her brethren in England who are still "under the boot of the reprobate king," Bethia says, "I pause to watch the splendid disc set the brine aflame and then douse itself in its own fiery broth." While Bethia's thoughts and words might seem mature by contemporary adolescent standards, her authentic seventeenth-century cadence, word choice, and honest emotion make her a compelling narrator.

As in her earlier novels, *Year of Wonders* (2001), *March* (2005), and *People of the Book* (2008), Brooks's central themes include sexism, prejudice, religious intolerance, and pedagogical practices.

In *Caleb's Crossing*, however, Christianity takes on an even more significant role, influencing the story like an antagonistic character. Unlike the benevolent deities of the Wampanoag, the Christian God is vengeful and all-encompassing. Bethia truly believes that the deaths of her parents and siblings are a direct result of her sins: in addition to her unholy friendship with Caleb, she speaks her mind, asks too many questions, basks in the natural beauty of the island, and despises the insufferable Makepeace. It does not help that she also sneaks away from her duties to watch Wampanoag ceremonies and tries a hallucinogenic drug-laced drink.

Following Tequamuck's curse, John Mayfield is killed in a shipwreck. Bethia and Makepeace are orphans and Bethia is fraught with guilt over her transgressions. The siblings learn that the only way to pay for Makepeace's Harvard education is for Bethia to become an indentured servant. Her guilt and lowly station ultimately, and perhaps predictably, lead her to accept the role, and she is forced to leave her beloved Martha's Vineyard for the "smear and stench" of "unlovely Cambridge." Caleb begs her to refuse the position. To the proud son of the Wampanoag, an indentured servant is comparable to a slave. But Bethia's Christian ethics require that she comply, thus driving the plot further along. Together, the now-sober youths travel to Cambridge, Bethia as a servant and Caleb as a scholar.

Bethia and Caleb cross the channel between Martha's Vineyard and the mainland of Massachusetts in a journey that is both literal and figurative, completing Caleb's transition into Bethia's world. Once in Cambridge, however, Brooks relates the fates of the characters in a summary format that is much less satisfying than the first two sections of the novel. Nevertheless, the friends strive to answer their spiritual questions and resolve their internal conflicts using what they have learned from one another.

Caleb's Crossing is a commanding novel of love, loyalty, and spirit. Well-researched and beautifully written, the story will engender a strong emotional response in readers. While one might question the story's predictability, the intricate balance of character and setting is extraordinary. This setting, grounded in history and research, becomes richer with the benefit of hindsight; readers will find that the historical issues and themes are elevated by Brooks's captivating prose. In the book's afterword, the author also reminds readers of the contemporary relevance of Bethia's story: in 2011, Tiffany Smalley became the first Martha's Vineyard Wampanoag to receive an undergraduate degree from Harvard since Caleb Cheeshahteaumauk in 1665.

Cheryl Lawton Malone

Review Sources

Barnes & Noble Review, May 4, 2011 (Web).
The New York Times Book Review, May 13, 2011 (Web).
USA Today, May 6, 2011 (Web).
The Wall Street Journal, May 3, 2011 (Web).
The Washington Post, April 28, 2011 (Web).

The Call

Author: Yannick Murphy (b.1962)
Publisher: Harper Perennial (New York).
 240 pp. paperback $14.95
Type of work: Novel
Time: Contemporary
Locale: Rural New England

This innovative novel draws on magical realism, mystery, and children's literature to present a moving and entertaining story of family love and community spirit.

Principal characters:
DAVID APPLETON, a quirky, compassionate
 veterinarian and family man
JEN, David's wife, chief cook and stay-at-home
 mother
SAM, their twelve-year-old son, who is in-
 volved in hunting accident
MIA, their six-year-old daughter
SARAH, their ten-year-old daughter
MARK HOWELL, a twenty-seven-year-old Spanish teacher from Philadelphia

With her latest novel, *The Call*, Yannick Murphy leaves behind the exotic locales of *The Sea of Trees* (1998) and the European countries of *Signed, Mata Hari* (2007) for a setting much closer to her home in rural Vermont: a New England community where farming, hunting, and raising horses are taken for granted amidst a landscape of mountains and valleys, forests and meadows. Murphy knows the setting intimately. She is aware of the privacy and the alienation that comes from living on several acres of land on the edge of the woods. The Appleton family observes deer, bats, owls, and other creatures in their native habitat and enjoys the beauty of rippling streams filled with trout and freshly fallen snows blanketing the tree limbs. It is against this serene natural setting that the bizarre and sometimes convoluted story takes place.

The characters all seem to be close to Murphy's heart. David Appleton, a veterinarian who makes house calls to treat sick and injured animals, was inspired by Murphy's real-life husband, Jeff Oney, a horse veterinarian. To learn how to administer vaccines to sheep or ease the colicky breathing of a horse, Murphy accompanied Jeff on his rounds. Raising their own three children gave Murphy the ability to write realistically about family dynamics and the parenting of the three fictional children. Even the Newfoundland dogs of the novel mirror Murphy's dogs in real life.

The innovative style of *The Call* also sets it apart from Murphy's previous works, giving the novel its unique patina. With an austere and undemanding choice of words,

Murphy tells the story from David's point of view, shaping the narrative in the form of a veterinarian's logbook or journal. Each bit of dialogue, action, and thought begins with a statement or declaration:

CALL: A cow with her dead calf half-born.
ACTION: Put on boots and pulled dead calf out while standing in a field full of mud.
RESULT: Hind legs tore off from dead calf while I pulled. Head, forelegs, and torso are still inside the mother.

Murphy then plays with this form, turning bits and pieces of action, description, or thoughts into declarations:

THOUGHTS ON DRIVE HOME WHILE PASSING RED AND GOLD LEAVES ON MAPLE TREES: Is there a nicer place to live?
WHAT THE CHILDREN SAID TO ME WHEN I GOT HOME: Hi, Pop.
WHAT THE WIFE COOKED FOR DINNER: Something mixed-up.

For those readers familiar with children's literature, this logbook form and its repetitious tags ("CALL," "ACTION," "THOUGHTS," "WHAT THE WIFE COOKED FOR DINNER") may suggest less a work of experimental fiction than a cumulative picture book or a pattern book written for children. As Murphy is also a children's author and references children's books throughout this novel, it is not too far-fetched to believe she may have gleaned some inspiration from picture books such as John Burningham's *Mr. Gumpy's Outing* (1970) or *The Gingerbread Boy* folktale, which also depend on the repetition of words, sounds, and actions to build momentum in the story and engage the reader. Murphy also seems to borrow from children's fantasy when she lightheartedly imbues inanimate objects and animals with human qualities, as in "WHAT THE MORNING SAID," "WHAT THE HOUSE SAYS," and "WHAT THE COYOTES SAID." Occasionally, the declarations are ridiculously long, "THOUGHTS WHILE WALKING WITH BREAD MACHINE FROM TABLE TO COUNTER TO PLUG IN BREAD MACHINE" or "WHAT SARAH IS READING NOW THAT SHE'S FINISHED WITH JANE EYRE: *Heidi.*" While these passages seem a bit silly, the overall warm and fuzzy feeling of the technique demonstrates not only Murphy's sense of playfulness, but her ability to make the novel's tragic plot accessible to all readers.

Other elements that resemble children's literature include the simplistic seasonal arrangements of chapters, and that Sam, a leading character, is just twelve years old. The focus on a traditional family is reminiscent of classic children's novels like Elizabeth Enright's *Thimble Summer* (1938) or Madeleine L'Engle's *Meet the Austins* (1960). If this were a children's novel, its young readers would probably relate especially well to the mother, as she nags repeatedly about the messy house:

WHAT THE WIFE SAID AFTER DINNER: Whose sneakers are these on the floor? Who left the butter out? Whose books are these? Whose sweater? Whose crumbs? Can't you clean up after yourselves? Don't leave a wet towel on your bed. Flush the toilet.

(© Clark Hsiao)

Yannick Murphy has published several novels, picture books, and short story collections. She is the recipient of a Whiting Writer's Award, a National Endowment for the Arts award, and a Chesterfield Screenwriting Award. Her stories were included in The Best American Nonrequired Reading *2009 and the* O. Henry Prize Stories *2007.*

However, the novel is not intended for a young audience, as it does contain some adult-oriented language and sexuality, as well as many sophisticated themes within its otherwise simplistic structure. The experimental form contrasts with the other traditional literary elements. The plot moves forward rather conventionally: a father takes his son hunting, and the son is accidentally shot by another, unknown hunter, ending up in a coma. The rest of the story finds the family wounded by anger and emotional suffering. A sub-plot involving a surprise visit from Mark Howell, a Spanish teacher, emerges less directly but in other ways is rather conventional also.

Most of the characters are portrayed as realistic, traditional New Englanders, although Murphy cleverly avoids stereotypes. David makes house calls for everything from sick alpacas to "depressed" horses competently and with just the right amount of emotional intelligence. When business is slow, he substitutes as a teacher in the local school, another sign of his dependability and the flexibility needed to survive in rural areas. Middle-aged, he suffers from many medical conditions, most likely high blood pressure and cholesterol, which he refers to simply as his "numbers" and fears will require surgery. While David appears stable and well adjusted from afar, his thoughts reveal otherwise. He feels as if "the world is closing in on him" and yearns for more privacy and protection than their wooded plot provides. He is constantly preoccupied with big issues, such as gravity, the Big Bang, time travel, and parallel universes, as well as the less important things, the "small stuff," to the point where he could clearly benefit from some stress management techniques. For example, he complains that the concave bottoms of peanut butter and mayonnaise jars represent a conspiracy among manufacturers to charge more for less product. And then there is the spaceship. Usually informed and intelligent, he occasionally seems as naive and innocent as the autistic fifteen-year old in Mark Haddon's *The Curious Incident of the Dog in the Night-Time* (2004).

David's wife, Jen, is portrayed as a busy, playful, and nurturing stay-at-home mother who tends to most household and child-rearing chores. She is emotionally available for David and offers sage advice when he cannot see clearly. When Sam, their twelve-year-old son, falls into a coma, Jen demonstrates her ability to hold things together emotionally while continuing to care for the family. On the other hand, David, used to solving problems with vaccines or stitches, comes close to an emotional breakdown.

Through David's veterinarian visits, the reader learns about the gentle folk who live in the community: Dorothy, who keeps a sheep named Alice in her house, the farmer who strokes the belly of his alpaca, and the family that is too poor to own the freezer needed to supply ice for their injured horse. As the plot unfolds, many of these rural characters show their appreciation and concern for their veterinarian, often in cleverly deceptive ways. This realistic portrayal of a small-town New England family and community is one of the novel's strengths, even as the presence of a fantastical element, a spaceship, pushes *The Call* into the realm of magic realism. Early on, David sees "bright lights in the sky, an object moving quickly back and forth." He catches a glimpse of the spaceship regularly, often circling his house, leading to incessant questioning of his customers and family. While he decides right away that it must be a military drone, he allows his imagination to wander: extraterrestrial beings, other worlds, and a path to escape his melancholy and earthly limitations. His wife plays into the fantasy, claiming to get "transmissions" from the aliens about their request for a "Head Potty Cleaner!" Complicating an otherwise transparent story, the mysterious lights can be interpreted from several different perspectives.

Humor keeps this novel from sinking under tragedy and grief. Murphy's sense of sweet and uncontrived humor is apparent from early on:

WHAT THE WIFE COOKED FOR DINNER: Nut loaf.
WHAT I ATE FOR DINNER. Not nut loaf.

Or in this scene:

CALL: Alpaca down.
ACTION: Drove to farm. Remembered not to look alpaca in the eye.
RESULT: Looked alpaca in the eye by mistake. Got spit in the eye.

Or this one:

WHAT I SAID TO THE WIFE IN BED: Am I getting grayer? The children told me I have more gray here. . . .
WHAT THE WIFE SAID: No, you don't have more gray than usual. It's just that the children are taller. They can see the gray they have never been able to see before."

Humorous scenes involving Gisela and Jürgen, characters from the instructional CD that David is using to learn German, tend to fall into an edgier type of humor, the kind that builds tension. As David becomes engulfed in grief and anger over his son's coma, Gisela becomes an almost tangible person, even assuming the position of a woman who threatens his marriage. This excerpt hints at both Gisela's increasingly real role for David's as well as his growing emotional instability:

WHAT GISELA SAYS WHILE I AM DRIVING HOME FROM A CALL: Where is the apothecary? I'd like to purchase some aspirin.
WHAT I PASS ON THE ROAD: A diner, a bowling alley, a car dealer, a tax-preparation office. Gisela doesn't need these things. What Gisela needs is an apothecary. I must find one for Gisela. Gisela feels *krank*.

The novel also contains elements of the mystery genre, as the story focuses on the search for the hunter who shot Sam. When the police fail to find the culprit, David takes it upon himself to track down the shooter. Rather than including dramatic chase scenes, Murphy takes advantage of her character's occupation and heightened sensitivities to create enough tension to keep the reader turning the pages. As each resident becomes suspected of being part of a community-wide conspiracy to keep the shooter's identity a secret, a different side of David emerges. Yet in the end, both David and Sam undergo major transformations rarely seen in mysteries. With its upbeat ending, *The Call* is reminiscent of happily-ever-after fairytales—additional proof that a contemporary novel can exist in more than one universe.

Sally S. Driscoll

Review Sources

Booklist 107, no. 22 (August 1, 2011): 20.
The Boston Globe, August 14, 2011, p. C7.
Library Journal 136, no. 10 (June 1, 2011): 93.
The Plain Dealer (Cleveland, OH), August 8, 2011.
Publishers Weekly 258, no. 16 (April 18, 2011): 29.
The Wall Street Journal, August 6, 2011, p. C6.

The Captain Asks for a Show of Hands

Author: Nick Flynn (b. 1960)
Publisher: Graywolf (Minneapolis). 104 pp.
$22.00
Type of work: Poetry
Time: The first decade of the twenty-first century
Locale: New Orleans; Abu Ghraib prison, Iraq;
Istanbul, Turkey

This fragmented and lyric collection of poems is Flynn's first book of poetry in nearly a decade. In language that draws freely from other poets, musicians, and government files, Flynn explores how language fails to adequately express the horrors of warfare and torture.

Nick Flynn's *The Captain Asks for a Show of Hands* begins by announcing itself as a failure with the title of the collection's first poem, "haiku (failed)." Even without such an explicit title, the poem's failure to adhere to the form's strict seventeen-syllable, three-line structure is obvious. Instead, it is written as a fourteen-line block of text spliced with forward slashes that suggest line breaks or interruptions to the thought process. In the poem, the speaker hopes to connect with another person, but language immediately escapes him or her, preventing that connection. As he or she begins, "The thin thread that hold us here, tethered / or maybe tied, together, what / do you call it—*telephone? horizon? song?*" The speaker is unable to find the words or the form that he or she wants, struggling to even articulate the companionship for which he or she needs to ask. Rhythmically surprising, the stuttering speaker pulls us along, punning and leaping from topic to topic, until he or she ultimately ends up alone.

This opening poem showcases some of Flynn's strengths as a poet while also setting in motion the important themes that will guide the rest of the collection. His first book of poetry in nearly a decade, *The Captain Asks for a Show of Hands* is a lyric exploration of the tragedies of the early twenty-first century. Focusing most often on the torture of prisoners by American soldiers at the Abu Ghraib prison in Iraq, Flynn is concerned not only with understanding the horrors themselves but also with exploring the limits and failures of language to describe and express such great human suffering. As a memoirist and a poet, Flynn has often written from his own perspective, carefully developing his persona on the page. With this collection, however, he relies heavily on the language of others, taking lines directly from poets, rock musicians, and those who have lived through extreme tragedy. He guides his reader through a world of torture and pain, urging us to confront this harsh reality and acknowledge our consistent inability to do better.

One of the most common forms of failing language in the collection occurs in four elemental poems, "earth," "fire," "water," and "air." All four poems are written as an address to the captain of the title, a figure who is at once a military leader and a father. However, he is not a figure who protects and supports his charges, but rather a mad, dangerous voice of authority, demanding violence and torture. In each of the elemental poems, the speaker addresses and acquiesces to this captain while considering the ways in which the four elements are used to torture prisoners. The captain, via authoritative language and memorandums, insists upon the torture of others. The speaker of the poem, often confused, does his or her best to meet these demands. As he or she says in "earth,"

(Geordie Wood)

Nick Flynn is the author of critically acclaimed poetry, drama, and nonfiction. His book Another Bullshit Night in Suck City *(2004) is a classic of contemporary memoir, while his poetry collection* Some Ether *(2000) was honored with the PEN/Joyce Osterweil Award.*

> if I understand the memo right, capt'n, we can use
> water, but we cannot use earth—that is,
> we can simulate drowning, but not
> burial—is that right, sir,
> capt'n? I've read
> the memos & I want to do
> what's right

When addressing the captain, the speaker is timid, cowering before the authoritative language. While the speaker's questions are clear and direct, the language itself fails, with the captain never answering and the speaker's rambling functioning more as a monologue than anything else. This failure of language, however, seems minor in comparison to the breakdown that occurs when the speaker attempts to address the prisoner. At these moments, the speaker stumbles, entering into lyrical nonsense. Trying to describe the experience of the prisoner whose face is pressed against the cell's tile, the speaker rambles, "yellow yolk yellow dead yellow / sulphur yellow." In this way, Flynn positions the speaker as both victim and victimizer. On the one hand, he or she is controlled by a demanding, authoritative voice that never responds to his or her concerns. On the other, he or she holds absolute power over another human, torturing the prisoner yet completely unable to make sense of the experience. In both regards, Flynn implicates language itself, questioning our ability to communicate with one another even as the poem itself attempts that task.

The breakdown of language in the face of war is perhaps most explicit in "seven testimonies (redacted)." In 2007, Flynn went to Istanbul, Turkey, to hear the testimonies of people who had been detained at Abu Ghraib. The testimonies themselves are horrifying, speaking of imprisonment, torture, and degradation. To compose the poem, Flynn took the testimonies and redacted them, erasing most of the text and leaving behind lyric and terrifying fragments of language. The process is similar to the redaction commonly done by governments, an act in which crucial details are removed from documents to protect sensitive or private information. Rather than hiding horrifying information, however, Flynn's redaction makes the language all the more nightmarish:

> remember
> waking up, somewhere
> a dog, I remember
> those days, two others
> were there, I remember
> two days

The language here is cyclical, repeating itself to the point of nonsensicalness. Flynn is at once giving voice to the detainees and silencing them. While his project is heavily concerned with their needs and humanity, he does not excuse himself or his reader from their torture. Instead, he implicates himself by removing their words, constraining them linguistically and making his reader tacitly complicit in the process. He further magnifies this horror by including the unedited testimonies at the end of the book, allowing readers to confirm that the experiences were just as awful as (and sometimes worse than) implied in Flynn's edited versions. The redacted texts, then, become some of the collection's most powerful examples of the failure of language. Flynn wants to share this horror with us, forcing us to face it head on, but is thwarted by the language itself, which is fractured and clouded by his own interference. For Flynn, it is ultimately impossible to truly communicate the experience of torture.

There are very few poems in *The Captain Asks for a Show of Hands* that do not borrow language from another source. While "seven testimonies (redacted)" is the most obvious example of this practice, the entire collection is scattered with the words of other people. Flynn includes language spoken by survivors of Hurricane Katrina, dialogue from documentaries on the Vietnam War, lyrics from Bruce Springsteen songs, and poetic lines from Walt Whitman, to name only a few of many sources. He is attempting to create a poetry that responds to the realities of modern warfare and torture, a task that is too big for his voice alone. As he says in "some notes" at the end of the collection, many of his lines are "pulled or twisted" from their original source before being inserted into his work. The resulting cacophony of phrases that are at once familiar and off key successfully communicates the inherent impossibility of Flynn's task.

While usually keeping an eye on his own failures and the failures of language, Flynn is not exclusively pessimistic. Instead, scattered throughout the collection are tantalizing reminders of pleasure, optimism, and the opportunity for human connection. For Flynn, these reminders are often physical rather than verbal, coming through the body rather than through language. The physical nature of human connection is hinted at in the opening poem when the speaker wonders if true companionship is "inside us, inside each / corpuscle." Though different poems appear to have different speakers, they still often seek this physical connection. As the poem "kedge" begins, "*ceaselessly*, I said, let's hold each other / ceaselessly." The speaker announces his or her need for comfort, and even finds it for brief moments, but then spins off into insecurity and fractured, unclear language. He or she begs, "can we start again— say // sorry dear ocean dear desperate dear boat," pleading for the chance to apologize to something as huge and uncaring as the ocean. The speaker of "forgetting something" oscillates between despair and optimism in a similar way. He or she suggests that they "make / a cage of our bodies—inside we can place / whatever still shines." The optimism and joy that might be found here and in other poems is fleeting and tinged with darkness; whatever light exists must be caged in the body, and the chance to hold someone is interrupted by the overwhelming need to apologize to the world. *The Captain Asks for a Show of Hands* is not a book that seeks to reassure or uplift the reader. Instead, it shows the pain and horrors of modern reality as starkly as possible, with pleasure being only a brief reminder that there could be a different world.

The Captain Asks for a Show of Hands is a report from the dark side of the twenty-first century. It is insistent and uncompromising, demanding that we look at the torture of modern warfare and refusing to forgive us (or the poet) for allowing torture to exist. Just as importantly, it is a book that wonders what poetry can be in such times, questioning the power of language to respond to inhumanity even as Flynn takes on that task. While the poems intentionally fall apart, repeat themselves, and grasp at other voices, Flynn maintains his lyric intensity and rhythmic ear. It is difficult, at times, to confront the horror that he enshrines in every page, but his poetic gifts transform the collection into more than a litany of tragedy. As he asks in "greetings, friend (mino-taur)," "O heart weighed down by so many wings / isn't it time to admit / we are more machinery than gods / that our house is more maze than temple . . . ." This is the challenge and the question of Flynn's poetry, demanding that we acknowledge the cruelty in our society and ourselves despite our need for love and human connection. We are not holy beings, gods living in temples, but rather complicated and flawed creatures, lost in the maze of our own lives. Flynn gives us a poetics to match this condition, as rich with failures as it is with beauty.

T. Fleischmann

Review Sources

Booklist 107, no. 12 (February 15, 2011): 43.
Library Journal 136, no. 2 (February 1, 2011): 63–64.
Publishers Weekly 258, no. 3 (January 17, 2011): 31.

The Chameleon Couch

Author: Yusef Komunyakaa (b. 1947)
Publisher: Farrar, Straus and Giroux (New York). 128 pp. $24.00
Type of work: Poetry

This poetry collection deepens Komunyakaa's enduring involvement with three elements of inquiry central to his writing: music, myth, and mystery.

The poem "Facing It," a striking work about a visit to the Vietnam Veterans Memorial featured in the Vietnam War–themed collection *Dien Cai Dau* (1988), stands as one of the most well-known poems by Yusef Komunyakaa, a poet whose military service in Southeast Asia gives readers a categorical location convenient for identifying him. Even at the time of the poem's initial publication, however, it was apparent that Komunyakaa's interests and poetic perspectives encompassed a much wider angle of vision than his experiences in Vietnam. His name, for instance, was chosen to reflect his admiration for his grandfather, a native of Trinidad, as Komunyakaa had been given the name James William Brown when he was born in Bogalusa, Louisiana. This alteration was not an erasure but rather an expansion or reclamation, part of a continuing process of self-exploration and an ongoing operation of self-creation that has shaped the poet's career. Komunyakaa's creativity and willingness to work with the materials of his craft have marked his writing from the beginning, and he has noted that he typically works on multiple poetry collections at once. The linguistic flux these factors create is evident in the poems collected in *The Chameleon Couch*, a volume that has been described by critics as both difficult and beautiful, garnering praise while demanding intellectual engagement.

While Komunyakaa's poems are difficult, this does not prevent them from connecting with an extensive readership. There is a pungency and directness to the poems in *The Chameleon Couch* that can immediately ensnare the reader. "A Translation of Silk," for example, begins with particularly evocative language:

> One can shove his face against silk
> & breathe in centuries of perfume
> on the edge of a war-torn morning
> where men fell so hard for iron
> they could taste it.

The actual intent of the poem does not become apparent until the entire poem has been experienced, but this is not a hindrance, as the power of the opening image is sufficient to capture attention and interest. The poems also frequently feature an intriguing personal declaration of direct participation by the speaker and a distinctive voice that has become increasingly recognizable with each volume that Komunyakaa publishes. The idea of a dual essence, a recurring theme in his work, is suggested in "Canticle," the first poem in *The Chameleon Couch*.

> Because I mistrust my head & hands, because I know salt
> tinctures my songs, I tried hard not to touch you
> even as I pulled you into my arms. Seasons sprouted
> & went to seed as we circled the dance with silver cat bells
> tied to our feet. Now, kissing you, I am the archheir of second
> chances.

In addition to the poet's striking invention of calling himself "the archheir," with its sonic resonance and somewhat puzzling connotations, the poem includes a juxtaposition of entities—head and hands, salt and songs, "not to" and "pulled you"—that is essential to the poet's methods. These contrasts generate energy through a kind of tension that is recapitulated but not resolved in the poem's concluding image of "the wet seam of memory & manna." The profusion of unusual physical and metaphysical imagery that contributes to the perceived difficulty of the poems can also be seen as one of its essential attractions, especially in conjunction with Komunyakaa's readiness to reveal dimensions of emotion.

"Canticle" depicts a couple "in the East Village as midnight autumn / shakes the smoke of the Chicago B.L.U.E.S. club from [their] clothes." Here, one of the central concerns of the volume can be seen: the music at the core of black culture. Komunyakaa is not particularly concerned with any one artist, although his knowing references to Lady Day (Billie Holiday), Bud (Bud Powell), Miles (Miles Davis), and Rahsaan (Rahsaan Roland Kirk) lend a sense of familiarity to many poems. His larger purpose is to link the jazz and blues cosmos to the entire human musical endeavor, seeing no reason to separate the jazz musicians he cites from classical composers such as Maurice Ravel (referenced in "The One-Handed Concerto"), Frédéric Chopin ("Aubade at Hotel Copernicus"), Johann Sebastian Bach, and Ludwig van Beethoven ("Gone"). Beyond this, he associates his calling as a poet with that of the legendary Greek musician Orpheus, an icon of inspiration that fuels Komunyakaa's determination to sing about all that he has seen. In "Orpheus at the Second Gate of Hades," the poet admits in direct, first-person cadences that his "lyre has fallen & broken," an admission of a debased condition. "But I have my little tom-toms," he says, conflating classical Greece with his African and Caribbean origins and insisting that he has not been disarmed. Likening Hades to a Holocaust concentration camp and making allusions to other historic forms of incarceration, Komunyakaa expresses his responsibility as an artist: "I knew I had to speak of what I'd seen." In a stirring paean to human endurance, he proclaims "If I never possessed these reed flutes / and drums . . . I shall holler to you through my bones, / I promise you."

Yusef Komunyakaa is an award-winning poet whose collections include Dien Cai Dau *(1988) and* Warhorses *(2008). He won the 1994 Pulitzer Prize in poetry for* Neon Vernacular: New and Selected Poems *(1993). He teaches at New York University, where he holds the position of Distinguished Senior Poet.*

Mythic allusions further inform Komunyakaa's investigation of the attributes of the muse, appearing alongside references to a wide range of international literary figures. While this lends a degree of detachment to some poems, the pattern of a recursive return to the personal, notably in poems in the second section of the volume, sustains the dynamic pulse of a deeply committed person. Wary of appearing too earnestly confessional or perhaps too eager to confide, Komunyakaa includes abstract images that raise more questions than answers, in keeping with his philosophy that poems are more effective when they pose questions. One such poem, "Ten or Eleven Disguises," actually comprises six parts with cryptic headings such as "I *Pretending to Be a Rock*," "III *Blush*," and "VI *Addendum to a Discourse*." Nonetheless, in poems from the middle of the collection, he offers direct insights into his "disguises" or poetic masques. In the last stanza of "Poppies," one of several poems to reference concentration camps, there is a signature statement that is close to the poet's heart: "I am a black man, a poet, a bohemian / & there isn't a road my mind doesn't travel."

Other bold declarations are interspersed throughout the collection, such as the claim in "Orpheus at the Second Gate of Hades" that the speaker "can make a lyre drag down the moon & stars," which is followed by the statement "but it's still hard to talk of earthly things." This pattern of exclamation and qualification is a fundamental part of Komunyakaa's strategy. In "When Eyes Are on Me," as a template for this trope, the poem begins with the declaration "I am a scrappy old lion," continues with the similar image of the speaker as a leopard, and later notes, "I am not / & I am." The poem and its implicit refrain come to an end, though not necessarily a conclusion, with the final stanza.

> I am a prodigal bird perched on the peak
> of a guardhouse. I have a message
> for fate. The sunlight has shown me
> the guns, & their beautiful sons are deadly.

The poem is a vision of the elusive, of revelation as a form of concealment, but it is so powerfully phrased that the "I" accrues presence. In this way, Komunyakaa mingles the personal with the mythic and mysterious, an important aspect of his presentation of the self with respect to the other key elements of his poetic explorations.

There is no title poem in the collection. "Ode to the Chameleon" is the seventh poem in the volume and the only one in which the word "chameleon" occurs. The first six poems are designed as a kind of preparation for its appearance. Following "Canticle," with its juxtapositions, "The Janus Preface" describes the natural world through contrasts observed in "a country between seasons." "Eclogue at Midnight" blurs the divide between the dream world and the waking world; "Ignis Fatuus," a phrase equivalent to "will-o'-the-wisp," extends the idea of duel essence; "The Story of a Coat" proceeds as a narrative of recollection based on a clash of binaries; and "Ten or Eleven Disguises" extends the motif of duality into a multiplicity of identities. In a candid commentary on the poet's fondness for flux, the "Ode to the Chameleon" is arranged as a genial meditation by the poet on a creature whose capacity for change is emblematic of the continuing fascination the poet has for the wonders of the world. Komunyakaa has noted that poetry helps him to understand himself, and his clear delight with the chameleonic images he proposes is crucial to the "I," the poetic speaker throughout the volume. He addresses the chameleon, which could be termed his avatar, attempting to understand the creature. Ultimately, he depicts the chameleon as the quintessence of transformation: a "little shape shifter" in a "little theater / of osmosis."

In the latter part of the collection, Komunyakaa begins "How It Is" with a statement about poetry and the poet's commitment: "My muse is holding me prisoner. / She refuses to give back my shadow." He admits, however, that even if he freed himself from his muse's hold, he would be unable to do anything but remain "in her ravenous light." The poet's shadow, referred to frequently in *The Chameleon Couch*, resembles the chameleon's variability; it is camouflage, protection for something vital and vulnerable. A fundamental part of the poet's nature that is contemplated, appreciated, and never quite completely understood, this shadow is a part of the mystery that makes Komunyakaa's poetry engrossing and in some ways difficult. In the presence of the poetic muse, Komunyakaa's shadow is brought to light.

Leon Lewis

Review Sources

Booklist 107, no. 12 (February 15, 2011): 43.
Library Journal 136, no. 2 (February 1, 2011): 67–69.
Los Angeles Review of Books, September 14, 2011 (Web).
Publishers Weekly 258, no. 12 (March 21, 2011): 55–56.

Changó's Beads and Two-Tone Shoes

Author: William Kennedy (b. 1928)
Publisher: Viking (New York). 336 pp. $26.95
Type of work: Novel
Time: 1936–1968
Locale: Havana, Cuba, and Albany, New York

This riveting novel, the eighth in Kennedy's Albany cycle, links such tumultuous events as the Cuban Revolution and the civil rights movement.

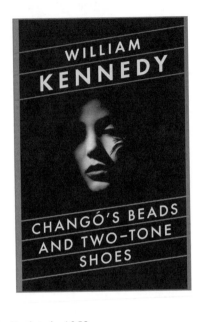

Principal characters:
DANIEL QUINN, a journalist from Albany, New York
RENATA SUÁREZ OTERO, a Cuban revolutionary who marries Daniel
GEORGE QUINN, Daniel's father
ERNEST HEMINGWAY, a famous American writer living in Cuba
FIDEL CASTRO, a Cuban revolutionary leader who overthrows the corrupt dictator Fulgencio Batista in 1959

Changó's Beads and Two-Tone Shoes is the eighth volume in what has been termed William Kennedy's Albany cycle, a series of novels focusing on crime, politics, and family life in Albany, New York. The cycle began with the 1975 novel *Legs* and expanded to include *Billy Phelan's Greatest Game* (1978), *Ironweed* (1983), *Quinn's Book* (1988), *Very Old Bones* (1992), *The Flaming Corsage* (1996), and *Roscoe* (2002). Place is of prime importance to Kennedy, and the city of Albany, his hometown and the state capital of New York, itself is a character in these novels. Kennedy's focus on a particular locale has garnered him comparisons to such writers as James Joyce and Charles Dickens, whose writings encapsulate and have almost come to define their respective cities, Dublin and London, during the eras in which they were writing. Growing up in a working-class neighborhood, Kennedy learned at an early age about the rough edges of the city, gaining an understanding of the effects of life on the streets and the political corruption for which the city was known. These elements of Kennedy's background further influence the Albany cycle, which concerns the lives of several generations of Irish American families. In *Changó's Beads and Two-Tone Shoes*, Kennedy chronicles the experiences of Daniel Quinn, the grandson of the Daniel in *Quinn's Book* and a minor character in *Billy Phelan's Greatest Game* and *Ironweed*.

The novel is divided structurally into three sections, each of which is set in a particular time and place denoted by the section's heading. The first part opens in Albany in 1936. A young Daniel encounters his father, the singer Bing Crosby, and some African

American men in a parlor. One of the men is the pianist Cody Mason, who plays as Crosby sings the minstrel song "Shine." This song has troubling racial overtones that Daniel does not understand, but they will reverberate later in the novel when Mason sings the song in his own way. This rich childhood experience has a strong impact on Daniel, and this opening chapter serves to set the tone of the novel through music and suggestions of social conflict. In the second section of the book, "Havana, March 12, 1957," the adult Daniel Quinn is a freelance journalist spending time in Havana, Cuba, where he hopes to meet and interview the larger-than-life writer Ernest Hemingway. He is largely unaware of Cuba's political instability, but the nation is on the brink of a revolution aimed at removing Fulgencio Batista from power. Daniel serves as the reader's eyes during the revolution. He is in Havana at the time of the attack on the Presidential Palace, a bloody event in which many students are killed. While in Havana, he meets and becomes attracted to the revolutionary Renata Suárez Otero. A follower of the religion of Santeria, Renata tells Daniel about Changó, a mythological "warrior king of kings." Both Daniel and Renata come to believe that this warrior has influenced their lives, and this influence is evident in the novel's title. Through his growing connection to Renata as well as his encounters with Hemingway and Fidel Castro, Daniel learns much and becomes increasingly involved in the brewing revolution.

The setting of *Changó's Beads and Two-Tone Shoes* next shifts to Albany in 1968. Daniel's father, George, is in the clutches of a growing senility, and the reader is provided with a view of the social and political landscape of Albany through George's muddled memory as he meanders around his old haunts. A connection is drawn between two-tone shoes and the opposing forces that inhabit Albany. In this final section of the novel, Kennedy links the revolution in Cuba with the civil rights movement in the United States. Kennedy has noted that he sees the civil rights movement as a "prolonged revolution against the US social order," in which an oppressed minority fought for the right to participate fully in the American system. Having witnessed the revolution in Cuba, Daniel now observes as the United States, and Albany in particular, is thrown into turmoil after the assassination of presidential candidate Robert Kennedy, a senator from New York. Racial tensions spill over into the streets, threatening the city and its residents.

Kennedy's prose is engaging and evocative, aptly transporting the reader between locations and time periods. The novel suggests a variety of influences, from the hard-boiled detective works of such writers as Raymond Chandler and Dashiell Hammett to the music of crooner Bing Crosby. Kennedy's novels have at times been criticized as confusing due to their scope and complexity, and this quality is somewhat evident in *Changó's Beads and Two-Tone Shoes* as well. The book depicts two events that are not typically thought of as connected, and Kennedy had to find a way to incorporate these events into a single cohesive novel. He does his best to juggle all of the characters and plot twists, but it is not always easy for the reader to keep track of the details. There is much for the reader to absorb in the novel, and at times, the number of side stories seems overwhelming. Nevertheless, Kennedy has made the story come alive, encouraging the reader to care about Daniel's experiences and depicting the revolution and the struggle for civil rights to great effect. The novel's level of detail and broad scope largely benefit the narrative, making it a meaningful exploration of life in two periods of social and political upheaval.

Kennedy worked as a journalist before establishing himself as a novelist, and this experience informs both his style of writing and the subject matter of some of his novels; in the case of *Changó's Beads and Two-Tone Shoes*, Daniel's career in journalism is essential to the plot. Kennedy's experience as a journalist is particularly evident in his use of realism. While there is a certain surreal flow to much of his richly inventive fiction, as he successfully mixes historical fact with mythical constructs, his writing is always rooted in a realism that draws the reader to sympathize with each character's predicament. Never one to restrain himself from exploring the more sensational aspects of city life, Kennedy does not shy away from depicting sex or violence. To some readers, this may come close to pandering, but it seems to be in keeping with the author's journalistic attention to detail. Holding back salacious or embarrassing facts in order to protect individuals or social and political organizations would be inconsistent with his mission as an author and reporter. Kennedy's experience as a journalist also has a great effect on his ability not only to create multidimensional fictional characters, but also to depict well-known historical figures in a vivid and factually appropriate manner. A meticulous researcher, Kennedy has gathered information for his Albany novels from books and newspapers as well as interviews with individuals who lived through the tumultuous eras he depicts.

William Kennedy is the author of numerous novels and nonfiction works, most of which concern life in Albany, New York. He was awarded the 1984 Pulitzer Prize in fiction for Ironweed *(1983), the third novel in his Albany cycle.*

Much of the novel, however, derives from Kennedy's own life experience. He has stated that he wanted to "write a novel about two of the most important things [he] covered as a reporter, the Cuban revolution and the civil rights movement." As a journalist, he wrote about events in Cuba for the *Miami Herald* during the 1950s and later had conversations with Fidel Castro. Daniel's experiences and the revolution as portrayed in the book clearly display the influence of Kennedy's personal history. While Kennedy emphatically claims that the novel is a work of fiction and nothing more, there are also similarities between characters in the novel and people close to the author. Daniel Quinn could be easily interpreted as a stand-in for Kennedy himself, while Renata could represent Kennedy's wife, Dana. Kennedy has dedicated the novel to several individuals, including his father, William Joseph Kennedy Sr., and the character George Quinn is like Kennedy's father in "certain ways," particularly in their shared experiences with the ravages of dementia. Despite these similarities, Kennedy cautions the reader not to assume that he is merely writing about his own life. In various interviews, Kennedy has made it clear that he has no desire to write about himself, as doing so would only result in a novel that is "dead on the page." Although Kennedy will not admit that he is writing directly about himself and his loved ones in *Changó's Beads and Two-Tone Shoes*, he will go so far as to state that this novel "is a bit more autobiographical" than his other books.

In addition to being the eighth installment of the Albany cycle, the novel also serves to continue the story that began in *Quinn's Book*, which also concerned a journalist named Daniel Quinn. Kennedy has expressed his belief that the 1988 novel was "an unfinished story," and in *Changó's Beads and Two-Tone Shoes*, he builds upon the themes and historical scope of the earlier work. The blending of fact and fiction found throughout the Albany cycle has served Kennedy well as a novelist. Despite the occasional confusion it elicits, *Changó's Beads and Two-Tone Shoes* is a riveting novel that delivers a magnificent view of historic events, depicting the many ways in which such events can affect nations, cities, families, and ordinary individuals.

Jeffry Jensen

Review Sources

Booklist 107, no. 22 (August 1, 2011): 32.
Library Journal 136, no. 14 (September 1, 2011): 100–101.
Los Angeles Times, October 16, 2011 (Web).
The New York Times Book Review, October 2, 2011, p. 1.
Publishers Weekly 258, no. 34 (August 22, 2011): 48.

Charles Dickens
A Life

Author: Claire Tomalin (b. 1933)
Publisher: Penguin (New York). Illustrated.
576 pp. $36.00
Type of work: Biography

Claire Tomalin presents a lively biography of Charles Dickens that balances an acute appreciation of the great novelist's literary output with an engrossing account of his complicated private life.

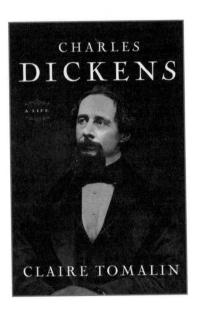

Principal personages:
CHARLES DICKENS (1812–1870), a prolific and
    beloved nineteenth-century English writer
CATHERINE DICKENS (1815–1879), his wife
JOHN FORSTER (1812–1876), his best friend and
    biographer
ELLEN "NELLY" TERNAN (1839–1914), his
    mistress

More than 140 years after his death, Charles Dickens still remains one of the world's most beloved writers. All his novels are in print, and the most popular of them continue to be adapted for film and stage. His *A Christmas Carol* is a holiday staple, and the notion of a "Scrooge" is a recognizable part of popular culture. The image of Dickens continues in large part to be that which he himself laboriously constructed: a benevolent crusader against the social and economic injustices of a rapidly urbanizing and industrializing Victorian England. Claire Tomalin is the author of eight previous biographies, including a study of the relationship between Dickens and his youthful mistress, Nelly Ternan; here, she provides her readers with a fascinating and fully rounded portrait of the only writer in the English language whose creative breadth and richness can rival that of Shakespeare.

Charles Dickens was born in 1812. His father, John Dickens, was an official in the Navy Pay Office at a time when the Royal Navy was winding down a long war with Napoleonic France and guarding the sea lanes of a burgeoning British empire. In his early days, Dickens lived an easy, secure life of genteel prosperity in tidy homes located near the naval stations where his father worked. Unfortunately for his family, John Dickens was a spendthrift, unable to live within his means. In class-conscious England, he aspired to a station in life he could not afford. Following a series of monetary embarrassments, he was arrested in 1824 and incarcerated in London's Marshalsea debtors' prison. John Dickens took his misfortune philosophically, later becoming the model for the famously sanguine deadbeat Mr. Micawber in *David Copperfield* (1850).

His father's financial ruin traumatized the young Charles. The comfortable circumstances of his early days gave way to increasingly dingy lodgings and dispiriting efforts to evade bill collectors. Worse, Charles, who had been raised to aspire to the status of a gentleman, found himself forced to work to help support the family. For a time he labored in a small factory that manufactured shoe polish, where his task was to label the bottles of shoe blacking. He regarded this job as degrading and was angered that his parents did not see things the same way. So insensitive were his parents to this that, much to his mortification, they occasionally brought friends around to watch him through the window of the workshop. Dickens would later transmute the pain of these youthful experiences into the many descriptions of childhood adversity that appear in his novels. The failure of his father to adequately provide for him and the stint in the blacking factory left Dickens with a burning need for control in his life. From this point on, he was determined to set the terms on which he would meet life. The steely will with which Dickens pursued this inner compulsion made him a remarkably disciplined and creative artist, but it also ultimately shattered his marriage and family.

Things eventually improved a bit for the Dickens family, and Charles was not destined for a life in the sweatshops of Victorian England that he would later evoke so memorably in his fiction. It was clear, however, that he would have to make his own way in the world. Dickens explored a range of possible careers early in his life: he clerked in a law office, learned shorthand and became a court reporter, dallied with the theater, and found success as a newspaperman covering Parliament and politics. It was his work as a journalist that eventually set Dickens on the path to his literary career. As he traveled around London and England, he was inspired to write short stories blending scenes and characters from his observations. At first these appeared anonymously, but as they grew in popularity, he adopted the pen name "Boz." The first collection of these, *Sketches by Boz* (1836), proved to be a publishing triumph and made Dickens a force to be reckoned with in the literary world.

Over the next two years, Dickens followed up his success with *The Pickwick Papers* (1837), a series of interconnected stories that gradually coalesced into something like a picaresque novel. *The Pickwick Papers* cemented Dickens's enduring appeal for his reading public, and the ongoing adventures of his endearing characters became sensationally popular. Each installment was published in paperbound pamphlets that were priced at a shilling, inexpensive enough to be accessible to most readers; for those who could not afford the price, copies were readily passed from hand to hand. The arrival of each new number became a literary event. People flocked to booksellers, clamoring for the latest chapters, and even butcher boys could be seen reading them in the streets. Dickens's course was now set. He would be a writer, popularly and critically acclaimed for the rest of his life. He dropped his pseudonym and began writing under his own name, producing all his longer works in serial form. Over the course of years, as one novel followed another, catching up on the latest episode from Dickens became an eagerly anticipated pleasure. But it locked Dickens into a grueling regimen of regular and inexorable deadlines, compelling him to create to an industrial timetable.

An almost superhuman energy enabled Dickens to meet the demands of his rigorous publishing program. Far from being an introspective and reclusive writer, Dickens threw himself into incessant rounds of activities that would last until his death. He was a gregarious man who socialized constantly, either having parties at his home or traveling in company with others. He made many friends and spent innumerable hours at gentlemen-only gatherings and dinners. In addition to his novels, Dickens generated a steady stream of articles, many for publications that he himself edited. He carried the

Claire Tomalin was the literary editor for the New Statesman and the Sunday Times in Great Britain before becoming a full-time writer and authoring eight acclaimed biographies. She has won numerous awards for her writing, including the James Tait Black Memorial Prize, the Hawthornden Prize, and the Whitbread Book Award.

social consciousness of his novels into his life and wrote about government corruption and the conditions of the working class. He often took an interest in unfortunate people he learned about and was always ready to raise funds to support the families of deceased friends and coworkers. He advised the heiress Baroness Angela Burdett Coutts on her philanthropies, and together they founded the Home for Homeless Women, which took in fallen women, including prostitutes and criminals, and prepared them for new lives in the British colonies. Dickens took a deep interest in this institution and visited it regularly for many years.

A great lover of theater, Dickens also wrote, produced, and acted in amateur theatricals that were publicly staged, occasionally before Queen Victoria. Later, as his fame grew, he began to give public readings, utilizing carefully crafted scripts drawn from his novels. This showcase gave Dickens a lucrative opportunity to combine profit with his passion for performance. Though the readings were physically and emotionally draining, Dickens continued them even as his health failed and he neared death.

Dickens's need for control in his life found its fullest expression in his family life. Here, a different Dickens emerged, one that contrasted with his public reputation as a humanitarian and reformer. At home, the sensitive creator of vulnerable characters scarred by the deprivation of love and kindness proved incapable of understanding or sympathizing with the feelings of his wife and most of his sons. The man who denounced tyranny in the realms of business and politics exhibited a domineering willfulness in his personal relations. Dickens yearned for a happy home life, but he failed to achieve the domestic harmony and peace that he celebrated in his fiction.

As his career as a writer took off in the mid-1830s, Dickens decided that he needed to settle down. Success for him meant making a home. For a wife, he chose Catherine Hogarth, the pretty daughter of one of his newspaper editors. Catherine was not his intellectual equal, but she was kind, devoted, and pliable, exactly what Dickens wanted in a spouse. He made it clear during their engagement that he would be the master in their relationship. For twenty-two years, Catherine would loyally follow him in his whims, from multiple moves to extended excursions on the continent. She accepted without complaint his platonic devotion to her sisters. When Mary Hogarth died suddenly, the grief-stricken Dickens declared that he wanted to be buried next to her; Catherine's other sister, Georgina, would remain with Dickens until his death. Dickens never wanted more than three or four children but did nothing to prevent regular additions to his brood, with the result that Catherine bore ten children in sixteen years.

He was a distant father, packing his sons off to boarding school as soon as decently possible.

As she aged, Catherine grew stout and matronly. Dickens increasingly complained to his friend John Forster that he was unhappy in his marriage. Then, in 1857, during the production of one of his plays, he met the teenage actress Ellen "Nelly" Ternan. Dickens fell in love with the young woman, though at first his attentions did not meet with full success. At home, Dickens ordered the construction of a divider in his bedroom, separating him from Catherine—just one of many cruelties.

Tomalin writes that some readers might feel the need to avert their eyes from much of what happened in Dickens's life in 1858. At forty-six, he finally gained nineteen-year-old Nelly Ternan's heart. His romantic success led Dickens to a decisive break in his life, which resulted in ruptures with family and friends that never healed. He cast off Catherine with a financial settlement, forcing her to return to her parents. He published a self-serving statement in the press that questioned her mental balance. He demanded that his children and friends sever their relations with Catherine; those friends who sympathized with Catherine, or who disapproved of his conduct, were cut from his life. Dickens was always determined that his life would be his own, and he defied both convention and decency to achieve this at last.

Nelly Ternan would remain Dickens's devoted mistress for the remaining dozen years of his life. While Dickens's relationship with Nelly Ternan was an open secret among the inner core of his friends and business associates, it was not known to the general public. Concealing what most would have regarded as a scandal added to the complexity of Dickens's busy life. He continued to drive himself hard, even as his health deteriorated. Dickens was churning out yet another popular serialized novel when he died in 1870 at the age of fifty-eight.

Claire Tomalin's biography brilliantly captures the rush and excitement of Dickens's crowded life. Her treatment is sympathetic but judicious; she describes a great man but does not shirk from discussing his flaws. Brief but authoritative, Tomalin's book should be the starting point for anyone newly interested in the life of Charles Dickens.

Daniel P. Murphy

Review Sources

Booklist 108, no. 2 (September 15, 2011): 11.
The Economist 400, no. 8753 (October 1, 2011): 88–89.
Kirkus Reviews 79, no. 17 (September 1, 2011): 1573.
Library Journal 136, no. 17 (October 15, 2011): 83.
The New York Times Book Review, November 6, 2011, p. 4.
Publishers Weekly 258, no. 32 (August 8, 2011): 39.
Time 178, no. 15 (October 17, 2011): 67.
The Times, October 1, 2011, p. 17.
The Washington Post, November 11, 2011 (Web).

China in Ten Words

Author: Yu Hua (b. 1960)
Translated from the Chinese by Alan H. Barr
Publisher: Pantheon (New York). 240 pp.
$25.95
Type of work: Essays, current affairs, history,
memoir, sociology
Time: 1960s to the present
Locale: China

*Yu Hua presents a series of personal essays
centered on ten key words: "people," "leader,"
"reading," "writing," "revolution," "disparity,"
"grassroots," "copycat," "bamboozle," and "Lu Xun."
As he meditates on each word, Yu Hua reflects
on the China of his boyhood and the China of
his middle age, describing the two eras' similarities and differences.*

Principal personages:
YU HUA (b. 1960), the author, a writer who grew up during China's Cultural Revolution
XU HUA (b. ca. 1958), the author's older brother
LU XUN (1881–1936), an influential Chinese writer in the 1960s and 1970s
WANG HONGWEN (1935–1992), a Chinese leader who both rose to power and fell
quickly
MAO ZEDONG (1893–1976), the leader of the Chinese Communist Party and father of
the People's Republic of China
JIANG QING (1914–1991), Mao's longtime wife who lost power after he died
DENG XIAOPING (1904–1997), a Chinese leader who advocated a more flexible eco-
nomic policy
ZHAO ZIYANG (1919–2005), a Chinese leader who was sympathetic to student demon-
strators in 1989

Published first in Chinese (though not in China) and then translated into English by
Allan H. Barr, Yu Hua's *China in Ten Words* is a peculiar book. Yu Hua, a prominent
Chinese novelist and intellectual, offers a series of ten essays, each revolving around
a significant word or term. Each word provides a theme for its accompanying essay,
and the book as a whole is unified in three ways: by its focus on Yu Hua's life, its
concern with China during the Cultural Revolution, and its attention to China in far
more recent times. Part memoir, part history, and part contemporary social analysis,
China in Ten Words combines the virtues of all these genres. This is, in short, a highly
personal book, unusual in its structure, purpose, and method, and valuable, in large
part, precisely because it is so distinctive. Readers looking for a well-documented

historical narrative or a deeply sourced contemporary analysis will not find either here. However, those looking for a unique and memorable reflection on China's past and present from a thoughtful observer will surely be fascinated by this engaging and thought-provoking work.

Yu Hua structures his narrative around the ten words mentioned in the title—people, leader, reading, writing, revolution, disparity, grassroots, copycat, bamboozle, and Lu Xun (a celebrated Chinese writer). These words form the framework of the book and allow Yu Hua to balance personal reflection with a discussion of China's politics, social conditions, economy, and history. The key words are seemingly innocuous on their own, but Yu Hua uses them to delve deeply into China's troubled past and present. With "people" he can discuss the People's Republic, protestors, and the government. With the word "reading" Yu Hua can reflect on education, censorship, and class. The final chapters—on the words "copycats" and "bamboozle" —are perhaps the most critical with their meditations on such issues as government propaganda, fraud, piracy, and the pervasiveness (and apparent acceptance) of crime in Chinese society. Whether his stories are based on his own life or rooted in China itself, they are astute and lucid descriptions of a country where a great deal has gone wrong.

China in Ten Words is in many ways a very daring book. Owing to its sensitive and occasionally unflattering subject matter, the book was—perhaps unsurprisingly—first published not on the Chinese mainland, but rather in Taiwan. Yu Hua continually draws parallels between China at the time of the highly destructive Cultural Revolution (1966–76) and China in the early twenty-first century. He lives and works in the so-called People's Republic, but surely some officials there will not be happy with what he has written. There are times, as readers make their way through this book, when many are likely to worry for Yu Hua's safety, especially if a crackdown similar to the one in Tiananmen Square in 1989 should ever occur again. Yu Hua, in fact, mentions the Tiananmen protests more than once and describes his own involvement in them. He sympathizes with the protestors who were brutally suppressed, yet he also raises the ironic possibility that greater political liberalization might have happened sooner in China if the protests had not occurred. As this example suggests, Yu Hua rarely seems rigid in his thinking (although he obviously detests the Cultural Revolution, having personally suffered from and through it). He knows that China is richer, freer, and more dynamic in the first decade of the twenty-first century than it ever was under Mao, but he still seems troubled by various recent trends and worried about his country's future.

Yu Hua's reflections on post-Tiananmen China may strike many readers as the most fascinating aspect of this book. He describes, for instance, a current China in which money rules, corruption is endemic, and social rage is bubbling just beneath the surface. A China that once had one clear leader—Mao—has been replaced by a China in which the very concept of leadership has been become both widespread and watered down. Huge economic gains have occurred, but often at enormous costs to the environment and with astonishing inefficiencies. At one point, for instance, Yu Hua reports that "An authority I respect has put it this way: China's model of growth is to spend 100 yuan to gain 10 yuan in increased GDP. Environmental degradation, moral

Yu Hua is a Chinese novelist, essayist, and writer of short fiction. His works— including the books To Live *(1992) and* Chronicle of a Blood Merchant *(1995)— have been translated into more than twenty languages. Yu Hua is a recipient of the Premio Grinzane Cavour award and was the first Chinese writer to win the James Joyce Foundation Award.*

collapse, the polarization of rich and poor, pervasive corruption—all these things are constantly exacerbating the contradictions in Chinese society. More and more we hear of mass protests in which hundreds or even thousands of people will burst into a government compound, smashing up cars and setting fire to buildings." Many readers will probably be quite shocked to learn just how fundamentally China seems to have changed in a few short decades. Yu Hua notes, for instance, how difficult it was to find anything worth reading when he was young, especially anything literary, whereas two hundred thousand new books were being published annually during the completion of Yu Hua's latest volume.

Nevertheless, Yu Hua's recurring argument is that China has not changed as completely as appearances might suggest. As Yu Hua's chapters weave back and forth between the years of his youth and those of his very recent past, he repeatedly stresses that, in some ways at least, the more things have changed, the more they have remained the same. Unnecessary ports, vastly under-used highways, ill-conceived and risky public loans, skyrocketing university tuition rates, a rapidly growing cadre of university students who cannot find jobs, a vast number of people in poverty, and a yawning income gap between the rich and the poor—these are just a few of the problems Yu Hua highlights. Many of them will seem familiar to American readers who face similar challenges. In general, though, Americans are used to hearing mainly about China's swift progress, not its ominous problems. The further one reads in Yu Hua's book, the more worried one becomes about China's potential social instability. After all, it possesses a very large army, a great stockpile of nuclear weapons, and an increasingly strong sense of its historical destiny.

Perhaps even more surprising than Yu Hua's accounts of China's economic problems are his depictions of its moral transformation. Some of the humor in this often-funny book results from Yu Hua's recollections of the sexual repressiveness of the society of his youth. He and his boyhood friends were delighted to discover an anatomy text that finally revealed some of the wonders of the female body, but that was about as far as their curiosity was allowed to go. The China of his youth was prudish to an extreme, and it is partly that prudery (he thinks) that helps account for the fact that the pendulum has recently swung so far in the opposite direction. Thus he notes that "These days pregnancies among high school girls have become so common they are no longer controversial, but it is still startling to find that some teenage girls actually show up for abortions in their school uniforms. I read that in one case the girl was escorted to the hospital by no fewer than four schoolboys. When the doctor said she needed a relative's signature, all four rushed forward." Yu Hua depicts a contemporary Chinese society that seems increasingly self-indulgent in almost every way.

Yet the anecdote about the girl getting the abortion, with four potential fathers in tow, all eager to claim paternity, is typical of an unsettling aspect of this book. The story sounds implausible, but Yu Hua claims to have read it. Where did he read it? He does not say. How typical is such behavior? Readers cannot know for sure. Yu Hua often reports statistics, but he cites few clear sources. He makes factual claims about both the distant and the recent past, but for the most part readers have to rely simply on his word if curious about the reliability of his assertions. Some of his anecdotes may occasionally leave readers wondering how seriously to take various claims made in this book. Endnotes would have added enormously to the credibility of Yu Hua's narratives.

But this is not a scholarly tome. It is, instead, a highly personal and very informal work, consisting of the kinds of essays one might find in popular publications. Perhaps, then, it is wrong to judge it by strict academic standards. Academics who have read and reviewed the book have been highly impressed. Yu Hua has won worldwide acclaim for the quality of his fiction, but he is also highly respected as a perceptive observer of his homeland. However factually dependable the claims in Yu Hua's book may or may not prove to be, this volume presents China as Yu Hua has experienced it and perceives it. For that reason alone, it is likely to be of interest to a wide range of readers, particularly to students of Yu Hua's writings in other genres.

Robert C. Evans

Review Sources

The Christian Science Monitor, December 8, 2011 (Web).
Kirkus Reviews, October 1, 2011 (Web).
Los Angeles Review of Books, November 2, 2011 (Web).
The New York Times, November 10, 2011 (Web).
Time, December 5, 2011 (Web).
The Wall Street Journal, December 7, 2011 (Web).

Civilization
The West and the Rest

Author: Niall Ferguson (b. 1964)
Publisher: Penguin (New York). Illustrated. 432 pp. $35.00
Type of work: History
Time: The sixteenth century to the early twenty-first century
Locale: Western Europe and most of the rest of the world

Ferguson argues that the countries of the West became dominant world powers because of six "killer apps" that other nations, particularly China, have now begun to "download": competition, science, the rule of law, modern medicine, consumerism, and the work ethic.

Principal personages:
KEMAL ATATÜRK (1881–1938), Turkish army officer and statesman, the first president of Turkey
SIMÓN BOLÍVAR (1783–1830), Venezuelan soldier and politician, liberator of South America
EDMUND BURKE (1729–1797), Irish politician and political theorist
FREDERICK THE GREAT OF PRUSSIA (1712–1786), Prussian king and military leader
JOHN LOCKE (1632–1704), English political philosopher who emphasized the "social contract"
KARL MARX (1818–1883), German political and economic philosopher
NAPOLEON BONAPARTE (1769–1821), French political and military leader, emperor of France
JEAN-JACQUES ROUSSEAU (1712–1778), Genevan philosopher and intellectual
ADAM SMITH (1723–1790), Scottish political and economic philosopher
MAX WEBER (1864–1920), German political economist and sociologist

In *Civilization: The West and the Rest*, historian Niall Ferguson argues that the West, particularly Western Europe and the United States, has been the dominant force in world affairs since around 1500. Rather than lament or apologize for this fact, he seeks to explain how Western dominance came to be, as well as how and why the balance of global power and innovation is shifting to the East. While China and other Asian countries are adopting and adapting many of the cultural traits that have given the West its enormous competitive advantages, the West is losing focus on, and even faith in, some of the values that once made it dominant. Ferguson suggests that these shifts may result in the loss of Western hegemony, or perhaps something far worse. Many past civilizations, he notes, have collapsed with astonishing speed, and he raises the alarming prospect that the West, including the United States, may be on the verge of just such a fall. The West may remain a strong force in global affairs, but its days of unchallenged supremacy seem to be over.

Written for a popular audience and particularly intended for use in secondary schools and universities, Ferguson's provocative book is the companion to a television series that aired in the United Kingdom. Ferguson recalls the stirring impact that a similar book and documentary series, Kenneth Clark's famed late-1960s volume and programs *Civilisation*, had on him when he was a child just beginning to develop an interest in history. Believing that present methods of teaching history leave much to be desired, Ferguson hopes to arouse the same kind of interest in young people with his own take on the subject. His book is written with considerable wit and verve, and he almost seems to enjoy mocking and challenging standards of political correctness. He argues, for instance, that the process of colonialism generally benefited the groups and nations colonized, introducing better medicine and education, more effective forms of government, and significant economic prosperity. Ferguson appears to delight in being the "bad boy" of academic history, and he cannot resist making jabs at leftists in general and communists in particular, somewhat limiting the audience for his work. Ferguson's politically and economically conservative beliefs are clearly evident, and the critical and public responses to the book have been significantly influenced by the degree to which the reader agrees or disagrees with his stance. One reviewer went so far as to compare the volume to the work of an early-twentieth-century white supremacist writer, a comparison to which Ferguson has strongly objected.

Few readers are likely to disagree with Ferguson's basic premise that the West has benefited enormously from six developments that the author, presumably in an attempt to appeal to younger readers, terms "killer apps": competition, science, the rule of law and representative government, modern medicine, consumerism, and the work ethic. Some readers may doubt the benefits of consumerism, but it is hard to dispute Ferguson's claims when considering them purely in economic terms. A professor of business as well as history, Ferguson places a great deal of emphasis on economic factors throughout the book. He makes clear that he is not discussing civilization as Clark conceived it: buildings, art, music, and other kinds of great cultural accomplishments. Instead, Ferguson thinks of civilization in mainly political and economic terms, considering such factors as land controlled, productivity per year, life expectancy, relative wealth, scientific innovation, and personal freedom. Without a solid economy and political stability, he suggests, civilization in Clark's sense is much less likely to develop.

Each chapter of Ferguson's book is carefully annotated, and the final bibliography is impressively long. This is less a book of original research, however, than one of careful synthesis. It obviously benefits from Ferguson's stature as a scholar, especially in its discussion of the nitty-gritty details of economics. Mostly, though, the book is what it was intended to be: a lively textbook offering well-written overviews of already familiar topics. Sometimes the connections between the stated topic of each chapter and its actual contents seem thin. The chapter on medicine, in particular, is

Niall Ferguson holds a double appointment in history and business administration at Harvard University and is also affiliated with Oxford University and the Hoover Institution at Stanford University. He is the author of numerous historical studies as well as several documentaries.

less an exploration of the numerous Western medical innovations and more a survey of political and military developments in nineteenth-century France. France, Ferguson shows, was one of many European powers to establish African colonies through military might, and he argues that this process of colonization brought the benefits of modern medicine to many indigenous peoples. Ferguson never denies and, in fact, often stresses the horrors of various colonial enterprises. However, he maintains his belief that colonialism often resulted in many positive changes in the lives of colonized peoples. This tendency to tout the achievements of empire is by far one of the most controversial aspects of the book.

Ferguson is at his most impressive when he is gathering and reporting reams of hard data. He has an excellent understanding of how to make such information seem interesting and important, and he exercises this skill by filling the book with facts and statistics. Thus, the reader learns that an early Chinese encyclopedia consisted of eleven thousand volumes, that some ancient Chinese gates were so large they could house three thousand soldiers, and that between 1330 and 1479, one-fourth of all deaths among the English aristocracy resulted from violence. Such facts help Ferguson make strong cases for most of his assertions, creating a work that is difficult to challenge not only in its sweeping scope but also in its depth of detail.

Typical of the method of this work is the chapter "Property," in which Ferguson argues that private property rights played a key role in the development of Western civilization. He compares and contrasts the colonies established in North America with those established in Central and South America, noting that British colonies were consistently more economically productive than those established by Spain and Portugal, even though there were sufficient natural and manmade resources in both areas. The crucial difference, he asserts, is that property was much more widely distributed in the north than in the south. The greater number of individual, upwardly mobile property owners in the north coincided with much greater religious diversity, and both factors helped promote the "creation of a society of merchants and farmers committed to religious as well as political freedom." Eventual efforts by Simón Bolívar to establish republican government in South America ultimately led not to democracy but to dictatorship, partly because in postrevolutionary Venezuela, almost all land was owned by only 1.1 percent of the population. Ferguson further notes that the apparent link between property ownership and economic and social success was not limited to the colonies that became the United States; widely dispersed ownership of land was also evident in Canada, Australia, and other British colonies, and these colonies would go on to contribute to the development of the West. Full of detailed facts used to support strongly argued claims and tinged with pride in the achievements of the British, this chapter is largely representative of *Civilization: The West and the Rest* as a whole.

The book's historical arguments are framed by chapters dealing with more contemporary interests and events. Ferguson repeatedly refers to news from as late as 2010, often making his contentions seem especially timely. He includes, for instance, projections that the United States' federal debt may exceed the gross national product in the near future, and cautions that even these sobering figures do not include the unfunded liabilities associated with Medicare and Social Security. All it may take, he warns, for the economy of the United States and the West as a whole to slip into a catastrophic and perhaps irreversible financial crisis is a sudden loss of fundamental confidence in the dollar. In the meantime, Ferguson foresees an inevitable and rapid decrease in US military commitments abroad, and he also expects China to simultaneously consume more, import more, innovate more, and invest more of its resources abroad. He questions arguments that China may also be headed for an economic collapse, suggesting that the nation's main social problem is a rapidly aging population. Some of the most sobering statistics in the whole book come in the final chapter, in which Ferguson notes that in the number of patent applications submitted, patents granted, and scientific papers published, China is now overtaking the West.

Ferguson seems certain that the period of undisputed Western economic superiority he chronicles in *Civilization: The West and the Rest* is coming to an end. Yet the specific consequences of this apparent decline are, he implies, difficult to foresee with any real precision. According to Ferguson, a steady decline of the West seems inevitable, but a calamitous collapse may still perhaps be averted.

Robert C. Evans

Review Sources

The Economist, March 12, 2011 (Web).
The Guardian, March 25, 2011, p. 7.
Independent, March 11, 2011 (Web).
Maclean's 124, no. 44 (November 14, 2011): 92–93.
National Post, November 18, 2011 (Web).
New Statesman 140, no. 5044 (March 14, 2011): 44.
The New York Times, November 15, 2011, p. C1.
Spectator 315, no. 9522 (February 26, 2011): 31–33.
The Telegraph, March 18, 2011 (Web).

Cloud of Ink

Author: L. S. Klatt (b. 1963)
Publisher: University of Iowa Press (Iowa
City). 84 pp. $17.00
Type of work: Poetry

*This varied collection of tight, clear, and de-
termined poems generally aims to understand
the world through the examination and presentation of small details, subtle surrealism, and
casual absurdity.*

L. S. Klatt's second collection of poetry, *Cloud
of Ink*, was one of two winners of the 2010 Iowa
Poetry Prize. Upon publication, the collection
received critical praise, earning Klatt comparisons to W. S. Merwin, James Wright, and Richard Hugo, among others. Robert N. Casper, writ-
ing for *Publishers Weekly*, wrote that "L. S. Klatt's new collection creates a taxonomy
of mystery, magic, and surprise. Like a cloud, it floats through the reader's mind with
playful shapelessness—but like ink, it leaves a darker, and lasting, impression."

Klatt's unique blend of the playful and the sinister can be seen in his fondness for
the strange, surreal, and sometimes absurd. In "Momentum," the setting is described
with a synesthesia reminiscent of that which Emily Dickinson employed in her poem
"I heard a Fly buzz – when I died," also about a fly:

> With this thread I tie myself to the fly
> for let us share chromosomes. I also drag
> behind me an iceberg on leash & our fondness
> for consuming. When
>
> I leave the horizon, a pyramid is buried
> upside down between dunes. Big lake, it tastes
> Like a fried egg, a blue one.

Klatt's settings range from the mundane to the classically sublime, from an airplane
cockpit and the open sky to Picasso's mindscape, the deepest ocean, or one's own back-
yard. They shuttle between the opposing poles of the gross or the startling (a cockroach,
a lonely suicide) and the lighthearted or childlike and often substitute the silly for the
somber. *Cloud of Ink* hunts wild pears instead of wild boars and situates the strange
within the everyday, the epiphany within the centerpiece on the kitchen counter.

The spirited surrealism that typifies Klatt's *Cloud of Ink* can produce vivid, surprising moments, as in "Liquefaction": "I found an octopus in the snow / And not knowing

what it was or why it was there, I gutted it / as if a hunter. / To me, up to my elbows in bladder, the ink was a surprise. / I wore it like opera gloves in the moonlight." Reviewers have noted Klatt's sharp vision and the precision and resonance of his images. The collection is aptly prefaced by two lines from Wallace Stevens: "In my room, the world is beyond my understanding; / But when I walk I see that it consists of three or four hills and a cloud." Stevens's epigraph highlights the friction between interiors and exteriors, the metaphysical and the physical, real and surreal, that drives Klatt's poetic project. His poems seem to dramatize the ways that experience distinguishes itself from imagination as well as the ways in which they may predicate one another.

Klatt's playfulness can be seen in his often-youthful wordplay and his examination of the word in the world. He imagines scenarios that align the written world with the actual world or makes language his apparent subject, as seen in "The Calm of a Thoughtful Sentence" or "Reading." The sky becomes a punctuated page, or the sea, like the page, becomes stained with ink. Klatt finds immense possibility in similes and metaphors that compare the textual world to the physical world, rendering them indistinguishable from each other. This merging of the textual and the physical can be found in "Aeronautics": "Whereupon you are alone / in a cockpit, a multitude behind you sealed tight, / & it occurs to you that you are in an updraft / of ampersands & colophons . . ." It also figures in his title, where *Cloud of Ink* could refer to the camouflaging plumes of a cephalopod, to a thunderhead, or to the ink-based flourishes of writers upon the page. The title itself is culled from a line from one of the poems in the collection, "Andrew Wyeth, Painter, Dies at 91," in which "A giant squid rises out of a hayfield, & the barn / is compassed in tentacles / then a cloud of ink."

Klatt's love of such wordplay was inspired in part by the avant-garde Language poets. "They were interested in the texture of language, its sonic qualities, its textual qualities, the way letters can be re-arranged to create all these wonderfully new meanings," he said in a 2010 interview with Calvin College's Myrna Anderson. "*Cloud of Ink* celebrates the versatility of language and, at the same time, explores its limits." Language is versatile, but it is this very versatility that can obscure a word's meaning. In "Liquefaction," for instance, members of the audience "were swimming in a maelstrom of inklings," which could mean meaning drops of ink, intuitive notions, or both. Images of clouds of ink, nebulae, and maelstroms also hint at Klatt's preoccupation with the confusion that is inherent in language.

Another limit of language that Klatt appears to explore is that of length. As poems go, those in *Cloud of Ink* are terse; most are no longer than a page. For those who are familiar with Klatt's first collection, *Interloper* (2009), his conciseness will not come as a surprise, for his poems do not seem to be belabored thoughts or hard-wrought lines, but rather are quick, smart jabs that carefully count the punches they pull. Perhaps fearful that they will say too much, the poems and the lines that constitute them end rather quickly, often concluding just as they seem to be conceptually beginning. Readers may wish Klatt would not limit his presentation to such an extent; often the need for more development is apparent, and his last lines sometimes do not satisfy enough to warrant the brevity. The poems do have a rich lyricism and their images can be stunningly beautiful and strange, but when they are so restrained, these noteworthy

(CG Clarke)

L. S. Klatt's poems have appeared in the Boston Review, Columbia Review, FIELD, Cincinnati Review, jubilat, Colorado Review, The Iowa Review, Eleven Eleven, *and* Verse. *His first book,* Interloper *(2009), won the Juniper Prize for Poetry.*

skills may escape the notice of some readers. In addition to their overall brevity, the poems of *Cloud of Ink* repeatedly entertain immense amounts of white space. Often taking just half a page to do their duty, the poems tend to luxuriously separate themselves into single-line stanzas that remind one of the self-confidence and independence that comes across in the formal choices of W. S. Merwin.

Klatt's surrealism and playfulness are often closely juxtaposed with seemingly mundane images from the Midwest. Poems like "Ohio" and "Semiconductors in the Breadbasket" expand on James Wright's poetic portraits of the region. Like Wright, it appears that Klatt sees great potential in poetic meditations on Ohio and its rivers, towns, and fields as a subject or a setting throughout *Cloud of Ink.* In poems like "The States of the Great Lakes" or "Berryman in Cincinnati," it seems clear than when Klatt's eye is not caught by the catalog and complexities of biology, he places just as much stock in plotting and pondering the rural, fields, livestock, crickets, tractors, and other Midwestern tropes that populate the rolling land of Ohio. His attention bespeaks a fondness for this kind of place and a call to consider its landscape of propane tanks, picket fences, and chickens to be just as surreal as anything his capable imaginative faculties could muster.

Throughout *Cloud of Ink,* Klatt's surrealism blends into more somber contemplations of mortality and one's relationship with the dead. Ghosts as characters and images are repeatedly present in *Cloud of Ink,* but the presence of the dead is particularly interesting as charted in two similarly titled poems, "Andrew Wyeth, Painter, Dies at 91" and "J. D. Salinger, Recluse, Dies at 91." In both, Klatt seems to chronicle the strange relationship that people sometimes hold with an aesthetic celebrity or hero, and what becomes of that relationship when an obituary presents itself in the morning paper. The poems that accompany these titles are hardly obituaries in the traditional sense, and they are not narratives of these figures' respective deaths. In "Salinger," Klatt depicts a snowshoe hare moving casually through the elements, whereas in "Wyeth" it is another typically surreal rural scene that Klatt presents. Both eponymous figures indicated in the titles are linguistically absent in the body of the poem, but because of Klatt's titling, they remain present, forced to hover at the edge of these poems. Life, and the life of the mind, goes on, Klatt seems to say, even when the great creators die. Death is no reason to conclude that they are not present, especially in the minds of those whom they have impressed.

Klatt pays tribute to the writers who have impressed him by listing them in the notes section at the back of the volume, where he has included a short narrative of inspiration and poetic motivation. It seems that Klatt has read widely from the best and the brightest, and this aesthetic star power shines light on his poems. He mentions Herman Melville, Joan Miro, Gertrude Stein, a *New York Times* story about the extended family of John Keats, Charles Darwin, Ralph Waldo Emerson, Flannery O'Connor, and John James Audubon.

However, Klatt also believes that, although such admiration might persist long after the poet has passed away, it is still inevitably fleeting. In his interview with Myrna Anderson, he discusses the comfort that writers might find in religious faith: "Poets especially want to memorialize themselves with words, but none of it is permanent. They may be remembered by their own generation or even subsequent ones, but history is the ultimate eraser. The comfort for the Christian writer is to understand that her words have not been wasted; for a time and for a season, the poems entertain, provoke. Perhaps God himself enjoys them." The poems in *Cloud of Ink*, with their playful surrealism, certainly entertain and provoke; readers can also rest assured that with Klatt's conciseness, no words are wasted.

Grant Klarich Johnson

Review Sources

Boston Review 36, no. 3 (May/June 2011): 75
Full Stop, April 13, 2011 (Web)
Publishers Weekly, March 21, 2011 (Web).

Coda

Author: René Belletto (b. 1945)
First published: 2005, in France
Translated from the French by Alyson Waters
Foreword by Stacey Levine
Publisher: University of Nebraska Press (Lincoln). 69 pp. $13.95
Type of work: Novella
Time: The present
Locale: Paris, France, and the surrounding suburbs; Spain; Cologne

In this French Voices Award winner, a widower father follows a strange sequence of events in the wake of his wife's mysterious murder. Along the way, he encounters old and new friends and has brushes with death and fate itself in an accidental quest for immortality.

Principal characters:
X, the narrator, a widower whose wife was mysteriously murdered
ANNA, his six-year-old daughter
MARIA, his deceased wife
MAURICE AND MAUREEN MICHELANGELI, his in-laws
LORIMA, the in-laws' housekeeper
HERVE MATHEAU, X's doctor
MAURICE DE VIL, the father of X's deceased school friend and his partner in the perpetual motion machine business
MARC KRAM, X's college friend
AGATHE KRAM, Kram's younger sister, a caring but psychologically troubled teacher
MARTHE, a mysterious, beautiful woman who is possibly fate incarnate
AMÉDÉE MARQUIS, an addled nephrologist who escapes from institutionalization

In this strange but straightforward short novel, Belletto's narrator, referred to several times simply as "X," tells the tale of how an unusual sequence of events in his otherwise mundane life gave birth to a world without death. The down-the-rabbit-hole narrative contemplates how chance events can change everything, including love and life after death. It is both a narrative of what happens to a family following the loss of a loved one (X's wife Maria) and the story of how the world arrived at a post-death era. In the end, one wonders how *Coda* reads in its original French, for in English it comes across as a sprightly folly that is a bit too literal. It is at times inventive, certainly, but as a whole possibly just too oddball to take with much gravity. Unselfconscious to a fault, *Coda* is confident about the story it tells, which is a quirky one, to be sure, but it ultimately fails to astound in matters of plot or style.

The story begins with X's dramatic claim that not only does humanity exist in an immortal state but the production of this altered state can be credited completely to him. He is a Parisian widower who lives with his six-year-old daughter, Anna. They survive his wife, Maria, who, while home alone at their former residence in Versailles, was shot by a robber who continues to evade detection and prosecution. They live off the profits X has made from the mildly successful commercial sale of one of his father's eight perpetual-motion machine prototypes, retrofitted to a mechanical illuminated aquarium. The machine stops its movement after twenty-four hours, but was successfully marketed as a toy for young children because of their willingness to set its ball bearings back in motion.

The actual story of the novella begins a year and a half after Maria's death, as X takes Anna to the home of her maternal grandparents. They are doting and supportive caregivers to the girl, and have invited her to stay for a month. The narrator exists in a state of constant antagonism and uneasiness around his in-laws. He is confident that they suspect him of being responsible for his wife's murder and are actively plotting to take Anna away from him permanently. After dropping Anna off and picking up some groceries, he returns home to his empty apartment and opens his supposedly empty freezer to find a package of frozen clams inside. X becomes engrossed in the strange appearance of the clams, both because they are a brand he does not recognize and because he is positive he did not buy them. He also finds a scrap of red fiber. He tracks down the clam supplier, which leads him to a former college acquaintance, Marc Kram. When he contacts Kram, he is invited to a party at his old friend's house, but does not tell Kram why he seeks the reunion. At the party, X meets Marthe, who immediately strikes him as benevolent but intoxicating, as if she has the power to psychically control his every move and emotion. She disappears before too long, and when X attempts to find her, no one at the party seems to have noticed her but him. He begins to question the reality of her presence, whether she represents something supernatural or otherworldly, or if she could possibly be a sorceress.

Searching for leads, X arranges to meet Marc's sister, Agathe, who is too ill to attend the party. They meet, and he is struck by a gesture she shares with Marthe, as well as the small red fiber he finds on Agathe's clothing. He wonders if Marthe holds some power over Agathe, imagining that they might be psychic doppelgangers. He suspects that Agathe broke into his apartment under Marthe's power and placed the startling frozen clams in his freezer, but to what end? He picks up Anna for an evening out and they encounter Marthe. Pressed by X to explain, Marthe claims to have attended Kram's party uninvited out of loneliness and the desire for company. She gets her wish when she and X go to dinner and later become intimate. Eventually, X confesses his elaborate suspicions, and Marthe laughs them off. He meets again with Agathe, who informs him that she is about to go on vacation with Marc in Saint Rometz, which she appears to be dreading. Again, X and Anna meet up with Marthe, who suggests that there is a dark secret society that congregates in Saint Rometz.

The next day, Anna is kidnapped while walking in the park with her grandparents' servant, Lorima. Panicked, X continues to play detective. A flier leads him to an organization called United Family, which he breaks into with Marthe; coincidentally, his key works on the door. There, X finds Marc Kram's name in a database. The next day, he receives a call from Agathe, who informs

The author of more than twenty books and screenplays, René Belletto has won the Prix Jean Ray award for fantasy literature for his first book, Le Temps mort *(1974), the* Grand Prix *for fiction for* Sur le terre comme au ciel *(1982), and the Prix Fémina for his novel* L'Enfer *(1986).*

him that Anna has been taken to a hotel in Saint Rometz. Suspicious, he rushes there with Marthe and arrives to find Anna safe and asleep on a hotel bed. X is overcome by the sense that Marthe orchestrated the entire sequence of events, from the clams to the kidnapping. Soon after they arrive at the hotel, Amédée Marquis, a deranged asylum escapee, barges into the room and fires a gun. Marthe sacrifices herself to shield Anna and is gravely wounded by the bullet. She is hospitalized as X and Anna return to the city. When news comes of Marthe's condition, reality suddenly begins to pivot. At the moment she appears to be on the verge of death, she inexplicably revives. X then attempts to tell Agathe of Marthe's death, but finds that Agathe is unfamiliar with the concept and that, in fact, "death" does not even exist in the dictionary. It seems that by way of Marthe's Christ-like sacrifice and the strange events that precipitated it, humankind has become immortal, freed from the realities of death. As the novel concludes, the perpetual motion machine has changed as well; no longer imperfect and prone to halting, it too has somehow found a way to sustain itself indefinitely.

The narrative within *Coda* is presented as an explanation for, and origin story record of, this revolutionary state of the world. X worries that if he does not document the story, death as a concept will be unknown without him. This is presumably why years appear to be redacted throughout the novel, indicating that an immortal world is also apparently a timeless one.

Coda's prose style is confident in its concision and sparsity. Almost shockingly efficient, the novella speeds along because it is essentially only plot. Sentences simply describe the events that carry X along, occasionally lapsing into a few refrains of internal angst over what is occurring. No word feels luxurious or extraneous. Belletto moves quickly from event to event, avoiding description almost entirely. This is not a book about how something came to pass or all the ways in which something may occur; *Coda* is, explicitly and tersely, just about what happened.

Mortality, immortality, and death are familiar themes. *Coda* reiterates these topics in a way that makes them feel more current, but it is unclear how humans who struggle with these themes outside the new reality presented by the novel should proceed. Clearly, within the world of the novella, as is often the case in this world, death is something to be dreaded and is a prospect that some would be grateful to have wiped from their consciousness. But ultimately, although it trades in generally serious and universal themes, *Coda* remains a light and frothy experience, with little possibility of the reader taking away a lesson for dealing with these momentous issues. Instead, one is free to take in the daydream for a bit and return to the real world generally unaffected. With its weird twists and its plucky yet easily startled protagonist, *Coda* is a bit of escapist melodrama that works effectively and briefly, like a soap opera or a public television miniseries one stumbles upon late at night. Though an interesting and truly engrossing experience, it is ultimately forgettable, revealing itself to be ridiculous when discussed out of context. On its own terms, *Coda* is a fun game, but when forced into the discourse of reality, it starts to sound too absurd.

    Coda is typical of Belletto's other fiction and part of a relatively large body of work. He is known in France for novels that blend elements of noir, science fiction, fantasy, mystery, and philosophy, and the genre-defiant *Coda* is in keeping with the rest of his oeuvre. *Coda*, with its coincidence-centered plotting, recalls the oddball confidence that characterized Thomas Pynchon's *The Crying of Lot 49* (1966), and it has also been described as akin to the works of Paul Auster.

Grant Klarich Johnson

Review Sources

Kirkus Reviews, December 15, 2010 (Web).
Publishers Weekly, January 3, 2011 (Web).

The Cold War

Author: Kathleen Ossip (b. 1959)
Publisher: Sarabande Books (Louisville, KY).
  96 pp. $14.95
Type of work: Poetry
Time: 1950s–2000s
Locale: Suburban United States

Ossip's poetry collection captures the latter half of the twentieth century in the United States: a time of progress and paranoia, change and conformity.

Principal personages:
RICHARD (BUD) and JOY, a suburban, middle-class married couple facing the stresses of upward mobility
WILL AND ARIEL DURANT (1885–1981; 1898–1981), spouses and coauthors of *The Story of Civilization* (1935–1975), an eleven-volume history of Western civilization
WILHELM REICH (1897–1957), a controversial Austrian-born psychiatrist
YVOR WINTERS (1900–1968), a poet and literary critic whose *In Defense of Reason* (1947) criticizes the work of T. S. Eliot and other modernist poets

The Cold War is a visceral, collage-like evocation of life in the United States during the second half of the twentieth century. While the historical Cold War is generally recognized as the period between 1946 and 1991, Kathleen Ossip's poems outline a series of American moments extending from the boom of post–World War II prosperity to the fear and paranoia following the terrorist attacks of September 11, 2001. Seamlessly shifting from free verse to traditional form and from persona poems to confessionals, *The Cold War* reflects facets of American history and myth, from the 1950s explosion of "goods and services—including television, miracle fibers, and vichyssoise" to the "half-mile circle of death and destruction" of a theoretical nuclear attack. Ossip has noted that part of her impetus for writing these poems was her desire to understand the repression of her parents' era, the 1950s, and to understand how that era led to the post–Cold War period. Borrowing freely from the Eisenhower-era bestsellers that lined her parents' bookshelves, Ossip juxtaposes the writers' attempts to order and classify the world through psychology, sociology, and history with the messiness and illogicality of reality. At once nostalgic and unsparing, Ossip's poems evoke the American dream while exposing the nightmares beneath its surface.

    The volume is divided into five sections, each with a thematic focus. The first section, dominated by quotes from psychiatrist Karl Menninger, evokes a witty, knowing nostalgia for a childhood far less innocent and more anxious than its outward signifiers would imply. "Things were different then," Ossip writes in "The Human Mind," a meditation on melancholy that recalls Menninger's influential 1930 work of the same name. Yet Puritan ghosts linger: pleasure is suspect, beauty vaguely subversive. "Art Project" captures the awkward guilt of an adolescent asking for a copy of Michelangelo's *David*: "What's it for?" demands the voice of adult authority. In "Ameri-deer," nature's intrusion into suburbia evokes an uneasy mixture of resentment and yearning, as the poem ends with three rearrangements of the phrase "It was so beautiful she wanted to kill it."

In the second section, Ossip explores the darkness found within the ideal 1950s suburban home. Two poems pay homage to *The Status Seekers*, Vance Packard's 1959 study of class in America. Packard's critique of social stratification became a handbook for social climbers, teaching them how to choose the "right" words, clothes, and countertops. The second and longer of the two poems follows suburban couple Bud and Joy from their hopeful young marriage to their later lives, filled with bitterness and tragedy. Bud is passed up for a promotion at work and is later found hanging in the basement; Joy survives alone, to raise "four girls in their Easter miniskirts."

The book's central section is the long poem "Document:," a fragmented and telegraphic re-creation of the anxious months after the September 11 terrorist attacks, composed in part of e-mails disseminated after the attacks. The poem evokes a feeling of danger as Ossip fuses social anxiety and mortal terror in a paean to paranoia. Closed in, Ossip's narrator seeks protection from a world of airborne particles, splashes of liquid, crops tainted by suspicious dust, and low-grade nuclear devices. Snippets of "expert" advice offer scant comfort: "You just gotta avoid inhaling dust that's contaminated with atoms that are emitting these things." A *New York Times* review identifies the narrative voice in "Document:" as that of a military weapons expert, but woven in with this voice is the nervous whisper of another narrator, an everywoman who still worries about her looks, her weight, and what people think of her, even in the face of chemical, nuclear, and biological warfare. She may escape mass destruction, but can she escape the public gaze, the expectations her culture has imposed?

In section four, Ossip looks inward with the self-questioning "Confession" and plays with traditional metered poetic forms in "Romantic Depot" and "Upon the Porch." The centerpiece of this section, "The Nervousness of Yvor Winters," combines biography, criticism, and ruminations on the nature of art and the mind. This long poem traces the source of literary critic Winters's scorn for modernist poetry to his youthful struggle with tuberculosis; following his stay in the "orderly, white, dry environment" of a sanatorium, he abandons the chaos of free verse for the order he finds in standard poetic forms. Winters is known less for his own poetry than for his vigorous criticism of experimental poets such as Marianne Moore, Ezra Pound, T. S. Eliot, and Wallace Stevens. Their work, he says, is not a new kind of poetry, but "the old kind of poetry with half the meaning removed." He argues that poems should proceed from thought, not emotion. Ossip attributes Winters's antipathy toward poetic ambiguity to fear, but she leaves readers with a significant question: "Do we want to understand poems, or do we want poems that understand us?"

(Jennifer May)

Kathleen Ossip's first book of poetry,
The Search Engine, *was published in*
2002. Her poems have appeared in many
collections and journals, including Best
American Poetry *and* Paris Review. *She*
teaches at the New School in New York
and is a founding editor of LIT *maga-*
zine and poetry editor of Women's Studies Quarterly.

Ossip again plays with literary theory and traditional rhyme in "Poetry is Sardonic. Business is Sincere." With wry humor, she imagines a romance between a poet and a gray-suited businessman and concludes that "what sells cannot be art." The final piece of the section, "The Senator and the Medical Intuitive," is an odd political fable. In a style reminiscent of a prose poem or flash fiction, Ossip describes an encounter between a United States senator and a "medical intuitive" who uses her psychic abilities to diagnose illness. The medical intuitive identifies the senator's malady as tragedy, and Ossip then imagines a series of possible endings to their story, ranging from melodrama to quiet despair.

The collection's fifth and final section begins with another long biographical poem, "American Myth," which connects the seemingly disparate life paths of Wilhelm Reich, a controversial psychoanalyst who touts the healing power of something he calls "orgone energy," and Will and Ariel Durant, self-made scholars who write *The Story of Civilization*. This eleven-volume history of Western civilization becomes a standard reference found in many public libraries, though a few dissenters find the work bland and oversimplified. Reich builds orgone accumulator boxes, which he claims harness a sort of cosmic energy that can cure cancer and improve orgasm. The Durants show society what it wants to see: history on its proud march forward, civilization becoming ever more civilized. Reich's eccentric individuality is viewed as bizarre, his ideas disturbing and easily mocked. For their efforts, the Durants receive prizes and honors; for his, Reich is investigated by the Food and Drug Administration, labeled a pornographer, and imprisoned. Ossip presents this juxtaposition without editorializing, an understatement that would no doubt have annoyed Yvor Winters.

"The Deer Path," a shorter poem that follows, portrays deer behaving badly: "I heard one buck fawn call his friend a FAG, in an unmistakably cruel way." Ossip's anthropomorphized deer, shouting obscenities from truck windows, provide a sly commentary on "civilized" human behavior. The title poem, "The Cold War," ends the volume in a confessional, self-questioning mode with a note of bittersweet nostalgia for the "crisp blue days" of an unexamined childhood and the "blue comfort" of the television. The poem acknowledges the conventionality of the Cold War era, the subtle discouragement of introspection, and the pressure to conform, yet Ossip finds much to miss about a time in which human interactions were real, not virtual. "In those days," she writes, "when you dialed the phone, / someone answered it." Pulled by the lure of the past, Ossip cannot unknow what she has learned. Such knowledge can be painful, but Ossip looks to art, not innocence, for salvation. In a nod to Dante Alighieri's *Inferno*, she ends the poem and the collection on a note of affirmation: "Craft will take us through this wood."

Ossip's work incorporates material from a variety of sources, mining found poetry from best sellers of the 1950s and anonymous messages forwarded through e-mail. A number of the poems are accompanied by epigraphs from texts such as Menninger's *The Human Mind*. In a note on her "borrowings," Ossip carefully documents her eclectic and multifarious sources, from French decadent poet Paul Verlaine to popular self-help books. Such cultural artifacts orient the collection in the era it depicts, enhancing Ossip's exploration of internal and external conflict.

The Cold War has drawn critical praise for Ossip's willingness to play with form and write with energy and wit. As a poet who faces, interprets, and reinterprets classic American myths, Ossip casts a postmodern eye upon the art and history of the modern age, mixing high culture with low and moving with ease from introspection to documentation. Her poetry can be intensely personal, even confessional, while at the same time socially engaged. Ossip's unconventional use of language may make *The Cold War* a difficult read for those unfamiliar with her style of poetry, but the compelling themes and playful stylistic experiments of her work might win some new converts to the poetic form.

Kathryn Kulpa

Review Sources

Huffington Post, July 2, 2011 (Web).
Library Journal 136, no. 10 (June 1, 2011): 104.
The New York Times, August 30, 2011, p. C4.
Publishers Weekly 258, no. 16 (April 18, 2011): 35.

The Color of Night

Author: Madison Smartt Bell (b. 1957)
Publisher: Vintage (New York). 224 pp. $15.00
Type of work: Novel
Time: September 2001; 1964–1969
Locale: Las Vegas, Southern California, and
New York City

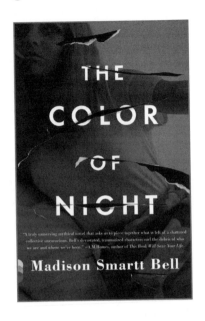

*The novel is a disturbing investigation into the
erotic thrill of violence in American culture
through the story of a fugitive killer who attempts to reunite with a former lover in New
York City following the terrorist attacks of September 11, 2001.*

Madison Smartt Bell

Principal characters:
MAE CHOREA, a blackjack dealer at a casino,
    wanted by the FBI for her participation in
    brutal killings nearly thirty years earlier
LAUREL, Mae's former lover, a New York City
    school administrator dying of ovarian cancer
PAULEY, Mae's acquaintance and occasional lover, an unscrupulous private investigator
TERRELL, Mae's sociopathic older brother who sexually abused her during her teen
    years
D——, a charismatic struggling musician in Los Angeles who leads a sex and drug
    commune in the late 1960s
O——, a successful singer-songwriter in the late 1960s Southern California folk-rock
    movement
EERIE, a bewitchingly beautiful starlet, O——'s love and muse

In the years since September 11, 2001, historians, pop culture commentators, theologians, and psychologists have catalogued the responses Americans have expressed
to the terrorist attacks on the World Trade Center and the Pentagon: outrage, sorrow,
vulnerability, practical concern for homeland security, heartfelt admiration for the
crews of first-responders, and patriotic reinvigoration among them. A reaction seldom
explored or even acknowledged is the voyeuristic hunger to watch the mayhem captured on film by hundreds of eyewitnesses. Catastrophe taps into an element of the
imagination that has featured in American literature across three centuries, from the
unsettling romances of Charles Brockden Brown to the apocalyptic parables of Cor-
mac McCarthy: namely, the erotic power of blackness, humankind's fascination with
the mesmerizing pull of violence and with those who perpetrate such heinous acts. It
is this fascination that supports the dark premise of Madison Smartt Bell's disturbing
novel *The Color of Night*.

Mae is a serial killer who has been on the run for more than thirty years, wanted by the FBI for her part in a home invasion in the canyon suburbs of Los Angeles that resulted in multiple grisly killings. Unaffected by guilt or remorse, Mae spends her nights toiling joylessly in the "fifth-rate hell" of a Nevada casino and her free time trekking through the desert, eying coyotes through the scope of her ever-present rifle. The attack on the World Trade Center disrupts this routine. Mesmerized by the news footage of the destruction, she fashions a crude two-hour VCR tape that allows her to loop the most destructive moments from the attacks and watch them over and over again. She does not feel compassion or outrage—for her, watching anguished New Yorkers staggering about in the smoke and ash is similar to watching the pixelated images in a video game. As she watches, she feels the reanimation of an erotic fascination with violence that dates back to her teen years in rural Appalachia. When she recognizes a lover from years before in the footage, she begins to recall without emotion the violent events of her adolescence.

For five years in the mid-1960s, Mae is physically, emotionally, and sexually abused by her older brother. After running away and working as a prostitute in several cities, she meets D——, a failed songwriter, petty criminal, and charismatic psychopath modeled on Charles Manson who senses in the homeless runaway a troubled spirit. She quickly becomes entangled in his commune, an abandoned desert ranch outside Los Angeles. There, amid its hedonistic environment of free love, Mae first meets intelligent, self-assured, beautiful Laurel, and they explore their attraction, heightening their passionate sexual experiences not only with a near-constant supply of drugs but also with the use of knives and the tasting of blood. On some nights, at the direction of D——, the members of the commune roam the neighborhoods of Los Angeles on what D—— describes as "slithers," choosing random homes to enter and vandalize. Eventually, this practice leads the group to brutally murder the residents of one of the homes.

Watching Laurel on her recorded tape in the narrative present, Mae relishes the memory of their passion. With the events of the 1960s reawakened in her mind, she decides to reconnect with Laurel and asks Pauley, a seedy unlicensed private investigator, to track her down. It turns out that Laurel is working as an administrator in an upscale private school in New York City under an assumed name. When Mae finally gathers the composure sufficient to talk to Laurel, she finds that Laurel wants only to forget their relationship and is dying of ovarian cancer. Several days later, Mae discovers that an FBI agent has come to the casino asking about her. When she returns to her trailer, she spies a man she assumes is the agent and kills him. Certain that law enforcement now knows where she is, she travels to New York to confront Laurel.

Bell explores the transfixing power of violence by connecting two events that tap into the dark heart of the American cultural imagination—the August 1969 Tate-La-Bianca murders by the followers of Charles Manson and the September 11 terrorist attacks. It is, at first glance, an uneasy parallel, equating the random murders of several individuals by drug-crazed cult members with the meticulously planned act of terrorism carried out by trained religious extremists. However, what Bell examines are not so much the acts as the reactions to them. In particular, he examines the fascination

Madison Smartt Bell is a professor of English at Goucher College in Maryland. His novels include Waiting for the End of the World *(1985),* Doctor Sleep *(1991), and* All Soul's Rising *(1996).*

that many have with such heinous acts that disrupt a seemingly complacent society. In doing so, Bell explores the complex conspiracy between the writer and the reader. Bell himself is haunted, as he admits in his acknowledgements, by demons sufficient to conjure and then record with lyric directness such acts of violence. "Surely it is the most vicious and appalling story ever to pass through my hand to the page," he writes. The reader, too, is drawn by violence and the voyeuristic appeal of reading about barbarity, irresistibly engaged by representations of depravity and the primal urge to hurt and kill.

One of the most striking qualities about *The Color of Night* is its unsettling protagonist. As the reader meets Mae through the claustrophobic intimacy of her first-person narration, it quickly becomes apparent that she is a repugnantly antisocial person with no interest in redemption or reclamation. She is coolly vicious, feral, predatory, and beyond the reach of therapy or salvation. Bell provides a reason for Mae's mental state: years of horrific abuse at the hands of a malignant older brother, himself a budding sociopath with a penchant for knives and torturing small animals. Yet, Bell never allows Mae to become a sympathetic victim. She is so casually savage, so erotically charged by acts of mayhem that, like the central characters of Truman Capote's true-crime *In Cold Blood* (1966), Bret Easton Ellis's *American Psycho* (1991), and the carnage epics of director Quentin Tarantino—works to which Bell's novel has been compared—she is ultimately unforgivable. Any sympathy extended to her is at best problematic and at worst a sign of a profound moral lapse. Bell teases the possibility of a redemptive ending for Mae, one in which she forgives her dying lover and leaves her in peace. She visits Ground Zero, slips past the barricade, sifts through the toxic dirt, and pauses momentarily over a locket she finds in the silt along with a burned human bone. It is a promising moment that presents the opportunity for Mae to be touched by the revelation of the humanity of victims. Nevertheless, her heartless depravity prevails, and redemption remains out of reach. Without pretense to offering any therapeutic or theological speculations that might give meaning to Mae's brutality, Bell suggests that in Mae, the reader encounters and confronts the darkest reach of humanity.

In addition to referencing the September 11 attacks and the murders carried out by the Manson "family," Bell incorporates classical allusions, contributing an additional layer of otherworldliness to a narrative already composed significantly of drug-clouded memories. Mae is fond of evoking a range of Greek mythological types to endow her repugnant narrative with classic grandeur. Perhaps most prominent is her evocation of the tragic tale of Orpheus and Eurydice. When the dazzling young nymph Eurydice dies after being bitten by a snake, Orpheus, a gifted musician, sings such beautifully desolate songs that the gods agree to let him descend into the underworld and retrieve his wife. However, his attempt is unsuccessful, and Eurydice is lost to him. The grief-stricken Orpheus is eventually torn to pieces by the female followers of the god Dionysus. One of the stories Mae recounts about her days in the commune centers on a handsome folk singer, whom she calls O——, and his obsession with a beautiful starlet named Eerie, whose violent death in a seedy hotel drives O—— to write some of his most evocative songs. After D—— and other commune members are arrested during a police raid looking for stolen cars that happens to occur the same night as the bloody slither at the canyon ranch, Mae and Laurel make their escape and share a hotel room with O—— for a night. Still grieving his dead lover, he is inconsolable despite Mae and Laurel's best efforts at seduction. High on drugs and frustrated by his persistent gloominess, Laurel and Mae finally attack O—— with knives, ritualistically stabbing the grieving lover to death. In their own way, these followers of D—— dispatch their Orpheus to the underworld. While the tragic story of O—— is similar to that of Orpheus, Bell emphasizes that Mae's own story is not some grand myth; rather, it is marked by shoddy, shabby faux grandeur. Try as she might, Mae cannot aspire to mythological heights. Instead, she represents violence unredeemed by any humanity.

Joseph Dewey

Review Sources

Booklist 107, no. 5 (November 1, 2010): 22.
High Country News 43, no. 15 (September 5, 2011): 22.
Kirkus Reviews 78, no. 22 (November 15, 2010): 18.
The New Yorker 87, no. 15 (April 12, 2011): 83.
Seattle Times, April 9, 2011 (Web).
The Washington Post, May 18, 2011 (Web).

Come and See

Author: Fanny Howe (b. 1940)
Publisher: Graywolf (Minneapolis). 80 pp.
$15.00
Type of work: Poetry
Time: The late twentieth and early twenty-first
centuries
Locale: Eastern Europe and the United States

*Showcasing her meditative and lyrical
strengths, Howe's collection of poems explores
perception, misperception, and social justice in
the rapidly changing world of the twenty-first
century.*

Having received extensive acclaim and significant awards for her many previous volumes
of poetry and prose, Fanny Howe was able to
spend some time traveling throughout Italy, Ireland, and particularly Russia while composing
her new collection, *Come and See*. In the acknowledgments, she describes this period
of her life as one in which she found herself becoming "a relic of the twentieth century
and its ceaseless wars, failures and technological advances." Howe's work has always
been focused on the tragedies of modern life, but her travels had an obvious impact
on this collection, as evidenced by its many references to the horrors of World War II,
the politics of both the Soviet Union and the Middle East, and Russian cinema. Just as
important is the landscape, so often covered in a silencing snow, which provides *Come
and See* with many of its central images.

Regarded as one of the more experimental writers of her generation, Fanny Howe
also has the unique distinction of being a widely read and respected poet; the Ruth
Lilly Poetry Prize, which she received in 2009 and whose previous recipients include
W. S. Merwin, John Ashbery, and Kay Ryan, awards poets for outstanding lifetime
achievement. The term "experimental," while regularly used to describe her work,
is itself rather vague, broadly signaling a tendency to use structures, forms, and languages that might seem unfamiliar to many readers. In Howe's case, this experimental
tendency takes the form of associative logic, shifts from one idea to another, and an
intentional lack of clear narrative connection. This style is often apparent in *Come
and See*, with certain lines reading like film criticism, while others are more akin to
personal recollection, spiritual revelation, or simply description of the natural world.
Howe does not favor one particular form throughout but instead adapts each poem's
form to the demands of its content, writing in prose poems, scattered stanzas, and
strings of sentences. The collection's tight thematic focus and immediate moral and
ethical center help it remain unified in spite of its dynamic formal variety. Though

challenging, this style allows Howe to surprise readers again and again with sudden insight and revelation.

Issues of social justice have appeared throughout Howe's poetry, from *The Wedding Dress: Meditations on Word and Life* to *The Winter Sun: Notes on a Vocation.* As a gesture toward those core concerns, Howe positions herself between the tragedies of the recent past and the uncertainties of the future, often bridging the two by way of the family unit, young children, grandparents, and other intergenerational links. The first poem of the collection, "This Eye," establishes the meditations and paradoxes that preoccupy the collection:

> Like the boy in a story
> he sees fire in wood and words
> in smoke and he is good, too good
> to be far from anyone old.

The boy and the poem's speaker face the same task: to make sense of disaster, to find "words / in smoke." Though he stands near the older generation ("too good / to be far from anyone old") and lives in the fractured world they have passed on, the boy must decide for himself what to do and what to believe. With each poem, Howe's speaker guides the reader through the same decision-making process and the many ethical complexities therein.

Throughout the collection, truth is evasive and untrustworthy, and rather than providing false truths or lies in response to history, Howe offers questions, meditations, and images. In "Passages," she addresses the security that people find in lies and "ruthless power": "People prefer the liar. // Honestly, with full knowledge." The poem finds its closing "by the nuclear power plant," the location announced in a stark, one-line stanza. The relationship between the liar and the power plant remains unspecified, except, of course, for the most unsettling of associations. Despite this, Howe ends on a hopeful note, with the speaker "Sitting on a wall / outside a bank, waiting for a child."

Unlike many postmodern poets, Howe does not respond with anger or outrage to the traumas and dilemmas of history. Rather, her sparse, measured lyricism goes hand-in-hand with her political and religious concerns, speaking to history rather than against it. "Correspondence," for instance, begins with a description of falling snow. In brief, beautiful language, Howe states that "In a land of troubles / every snowfall is the same." While the poem introduces an element of unease early on, the majority of the poem is purely lyrical, as the speaker imagines the pollen of summer as a kind of snow. Only in the last line does Howe reveal that the snow-like pollen is falling outside Chernobyl, Ukraine, the site of a major nuclear disaster in the 1980s. With this revelation, the beautiful landscape adopts unexpected associations of trauma and death. Howe avoids direct comment on the incident, instead offering this curious and disarming observation of the pollen: "Some say they're bad. / Some say they're pretty."

As the title, *Come and See*, suggests, these poems often operate in terms of sight and perception, such as in "Correspondence," where vision unfolds into memory and memory into trauma. In "This Eye," the title phrase is a pun that conflates the subject "I" with the

(Ben E. Watkins)

Fanny Howe is one of the most popular contemporary poets in the United States. Her writing spans a wide range of genres, from experimental poetry to narrative prose, but consistently explores matters of faith, morality, and social justice. She has won many major awards, among them the Lenore Marshall Poetry Prize and the Griffin Poetry Prize,

seeing "eye," thereby defining the speaker by what she observes. Sight is important to Howe as it relates to acquiring information and coming to a deeper understanding. She is especially interested in misperception, as in instances when the material world seems discordant with spiritual experience. In such cases, Howe suggests, seeing can be dangerous. "Written on Steps in Winter" begins with a young boy who "spent his childhood on his mother's bed watching pornography and murder." While the boy does not personally experience actual violence, Howe posits that in observing great violence, he has still experienced it in a significant sense. The speaker does not "blame the children for anything," as the horrors of their futures have been prescribed by what they have seen of the past. While this instance of sight seems to have damaged the boy, however, the act of seeing is not in itself culpable, and indeed, sight remains an important tool for dealing with tragedy. Later, and in the same poem, the speaker describes herself as

> one of the lucky ones,
> privileged to live a few decades in peace,
> if without stature or particular beauty or grace or fame, just watching
> and taking notes

She calls herself "lucky" not to have directly experienced the violence that many others—the personages of her poems, for example—experience as part of their daily lives. While the poem suggests that her luck is circumstantial and relative, it still assists her in "watching" and, ultimately, in making sense of what she has observed. Watching is not simply a passive activity but rather an urgent task, allowing Howe to discern history, meditate upon its images, and try to make sense of them in poetry. The poems themselves become a second glance, a recollection or a review. While Howe's stance is that of the observer, her act of observation fosters, within her speaker and within the reader, empathy and knowledge that did not exist before. Observation, then, transmits histories lived and not lived, as well as beginning the process of making sense of the past.

The link between perception and poetry becomes particularly evident in the several poems that focus on works of art. Throughout *Come and See*, Howe turns many times to paintings and films for her subject matter, selecting works that, as she explains in the acknowledgments, "gave me a meditative and focal point for my sense of things." These works echo some of the most important themes in the collection, such as the suffering and martyrdom represented in Larisa Shepitko's films about Nazi Germany. Howe joins these artists in the process of taking the tragedies of modern history and rendering them as art, hoping to make sense of the human spirit and gain some perspective as they do so. This process is perhaps most clear in the poem "What Did You See?," in which Howe describes the experience of viewing new paintings by Peter Sacks, a popular visual artist and poet. Sacks's paintings are abstract, often composed in gray and white color schemes, and are themselves known to depict the confluence of poetry and painting. Amongst their blotches of color, bits of fabric, and historical text, Howe sees "shrouds of prisoners," a recognition of the misery in human history and the chance for spiritual redemption, the shroud being a symbol of sainthood or martyrdom. Although Sacks, a native of South Africa, uses historical texts to reference specific events, the majority of his work is imagistic and abstract, allowing Howe to see the whole span of modern history in its muted colors. The poem moves quickly, observing the paintings' religious imagery, suggestions of historical tragedy, and bodily detail. In the end, it is via perception that Howe manages to bring together the material death and spiritual crisis of the history at hand. She wonders,

> Angels die?
> It's a frightening-miracle
> because here they are.
> The Upper God
>
> has let them drop
> like centuries into space.
>
> And I recognize them!

    This final realization, the shock of "I recognize them," signals a kind of empathic perception—a moment where the speaker is perhaps closer to the subjects than the old men of previous generations. This moment is one of the most lasting impressions of the collection. *Come and See* is a far-reaching book, one that contemplates some of the weightiest questions and most traumatic issues of recent history. It demands the reader's involvement in the examination of history's failings and cruelties. Yet Howe's lyrical language also inspires awareness of beauty. She invites the reader to bear witness to the complicated and often paradoxical realities of human life, a meditative process that rarely offers answers. Even as the act of sight leads to an image that may seem incomprehensible, what Howe calls a "frightening-miracle," the reader is encouraged to consider the image as truth. The challenge of *Come and See* is this: to see the world in all its suffering, then to feel it.

T. Fleischmann

Review Sources

Booklist 107, no. 18 (May 15, 2011): 11.
Library Journal 136, no. 10 (June 1, 2011): 104.

Confessions of a Young Novelist

Author: Umberto Eco (b. 1932)
Publisher: Harvard University Press (Cambridge, MA). 240 pp. $18.95
Type of work: Literary criticism, essays

This collection of lectures can be read as a memoir, a guide to novel writing, and a treatise on literary theory that provides insight into Eco's mind and career as well as the art of writing.

Confessions of a Young Novelist collects four essays based on lectures that Umberto Eco presented as the Richard Ellmann Lecturer at Emory University in Atlanta, Georgia. Established in 1988, the Richard Ellmann Lectures in Modern Literature have featured appearances by such well-known authors as Seamus Heaney and Salman Rushdie. In 2008, Eco presented the lectures "How I Write," "Author, Text, and Interpreters," and "On the Advantages of Fiction for Life and Death" as a lecture series titled "Confessions of a Young Novelist." In choosing this title for the series of lectures and the collected volume based on them, Eco has adeptly linked the work to a vast body of texts ranging from religious works such as the fourth-century *Confessions of St. Augustine* to personal memoirs such as Jean-Jacques Rousseau's *Confessions* (1782, 1789) to twenty-first-century texts recounting the confessions of shopaholics, escorts, and public speakers. With his title, Eco subtly emphasizes the diversity and complexity of his text, which combines autobiographical details, an account of his writing process, and concepts drawn from literary theory. Although his work is complex and erudite, he imbues his essays with an approachable, often whimsical tone.

The title of the first essay, "Writing from Left to Right," immediately sets the tone of the piece, indicating that Eco is gently teasing or playing with the reader. He later notes that "from left to right" is his typical answer when he is asked how he writes his novels, thus lending the title additional significance; it emphasizes the power of the writer, who can choose what to reveal about his methods and what to keep secret. Eco begins by addressing the complexity of the meanings of words. Meaning varies in different contexts; what is stated may not be totally true, and words are always open to interpretation. For a man of Eco's age to refer to himself as a young novelist, as in the title of the collection, seems highly contradictory. However, Eco explains that while he is no longer in his youth, he has been a novelist for a relatively short time, only since the publication of *Il nome della rosa* (*The Name of the Rose*) in 1980. "I consider myself a very young and certainly promising novelist," Eco writes, and while he has published few novels throughout the subsequent decades, he asserts that he "will publish many more in the next fifty years." This humorous explanation establishes two important notions that play an important role in Eco's fiction: Narrators are not always reliable, and what is written is not necessarily governed by the truths of the real world.

Eco proceeds to discuss the nature of creative writing and the process of writing a novel, drawing examples from his own personal experiences as a novelist and from his own work. He rejects the idea that writing emerges from a mysterious artistic inspiration that suddenly fills the writer's mind with the entire text. In contrast, he emphasizes the importance of researching all aspects of the novel and of constructing the fictional world in which the novel's plot unfolds. He clarifies that *The Name of the Rose*, a mystery novel set in a fourteenth-century monastery, was written neither from pure inspiration nor with a computer program, as was attested by various critics, much to his annoyance. Rather, the novel was the product of two years of work on a topic that took minimal research, given his extensive knowledge of the Middle Ages. For Eco, the writing of a novel is a long process that begins with a seminal idea or image around which the writer constructs a detailed, precise fictional world.

"Author, Text, and Interpreters" discusses the roles of and relationships between authors and their readers, the limits of textual interpretation, and the rights of the text versus those of the reader. This essay differs considerably in tone and style from the first. It is far less personal and lacks the first's light, teasing tone; however, it remains accessible for the reader, as Eco provides thorough and clear explanations of the literary terms used. While Eco continues to draw many examples from his own texts and incidents of interaction with his readers, he also includes numerous examples from works by other authors. Eco builds upon a concept mentioned in his discussion of creative writing: the distinguishing factor separating creative writing from other writing is the response to interpretation available to the author. Drawing upon his own work in semiotics and literary theory, he further supports his argument through references to the works of thinkers such as philosopher Jacques Derrida. Eco presents a text as an entity in its own right, and while he views a text as open to interpretation, he does impose limits upon such analysis. For him, an interpretation of any portion of a text must be supported by all parts of the text and by the text as a whole for it to be accepted as valid.

The third essay, "Some Remarks on Fictional Characters," addresses the strange way in which fictional characters seem to move outside of their fictional worlds and become part of the real world, often garnering more attention than real historical figures. In order to solve this curious puzzle, Eco minutely investigates the characteristics and properties of fictional characters, whom he defines as mind-dependent objects in contrast to physically existing objects. There is no object in the real world that can be identified as a particular fictional character; no one is going to encounter a living Anna Karenina, Madame Bovary, Sherlock Holmes, or Superman, nor are there facts to be discovered that will disprove or change what is known about such fictional characters. Such characters live in a fictional world that the reader and writer pretend is an existing or real world, having entered into an implicit agreement to do so. What is true or untrue, relevant or irrelevant in this world is determined by the text itself. Within this world, fictional characters are given certain essential distinguishing features that Eco terms diagnostic properties. The characters' actions and fates are governed by the narrative, regardless of the reader's desired outcome. Eco suggests that it is this aspect of fictional characters that permits certain of them to become part of the real world and elicit emotional reactions. He proposes that

Umberto Eco, professor emeritus at the University of Bologna, is a semiotician, philosopher, medievalist, literary theorist, and novelist. He has written such novels as The Name of the Rose *(1983;* Il nome della rosa, *1980) and numerous books on semiology and literature.*

readers see in these characters and their limited worlds a reflection of themselves, their world, and their attitude toward their world. Consequently, fictional characters become part of the real world as significant examples of the human condition.

The final and longest of the essays is "My Lists," in which Eco returns to the very personal, autobiographical tone of "Writing from Left to Right." He explains that, growing up as a Roman Catholic, he was from childhood exposed to lists in the form of litanies. He has realized the importance of lists to him after writing several novels—an importance he further explores in his book *The Infinity of Lists* (2009; *Vertigine della lista*). Once again joking with the reader, he states that to prove how humble he is, he is going to compare his lists with some of the greatest lists to appear in the literature of the world. Indulging his fascination with the form, Eco introduces the reader to the wonders and usefulness of lists and distinguishes between practical lists that serve definite purposes, and poetic lists that have myriad functions, properties, and uses. Eco examines the use of lists in literature and includes sections on the rhetoric of enumeration, the forms that lists may take, and the way in which lists may represent the ineffable or the infinite through their incompleteness. The final lists included in the essay are catalogs of books, and Eco follows the final list with a simple "Amen." While he has moved beyond the litanies of his childhood, Eco continues to acknowledge the almost spiritual power of the list.

As a volume in the Richard Ellmann Lectures in Modern Literature series, which also includes such works as Mario Vargas Llosa's *Wellsprings* (2008), David Lodge's *Consciousness and the Novel* (2004), and A. S. Byatt's *On Histories and Stories* (2002), *Confessions of a Young Novelist* is significantly based on the original lectures. While the essays do not differ greatly in form or style from works that were not originally intended for oral presentation, they are largely rooted in 2008 despite the book's publication in 2011. Thus, the later, related work *The Infinity of Lists* is mentioned only in the notes despite the presence of "My Lists," and Eco's references to his age and number of published novels have since become out-of-date. Nevertheless, the extensive endnotes serve to expand the work's scope somewhat, referencing several works by Eco and others published after his lectures at Emory.

Confessions of a Young Novelist has been well received by critics and praised for its vivacity, wit, and charm. While some critics have noted that it seems to repeat topics discussed in Eco's previous books, the work's origin as a series of lectures and status as a sort of memoir, a summary of a novelist's experiences and discoveries in a world of words, lend it additional significance. Eco's text is complex and includes discussions of literary concepts familiar to a limited audience of scholars, literary theorists, and writers; likewise, his references to his own novels may be best understood by regular readers of his work. Yet, his personal, humorous tone is welcoming, and his literary and semiotic terms are always accompanied by examples from a range of works. Just as his Richard Ellmann Lectures were open to the general public, *Confessions of a Young Novelist* is accessible to general readers unfamiliar with Eco's work.

Shawncey J. Webb

Review Sources

Booklist 107, no. 14 (March 15, 2011): 14.
Library Journal 136, no. 2 (February 1, 2011): 60.
Publisher's Weekly 258, no. 2 (January 10, 2011): 39.
Times Literary Supplement, no. 5642 (May 20, 2011): 10–11.

Conversations with Scorsese

Author: Richard Schickel (b. 1933)
Publisher: Alfred A. Knopf (New York). Illustrated. 448 pp. $30.00
Type of work: Autobiography, biography, film, media
Time: 1942–2010
Locale: The United States

Schickel interviews noted filmmaker Martin Scorsese, eliciting detailed comments about his early life and film career and his thoughts on art, morality, religion, and life.

Principal personages:
MARTIN SCORSESE (b. 1942), an award-winning film director and screenwriter
ROBERT DE NIRO (b. 1943), an actor who has starred in many of Scorsese's films, including *Raging Bull* (1980) and *Goodfellas* (1990)
LEONARDO DICAPRIO (b. 1974), an actor who has starred in several of Scorsese's films, including *Gangs of New York* (2002) and *The Aviator* (2004)
JOHN FORD (1894–1973), a director much admired by Scorsese
HARVEY KEITEL (b. 1939), an actor who has appeared in several of Scorsese's films, including *Mean Streets* (1973) and *Taxi Driver* (1976)
JACK NICHOLSON (b. 1937), an actor who starred in Scorsese's film *The Departed* (2006)
JOE PESCI (b. 1943), an actor who has appeared in many of Scorsese's films, including *Casino* (1995)

Conversations with Scorsese, Richard Schickel's lengthy, handsomely produced collection of interviews with the accomplished director and screenwriter Martin Scorsese, is at once the chronicle of one man's life and career and an examination of the development of film in the United States. The book explores Scorsese's creative process, from the development of his vision for a film through the process of filming and editing, and provides a great deal of insight into his aesthetic and thematic concerns. A noted film critic and a knowledgeable film historian who has known Scorsese since 1973, Schickel approaches the films and other subjects discussed within the book not as a starstruck fan or a detached biographer but as Scorsese's friend and equal, creating a compelling portrait of one of the great figures of American film.

This engaging book begins with Schickel's introduction, in which he recounts his early meetings with Scorsese and comments on the director's personal history and character. The introduction is one of only two sections of the book to be written in a style reminiscent of a standard biography. As suggested by the title, the rest of the book consists of written transcripts of conversations between Schickel and Scorsese, informal interviews that begin with questions about Scorsese's childhood and move steadily forward through his subsequent life and career. Later chapters deal with such broader topics as the use of drawings, color, and music in filmmaking, methods of filming and editing, and ways of working with actors.

Schickel devotes more than thirty pages to discussion of Scorsese's early life in the chapter "Little Italy," the longest single section in the book. As with the rest of the volume, this chapter is illustrated with numerous photographs, making it possible to see as well as read about the evolution of Scorsese's life. *Conversations with Scorsese* continually emphasizes the enormous impact that Scorsese's childhood had on his life and on the subjects and methods of his films. Raised in a working-class Italian American neighborhood in New York, Scorsese encountered the pervasive and threatening presence of the Mafia early in life. He notes repeatedly that people in his neighborhood never knew when deadly violence might suddenly occur, often for no apparent reason. "On a certain level you grow up full of mistrust," Scorsese tells Schickel. These circumstances, possibly the source of the sense of paranoia that the two men later discuss, had a clear influence on Scorsese's later work on Mafia films such as *Goodfellas* and *Casino*, as well as the nineteenth-century gang epic *Gangs of New York*.

An asthmatic child, Scorsese was unable to play sports like the other boys in his neighborhood. Instead, he was drawn to film from a very early age, finding in films a refuge from his surroundings. By the time he was ten years old, he had already begun imagining films of his own and making elaborate drawings of them. Some drawings are reprinted in the book, including a storyboard from an imagined epic about ancient Rome titled *The Eternal City* that displays the credit "Directed and Produced by Martin Scorsese."

The next chapters explore Scorsese's admiration for directors such as John Ford, his time in film school and the influence of some of his teachers there, and his eventual move to California. The conversation then shifts to chapter-by-chapter discussions about each of Scorsese's films. Schickel asks probing questions, prompting Scorsese to reveal each film's origins, strengths and weaknesses, and themes. Betrayal is a theme strongly emphasized in a number of different works, another thematic concern that Scorsese links to his childhood experiences. Having worked with some of the most notable actors in the United States film industry, Scorsese provides memorable anecdotes about such actors as Robert De Niro, Harvey Keitel, Jack Nicholson, and Leonardo DiCaprio.

Of particular interest is the chapter on the 1980 film *Raging Bull*, which stars De Niro as boxer Jake LaMotta. Considered by many critics to be one of the most important films of all time, *Raging Bull* won two Academy Awards and contributed to Scorsese's reputation as a talented filmmaker. The director reveals to Schickel that De Niro was the original force behind the project, as Scorsese himself was initially unsure whether he wanted to be involved. A difficult period in his life eventually led to him to identify with the struggles of the film's protagonist. He comments, "I couldn't understand Bob's obsession with [the film] until I went through that rough period of my own. Ever since then—like they always say, but it's true—every day is special. You always have to remember that every day is kind of a gift." The book mentions but

Richard Schickel, noted critic and author of more than thirty books, is a filmmaker and film historian. He is the winner of various awards, including a Guggenheim Fellowship.

does not discuss in any real depth Scorsese's struggles with illness and drug use prior to the making of *Raging Bull*; nevertheless, even the brief references to such human experiences provide additional insight into the filmmaker's psyche.

Another notable topic of discussion is Scorsese's financial situation. Not an enormously wealthy man, he often uses the profits from one film to support his next project or to fund his film preservation efforts, and as Schickel notes in the epilogue, Scorsese is concerned about providing his children with a secure financial future. This concern, typical of many parents, further illuminates Scorsese as a person. The book emphasizes the fact that making a film is often a huge financial gamble as well as an extremely complicated collaborative process involving diverse and often conflicting personalities. However, Scorsese's talent and training as a director and screenwriter have helped him to succeed in creating critically acclaimed and financially successful films, as has the continuing loyalty he has inspired in the actors who have appeared in many of his films, notably De Niro, Keitel, DiCaprio, and Joe Pesci.

The book concludes with an epilogue in which Schickel discusses several of Scorsese's later projects, most of which were, at the time of writing, yet to be filmed, completed, or released. These include the documentaries *Public Speaking* (2010) and *George Harrison: Living in the Material World* (2011), the 3-D fantasy film *Hugo* (2011), and two proposed future projects, one about missionaries in seventeenth-century Japan and one about Frank Sinatra. In addition to providing an expanded view of Scorsese's filmography, this epilogue emphasizes the ongoing nature of his career. He is not a former director interviewed long after retirement; rather, he is a working filmmaker whose career is continuing to develop, shaped by his early experiences, his many films, and the possibilities presented by new film technology.

A highly reflective book, *Conversations with Scorsese* provides Scorsese with the opportunity not only to recall his past but also to meditate on the ways in which his past experiences have influenced his life and films. As the book explores his life from childhood to late middle age, it serves, in a way, as an overview of human life itself, emphasizing common human experiences, concerns, and feelings. Scorsese is focused as much on the meanings of life as on the technical details of filmmaking. He cares deeply about such details, a fact that becomes evident throughout the interviews as he speaks with great enthusiasm about how to position actors within frames, how actors should move, how transitions should be made from one scene to the next, and how a film should be edited. He is also focused on and highly knowledgeable about the use of color, an important factor in many of his films. Yet for Scorsese, filmmaking does not seem to be an end in itself. Instead, he uses films to explore social, moral, and spiritual issues he considers important.

Throughout these question–and–answer sessions, which resemble one long conversation, Scorsese is presented as a thoughtful, articulate, and unpretentious man whose love of films and filmmaking is apparent above all else. Readers interested in exploring the dark side of Scorsese or examining his less successful films will likely go unsatisfied, as the nature of the book allows Scorsese to avoid any topic he prefers not to discuss; "I don't even want to talk about it because it's like I can't handle any more criticism of it," he says of the somewhat unsuccessful *Shutter Island* (2010). Nevertheless, Schickel is an effective interviewer. He is thoroughly familiar with Scorsese's work and asks relevant questions, and although he has his own theories about Scorsese, for the most part he simply encourages Scorsese to talk, something the director does very well. One of the most enjoyable aspects of the book is the enthusiastic way in which Scorsese and Schickel discuss films, exclaiming that one film after another is "wonderful" or "beautiful." The breadth of knowledge each displays is impressive, and they seem to possess detailed recollections of individual scenes, editing techniques, and performances. Readers of this book will likely come away with a long list of old and sometimes obscure films that they will want to watch for themselves, especially after reading Scorsese's and Schickel's complimentary comments. In some ways, *Conversations with Scorsese* is a history not only of Scorsese and his films but also of the film industry itself.

Robert C. Evans

Review Sources

Booklist 107, no. 12 (February 15, 2011): 38.
Kirkus Reviews 79, no. 1 (January 1, 2011): 45–46.
Library Journal 136, no. 2 (February 1, 2011): 63.
Publishers Weekly 258, no. 2 (January 10, 2011): 41–42.
Toledo Blade, April 3, 2011 (Web).

The Convert
A Tale of Exile and Extremism

Author: Deborah Baker (b. 1959)
Publisher: Graywolf (Minneapolis). 256 pp.
$23.00
Type of work: Biography, religion, history, psychology
Time: 1934–2009
Locale: New York and Pakistan

Baker narrates a primarily factual story about an ethnically Jewish woman from suburban New York City who converted to Islam, moved to Pakistan, and wrote in support of her new religion in its struggle against the West. Her unusual life story raises numerous questions about the relations between East and West and about the nature of truth.

Principal personages:

MARGARET "PEGGY" MARCUS / MARYAM JAMEELAH (b. 1934), a socially awkward, emotionally troubled Jew who became a Muslim, changed her name, and immigrated to an Islamic country

ABUL ALA MAWDUDI (1903–1979), the *mawlana* (Islamic scholar) in whose home Jameelah lived briefly after her arrival in Pakistan

HERBERT MARCUS, Margaret's father, a resident of Mamaroneck, New York

MYRA MARCUS, Herbert's wife and Margaret's mother

MOHAMMAD YUSUF KHAN, Jameelah's husband and publisher

DEBORAH BAKER, the author who tries to understand Peggy Marcus / Maryam Jameelah

Like most other persons outside Islam, Deborah Baker had never heard of Maryam Jameelah when she found Jameelah's name standing out among others in a list of papers deposited in the New York Public Library. In *The Convert: A Tale of Exile and Extremism*, Baker details how Margaret Marcus, born in 1934 in Westchester County, New York, to a secular Jewish family, converted to what she considers the true religion, became a secluded wife of a Pakistani Muslim, and gained a reputation as a strident voice of anti-Western Islam. In many respects, the book represents more strongly Baker's attempt to understand a woman who tried to start a new life for herself in exile from the homeland in which she felt foreign.

Margaret Marcus's parents, Herbert and Myra, wished to assimilate. Peggy, as they called their daughter, grew up celebrating Christmas and Easter, believing that Santa Claus visited her home and the Easter Bunny brought chocolate eggs. She was unaware of a religious difference between herself and other children until the 1939–40 school year; it was during the spring of 1940, she claimed, that Catholic fourth graders threw stones at her, calling her "Christ killer." In October 1943, Peggy's parents enrolled her in Sunday school classes at a liberal synagogue, but other children's misbehavior upset her. Ultimately, neither she nor her family would return to their ancestral religion, although shortly after World War II, she became fascinated by photographs of Jews in Nazi concentration camps.

Arabs fascinated her as well, and as an imaginative child, Peggy pretended to be an Arabian hero. As a questioning and fearful child, she wanted assurance from her parents that she would not die, but all they could tell her truthfully, from their viewpoint, was that medicine was progressing so fast that she might live more than a century. That response was unsatisfactory, as was the perceived nationalism of the Jewish faith, because she had come to believe that God, if real, must be universal. As for the newly reestablished state of Israel, she came to oppose it, to her parents' dismay, because she believed that Jews were stealing the land from Palestinians. Islam was becoming attractive to her, but in her loneliness, the socially maladroit teenager found solace in painting pictures of people—a practice forbidden in strict interpretations of the Qur'an.

After high school, Peggy Marcus tried college unsuccessfully. Apparently stricken with mental illness and given to fits of rage, she remained single, lived in near isolation with her parents, and did not work for a living. Eventually diagnosed with schizophrenia, Marcus says that she considered suicide but the fear of hell kept her alive and inspired her to begin praying to Allah. Her troubles continued, however. Beginning in 1957, she spent fifteen months at a private psychiatric hospital and then, with hardly a break, entered a state-run institution. In her account of Marcus's ordeal, Baker expresses her own low opinion of American psychiatry in particular and America in general during the 1950s and suggests that Marcus's crisis may have been spiritual rather than psychiatric. According to Baker, Marcus knew that she had a bad temper and strong desires and tried to stay on the right path by committing herself to all-encompassing, uncompromising Islam.

As restricted as her life was, one thing that Marcus could do, besides draw and paint, was write, and she became a prolific letter writer. December 1960 marked the beginning of her correspondence with Abul Ala Mawdudi, a native of Aurangabad, India, and an eminent Islamic scholar living in Lahore, Pakistan. Mawdudi had gained the title of *mawlana* through his followers' respect for his Islamic learning. Opposed to the partition of British India and to secularism and nationalism, he advocated Islamic rule over all India. Moving in 1947 to Pakistan when the subcontinent was divided despite his wish, he became the leader of Jamaat-e-Islami, a religious and political party, and longed for the establishment of Islamic law in the newly established, overwhelmingly Islamic nation. At the end of Ramadan in 1961, a few months after their correspondence had begun and one day after her twenty-seventh birthday, Marcus formally converted to Islam at the Islamic Mission of America in Brooklyn, New York. Then, in light of her parents' plan to relinquish the lease on their apartment, tour the world, and stop supporting her financially, Peggy Marcus boarded a freighter in 1962 that would take her to Pakistan. There, accepting the *mawlana*'s invitation, she intended to make

(Julienne Schaer)

Deborah Baker is a biographer who divides her time between Brooklyn and India. She has also written the Pulitzer Prize–winning In Extremis: The Life of Laura Riding *(1993) and* A Blue Hand: The Beats in India *(2008).*

her home with his family and, as Maryam Jameelah, live a thoroughly Islamic life away from American decadence.

Leaving the West behind, however, did not mean that Jameelah left her behavioral quirks behind, as Baker clearly shows. Despite her cheery letters to her parents, she wore out whatever welcome she had in Mawdudi's crowded house. As close as her ideas were to the *mawlana*'s and as famous as she became in Pakistan as an American Jew who had accepted Islamic truth and wrote for Allah's sake, she appeared ignorant and crazy to Mawdudi and his family. After a month, Mawdudi, her disappointed guardian, sent her to live with a childless couple in the town of Pattoki. When, after about eight months, Jameelah hit the woman of the house with a skillet, Mawdudi had her brought back to Lahore to a psychiatric hospital.

Not until August 2, 1963, did Jameelah leave the hospital. Within the month, she married Mohammad Yusuf Khan, a member of Jamaat-e-Islami who already had a wife and children. Whether she asked her guardian's permission to marry is uncertain: in a 1963 letter, Jameelah says she did; however, in 2007, Baker heard one of the *mawlana*'s sons say that his father gave no such permission and was outraged by the news, as was Mohammad Yusuf Khan's first wife. Whatever the truth behind it, the deed was done, and the American-born woman of Jewish descent began living in traditional Islamic seclusion at 15/49 Sant Nagar in Lahore.

Jameelah continued to write for Islam and against the West. Among her books were *Islam versus the West* (1962), published before her marriage, and numerous books published by her husband, including *Islam in Theory and Practice* (1967), *Islam and Orientalism* (1971), *Islam and the Muslim Woman Today* (1976), and *The Resurgence of Islam and Our Liberation from the Colonial Yoke* (1980). In addition, prompted by the Soviet invasion of Afghanistan in 1979, she wrote pamphlets praising jihadis of ages past.

Besides writing, she bore five children, three daughters and two sons. While Jameelah lay psychosomatically ill, her oldest child died from malnutrition four months after her birth. Jameelah's co-wife was essential in raising the other four, because, as Jameelah acknowledges, she was unhappy and incompetent at motherhood. She had wanted an intrauterine device, but her husband was too strict a Muslim to agree. He was also too opposed to Western science and industry to comply with Jameelah's ideologically inconsistent wish that her children receive vaccinations. By the time Baker interviewed Jameelah in Lahore late in 2007, her sons had served the Islamic cause against the Soviets in Afghanistan and had moved to the United States. Her surviving daughters were living some distance from her, and she spent most of her time in her upstairs bedroom, where she hid photographs of her children and grandchildren out of the belief that for devout Muslims, photography was sinful. She also used an air conditioner and had resumed drawing without her husband's knowledge or consent, but otherwise she remained as strongly pro-Islamic and anti-Western as before.

Such, then, is Maryam Jameelah's life, according to Deborah Baker in *The Convert*. It is, as Baker suggests, a life that challenges Western understanding and that challenged her as a biographer. The front of the dust jacket on the first edition of the book shows at the bottom what appears to be a 1940s-era photograph of the shoes, socks, legs, and skirt of a Western schoolgirl. Above a band containing the title, subtitle, and author's name, there is a waist-up photograph of Jameelah in 1962 after her arrival in her adopted country, in which she wears a burqa that reveals only her hands and lower forearms. That is just what she wanted to reveal, and according to Baker, Jameelah's letters sometimes similarly reveal only what she wanted to reveal, as in a letter to her parents that pleasantly announces her move to Pattoki as if Mawdudi had not evicted her. There is also, says Baker, the probability that Jameelah wrote two dozen letters not to the persons nominally addressed but to a broad future audience.

Further complicating the problem of interpretation is the unconventional use Baker makes of Jameelah's letters, which seem to be copied in the book. Yet Baker hints in the final chapter and states explicitly in "A Note on Methodology" that she has not used Jameelah's exact words except within quotation marks. In many other instances, she has condensed and revised what Jameelah actually wrote, occasionally reworking a passage from an essay and inserting it into a letter or moving an idea or brief story from one letter to another. To defend herself against the charge of deliberately misleading her readers, Baker argues that she has done what she needed to write intelligibly about Jameelah's life and her own reaction to it in the early twenty-first century. She assures her readers that the "tale," as her subtitle says, is basically factual.

However close to perfect fact Baker comes, she has not told the easiest of tales to follow or written the easiest of books to read. Her deviations from a straight chronological narration doubtless create the effect she wishes as she shows her own struggle to understand a woman she perceives as strange. Even so, many readers would not have felt that Baker was insulting their intelligence had she provided a timeline of Marcus / Jameelah's life and a selected bibliography of her numerous Islamic publications. To go along with the seventeen pages of endnotes, an index to the persons and places mentioned in the book would have been welcome as well.

If the deficiency in orthodox scholarly apparatus is a shortcoming at all, some readers will find a more troublesome one: when presenting her own ideas about historical events, Baker tends merely to assert rather than to argue. For instance, as she contemplates whether the United States effectively eliminated parts of its constitution in the wake of the September 11 terrorist attacks, Baker casually mentions several specific government actions but does not delve into what restrictions of civil liberties or constitutional rights they might impose or address indeed any specifics.

While Baker recognizes the danger that Muslims reading the works of Mawdudi and Jameelah might use airliners as bombs to kill Americans, she also argues that Westerners usually see only the worst of Islam, just as Muslims usually see only the worst of the predominantly secular West. Yet despite this flicker of broader intercultural awareness, in *The Convert*, Baker presents no faithful, nonviolent Muslims who are clearly willing to acknowledge the rights of persons of other religions or of no religion. As Baker mentions in this book, she lost the Christian faith of her childhood and, as Marcus did, she longs for the absolute. Unlike Maryam Jameelah, Deborah Baker, declaring herself emotionally exiled from the United States, has failed to find a solid faith. It seems that in Baker's quest to understand and document this one woman's personal spiritual journey, she has failed to find a balanced, more nuanced vision of Islam to offer her audience.

Victor Lindsey

Review Sources

Booklist 107, no. 15 (April 1, 2011): 6.
Christian Century 128, no. 14 (July 12, 2011): 41.
Library Journal 136, no. 7 (April 15, 2011): 99.
The New York Times Book Review, May 22, 2011, p. 17.

A Covert Affair
Julia Child and Paul Child in the OSS

Author: Jennet Conant (b. 1960)
Publisher: Simon and Schuster (New York).
416 pp. $28.00; paperback $16.00
Type of work: History
Time: 1930s–1960s
Locale: Southeast Asia, Paris, and the United
States

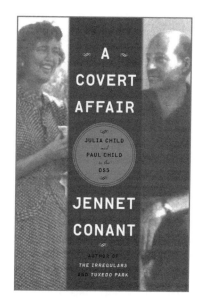

*A historical account of Jane Foster, an artist
and employee in the United States Office of
Strategic Services (OSS) who was accused of
working as a Soviet spy during World War II.
The book discusses her life in the 1940s and
1950s, during which time she was friends with
iconic chef Julia Child and her husband Paul.*

Principal personages:
JANE FOSTER (1912–1979), an artist and OSS
agent indicted as a Soviet spy in 1957
JULIA CHILD (1912–2004), a chef and author who worked with the OSS during World
War II and was friends with Jane
PAUL CHILD (1902–1994), Julia's husband, an OSS and US Foreign Service employee
who was friends with Jane

Before living in Paris, where she first mastered the art of French cooking, Julia Child
and her husband Paul lived in Southeast Asia. There, instead of unlocking culinary
secrets, they spent their days working with military intelligence. Now remembered as
a legendary chef, Julia first met her husband in Ceylon when they were working for the
United States Office of Strategic Services (OSS) during World War II. Author Jennet
Conant follows their lives from World War II through the early years of the Cold War
in this meticulously researched spy story. The title is misleading, however; the scope
of the book goes beyond the Childs to focus on the story of their friend Jane Foster, an
alleged Communist spy.

Conant's book immediately creates an atmosphere of uncertainty that captures the
McCarthy-era world of hierarchy, secrecy, and propaganda. She dramatically opens
the story in 1955, when OSS employee Paul Child was recalled to the United States
from Europe by a mysterious telegram. The telegram, which Julia assumed preceded
a job promotion for Paul, instead marked the beginning of a long and convoluted investigation into the Childs' former OSS colleague Jane Foster. With this framework
established, Conant tells the story of Julia, Paul, and Jane in the decades during and
after the war, creating a bracing narrative about friendship, loyalty, and history.

In the early chapters of *A Covert Affair,* Conant works to reconstruct the story of Julia's entry into the OSS, describing the events of her transfer to the Far East and her association with Jane in Indonesia. Conant then shifts focus from Julia to Jane, the real subject of the book, and describes her contributions to the war effort in the Pacific. Jane was involved in Indonesian resistance against Japanese forces, and while she was developing and implementing communication strategies, she became passionate about the Indonesian cause. She was in her office when she heard about the atomic bomb being dropped on Hiroshima; two days later, the Soviet Union declared war on Japan. After the second bomb landed on Nagasaki, Japan surrendered to the Allied forces and Jane's role in the war changed.

With the end of combat, Jane was summoned to the island of Java to report. She was briefed on the details of the newly formed Republic of Indonesia; with the Japanese gone, Indonesians were in full revolt against Dutch colonial rule. Jane's work was crucial in the shifts in foreign policy that followed the death of President Franklin Delano Roosevelt and the transfer of the presidency to Harry Truman. The OSS removed Foster to Saigon, Vietnam, and then later to Bangkok, Thailand, before she returned to the United States in 1946. She resigned shortly after her return and debriefing, citing frustrations and disillusionment with the State Department's views on Indonesian independence and conditions in Indochina. She was outspoken about her displeasure with the government's treatment of Southeast Asia. In these chapters about the end of World War II, Conant also describes changing attitudes toward communism in the United States. She describes the shift of American interest away from Asia and toward free elections and self-government in Eastern Europe. As anti-Communist policy came to the forefront of government, the OSS fell out of favor and the work of its agents also became undesirable.

Jane, angry about her debriefing, spoke to the press about conditions in Indonesia, even handing out her top-secret reports to the press. Her public lectures gave rise to the San Francisco Committee to Free Indonesia, as well as to picketing outside the British and Dutch embassies. The State Department forced the cancellation of future talks, as the Dutch deemed Foster's public remarks offensive. Outraged, she wrote to the *New York Times* disputing its editorial claims about Indonesia. During this time, Jane took shelter with her Russian lover George Zlatovski, whom she had married in secret, becoming Jane Foster Zlatovski.

While Jane was growing depressed about postwar American policy, Julia and Paul were growing happier in their personal lives. After the dissolution of the OSS, the couple got married. Conant uses quotes from Julia's famous correspondence to describe the pair's courtship and marriage. Paul eventually joined the United States Foreign Service and the Childs moved to Paris in 1948. There, as many readers will know, Julia began to attend cooking school. At the same time, Jane traveled to Paris for an exhibition of her art. The two women met and talked about red-baiting and anti-Communist politics, noting that they had seen similar acts of character assassination in President Truman's treatment of OSS members in 1945.

When Conant's story enters the 1950s, she vividly describes the nightmarish era of McCarthyism, book burning, and the witch hunt for Communists. Julia and Paul learned that Jane went home to the United States and was not allowed to return to Paris; the State Department restricted the travel of anyone suspected of being a Communist sympathizer, and Jane's passport had been seized. Jane faced several charges at the passport division of the State Department, and her attempts to leave the country were blocked. She wrote to the Childs that she was being followed by government agents and that "men in a parked car began calling her names—yelling 'Spy! Spy!' at the top of their lungs."

In March of 1955, Jane appeared before the Board of Passport Appeals. There, she lied under oath when asked about her membership in the Communist Party, her views on Communist ideology, and whether she knew if the former friends and acquaintances whose names she was presented with were Communists. She had no intention of informing on her friends and, after her hearing, fled to New York City. Her lawyer later told her that her application for a passport had been denied because she had joined the Communist Party in the 1930s. Eventually, Jane's mother found another lawyer to take the

Jennet Conant is an American journalist and the author of three best-selling nonfiction books about World War II. She has also contributed to numerous publications, including Esquire, Newsweek, *and the* New York Times.

State Department to court for being unconstitutional; the case was dropped and Jane was given her passport and allowed to return to France.

It was during this time that Paul Child, as described in the book's opening pages, was called to the United States to answer questions about Jane. After Paul was cleared and while Julia was working on *Mastering the Art of French Cooking* (1961), the couple saw their old friend and her husband, George Zlatovski, mentioned in the *New York Times*. They had been indicted for membership in a Communist spy ring and had been connected to the Kremlin. Jane and George remained front-page news for the entire summer of 1957. Americans were transfixed by stories about spies and were especially fascinated by Jane and George, even though the couple denied the charges and refused to talk to reporters.

Later, a Federal Bureau of Investigation (FBI) double agent named Boris Morros claimed to have interacted with Jane when posing as a Russian spy. Jane and George went to their lawyer out of fear and were arrested by French policemen and interrogated. They were not tried, but agreed to confess everything they knew about Soviet espionage in France and name anyone they knew who was involved with communism. Drawing from Jane's posthumously published memoir, *An Unamerican Lady* (1980), Conant examines Jane's rationalizations for her subversive activities and the painful act of naming names. The interrogations continued for weeks and culminated with

Jane's hospitalization after she suffered a breakdown. After she had spent two weeks in the hospital, American officials came from the attorney general's office to ask Jane to return to the United States to testify. She refused and slit her wrist shortly after in a suicide attempt. Though she survived, she felt that her actions demonstrated that she "would rather die by her own hand in France than return to the United States to die in the electric chair."

When Jane got out of the hospital, she retreated back into her Paris home, surrounded by an encampment of hostile reporters that was permanently outside her building. Her lawyer sent her the American indictment, which she refers to as "THE BIG LIE" in her memoir. Jane maintained that the charges against her were based on innuendo and ignorance, stating that they were filled with "glaring inaccuracies and discrepancies." She resigned herself to a life in exile, living as a political prisoner in France until she died at the age of sixty-seven.

Conant's views on Jane's guilt remain somewhat ambiguous, and it is unclear to what degree she was a victim of McCarthyism and the Red Scare. While it is clear that Conant sympathizes with Jane's plight, the author knows that Jane is not blameless in her predicament and finds fault with her many denials and evasions. Although Conant draws heavily from Jane's memoir, she also references declassified files, letters, interviews, and government documents, many of which are cited or included in the book's appendix and bibliography, to recreate a well-rounded story of Jane's life during and after World War II.

Critics have faulted Conant for using Julia and Paul Child to market a book that is so clearly about another, lesser-known figure. Some readers will undoubtedly be disappointed that, while the Childs knew and supported Jane, Julia and Paul are not central to this otherwise fascinating story. Jane will be an unfamiliar subject to most; it is, therefore, fortunate that Conant so vividly describes the enigmatic and misunderstood woman. Regardless of their views on foreign service, communism, American history, or even Julia Child herself, readers will find Foster to be a fascinating character who led an extraordinary life. Few readers will question Julia Child's contributions to culture, but after reading *A Covert Affair*, some might wonder why her friend Jane was sidelined in the annals of American history.

Batya Weinbaum

Review Sources

Los Angeles Times, April 28, 2011 (Web).
The New York Times Book Review, April 1, 2011 (Web).
Seattle Times, March 26, 2011 (Web).
USA Today, April 5, 2011 (Web).

Crazy U
One Dad's Crash Course in Getting His Kid into College

Author: Andrew Ferguson (b. 1956)
Publisher: Simon & Schuster (New York).
 240 pp. $25.00; paperback $16.00
Type of work: Education, memoir
Time: 2007–2009
Locale: Virginia

With self-deprecating humor and critical scrutiny, Ferguson and his oldest child struggle through the college application process, uncovering research on the SAT, college rankings, and admissions.

Principal personages:

ANDREW FERGUSON, a journalist who tries to help his college-bound son through the application process

GILLUM FERGUSON, Andrew's son, a suburban high-school student with a good but not spectacular record

DENISE FERGUSON, Andrew's wife and Gillum's mother, who refuses to mourn her son's departure for college

EMILY FERGUSON, Andrew's daughter and Gillum's sister, the next family member who will apply for college admission

KATHERINE COHEN, an independent college admissions counselor who charges a large fee

BOB MORSE, the overseer of college rankings for *U.S. News*

BOB SCHAEFFER, the director of public education at the National Center for Fair and Open Testing, which opposes the SAT

ROB, Andrew's friend, who goes through the college admissions process with his own son

RICHARD VEDDER, an economics professor at Ohio University who has upset college administrators by investigating college tuition

In *Crazy U: One Dad's Crash Course in Getting His Kid into College*, Andrew Ferguson takes on the topic of college admissions in the United States, telling a personal narrative about his son's transition from a suburban high school to a highly selective university. Beginning with the brochures, or viewbooks, that colleges provide to prospective students, Ferguson describes how colleges advertise themselves and attempt to attract as many first-year applications as possible. Gillum, who boasts a good but hardly exemplary student record, is by no means guaranteed admission into the schools of his choice. In spite of his feigned nonchalance, getting into college is difficult for him, and likewise for his father, who struggles alongside him throughout the admissions process.

Throughout the book, Ferguson recognizes that acceptance into a prestigious college is far from the gravest concern in the world. The Fergusons' perspective and attitude of good humor helps *Crazy U* appeal to readers who might otherwise find college admissions to be an unworthy topic for a book. The reader is hard pressed not to find amusement in Gillum's suggestion that his parents get divorced and provide him with a psychological trauma on which to write his admissions essay. Similarly endearing is Ferguson's discovery, as a senior at Occidental College in 1978, that he has no employable skills and should therefore become a journalist. And it is difficult not to find humor in the story of a woman at a party who writhes until another parent gives her a semipolite chance to brag about her daughter's perfect SAT scores.

Although it is a memoir, *Crazy U* takes certain precautions to protect the identities of Ferguson and his family. Nowhere in the body of the book does Ferguson name his wife, son, or daughter. He dedicates the book to people he later identifies in the acknowledgments as his children, Emily and Gillum, and only there does he reveal his wife's name, Denise. A friend of Ferguson's is given the name "Rob," and similarly, the university where his son eventually enrolls is named "Big State University," or BSU, and located in "Collegetown." Ferguson never states what many readers might suspect: BSU is the University of Virginia, and Collegetown is Charlottesville.

Throughout the family narrative, and bolstered by his exhaustive research, Ferguson argues that American colleges are first of all a competitive business, seeking income, high enrollment, and prestige, regardless of what they may otherwise claim. Independent admissions counselors, such as Katherine Cohen of New York City, help families navigate and enter into the business of American colleges. Although he cannot afford Cohen's services, Ferguson interviews her, and he is informed that by only beginning preparations for college during Gillum's third year of high school, he has made a grave error. Resilient, Ferguson attempts to evade the pitfalls of neurotic, obsessive parents by reassuring himself that his son's happiness does not depend on admission to a particular school. However, he cannot avoid parental madness for long.

Ferguson interviews Bob Morse, who oversees the annual college rankings published by *U.S. News*, a widely read and prestigious resource. He finds that although college administrators disparage the rankings as a nearly worthless measure, they still do their best to rank high, even if they must manipulate their figures to do so. For instance, Ferguson says that Clemson University in South Carolina adjusts class sizes to look good in the eyes of *U.S. News*; similarly, Harvard University in Cambridge, Massachusetts, keeps its acceptance rate low by routinely soliciting applications from students it will likely reject in the interest of bolstering its reputation.

Then there is the SAT, the standardized test taken nationwide by high school students seeking admission into highly selective colleges. While Gillum completes the SAT at a testing site, Ferguson takes a practice test at home and scores comically low. Ferguson interviews one of the SAT's most outspoken opponents, Bob Schaeffer, who directs public education at the National Center for Fair and Open Testing in Massachusetts. Schaeffer claims that the SAT was designed to favor men from rich families and to

(© Jack Shafer)

The author of Fools' Names, Fools' Faces *(1996) and* Land of Lincoln: Adventures in Abe's America *(2007), Andrew Ferguson works as a senior editor for* The Weekly Standard. *He has written for* Time, National Review, *and other periodicals, as well as for President George H. W. Bush.*

work against Jews, women, and racial minorities. Based on research of his own, Ferguson disagrees, finding that the SAT was instituted in the 1930s to ensure fairness in college admissions. He finds no ethnic bias in the test's wording and discovers that students from rich families score higher on average. Students of Asian ancestry score the highest, followed by whites, then Latinos, then African Americans. Men generally outscore women in mathematics, while women outscore men in verbal sections. Despite these differences, Ferguson observes that the test indicates a student's chance of academic success in college fairly well, casting the measures some colleges have taken to avoid using the SAT in a questionable light.

With the SAT out of the way, Gillum then turns his attention to applications, which require him to supply personal information and compose the dreaded admissions essays. He resists the essay prompts, which would require him to display his private thoughts to strangers and which, the Fergusons observe, favor emotionally troubled applicants and betray colleges' desire to remake rather than educate students. Vexed, Ferguson buys a personalized sample essay online. Although he does not intend for his son to submit the sample, he notes that it would suit the administrators' demand for exhibitionist self-flattery.

Much to Ferguson's relief, Gillum eventually submits his applications, but he soon learns that applying for financial aid can be worse than applying for admission. There is plenty of money available for student aid, but the listed cost for in-state students at public institutions is high, and the cost of private institutions is even higher. Here, Ferguson turns his attention to the Free Application for Federal Student Aid (FAFSA), the College Scholarship Service (CSS) Profile, and the Expected Family Contribution (EFC). He complains about this time-consuming paperwork until he considers that maybe it should be hard to get money for free. One question, however, comes up repeatedly for Ferguson and his friend Rob: Why does a college education cost so much? According to Richard Vedder, a professor of economics at Ohio University, the simple answer is that colleges keep raising tuition because nothing stops them. College presidents want to keep their various constituencies happy, and the cost of keeping them happy is higher spending. Ferguson suggests that while the market would slow the rise of tuition on its own, third-party and government payments negate this, with subsidies rising as tuition rises. The cost of a college education has far outpaced inflation in the United States.

Ferguson finds an imbalance between the cost of college and the education offered there, agreeing with Vedder that a bachelor's degree no longer guarantees an education of verifiable quality. Instead, Ferguson opines that the primary service of a degree is to communicate to employers that its holder also can hold a job. It is a costly signal, to be sure, but Ferguson acknowledges that as a father he is too invested in the American educational system to condone his son's dropping out.

Though he is a caustic critic, Ferguson reconciles himself to the system and does not stand in his son's way. If the book has any weakness—from the viewpoint of parents and students, not college administrators or the US Department of Education—that weakness lies in what the author omits, and he could hardly have included everything in a moderately short personal account. Nevertheless, besides an explanation of how his son's application to Vanderbilt seems to lead to his acceptance at Villanova, with Vanderbilt forgotten, Ferguson may leave his reader wishing for a longer explanation of how ethnic diversity influences the way admissions offices decide the makeup of a freshman class. He observes the irony of the recent admissions situation wherein males, mostly white males, have benefited from colleges' attempts to achieve an approximate gender balance, despite the larger number of female applicants with exemplary high school records. Ferguson also refers to an apparent obsession with affirmative action among some contributors to the website College Confidential, but he could have written more to refute the common argument that, after athletes and the children of alumni, elite colleges next try to admit applicants of Latino and African ancestry, doing so at the expense of applicants of European and Asian ancestry. Instead, Ferguson's idea of an applicant who would receive automatic admission to a top-tier college is somebody of Haitian descent.

Factors of race and ethnicity aside, Gillum is accepted into the freshman class at BSU. Ferguson's story is intensely personal from start to finish, reflecting the relatable event of a child's leaving home and entering adulthood, as well as the conflicted feelings of parents toward the American rite of passage that is leaving home for college. The book ends with Ferguson's son at BSU, his daughter almost old enough to go to college herself, and his wife still refusing to grieve her son's leaving home. Ferguson's journey ends at a gas station in Collegetown, where he finds himself gripped by many emotions at once. With the gas nozzle still in the tank, he gets into his car and obliviously tries to drive away.

Victor Lindsey

Review Sources

The American Spectator 44, no. 5 (June 2011): 78–81.
Kirkus Reviews 78, no. 23 (December 1, 2010): 1196.
National Review 63, no. 7 (April 18, 2011): 48–50.
The New York Times, March 4, 2011, p. C1.
Publishers Weekly 258, no. 2 (January 10, 2011): 43.
The Wall Street Journal, March 5, 2011, p. C8.

Culture of One

Author: Alice Notley (b. 1945)
Publisher: Penguin (New York). 160 pp. $18.00
Type of work: Poetry
Time: The present
Locale: The American Southwest

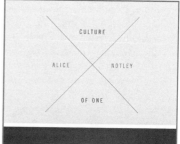

This innovative collection of poetry tells the story of Marie, a woman living in a desert town in the American Southwest.

Principal characters:
MARIE, an artist who lives in a dump
LEROY, her friend, a compulsive liar who
    works in the Buy-Rite store
EVE LOVE, a rock star
RUBY, Leroy's wife, who dies of cancer
THE MEAN GIRLS, girls who live in town and
    persecute Marie by burning her shack and
    killing her dog
MERCY / TARA, goddess of compassion

In a 2009 interview with the *Kenyon Review*, Alice Notley described her life at her home in Paris as an "intense solitude," in which she is disconnected from the dominant culture around her. Fittingly, the title of her latest book describes not only the life of Marie, the main character, but also the life of the poet, an immigrant who lives segregated from the mainstream in her new environs. On a broader level, *Culture of One* is both the chronicle of a woman's choice to live outside the mainstream and a meditation on the lived realities of alienation and imagination that go hand in hand with that separation. A cross-genre book written in verse, *Culture of One* consists of page after page of a stacked series of poems, printed one after the other without page breaks or interruptions, fostering a kind of continuous reading experience. This technique suits the underlying narrative structure, which is that of a novel, though Notley's critics have also described the form as a "verse narrative" and "a novel in verse." Notley has developed a reputation as a poet of a uniquely lyrical and experimental sensibility, and critics find this collection to be no exception.

In the first part of the book, a group of characters is developed; later, their stories are complicated by environmental and existential problems. In the second part, the narrative reaches a climax and, finally, a series of resolutions. As is the case in many of her works, Notley breaks with traditional conventions, taking the opportunity to push the boundaries of what a novel is expected to be. In her own words, she is "altering / the syntax of narration, its pace and vocabularic exigencies." She declares, "I stopped caring what you wanted me to say; I stopped / caring what you wanted me to do."

Alice Notley is the author of more than thirty books of poetry, including Grave of Light: New and Selected Poems, 1970–2005 *(2006) and the Pulitzer Prize finalist* Mysteries of Small Houses *(1998). She has won numerous awards and grants from the Poetry Society of America, the American Academy of Arts and Letters, the Academy of American Poets, and the National Endowment for the Arts.*

As a poet, Notley has always remained on the edges of any school or rigid conceptual framework, insisting that readers meet her work on her own terms. In part, *Culture of One* is about how Notley lives the life of her poetry: in the margins, inventing the culture that defines her. Notley's textual doppelgänger describes herself as "more powerful than a president; I am a charmed and desperate / poet speaking to everyone."

Each of the characters in *Culture of One* is an embodiment of the poet. "I couldn't stop being Marie— / or Eve Love—even in Paris. I couldn't stop being Mercy, or Leroy," Notley writes. Based on a real person from Notley's youth, Marie lives in a dump outside of a depressed desert town in the American Southwest and makes art from old scraps. Her home is a shack constructed from rubble and is repeatedly burned down by the mean girls in town. Marie's culture stands in opposition to the culture of the mean girls. While they focus on destruction and desperately seek the love of the violent men around them, Marie is a creator who rejects the mainstream, choosing only a pair of friends: Leroy, a compulsive liar who works at the Buy-Rite and supplies Marie with water and food, and Eve Love, a rock musician who struggles with self-mutilation.

Each of these characters is a mask that one can wear, or, more importantly, a mask that the author wears. For Notley, the mask is not a fiction: "The mask is what you use; it isn't a fake, it's a mask." The mask is the self; it is culture, what people make. At its core, *Culture of One* is about the creative act. By assembling various fragments of character, narrative, and verse, the book is Notley's vehicle for both describing and using a technique of self-creation. Marie authors her own culture from the discarded artifacts of other people's lives that she finds in the dump where she lives. "Where does culture come from?" Notley asks. "It comes from the materials you do it with." She refers to Marie's creation as her "codex," a formal word that is used to describe an ancient manuscript or book of laws. Marie's codex is collage, painting, and pictures; the one thing that Marie does not include is writing, for only Notley is the writer in this world, a theme she returns to again and again throughout the book. As the author of the book, she constructs her own culture, inventing and reinventing her self from salvaged and recovered pieces of observation, just as Marie does each time her home is destroyed.

There are several instances throughout the book of characters making marks upon themselves and the world around them, and this process of making a mark often appears in tandem with the theme of creation. There are the marks that Marie makes in her codex, and there is the text of *Culture of One* itself. Both of these processes can be viewed as methods of recording. Another important document is the scar, which appears with regard to Marie and Eve Love, two scarred characters. The web of white scars that covers the front of Marie's body is evidence of the fire that took her baby. Similarly, the scars on Eve Love's thighs bear witness to her struggle with self-mutilation, although in her case, they are marks of which she is the author. "There are adventures recorded in my scars," Marie says to Leroy, equating her scars with her mind. They are a lasting record of memories that the characters struggle to erase. The books, on the other hand, are the memories they try to create: "When I die I will be my book and / the spirit of creation."

Looming over the book's many characters is the spiritual figure Mercy, who is introduced on the first page:

> I am mercy; I have no understanding of who I am;
> though, with my thousand arms, I have written of my own
> nature since writing began. I inhabit you and you write about me again.

Mercy, also referred to as Tara, is a mystical figure who appears throughout the book. A symbol of feminine strength and compassion, she is based on a goddess concept that is present in a number of different cultures. She appears as energy, a kind of force field that moves through the characters in turn. "It was all about power," Notley writes in "Obsidian Necklace." "Have / you ever noticed that Mercy doesn't have any?" The theme of power emerges throughout the book as well, often as power lying in the hands of men that Notley declares she can "never vote for" again. Conversely, Mercy is an embodiment of female power, the flip side of the destructive power that the mean girls use to torment Marie and destroy the things she loves. Mercy has a spiritually transformative and healing power, and it is this power that propels the transformations of Notley's characters. Her thousand arms imply different forms of energy in their various positions: folded, opening a door, moving automatically, trying to put a fire out, and beating a drum.

Further complicating these intertwined themes of imagination, creation, documentation, and destruction is Notley's grappling with the concept of truth. Notley sets up her text as a piece of fiction at the outset, calling into question her own reliability: "I mean *everyone* lies about Marie. I'm lying about her right now." Shortly after, in a uniquely frank and direct moment, Notley inserts her "true" self into the text:

> I live in Paris, France, but I spend some time each year
> in the Mohave Desert in the U.S. Improbable? This is the only
> true thing I have to tell you. The only really true thing.

Late in the book, Notley reinforces the view of her own text as a fabrication in the poem "Far from Thought," in which "most of what happens is a lie. There is no record / but lies." Where, then, is truth? What does it mean that Notley has based her collection on a real person? In "Diamond," she offers a possible answer: "The words say, We are not untrue; we are words. Try us / again." The reader might take this passage as a gesture of resolution on the author's part. Yet Notley ironically delivers this message from the mouths of words themselves, those objects that she has implied the reader should doubt. In fact, the words have lives, as demonstrated by the letter *R* that Marie paints on the bathtub. In passages that are entirely devoid of humor, the letter *R* talks, bathes, mocks Marie, and murders her baby. Clearly, works of creation are as powerful for Notley as the characters in her story.

As much as *Culture of One* is the story of its characters, it is also a philosophical meditation on language, poetry, and human invention, as well as an exploration of Notley's deeply personal worldview. By reinventing her poetics, Notley has devised a method for asking questions about the consequences of individualism and the globalization of culture, questions that need not, and indeed cannot, be resolved with easy answers. She writes in the end that "the lies were half-true." Nevertheless, *Culture of One* makes important and relevant inquiries into what it means to create, reminding readers of the choices that are involved in self-invention, choices that can lead to acts of violence and destruction as well. The creative act, Notley reminds her readers, possesses a unique transformative power, though the pursuit of this type of power is something that Notley simultaneously laments and hopes for:

> There is no culture anywhere, in these countries I almost
> live in; though there is history. And there was once—but
> now only monolithic companies. I drove through
> town—nothing left . . .

Amira Hanafi

Review Sources

Library Journal 136, no. 6 (April 1, 2011): 92.
Publishers Weekly 258, no. 16 (April 18, 2011): 34–35.

The Curfew

Author: Jesse Ball (b. 1978)
Publisher: Vintage Contemporaries (New York). 194 pp. $15.00
Type of work: Novel
Locale: The city of C

Jesse Ball's third novel takes place in a totalitarian state and follows a father's dangerous night journey through the city after curfew while his daughter waits his return at home and imagines, reinvents, and possibly retells their past, present, and future.

Principal characters:

WILLIAM DRYSDALE, a twenty-nine-year-old former concert violinist who now works as an "epitaphorist" in the city of C and mourns the loss of his wife at the hands of the government

MOLLY DRYSDALE, a schoolchild and William's eight-year-old mute daughter

MRS. GIBBONS, the elderly neighbor of the Drysdales who agrees to look after Molly for the night

MR. GIBBONS, husband to Mrs. Gibbons and former puppeteer

LOUISA DRYSDALE, William's wife, who has disappeared

GERARD, former friend of William and Louisa Drysdale, currently a leader of antigovernment activity

An old woman is shot in the street. The gunshot resounds in a bedroom where William and Molly, father and daughter, sleep as if nothing happened. So begins Jesse Ball's *The Curfew*, a novel of love, imagination, and survival in the face of meaningless violence within a dystopian society.

The residents of the city of C live in fear under an "invisible state," an anonymous police force whose tyranny is enforced through surveillance, anonymity, and murder. Ball's narrative evokes the dystopia of George Orwell's *Nineteen Eighty-Four* (1949) or Ray Bradbury's *Fahrenheit 451* (1953) in providing a snapshot of what readers assume is a future city where societal advances have failed to improve life and instead have caused total collapse. The city's inhabitants are left with a totalitarian existence where individual will and spirit have been depleted. In the novel's opening scene, readers learn that the residents have not only grown accustomed to, but have come to accept a life filled with violence, unexplained deaths, and the absence of music. Forces real and imagined, literal and internal, rule the society of *The Curfew*. Setting his novel in a climate of fascist hegemony, Ball shows how fear of what one cannot see (the government itself, in this case) inspires control of the fearful. This relationship suggests, as Ball's fiction often does, that reality is only as significant as the imagination permits. For the central characters of *The Curfew*, however, the virtues of imagination are threatened by the cruelty of reality.

Jesse Ball is the author of two previous novels, The Way Through Doors *(2009) and* Samedi the Deafness *(2007) and several books of poetry. His work was included in* The Best American Poetry, *2006, and his short story, "The Early Deaths of Lubeck, Brennan, Harp and Carr" won the Paris Review's Plimpton Prize in 2008.*

"I shall introduce this city and its occupants," the narrator announces early on, "as a series of objects whose relationship cannot be told with any certainty." An aesthetic of uncertainty guides the formal design of *The Curfew*—with its imagined histories, reluctant narrators, and poetic logic. Yet, it is the search for certainty that motivates the novel's story. Risking death, William sets out after dark to find Gerard, his former friend, who is now an antigovernment activist and offers William information on the fate of his wife, Louisa. While William navigates the city streets evading the police, his daughter, Molly, is at home and being cared for by neighbors, the Gibbons. Molly fashions a puppet play in which she imagines her parent's history. She goes on to imagine her father's trip through the city, his ultimate fate, and hers as well. Molly's play—executed with the help of Mr. and Mrs. Gibbons—is both an act of certainty, in that the puppet play can progress and end any way that Molly and the Gibbons decide, and a concession to the bleakness of uncertainty, for neither Molly nor the Gibbons truly know how this night will end. Remembering her parents' love is in many ways a defense against the uncertainty. The puppet play ends and reveals questions that will loom for the reader throughout the novel, allowing life to imitate art. Readers are just as curious and uncertain as Molly, the Gibbons, and William. Readers are also prompted to ask how much of Molly's play is real and, in considering the violent world outside, what the significance of Molly's invented story is in the world beyond the pages of the book.

Sometimes called a modern Franz Kafka, Jesse Ball delights in narrative digression, systems of control and chaos, and dream-like passages. In addition to writing fiction, Ball is also an accomplished poet. As such, his novels may pose a challenge to readers seeking strictly conventional fiction that is composed of discrete characters and coherent plots ("sly" is a word typically used by critics regarding Ball's work). The subject of Ball's novels is often storytelling itself. For example, in his previous novel, *The Way Through Doors* (2009), a woman loses her memory in a car accident, and a playful government agent decides to fabricate and then recount to her the story of her life. What follows is a circuitous, surreal journey involving "guess artists" and staircases that lead deep underground. *The Curfew*, while certainly containing many of these furtive tendencies critics have alluded to, is firmly grounded in the emotional stakes of its characters. In this way, the novel is wholly accessible fiction, captivating and powerful in spite of (and perhaps because of) its experimentation. Only occasionally does the font on the page grow to thirty-six-point size, and when, toward the end, the novel takes a self-referential and metaphorical turn, the story justifies what some critics might call indulgence.

The emotions and metaphors of *The Curfew* are a facet of the story, stemming as they do from the narrator's opening statement that nothing "can be told with any certainty" and that events "in process cannot be judged." An aesthetic of ambiguity and absence most obviously defines the government, but it also permeates the life William and Molly have made, which can be seen, for example, in William's job as an "epitaphorist," a writer of tombstone epitaphs. He meets with the families and loved ones of citizens who have passed away, and the pure invention of this work emerges quickly. By omission and fabrication of the deceased's life, actual history is distorted. The parents of a dissenting government official, for instance, ask William to compose: "Dutiful husband, Devoted son." At the request of a woman whose husband died of natural causes at the age of ninety-two, William writes: "Died before his time." William alters history willingly, even happily, and Ball may be suggesting that memory is amenable to whimsy and is in no way obliged to history. The citizens of C have elected to remember their loved ones not as they were, but as they would like to imagine they were, and William proves the vehicle through which their memories can remain altered and intact.

William and Molly adopt this same ethic of uncertainty in a scene that finds them casually reading the newspaper. Unsatisfied with an article's content, they embellish by changing uncertain facts to proven facts and thereby dispose of reality for fancy. A man does not claim to have been asleep inside a hill for fifteen years, as the article reports; when William rereads the article for Molly, the man was not only actually asleep inside the hill, but was there for twenty years. Imagination, then, is not merely the means by which the totalitarian government functions; it is also the means by which family functions, loves, and remembers. This is the case for William and Molly, and also for Mr. and Mrs. Gibbons, the elderly couple that lives downstairs and hides Mr. Gibbons's puppeteer equipment in the corner of their apartment.

Having lost his wife, though, William cannot find true solace in his imagination. He races through the night to learn more about Louisa's fate. "All his inquiries to find her had met with no success." William remembers, "Louisa Drysdale? We have no record of a Louisa Drysdale." In the face of grief, the whimsical outlook William and Molly have built breaks down. Later, in the context of her puppet play, Molly's own imagination breaks down as well. For the reader, this is the point in the novel where Ball's narrative and Molly's play become inextricable.

Awaiting her father's return, Molly resolves to tell her parents' history herself. With the help of Mr. Gibbons, she assembles an elaborate play that recounts how her parents met, how they raised her, and what might ultimately happen to her father on his journey home. Near the end of the novel, the main narrative steps aside. Molly's puppet play takes over, and the imaginary story emerges as either the only story available or the only story that matters for Ball and his reader. The barrier between the play and the actual novel, between fantasy and reality, begins to blur as Ball confuses the reader's sense of real and imagined action.

At one point, Molly (in the puppet play) asks her father if the world can be changed. The William puppet responds in the negative, "I don't know that I would want to live in a world where things had become better, but your mother was gone." This raises the question: Does one dare imagine a different world when the real world contains such cruelty and loss? Ultimately, *The Curfew* seems to suggest that some losses are so harshly felt and are so real that even the imagination suffers the repercussions of intense pain. Perhaps, contrary to what William's epitaphs would suggest, certain losses can only be remembered exactly as they happened.

Ball closes his novel with the play's puppet-jester calling Molly's name and proffering a metaphor, perhaps, for memory and history. The act of remembering, finally, is what Ball offers readers, but even this bears the scars of what has passed away.

Ball's novels and poetry are filled with the unnatural but are presented in a natural way that allows readers to feel that they are walking arm-in-arm with Ball through the darkness and absurdity. His prose reads like poetry and is often typeset on the page to look like a poem. There is a feeling of calm, however, as one reads Ball's prose, which allows readers to experience the intense and often disturbing subject matter and insights in a way that can be digested easily, all the while wanting to go back for more.

James Flaherty

Review Sources

Millions, June 22, 2011 (Web).
The New York Times Book Review, August 28, 2011, p. 17.
NPR. June 27, 2011 (Web).

Dante in Love

Author: A. N. Wilson (b. 1950)
Publisher: Farrar, Straus and Giroux (New York). Illustrated. 400 pp. $35.00
Type of work: Literary biography
Time: Late thirteenth century to early fourteenth century
Locale: Italy

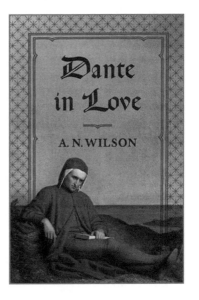

Wilson offers a detailed overview of Dante's life and the political and religious conflicts, cultural concepts, and historical events that informed The Divine Comedy.

Principle personages:
DANTE ALIGHIERI (1265–1321), an Italian poet
THOMAS AQUINAS (1225–1274), a Roman Catholic theologian
POPE BONIFACE VIII (1235–1303), the leader of the Roman Catholic Church from 1294 to 1303
FRANCESCO DELLA SCALA (1291–1329), also known as CAN GRANDE, the patron of Dante
GUIDO CAVALCANTI (ca. 1250–1300), a poet and important friend of Dante
GEMMA DONATI (ca. 1265–ca. 1342), Dante's wife
GIOTTO DI BONDONE (ca. 1267–1337), a famous painter and architect and friend of Dante
EMPEROR HENRY VII (ca. 1275–1313), the ruler of the Holy Roman Empire during much of Dante's life
BEATRICE PORTINARI (1266–1290), the inspiration for much of Dante's poetry
VIRGIL, born PUBLIUS VERGILIUS MARO (70 BCE–19 BCE), a Roman poet and Dante's guide through hell and purgatory in *The Divine Comedy*

"Dante believed that Love encompassed all things," A. N. Wilson writes in the first chapter of *Dante in Love*, explaining that his text is not a study of Dante's romantic life but rather an exploration of Dante as he fit into his contemporary world. In this literary biography, Wilson presents an enthusiastic yet frank and multifaceted depiction of Dante as a human being. Chronicling Dante's life and posthumous reception, Wilson explores the world in which the poet lived and wrote, providing crucial context for his works and an understanding of the development of Dante's reputation as one of the greatest European poets.

Structurally, *Dante in Love* is divided into twenty-one chapters that outline Dante's life and proceed largely in chronological order. The chapter titles are clear

A. N. Wilson is the author of many novels, including the five volumes of the Lampitt Chronicles *(1988–1996) and* Winnie and Wolf *(2007), as well as studies of John Milton, Leo Tolstoy, C. S. Lewis, Iris Murdoch, and the apostle Paul.*

and straightforward, allowing the reader to navigate through this complex work; there is no question about the topic of chapter 5, "Dante's Education," for instance. The bulk of the book's information is found within these chapters, but the back matter may also be of interest to many readers. Endnotes rarely expand upon Wilson's arguments, but they provide clear sources for the text's many quotations and clarify certain points, noting in particular when dates or other historical details are uncertain. Wilson provides readers who wish to learn more about Dante with a substantial selection of further reading in the bibliography, which lists many translations of Dante's works as well as wide variety of primary and secondary sources. The extensive index is a valuable tool in a text as detailed as this.

Following Wilson's explanation of the book's purpose, he begins his examination of Dante's life in the spring of 1300, at which time Dante, like many Catholics, was visiting Rome as a pilgrim during a holy year. In *The Divine Comedy*, the three days between Good Friday and Easter of 1300 become the period in which the fictionalized Dante makes his journey through hell, purgatory, and heaven. For the real Dante, 1300 had life-changing significance as well; the year of his spiritual journey was also the year that set in motion a series of events resulting in his exile from his home, the city-state of Florence. Wilson refers to this significant year frequently while chronicling Dante's life, moving from his childhood to his eventual death in exile. As in any biography of Dante, the poet's nearly lifelong fascination with Beatrice Portinari is of great importance; Wilson devotes a great deal of discussion both to the woman herself and to the allegorical figure she becomes in Dante's work.

One of the most fascinating chapters of the text appears after the end of the main narrative. "Dante's Afterlife" explores the poet's historical reputation, chronicling the ways in which critical and popular responses to his work changed over time. It is surprising, for instance, to learn that his status had begun to decline by the time of the Renaissance, even in Italy; Wilson notes that by the seventeenth century, the works of later poet Petrarch had surpassed those of Dante in popularity and reputation. In a book on Italy, English writer Joseph Addison ignored Dante. French thinker Voltaire despised *The Divine Comedy*, and German writer Johann Wolfgang von Goethe found the work unworthy of his time. It was not until an obscure English clergyman named Henry Francis Cary produced a translation of *The Divine Comedy* that Dante's work reentered the public consciousness to a significant extent. After reading this translation, poet Samuel Taylor Coleridge began to lecture on Dante, thus beginning the nineteenth-century Dante craze in England. Wilson goes on to note that this translation went on to inspire poets John Keats and Alfred, Lord Tennyson, art critic John Ruskin, and many others.

Wilson calls Cary "an excellent translator," but he is far less complimentary about the translation by Henry Wadsworth Longfellow. Wilson comments that some translators have attempted to write in the extraordinarily demanding confines of *terza rima*, seeking to replicate the rhyme scheme of the original work, but he argues that many such translators lacked the expertise to do so properly. While he considers many translations of *The Divine Comedy* to be inadequate, Wilson recommends the facing-page version by Robin Kirkpatrick as well as the renderings by Allen Mandelbaum, Robert Pinsky, John Ciardi, Mark Musa, and J. G. Nichols. As Wilson lists one "superb" translation after another, his sheer love for Dante becomes apparent; his deep desire to spread his appreciation of Dante to readers relies on the existence of quality translations.

A highly personal volume that clearly reveals its author's enthusiasm for Dante and his works, *Dante in Love* is an engaging narrative characterized by its autobiographical reminiscences, very personal tone, and attention to detail. Some chapters become small essays in themselves, discussing at length such topics as courtly love and the development of the Italian language. The book progresses at a leisurely, sometimes rambling pace, following the basic contours of Dante's life and placing him squarely within the historical developments of his time. The reader is introduced not only to a single major poet but also to the socially and politically complex age in which he lived. Political corruption within the Roman Catholic Church is emphasized, as are factionalism within Florence and the other Italian city-states and relations between the Church, the Italian states, and the Holy Roman Empire. Wilson considers such data crucial to understanding Dante's life and work, and he demonstrates the extent to which Dante was influenced by his sociopolitical environment. *The Divine Comedy*, in particular, includes numerous references to the political and religious figures of Dante's time, and to understand their significance within the work, the reader must have a general understanding of their roles in Dante's world. Wilson provides this background knowledge, allowing readers to better understand the mind of the great poet.

Wilson repeatedly confesses that he is an amateur in Dante studies, giving himself far too little credit in this respect. It is clear that he has read widely in both the primary and secondary literature, and he is always appealingly generous and respectful when he cites other scholars. He has his own theories about certain aspects of Dante's life and writings, yet he never seems to be arguing in favor of some pet theory of his own. Just as Wilson is a bit more than the "amateur Dantean" he claims to be, *Dante in Love* is a text somewhat above the amateur level. The ideal reader of Wilson's volume is a person very much like Wilson himself: curious, thoughtful, well educated, and well read in both medieval and later literature. For those readers who know Dante and Dante scholarship less fully than Wilson himself obviously does, the competing views on particular issues and the reasons for and against various scholarly positions are somewhat unclear. Wilson does elaborate on interpretations by some critics, but readers unfamiliar with Dante studies will have to take on faith some of his individual assertions.

Similarly, while the historical intricacies of Dante's society are undoubtedly of great value, Wilson focuses on such details in lieu of explaining the artistic strengths of Dante's work, particularly *The Divine Comedy*. An explanation of what makes Dante "the greatest poet of the Middle Ages" and arguably "the greatest of all European poets" would have served to balance the discussion of Dante's historical reception;

as noted in "Dante's Afterlife," readers and writers for several centuries were largely indifferent to his work. Wilson's palpable enthusiasm for Dante makes the book a pleasure to read, but it seems at times that he is so convinced of the overwhelming power of the poetry that he thinks it unnecessary to demonstrate this power. Often he simply asserts the splendor of a particular passage, quotes it, and then moves on, leaving the reader unsure of why that specific excerpt so impresses him. Wilson refers to one lengthy quotation as "the most famous and most haunting passage in the *Inferno*," but without substantial further comment, it is difficult to determine what makes the extract particularly memorable or "haunting." While *Dante in Love* is an effective and engaging portrayal of a complex poet and his equally complex society, further examination of the artistic value and technical aspects of his poetry would make the book more accessible to readers less familiar with Dante and his works.

Presenting a detailed and layered portrait of one of the most significant poets in Western culture, *Dante in Love* is a successful exploration of the relationship between an artist and his society. Wilson places Dante and his works in a historical context that illuminates not only the significance of people and events within the poems but also the development of European literature, the origins of the Italian language, and the political machinations of the Italian city-states. Wilson's infectious love for Dante and his writings is apparent throughout, and many readers will leave this volume with an intense desire to turn to *The Divine Comedy*, whether for the first time or to renew an old acquaintance.

Robert C. Evans

Review Sources

Booklist 108, no. 3 (October 1, 2011): 16.
Kirkus Reviews 79, no. 18 (September 15, 2011): 43.
Library Journal 136, no. 13 (August 1, 2011): 100.
Publishers Weekly 258, no. 28 (July 11, 2011): 43.

Devotions

Author: Bruce Smith (b. 1946)
Publisher: University of Chicago Press (Chicago). 104 pp. $18.00
Type of work: Poetry

In the tradition of Walt Whitman, Bruce Smith's sixth collection is an expansive, celebratory portrait of the United States.

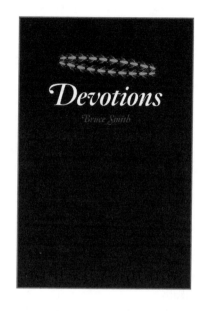

While Bruce Smith has always written in the tradition of Walt Whitman, his latest collection links him to the Whitmanesque more explicitly than ever. Some poems go so far as to directly quote Whitman's *Leaves of Grass* (1855), a collection widely considered to be one of the first masterpieces of American poetry. Both writers are interested in describing and performing the United States, using their verse to encompass the rural and the urban, the commonplace and the mystical, warfare and domestic life. Both writers proudly and sometimes defiantly write from the perspective of working-class white men, although their takes on the United States include many reasons to explore the experiences of other social groups. Smith is also a stylistic descendant of Whitman, preferring long lines and phrases that seem to tumble forward, listing as many images as possible while still maintaining the music and rhythm of verse. *Devotions* is one of the Smith's most successful books yet, having gained as much critical attention as his previous collection, *The Other Lover* (2000). It is, like its topic of the United States, firmly rooted in history and unflinchingly focused on the present, bringing the lyricism of American poetry to contemporary grounds.

One of the best ways to understand the world of *Devotions* is to look at the poems' physical settings. Verses are set in cheap motels, chain restaurants, and laundromats, beside highways and on baseball fields. While perhaps unglamorous, these are not landscapes of despair or squalor. Instead, Smith finds in them the exultation that drives the collection's music, even as he also sees the problems and challenges that America faces. As he says in "Devotion: Red Roof Inn," "The Red Roof Inn hath me in thrall. The highway sounds / like the sea in storm." The setting of the motel might seem dull and mundane, but Smith finds inspiration in it. His language even shifts; by using the archaic "hath" and comparing the modern highway to the classical image of the stormy sea, he links his own enthrallment with the spiritual and revelatory revelry of earlier poets, particularly the romantics. As he says earlier in the poem, "The remote is toxic," a pun in which he encourages the reader to find beauty and passion in what is nearest at hand, regardless of what that happens to be. Heeding this advice, Smith is able to find a moment of complex, creative inspiration in a cheap motel.

The subjects of Smith's poems vary, but they are all given the same basic treatment. Every poem in the collection is called a "devotion," a title that carries several meanings. It has a spiritual or religious resonance, devotionals being hymns that promise their singer to a god. It also implies a loving commitment, as one is devoted to a lover or partner. A devotion is a promise to never abandon something, a promise that Smith makes to a host of gritty topics (smoke, high school, a car wreck) as well as to loftier subjects like Rimbaud, Paris, and Emily Brontë's *Wuthering Heights* (1847). Such a range of topics has the effect of leveling them individually, as Smith implies the same caliber of devotion to the riffraff of modern life as to romances and literary allusions, topics more commonly found in poetry. They are all spiritually equal, Smith promising himself to them all.

Bruce Smith's The Other Lover *(2000)* *was a finalist for both the National Book Award and the Pulitzer Prize. His work has been widely anthologized and is noted especially for its portrayal of modern life in Alabama and New York State.*

(University of Chicago Press)

Smith enacts this devotion largely via form, expressing it through the long lines and lists that are present on almost every page. He explains this desire to list in "Devotion: Soup," a poem that in many ways describes the book itself:

> Wanting to use everything, wanting to be beautifully used . . .
> Rind, pith, placenta, the orts, the scourings, the skimmed
> solids, skin rotted and bruised because of you and September.
> The globe of the peach has its North America darkened, sweet,
> too sweet, and I eat it on my way to other eating, pleasure monster
> that I am.

His interest is in using every part of life, devouring the bruised side of the peach (which he equates with North America) just as he devours the rest of its flesh. By giving importance to every detail, he can more fully "engross the present" and so more fully understand the world he lives in. These lists also provide the collection's musical backbone. They are filled with repeated words, sounds, and grammar, so that "Rind, pith, placenta, the orts" is not simply a list but a line singing with subtle rhythms. Every detail is made musical and linked to every other detail, allowing Smith to see an aspect of the lyric world even in rotten food. If these gritty details are musical, musicality and beauty can likewise become gritty and unpleasant. The poem "Devotion: Hörlust" is about the pain that comes from living in a world so filled with imagery and sound. In it, the young musician Pyotr Illyich Tchaikovsky screams in his bed, trying to block out the music he hears when his mother speaks or his father rises from a chair; Smith, also, is desperate to block out "the plain / song of the mosquito, the pandemonium of car alarms." This collection overflows with sound, with long lists detailing the imagery of life. It is in this cacophony that Smith finds beauty, but it is also the very thing from which he needs relief.

While long lines and complicated grammar are Smith's usual mode, he does occasionally break away. A few poems within the collection rely on the sonnet form, rhymes, and pithy language. Poems like "Devotion: Syracuse" stand out for sparse lyric lines in which an entire stanza is devoted to the sentence "Not a siren but a dial tone." These stylistic switches offer a relief from the sometimes exhausting lists while still retaining the devotional form. Smith is just as inspired by Syracuse as by his other subjects; he simply describes it in a sparser, sadder voice.

Although Smith's focus is on the contemporary American landscape, the landscape is itself informed by other locations. Although he has never served in the armed forces himself, Smith maintains an awareness that for much of his life the United States has been involved in some form of warfare. Often, the reality of war enters the landscape in surprising ways, complicating his praise of masculine topics. The poem "Devotion: Baseball" begins by speaking fondly of the sport:

> for doing things fairly—one out of three
> swipes at the ball and a flare to right, a dying quail, a 3-
> 2 change popped up with a *shitfuck*, handcuffed, tomahawked
> the high hard stuff or took a backwards K when made to look ugly
> as we often were: Humility 3 Arrogance 1 after seven innings. And all
> America around us in the sentimental vaudeville.

Playful and celebratory in his description of the game, Smith still includes loaded language, the "handcuffed" and "tomahawked" implying violence. The depiction of America as being in "sentimental vaudeville" is also loaded, suggesting that something is insincere or exaggerated in the culture of the United States. All of this stays beneath the surface until the final line, when Smith concludes with the terse declaration that "Boys my age were dying in Khe Sanh," a reference to a famous battle in the Vietnam War. This ending is shocking for many reasons: the intrusion of Vietnam, the butting up of warfare against a game, and the contrast between the unambiguous closing statement and the exuberant, elaborate lines that come before. More than shock, however, it supplies the intellectual and emotional core of the poem. The culture and life that Smith is describing are themselves complicated, and he finds it impossible to write a poem in praise of an American sport without acknowledging the darker and more dangerous flip side of modern life.

The ability to hold both international warfare and a wholesome game within the same poem is characteristic of Smith's strengths. His devotions resist single topics in the same way they resist short lines. They include multiple, often contradictory emotions. The grandiose nature of his reach can sometimes prove exhausting, the lists piling up and the poems turning into an avalanche of phrases, but it is also the reason that he is able to witness the United States as fully as he does. He reaches freely into the legacies of American culture, comfortably moving from Emily Dickinson and

Langston Hughes to the hip-hop musician Grandmaster Flash within the same few lines. He is a white poet who regularly writes about African American cultural figures, who crafts a poem about the September 11 terrorist attacks in New York City from the perspective of his home in Alabama. While Smith's lyric strength and rhythmic ear immediately stand out, it is his insistence on taking in as much as possible that ultimately becomes the point. He rejects any easy understanding of modern life, embracing instead something sprawling and contradictory. As the poem "Devotion: Futurismo" describes,

> We entered the future backwards, not aliens, not robots,
> more like workers with dispensable shovels rising into the blasted
> new/old country, becoming the bosses of ourselves, firing ourselves,
> grumbling about the work.

The country is at once new and old, a place blasted apart where everyone is a worker tasked with making it new again. He declares us to be our own bosses, an act that both frees people and makes us our own enemy, "firing ourselves, / grumbling about the work." We are as complicated and contradictory as the culture we recreate, and Smith declares that

> my country will suffer and murmur and shit
> and go blind. The beautiful obliterating snows will drift and melt
> and freeze and ravish the surface and light will glaze the trash—
> the most meager skin made magnificent.

At once optimistic and pessimistic, the world of *Devotions* is one where trash and destruction lead to beauty. There is a promise here that even as we "shit / and go blind," we still move toward a time when "the most meager skin [will be] made magnificent." This is the promise to which Smith is devoted. He holds himself to the grit and gristle of the world and promises himself to the spirituality and redemption that must reside there. For readers who give themselves over to these sprawling lines, Smith offers a uniquely honest embrace of modern life.

T. Fleischmann

Review Sources

The New York Times Book Review, August 4, 2011, p. 16.
Publishers Weekly 258, no. 12 (March 21, 2011): 54.

Don't Shoot
One Man, a Street Fellowship,
and the End of Violence in Inner-City America

Author: David M. Kennedy (b. 1958)
Publisher: Bloomsbury (New York). 320 pp.
  $28.00
Type of work: Sociology
Time: The present
Locale: Boston and other American urban centers

A self-trained criminologist offers a possible solution to the problem of gang-related homicides in America's inner cities.

Principal personages:
DAVID KENNEDY, a self-taught criminologist
PAUL JOYCE, a police lieutenant, head of Boston's gang unit
MARK MOORE, Kennedy's school professor, who introduced Kennedy to the study of urban violence
JAMES FEALY, a police chief in High Point, North Carolina
MARTY SUMNER, a police drug-market strategist in High Point
FREDDIE CARDOZA, a gang member who received an extended jail sentence

Crime remains a major problem in contemporary America. Despite innumerable laws and billions of dollars spent on enforcement, many citizens still feel they are not safe, as daily news reports bombard viewers with stories of lawlessness. Although certain types of crime, such as identity theft, are on the rise, murder rates have slowly dwindled over the past few decades. Most Americans are safer today than they were thirty years ago. However, one segment of America's population faces a different reality. Young black men living in poor urban environments, where drugs and guns are commonplace, confront shockingly high murder rates that seem to inch higher every year. This world provides the backdrop and the research group of David Kennedy's provocative book *Don't Shoot: One Man, a Street Fellowship, and the End of Violence in Inner-City America.* Kennedy's story underscores the need for the continual reevaluation of policing practices and the need to forge bonds of respect between law enforcement, criminals, and the noncombatants who reside in urban zones terrorized by violence.

Kennedy's involvement with crime happened by accident. While writing case studies for public policy faculty at Harvard University's Kennedy School of Government in the early 1980s, he became involved in a sweeping investigation of police practices. Although originally tasked with writing field reports, Kennedy soon found himself heading down a path that would dramatically change his future plans. Before long, the author was visiting the Nickerson Gardens housing project in Los Angeles, which adjoined the notorious Compton neighborhood, a location considered by many experts as "ground zero" of the crack epidemic. What he saw in this and other drug-infested urban communities caused Kennedy to ultimately change both his career path and his views on law enforcement. He traveled to the poorest neighborhoods of Houston, Texas; New York City; Washington, DC; and many locations in between. Each community had a problem with young men killing other young men, and likewise, each community contained an overwhelming majority that did not break the law. As Kennedy saw it, the senseless loss of life in poor black neighborhoods, in conjunction with the scores of innocents picked off in gang cross fire, created a climate in which men expected to die young, while those not involved in the city's nightly gunplay lived in fear that either they or their loved ones would be the next victims.

Urban violence is not a new phenomenon, but criminologists agree that the emergence of crack cocaine did much to foster the disdain for life found among small groups of lawbreakers in poor neighborhoods. At times, Kennedy makes claims that may seem contradictory regarding the deleterious consequences of the drug. Early in the book, he proffers the theory that the government misrepresented the threat posed by crack, exaggerating its dangers and targeting all those associated with the drug, even common users, a tactic Kennedy deems fruitless. Several pages later, he labels the drug as the principal culprit in the nation's mounting youth homicide rates, supporting the notion that crack often catalyzes large urban drug markets, which in turn become hot zones for homicide. How can crack cocaine's consequences be exaggerated if the drug is so clearly linked to the issues Kennedy describes?

These inconsistencies aside, Kennedy, along with his criminal justice cohorts and almost all the law enforcement officials who assisted in the investigation, believe that the best way to combat urban crime is to alter policing patterns. In its most basic form, the Harvard study revealed that all crime, even violent crime, tends to decline when law enforcement officers are a visible presence in a neighborhood. When patrolmen walk the same beat every day, they become a part of the community, making people feel safer and encouraging those who want violence-free streets to give them tips regarding illegal activity. Kennedy does not dismiss the notion that strained race relations play a role in the distrust of the police found in many black communities and the similar attitudes toward perpetrators found in local precinct houses. He does, however, present a far more complimentary picture of law enforcement than one would expect, given the current tendency to sensationalize rogue police officers. Most law enforcement agents care about the communities they work in and are genuinely trying to make things better. African Americans are disproportionately stopped by police, Kennedy asserts, not because all cops are racist, but because poor blacks tend to live in locations where violent crime is most prevalent. Racism certainly plays a role in how the nation's drug problem is portrayed and often how it is attacked, but racism is not the cause of the violence.

Despite the evidence that Kennedy and his associates gathered, few communities embraced their conclusions. Violent crime continued to mount. In a pose that is

(Bloomsbury Publishing Plc)

David M. Kennedy is a professor of criminal justice at John Jay College and director of the Center for Crime Prevention and Control. He served for over a decade at Harvard's Kennedy School, where he worked as a consultant for local, state, and federal agencies.

often affected throughout the book, Kennedy found himself worked into a state of "desperation" as his possible solution to urban violence went ignored. Becoming a one-man agent for change, he refused to let the lessons go to waste. Most criminologists miss the boat, Kennedy argues, but many in the law-enforcement community already understand the forces that produce most urban homicides. Drugs such as crack help support local strongmen, who control drug distribution in a specific territory through gang activity. Despite the perceived prevalence of crime in areas where murder rates are highest, only a small minority is responsible for most homicides. More importantly, the criminals behind the shootings are on the radar of local police and evade arrest only because they have underlings who do most of the dirty work. The communities directly impacted by the violence are filled with good people who want nothing more than to live free of fear.

With these factors highlighted, Kennedy advances a solution that the establishment, which has tried everything from massive incarceration to crackdowns on all offenders, even minor ones, has overlooked for decades. The communities directly or indirectly involved in the violence merely need to sit down and talk—a seemingly simple solution to what has been described as a complex and unsolvable problem. Kennedy has reduced one of the great law enforcement mysteries of the modern era to its simplest terms. He states with certainty that his theory, based on its proven track record and if implemented exactly as he describes it, is more aptly defined as a law. Based on his extensive interaction with gang members, he believes that rational decisions inform their actions, and a rational person, if confronted with logic, will chose the correct path.

Armed with twenty years of investigation and research, Kennedy came to the attention of the Boston police department, which was struggling in the mid-1990s to thwart the proliferation of urban homicides. In what was known as Operation Ceasefire, gang leaders were called to a town-hall meeting in which they and their cohorts could engage in dialogue with law enforcement officers and community members. This was no ordinary civilian give-and-take session. Law enforcement officers made it clear that they were about to embrace a zero-tolerance policy for all crimes if the violence did not cease. Even small violations would result in extensive prison terms. At these gatherings, employment counselors were often on hand to guide young gang members toward legal means of making money, while community workers reiterated the police's mantra that if the violence continued, so would the pressure and so would the extended prison sentences. As Kennedy argues, the "rational" gang leaders called off their wars with rival gangs when faced with the prospect of lifetime in prison.

When word spread of Kennedy's success with the notorious Vamp Hill Kings gang, his services were requested in other blood-soaked Boston neighborhoods, with similar results. Murder was going down across the city, and Ceasefire was soon heralded as the Boston Miracle, a term Kennedy despises for its implication that something other than hard work led to the gang cease-fires. Taking the basic principles utilized in Boston, Kennedy expanded the program in an effort to dismantle the drug markets that destroyed the social fabric of communities. His mantra is simple: "Don't hurt people." Success followed most of his initiatives, while he promptly dismisses his program's failings as the fault of short-sighted bureaucrats or others with conflicting interests.

Evidence suggests that when it comes to gang-related violence, Kennedy's strategy is an effective one. As for his system's applicability to other crimes, the verdict is still out. So long as there continues to be a demand for drugs, such street bazaars will remain. A program like Ceasefire might convince leading dealers to stop selling in certain ravaged neighborhoods, but the likelihood remains that these operations will simply relocate elsewhere. The problem may disappear in one portion of the city only to reemerge in another. Although Kennedy dismisses the need for cracking down on drug abusers, the cautious citizen would be wise to pause before embracing this philosophy. Many addicts can sustain their habits without resorting to crime—discounting, of course, the initial purchase and possession—but other users are not so adept, and it is this latter group that will commit the burglaries and armed robberies that send communities into panic. Users are inherently irrational, at least while under the influence, a fact that strains a critical premise of Kennedy's crime-prevention paradigm. If a criminal is not rational, then efforts at convincing said criminal with logic will yield imperfect results.

No theory is flawless, and when it comes to something like violent crime, no theory should be dismissed without being given a fair test. Skeptics might find Kennedy's assertions impossible to believe, but it is hard to deny that he has found success in many locations. Perhaps Kennedy's word is not the last on the subject. Still, if his program works, to one degree or another, it should be implemented posthaste. It is imperative that America transform its urban war zones back into the peaceful communities they once were and the majority of their inhabitants wish them to be again. *Don't Shoot* offers a road map that just might make this happen.

Keith M. Finley

Review Sources

The Boston Globe, September 30, 2011 (Web).
New Republic, October 6, 2011 (Web).
Seattle Times, October 1, 2011 (Web).
The Washington Post, November 18, 2011 (Web).

The Drop

Author: Michael Connelly (b. 1956)
Publisher: Little, Brown (New York).
   400 pp. $27.99
Type of work: Novel
Time: The present
Locale: Los Angeles, California

The seventeenth entry of the Harry Bosch police procedural series follows the detective on a baffling cold case and an apparent suicide, two cases that present a multitude of political implications.

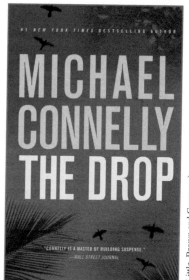

(Little, Brown and Company)

Principal characters:

HIERONYMUS "HARRY" BOSCH, a sixty-one-year-old single parent and homicide detective who has served with the Los Angeles Police Department (LAPD) for three decades

DAVID CHU, a former member of the LAPD Asian Gangs Unit and Harry's current partner

KIZMIN "KIZ" RIDER, a friend of Bosch and former partner, now a lieutenant in a public relations role with the Office of the Chief of Police

IRVIN IRVING, a seventy-year-old former LAPD officer and old nemesis of Bosch, now a member of the city council

GEORGE IRVING, Irvin's forty-eight-year-old son, a former police officer and lobbyist, who is found dead outside the Chateau Marmont Hotel

DEBORAH IRVING, George's attractive, blonde, forty-something widow

MADDIE BOSCH, Harry Bosch's fifteen-year-old daughter, who has aspirations of following her father into law enforcement

CLAYTON PELL, a twenty-nine-year-old felon connected to a 1989 cold case

DR. HANNAH STONE, an attractive divorcée in her mid-forties employed as the rehabilitation program director of a Buena Vista halfway house

CHILTON "CHILL" AARON HARDY JR., a suspect in the cold case murder

Since the introduction of Hieronymus "Harry" Bosch in Michael Connelly's *The Black Echo* (1992), readers have come to learn a great deal about the LAPD homicide detective. He is the illegitimate son of a high-powered attorney and a murdered prostitute and the half brother of the slick, Los Angeles lawyer Mickey Haller, the hero of another popular Connelly series. Having spent his childhood in orphanages and foster homes, Bosch ran away as a teenager to join the US military and serve as a tunnel rat in the Vietnam War. During his three-decade career with the police, Bosch has often come

(Little, Brown and Company)

Michael Connelly is the best-selling author of the Harry Bosch and Mickey Haller detective series. His first entry in the Bosch series, The Black Echo *(1992), won the Edgar Award for Best First Novel. His award-winning novels have sold more than forty million copies worldwide and have been translated into dozens of languages. His novels* Blood Work *(1998) and* The Lincoln Lawyer *(2005) have been adapted for film.*

into conflict with authority, likewise during his brief retirement from the department, when he worked as a private eye. Faithful readers know all the trivia: that Bosch has been shot in the line of duty, that he is left-handed, that he has a tattoo, that he is a jazz fan, and that he lives in a stilted house on Woodrow Wilson Drive. Most of all, readers know that Bosch is wholly dedicated to his profession and works by a simple credo, "Everybody counts or nobody counts." To Bosch, all victims of murder deserve the same high level of commitment from the law enforcement, regardless of race, religion, national origin, profession, or social status. He speaks for the dead whose voices have been stilled. He is savvy, thorough, and relentless in his pursuit of the guilty, and *The Drop* continues Bosch's single-minded quest for justice for the victims of violent crime.

The novel opens to find Bosch as a member of the LAPD Open-Unsolved Unit, but he soon learns that thanks to the Deferred Retirement Option Plan (DROP), he has just thirty-nine more months of service before he must face mandatory retirement. Not surprisingly, Bosch wants to make the most of his remaining time. He and partner David Chu receive their monthly unsolved assignment, a seemingly botched cold case from 1989, wherein forensic evidence connects convicted felon Clayton Pell, eight years old at the time of the crime, with the rape and murder by strangulation of Lily Price, a nineteen-year-old student. Bosch and Chu have just begun to investigate the unusual case when Bosch is ordered to take over a new, high-profile and high-priority case in Hollywood. George Irving, the son of Bosch's longtime nemesis Irvin Irving, the former assistant police chief and current city councilman, has been found dead. Despite his animosity for Bosch, Councilman Irving respects the detective's integrity and persistence, and he demands Bosch lead the investigation. Did George Irving accidentally fall? Did he jump? Or was he pushed from the seventh floor of the posh Chateau Marmont to the sidewalk below? Whatever the eventual conclusion, Bosch knows that the Irving case is fraught with "high jingo," police slang for a situation that, no matter how it turns out, will present political and public relations problems for the department. Regardless of these consequences, Bosch takes full charge of the investigation, ordering the grumbling detectives Solomon and Glanville, nicknamed "Crate & Barrel" for their blocky physiques, to conduct canvasses of hotel guests and neighboring residences while he and Chu interview the surviving family members and acquaintances of the dead man.

Facing constant pressure from police and political hierarchies, Bosch continues to explore the cold case and investigate the death of George Irving simultaneously, sometimes doing so in concert with Chu and sometimes leaving his young partner in the dark. As in the best Connelly mysteries, these cases take multiple twists and turns, as Bosch follows false leads, dead ends, mistaken information, and incorrect assumptions, all the while spiraling slowly closer to the truth. He learns that George was more a fixer, bagman, and influence peddler than a lobbyist, and he also learns that George had enemies. With his father's assistance, George had used devious methods to help a taxicab company establish a lucrative franchise in Hollywood at the expense of another cab company, whose drivers had been routinely picked up for driving while intoxicated in order to discredit their bid for service. Bosch learns that George's supposedly ideal life was not so happy and that his wife of twenty years was planning to leave him. The death, which appeared to be a simple suicide at first, then an accident, begins to look more and more like a homicide. In the course of the investigation, Bosch is startled to discover that Chu, angered at his lone-wolf tactics, has been providing inside information about the progress of the Irving case to a reporter with whom he has a sexual relationship. Bosch decides that once the current cases have been completed, he and Chu will be finished as partners.

Meanwhile, the cold case from 1989 begins to take shape as well. Clayton Pell, a homosexual and a pedophile whose blood was found on the murder victim, reminisces about his troubled and brutalized youth at the advice of his psychological therapist, Dr. Hannah Stone. Pell reveals that as a boy he was frequently beaten with a belt by a man named Johnny, a sadist who lived with his prostitute mother. This revelation accounts for the discrepancy of the forensic evidence: Pell's blood, drawn during Johnny's whippings, was transferred to Lily Price from the belt, which was used on her as a ligature. As a search begins for the mysterious Johnny, Bosch and Dr. Stone, having become attracted to one another, begin a tentative romantic relationship. Fans of Connelly's previous mysteries need not worry that the romance will distract from the investigation, as Connelly leads his hero ever closer to the elusive killer, who may be responsible for additional murders. By the conclusion, major issues have been resolved, though a few narrative threads—Bosch's new romance, the conflict between Bosch and Councilman Irving, and the wounded relationship of Bosch and Chu—are left dangling, in all likelihood to serve as lures for the next entry in the series.

The Drop is a worthy and satisfying addition to the best-selling, award-winning Harry Bosch series and a step-up from Connelly's less-admired recent novels. Realistic in its depiction of the techniques and protocol of homicide investigations, the behind-the-scenes political infighting, and the social issues at play in Los Angeles, the suspenseful novel is smoothly and confidently written, even as it delights in police acronyms and jargon—readers are sure to note how frequently Connelly uses such phrases as "high jingo." A former crime reporter, Connelly has an uncanny ability to capture the imagination at the very beginning and hold the reader's attention throughout, presenting and then unraveling, strand by strand, knotty cases that offer no easy solutions. The author's crisp and relatively unadorned prose delineates fully rounded and complex characters that speak as living, breathing people and exhibit the full range of qualities to which real humans are subject: pettiness, jealousy, ambition, lust, hatred, fear, guilt, and greed. As is the case in previous entries in the Bosch series, the roadblocks to justice are often petty, and even more often they are rooted in the bureaucracy of the police establishment itself. Part of the appeal of Bosch's character is his willingness to fight his own system in the pursuit of justice, and this quality is certainly on display here.

The novel's title resonates on several levels. "Drop" refers not only to the acronym of the police retirement program, or the manner of George Irving's death. The word also relates to trumpeter-singer and drug addict Chet Baker, one of Bosch's favorite jazz musicians; Bosch has mystery writer John Harvey's poem about Baker hanging on a wall in his home. Baker himself fell to his death under mysterious circumstances in Amsterdam, Netherlands, in 1988.

Much to the chagrin of fans, *The Drop* foreshadows the potential conclusion of the Bosch series, hinted at in the detective's impending forced retirement. However, in the fictional world, such an end can be delayed indefinitely. For compensation, readers can turn to the author's other series, such as the Mickey Haller series, which began in 2005 with *The Lincoln Lawyer*, or they can watch for further entries in the Jack McEvoy series, which started in 1996 with *The Poet*. Connelly has indicated in interviews that in the future he could continue writing about his iconic detective in any of a variety of ways. The possibilities include having Bosch investigate crimes out-of-state or taking the series back in time to focus on crimes from earlier in Bosch's career. Much like the popular Inspector Wallender series by Swedish crime author Henning Mankell, Connelly has even suggested that he may pass the investigative baton on to Maddie, Bosch's daughter, thus initiating a Bosch series for a new and younger generation.

Jack Ewing

Review Sources

Booklist 108, no. 5 (November 1, 2011): 26.
Entertainment Weekly, no. 1183 (December 2, 2011): 10–11.
Kirkus Reviews 79, no. 20 (October 15, 2011): 1860–61.
USA Today, December 8, 2011, p. D6.
The Wall Street Journal, September 9, 2011, p. D5.

A Drop of the Hard Stuff

Author: Lawrence Block (b. 1938)
Publisher: Little, Brown (New York).
  336 pp. $25.99
Type of work: Novel
Time: 1980s and 2010s
Locale: New York City

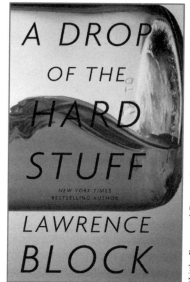

(Little, Brown and Company)

In the seventeenth entry in the Scudder crime series, private investigator Matthew Scudder tells the story of his childhood friend and reflects on how their lives were entwined despite their being on opposite sides of the law.

Principal characters:
MATTHEW SCUDDER, a retired police officer turned private investigator and a recovering alcoholic
MICK BALLOU, a former gangster and the current proprietor of a bar in Hell's Kitchen
JACK ELLERY, Scudder's childhood friend, a career criminal and an alcoholic with two years of sobriety
JAN KEANE, Scudder's girlfriend
JIM FABER, Scudder's Alcoholics Anonymous (AA) sponsor
GREGORY STILLMAN, Ellery's AA sponsor

With its opening line of dialogue, "I've often wondered how it would all have gone if I'd taken a different turn," *A Drop of the Hard Stuff* begins its exploration of the roles of destiny and choice in people's lives. Sitting in a gentrified bar in Hell's Kitchen, two aging friends—Matthew Scudder, a former police officer turned private investigator, and Mick Ballou, a former gangster turned respectable bar owner—muse about the turns in their lives and wonder what they would be like had they had made different choices. Recalling a childhood friend, Scudder tells the story of low-end career criminal Jack Ellery and how their paths diverged and crossed through the years as their choices played out.

    After parting many years earlier as children, Scudder and Ellery first cross paths again in the early 1970s when Scudder, a detective with the New York City Police Department (NYPD), sees Ellery as a suspect in a police lineup. Ellery walks free after the crime victim fails to identify him and it is several years until they meet again. By this time, Scudder is no longer on the police force and he spends his days wandering from AA meeting to AA meeting, occasionally doing detective work as favors for others. He meets Ellery, now an ex-convict and an alcoholic, at an AA meeting. While

Scudder has less than a year of sobriety under his belt and is taking it one day at a time, Ellery has been in the program longer and is actively going through AA's twelve-step program. He possesses what Scudder lacks: confidence, conviction, and the determination to make amends to those he wronged in the past.

Scudder has no strong desire to reconnect with his old acquaintance, but has no reason to avoid Ellery either. They run into each other at occasional meetings until one week when Scudder misses several telephone calls from Ellery. They never get the chance to speak because the next time Scudder sees Ellery, he is a corpse on a slab in the morgue, having been shot once in the forehead and once in the mouth. Curious, but not curious enough to investigate further, Scudder is willing to leave the unsolved murder alone until he is approached by Gregory Stillman, Ellery's sponsor. Stillman fears that Ellery was killed in the process of fulfilling AA's ninth step: making amends. Ellery made a list of those he had wronged and Stillman suspects that someone on that list is the killer. He hires Scudder to either eliminate suspects from the list or provide potential names to the police. Scudder reluctantly accepts this task and begins to investigate those who Ellery had wronged. As more bodies begin to turn up, Scudder takes on the task of finding the murderer himself as he traces Ellery's quest for atonement.

Moving at a slow pace, the story shifts between the search for the killer and the more immediate and pressing needs in Scudder's life: staying sober, resisting temptation, and maintaining his equilibrium. Just a year or so out of the NYPD, Scudder is adrift and his current path is uncertain; he has yet to make a career of being a private investigator, while his relationship with his girlfriend, Jan, is unstable and he does not know what he wants from it. He envisions the future with equal amounts of anticipation and fear.

Scudder's life is marred by such contradictions, fraught with doubt and the uneasy feeling that he is doing something wrong. He happily envisions a future with Jan one minute and dreads the sameness of such a future the next, wondering if that is all his life will amount to. After his girlfriend breaks up with him, Scudder is filled with both relief and a sense of betrayal, saying, "I didn't know whether I wanted to thank her or kill her."

Scudder's ambivalence hangs like a miasma over his life, but he never gives in to despair. He concentrates on what is within his reach and lives by the mantra of his sponsor, Jim Faber: "One day at a time." Block captures the tension of Scudder's inner struggle with the endless rounds of AA meetings, talks with Faber, and empty nights. With minimal action and sparse dialogue, the story focuses not on the interaction between the characters or on a series of events but on what is happening within Scudder. His internal dialogue and inner conflicts dominate the story, while the mysterious murders serve as a backdrop for his personal journey.

While some critics found this book less appealing than earlier installments in the series, others commended its themes of redemption and transformation. Although lacking in action, the novel still has plenty to say. Block has moved his story away from actual events and toward what lies behind them, examining what makes one person become a cop and the other a criminal and whether there is that much difference between the two. When Scudder recalls his wrongdoings in law enforcement, he does not use the good he did to justify them. He acknowledges that he stayed out of prison but does not assume any moral superiority for doing so. Like Ellery, he has his own amends to make. He knows that the line between right and wrong can be blurred and that the differences between people are not always clear cut. He thinks that he is different from Ellery, but is he really, and in what way? Are these differences the result of conscious decisions or of factors beyond their control?

Scudder does not have these answers, and his search for them is ultimately more important than his search for Ellery's killer. *A Drop of the Hard Stuff* is a story about the course of a life and how it is determined. It is a story about two boys from the same neighborhood who grew into men living on opposite sides of the law. It is a story about fate and chance and how forces can shape a person. But it is also a story about the need to make decisions and take action rather than submit to fate.

For Scudder, these ever-present philosophical musings run parallel to his search for the killer. Over and over again, he contemplates the role destiny plays in life and whether de-

(Little, Brown and Company)

Lawrence Block has received many awards for his contributions to detective fiction, including the Lifetime Achievement Award from the Private Eye Writers of America in 2002 and the Diamond Dagger from the Crime Writers of America in 2004. He was named a Grand Master of the Mystery Writers of America in 1994.

cisive action makes a difference. Block captures this inner debate through terse dialogue that illustrates Scudder's state of mind: "Maybe I'd call Redmond, I thought, and maybe I wouldn't. I couldn't see that it made much difference either way."

In embarking on his search for Ellery's killer, Scudder begins to resolve his own inner conflicts. He refuses to cede control of his life to fate and determines that action, regardless of its outcome or effectiveness, is the option he must choose. As Stillman tells him, in the end it does not really matter who killed Ellery. The fact that Scudder does everything possible to find out—that he takes action, not where that action leads—is what is important.

A Drop of the Hard Stuff is a masterpiece of character study. Block is at his finest in creating intimate and realistic portrayals of his characters. His characterization of Scudder captures the egocentrism of every human without portraying Scudder as a self-centered, arrogant individual. His characters and their relationships are full of contradictions, deftly depicting real people who are multifaceted and flawed. The plot lacks the drama of many detective thrillers, but it captures the reality of ordinary life with its lulls, mundane activities, and occasional moments of excitement. By the time readers finish the novel, they know Matt Scudder well.

This novel will also resonate with readers familiar with AA, not so much for its references to the organization's tenets, but for its careful depiction of what it is like to face addiction and the demons that accompany it. Familiarity with AA is no prerequisite, though. Any reader who has struggled with an inner dilemma will find much to identify with in Matt Scudder's tale of his first year of sobriety.

The flashback format of the story allows readers to eventually learn the outcome of Ellery's mystery and the identity of the killer. It also provides some resolution to Scudder's struggle with alcohol within the context of both *A Drop of the Hard Stuff* and the series as a whole. The older Scudder telling the story to Mick Ballou in a bar is comfortable and relaxed, at ease with the world, though he still ponders the roles that choice and destiny play in his life. Both new readers and longtime fans of Matt Scudder will enjoy this book, the newest entry in the series after a lull of six years.

Barbara C. Lightner

Review Sources

Booklist 107, no. 13 (March 1, 2011): 31.
Kirkus Reviews 79, no. 4 (February 15, 2011): 259.
Library Journal 135, no. 20 (December 1, 2010): 84.
Library Journal 136, no. 1 (January 1, 2011): 80.
The New York Times Book Review, May 20, 2011, p. 22.
Publishers Weekly 258, no. 10 (March 7, 2011): 41.
The Wall Street Journal, May 7, 2011 (Web).

The Eichmann Trial

Author: Deborah E. Lipstadt (b. 1947)
Publisher: Schocken (New York). 272 pp.
$24.95
Type of work: History
Time: Twentieth century
Locale: Mostly Jerusalem, Israel

Lipstadt provides an account and analysis of the 1961 trial in Jerusalem that brought SS Lieutenant Colonel Adolf Eichmann to justice.

Principal personages:
ADOLF EICHMANN (1906–1962), a German Nazi charged with facilitating the transport of Jews to extermination camps during the Holocaust
GIDEON HAUSNER (1915–1990), the Israeli attorney general who headed the prosecution
HANNAH ARENDT (1906–1975), a German American journalist and critic, the author of *Eichmann in Jerusalem*
DAVID IRVING (b. 1938), a British historian discredited for racism and anti-Semitism
DAVID BEN-GURION (1886–1973), Israel's first prime minister

In the introduction of Deborah Lipstadt's *The Eichmann Trial*, a new contribution to twentieth-century Jewish history, the author remembers back to fifty years earlier, when she watched the televised trial. Dinner had been timed so that her family could watch news clips from Jerusalem. Thirteen years old at the time, Lipstadt was "intrigued that something so profoundly connected with Jews had been featured so prominently" as to be the lead story in the day's *New York Times*. The trial entered Lipstadt's life at a time when, according to her, she was naive about the world, believing it simply divided into Jews and non-Jews. She would later pursue the subject of the Holocaust in her book *Denying the Holocaust: The Growing Assault on Truth and Memory* (1993), which would provoke a libel suit from one of its principal targets, the British historian and well-known Holocaust denier David Irving. Many were shocked by the absurdity of a denier suing a historian, including many Holocaust survivors, who approached Lipstadt and sent "notes, letters, and copies of their books," begging her to "stand up for us."

The British press drew parallels between the libel trial and the Eichmann trial, which eventually led Lipstadt to write on the subject of Adolf Eichmann. As part of her defense, she asked for the release of Eichmann's memoir, which the Israeli government had kept since his execution. Lipstadt intended to use the memoir only to argue her case, but she soon began comparing what she was experiencing with what

Deborah E. Lipstadt is the Dorot Professor of modern Jewish history and Holocaust studies at Emory University. She won the National Book Award for History on Trial: My Day in Court with David Irving *(2006). Her other books include* Beyond Belief: The American Press and the Coming of the Holocaust, 1933–1945 *(1986) and* Denying the Holocaust: The Growing Assault on Truth and Memory *(1993).*

happened in Jerusalem in 1961. Adolf Eichmann had facilitated the murder of one-third of the world's Jewish population, while David Irving had dedicated himself to denying the whole matter. In both cases, survivors wished to communicate their true stories.

From the response of historians to Lipstadt's legal battle to her decision to explore what transpired in Jerusalem years before, this history covers a wide range of perspectives, both personal and historical.

The book considers the dramatic newspaper accounts of Prime Minister David Ben-Gurion's announcement on May 23, 1960, that war criminal Adolf Eichmann was under arrest in Israel. Eichmann had been captured once before but had escaped to Argentina; Lipstadt recounts his second arrest, including details about how his Israeli captors drugged Eichmann and dressed him in a phony El Al uniform to get him out of the country. She describes the controversy surrounding the abduction in terms of diplomatic relations between Israel and Argentina, including a barrage of anti-Semitic attacks on Argentina's Jewish community, despite both countries being part of the United Nations. Debates ensued about where the trial should be held, some arguing for Germany over Israel, as the trial was for international crimes against humanity, not against Jews exclusively.

Lipstadt recounts how the legal team was assembled and the location selected. Although an interrogator was assigned, Eichmann spoke freely, declaring himself prepared to say anything he knew of all events, even offering to hang himself "in public as a deterrent example for future anti-Semites of all the countries on earth." Yet Eichmann declined to acknowledge personal guilt, claiming he was just a "little cog" and "exclusively a carrier out of orders." He bemoaned that he was too loyal to his superiors, while "those who planned, decided, directed, and ordered the thing have escaped responsibility." The book goes on to include many humanizing touches that suggest how his interrogators and kidnappers felt about him. They reported surprise at finding him little, meek, and balding, not a powerful, intimidating Nazi. The man hardly seemed capable of murdering millions, as he was afraid to do anything without permission, wore dentures, cowered, and acted compliantly.

Lipstadt relays Eichmann's history, portraying him as a young man who worked for an oil company in Austria and, lacking any deep anti-Semitic sentiments, became involved with the Nazi party only circumstantially. After losing his job, he lied to Nazi officials that his termination was due to his party membership. He was only a "weekend Nazi," on call for street brawls with anyone who denigrated national socialism. In short, he was a thug. Subsequently, he was put to work monitoring Jewish organizations and told to study Zionist organizations. These materials and more were used in the charges against him, including the charge of facilitating the murder of millions of Jews and Gypsies, as well as more than a half-million Polish non-Jews, people murdered and deported under conditions of "servitude, coercion, and terror." But when

Eichmann was ushered into the glass booth in Jerusalem, a group of reporters that included Elie Wiesel and C. L. Sulzberger had trouble believing that this normal-looking man, who even looked Jewish, could be responsible for the deaths of millions.

Next, the book focuses on the different tensions that surrounded Israel's jurisdiction in the trial. Conflict ensued regarding the language of the trial and the bulletins made available, particularly concerning why nothing was done in Yiddish, the language of Eichmann's victims. The state of Israel upheld the position that all should learn Hebrew. Eichmann's defense lawyer argued that "the court lacked jurisdiction, because these crimes were committed prior to Israel's existence, on foreign soil, and against people who had no connection to Israel." He raised the illegality of the abduction and the complication that colleagues whom Eichmann might wish to call to his defense could not enter Israel without immediately facing arrest. Finally, he questioned whether the judges, as Jews, could guarantee impartiality.

In the end, the international press was persuaded that even in Israel Eichmann could be fairly tried. Nonetheless, it took four days to reject the objections of Robert Servatius, Eichmann's lawyer. Referencing the story of Cain and Abel, as well as the Dreyfus affair of the late nineteenth century, Gideon Hausner gave his opening address, which political theorist Hannah Arendt dismissed as cheap and bad history but which left many moved. He invoked the six million accusers who could not speak:

> Now, for the first time, the Jewish people, who during the war had looked this way and that for someone to speak on their behalf, had risen, not to implore others to save them, but to prosecute. Here was a representative of the Jewish people speaking, not as a supplicant for help, but as a government for justice demanding long-delayed justice.

Although his speech got some history wrong, it was followed by the testimony of one hundred Holocaust survivors, whose concentrated stories were heard by a broad international audience. Hausner also introduced interrogation tapes in which Eichmann had freely described his experiences, introducing his own testimony into the public arena as well.

What follows is Lipstadt's account of evidence and testimony, including a number of lurid details. One letter entered as evidence contains Eichmann's boasting about the pleasure he took in controlling the Jewish community. He had been elated that they "dare not take a step without first consulting me." Witnesses of the murders of the Final Solution were also called, such as a woman who relayed how a German soldier debated in front of her whom he should shoot first, her or her child. After he shot the child, she fell into the pit where the rest of her family's bodies were, later crawling out. Lipstadt analyzes popular reactions to Hausner's questioning of survivors and the questioning itself (why did they not fight back and try to escape?). Another controversy of the trial involved Hausner including testimonies of questionable relevance, such as those of resistance fighters. Judge Moshe Landau attacked Hausner for introducing irrelevant testimony, but conflict regarding the relevance of testimonies continued throughout the trial, one example involving Eichmann's off-again on-again commitments to negotiations with Jewish national leaders.

The trial was marked by the reading of letters that had been thrown from trains bound for Auschwitz and disruptions about how family members had been murdered; at one point, even Judge Benjamin Halevi asked why a witness had not considered assassinating Eichmann. Then Eichmann took the stand, testifying that he was following orders and that documents had been altered by Nazi higher-ups to shift the blame onto him. His memory failed him on numerous charges. He was not an anti-Semite, he claimed. This was greeted with laughter. Eichmann remained oblivious to how strange many of his explanations sounded, the most incredulous being that he was "just an observer" who was supposed to keep his bosses informed. Lipstadt includes newsmagazine responses to Eichmann's testimony and the battering he underwent under Hausner's cross-examination. She also covers the battering that Hausner underwent for exploding at the witness and being rude to the defense lawyer. According to Lipstadt, the crux of the matter was that "Hausner wanted to tell the entire story of the Final Solution. They [the judges] wanted a narrowly constructed judicial proceeding that focused on Eichmann's misdeeds, whereas Hausner wanted a broad educational exercise." In spite of Eichmann's appeal and the fact that many survivors supported granting him clemency, the protests within Israel won out.

Following Lipstadt's recounting of Eichmann's execution, she then turns her attention to Hannah Arendt's *Eichmann in Jerusalem: A Report on the Banality of Evil* (1963), in which the German American Arendt critiques Israel and the relationship between Nazis and Jews. Lipstadt discusses the criticism that Arendt received for her insinuations that Zionists were collaborationists and her critique of the cooperation of Judenräte (Jewish councils), which she held responsible for the death of millions. Questioning why Arendt chose to air Jewish dirty linen in public, so to speak, Lipstadt argues that Arendt was wrong in many of her criticisms and notes that many readers "probably found her insistence that anti-Semitism was not at the heart of the Holocaust particularly appealing," as they "welcomed a universal explanation for genocide that freed them from having to grapple with the anti-Semitic legacy of a European culture they extolled." She also questions why *Eichmann in Jerusalem* was presented as a journalistic account when Arendt was not even in the courtroom during much of the trial.

Lipstadt concludes the book with an exchange she had with Rwandan survivors of genocide, who met with Holocaust survivors at Yad Vashem. She sees this bonding as the most enduring legacy of the trial, creating community and continuity between generations.

Batya Weinbaum

Review Sources

The New York Times Book Review, April 8, 2011 (Web).
NPR, March 27, 2011 (Web).
Publishers Weekly 258, no. 3 (January 17, 2011): 41.
The Washington Post, April 22, 2011 (Web).

1861
The Civil War Awakening

Author: Adam Goodheart
Publisher: Alfred A. Knopf (New York). 481 pp.
$28.95
Type of Work: History
Time: 1860–1861
Locale: South Carolina, Illinois, Washington, D.C., and various other locations in the United States

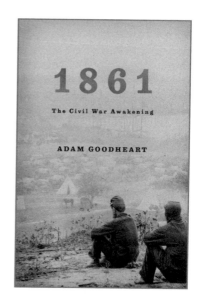

Goodheart describes events that took place during the first months of the American Civil War, primarily from the perspectives of lesser-known historical figures.

Principal personages:
ABRAHAM LINCOLN, president of the United States from 1861 to 1865
ROBERT ANDERSON, major of the Fort Sumter garrison, the target of the opening salvos of the war
ELMER ELLSWORTH, colonel of First New York Volunteer Infantry regiment (the Fire Zouaves), the first notable casualty of the war
JAMES GARFIELD, a professor and state legislator who would become a Civil War general, later president of the United States

The Civil War and Abraham Lincoln represent two of the most common subjects about which American history is written, and one might ask whether and how the latest book by Adam Goodheart differs in a significant way from those that preceded it. Goodheart's approach is to place less emphasis on the individuals who guided both the North and South through the war—Robert E. Lee, Jefferson Davis, Ulysses Grant, and of course Abraham Lincoln himself—and instead to describe the story as viewed by individuals who only later would become better known, either in their own right or with the help of historical hindsight.

Most histories of the war begin with the opening shots fired at Fort Sumter off the coast of Charleston, South Carolina. Goodheart's story begins earlier, during the fall of 1860. James Buchanan was still president, and American army garrisons under the command of Major Robert Anderson manned sites on the two major islands in Charleston Harbor: Fort Moultrie and Fort Sumter. On December 20, 1860, an ordinance was passed in Charleston that declared the secession of the state. Anderson's quandary was whether to surrender the forts to Southern forces in the city or to defend them in the event of attack. Buchanan's secretary of war, John Floyd—a Virginian,

a Southern sympathizer, and a future Con-
federate general—hinted at the forts' surrender. Instead, on the evening of December 26,
Anderson ordered the garrison at Moultrie
to spike the cannons, remove the American
flag, destroy the flagpole, and move to Fort
Sumter, where he raised the flag in defiance
of the Southerners. Goodheart points out the
symbolism of Anderson's act, the intention
of Anderson to preserve his and his men's

*Adam Goodheart is the director of Wash-
ington College's C. V. Starr Center for
the Study of the American Experience.
His written works include articles for*
Smithsonian, *the* Atlantic, National
Geographic, *and the* New York Times
Magazine. *He is a regular contributor
to the* New York Times' Civil War series,
Disunion.

honor, and how he inadvertently set in motion events that culminated in the first shots
of the war originating from the South.

Rather than simply presenting events taking place during the first months of the war
in chronological order, the manner in which most histories are described, Goodheart
has written each chapter to describe the impact of slavery on lesser-known individuals.
For example, in the first chapter, entitled "Wide Awake," Goodheart presents the story
of Ralph Farnham. At 104 years old, Farnham had been present at the Battle of Bunker
Hill in Boston in 1775. While he did not actively participate in that battle, subsequent
writers embellished his story such that, in their versions, he all but won it single-handedly. Farnham had been present at one revolution and was now witness to a second.

Goodheart expands the story to include events taking place far from Farnham's
Boston as well. He describes conditions in Texas, where drought and fires fed the hate
that resulted in the lynching of both African Americans and whites perceived to support abolition. Meanwhile, that November, Lincoln was elected president. The chapter
closes by noting that on the same day newspapers reported the story of Anderson's
move from Moultrie to Sumter, they also reported the death of Ralph Farnham, the
last hero of Bunker Hill.

Elmer Ellsworth was typical of the young, idealistic men who enlisted following
Lincoln's call for volunteers to suppress the South's rebellion. Twenty-four years old
at the onset of the conflict, Ellsworth was born in upstate New York into a struggling
family. As a boy, he spent much of his spare time playing soldier and building forts,
likely inspired by the nearby military academy at West Point. Eventually, he moved to
Chicago and joined a local militia, in which his leadership qualities resulted in rapid
advancement. While there, he also met a French fencing instructor who had served
with the elite French Zouaves during the Crimean War. Ellsworth quickly became
proficient as a fencer and gymnast, adding to his ability as a drill instructor for a sixty-
man unit called the Chicago Zouaves. Following the fall of Fort Sumter, Ellsworth
mobilized a group of recruits into a New York Volunteer Infantry Regiment of Fire
Zouaves, with himself as the colonel, and went looking for a fight.

Unfortunately, reality dispelled any romantic notions Ellsworth might have had
about the fight. After Virginia seceded in May 1861, Northern troops, including those
led by Ellsworth, crossed the Potomac River into Alexandria, Virginia. While leading
a small contingent into the town, Ellsworth observed a rebel flag flying from the top
of a local tavern. He climbed to the roof and pulled down the flag, but was shot by the

tavern owner, a secessionist named James Jackson, while he was coming down the stairs. Jackson was himself was shot immediately after. Ellsworth and Jackson—one a Northerner, the other a Southerner—became two of the first casualties of the war.

Goodheart continues his description of events during the early months of 1861 by depicting Lincoln's travels through the Midwest from his home in Springfield, Illinois, on the way to Washington. In the months immediately following Lincoln's election, President James Buchanan appeared to deal with the crisis of secession largely by doing nothing. Those who had voted for Lincoln the previous November were looking for a decisive leader who would know how to address the impending crisis. Yet, during this period, Lincoln was clearly still unsure how to deal with the events rapidly unfolding. This was not the decisive Lincoln whom history would later remember as president; he seemed almost unable to grasp the seriousness of the situation. Goodheart provides excerpts from the president-elect's speeches, in particular one delivered in Columbus, Ohio, in which Lincoln seemingly ignores both the financial implications of a possible war and even the very existence of a growing rebel army in the South.

Among the dignitaries who met with Lincoln in Columbus was James Garfield, a young state senator and a college professor at Western Reserve Eclectic Institute. Here, Goodheart intersperses his discussion of Lincoln with a biography of Garfield, a man on the rise in the Republican Party. Like Lincoln, Garfield was born in a log cabin. Both men had parents who participated in the western migrations during the nineteenth century, though a generation apart. Garfield's views were significantly divergent from those in the mainstream population. He supported abolishing the death penalty, supported women's rights, and, in a vote that could easily have ended his political career, voted against a bill that would outlaw interracial marriage.

Garfield's education included the study of both the Old and New Testaments, Greek and Roman classics, geology texts, and Charles Darwin's controversial book *On the Origin of Species* (1859). He had the opportunity to present his views at an Independence Day picnic on July 4, 1860, during which he compared the United States to the sea, noting that both are in constant motion and undergoing constant change. Individual freedom would be the driving force of this constant change within the country. Lincoln himself appeared to Garfield as an exemplar of this change: the dynamic leader of a new generation, addressing the issue of slavery.

Garfield was no radical on the issue of slavery; he had even forbidden abolitionists from holding a rally on the Institute campus. He was convinced, however, that while slavery would eventually disappear, it would only end with the shedding of blood. His views gradually became more radicalized in the months after Lincoln's election; he slowly developed the notion that evolution applied not only to Darwin's finches but also to the divergence of the North and South as well. The attack on Fort Sumter would settle the issue for Garfield, as it would for most Northerners: the country would have no choice but to go to war.

As March came to a close, Lincoln realized that war was inevitable. The question remained of how to address the issue of Fort Sumter. Here, Goodheart provides an example of how Lincoln maneuvered and manipulated the South into becoming the aggressor. The president notified South Carolina governor Francis Pickens of his intent to resupply the fort with provisions, not arms, knowing this would be refused and would likely result in hostilities.

The ploy worked. An hour before dawn on April 12, batteries around Charleston began firing on Sumter; the war had begun. The siege was unlike any in history. The two commanders—Major Robert Anderson in the fort and General Pierre Beauregard in Charleston—had been friends since their days at West Point, and Beauregard had even studied under Anderson. Prior to the bombardment, Beauregard had sent Anderson cigars and brandy. The nine officers at the fort presented an interesting contrast, something Goodheart takes pains to point out. Major Anderson was a Kentuckian like Lincoln, but, unlike the president, he was a supporter of slavery. By contrast, Captain Abner Doubleday from Auburn, New York, second in command in the garrison, was a strong opponent of the practice.

The cliché is that history is written by the victors. In *1861*, Goodheart has provided the story of the opening months of the Civil War largely from the perspectives of less familiar individuals, albeit those whom posterity has declared to have been on the right side of history. Their stories are important, but those who supported the South— whether because they supported the concept of slavery or because they "merely" believed their state had the right to secede—were just as idealistic and self-righteous as those they opposed. Their stories are not here.

What is here, however, is a thought-provoking and ambitious work that highlights some of the minor characters in a major chapter of American history. Though it is one among thousands of books about the Civil War, Goodheart's stands out for its intimate study of almost-forgotten, but nevertheless important, figures in the conflict's first months. Though somewhat unconventional in its structure and perhaps too narrow in its focus on the Union, *1861: The Civil War Awakening* is a notable addition to the canon of American Civil War literature.

Richard Adler

Review Sources

Booklist 107, no. 16 (April 15, 2011): 17.
Kirkus Reviews 79, no. 6 (March 15, 2011): 467.
The New York Times Book Review, April 24, 2011, p. 1.
Publishers Weekly 258, no. 9(February 28, 2011): 49.

Electric Eden
Unearthing Britain's Visionary Music

Author: Rob Young (b. 1968)
Publisher: Faber and Faber (New York).
672 pp. $25.00
Type of Work: Music, history
Time: Twentieth century
Locale: Great Britain

Young provides a historical overview of the mid-twentieth-century folk music revival in Great Britain that examines the genre's roots as well as its culture, contributors, and legacy.

Principal personages:
CECIL SHARP (1859–1924), a music collector of folk songs whose records and publications helped preserve traditional English folk music
PEGGY SEEGER (b. 1935), an American folksinger who participated in the British folk revival
EWAN MACCOLL (1915–1989), a Scottish folksinger, record producer, and cofounder of the Workers Experimental Theater
THE INCREDIBLE STRING BAND, a Scottish psychedelic folk band from 1966 to 1974
SHIRLEY COLLINS (b. 1935), a British folk singer in the 1960s and 1970s
FAIRPORT CONVENTION, an English folk rock band that formed in 1967
RICHARD THOMPSON, an English songwriter and guitarist for the folk band Fairport Convention
ALAN LOMAX (1915–2002), an American folk music collector and musicologist
NICK DRAKE (1948–1974), an English singer and songwriter
KATE BUSH (b. 1958), an English musician and music producer

In this comprehensive account of the twentieth-century British folk revival, author Rob Young examines the history of the movement and its mythical and visionary roles in changing musical expression. Young studies traditional folk music through its dalliances with electrification, drug experimentation, and phases related to mysticism and paganism. In addition to its study of the changing music itself, this sizeable text also examines the musicians as they struggled to define themselves through their lyrics, instruments, spirituality, and dress (or, in some cases, their nudity). This ambitious book is a labor of love from Young, a music journalist himself, and both his passion and his vast knowledge shine through the text.

In this meticulously researched book, Young uses pictures and other visual records to ground his often-nostalgic study in a proper historical context. These include the first page of the original script of a groundbreaking 1957 ballad by Charles Parker and Ewan MacColl, a flyer for the Singer's Club in 1961 where Peggy Seeger performed, and a 1957 handbill for a Sunday hootenanny at a music club. The collected images effectively document how distinctly British the music scene of the 1960s was. In addition to the book's visual matter, its resources also encourage readers to take the subject seriously; Young includes nineteen pages of organized notes that draw from a range of materials, such as quotations, interviews, and lectures. He also includes a bibliography and a thirteen-page musical and discographical timeline that lists recording artists, albums, and dates for significant releases, beginning with Arnold Bax's "A Celtic Song Cycle" in 1904 and ending with Richard Young's "Under Stellar Stream" in 2009.

Originally intended as a story about British folk rock's high watermark—"music born out of the battle between progressive push and nostalgic pull"—it became, as the author writes, the story of people who have treated the well of British folk tradition as "an oasis from which to refresh their own art." Young came to understand folk as only one of the many ingredients in the canon of British music and saw that it came to the forefront only when people believed that it was at risk of disappearing. Citing Karl Marx, Young reminds readers that "links in the chain of tradition have been forged by revolutionaries," and that folk is not only about remembering and preserving the past but also about the present. He notes that grasping this broader view of music led him to increase the scope of the book.

Young moves on from this ambitious statement of intent in the book's prelude and begins the first chapter with the story of recording artist Vashti Bunyan. The author sets the scene by describing a day in 1969 when Bunyan wandered through the Scottish countryside with her artist friend Robert Lewis and her dog Blue, the three of them on their way to Skye, an island with a strong folk tradition. They were off to a place where they had heard Donovan, a singer and songwriter at the height of his fame, had established a commune for artists like themselves. Having recorded some singles on various labels, Bunyan had decided to embark on a pilgrimage to Donovan's rural cottage. Inspired by Jack Kerouac's *On the Road* (1951), she and Lewis made their eighteen-month trip with a horse-drawn cart. In describing their pastoral journey, Young reflects on author William Morris and other nineteenth-century writers, noting their role in the roots of British folk music.

In his discussion of Bunyan's travels, Young also cites other wanderers, some from centuries earlier, who walked through the same settings. He includes anecdotes about musical influence, musical technique, and the musical instruments employed; he also describes the style of dress, community reception, and role of socialism in previous journeys of music collection. Young pays particular attention to musicologists such as Carl Engel in his discussions about the preservation of song and dance in rural England. He also includes an homage to laborer John England, whom he describes as the "man who inadvertently triggered the twentieth-century folk song revival" when music collector Cecil Sharp overheard him singing folk songs in his garden.

Young's writing demonstrates his respect for Sharp and his decades of work collecting English folk music. Sharp's meticulous research is evident as Young describes the process of transcribing such songs as "The Golden Glove" in 1910 or explains the

*Rob Young is a British journalist and ed-
itor-at-large for the* Wire, *an experimental music magazine. He has contributed
to numerous publications, including the*
Guardian, Jazz Times, *and* Art Review.

publication of the volumes of folk songs between 1904 and 1909. The author's text artfully depicts how the folk songs, existing in
a state of constant transformation, could be a
living example of "an art form in a perpetual
state of renewal." Young's dynamic depiction of the genre enhances readers' appre-
ciation of the later movement of artists he chronicles, including such icons as Peggy
Seeger. Seeger, half sister of singer Pete Seeger, made twenty-two solo recordings and
participated in more than one hundred collaborations; she is considered by Young to
be a voice of antiauthoritarian protest that successfully drew on Sharp's folk roots in a
different historical moment.

Having established that basis, Young shifts his narrative from the country to what
he calls the "folk rock boom," which was predominantly city based and emanated
from urban centers such as London, Birmingham, Cambridge, and Canterbury. He
analyzes song lyrics of the late 1960s, noting that they read "like a recipe for rural
enlightenment" with elemental ingredients of rivers, sun, and rain; these songs com-
plain that cities bleed the soul, and that they are inhabited by clock-watchers, losers,
squares, and The Man. This sets up Young's shift to the counterculture associated with
the movement as he discusses exploration of drugs and spiritualism.

The author explains the contributions of the Glastonbury performing arts festival
in particular. The 1971 festival—the first to include the Pyramid Stage, designed to
stimulate the earth's nervous system—is recorded in photographs that include a quintessential image of the event: a man wearing nothing but a flowered jock strap, dancing
in a field of flowers, next to a man in a posture of prayer with his hands to the sky. The
festival, financed by donations, served only vegetarian food and encouraged strangers
to break bread together with the intent of experiencing a new way of life. Subsequent
chapters of *Electric Eden* include coverage of this pageant and others. Young reproduces posters for the second Windsor Free Festival in 1973 and the Stonehenge Free
Festival from 1975 to 1984. These provide valuable records of the visual culture of the
period. Photographs of the tepees and megaliths constructed at the Stonehenge Free
Festival are valuable for recording material culture of the era.

Throughout the book, Young makes connections to classic pieces of British literature, such as the depiction of Earthly Paradise in John Donne's *Paradise Lost* (1667).
He does so to establish the connection between the unique experimental period of the
1960s and 1970s and the roots of British dominant culture. He calls upon classical
texts in British literary history that address the loss of innocence, weaving a revolutionary spin on Temptation and the Fall to establish a precedent for the extraordinary
developments of the folk era in an attempt to normalize them.

This folk era, perhaps best known for its hippie subculture, was met with a wide
variety of reactions from people both within and outside of the music industry.

In addition to connecting the folk resurgence to literature, Young also discusses its
relationship with religion. He describes the ties between Christianity and folk music,
noting how a new form of religious music resulted from the era. Young uses examples

like *A Folk Passion*, a concept album based on the last days of Christ's life, and an uncredited compilation called *Sounds of Salvation*. The latter was commissioned by the Methodist Missionary Society with the intent of being distributed at the Nineteenth General Assembly of the World Council of Churches.

Throughout *Electric Eden*, Young discusses the careers of dozens of folk artists, some better known than others. He describes early pioneers like Davey Graham, Shirley Collins, and Richard and Linda Thompson, as well as groups like Pentangle, the Incredible String Band, and Fairport Convention. He traces the participants from the movement's early days through its later iterations in the 1970s. With the swift social changes that occurred during these decades, Young is always careful to ground these artists in historical context. This allows readers to see how issues like war, politics, drugs, civil rights, and the environment changed musicians' outlooks and creativity.

The notion of creation is essential to *Electric Eden*, and Young's profound respect for, and appreciation of, these folk artists is palpable in its pages. For the artists whose work Young chronicles, creation was their tie to the earth and to the real and imaginary gardens they were cultivating. Folk music was a link to an earlier time that these artists saw as idyllic and utopian, a far cry from the increasingly turbulent urban world of the 1960s. The folk music revival began rooted in the past, eventually growing to embrace world music, drugs, and innovations like electric instruments. Though the folk revival ran parallel to another, more popular music movement, most notably exemplified by the rock-and-roll music of the Beatles, it nevertheless played a significant role in the British cultural canon.

Young's enthusiasm for music and his attention to detail make this sprawling book readable and engrossing. Despite its heft, occasional tangents and digressions, and nonlinear storytelling, readers will be entertained and educated by *Electric Eden*. More than just a critical history of the genre, Young has also created a poignant and illuminating record of an enduring folk tradition and the era it defined.

Batya Weinbaum

Review Sources

Austin Chronicle, July 15, 2011 (Web).
Driftwood Magazine, September 30, 2011 (Web).
New Statesman, August 2, 2010 (Web).
The New York Times, June 2, 2011 (Web).

11/22/63

Author: Stephen King (b. 1947)
Publisher: Scribner (New York). 864 pp.
$35.00
Type of work: Novel
Time: 1958–1963, 2011
Locale: Lisbon Falls and Derry, Maine; Jodie,
Fort Worth, and Dallas, Texas

*King conjures up an intriguing time-travel tale
about an English teacher from Lisbon Falls,
Maine, who journeys from 2011 back to 1963
in order to stop the assassination of President
John F. Kennedy.*

Principal characters:

JAKE EPPING / GEORGE AMBERSON, a high school
English teacher who has been recruited to
kill Lee Harvey Oswald
AL TEMPLETON, a terminally ill time traveler
and restaurant owner who convinces Jake to take on the task of preventing Kennedy's death
HARRY DUNNING, a high school janitor enrolled in Jake's GED class
FRANK DUNNING, Harry's father
SADIE DUNHILL, a high school librarian in 1958, Jake / George's lover
LEE HARVEY OSWALD, a Communist sympathizer and alleged assassin of President
Kennedy
MARINA OSWALD, Lee's wife
YELLOW / BLACK / GREEN CARD MEN, guardians of the time portal

November 22, 1963—the date looms large in the annals of American history as the day
President John F. Kennedy was fatally shot by alleged assassin Lee Harvey Oswald
in Dallas, Texas. In the hours that followed, a traumatized nation came to a standstill.
Students were released from school early; people gathered in stores, neighborhood
bars, and other public places to share their disbelief and grief; and the media reported
every detail of the murder. The unforgettable photograph of the president's elegant
widow, Jacqueline Kennedy, dressed in a bloodstained pink Chanel wool suit, standing beside Vice President Lyndon B. Johnson as he took the oath of office is one of the
iconic images of the time. The Kennedy assassination was such a defining moment for
baby boomers that when they are asked "Where were you when you heard Kennedy
had been shot?" most people can supply a detailed answer.

The United States faced many difficult changes in the years following the assassination, and it is a matter of debate as to what differences Kennedy's sudden death made

(© Shane Leonard)

Stephen King is the author of more than fifty novels, including The Shining *(1977),* Misery *(1987), and the* Dark Tower *series (1982–2012), as well as his acclaimed nonfiction book* On Writing *(2000). He was awarded the National Book Foundation Medal for Distinguished Contribution to American Letters in 2003 and was inducted as Grand Master of the Mystery Writers of America in 2007.*

to the historical direction America traveled in the 1960s. But what if Kennedy had survived the assassin's bullet? This question lies at the center of Stephen King's novel *11/22/63* and is highlighted by two simulated newspaper stories on the book jacket. The front cover displays a color photograph of President and Mrs. Kennedy riding in an open car with Texas governor John Connally and his wife. Above the photo, the words "JFK Slain in Dallas, LBJ Takes Oath" appear in a large headline. On the back cover, a black-and-white image of the presidential couple walking through an airport is accompanied by the headlines "JFK Escapes Assassination, First Lady Also OK!" and "Americans Breathe a Sigh of Relief." Throughout his narrative, King incorporates the observation that "life turns on a dime." The back cover headlines and photo are a jarring yet poignant illustration of what could have been had the fateful bullet missed its target.

The alternate history portrayed on the back cover is the focus of King's novel. A combination of historical and science fiction, *11/22/63* is a time-travel story set between 1958 and 1963. The novel is told in the first person by high school teacher Jake Epping, a divorced man in his thirties who teaches GED classes in Lisbon Falls, Maine. When he asks his students to write about an event that changed their lives, he receives mostly run-of-the-mill essays, with one exception. The school janitor, Harry Dunning, pens an account of a night fifty years before when he witnessed his drunken father, Frank, brutally beat his mother and siblings to death with a sledgehammer. The normally composed Jake is horrified and haunted by Harry's account, and he becomes a mentor to his troubled student.

At the end of the school year and in honor of Harry's graduation, Jake treats him to lunch at Al Templeton's diner, where Al takes a picture of Harry in his robes and hangs it on his wall. Two years later, Al places an urgent call to Jake, asking him to come to the diner right away. When Jake arrives, he finds Al wasting away from lung cancer. At first he is astonished and mystified, because Al appeared to be fine the night before. Taking Jake to his back storeroom, Al shares his secret. He has actually been gone from the town for four years after stepping through a "rabbit hole," or time portal, that always leads to Tuesday, September 9, 1958. When Al convinces him to descend the stairs into the portal, Jake finds himself in the Lisbon Falls of fifty-three years before, where he meets an apparently drunken man with a yellow card stuck in his hat who seems to be guarding the time slip.

When Jake returns to 2011, he is merely intrigued by his experience. Al, however, has an ulterior motive for introducing Jake to the rabbit hole; he is determined to prevent the Kennedy assassination, believing that if the president had lived, the Vietnam War could have been avoided. Because of his terminal illness, Al enlists Jake's aid to complete the mission, which involves killing Lee Harvey Oswald during his attempted murder of General Edwin Walker in April 1963.

Jake reluctantly accepts the assignment on one condition: that he can test Al's theory by traveling back in time to save Harry Dunning's family first. Once back in 1958, Jake, now calling himself George Amberson, travels to Derry, Maine (a fictional town that has appeared in four of King's previous novels). He keeps Frank under surveillance until Halloween night, the date of the attack, then kills Frank before he can commit the murder. When he returns to 2011, Jake discovers that he has indeed changed history—but not in the way he intended. Harry's picture has disappeared from Al's wall, and Jake learns that although Harry and most of his family survived, Jake's actions in the past have actually cut Harry's life short; instead of growing up to become a high school janitor, Harry died in Vietnam.

While Jake is trying to make sense of his experience, Al commits suicide. Al's death motivates Jake to finish what Al started, so he steps through the rabbit hole once again and begins life in a very different world from the one he knows in 2011. There are no cell phones, websites, or personal computers. Instead, Eisenhower is nearing the end of his presidency, Americans are enjoying peace, prosperity, and prestige, and the world is living in fear of a nuclear holocaust.

After a series of false starts, Jake, once again using the alias George Amberson, settles in the small town of Jodie, Texas, a few hours' drive from Dallas. There he puts down roots as a high school English teacher and outwardly lives a normal life. His students and fellow faculty members respect him, and he wins the heart of Sadie Dunhill, the school librarian. At the same time, he remains focused on his mission and is intent on keeping tabs on Lee and Marina Oswald. Eventually, Jake informs the school's principal that he intends to resign his position to work on a novel. Instead, he leaves Sadie and rents an apartment downstairs from the Oswald family.

As the date of Oswald's attempt on Walker's life draws near, inexplicable obstacles prevent Jake from eliminating Oswald. He has sensed before that "the past is obdurate," and it is this uncompromising quality that asserts itself whenever major events are targeted for change by interfering time travelers. Jake's plans to do away with Oswald are repeatedly foiled, until finally November 22, 1963, arrives. This time, Jake succeeds in killing Oswald before he can shoot Kennedy. In saving the president's life, however, Jake unleashes a new set of circumstances that lead to near disaster for the country, the world, and his personal life. In order to try to put things right, he must use time travel once again.

The consequences of time travel can be mind-bending for the characters in science-fiction stories. The different men guarding the portal to 1958 Lisbon who wear yellow, black, and green cards in their hats (the colors denote the health of that particular branch of alternate reality) have such difficulty keeping track of possible histories that they are driven to madness. Similarly, the authors of such stories are no doubt challenged by the possible inconsistencies and paradoxes that can become evident as they pen their tales. In competent hands, however, loose ends in such stories are deftly tied and knotted. In King's case, he draws on the work of Richard Matheson and the late John Finney for inspiration. In his afterword, King calls Finney "one of America's great fantasists and storytellers" and cites his novel *Time and Again* (1970) as "*the great time-travel story.*" Elsewhere, King has noted that the writer who has most influenced him is Richard Matheson, the author of *Bid Time Return* (1975).

Writing a time-travel novel is a new venture for King, but the "what if" scenario concerning a time traveler racing to stop the Kennedy assassination has appeared before in film, in print, and on television; a 1985 episode of the *Twilight Zone*, the 1990 movie *Running against Time*, and Greg Ahlgren's 2006 novel *Prologue* are just a few examples of this conceit. Because the material has been covered before, the question arises of what makes King's novel different from other portrayals. Taking a page from Finney, who in *Time and Again* paints a vivid portrait of life in New York City in the 1880s, King carefully crafts a detailed picture of what life was like in the late 1950s and early 1960s. The mentions of drinking a ten-cent root beer at a soda fountain, singing along to hit songs such as "Purple People Eater" and "Hang on Sloopy," and watching *Howdy Doody* on black-and-white television will evoke nostalgia in baby boomers and provide a history lesson in mid-twentieth-century popular culture for younger readers.

Although King is a baby boomer himself, he refreshed his memory by conducting meticulous research into American life before and during the Kennedy era. The knowledge he gleaned from reading a variety of books on the assassination, including William Manchester's *Death of a President* (1996) and *Case Closed* (2003) by Gerald Posner; consulting historians like Doris Kearns Goodwin and her husband, former Kennedy aide Dick Goodwin; touring sites in Dallas such as the Texas School Book Depository; and interviewing museum directors and other scholars brings historical depth and a sense of immediacy to this work of fiction. A case could be made that the story is too long and lags in the middle. King does indeed seem enamored with the period and spends a lot of time exploring life in 1958 Texas, as well as the relationship between Jake / George and Sadie. Yet it is a mostly pleasant interlude, not unlike the idealized memories many people who grew up in that era still cherish. King succeeds brilliantly in not only opening a window on a time that now seems mythical but also bringing to life a crucial period in American history.

Pegge Bochynski

Review Sources

The Christian Science Monitor, November 22, 2011 (Web).
Kirkus Reviews 79, no. 20 (October 15, 2011): 1866–67.
Library Journal 136, no. 15 (September 15, 2011): 69.
The Wall Street Journal, October 28, 2011, pp. D1–2.

Elizabeth Bishop and the *New Yorker*
The Complete Correspondence

Author: Elizabeth Bishop (1911–1979)
Editor: Joelle Biele (b. 1969)
Publisher: Farrar, Straus and Giroux (New
York). 496 pp. $35.00
Type of work: Letters
Time: 1933–1979
Locale: United States

Spanning from 1933 to 1979, the correspon-
dence between poet Elizabeth Bishop and her
editors at the New Yorker *illustrates details of*
Bishop's life and writing process and gives new
insights into the background and inspiration
behind many of her poems.

Principal personages:
ELIZABETH BISHOP (1911-1979), a United States
poet laureate, two-time Guggenheim fellow, and Pulitzer Prize winner, regarded as
a major force in the development of contemporary and feminist literature in the
twentieth century
KATHARINE S. WHITE (1892–1977), author and fiction editor of the *New Yorker* from
the 1920s until 1960, wife of celebrated American author Elwyn Brooks (E. B.)
White
HAROLD ROSS (1892–1951), American journalist who founded the *New Yorker* in
1925 and served as one of its managing editors until his death in 1951
HOWARD MOSS (1922–1987), American poet, writer, and drama critic, the poetry editor at the *New Yorker* from 1950 until his death in 1987

Poet Elizabeth Bishop published just over fifty poems in the *New Yorker* between 1940
and her death in 1979, helping to cement her reputation as one of the most skillful
poets of her age, while the magazine gradually increased its reputation for publishing
quality fiction and prose. In *Elizabeth Bishop and the "New Yorker": The Complete
Correspondence*, poet Joelle Biele has collected dozens of letters that represent more
than forty years of correspondence between Bishop and her editors at the *New Yorker*
and contain the record of Bishop's difficult, though often loving, relationship with
editors Katharine White, Howard Moss, and others at the magazine. This publication
is one of several covering aspects of Bishop's life and work to have arrived in the
last couple of years, and while it is perhaps not of substantial interest to the lay fan
of Bishop's work, the book reveals aspects of her writing process and personality that
may give readers new insights into her poems.

Joelle Biele is an essayist, playwright, and poet whose poetry collection White Summer *(2002) won the 2001 Crab Orchard Review First Book Award. She was a Fulbright scholar in both Germany and Poland.*

Details of Bishop's biography are only briefly covered in the book, but they are helpful for understanding aspects of her personality that color the collected letters. Bishop was a lesbian, but she did not consider this aspect of her life to be predominant in her work. Her style was neither confessional nor deeply intimate, and she preferred to write from a removed vantage point, often writing about everyday items, unusual locations, or issues facing humanity on a more general level.

Over the span of her career, Elizabeth Bishop won several of the highest accolades awarded for literary talent. She was US poet laureate from 1949 to 1950, and a collection of her poems, *Poems: North and South; A Cold Spring* (1955), won the Pulitzer Prize for poetry in 1956. *The Complete Poems* (1969) won the 1970 National Book Award. Her 1976 collection of poems, *Geography III*, won a National Book Critics Circle Award, and that same year, she became the first American and the first woman to win the Neustadt International Prize for Literature, considered to be the second-highest award for literary achievement after the Nobel Prize.

Bishop was born in Worcester, Massachusetts, in 1911 but spent much of her childhood with relatives in Nova Scotia, Canada. Bishop's father died shortly after her birth, after which her mother suffered a mental breakdown that led to her permanent institutionalization in 1916. Bishop attended Vassar University, where she met and befriended poet Marianne Moore, who became her role model and convinced her to pursue a career in writing and poetry.

Bishop's father left her a sizable inheritance, and she was able to live frugally without needing to find additional employment. After graduating from Vassar with a degree in English, she traveled extensively in North America and Europe. In 1938, she moved to Key West, Florida; it was during this time that she developed her publishing relationship with the *New Yorker*, which would continue until her death in 1979. In 1944, Bishop moved to Brazil, where she lived until 1967, much of that time spent in the city of Petropolis. While there, she began a relationship with prominent French Brazilian architect Lota de Macedo Soares, the designer of Flamengo Park in Rio de Janeiro. Soares, who suffered from depression, took her own life in 1967 while she and Bishop were visiting friends in New York. Bishop later moved to Massachusetts and took a teaching position at Harvard University. Later in her life, she began a relationship with Alice Methfessel, who would remain her partner until Bishop's death in 1979.

Bishop had a knack for correspondence, and hundreds of her letters were left in the care of Alice Methfessel, who became executor of Bishop's estate after her death. Bishop was a close friend of poet Robert Lowell's, and the two corresponded from their introduction in 1947 until Lowell's death in 1977, producing a series of intimate, charming, and often hilarious letters that have been collected in the book *Words in the Air: The Complete Correspondence between Elizabeth Bishop and Robert Lowell* (2008). In *Elizabeth Bishop and the "New Yorker,"* readers come to know the business side of Bishop, including the way she treated those charged with judging her work and ultimately determining if it would find its way to print.

As the subtitle of the book asserts, this is the complete correspondence, and the letters contained have not been restricted to only those with artistic merit or eloquence. Occasionally, an interesting exchange between Bishop and one of the editors regarding stylistic choices gives some insight into the way that she thought about her work. On numerous occasions, for instance, her editors attempted to insert commas into her submissions, while Bishop countered that she preferred to leave the lines without, a choice that she felt enhanced the fluidity of her poems.

Also interesting in *Elizabeth Bishop and the "New Yorker"* are the relationships that develop between Bishop and her various editors. Most notable perhaps is Bishop's relationship with editor Katharine White, who accepted many of her early poems and was a strong supporter of her work. According to Biele, White took on a mentor-like role in Bishop's life at approximately the same time that Bishop's friendship with Marianne Moore ended, and she was instrumental in bolstering the poet's confidence. Bishop was not prolific and tended to work on a poem for months or years before submitting it for publication. Biele suspects that the encouragement of White and other editors gave Bishop a reason to keep working when she might otherwise have kept much of her material stashed away indefinitely.

While Bishop enjoyed considerable success publishing with the *New Yorker*, she suffered her fair share of rejections as well. Bishop's letters to friends and colleagues indicate that she was often vexed by the magazine's standards, which she felt forced poets and other writers to spare their best material and only send in submissions that fit into the magazine's rather narrow definition of publishable work. Bishop's poems were rejected with phrases like "a little too remote" and "doesn't seem quite precise enough." On one occasion, she received a rejection that included the phrase "it may be our denseness, rather than a real ambiguity in the poem, that led to a negative vote."

As to these rejections, it would be far too simple to blame the magazine's picky appetite on its editorial staff, many of whom were poets and authors themselves who felt similarly about the magazine's standards. These standards were largely influenced by just a few editors whose personal tastes dominated editorial policies for decades and who believed that the *New Yorker* should avoid any work with hints of radicalism or eroticism. Though Bishop was always friendly in her correspondence, she did not shy away from expressing annoyance at the way the magazine handled her work. In the early 1960s, she decided to stop publishing in the *New Yorker*, in part to protest standards that she thought were unreasonable. Little was written about her absence, though it is clear that Bishop began submitting poetry to the magazine again a few years later and continued to do so until her death.

While *Elizabeth Bishop and the "New Yorker"* provides an interesting look into the thought process and writing habits of one of the nation's seminal poets, those most interested in the book will likely be avid fans and scholars looking for minute biographical and historical details of her career. Long passages of the book may pass by with the only development being Bishop's decision to add a comma or change a single word. This book, then, is a relatively esoteric work of literary significance, but one that can hold the interest of any reader interested in gaining a deeper understanding of Bishop's personality or investigating the story of the *New Yorker* and the role it played in finding, nurturing, and supporting American literary talent over its many years of publication.

While many of the poets of her age, including her good friend and confidant Robert Lowell, wrote in a confessional, highly personal style of poetry, Bishop focused on the poetry of the world around her. Through her observations of the natural world, she found a road that led finally to a more subtle sense of introspection. This style made her a favorite at the magazine, as the editors rarely had to worry that a submission from Bishop would be too racy or too radical for publication. She had an immense skill with language that enabled her to find ways to conflate the ordinary and extraordinary in a single sentence, moving from banal to brilliant as she wrote. A section from one Bishop's poems published in the *New Yorker*, entitled "At the Fishhouses," illustrates these elements of her style. In this section, she writes about what would happen if the "you" of the poem dipped a hand in the sea:

> your wrist would ache immediately,
> your bones would begin to ache and your hand would burn
> as if the water were a transmutation of fire
> that feeds on stones and burns with a dark gray flame.
> If you tasted it, it would first taste bitter,
> then briny, then surely burn your tongue.
> It is like what we imagine knowledge to be:
> dark, salt, clear, moving, utterly free,
> drawn from the cold hard mouth
> of the world, derived from the rocky breasts
> forever, flowing and drawn, and since
> our knowledge is historical, flowing, and flown.

Though they occasionally disagreed, Bishop and the editors at the *New Yorker* offered mutual assistance to one another. The magazine played a role in eliciting some of Bishop's best-known compositions, and she in turn helped it achieve stature as a publisher of quality work. Bishop's life and artistic output have been studied from every possible angle by critics, fans, and academics. Since her death, she has come to be recognized as one of the country's premier poets. In *Elizabeth Bishop and the "New Yorker,"* Biele, who has spent much of her career writing about and studying Bishop, provides a view of the author's professional life and a rare glimpse into the business of poetry told through the words of one of the country's most singular talents.

Micah L. Issitt

Review Sources

Columbia Journalism Review, February 17, 2011 (Web).
Globe and Mail, March 21, 2011 (Web).
New Republic, March 7, 2011 (Web).
The New York Times, February 8, 2011 (Web).
Publishers Weekly, November 15, 2010 (Web).
The Wall Street Journal, February 5, 2011 (Web).

Embassytown

Author: China Miéville (b. 1972)
Publisher: Del Rey (New York). 368 pp. $26.00
Type of work: Novel
Time: The future
Locale: Embassytown, on the distant planet of
Arieka

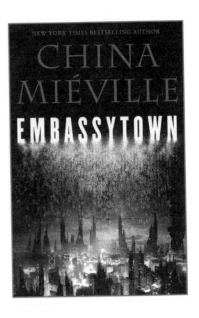

*When a human's voice has unexpected effects
on an alien race, a group of humans and Ariekei must find a new way to use language to
save their society.*

Principal characters:

AVICE BENNER CHO, an Embassytown native,
an immerser and a simile
SCILE CHO BARADJIAN, her husband, a linguist
EHRSUL, her best friend in Embassytown, an
autom
BREN, the surviving half of an Ambassador pair
WYATT, a political representative of Bremen
CALVIN, an Ambassador, Avice's ex-lovers
EZRA, an Ambassador created outside Embassytown whose speech has an unusual
effect on the Ariekei Hosts
YLSIB, a renegade Ambassador
SURL TESH-ECHER, a Host who leads a group of Ariekei attempting to learn to lie
"SPANISH DANCER," one of Surl Tesh-echer's followers, an Ariekes
THEUTH, a Languageless Ariekes

China Miéville's ninth novel, *Embassytown*, is set in the eponymous city, an outpost at
the edge of known space on the planet of Arieka. Arieka's residents, the Ariekei (politely called Hosts), are an intelligent insectile species with a unique language. "Words
don't signify," one character says of Language, "they *are* their referents." The Ariekei
have no metaphor or abstract speech, and they lack the ability to lie. This alien language
implies a very literal take on linguistic relativity, the concept by which categories of
language influence thought. While extreme forms of this concept are no longer popular
among linguists, what if alien language could shape alien thought? Complicating matters, Language is spoken through two orifices, each word a pair of simultaneous sounds.
The Ariekei cannot understand mechanical speech or speech with nonsynchronous
minds behind it; as a result, in order to communicate with the Ariekei, humans have
developed techniques for raising paired human doppels and synchronizing them via
training and technology so that the Ariekei will understand them. These Ambassadors
are crucial to human-Ariekei relations, making trade and other negotiations possible.

As a child, Avice becomes a simile in Language; that is, she consents to the Host's enabling her to express something previously inexpressible in Language. She is referred to as *the girl who was hurt in darkness and ate what was given her*, often abbreviated as *the girl who ate what was given her*. After leaving Arieka, Avice returns to Embassytown years later with Scile, her husband. She is a minor celebrity among humans for her status as an "immerser," one who navigates ships through the dangerous immer that binds the universe together. In Host circles, as a popular simile, she has a front-row seat to the events that soon unfold. EzRa, a new Ambassador, arrive from Bremen, the distant imperial center of which Embassytown is a colonial outpost. Unlike the homegrown Ambassadors, EzRa are not doppels, and although they score well on the synchrony test and are fluent in the human approximation of Language, their speech has a terrible effect on the Host. As human and Ariekei society begins to unravel, Avice and a small group of others must find a way to save their city.

Embassytown could be described as China Miéville's attempt at space opera, but like all of his previous works, this novel deconstructs and subverts the clichés of the science-fiction genre, at the same time exploring themes of language, identity, narration, and imperialism. As the narrator, Avice serves primarily as an observer. She plays an important if reluctant part in many of the novel's events, making *Embassytown* as much her memoir as it is a novel. There is little linear plot, and Miéville takes many pages before he reveals the sources of tension. At first, the novel reads merely like Avice's disconnected memories of childhood in Embassytown, how she came back to the city even though she swore she would not. There are no clear instances of Avice's narration being unreliable, but she does narrate several key scenes with the side note that she was not actually present, reminding the reader that she is selective about what to relate. "It's unfair to insinuate that all Hosts cared about was Language," she says, "but I can't fail to do so. This is a true story I'm telling, but I am telling it, and that entails certain things."

Avice's "memoir" is studded with scenes whose importance becomes clear only later. Terms such as turingware, exoterre, immer, and autom are introduced with little to no explanation, leaving the reader to infer their significance from context, word roots, and obscure references. Much of this might prove opaque to the occasional science-fiction reader. Even the importance of Avice's role as a simile in Language remains unknown until late in the novel. In less skilled hands, withholding so much information would result in a dull, impenetrable text. But Miéville's willingness to play with the structure of the novel, drawing the reader in only to point out the degree to which the narrative is subjective and unreliable, pays off. Despite its nontraditional structure, or perhaps because of it, *Embassytown* flows naturally and inexorably toward its conclusion, though not always in the ways readers may expect at first. Miéville is well aware of the clichés and tropes of the genre, subverting them at every turn.

The world of *Embassytown* is extremely complex, both socially and functionally, yet Miéville narrates through Avice so naturally that it is easy to follow musings on such lofty subjects as the nature of language and thought. While it is impossible for humans to truly conceptualize an alien species, the Ariekei feel convincingly alien; their society is as elaborate a mixture of genetic programming and socialization as human

Although China Miéville has written in many genres, all of his novels contain elements of the fantastic. He has received the Hugo Award, the British Science Fiction Award, the Arthur C. Clarke Award, and the World Fantasy Award for his work, which includes Perdido Street Station *(2000),* Un Lun Dun *(2007),* The City and the City *(2009), and* Kraken *(2010).* Embassytown *is his ninth novel.*

society, while humanity, in Miéville's novel, has itself become something quite different. The Ariekei are not passive victims but beings with agency and their own values and priorities.

Embassytown is also a novel about imperialism, and it is easy to draw parallels between the addictive effect of EzRa's voice on the Ariekei (the *god-drug*) and the role of opium and alcohol in the history of imperialism. Scile and other humans place the Ariekei and Language on a pedestal, regarding them as something culturally and linguistically pure, untouchable by history; yet the Ariekei are already part of history, changed from their first interaction with humans just as they in turn have changed human culture. The seemingly benign impulse to preserve the culture of the natives is itself an imperialist goal. In addition to the tensions between humans and the Ariekei, Embassytown's relationship with its parent Bremen is deeply troubled. As the motivations behind Bremen's creation of Ambassador EzRa are revealed, tensions grow between distant Bremen and its colony. Embassytown wants independence, whereas Bremen wants a port on the way to further reaches of space, even at the cost of the city's fragile society. Regarding the darker actions of Embassytowners, Avice herself is not entirely innocent, but her complicity makes her later decisions more dramatic.

The novel's denouement calls into question the possibility of preserving cultural and linguistic purity, while at the same time acknowledging the difficult choices and inevitable losses that result from imperialism. Avice draws a distinction between colony and empire, even as there is also a distinction between colony and local culture. In the case of *Embassytown*, the Ariekei are not exactly colonized; they retain their autonomy, though it remains clear throughout that distant Bremen has the weaponry to commit genocide should they decide the Ariekei are no longer useful partners for further space exploration.

The conclusion of the novel suggests the future development of a more collaborative culture in which Host, human, and the other exots might work together in pursuit of greater goals, retaining functional independence from Bremen. However, this culture will not be born without a price. The novel does not consider this price from the point of view of the Ariekei, who must eventually pay it, but instead from the point of view of Avice, who is a part of the imperialist culture whether she approves of imperialism or not. *Embassytown* tackles the subject from a self-consciously postcolonialist perspective, perhaps, but the perspective is also that of the imperialist power. It is a morally uncomfortable point of view from which to narrate a novel, and much of the subtext remains between the lines for the reader to find.

While *Embassytown* is a strong novel overall, Avice is a curiously distant narrator, sometimes seeming emotionally disengaged from the events around her and entering the action of the novel only reluctantly. Her evolution as a character arrives late and lacks drama. Avice's relative flatness prevents the book from being truly character driven, and given the lack of a standard plot, this leaves the novel's ideas as its primary source of energy. In general, idea-driven novels, especially ones so full of terminology and indirect information, can be difficult to follow initially or engage with emotionally. There are also some puzzling logical holes in the world Miéville has built. For instance, it is never clear how the perfectly literal Ariekei are able to conceptualize and communicate not-yet-existing similes in Language to the Ambassadors, who then find humans willing to become those similes. Yet these flaws seem minor when compared with the ambition of Miéville's ideas and the clever use of language and reference throughout, fitting for a book that is ostensibly about language.

In the end, *Embassytown* raises more questions than it answers about big concepts such as the role of language in culture, the gift and price of change, the nature of responsibility, and even issues of theology. Perhaps it is better to leave these questions open for the reader, as not having simple answers is what makes them big in the first place. The novel works on multiple levels simultaneously: as an exploration of abstract issues, as a musing on imperialism and cultural purity, and as a gripping political thriller that just happens to be set in the distant future.

Melissa A. Barton

Review Sources

Barnes & Noble Review, May 17, 2011 (Web).
The Guardian, May 6, 2011 (Web).
Kirkus Reviews 79, no. 7 (April 1, 2011): 548.
London Review of Books 33, no. 12 (June 16, 2011): 21–22.
The New York Times Book Review, June 5, 2011, p. 43.
Publishers Weekly 258, no. 12 (March 21, 2011): 60.

Emily, Alone

Author: Stewart O'Nan (b. 1961)
Publisher: Viking (New York). 255 pp. $25.95;
  paperback $15.00
Type of work: Novel
Time: 2007–2008
Location: Pittsburgh, Pennsylvania

Stewart O'Nan chronicles a year in the life of eighty-year-old Emily Maxwell as she tries to cope with declining health, loneliness, a constantly changing world, and memories of the past. The novel provides an objective and perceptive look at a period of life not often treated in fiction.

Principal characters:

EMILY MAXWELL, an eighty-year-old widow
  who lives alone with her dog, Rufus
ARLENE MAXWELL, Emily's sister-in-law and
  friend
RUFUS, Emily's very old dog
HENRY MAXWELL, Emily's deceased husband, who is ever-present in her memories
MARGARET, Emily's daughter, who struggles with alcoholism
KENNETH, Emily's son
BETTY, the woman who cleans for both Arlene and Emily, also a friend
JIM COLE, Emily's helpful neighbor, a university professor
MARCIA COLE, Jim's wife, who also helps Emily

Emily, Alone, the sequel to Stewart O'Nan's successful 2003 novel *Wish You Were Here*, is the story of a year in the life of Emily Maxwell, an eighty-year-old widow who lives alone with her old dog, Rufus, in Pittsburgh, Pennsylvania. She still resides in the family home in which she and her late husband, Henry, reared their two children, Margaret and Kenneth. O'Nan's novel follows Emily through her quiet daily life as she deals with the vicissitudes of aging and recollects the people and events of her past. It proceeds slowly, allowing the story to reflect the pace of this stage of life as it unfolds.

Emily's life has become static and much of her time is spent waiting and remembering. When the novel opens, she is waiting at the window for her sister-in-law Arlene to pick her up so they can go to the Eat 'n Park, a local restaurant, for a buffet breakfast. After two accidents with Henry's Oldsmobile, Emily no longer drives. She is dependent on Arlene for transportation and her personal life is severely limited by her lack of independence.

While at the restaurant, Arlene suddenly suffers a stroke and must be hospitalized. Without Arlene to drive her and too frugal to pay for a taxi, Emily reluctantly resumes driving herself, a small but significant change that allows her to regain some of her lost autonomy and agency. While she is still an old woman for whom death is a constant reality, this development prevents the novel from becoming a bleak portrayal of life for

Stewart O'Nan holds a BS from Boston University and an MFA from Cornell University. He is the author of thirteen novels, a collection of short stories, and several works of nonfiction. He has won numerous awards, including the 1993 Drue Heinz Literature Prize, and was named one of America's best young novelists by Granta magazine in 1996.

the elderly. O'Nan objectively and realistically presents Emily's loneliness, her nostalgia, and her regrets without satirical or comic undertones about old age.

The novel's exceptional utilization of third-person narration is perhaps its greatest strength. This style of writing allows the reader to observe Emily in her everyday life while also gaining insight into her thoughts and memories and seeing events and characters through her eyes. The plot is centered on Emily and she is the lens through which readers view her world. By using the third-person narrator, O'Nan also lets the reader see Emily as a character who is defined by the actions of her daily life. Despite her reclaimed mobility, Emily spends much of her time alone in the house with Rufus. She listens to classical music, goes up and down the stairs, does crossword puzzles, lets Rufus in and out, sorts through the things she has accumulated during her life, looks at old pictures, and keeps herself busy. She spends a considerable amount of time with Arlene, going with her to the country club, the Eat 'n Park, flower shows, and the funerals of friends. Betty comes to clean Emily's house every Wednesday; Emily likes her and enjoys the time she is there. Emily is also friendly with her neighbors, Jim and Marcia Cole, and occasionally asks them to help her as well. It is in this manner that the narration chronicles the mundane tasks and minutiae that make up Emily's life.

The narration also reveals Emily's attitudes and opinions as she passes her days. While she is grateful for Arlene's company and likes her well enough, she is also critical of her sister-in-law. Emily thinks that Arlene is overly fastidious, wears too much makeup, and brings up the subject of Emily's neglectful children just to be annoying. Emily's children and grandchildren fail to live up to her expectations; she cannot understand why her daughter and son are always busy and she wonders why they seem to have so little interest in spending holidays with her. Even Rufus is unruly and difficult, but she dreads the thought of losing him as her companion.

Emily plays an important role in her own development as a character by continually engaging in self-analysis. In this way, she exposes herself as a practical, realistic, and self-disciplined individual. Her tenacity is apparent in her adherence to social etiquette and protocol; for example, though she has little interest in writing Christmas cards, she nonetheless sets about the task. Even though she misses Henry constantly and often lacks the energy and agility she would like to have, she does not permit herself to indulge in self-pity. She accepts her eighty years of age and her life as it is. This pragmatism contributes to Emily's appeal and enhances O'Nan's realistic portrayal of old age as a normal stage of life that, though often difficult, is still manageable.

O'Nan uses his title character to address many issues affecting old age and the problems that arise between generations within a family. Change is an important subject for Emily. Neither her neighborhood nor the city of Pittsburgh is anything like it was when she was raising her children; familiar landmarks are gone and new families have replaced old neighbors. Many of her friends are either in nursing homes or have died. Even Henry's Oldsmobile is no longer a sensible car to drive. Emily also dwells on her physical decline; she has had to learn to accept help cleaning and maintaining her house, as she is no longer capable of doing so herself. Indeed, even planting flowers on a grave is now almost a life-threatening challenge.

In addition to these external changes, Emily also reflects on how her personal relationships have shifted over time. Her thoughts often return to mother-daughter relationships. She and Margaret agree on very little and Margaret blames her mother for many of her problems. Emily believes that she could have been a better mother, acknowledging the constant arguing that shaped her relationship with her own mother as well. O'Nan also uses Emily's voice to address the problem of generations not placing the same values on family possessions. Emily cannot understand why Kenneth did not want Henry's Oldsmobile when she thought it represented a father-son bond. Her children even seem disinterested in family pictures, though Emily continues to sort and share them.

Just as O'Nan uses Emily to develop his other characters, he also uses them to enrich his portrayal of her. Emily's dog, Rufus, is in many ways a reflection of his owner. Rufus, too, is older and physically infirm but refuses to give up his usual habits. He still eats well, goes upstairs, barks and growls when someone comes to the house, insists on riding in the car, and follows Emily around the house. Arlene is used to provide a contrast to Emily that emphasizes Emily's balance and practicality. Where Emily takes more measured action, Arlene tends to overcompensate. She realizes that she needs to exercise more caution when driving and consequently drives at a snail's pace. She wears brighter lipstick and has her hair garishly colored to make up for her aging appearance. Additionally, Emily's strained relationships with Margaret and her late mother provide the reader with insight into Emily as both a child and young woman.

Inanimate objects also play an important role in the novel, as they repeatedly elicit memories of Emily's past. These objects provide her with a physical connection to the past, whether they are empty whiskey bottles that remind her of a party or a set of luggage that is linked to memories of travel. However, they can also demonstrate Emily's willingness to live in the present. When the set of luggage is about to be discarded after a rummage sale, she resists the urge to retrieve it, realizing that it has no place in her life. When the Oldsmobile is wrecked, she decides not to have it repaired, even though it was one of Henry's prized possessions; instead, she buys a Subaru, a practical car designed for driving in the modern era. It is the Subaru that enables Emily to return to an active and independent life, and it is the Subaru that ultimately represents promise and optimism for her remaining years.

O'Nan has crafted this engaging and thoughtful novel as a meditation on the aging process as a whole. His main character is an ordinary woman who can be seen as representative of an entire social class. By choosing to situate his story in an upper-middle-class milieu, O'Nan has eliminated issues such as poverty that might overshadow his other themes. He is instead able to concentrate his story on the elements that universally accompany the aging process: the advancing decline in physical and mental abilities, the loss of contemporaries in the form of both family and friends, the difficulty of living in a changed world, and the acceptance of one's own mortality as a very present reality.

Emily, Alone will engage readers with its unsentimental exploration of aging as an inevitable fate. The book's quiet examinations of family, friendship, memory, and change reveal the significance in the seemingly mundane. Through his use of quotidian detail to create an authentic character, O'Nan has skillfully painted the portrait of a woman all too aware of her decline and uncertain of her place in a world that is moving on without her. Often funny, typically candid, and eminently human, Emily is a memorable character who will resonate with readers. *Emily, Alone* has earned high praise for Stewart O'Nan and has contributed considerably to his recognition as a talented novelist. In this short sequel to *Wish You Were Here*, O'Nan once again demonstrates his ability to tell riveting stories about ordinary people living ordinary lives.

Shawncey J. Webb

Review Sources

The Boston Globe, March 20, 2011 (Web).
Los Angeles Times, April 17, 2011 (Web).
Miami Herald, April 3, 2011 (Web).
The New Yorker 87, no. 7 (April 4, 2011): 75.
San Francisco Chronicle, April 17, 2011, p. GF-7.

An Empty Room

Author: Mu Xin (1927–2011)
First published: Stories selected from three sources: *Sanwen yiji*, 1983, in Republic of China (Taiwan); *Wensha muyuan*, 1988, in Republic of China; *Balong*, 1998, in Republic of China
Translated from the Chinese by Toming Jun Liu
Publisher: New Directions Books (New York). 192 pp. $13.95.
Type of work: Short fiction
Time: 1824–1832, 1930s–1980s
Locale: China, England, Germany, New York City

The thirteen short stories of this collection span life experiences from childhood to death, reflecting on lives shaped by family and history.

Principal characters:

THE FIRST PERSON NARRATOR, an unnamed male who narrates nearly every story

THE NARRATOR'S MOTHER, an upper-class woman who is fiercely protective of her children and appears in the first two stories

XIA MINGZHU, the college-educated mistress of the narrator's father in the second story

LIANG and MEI, enigmatic lovers in the title story

ALICE, the English narrator of "Quiet Afternoon Tea"

FONG FONG, the narrator's lover in "Fong Fong No. 4"

LI SHAN, a bus driver bullied by his academic passengers in "Eighteen Passengers on a Bus"

JOHANN WOLFGANG VON GOETHE, a historical nineteenth-century German writer who features in "Weimar in Early Spring"

HEINRICH HEINE, a historical nineteenth-century German poet who features in "Weimar in Early Spring"

SANDRA, the narrator's lover in "The Windsor Cemetery Diary"

A child and teenager during the Sino-Japanese War and World War II and an adult during the Cultural Revolution, writer Mu Xin experienced many of the hardships that affected the people of China during these turbulent periods, including imprisonment by the Communist government and the destruction of much of his writing and artwork. The influence of this personal and national history is readily apparent in the thirteen stories collected in *An Empty Room*. Selected from various collections published in the Republic of China, the stories derive significant narrative power from the juxtaposition and blending of specificity and universality. Most of the stories are set in China during distinct periods of the twentieth century, grounding Mu Xin's narratives in a concrete space and time. Yet, these stories reflect universal human themes, each offering poignant insights into diverse aspects of human life. Individual stories deal with the challenges of growing up, the power and potential tragedy of love, the force and nature of memory, and the mysteries of religion and death. The seemingly personal nature of the stories is emphasized by the use of first-person narration; however, the character of the narrator seems to shift between stories, creating the impression of a collective experience. Arranged in a generally chronological fashion, the stories depict stages of life from childhood to death and form a deliberate cycle that begins with a Chinese temple and ends with a monastery in New York City.

An Empty Room opens with the story "The Moment When Childhood Vanished." The story is set in late republican China just before the outbreak of the Sino-Japanese War in 1937. The ten-year-old male narrator is forced to attend a religious ceremony for his ancestors by his upper-class mother and her female relatives. Already aware of the principles of Buddhism, the narrator is startled to find monks present at a nunnery. He is equally puzzled that a monk shows keen knowledge of cigarette brands, contravening his supposed rejection of worldly concerns. Having accidentally left his gift of a ceramic bowl at the religious site, the narrator convinces his companions to wait while a servant retrieves it. He soon learns, however, that while adult humans may do his bidding, the larger universe will not do so. The second story, "Xia Mingzhu: A Bright Pearl," reflects the uncertain status of women in postimperial, republican China. A young, college-educated woman, Xia Mingzhu falls in love with the narrator's married father, who takes her as his mistress. When the wealthy father dies, the narrator's mother refuses to associate with Xia Mingzhu. In doing so, she saves her immediate family from a terrible fate, at the price of solidarity with a brave but unfortunate woman.

The title story, "An Empty Room," is an enigmatic love story that takes place in China just after the end of World War II. The narrator comes upon a recently vacated room in a deserted temple. In this otherwise empty room, he finds scattered love letters and empty boxes of Kodak film. From the letters, the narrator learns the names of the lovers, but he is unable to determine what happened to them and why they left behind their letters and film boxes. A sort of antidetective story in which the mystery goes unsolved, the story serves as a poignant meditation on the unresolved mysteries of human life. Similarly, "Fong Fong No. 4" tells a bittersweet love story that chronicles the personal development of a headstrong young woman, the narrator's lover. Fong Fong is known as "No. 4" due to her rank among similarly named women within her traditional family, and her life progresses through four stages throughout the story. At first, the narrator dismisses the younger Fong Fong as a romantic interest, and though they later form a romantic relationship during Christmas, their time together is fleeting. Taking place during the Cultural Revolution and afterward, the story explores the ways in which individuals could be shaped by this turbulent period of Chinese history.

"Notes from Underground" is one of the most overtly autobiographical stories in the collection. The multilayered story's title alludes to Fyodor Dostoyevsky's famous novella *Zapiski iz podpol'ya* (1864; *Notes from Underground*), the fictional memoir

Mu Xin, born Sun Pu, has authored more than twenty books published in the Republic of China (Taiwan) and the People's Republic of China. An Empty Room is the first collection of his writing to be published in English.

of a reclusive retiree in czarist Russia. The narrator's friend is imprisoned in an underground air-raid shelter during the Cultural Revolution, as was Mu Xin himself. The authorities supply the prisoner with paper on which to write self-criticism, but he is able to steal some and record his true thoughts despite his oppression. The story celebrates self-assertion and affirmation of identity, as represented by the prisoner's secret writing. The stories "The Boy Next Door" and "Eighteen Passengers on a Bus" similarly examine human issues through the lens of Chinese history. The question of memory and remembrance is addressed in "The Boy Next Door," in which the middle-aged narrator proposes replacing the lost photographs of his own boyhood with pictures of a boy who resembles himself as a child. In "Eighteen Passengers on a Bus," bus driver Li Shan is mercilessly bullied by his passengers, with the exception of the sympathetic narrator. The driver's eventual response to this treatment calls attention to the extremely negative effects that such hostility, whether on a personal or national level, can have on individuals. The setting of a bus is again used in "Fellow Passengers," placing a variety of human characteristics and actions on display.

In "Quiet Afternoon Tea," the first-person narrator is not the Chinese man or boy of the previous stories. Rather, the story is narrated by Alice, an Englishwoman who lives with her uncle and aunt. The story concerns the aunt's obsession with the uncle's four-hour absence in the aftermath of an air raid during World War II, forty years prior. While the characters are English, their sentiments could just as easily apply to a Chinese family suffering through a similar postwar situation. One of two stories that seem largely disconnected from the setting and historical context of the collection as a whole, "Quiet Afternoon Tea" emphasizes the universality that is apparent throughout the various stories. "Weimar in Early Spring" similarly expresses a universal theme while exploring European history and culture. While reflecting on the mystery of spring, the narrator tells the story of the death of the German writer Johann Wolfgang von Goethe, who dies of a spring cold in Weimar in 1832. Next, the story depicts a springtime meeting between Goethe and fellow German writer Heinrich Heine in 1824. Both writers are working on plays with similar subjects, but they part politely, each wishing the other good luck. Their polite and reasonable behavior is presented as an alternative to the often-cutthroat climate of the literary world and society in general.

"Halo" and "Tomorrow, I'll Stroll No More" reflect on some of the differences and similarities between Asian and American cultures. The first story examines the apparent differences in the visual portrayal of the halos of saints in Christian and Buddhist religious art, leading the narrator to conclude that both methods have their flaws. Salvation comes only to those who remain committed to their art in the face of obstacles such as imprisonment. Similarly, in the next story, the narrator compares the flowers of China with those encountered on a stroll through the garden-lined streets of the Jamaica, Queens, neighborhood of New York City. He concludes that in both countries, life is characterized by uncertainty.

The final story, "The Windsor Cemetery Diary," is a sort of mystery narrative that, like the somewhat similar mystery in "An Empty Room," remains unsolved. While his lover, Sandra, is living in Switzerland, the narrator visits the cemetery of a monastery in New York City. On a whim, he flips over a coin that is lying on a tombstone. When he returns another day, someone has turned the coin over again. The narrator and his unknown counterpart continue to play this game until one snowy evening in February, when the narrator sees a light in one of the monastery's windows. While the narrator seems to find some sort of resolution, from the reader's perspective, the mystery remains a mystery.

In addition to being a writer, Mu Xin was a visual artist whose painted landscapes display the influences of both Chinese and Western art and culture. Like these paintings, the stories in *An Empty Room* transcend cultural boundaries while simultaneously depicting concrete eras and events in Chinese history. Mu Xin skillfully represents such conflicts as the Sino-Japanese War and the Cultural Revolution while making the universal themes and concerns related to such events accessible to readers who did not experience them. Translator Toming Jun Liu worked closely with Mu Xin to ensure the stylistic accuracy of the translation, to great effect. With vivid, engaging language, Mu Xin's collection succeeds brilliantly in examining the course of human life through a cycle of loosely related short stories.

R. C. Lutz

Review Sources

Library Journal 136, no. 10 (June 1, 2011): 96.
Publishers Weekly 258, no. 13 (March 28, 2011): 36–37.

Endgame
Bobby Fischer's Remarkable Rise and Fall—
From America's Brightest Prodigy to the Edge of Madness

Author: Frank Brady (b. 1934)
Publisher: Crown (New York). Illustrated. 402
pp. $25.99
Type of work: Biography
Time: 1943–2010
Locale: The United States, primarily New
York, as well as Cuba, Iceland, Russia, Hun-
gary, and the Philippines

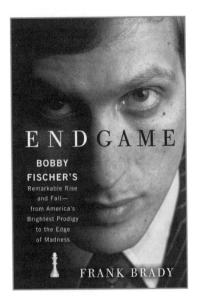

This comprehensive biography of controver-
sial world chess champion Bobby Fischer uses
new information from friends, family, and FBI
and KGB documents to build a more complete
picture of Fischer as a person. Endgame *fo-*
cuses on Fischer's personality and personal
relationships more than the details of his chess
games.

Principal personages:
ROBERT JAMES "BOBBY" FISCHER (1943–2008), chess prodigy and eleventh world
  chess champion
REGINA WENDER FISCHER (1913–1997), teacher, nurse, physician, activist, and mother
  of Bobby Fischer
JOAN FISCHER TARG (1938–1998), older sister of Bobby Fischer and a computer edu-
  cation pioneer
CARMINE NIGRO (1910–2001), Bobby Fischer's first chess teacher
JOHN WILLIAM "JACK" COLLINS (1912–2001), American chess master and influential
  teacher
BORIS SPASSKY (b. 1937), Soviet-born chess grand master and tenth world chess champion
ZITA RAJCSANYI (b. 1973), seventeen-year-old fan of Fischer and Hungarian junior
  chess champion who convinced Fischer to rematch with Spassky in 1992
MIYOKO WATAI (b. 1945), president of the Japanese Chess Association, who claimed
  to be married to Fischer, although the legality of the marriage was disputed

In writing about the life of chess prodigy Bobby Fischer, a biographer has the option to focus on the technical aspects of Fischer's chess brilliance and his notable
games or on his troubled personal life and increasingly violently expressed political
views. With *Endgame: Bobby Fischer's Remarkable Rise and Fall—From America's
Brightest Prodigy to the Edge of Madness*, author Frank Brady chooses to emphasize
Fischer's personality and relationships with family, friends, colleagues, and rivals over

the details of his chess playing. For readers seeking insight into Fischer's playing style or techniques, *Endgame* provides almost no detail, although it does touch on key highs and lows of Fischer's career.

Where *Endgame* shines is in its comprehensive portrayal of Fischer as a person. It highlights particularly his unusual childhood with his intellectual mother and sister, an experience of frugal poverty that may explain his later emphasis on the financial compensation for his chess matches (although he also turned down numerous financial opportunities, in particular those that would have used his name and image to sell products). *Endgame* also details the last years of Fischer's life, as an international fugitive from the US government, in ill health but mistrusting doctors, and vociferously declaring his anti-Semitic and anti-American views.

Brady, who also wrote *Bobby Fischer: Profile of a Prodigy* (1989 rev. ed.), focusing on Fischer's early years, spent decades studying Fischer's life, collecting stories and anecdotes from those who met him and digging through untouched records for new information. Although many of the anecdotes could not be journalistically confirmed, Brady was able to create a much more complete picture of Fischer's life than any previously published. To form his narrative, Brady drew upon such sources as FBI and KGB records; correspondence between Fischer and his mother, friends, and teachers; Fischer's own anti-Semitic and anti-American radio broadcasts; an autobiographical essay written by a teenage Fischer; and discussions with many of Fischer's chess teachers, colleagues, and rivals, including Soviet grand master Boris Spassky, whose world chess champion title Fischer took in 1972.

The use of anecdotes and unusual details, as well as direct quotations from many of Fischer's chess colleagues, gives *Endgame* an almost novelistic feel at its best, setting vivid scenes instead of merely reciting dry facts and events. The effectiveness of this technique varies: While it can draw readers into the narrative more deeply, it also raises questions about where and how significantly Brady embellishes the facts for dramatic effect. A little description of traffic noise is one thing, but speculations on Fischer's thought processes tread dangerously close to fiction at times.

Endgame can be roughly divided into thirds: Fischer's childhood and emergence as a chess prodigy (he was the youngest American master at thirteen and the youngest international grand master at fifteen); the height of his career, leading to his 1972 match against Spassky for the World Chess Championship, which he won; and his "wilderness years," when he withdrew from chess. This latter period was punctuated by his reemergence in 1992 for a rematch with Spassky. Afterward, however, he declined again, becoming an international fugitive for tax evasion and violation of US economic sanctions for playing the 1992 rematch with Spassky in Yugoslavia during the Bosnian War.

Fischer's childhood is perhaps the most clearly portrayed and interesting portion of the book, perhaps because much of it was drawn from Fischer's autobiographical essay and from family and teacher correspondence. Counter to prevailing belief, Fischer's mother, Regina, as shown by Brady, was caring and concerned for her children's well-being, but she was forced to work extremely long hours away from home. Despite this, she strongly supported Fischer's interest in chess and attempted to foster other intellectual interests in him as well.

As the narrative progresses through Fischer's early career, the sporadic use of dates sometimes makes it difficult to follow events. Brady provides almost no information about key games and tournaments, sometimes neglecting even the final score. While this was done to keep the text accessible to readers with no chess background, it results in a text that tells but does not show that Fischer was a chess prodigy.

While undoubtedly important and a portion of Fischer's life not covered by other biographies, Fischer's decline is less interesting and more sketchily drawn, largely because reliable sources for this period of Fischer's life are limited. Although Brady interviewed a number of people who had known Fischer, there are some surprising gaps in this section of the narrative. Most notably, he did not include any interviews with Fischer's wife, Japanese chess player Miyoko Watai.

Where *Bobby Fischer: Profile of a Prodigy* was more apologetic about Fischer's notoriously outrageous, unpleasant behavior in

(Richard Rex Thomas)

Frank Brady has authored numerous biographies, including Citizen Welles *(1990),* Onassis: An Extravagant Life *(1978), and* Bobby Fischer: Profile of a Prodigy *(1989), the last of which focuses on Fischer's youth. He is the chair of the communications department at St. John's University, president of the Marshall Chess Club, and founding editor of* Chess Life *magazine.*

his early years, some temporal distance and perhaps the cooling of Brady's respect for Fischer, as well Fischer's increasingly hostile political views in his later years, make *Endgame* a more neutral review of Fischer's life, with some attempt to explain his behavior. *Endgame* paints a vivid portrait of a highly intelligent person with social difficulties, one who might be diagnosed with Asperger's syndrome today. Chess clearly seemed to help Fischer function; in the chess world, he found people who could handle his sometimes obnoxious manner and appreciate his brilliance. When he left the chess world, he grew increasingly paranoid—about the Soviets, the US government, doctors, Jews, Christians, and many other groups—constantly seeking direction from various religious sources.

Fischer did not unravel dramatically until after the 1972 match, and when he reemerged in 1992, he seemed collected and relatively contained, at least for the duration of the match. For many chess enthusiasts and members of the general public, Fischer's lowest point was a violently anti-Semitic rant on a Filipino radio station following the terrorist attacks of September 11, 2001, in which Fischer suggested that the US military should take over the United States by force and kill hundreds of thousands of Jews. Yet *Endgame* never quite explicitly makes the connection between Fischer playing chess and his ability to function in society. Indeed, it was love of the game that for many years allowed Fischer to maintain friendships with many Jewish chess players despite his anti-Semitic views.

In the end, while *Endgame* brings insight into Fischer's character and his declining, postchampionship years, it leaves a number of questions frustratingly unanswered. Some, like the state of Fischer's mental health, can never be answered. However, there are other puzzling gaps in the narrative, such as the hostile, uncooperative behavior of Fischer's second (his attendant) at the Candidates Tournament in Yugoslavia, which is insufficiently explained. Brady also somewhat glosses over some aspects of Fischer's life, such as his womanizing in later years. Although Brady discusses this in general terms, he downplays Fischer's more obnoxious behaviors toward women and never really posits a full explanation for Fischer's shift from disinterest in women to quite the opposite. Brady also makes no attempt to answer the question of who Fischer's biological father was.

The chess analysis present in *Bobby Fischer: Profile of a Prodigy*, which has been criticized by some chess enthusiasts as superficial, is completely absent from *Endgame*, which is aimed at a general audience. However, in downplaying chess, the book obscures somewhat the reasons people tolerated Fischer and his erratic behavior and does not leave general readers with a clear idea of what Fischer contributed to chess. Perhaps the book's biggest flaw is its lack of a clear timeline for Fischer's chess career and his life in general; it is sometimes difficult to determine the order of events from the narrative, which is occasionally disjointed.

Endgame succeeds, however, in presenting a portrait of Fischer's life from birth to death, his rise and fall as a chess player, and some of his complicated relationships with others. It sheds some light on his behavior, perhaps as much as can be understood posthumously. Since the publication of the book, an Icelandic court declared Watai to be Fischer's heir, resolving the final question of the last chapter as to whether the US government would finally claim Fischer's back taxes or whether his estate would go to Watai or to his sister's children.

Brady concludes with his own mixed feelings about Fischer: He has respect and awe for his genius but disgust for his beliefs and some of his behavior. The book is likewise mixed in its success. It is a fine portrait of a complex person but does not contain quite enough explanation of his impact in the chess world. In trying to write a book for a general audience, Brady may have removed a little too much of the chess to fully convey Fischer's historical significance. All the same, *Endgame* is perhaps the most comprehensive attempt at understanding Fischer's entire life and well deserves its place in biographical literature as a thought-provoking, compelling tragedy.

Melissa A. Barton

Review Sources

American Spectator 44, no. 4 (May 2011): 69–70.
Library Journal 136, no. 3 (February 15, 2011): 117.
Maclean's 124, no. 7 (February 28, 2011): 60.
National Review 63, no. 5 (March 21, 2011): 50–52.
The New York Times Book Review, February 13, 2011, p. 24.
Salon, January 30, 2011 (Web).

The Evolution of Bruno Littlemore

Author: Benjamin Hale (b. 1983)
Publisher: Twelve (New York). 592 pp.
   $25.99
Type of work: Novel
Time: The present
Locale: Chicago, Colorado, New York City,
   and Georgia

Author Benjamin Hale presents the fictional
memoir of an erudite and loquacious talking
chimpanzee, who reflects on his life and on
the nature of being human.

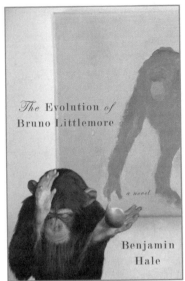

(Little, Brown and Company)

Principal characters:
BRUNO LITTLEMORE, the narrator, a chimpan-
   zee who has learned to talk and read
GWEN GUPTA, the research assistant to whom
   Bruno dictates his story
LYDIA LITTLEMORE, a University of Chicago
   researcher who raises and cares for Bruno, eventually his lover and the mother of
   his humanzee child
NORM PLUMLEE, the head of the University of Chicago research program, Lydia's boss
   and Bruno's nemesis
HAYWOOD FINCH, a night janitor who teaches Bruno to speak
TAL, Lydia's lover, variously a rival to and a supporter of Bruno
THE LAWRENCES, philanthropists who host Lydia and Bruno on their ranch
LEON SMOLER, an actor who befriends Bruno in New York City
CELESTE, ROTPETER, CLEVER HANDS, AND VARIOUS OTHER CHIMPANZEES, apes that cannot
   speak or understand language but nevertheless have meaningful relationships with
   Bruno

At times both rambunctious and meditative, *The Evolution of Bruno Littlemore* is a fictional memoir narrated by a highly intelligent talking chimpanzee named Bruno who
has spent most of his life trying to become more human. Bruno is dictating his story
to a research assistant at the Zastrow National Primate Research Center in Georgia,
where he has been confined. Now well past the age of twenty-five, Bruno is reflecting
on his own life and on the nature of language, love, art, and learning. This daring debut
novel from newcomer Benjamin Hale will invoke similar reflections from readers as
they confront questions about humanity.
   Removed from Lincoln Park Zoo as a preadolescent, Bruno is made a participant
in a University of Chicago experiment to teach chimpanzees to understand spoken language. Bruno surprises the researchers by secretly learning how to speak. It is not the

scientists who surround him by day who accomplish this feat, but rather a night janitor who spends an hour each evening communicating with Bruno in a series of simian hoots and English words. Now able to communicate, Bruno forms a tight bond with scientist Lydia Littlemore. Lydia eventually brings him home to live with her, ferrying him back to the lab each day for research.

Bruno plays a number of roles in Lydia's life. At first, theirs is a mother-and-child relationship, and Bruno lives in the room that had been intended for Lydia's son, who died at birth. Later, as Bruno grows older and Lydia's personality and behavior become increasingly erratic, they begin a sexual relationship. Hale's description of Lydia and Bruno's coupling is graphic and detailed, and even the most seasoned reader may be taken aback at its explicit nature. These scenes of bestiality, particularly Lydia and Bruno's first sexual encounter, have an element of shock value to them and may be an example of a first-time novelist showing just how outré he is willing to be. But they might serve a further purpose as well in calling on the reader to ask again where the line between animal and human should be drawn.

After Bruno reverts to animalistic behavior at an art gallery opening featuring his paintings, he and Lydia lose their respective jobs as research subject and researcher. The two find a safe haven with the Lawrences, wealthy eccentrics who use their ranch as an animal rescue center. Here, away from the pressure of the laboratory, Bruno truly finds his voice and begins to speak fluently. He learns to read as well, studying in the Lawrences' library and learning philosophy and literature in their makeshift classroom.

Bruno and Lydia's eventual return to Chicago is disastrous, as the news that Bruno can speak is eclipsed by the revelation that Lydia is carrying his half-human, half-chimpanzee child. Lydia is soon diagnosed with a brain tumor, which results in a condition of aphasia. Bruno and Lydia's relationship is inverted; Bruno can now communicate with assurance, whereas Lydia is gradually losing her ability to speak at all. While Lydia once supported Bruno, now Bruno must find work to support her. He returns to the lab in a hybrid role as both research subject and paid employee, or "indentured servant," as Bruno describes his position. In this reversal of roles, Lydia is forced to confront the place of words and their meanings in her life. If the ability to use language is a distinctly human trait, then what does it mean for Lydia and Bruno that the chimpanzee can speak and the human no longer can?

After a series of further complications, Bruno finds himself alone in New York City. Sporting a disguise that thinly veils his true nature, he falls in with a group of actors, including street performer Leon Smoler. When Leon stages a performance of *The Tempest*, Bruno, of course, plays Caliban. It is during his time away from Lydia that Bruno's story (and Hale's novel) is at its most episodic. The time in New York feels like a series of colorful vignettes that are somewhat irrelevant to the main arc of the story. Here, too, the reader is asked to suspend a great deal of disbelief over whether a chimpanzee, regardless of how upright he holds himself and how well he can speak, could truly pass for a human. One character after another responds to Bruno as if he is a small, odd-looking man rather than a primate. Yes, his hair has fallen out and he has had rhinoplasty to reshape his nose, but these encounters still strain credulity. The

convincing descriptions of Bruno's physi-
cality in the first half of the novel, such as
references to his "long purple fingers" and
depictions of him "brachiating from canopy
to canopy," are hard to undo, and the uncon-
cerned reactions of New Yorkers to his appearance feels like an exigency of plot.

*Benjamin Hale graduated from the Iowa
Writers' Workshop, where he was the
recipient of the University of Iowa Pro-
vost's Teaching-Writing Fellowship and
the Michener-Copernicus Award. He
was also awarded the Bard Fiction Prize
for 2012.* The Evolution of Bruno Littlemore *is his first novel.*

While the long New York interlude may
ramble, by novel's end, the main storyline
comes back into focus as Bruno returns to Chicago and to Lydia. After committing a
crime of passion, he finds himself again imprisoned, this time in the confining halls of
the primate center where he is telling his story. But perhaps this makes no difference to
Bruno; as he says, riffing on Hamlet, "if we think of the whole world as a prison, then
there's no such thing as a cage-free animal."

The strongest element of Hale's novel is neither its plot nor its characters, but rather
Bruno's narrative voice. A voracious reader, Bruno is an impressively urbane and sophisticated individual. His world-weary lassitude, his penchant for making literary
references, and his startling narrative unreliability all bring to mind the protagonists
of Vladimir Nabokov. In fact, some of the funniest and most original passages in *The
Evolution of Bruno Littlemore* come from the contrast between Bruno's cosmopolitan
self-representation and his occasionally animalistic nature (and for that matter, the
same might be said of Nabokov's Humbert Humbert, the narrator of *Lolita*); Bruno's
obfuscations regarding an incident in which he bites off a lab assistant's finger come
to mind. These gaps and contradictions are a rich vein that Hale mines for both comedy and pathos. But invoking Nabokov works against Hale, too, as the urbanity of
characters like Humbert Humbert or the narrator of *Pale Fire* is grounded in a European education and culture that Bruno lacks. The chimpanzee's literary and cultural
references are those of a precocious English major, and at times seem too predictable
and programmatic. In fact, while Bruno describes himself as an autodidact, there is
a canonical homogeneity to his allusions that is in keeping with a student who has
taken numerous survey courses and introductory classes. Nevertheless, Bruno has an
unusual lens on the Great Books: he is drawn to representations of the bestial, from
John Milton's Satan to Shakespeare's Caliban. Literature may be the study of the human condition, but from Bruno's perspective, this condition is often defined by what it
is not. Bruno sees himself in the classic literary representations of the nonhuman and
the other—the talking serpent, the naked islander—and the subjects of this tradition
become markers for him to navigate his passage from primate to man.

Bruno is also preoccupied with the nature of language itself. The book is peppered
with his meditations on the value and meaning of words, speech, and communication.
Of his hooting, exuberant exchanges with Haywood, the janitor who first taught him
to speak, he says, "language for the sake of communication follows languages that is
noise for the sake of fun—that is, music—and—this I truly believe—all truly beautiful
language is for the sake of both: communication and music." Like so many of Bruno's
disquisitions, this is as much the novelist's credo as it is the chimpanzee's. It is this

element of music and joy, not the measured experiments of Dr. Plumlee, that leads Bruno to master speech and reading. This joy in words is evident in the many lists, catalogues, and detailed descriptions that fill Bruno's narrative. Yet Bruno's account of how he learned to speak and read can feel evasive; regarding the time on the Lawrence ranch, for example, he says, "my vocal capacities exploded. How can I describe this? How can I possible narrate it? Describing the process of learning to speak is like trying to bite your own teeth." Because the novel is written in Bruno's literate voice, the text itself never really reflects the process by which language is acquired. And because of his love of literature, philosophy, and rhetoric, Bruno always seems happy to escape into abstractions and parables. Thus, it is never entirely clear why Bruno can learn to speak, read, and write while the chimpanzees around him remain shut off from language. At times, Bruno's ruminations may not pass an acid test, and some of his theorizing would not be particularly worthwhile if it were voiced by a human instead of a chimpanzee. At their best, however, Bruno's reflections on language are insightful and moving.

Like its eponymous narrator, *The Evolution of Bruno Littlemore* is joyful, ambitious, and overreaching. A long and loosely structured novel, it may at times exhaust its reader and lose its own narrative thread amid its many allusions and existential musings. But Hale's audacious first book is nevertheless quite an accomplishment. It is a bold, evocative examination of humanity and consciousness, featuring a narrator with a distinct and unforgettable voice.

Matthew J. Bolton

Review Sources

Barnes & Noble Review, February 2, 2011 (Web).
Los Angeles Times, February 17, 2011 (Web).
The New York Times Book Review, February 4, 2011 (Web).
The Washington Post, February 8, 2011 (Web).

The Fates Will Find Their Way

Author: Hannah Pittard (b. 1979)
Publisher: Ecco (New York). 256 pp. $22.99;
paperback $14.99
Type of work: Novel
Time: Late twentieth and early twenty-first centuries
Locale: American Mid-Atlantic suburbs, Arizona, and Mumbai

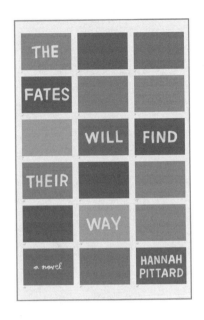

In this debut novel, sixteen-year-old Nora Lindell is missing and missed. The story that follows, narrated by the boys she left behind, imagines where she may have gone and what her disappearance might mean.

Principal characters:
NORA LINDELL, a sixteen-year-old girl who
    disappears
SISSY LINDELL, Nora's promiscuous younger
    sister, who similarly inspires adoration
HERBERT LINDELL, Nora's widower father
SARAH JEFFREYS, a rape victim who, like Nora, disappears
DREW PRICE, a neighborhood boy who claims to have seen Nora at bus station
TREY STEPHENS, a public school student who claims to have slept with Nora
PAUL EPSTEIN, another neighborhood boy
MRS. DINNERMAN, a local Eastern European mother who is the object of the boys'
    fascination and lust
THE MEXICAN, Nora's hypothetical male caretaker and lover in Arizona
ABJA SAFIA, Nora's hypothetical female lover in Mumbai

The Fates Will Find Their Way begins with the mysterious disappearance of sixteen-year-old Nora Lindell from her suburban neighborhood one Halloween. The novel that follows is narrated by the adolescent boys she leaves behind, made up of the stories they imagine to fill in the blanks—blanks formed by loss, obsession, and simply growing up. The collective narrative voice, the disembodied "we," meanders from speculation to speculation, revealing the boys' youthful curiosity as it gradually becomes a fixation that will stay with them into middle age. In an America quick to panic over the possibility of childhood abduction, *The Fates Will Find Their Way* could have easily succumbed to abduction thriller or crime potboiler clichés. Instead, Pittard treads lightly when it comes to the grieving Lindell family, scarcely mentioning the police and newscasters who presumably attempt to track down Nora. The novel does not dwell on the headline-nabbing themes of kidnappings or pedophilic predators. Rather, it uses their power to frame a more general meditation on desire for the unattainable, a desire that blossoms in youth and refuses to go away. Such a longing motivates Pittard's chorus of boys, stuck in arrested development as they imagine Nora's fate at the expense of their own lives.

This is not to imply that *Fates* is a wholesome morality tale. As one would expect of a story that springs from the minds of teenage boys, sexuality is most certainly involved, and in ways that may alarm some readers. The boys speak of Nora in brazenly sexual terms, heedless of the fact that none of them knew her in such a way prior to her disappearance. Rumors of Nora's sexual history spread, and in the boys' imaginations, we see the power of suggestion and hearsay, as well as the role such power plays in the construction of figures of lore; consider, for instance, the sexual threat of a mystery man in a Catalina, or the dubious account of Trey Stephens.

With the exception of Nora, the novel is almost consumed with sexual deeds and musings. A conflicted sexual imagination, at once hungry and suppressed, colors the boys' perspective throughout. Their narrative focus is quick to dwell on a hemline across a bare thigh, but no less quick to recognize these thoughts with shame. The reader is given the impression that this shame has been communally conditioned, their mothers disapproving, their girlfriends modeling resistance and restraint. Pittard suggests that the boys' conflicted sexuality is shaped by both teenage hormones and the expectations of mild-mannered suburbia. As friends and neighbors enact sexual horrors that demonstrate the malicious capacity of the lustful male, the boys recoil with mixed feelings. One passage in particular, in which a group of young boys commits an outlandish act of public masturbation, will attest to readers that sexuality is central to Pittard's concerns, both plot-wise and with regard to her themes. Any thought, Pittard suggests, can become a sexual thought, and any sexual thought risks erotic impropriety. Even crumbs in the carpet, if handled in a certain way, can take on a sexual cast. The novel reveals a communal psyche in which biology is at odds with society, torn as to whether sexual urges (and their potentially messy consequences) should be rejected or simply accepted as an inherent aspect of humanity.

In its premise, setting, and first-person plural narration, *The Fates Will Find Their Way* brings to mind Jeffrey Eugenides's *The Virgin Suicides* (1993), another novel narrated by a troupe of fixated suburban boys, here speculating about five young sisters who all mysteriously take their own lives. As with *Fates* for Pittard, *The Virgin Suicides* was Eugenides's first novel and received great acclaim. Both novels attempt to plot the dark perversity of American suburbia. For both Eugenides and Pittard, the suburbs are a nostalgic place of phone trees and adolescent parties in carpeted basements, but they are also a place of suicide, rape, maliciousness, and inescapable ennui. Both novels leave the reader somewhat empty-handed in their closing pages. Aside from these details, though, the resemblance is a general one. Pittard's book is sparse and quick, unlike Eugenides's calculated, delicate wading pool. Pittard's style and diction lends her novel a collective voice that feels necessary and simple. Though the novel's issues are certainly complex, the underlying prose is straightforward, efficient, immediate, and almost austere, as if fearful of unnecessary flourishes or lavish description. Ultimately, Pittard's work charts new ground in its investigation of

(© 2010 Joe Wigdahl)

Hannah Pittard earned her MFA in creative writing from the University of Virginia and teaches fiction at DePaul University. She has published short fiction in McSweeney's, The Oxford American, BOMB, Nimrod, *and elsewhere, and was the winner of the McSweeney's Amanda Davis Highwire Fiction Award in 2006.* The Fates Will Find Their Way *is her first novel.*

sexual fantasy as a narrative motivation, as well as its exploration of an obsessive kind of psychology. Pittard reveals the world and longing of teenage boys, rendering the boys' imagined stories of Nora's possible life with as much vibrancy as she does the reality that Nora leaves behind. In its quick pages, *Fates* chases what we cannot know for sure and asks what is so tempting about this kind of knowledge.

After tracing the boys' various recollections of the day Nora disappeared, each with its own conflicting account of where she was last seen, the novel moves in a more unpredictable direction as the boys begin to imagine hypothetical scenarios. The narrative sweeps across gulfs of time and place, meandering from episode to imagined episode in an attempt to fit everything together in the wake of Nora's disappearance. The boys wonder, for example, what if Nora left town with a man in a Pontiac Catalina? The man they fashion, the hypothetical driver, is at turns strange, threatening, and benevolent. He drives Nora far into the wilderness, then lets her out of the vehicle and encourages her to run into the woods. She may have gotten lost in those woods and died. Alternatively, she could have returned to the car, or never left the passenger seat to begin with. The man may have simply given her a free ride to the airport. Perhaps, the boys speculate, she then flew to Arizona. Pittard follows this possibility through one of the novel's longest and most emotionally accessible scenarios: there, pregnant with twins, Nora works as a waitress and starts a relationship with a benevolent man referred to as simply "the Mexican." Together, she and the Mexican raise a family until, according to the possibilities the boys envision, one of two things happens: either Nora dies in childbirth, or she merely decides to leave. The second scenario then follows Nora to the tumultuous Indian city of Mumbai, where she begins a love affair with an Egyptian woman named Abja. In the end, it may be that Nora dies of cancer, or possibly she is killed in a terrorist bombing; the boys are unsure.

The novel continues to proceed in this way: one possible story is offered, followed by another, and another, as the narrators continue their fascination with the duality of incommensurable truths versus endless possibilities. Themes of fact versus fiction clearly intrigue Pittard, as her narrators ponder the act of storytelling itself. They lust after the allure and imagination of a good story while their mundane lives gradually encroach and surround them, seemingly without their knowledge. Increasingly, the boys' fixation on Nora rationalizes the transgressions and decisions of adulthood.

The reader can certainly detect that beneath the many hypothetical fantasies of exotic lovers and distant worlds lies a simple narrative projection of the boys' own desires, both to care for Nora and to know her in the context of places and events they will never themselves experience. These fantasies also seem to suggest the boys' attempts to reconcile themselves with their own sexuality. While Nora's imaginary companions all feature sexual characteristics, their sexuality has been rendered beneficent, kind, and acceptable: the benevolent predator, the asexual and generous Mexican, and the lesbian who offers sexuality without masculinity.

The boys derive these narrative fantasies from scraps and shards of information that they come across over the years: an airline stewardess who claims to have spoken to a young girl fitting Nora's description, a man who swears he saw Nora in the Phoenix airport, a newspaper photograph of a bombing in Mumbai that features a woman resembling Nora. The boys even take Mundo, the Mexican nurse who appears with three little girls at Mr. Lindell's funeral, as a clue. In Pittard's world, mere snippets of reality drive the creation of stories, highlighting the unsubstantiated quality of narrative and suggesting that a consuming and compelling tale does not require thorough research to take hold. The tension is that between fantasy and reality, demonstrating the lengths storytellers are willing to go to in order to reconcile the two.

While Pittard singles out and tells the stories of many individuals in the boys' group, the novel's narrative perspective proceeds from a kind of chorus, disembodied and general. Pittard spends little time with individual characters before quickly shifting focus to another storyline. One negative consequence is that readers may occasionally find it easy to confuse these characters, mistaking one boy for another or conflating the town's mothers into one vast, overly concerned figure. Ironically, and perhaps intentionally, it is Pittard's hypothetical characters—the post-disappearance Nora, the Mexican, and Abja—who receive deliberate amounts of narrative space and time, as if it is only imagined, fabricated characters, born exclusively of the mind, that we can truly know. The novel's hypothetical scenarios, particularly Nora's relationship with the Mexican, provide the novel's only positive reflections on sexuality and love, suggesting that, for the boys, love is a thing more successfully imagined than attained.

Grant Klarich Johnson

Review Sources

The New York Times, January 28, 2011 (Web).
The Washington Post, January 25, 2011 (Web).

The Fear
Robert Mugabe and the Martyrdom of Zimbabwe

Author: Peter Godwin (b. 1957)
Publisher: Little, Brown (New York). 372 pp.
$26.99; paperback $15.99
Type of work: Current affairs
Time: 2008 and 2009
Locale: Zimbabwe

Godwin describes an extended trip back to his native country of Zimbabwe to observe the change of government after the violently disputed 2008 presidential and parliamentary elections.

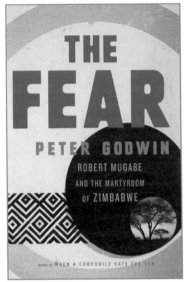

(Little, Brown and Company)

Principal personages:
PETER GODWIN, a Zimbabwean journalist living in New York
GEORGINA GODWIN, his sister
ROBERT MUGABE, president of Zimbabwe and leader of its main political party, the Zimbabwe African National Union-Patriotic Front (ZANU-PF)
MORGAN TSVANGIRAI, leader of the main opposition party, the Movement for Democratic Change (MDC)
ROY BENNETT, treasurer of the MDC and a member of Parliament, persecuted and imprisoned under Mugabe's orders
JAMES MCGEE, United States ambassador, based in Harare, Zimbabwe

Zimbabwe, formerly Southern Rhodesia and Rhodesia, is one of a number of former colonies that have struggled to achieve independence and faced considerable obstacles in overcoming despotic regimes. By the end of the nineteenth century, Southern Rhodesia had been established as a British colony with a largely black African population, as well as a substantial number of white settlers who moved up from South Africa to settle the land.

Toward the end of colonial rule in the 1960s, these settlers initiated a period of autonomous rule led by a Unilateral Declaration of Independence (UDI) under Premier Ian Smith, interrupting the country's transition to true independence. Neither Britain nor the rest of the world recognized this de facto government, but, apart from imposing economic sanctions, they did nothing to hinder it. A number of African insurgents began to resist Smith's government through guerilla warfare. One of the guerilla factions was led by Robert Mugabe, an ex-schoolteacher.

Eventually, the Smith regime had to negotiate. The terms of the 1980 Lancaster House Agreement gave the newly formed Zimbabwe a black majority government with reserved seats for the white settlers. The agreement also gave the country international recognition and generous aid packages. A period of prosperity and hope ensued, and Zimbabwe's new currency was among the most stable in Africa. Robert Mugabe's ZANU party (later the ZANU-PF) won the 1980 elections and Mugabe was elected the first government's prime minister.

This background needs to be understood in order to make full sense of Peter Godwin's gripping account of the 2008 election in Zimbabwe, in which Mugabe's ZANU-PF sought to retain the power it has held, unbroken, since that first election. The ZANU-PF was being challenged by the MDC, a party formed in 1999 to try to restore some sense of democracy to a country that had lost it under what had become a single-party state.

It is also important to understand Mugabe's early suppression of his political rivals: the Zimbabwe African People's Union (ZAPU), whose power base was the Ndebele people of the Matabeleland region, and its leader, Joshua Nkomo. From 1981 to 1987, there was a period of *gukurahundi*, or ethnic cleansing, culminating in widespread massacres of the Ndebele in 1983–84 that resulted in over twenty thousand deaths and the elimination of the ZAPU. The remnants of ZAPU joined ZANU, the party of the Shona people, in December 1987, forming a single-party state. Mugabe had himself made executive president and most of Parliament's power then flowed to him, including direction of the armed forces and the police.

Peter Godwin was raised on a large white-owned farm in Zimbabwe. These farms were the basis of Zimbabwe's economic prosperity, producing huge tobacco exports and feeding the rest of the country. Godwin was conscripted into the Smith regime's police force in the 1970s, and he fought in the Rhodesian Bush War against the guerrillas before eventually going to university in the United Kingdom.

At independence, Godwin had hurried back as a reporter for the London *Sunday Times*. But his frank reports of the *gukurahundi* earned him Mugabe's displeasure and he was considered an enemy of the state, forced to leave the country or face charges. Later, all foreign journalists were banned from the country.

It was thus an act of some personal bravery for Godwin to travel back to Zimbabwe in 2008 with his London-based sister, Georgina. He had no idea if he would be allowed into the country at all, but under the pretext of visiting his parents' property and his father's grave (his mother was living in London), he and his sister were granted entry. Godwin's opening pages show his hope that the Mugabe regime would fall at last as a result of the elections, which were held on March 29, 2008.

Godwin and Georgina arrived five days after the elections, and these hopes were quickly dashed. They heard stories of "Operation Mauhotera-papi" (Who did you vote for?), in which ZANU gangs, usually consisting of ex-guerrilla fighters, youths, and party officials, systematically beat up those who they thought had voted for the MDC. There was a deliberate delay in announcing the election results, and despite international observers from other African states declaring the election essentially fair, it soon became apparent that it had been heavily rigged. Even so, the MDC fared better than the ZANU, both in the presidential race and in parliamentary elections. The delay was a ploy by Mugabe to see how MDC voters could be intimidated into changing their vote in the presidential runoff elections, slated for June 27, 2008.

Godwin and his sister discovered that this was only one of a number of interlinked problems in the government's abuse of power. The physical beatings were the climax of a long history of violence against opponents of any kind, which includes the use of torture camps. Over a third of the population had already fled the country for political and economic reasons, many of which were connected to the atmosphere of violence. It was apparent to Godwin that the strategy of Mugabe's regime was to beat up opponents rather than kill them, burn down their houses, and attack their families. The maimed victims would then return to society, so everyone could see the consequences of opposing ZANU. This was called *chidudu*, "the fear."

Godwin and Georgina went on tour, meeting old family and personal friends. Most of their white farmer friends had been dispossessed of their farms, which now lay

(Little, Brown and Company)

Peter Godwin has worked as foreign correspondent for the Sunday Times *and contributed many pieces to New York journals. He has written two memoirs of his life in Zimbabwe. He received a Guggenheim Fellowship in 2010.*

unproductive, being reclaimed by the bush. ZANU gangs made a practice of arriving on a farmer's property, taking over the house, looting it, and then possessing the land; because they had no agricultural skills, however, the harvest of grain and tobacco fell and the country became more and more impoverished.

This led to rampant inflation, sending the Zimbabwean dollar into free fall. The consequent state of hyperinflation resulted in the creation of currency notes for billions and even trillions of dollars. Financial savings had long ago disappeared, as had the value of any fixed pensions. Retired people were dependent on charities or relatives abroad and many black families were dependent on family members working in South Africa.

The book consists largely of the narratives of the victims, both black and white, past and present. Many of the stories are quite horrific. Godwin does not avoid sharing details of the unimaginable cruelty inflicted on defenseless men, women, children, old people, and even animals. Yet in the midst of this savagery, there are two things that stand out. The first is the bizarre sense of normalcy that exists side by side with the grotesque injustice; next door to a hospital overflowing with victims of violence is a racetrack meeting, where people place bets and socialize as if nothing is awry. Second, there is an emerging group of people who have moved beyond fear. They have been beaten but their spirits have not been broken. Their beatings unite them and make them more determined than ever to support the MDC and defy Mugabe. The book's closing episode features a support group of torture and rape victims seeking to bring healing to each other through shared narratives and rituals.

The book's forty-one chapters follow Godwin and Georgina's travels around Zimbabwe interviewing victims. Godwin attends his parents' Anglican church, only to find it divided between pro- and anti-Mugabe congregations. The police arrive to drive away the hymn-singing opponents, Godwin among them. Finally, the secret police confront the pair and a friendly police officer advises them to leave the country. Godwin goes briefly to South Africa, then returns to the United States, where he solicits support from the government

Ultimately, the MDC leader, Morgan Tsvangirai, withdraws his candidacy in the runoff election to try to stem the killing, beating, and torture of his party members. Mugabe is therefore reelected president, but with so little credibility or international recognition that he has to agree to Tsvangirai becoming prime minister in a power-sharing government. In February 2009, Godwin returns to Zimbabwe to observe the formation of this new government.

The beginnings of the new government are slow and difficult. In additional to economic troubles, the country faces health crises such as epidemics of cholera and AIDS. Godwin also raises issues related to the persecution of politician Roy Bennett and allegations of the use of "blood diamonds" to fund violence. Despite these obstacles, Godwin acknowledges improvements to the economy following the abandonment of the Zimbabwean dollar in favor of foreign currency. He also highlights the role of foreign embassies in the protection of victims of political violence.

Godwin's dramatic and detailed account reveals a beautiful and sad country that is as full of brave, patiently suffering people as it is of their violent tormentors. Whereas in some brutal dictatorships, the moral forces of civil society have been corrupted almost beyond repair, here in Zimbabwe that is not the case. There are still pastors, educators, farmers, activists, and organizations actively trying to stem the tide of evil at great cost and through countless small acts of strength.

In *Fear*, Godwin expects his readers to know more about Zimbabwe than most will at the outset. Those familiar with his previously published memoirs, *Mukiwa: A White Boy in Africa* (2004) and *When a Crocodile Eats the Sun: A Memoir* (2008), will understand more of the references. Other questions go unanswered as Godwin often neglects to share logistical details. For example, how does he manage to drive around the country several times when everything is in desperately short supply? How can a country abandon one form of currency for another when it has no currency reserves?

The book received high praise when it was first published in mid-2010, first in the United Kingdom and then shortly after in the United States. A slightly revised paperback version with a new subtitle, *The Fall of Robert Mugabe*, was released in 2011 to equally positive reviews. Because foreign journalists had been banned from Zimbabwe for some years, Godwin's firsthand account gave substance to many of the secondhand reports circulating via reporters in South Africa or through the diaspora. His knowledge of the country and the breadth of his acquaintances make this book both an authentic plea for justice on behalf of the victims and a documentary worthy of bringing Mugabe to international justice.

At the end of the book, Mugabe is still in power. But the book is part of an ongoing narrative, with the final outcome still far from certain.

David Barratt

Review Sources:

The New York Times, May 23, 2011, p. C1.
The Observer, November 28, 2010, p. 45.
The Sunday Times, October 3, 2010 (Web).
The Sunday Times, July 24, 2011 (Web).
The Wall Street Journal, April 2, 2011 (Web).
The Washington Post, April 10, 2011 (Web).

Feeding on Dreams
Confessions of an Unrepentant Exile

Author: Ariel Dorfman (b. 1942)
Publisher: Houghton Mifflin Harcourt (New York). 332 pp. $27.00
Type of work: Memoir
Time: 1973–2011
Locale: Chile; Argentina; Paris, France; Amsterdam, Netherlands; Washington, DC; and Durham, North Carolina

This memoir relates the experiences of loss, exile, and self-discovery of Ariel Dorfman after his flight from Chile. Dorfman's book makes an important contribution to the area of human rights by insisting on the necessity of valuing human community over membership in political parties.

Principal personages:
ARIEL DORFMAN, an author and a human-rights
    activist; former cultural adviser under the administration of Salvador Allende
ANGÉLICA DORFMAN, his wife, also a human rights activist
RODRIGO DORFMAN, his son, born in Chile
JOAQUIN DORFMAN, his son, born in Amsterdam
SALVADOR ALLENDE, Chilean president overthrown by Pinochet
AUGUSTO PINOCHET, extremely brutal Chilean dictator whose overthrow of Allende
    forced Dorfman to flee his homeland

Feeding on Dreams: Confessions of an Unrepentant Exile is Ariel Dorfman's second memoir. In his first memoir, *Heading South, Looking North: A Bilingual Journey*, published in 1998, Dorfman relates the story of his childhood and his life up to the military coup of 1973 that forced him to flee from Chile. In *Feeding on Dreams*, Ariel Dorfman recounts his years of exile after the overthrow of Salvador Allende's government by General Augusto Pinochet in the military coup of 1973. He also tells the stories of numerous individuals whose lives were severely damaged or destroyed by the Pinochet regime. Dorfman focuses his memoir on both his own inner life and that of the people whose stories he tells. He emphasizes his intense love for Chile and his overwhelming desire to return there. He explains that the dictatorship deprived Chileans of their country whether they fled or remained in the country.

Dorfman's text does not follow a chronological order of events. It is symbolically liberated from the constraints of logical order and time sequence. As he states, the text is a memoir and the mind is free to remember in a disordered fashion that defies strict organization. He admits that this method of narration can cause problems for the reader, and so he includes a useful timeline at the end of his book. The book is divided into three sections—"Arrivals," "Returns," and "Departures"—along with an introduction and an epilogue. Interspersed throughout the text are fragments from the diary he wrote during his return to Chile in 1990. These are also out of chronological order and give the text a sense of circularity and return, however impermanent.

In his introduction, Dorfman summarizes his life of exile and the loss that it has generated, explaining to the reader his preoccupation with death that began when he was very young. As a child, he fantasized about hovering above his dead body, waiting for just the right moment to return to life. In his adult life, death becomes an ever-present, oppressing threat beginning with the military coup of September 11, 1973. Death becomes a destructive force that deprives him of many friends and forces him into exile. Here, Dorfman also introduces the role of language in human life. For him, language exists as a realm, as a means of realization of existence and as a complex tool of interaction between both benevolent and sinister human beings. He also tries to explain the genesis of his text. He proposes that writers do not choose their books, but are rather chosen by them and led to write them at the right time.

In the main three sections of the book, Dorfman elaborates on the titular themes of arrival, departure, and return. He discusses exile, isolation, loss, language, the vocation of the writer, the devastating effects of violent revolution and dictatorship, the complexity of human relationships, and the value of political systems. As the book progresses, he delves ever deeper into the human condition.

Dorfman's exile leads him to Buenos Aires, Argentina, where he was born but is not welcome to stay. Upon arrival, he is immediately subjected to innumerable hours of interrogation and warned that revolutionaries are not welcome. Threatened for his life, he is once again forced to flee. His exile takes him to safe houses first in Paris, then in Amsterdam, and eventually to the United States, where he became the Walter Hines Page Professor of Literature and Latin American Studies at Duke University, a teaching position he still held while writing *Feeding on Dreams*.

Dorfman addresses a considerable number of issues in his book; some surface as he attempts to discover himself, others as he relates stories about his friends and comrades and the effects of revolutionary resistance to dictatorship. The most significant personal issues for Dorfman are his suffering in exile, the way his bilingualism divides him, and his final acceptance of the fact that he is different from the *pobres*, the poor Chileans he wants to help. Further discoveries Dorfman addresses in the memoir include the realization that his enemies can share his tastes in the arts and that party loyalty and morality are often incompatible. Throughout his text, Dorfman emphasizes how out of place and alienated he feels. His sudden impoverishment and struggle to live without secure employment, as well as the control that the resistance group has over his life, create an environment of tension and desperation. He despises Paris, where his group has sent him and his family. Their life in France is almost unbearable because of the linguistic and social challenges they face. Although life is better once he and his family have moved to Amsterdam, Dorfman is still tormented by his desire to return to Chile.

© Les Todd

Ariel Dorfman, a professor at Duke University, is a Chilean American writer and human rights activist. His work has been translated into over forty languages, and his plays performed in more than one hundred countries. He has won numerous awards for his novels, plays, poetry, and essays, including the Sudamericana Award and two Kennedy Center theater awards.

One theme running throughout the text is Dorfman's need to use his talent as a writer to tell the story of the victims of oppression, coupled with his inability to do so and the way he works his way back to writing both in English and in Spanish. As a speaker of both Spanish and English, Dorfman experiences a long period of conflict. For him, the two languages exist as living entities; he feels that speaking English is a betrayal of Spanish, his true language. Eventually, he accepts himself as a bilingual individual and realizes that both languages are part of who he is. In *Feeding on Dreams*, Dorfman writes primarily in English, but the text is speckled with Spanish words and phrases. Throughout his seventeen years of exile, Dorfman dreams of returning to Chile, and he deceives himself into believing that both he and Chile will be as they were when he was a young idealistic supporter of Allende. Finally, after his returns to Chile in 1983 and again in 1990, he accepts the fact that the country has become a different Chile, marked by the suffering it endured under Pinochet and by the affluence of those who profited financially from the dictatorship. Dorfman also realizes that he is unable to be one with the *pueblo* (the people) of Chile, because he is separated from them by the privilege of his European ancestry, his education, and his position as a writer.

While the memoir is focused on Dorfman's own life and the role that revolution, resistance to dictatorship, and exile have played in his own life and in that of his wife and their two sons, the memoir is also a strong condemnation of any government or political system that depends upon fear, brutality, and oppression to maintain its control. Dorfman asserts that the fear instilled in people by such a regime continues to control their lives long after the oppressive government is no longer in power.

Dorfman devotes a considerable portion of his book to examining the effects of revolution and resistance to dictatorship on women. As he recounts his own journey of exile, he also relates that of his wife, Angélica, emphasizing her resiliency and her willingness to accept a secondary role as she follows wherever the resistance committee sends her family. She also suffers loss as she is separated from her extended family and her country. In addition, Dorfman considers how totalitarian regimes and violent revolutions violate women both in their persons, through acts of rape and torture, and in their emotional lives, through the brutal murder or disappearance of the men in their families.

Dorfman is especially skillful in his use of description to convey ambiance and intense emotion, particularly fear. He recounts a night in Santiago, Chile, when he is walking in the streets and suddenly a car surrounded by guards on motorcycles passes by. A white-gloved hand emerges from the car and waves. It is Pinochet reinforcing his presence and his control over the life of each and every Chilean. For Dorfman, Pinochet is always there in the darkness, menacing and emptying the lives of the victims of his dictatorship.

Dorfman also offers a compelling description of the existence of a political prisoner. He may actually be a political dissident or only a purported revolutionary, but either way, he experiences horror and suffering. Dorfman describes how the blindfolded or hooded prisoner knows where he is being taken only by whether he is led upstairs or downstairs and by how many steps he must take. Sometimes he is led to the bathroom, other times to the torture room.

Dorfman's writing creates lasting images in the reader's mind, illustrating what he believes to be the realities of the world in which we live and explaining the complexities of life. When his son Rodrigo is taken to jail as an adult, he is able to avoid transfer to the penitentiary because he, like the police lieutenant, is plainly of European ancestry. He convinces the lieutenant that neither he nor the lieutenant belong there surrounded by the darker-skinned Chileans with their dark eyes; he and the lieutenant are superior. Similarly, Dorfman recounts how wearing a sumptuous camel hair coat left to him by a Yugoslavian dissident and fellow exile repeatedly opens doors for him because it declares his high social rank. Stories about Rodrigo's strong attachment to his toys, and easy acceptance of their loss, illustrate how exile changes even children.

Feeding on Dreams: Confessions of an Unrepentant Exile has been highly praised as a masterfully written text. Reviews also speak favorably of its sensitive portrayal of exile, loss, self-realization, and acceptance. An occasional critic has found the memoir to be too focused on Dorfman's life as a writer, but in general, *Feeding on Dreams* has been received as a perceptive investigation and portrait of the devastating effects of exile and of the losses citizens suffer when their rights are denied them.

Shawncey J. Webb

Review Sources

The Boston Globe, September 26, 2011 (Web).
Kirkus Reviews 79, no. 13 (July 1, 2011): 1107.
Law Professors, September 23, 2011 (Web).
The New Yorker 87, no. 33 (October 24, 2011): 81.

Field Gray

Author: Philip Kerr (b. 1956)
Publisher: G. P. Putnam's Sons (New York).
448 pp. $26.95
Type of work: Novel
Time: 1954
Locale: Havana and Guantánamo, Cuba; New
York City; Paris, France; Göttingen, Frank-
furt, Munich, and Berlin, Germany

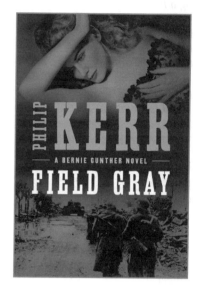

*The seventh novel in the popular Bernie Gun-
ther detective series finds the hero hiding in
Cuba, but he is soon forced back to Europe to
confront his checkered past.*

Principal characters:

BERNHARD "BERNIE" GUNTHER, a fifty-eight-
year-old police detective and former Nazi
soldier

MELBA MARRERO, a young, beautiful Cuban prostitute and fugitive wanted for murder

JERRY SILVERMAN, an American interrogator for the Office of the Chief Counsel for
War Crimes in Germany

GENERAL REINHARD HEYDRICH, the cruel leader of the *Schutzstaffel* (SS), assassinated in
1942

GENERAL ARTHUR NEBE, the former Berlin police chief, later a mass murderer and
coconspirator in plots to assassinate Hitler

ERICH MIELKE, a German communist whom Gunter first met in 1931, later head of
East German secret police

ELISABETH DEHLER, an attractive brunette seamstress, later the manager of a Berlin
nightclub and Bernie's love interest

PAUL KESTNER, a schoolmate and former friend of Gunther's from the Berlin police who
became an SS officer and deputy commander of Poland's Treblinka death camp

NIKOLAUS WILLMS, a former vice squad policeman who, as an SS officer, ran a prosti-
tution ring in wartime Paris

RENATA MATTER, a young Swiss housemaid in a Parisian hotel who once saved Bernie's
life

PHILIP SCHEUER, an agent with the Central Intelligence Agency who questions Gunther in Germany

JIM FREI, another CIA agent who questions Gunther

Complex and dense, Philip Kerr's *Field Gray* is part thriller, part crime fiction, and
part spy novel. By any label, it is a worthy continuation of the compelling and thought-
provoking Bernie Gunther series, which began with *March Violets* in 1989. Like its

Best-selling author Philip Kerr has won numerous honors for his work, including a Prix du Roman in 1993 for March Violets *(1989). His novel* If the Dead Rise Not *(2010) received the Le Point Prize, the RBA International Prize for Crime Writing, and the Crime Writers' Association Ellis Peters Historical Dagger Award in 2009, as well as the Barry Award for Best British Crime Novel in 2010.*

predecessors, *Field Gray* is a plausible and seamless weave of crime fiction within a factual backdrop, featuring actual historical figures and genuine landmarks. The novel creates a stark tapestry, depicting a volatile and horrific period of twentieth-century history and illuminating what people will resort to when faced with the need to survive.

In *March Violets*, the year is 1936 and police detective Bernie Gunther, an Iron Cross–awarded veteran of World War I, is called upon to solve murders committed during the Berlin Olympics. This novel alludes to Bernie's mettle as an investigator, frequently proven during his many years on the force. Resourceful, indefatigable, cynical, and caustic, Bernie is a hero in the hard-boiled, noir-flavored tradition that includes such characters as Sam Spade, Mike Hammer, and Philip Marlowe. In subsequent novels in the series, Kerr follows Bernie's suspenseful and convoluted exploits before, during, and after World War II as he demonstrates his investigative prowess working as a private eye and a hotel detective. He is eventually pressed into service as a reluctant officer in the Nazi SS, which controlled the *Sicherheitsdienst* (SD, the Security Service), the *Geheime Staatspolizei* (Gestapo, the secret state police), the *Kriminalpolizei* (Kripo, or criminal police) and the *Ordnungspolizei* (Orpo, or Order Police) during the early 1940s. Throughout his physically risky, soul-battering experiences, Bernie clings to his principles, holding himself firmly to morality and sanity in an ocean roiling with evil and madness. Though he must resort to violence in order to survive, and though he uses dubious or illegal methods to achieve his goals, he retains his humanity, often feeling the weight of his actions on his conscience. Having endured the ruthless new world order that attended the rise of the Nazi party in Germany, Bernie is well suited to his new life of living undercover in 1954, when *Field Gray* begins.

Hiding in Cuba under a fake name, Bernie enjoys the distance of time and geography that separates him from his previous life. In the late 1940s, he fled Germany to Argentina (via an ex-Nazi network, ironically) and since then has worked his way to Havana, Cuba. Posing as an Argentine named Carlos Hausner, he leads a comparatively untroubled life. Kerr details much of this in the novel *If the Dead Rise Not* (2010). With an apartment, money in the bank, an automobile, a boat, and a cushy job at a casino owned by the American mobster Meyer Lansky, Bernie enjoys an idyll that, in Kerr's world, cannot last forever.

Bernie is soon persuaded to accept the questionable assignment of sailing a young prostitute name Melba Marrero to Haiti to save her from punishment for killing a Cuban policeman. En route, a US patrol boat intercepts them, and Bernie is imprisoned and questioned at Guantánamo, Cuba. Weeks later, he is transferred to Castle Williams, a military prison in New York City, where agents from the Federal Bureau of Investigation (FBI) further interrogate Bernie about his past. Suspected of being a war criminal, he is flown to Landsberg Prison in Germany, where he is placed in the same cell Hitler occupied when he wrote his memoir and manifesto *Mein Kampf* (1925–26). Here, Americans from the War Crimes Office continue to grill him about his wartime activities. To convince his captors that he is not a Nazi sympathizer, Bernie is forced to recall unpleasant memories from the past. Although he is initially cleared as a war criminal, members of the Central Intelligence Agency (CIA) begin the interrogations anew, this time regarding Bernie's association with his ally and sometimes-foe Erich Mielke, a German Communist politician and the head of East German secret police.

In a series of flashbacks, Bernie relives key incidents from the previous twenty years, particularly concerning his complicated relationship with Mielke, whom he saved from being killed by Nazi thugs in 1931. Suspected in the murder of two Berlin policemen, Mielke leaves Germany for Russia, but Bernie tracks his friend's whereabouts and activities during his several stints as a police detective as Mielke engages in various acts of espionage. Bernie and Mielke cross paths repeatedly over the years, twice at prisoner-of-war camps, where Mielke, now a Soviet, returns Bernie's loyalty by making an attempt on his life. Still, the plucky detective foils the assassination attempt and returns to Germany unscathed. Mielke subsequently avoids Russian purges and is elevated in the ranks of Communist hierarchy until he becomes the deputy chief of the secret police, *Ministerium für Staatssicheerheit* (State Security, called "Stasi"), in East Germany. Kerr develops an intriguing relationship between the two characters, portraying both as survivors with murky moral codes.

Back in the central storyline, the CIA turns Bernie over to French security forces, who take him into custody for different war crimes: the alleged murder of concentration camp prisoners. Now with a passport that identifies him as Sébastien Kléber, Bernie bargains for his freedom and accompanies the French agents to Hannover, Germany, to identify a French war criminal among a mass of prisoners of war being repatriated from Russia. Meanwhile, Bernie reunites with Elisabeth Dehler, whom he has not seen in seven years, in the American sector of West Berlin. She has endured much, including gang rape by the Russians, abuse at the hands of the American occupation, and the death of a child from meningitis. With nothing to lose, Bernie and Elisabeth make arrangements to marry. Before the wedding, however, the CIA spirits Bernie away to Frankfurt. In return for his freedom, and a large monetary reward, he agrees to help capture Erich Mielke, whom the CIA hopes to pump for information about future Communist plans. The capture is to be staged in Berlin, where Mielke purportedly visits his ailing father on a regular basis. But Bernie, who never enjoys being forced to work for people he does not like, has made his own plans in secret with Mielke, and the outcome of the scheme is vastly different from what anybody expects.

Unlike the previous novels in Kerr's series, which are presented in straightforward chronological fashion, a major portion of *Field Gray* revisits the past, unfolding in chapters of extensive flashback. These chapters serve not just to dramatize incidents that would otherwise be described only in dialogue but also to expand upon incidents obliquely referred to in other books in the series, adding further dimension to the central character.

As in all of the novels, the antiheroic protagonist Bernie Gunther serves as the first-person narrator. Scarred by the circumstances of his tumultuous life, and with a personal agenda often at odds with prevailing wisdom, Bernie is not always a reliable narrator. He is honest with himself but seldom with others. He knows that those with whom he deals will not always disclose the full truth, and to protect his own interests he does not feel obliged to do otherwise himself. While his sense of honor remains constant, his sense of justice is ruled by expedience and varies according to the particular occasion. Even the novel's title has shifting shades of meaning: "field gray" was the color of Gestapo uniforms because, according to Bernie, gray does not show the dirt its wearers wallowed in. Gray is also an appropriate metaphor for the morally ambiguous twilight zone in which Bernie usually operates, somewhere between the whites and blacks of absolute good and evil. In Bernie's universe, it is difficult to distinguish between the good guys and the bad guys. Those characters who traditionally wear the white hats, like the British and Americans, are frequently just as ruthless as their black-hat counterparts. Symbolic of Bernie's independent and conflicted character is his good-luck charm, a broken chess piece made of bone. This material can be taken to represent the millions of lives that were lost during Nazi Germany's rise and fall, to which Bernie has contributed a share. Importantly, the knight is the only chess piece that does not move in a straight line, a path its owner emulates. With the symbol of the black knight, Kerr reminds his protagonist and readers both that no matter what, Bernie will never be anybody's pawn.

Jack Ewing

Review Sources

Booklist 107, no. 15 (April 1, 2011): 30.
Kirkus Reviews 79, no. 4 (February 15, 2011): 265.
Library Journal 135, no. 19 (November 15, 2010): 45.
Library Journal 136, no. 3 (March 15, 2011): 108-9.
The New York Times Book Review, April 24, 2011, p. 15.
Publishers Weekly 258, no. 8 (February 21, 2011): 110.

The Fifth Witness

Author: Michael Connelly (b. 1956)
Publisher: Little, Brown (New York).
448 pp. $27.99; paperback $14.99
Type of work: Novel
Time: The present
Locale: Los Angeles, California

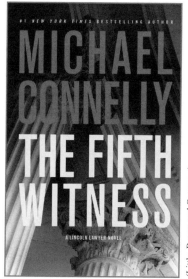

Mickey Haller, the hero of Michael Connelly's popular Lincoln Lawyer series, returns to criminal law to defend a client who has been accused of murder.

Principal characters:

MICHAEL "MICKEY" HALLER, a criminal defense attorney who ordinarily works out of the front seat of an armored Lincoln automobile

MAGGIE MCPHERSON, Haller's ex-wife

HEATHER HALLER, Haller's teenage daughter

LISA TRAMMEL, Haller's client, an anti-foreclosure advocate and the defendant in the murder trial

JENNIFER ARONSON, Haller's junior associate, a young, idealistic law school graduate

CISCO WOJCIECHOWSKI, Haller's investigator, also a member of a motorcycle club

MITCHELL BONDURANT, the victim, a senior vice president of the mortgage company

LOUIS OPPARIZIO, the CEO of ALOFT, the company that performs foreclosures for the bank

HERBERT DAHL, a filmmaker

(Little, Brown and Company)

The legal procedural thriller is a popular subgenre of the mystery novel, with literary roots going back at least to the early twentieth century. Some of its best-known examples are Dorothy Sayers's *Strong Poison* (1930) and *Clouds of Witness* (1926), Meyer Levin's *Compulsion* (1956), and Robert Traver's *Anatomy of a Murder* (1958). Since then, the genre has exploded in popularity, with novelists such as John Grisham, Scott Turow, and Michael Connelly reigning supreme among their American contemporaries. Connelly's latest novel, *The Fifth Witness*, is the fourth book in his Lincoln Lawyer series, and, like many such novels, it revolves around a trial for murder. Mickey Haller is the eponymous Lincoln lawyer, doing business from the back seat of a bulletproof Lincoln Town Car—which, notably, he obtained from the widow of a gangster as payment for his services.

As the novel opens, Haller finds that criminal defense does not pay like it used to; the economic downturn has hit his potential clients in Los Angeles just as hard as everyone else. Fortunately, Haller has discovered lucrative business in foreclosure defense, preventing his clients' home mortgage foreclosures, at least for a while. Like many recent cases of foreclosure in the United States, these cases are shown to be slipshod, even fraudulent, and Connelly uses Haller as a mouthpiece to comment on the corporate greed and carelessness that have produced the problem. This lends the plot a timely kind of urgency, as the central conflict arises from widely felt anxieties and issues in American society.

Haller is just closing his deal with a foreclosure client when he is suddenly catapulted back into criminal law. His very first foreclosure client, Lisa Trammel, has been arrested for the brutal murder of Mitchell Bondurant, one of the officers of Westland Financial, the corporation that previously foreclosed on her home. Following the foreclosure, Trammel turned to activism, organizing Foreclosure Litigants Against Greed (FLAG), a group whose street demonstrations and picketing against foreclosures have received significant publicity. By appearing online and in television interviews, she has become a widely recognized political figure, a recognition that proves problematic for her case.

Complicating the defense is an antagonistic filmmaker, Herbert Dahl, who puts up Trammel's bond and stands to gain exclusive book and movie rights to her story. Against Haller's advice, Dahl encourages Trammel to talk to the press, a poor course of action for the defendant in a murder trial. Haller manages to limit this potential damage by excluding Dahl from client and staff discussions of the investigation, trial, and defense strategies.

As the arraignment proceeds and the trial begins, the state makes its case against Trammel, with Connelly building courtroom suspense in a way that fans of his previous work will appreciate. The prosecution's case includes eyewitness testimony that places Trammel near the site of the crime around the time it was committed. To make things worse, detectives have discovered traces of the victim's blood on Trammel's gardening shoes and on a hammer in her garage. The prosecution then puts forward Trammel's political involvement and well-known opposition to the bank and mortgage company as a potential motive. The case against her seems strong, but in order to get an acquittal, Haller merely needs to convince the jury of reasonable doubt regarding her supposed role in the crime. In this way, Connelly raises a fascinating issue of legal practice and a compelling element of suspense. Under the ethical canons of the American Bar Association, a lawyer may not adduce facts that he or she knows to be false. A defense lawyer is sometimes handicapped if too much is known; it is important that the client not tell her attorney the details of the crime, for if she does, all defenses that rely on alternate theories cannot be raised. Haller often silences Trammel out of fear of such a risk, so that he may suggest an alternate theory to the jury.

Much of the suspense of *The Fifth Witness* lies in its description of the strategies and tactics that Haller uses to establish reasonable doubt for the jury. He hints that the eyewitness, a short woman, would have had difficulty identifying Trammel from across three lanes of traffic. Similarly, he argues the improbability of Trammel, who is only five feet three herself, being able to hit a man who is six feet tall on the top of his head with a hammer. The garage in which the incriminating blood evidence was found, Haller points out, was unlocked. While these points are not sufficient in

Michael Connelly is an American author of detective novels and other crime fiction, notably those featuring LAPD detective Hieronymus "Harry" Bosch and criminal defense attorney Mickey Haller. His books have received many awards. Connelly was president of the Mystery Writers of America from 2003 to 2004.

and of themselves to destroy the prosecution's case, they do cast an element of doubt. Finally, Haller deploys a technique that is a staple of legal procedural novels, presenting the jury with a possible alternative solution to the case. He tries to suggest that Louis Opparizio, the CEO of the foreclosure firm, had motive and opportunity to commit the crime, and Haller devises a superb scheme to serve Opparizio with a subpoena. Eventually, and against the prosecution's fierce opposition, Haller succeeds in forcing Opparizio to testify, and it emerges that he has ties to organized crime in New York City. As Haller cross-examines him, the meaning of Connelly's title becomes apparent when Opparizio desperately claims Fifth Amendment protection against further testimony.

Connelly reveals nearly all of these events in the context of the trial itself, advancing the plot through the examination and cross-examination of witnesses. While Haller propels the story line in the courtroom, however, significant events transpire outside it as well, as staff investigator Cisco Wojciechowski provides the factual ammunition that Haller needs in court. Also among the conflicts that take place outside of the courtroom is the severe beating that Haller suffers at the hands of a couple of thugs who are trying to warn him off the case. The assault helps to persuade Haller that there may be some truth to his alternate theory of the crime. When he learns the identity of the person who hired the thugs, the resolution of this subplot proves important in the novel's denouement.

Beyond its gripping storyline and courtroom intrigue, *The Fifth Witness* raises several serious ethical and personal issues. The novel is narrated in the first person from Mickey Haller's point of view, providing the reader with immediate access to his ambivalence about the responsibilities of his job. While he understands that all criminal defendants are entitled to a vigorous legal defense, he remains unsure about the ethics of using the rules of the system to potentially let murderers escape punishment. His idealistic junior associate, Jennifer Aronson, believes that rather than manipulating the system, lawyers should simply use it to discover the truth; Haller thinks she does not understand that both sides are guilty of manipulation, as demonstrated by the tactics of both prosecution and defense. Still, as Jennifer registers her distress at Haller's tactics, Haller himself feels a growing unease. Although his inner turmoil diminishes as the trial wears on and he becomes more and more convinced that his client is actually innocent, Connelly succeeds in raising a critical awareness of the many interests at play in the justice system.

Haller's concern for his role deepens once issues arise regarding his relationships with Maggie, his ex-wife, and Heather, their teenage daughter. Maggie is also an attorney, but she works for the district attorney. Although she is not directly involved with the case, she and Haller find themselves at different ends of the legal spectrum: her job is to put criminals away, while his job is to defend them. Though this underlying conflict has wrecked their marriage, they remain drawn to one another and committed to their daughter, with Haller hoping to reestablish their marriage one day. Haller fears that the better he is at his job, the less likely it is that he and Maggie will be together again permanently. This tension weighs on him throughout the course of the trial, his desire for Maggie's approval playing an influential part in some of his choices in the courtroom.

The trial's end sets the stage for the novel's denouement. There are some plot twists that defy prediction but which fit so cleverly and persuasively into the overall story that the reader is practically left gasping. Here, Connelly demonstrates his greatest gift as a novelist, his ability to keep the action moving until the very end. The reader also finds that Mickey Haller, whom Connelly is sure to revisit in future installments, has changed. The novel ends as he embarks on a new direction in life, one that is probably more likely to restore his relationship with Maggie and, perhaps, to resurrect his marriage.

The noir mystery has its conventions. There is always a detective or police officer with a drinking problem, a secret sorrow, or a broken romantic relationship, and this protagonist is typically at home in the seamiest and most disgusting venues of society. While Mickey Haller's drinking has been under control for two years, he otherwise fits this profile perfectly. The legal procedural subgenre employs these conventions as well, and *The Fifth Witness* is no exception. Readers who are tired of the clichés of the genre might be inclined to ignore *The Fifth Witness*; that, however, would be a mistake, for the novel represents Connelly at his most exciting and engaging. The clarity of Connelly's writing (especially in dialogue), his brilliant plots, and his main character's emotional journey make this novel an irresistible page-turner, both fascinating and worthwhile.

Robert Jacobs

Review Sources

Chicago Sun-Times, April 7, 2011 (Web).
Kirkus Reviews 79, no. 3 (February 1, 2011): 154.
Los Angeles Times, April 5, 2011 (Web).
The New York Times Book Review, April 8, 2011, p. 23.
Oregonian, April 9, 2011 (Web).

The Forgotten Founding Father
Noah Webster's Obsession and the Creation of an American Culture

Author: Joshua Kendall (b. 1960)
Publisher: G. P. Putnam's Sons (New York).
368 pp. $26.95
Type of work: Literary biography
Time: 1758–1843
Locale: Throughout the American East Coast

This biography of Noah Webster offers a color-ful portrait of the man who compiled the first American English dictionary and helped the country discover its national identity.

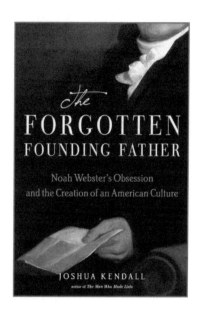

Principal personages:
NOAH WEBSTER JR. (1758–1843), lexicographer, educator, political activist, journalist, and editor
REBECCA GREENLEAF WEBSTER (1766–1847), his loyal wife
NOAH WEBSTER SR. (1722–1813), his emotion-ally distant father
MERCY STEELE WEBSTER (1727–1794), his emotionally distant mother
JOEL BARLOW (1754–1812), an early American poet and Webster's best friend at Yale University
BENJAMIN FRANKLIN (1706–1790), a writer and inventor, an early supporter of Webster's career

As Joshua Kendall's title suggests, Noah Webster may be the least known of the fig-ures who founded the United States, but this comprehensive biography should help to restore him to his rightful place in history. He deserves the spot for his *American Dictionary of the English Language* (1828) alone, the work that first catalogued the new nation's distinctive language and helped bring the country together both culturally and linguistically. As Kendall shows, however, Webster was much more than simply a compiler of words; he was an early American Renaissance man who made contribu-tions in half a dozen fields, from journalism and politics to medicine and education. Kendall also reveals the troubled and compulsive personality—vain and ambitious, self-critical and self-promoting—behind so many of Webster's achievements. Like his early mentor, Benjamin Franklin, Webster was a complex personality whose multiple achievements make their creator difficult to capture, though in this new biography he emerges vividly.

Webster was born in 1758 in Hartford, Connecticut, of pure Yankee stock; his moth-er's family traced their roots back to William Bradford, one of the original *Mayflower* settlers and the author of the first account of their settlement in *Of Plymouth Plantation.* Webster enrolled in Yale University at the age of fifteen, where he joined a distinguished company that included Joel Barlow, Timothy Dwight, and John Trumbull—the main members of the poetic circle later known as the Connecticut Wits, which helped establish early on an American literary tradition. Webster's education, like the college's schedule, would be disrupted by the Revolutionary War; just as he enrolled in the fall of 1774, the First Continental Congress was convening in Philadelphia. Webster graduated in 1778, the same year in which the fledgling nation emerged, and drifted through his first years after the war, teaching and practicing law without much success in either field. What did come out of these early struggles was Webster's first best seller, a speller for children (1784; renamed *The American Spelling Book* in 1787), which became an instant sensation. The volume would go through eighty-eight editions in two decades and sell thirteen million copies during Webster's lifetime; over the next century, it would be outsold only by the Bible. The success of this volume, and of Webster's accompanying reader (a third grammar volume of his did less well), can be explained in part by its simple, practical approach to pedagogy that incorporated American names and authors as its examples—qualities that would later make his dictionary successful as well. Even in the years after the nation's founding, textbooks were often British and carried English names, locations, and selections. Through his publications, Webster was changing education in the United States, slowly enabling Americans to think of themselves as a distinct and independent nation. Thanks to Webster, spelling bees became the United States' first national pastime, as evening "spelldowns" were commonly held in New England towns.

After this early success, Webster's career failed to take off, proceeding only in fits and starts throughout his life. He assured his wife's socially prominent family that he would give up his literary career to be a law professor, and for the next decade, he struggled to make a living from legal work. However, he continued his literary career and, according to Kendall, became America's most prolific freelance journalist, specializing in political commentary and anonymous articles; much of this work was later collected in a volume titled *The Prompter; Or, A Commentary on Common Sayings and Subjects* (1791). Webster also traveled the country peddling his speller and giving talks about the United States and its language, thus creating the first promotional book tour and becoming the nation's first celebrity speaker, though admittedly he was far less successful than Mark Twain would be in the century that followed.

In 1793, Webster finally gave up law to become the editor of the country's first daily newspaper, *American Minerva,* which he ran successfully for five years before giving it up and moving to New Haven. There, he continued his freelance career, often supporting Federalist positions on central government, among other issues. In 1800, he began serious work on his dictionary. Again, his progress would not be direct or swift; work on the dictionary would take nearly thirty years to complete, disrupted by a number of self-inflicted delays. His growing family (the Websters would eventually have six children) was one distraction, although Webster was an authoritarian husband and father who often isolated himself in a soundproofed study to work.

Joshua Kendall is an award-winning journalist whose writing has appeared in the Boston Globe, *the* Los Angeles Times, *and the* Wall Street Journal. *He is the author of* The Man Who Made Lists: Love, Death, Madness, and the Creation of Roget's Thesaurus *(2008).*

Webster continued to work on other projects during this time. After yellow fever spread across the country in the 1790s, he published a book on epidemics, in which his citation of possible environmental causes came close to identifying the fever's actual origins (mosquitoes); and in 1806, he published the *Compendious Dictionary of the English Language,* a preview of his later and longer dictionary, in which he began to regularize American spelling. Webster did much to create a unique American language—he dropped the "u" in "favour," for example, and the "k" in "musick"—but was also occasionally prone to heading in the wrong orthographic direction: he recommended the spelling "wimmen" for women, "tung" for tongue, and "wether" for weather. The lexicographer he was trying to match was the British writer Samuel Johnson, whose *Dictionary of the English Language* (1755) provided the model for dictionary makers for centuries. Like Johnson, Webster also fought a lifelong battle against mental illness, finding a solution in compulsive work. The personality defects he suffered from, such as his obsessive behavior, would make him a perfect lexicographer.

Webster's distractions continued as well. He spent a decade on a misguided attempt to prove a systematic universal etymology in *A Synopsis of Words in Twenty Languages* (1817), but he did not know these languages well enough to master comparative linguistics. He uprooted his family to Amherst, Massachusetts, in 1812 and returned to work on the dictionary in 1817. In 1822, the Websters returned to New Haven, where Noah hurried toward the finishing line. He traveled to Europe to complete the remaining linguistic research with his son, William, and then spent two years editing the work. In 1828, the two volumes of the *American Dictionary of the English Language* finally appeared, including thousands of commonly used American words such as "squash," "moose," and "skunk." Kendall describes Webster's achievement as extraordinary, saying that the "comprehensiveness of Webster's *American Dictionary* was breathtaking":

> It contained seventy thousand words, some twelve thousand more than the 1818 version of Johnson edited by Henry John Todd. Webster succeeded in forever expanding the scope of the dictionary. After Webster, all English lexicographers felt duty-bound to capture the language not just of literature, but also of everyday life. According to Webster's estimate, he added at least four thousand new scientific terms, including, for example, "phosphorescent" and "planetarium." . . . In perhaps his greatest contribution, Webster transformed definitions from little more than lists of synonymous terms to tightly-knit mini-essays, which highlighted fine distinctions.

Thirty years earlier, Webster had been attacked for his attempts to regularize American English; now, at the beginning of the populist presidency of Andrew Jackson, Americans were apparently more ready to recognize the distinctive characteristics of their own language and give up their reliance on British models, applauding a work that used American locales and founders as examples and authors. By the time the first edition of twenty-five thousand copies had sold out, Webster was already working on a revision. After he died in 1843, the rights to the *American Dictionary* were bought by the publishing company that would be known from that date on as Merriam-Webster. The *Dictionary* has been in print ever since, with sales in the millions and through countless editions, such as *Webster's Third New International Dictionary* in 1961, which revolutionized modern English by including numerous slang and colloquial terms as standard English, and the Collegiate edition, which has sold fifty-six million copies since it began in 1898.

Kendall's study is more than a biography of a lexicographer and more than a history of his dictionary. As the subtitle hints, the man and his book helped to create a distinctive American culture. At a time when the nation was anything but unified, Webster gave this ethnically and religiously diverse country a common language for expressing the unique social and political experiment of the United States and the culture that arose from it. There were only thirteen million Americans when the *Dictionary* appeared, and they were divided by class, region, speech, and habit, as the Civil War would prove a few decades later. Many Americans owned few books aside from the Bible and a copy of Shakespeare's plays. Webster gave them a volume that defined their own country in language they already knew, confirming their emerging history and culture. It was an astounding accomplishment. Kendall sketches out the historical and political background all along the way, explains the fundamental issues of the time, and delineates how Webster's political journalism and editing also helped define the course of the nation, its peculiar government, and its cultural institutions. Kendall shows that Webster deserves to stand next to Washington, Jefferson, Franklin, and the other founders of the nation, as his contributions to the nation's establishment were certainly as important as theirs, and in some ways were longer lasting. Readers may have to work to remember the contributions of Alexander Hamilton, but every time they consult a dictionary, they are reaching out to Noah Webster Jr.

David Peck

Review Sources

Booklist 107, no. 14 (March 15, 2011): 8.
Kirkus Reviews 79, no. 3 (February 2, 2011): 186.
Library Journal 136, no, 5 (March 15, 2011): 122.
Los Angeles Times, May 8, 2011, E12.
The New York Times Book Review, May 27, 2011, p. 17.
Publishers Weekly 258, no. 6 (February 7, 2011): 45.
The Wall Street Journal, April 14, 2011, p. A15.

Founding Gardeners
The Revolutionary Generation, Nature,
and the Shaping of the American Nation

Author: Andrea Wulf (b. 1972)
Publisher: Alfred A. Knopf (New York). 352 pp.
$30.00
Type of work: History
Time: 1776–1836
Locale: The United States

*Author Andrea Wulf examines the botanical in-
terests of America's founding fathers and how
those interests shaped their political endeavors.*

Principal personages:
GEORGE WASHINGTON, the first president of the
United States, commander in the Revolu-
tionary War
JOHN ADAMS, the second president of the Unit-
ed States, a prominent Federalist statesman
THOMAS JEFFERSON, the third president of the
United States, architect of the Monticello estate
JAMES MADISON, the fourth president of the United States, early American conservationist

Andrea Wulf's extensive scholarly and literary expertise is on full display in *Founding
Gardeners: The Revolutionary Generation, Nature, and the Shaping of the American
Nation*. Having chronicled eighteenth-century gardening in *The Brother Gardeners:
Botany, Empire, and the Birth of an Obsession* (2008), the horticultural historian now
takes her readers on a journey through the foundation of the United States, illustrating
how many of the founding fathers were avid gardeners for whom horticultural traits,
peculiarities, and skills were directly involved the political process. *Founding Gardeners* is a brilliant addition to the already considerable scholarly work available on these
figures. Although their interest in horticulture and gardening has not been ignored in
the past, the recasting of such characters as independence revolutionary and first president George Washington and founding republican Thomas Jefferson as obsessive and
neurotic gardeners is both entertaining and revealing.

Readers encounter these well-known figures as they discuss the seeds and foliage
of the new continent, swapping cuttings and dried specimens and musing on the possibility of new indigenous crops, the discovery of which could help the burgeoning
nation find economic independence. Jefferson faced the threat of the death penalty
in Italy for having stolen as much local rice "as my coat and surtout pockets would
hold." The risks were worth it, according to Jefferson, who wrote that agriculture was
"the surest road to affluence and the best preservation of morals." The unique land

and its spoils, the founding fathers believed, could forge a path of independence for the new nation.

Wulf argues that the notion of agriculture leading to a pious and prosperous nation was hardly new; in fact, it can be traced back to antiquity. The Greek philosopher Aristotle claimed that for a republic, "an Agrarian people is the best," and similarly, the Roman poet Cicero wrote that "of all the occupations by which gain is secured, none is better

Andrea Wulf's first book, The Brother Gardeners: A Generation of Gentlemen Naturalists and the Birth of an Obsession *(2008), won the American Horticultural Society Book Award in 2010 and was long-listed for the Samuel Johnson Prize in 2008. She also coauthored* This Other Eden: Seven Great Gardens *and* 300 Years of English History *(2005) with Emma Gieben-Gamal.*

than agriculture, none more profitable, none more delightful, none is more becoming to a freeman." These ancient ideals are espoused throughout the book, as Wulf's clear and concise writing style combines history with vivid description of the scenery and foliage of the largely untouched American continent.

Benjamin Franklin, the earliest founding father discussed, is often portrayed as a jack-of-all trades. Here, Wulf presents his botanical side, depicting Franklin as he swapped seeds with British dignitaries during visits across the Atlantic Ocean. The trips through the British countryside that Jefferson and John Adams took together illustrate how the two soon-to-be founding fathers, later political enemies, found peace and solitude in the peace and quiet of gardens. Wulf recounts other botanical tours, such as when Jefferson and James Madison delayed discussions regarding the creation of the Federal Bank—an issue that would tear the friendship of Jefferson and Adams apart—to tour the farms of Vermont. Wulf describes how these trips, while providing welcome relief from politics, were also deeply intertwined with the political situation of the day. Arguably, Jefferson and Adams's trip sowed the seeds that would eventually flourish into the modern-day Republican Party. Differences of opinion eventually destroyed the friendships of some of the founding fathers, but as Wulf observes, "Agriculture and its importance for the future of the United States of America remained the one topic all four agreed upon and continued to correspond about."

Much like her politician subjects, Wulf demonstrates a hands-on approach to her work. While collecting primary evidence for the book, she found herself living and working in the homes of the founding fathers, running her hands through the same soil that so captivated her subjects two hundred years earlier. This approach has no doubt helped to illuminate Wulf's vivid recreation of the stately homes and gardens in which the founding fathers lived. Washington's Mount Vernon, Jefferson's Monticello, James Madison's Montpelier, and Adams's Peacefield are described so vibrantly that the reader can picture the men themselves roaming through tumbling forests, manicured vegetable plots, and structured orchards.

According to Wulf, even in times of extreme political turmoil, the founding fathers found their way back to the land. For example, as 140 British ships sailed into New York Harbor under Lord William Howe, George Washington, the figurehead of the burgeoning American independence movement, took time off to write to his estate manager at Mount Vernon and ask how the gardens were coming along. Wulf describes Washington as "the Cincinnatus of the West," after the Roman dictator who was pulled away from his simple farming life to save the Roman people from intertribal squabbling. The analogy fits Washington perfectly; after sealing the independence of the American people and serving two terms as president, he relinquished power so he could return to the simple agrarian pleasures of his Mount Vernon estate. This instance of political selflessness set a precedent for American politics, as a two-term limit per president was eventually set down in the Constitution.

Rather than simply reading politicians' attitudes and the overall political ethos through agricultural metaphors and examples, Wulf instead describes how important decisions, such as the founding of the new capital city of Washington, DC, could be viewed through a botanical prism. She writes:

> That the seat of government should have been situated in such an uninspiring location, somewhere in the middle of nowhere, was a reflection of the tensions within the Union—between the North and the South, the rural and the urban, the farmer and the merchant, as well as the wider differences between Federalists and Republicans.

Furthermore, the situation on James Madison's Montpelier estate, where slaves and the former president lived side by side in a village-style living arrangement, illustrated the changing race relations of early nineteenth-century America. During this historical period, the country was in a state of constant evolution, allowing Wulf to relate many of these changes back to horticultural and agricultural examples at will.

Drawing upon thorough research, Wulf quotes politicians and their families and colleagues in a way that brings attention to the use of botanical and horticultural analogy in everyday language. Abigail Adams, the wife of John Adams, is quoted as saying that her husband "is made of oak instead of willow . . . he may be torn up by the Roots, or break, but he will never bend." Wulf also quotes J. Hector St. John de Crèvecœur's best-selling book *Letters from an American Farmer* (1782), which states that "men are like plants. The goodness and flavour of the fruit proceeds from the peculiar soil and exposition in which they grow." Jefferson himself is quoted as saying, "Our seventeen states compose a great and growing nation . . . their children are as the leaves of the trees, which the winds are spreading over the forest."

Although the transcendentalist philosophy of American poet and philosopher Henry David Thoreau evolved a generation later, Wulf makes a case that politicians such as Jefferson and Madison were among the first American conservationists. Compellingly, she describes Madison's *Address to the Agricultural Society of Albemarle* (1818), inspired by the thoughts of French philosopher Denis Diderot and British economist Thomas Malthus, as tackling the need for better management of soil and livestock many years before these issues became widespread and popular. Every enlightened farmer in the United States read Madison's treatise, and his views on returning vegetation to the soil reiterates Wulf's playful statement that "somewhat ironically . . . steaming piles of dung became icons of the founding fathers' agricultural vision."

Although the US government would not announce its first protected national park until 1870, Wulf reveals how the founding fathers played a related role in providing private conservation estates. She views Jefferson's Poplar Forest through a political analogy, describing the enclosure as the

> perfect republican retreat: far away from the commercial centers, turned toward the west, intimate, set amid agricultural activity and inspired by Palladio's country villas. Exactly what Jefferson had envisaged for the President's House and garden: his republic ideal writ into bricks, earth and trees.

Jefferson was not alone; Madison's two-hundred-acre deciduous Landmark Forest still stands as a symbol of the private conservation ethos of the founding fathers.

Whether drawn to history or horticulture, readers of *Founding Gardeners* will find the book a qualified success. Vivid descriptions of the landscape and foliage, detailed appendices, and maps of the gardens themselves will appeal to fans of gardening and horticulture. The description of historical events and anecdotes that depict the founding fathers' fascination with plants will engage even the most well-read fans of American history. The specific anecdotes, such as the Federalists' vandalism of the White House trees after Jefferson's election (Jefferson having described cutting down trees as "a crime little short of murder"), are both entertaining and educational, portraying well-known historical figures in a rarely seen light.

Wulf's central claim throughout *Founding Gardeners* is that "the first four presidents of the United States saw themselves first and foremost as farmers and gardeners," and she goes a long way to support and defend this point of view. Perhaps Wulf is only slightly exaggerating here, since Madison, Adams, Washington, and Jefferson all could have anticipated that their lasting legacy would consist of their political contributions to the independence and prosperity of a new nation, not their agricultural endeavors. Historians are likely to find that *Founding Fathers* could have been improved with more analysis given to classical conceptions of farmers and gardeners and the pre-American development of these notions. Likewise, horticultural fans may find that the book could have gone into greater detail regarding discoveries and the subsequent importance of American foliage. As it stands, Wulf's book successfully and expertly brings together these two fields of study into a piece that many readers are sure to enjoy.

Nicholas A. Kirk

Review Sources

Denver Post, April 20, 2011 (Web).
The New York Times Book Review, May 6, 2011 (Web).
Publishers Weekly 258, no. 8 (February 21, 2011): 125.
San Francisco Chronicle, April 10, 2011 (Web).
Seattle Times, April 16, 2011 (Web).
The Telegraph, February 13, 2011 (Web).
The Washington Post, April 15, 2011 (Web).

1493
Uncovering the New World Columbus Created

Author: Charles C. Mann (b. 1955)
Publisher: Alfred A. Knopf (New York). 560 pp.
$30.50; paperback $16.95
Type of work: History, natural history, anthropology
Time: 1493–1979

Using the background of Christopher Columbus's voyage to the Americas, Mann describes the impact of European exploration not only in the West but also on global changes and events.

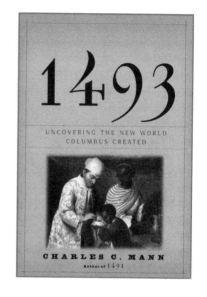

Principal personages:
CRISTÓBEL COLÓN / CHRISTOPHER COLUMBUS (ca. 1451–1506), Italian explorer whose four voyages to the Americas opened up those continents to European exploration
MIGUEL LÓPEZ DE LEGAZPI (1502–1572), Spanish explorer and conquistador who was the first governor-general of the Philippines, the center of the Spanish East Indies
HERNÁN CORTÉZ (1485–1547), Spanish conquistador who destroyed the Aztec empire and brought much of the Americas under Spanish control
HENRY ALEXANDER WICKHAM (1846–1928), British "bio-pirate" and entrepreneur, credited with bringing rubber-tree seeds from Brazil to England

Charles C. Mann's *1491: New Revelations of the Americas before Columbus* (2005) provided the story of the indigenous (Native American) peoples of the Western Hemisphere prior to their discovery by European explorers. His new book, *1493: Uncovering the New World Columbus Created*, expands the story by describing the global significance of Christopher Columbus's voyages and particularly their effects on trade, focusing on edibles such as corn and potatoes, the movement of precious metals such as gold and silver, and the evolution of the slave trade. His expeditions had a profound impact on the spread of diseases as well. In *1491*, Mann speculated on the possible evolution of the sexually transmitted disease syphilis, initially a relatively mild endemic illness in the Western Hemisphere, into a highly virulent form possibly introduced into Europe by Columbus's men. Conversely, in *1493*, the significance of African and European diseases such as malaria and smallpox and their effects on native peoples in the Americas is extensively discussed.

Mann's story begins with that of Columbus himself. Born into a family beset by debt, Colón, or Columbus as he was known to later historians, believed that by opening trade with China, he could amass a fortune for himself while providing funds for a new crusade to retake Jerusalem from the ruling Muslims. Contrary to what is often taught about Columbus, he did not believe the earth was perfectly round, nor did he believe it was as large as it is. Why did he and other explorers focus much of their travels on China? During that era, China was a mercantile power, a source of precious stones, spices, and in particular high-quality silk. Since much of the region between Europe and Asia was controlled by Muslims, the enemies of European Christianity, the only practical means of trade with China was by sea. The monarchs of Spain who ultimately backed Columbus saw his explorations as a means to gain access to Chinese trade. Columbus died believing he had succeeded in his goal, though it quickly became apparent to the European explorers who followed that he had not. Nonetheless, as a result of Columbus's voyages, innumerable species of foods as well as insects, quite possibly earthworms, and assorted invasive plant species, to say nothing of diseases, spread from Europe to the Americas. In turn, the Native American peoples provided Europeans with foods such as maize (an ancestor to modern corn), sweet potatoes, tobacco, and—to their own detriment—silver. The Columbian Exchange, as it was termed by historian Alfred Crosby, resulted in a new era of increasing biological homogeneity: the Homogenocene.

Historians have largely focused on the epidemic diseases introduced into the Americas by Spanish conquistadors and explorers, particularly measles and smallpox. There is no disputing the havoc and devastation that these diseases wreaked on the native populations. Mann contributes to this story of diseases of European and African origin by focusing on the endemic diseases that were also brought to the Americas during this period, malaria and yellow fever. The differences between epidemic and endemic diseases lie in their long-term effects on the population. Epidemic diseases run their course, albeit leaving hundreds of thousands or even millions dead in their wake, but nearly disappearing for a generation once those most susceptible have died, while endemic diseases find a reservoir in human or animal populations and are maintained within the population. Malaria is a prime example of such a disease.

Mann has partially divided his story into two portions, reflecting the movement of events, with the Caribbean at the core: Atlantic voyages and Pacific voyages. He introduces malaria in the former. The term "malaria" is derived from *mal aria*, "bad air," reflecting the belief that the disease was the result of emanations from swamps. It is unclear exactly when malaria first appeared in the Americas. Mann quotes excerpts from letters and reports believed to originate with Columbus during the 1490s in which the writer describes a "tertian fever" that caused his men to suffer intermittent chills and fever, symptoms that are typical of malaria. Since there was no evidence of the disease prior to Columbus's voyages, Mann suggests that it was brought to the Americas during these voyages.

Mann concedes that his evidence to support this hypothesis is largely speculative. He explains the disease is caused by two species of a bacterial parasite: *Plasmodium vivax*, which is highly sensitive to colder temperatures, and *Plasmodium falciparum*, which can better withstand the cold. The vector of transmission for each is the mosquito of the genus *Anopheles*. Mann suggests that the characteristics of the disease that became endemic in tropical regions, such as the southern portion of North

America (south of the present-day Carolinas) and South America, resembled the disease as found in Africa, while characteristics of malaria in less tropical regions north of present-day Virginia resembled the disease as found in Europe and England, the areas from which settlers in Jamestown and New England originated.

Mann's hypothesis linking the slave trade with the introduction of malaria is even more speculative. In making this link, Mann addresses the question of why slavery replaced the use of indentured servants in maintaining

Charles C. Mann has authored six books and written for numerous prominent media publications, including the New York Times, the Washington Post, Fortune magazine, and the Smithsonian. His work has gained recognition from the Alfred P. Sloan Foundation, the American Institute of Physics, and the National Academies Keck Futures Initiative, which named his previous book, 1491: New Revelations of the Americas before Columbus *(2005), best book of the year.*

the farms and plantations. He quotes British economic theorist Adam Smith, who in *Wealth of Nations* (1776) argued that freemen, including indentured servants, would ultimately be a cheaper investment than slaves. Mann's conclusion is that since malaria was an endemic disease in those regions of Africa that supported the slave trade, African slaves would have had more natural immunity to the bacteria and would therefore exhibit a lower mortality than indentured Europeans. He does not indict malaria as the primary reason for the development of slavery in the Americas but suggests it could have been a contributing factor.

Perhaps the earliest lucrative product brought from the Americas by European traders was tobacco. Arguably, tobacco was the first global commodity to originate in the West, as it was traded not only in Europe but also in eastern lands such as Japan and China. Two species of the tobacco plant existed in the Americas during the earliest Spanish conquests: *Nicotiana tabacum* in the Caribbean, where the dried leaves were smoked by the native population, and *Nicotiana rustica*, which was brewed as a tea by Native Americans in the area of present-day Virginia. The leaf was dispensed by both Spanish and Portuguese traders to China, where it rivaled silver in importance as a commodity for trade. Addiction to tobacco soon became so pervasive that the ruling khan of Manchuria forbade smoking after he learned his soldiers were trading their weapons in order to procure tobacco. Likewise, in Europe, the Vatican received reports that even priests were addicted, often celebrating Mass while smoking cigars, leading Pope Urban VIII to prohibit the use of tobacco in church.

It is likely that the ability to grow tobacco was a critical factor in the survival of the first English colony in the Americas, Jamestown. The Jamestown colony was established in 1607 on land long farmed by Native Americans, then led by an elderly ruler named Powhatan, a name also associated with the nearby village and peoples. The story of the colony is a staple of early American history, albeit much of it mythologized. As Mann correctly describes, the colony barely survived, and it was only with the aid of the Powhatan people that they were able to do so. Tobacco, a crop initially obtained from the Native Americans, became the first important export from the colony, the English contribution to the Columbian Exchange, and ultimately played a significant role as a source of revenue for the Jamestown survivors.

Among the primary factors driving Spanish exploration during the sixteenth century were exploration, colonization, and access to trade with China. China during this era ranked among the world's wealthiest and strongest nations. The most desired exports from China were silk and porcelain, and European nations were willing to pay a premium for each. In turn, the Spanish possessed something highly desired by the Chinese: silver. It was this exchange, silver for silk and porcelain, that was at the heart of what became known as the "galleon trade." Mann's account of the Pacific voyages provides much of the history linked to this exchange, including the role played by slaves in the Americas who mined the silver, and ultimately its relationship to Spanish settlements in the Pacific.

Mann opens his story with a discussion of two monuments, one erected in Spain in honor of Columbus and the other in Manila, the capital of the Philippines, dedicated to Spanish conquistador Miguel López de Legazpi and his navigator Andres Ochoa de Urdaneta y Cerain. Legazpi and Urdaneta landed on the island of Cebu in early 1565, establishing a Spanish settlement in what became a portion of the Philippines. Further northward exploration led to the discovery by Legazpi of Chinese merchants who had long plied their trade with the native peoples. Taking control of the area and establishing the town of Manila because of its safe harbor, Legazpi opened the galleon trade between China and Spain. Not only silver arrived from the West; in time, both sweet potatoes and maize would also be traded. The impact on Asia would be significant. Since these crops could be easily grown in the dry uplands of China, farmers moved to these areas, destroying the forests to clear the land and unwittingly allowing for both erosion and flooding.

The key factor for the Spanish in maintaining the galleon trade was silver. Mann begins this history with Diego Gualpa (Hualpa), who, in 1545, while walking in the Andes Mountains in southern Bolivia, literally stumbled upon a ledge of almost pure silver ore. Andean natives at the time had some of the most advanced methods in metallurgy, using smelters fueled by burning dry grass and llama dung to refine the ore. The result was one of the first "boom towns" in the Americas, Potosí, the population of which grew to 160,000 persons within seventy years, nearly all associated with silver mining. Unlike the natives, the Spanish used mercury, also found in a large nearby deposit, as a means to purify the ore. The methods used in mining both silver and mercury created an appalling mortality rate among the natives who were forced to work in the mines; some four thousand native men were forced into the mines each week, and by some estimates, the death toll rose into the millions.

Based on his sources, Mann estimates that over 150,000 tons of silver were extracted from South America between the sixteenth and eighteenth centuries, representing 80 percent of the world's output. Since the silver supply was unregulated, the resultant inflation caused the collapse of numerous European economies, a contributing factor in subsequent European wars.

Mann concludes his story with a summary of the impact of the homogenization of cultures and trade that began with Columbus and continues hundreds of years later. In many places, he draws on first-person accounts, including some of his own visits to many of the places he describes.

Richard Adler

Review Sources

Booklist 107, no. 22 (August 1, 2011): 15.
Kirkus Reviews 79, no. 13 (July 1, 2011): 1116.
Library Journal 136, no. 13 (August 1, 2011): 110
New Scientist, no. 2824 (August 6, 2011): 46.
The New Yorker 87, no. 27 (September 12, 2011): 85.
Publishers Weekly 258, no. 27 (July 4, 2011): 59.

The Girl in the Blue Beret

Author: Bobbie Ann Mason (b. 1940)
Publisher: Random House (New York). 368 pp.
$26.00
Type of work: Novel
Time: 1944 and 1980
Locale: Throughout Europe; New Jersey

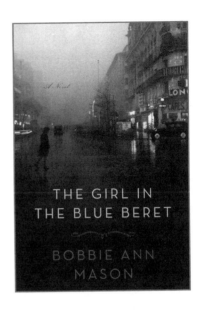

An American pilot reevaluates his life while searching for the resistance workers who helped him escape from Nazi-occupied Europe.

Principal characters:

MARSHALL STONE, a sixty-year-old American
World War II veteran and retired commercial pilot

LUCIEN LOMBARD, a Belgian octogenarian
who witnessed the B-17 crash in 1944 and
brings Stone to the site in 1980

LORETTA STONE, Stone's deceased wife

PIERRE ALBERT, the French Resistance operative who hid Stone during the war

NICOLAS ALBERT, Pierre's son, who as an adult conducts research locating people for
Stone

ROBERT JULES LEBEAU, a French Resistance worker who helped American aviators

ANNETTE VALLON BOUYER, the teenaged guide whose family hid Stone in their Paris
home and with whom he later reunites

CAROLINE, Robert Lebeau's daughter, who owns a Parisian grocery store where Stone
shops

LAWRENCE WEBB, B-17 captain

HOOTIE WILLIAMS, B-17 left waist gunner

BOB HADLEY, B-17 radio operator

Memories deceive protagonist Marshall Stone, an American veteran and pilot in *The
Girl in the Blue Beret*, a historical novel shaped by characters' concepts of heroism and
duty. As he nears his sixtieth birthday in 1980, Stone reluctantly approaches retirement
from his job as a commercial airline pilot. Recently widowed after his wife Loretta's
death, Stone ponders what he will do as he adjusts to his freedom from domestic and
professional demands. Before his last flight home from Paris, however, he reminisces
about serving as a World War II pilot. Accompanied by elderly Lucien Lombard, he
visits the site in Belgium where he crash-landed the B-17 Flying Fortress bomber
Dirty Lily on January 31, 1944. Lombard had helped the crew escape. For Stone, a
tree which has grown in the field after the crash represents survival. He cries and is
overwhelmed as Belgians greet him, praising his wartime bravery. He is amazed that

they have such vivid memories of the incident. Stone learns of the Belgians' sacrifices, such as when a man transported an airman on his bicycle only to be shot by the Nazis. Stone is embarrassed for not returning sooner to thank everyone who helped him escape from enemy territory.

Themes of transition and movement develop the novel's plot and characterizations. Emotionally estranged from his children, Mary and Albert, Stone realizes that he spent the majority of his career away from his New Jersey home. He reexamines his relationship with Loretta, acknowledging that she had raised their children and managed their home by herself, including the yard, which Stone neglects. Agitated and mourning his career, Stone hangs up his uniform, wanders through his house, and sorts through letters from the Alberts, the French family that concealed Stone from the Nazis. Stone is ashamed for having ceased contact with the family, after whom he named his own son, but he is also curious about his other rescuers. His most vivid memory of the experience involves a teenage girl wearing a blue beret, Annette Vallon, who taught Stone how to blend in, led him to her family's home where he hid in an armoire, and secured his false documents, cleverly identifying him as a stonemason named Julien Baudouin. He remembers visits from Robert Jules Lebeau, who brought the Vallons fresh food, scarce in Nazi-controlled Paris, and accompanied Stone as he began the journey south toward the Pyrenees Mountains between France and Spain.

Stone decides to become an expatriate in Paris, so that he can search for and express gratitude to the people who saved his life. Reading letters he wrote to Loretta during the war, he refreshes his memory and envisions how to proceed. Apprehensively he follows an address from his last letter from Pierre and Gisèle Albert to Chauny, France. There the Albert son, Nicolas, only a schoolboy in 1944, greets Stone and reunites him with the elder Alberts. Stone enlists the help of Nicolas, who eagerly makes inquiries in archives, and in Paris, Stone meets Robert's daughter, Caroline. Contrary to Stone's impressions of Robert as a admirable and heroic man, Caroline portrays him as an abusive father, who juggled two sets of children, one born to his wife, the other to his mistress, Caroline's mother.

Alternating chapters set in 1944 and 1980 gradually reveal aspects of Stone's experiences during the war. As he moves through the French landscape, Stones recalls in flashbacks the many selfish, immature, and impulsive indulgences and infidelities that he savored as a twenty-three-year-old pilot at his English base. Preparing to fly bombers into Germany, all went well until the tenth raid. Images of the crash cycle through Stone's mind: the German fighter jet flying by, the realization that the B-17 pilot, Lawrence Webb, had passed out, and finally landing the plane. Guiltily Stone recalls pulling wounded crew members from the wreckage before abandoning them, fleeing from approaching German soldiers with Bob Hadley, the radio operator. Stone soon separates from Hadley, who thinks they should travel north toward the English Channel, and proceeds south. Lost, he finds refuge in a barn and comes under the protection of resistance workers, including the Alberts and Vallons, prior to taking trains into the Pyrenees Mountains. Fear permeates these scenes, as Stone must trust strangers and ponder every turn. Upon crossing the Pyrenees, he is ecstatic to reunite with Hootie Williams, whom he had saved from the crash. Stone follows a guide through snow drifts and across a rope

Bobbie Ann Mason writes novels, short stories, and nonfiction. She has received the Southern Book Critics Circle Award, the PEN/Hemingway Award, and the Pushcart and O. Henry Prizes. Her works have been finalists for the Pulitzer Prize, the American Book Award, the National Book Critics Circle Award, and the PEN/Faulkner Award.

bridge, the rugged conditions symbolizing the seemingly endless hostilities of wartime. Stone is devastated when Hootie disappears after Germans fire upon the airmen during the crossing into Spain.

Stone writes the surviving crew of the B-17, describing his experience returning to the crash site and his efforts seeking his protectors. The responses vary, alerting Stone of the diverse reactions and profound personal changes that resulted from the crash, such as one crew member's new religiosity. Stone questions his memories as he reads the men's accounts of the crash and their return to civilian life. He meets with the children of deceased crew members, such as Webb's arrogant son, who believes his father landed the plane.

The novel's tone shifts when Stone locates the girl wearing the blue beret, themes of survival, grief, and healing dominating their interactions. The widow of the veterinarian Dr. Bouyer, Annette tends horses, dog, and poultry on their farm in the French countryside. Stone, who had been entranced by the teenager's spirited and defiant behavior during the war, nervously wonders how Annette will receive him. She embraces him, providing him food and wine and escorting him around her land, mirroring how she had led him through Paris when they were young.

Gradually, Stone and Annette confide details of their wartime experiences. The blue beret he had remembered, she tells him, had been what she wore to school and had served as a convenient signal to aviators looking for their contact. She also wore distinctive socks and scarves to alert American airmen to follow her to safety. She says that Stone was one of fifty aviators her family assisted. The French had been grateful to see Allied planes fly above because those aircraft symbolized hope that the war would soon end. Stone assumes that they continued their work after he left, but her revelations concerning the arrest of the Vallons and Lebeau families stuns him. Annette and her mother were separated from Robert and her father and incarcerated with other female resistance operatives, and from there they were transferred to a German concentration camp at Ravensbrück, then a work camp at Koenigsberg-sur-Oder in Poland. She describes deprivation and brutal treatment in the bitterly cold conditions, in which she witnessed friends' deaths from starvation and exhaustion. Alliances between prisoners helped Annette protect her fragile mother. The theme of resiliency resonates throughout the women's physical and emotional survival, their return home, and their recovery. Annette describes their losses: her father's life and Robert's sanity. In this way, Stone understands the cause of his hero's transformation.

Stone remains at the rural home, where he and Annette enjoy a romantic relationship. Annette tells Stone her widowed mother resides in Normandy, a motif used in the text to represent characters' freedom. He is amazed by her joyfulness, though she often admits to feeling *désolée* regarding her past, even referring to Stone as one of the many ghosts in her life. Annette acknowledges she should prepare school presentations about her experiences to ensure that future generations will know what happened and never forget history. Together, they plan to hike on a Pyrenees mountain trail into Spain wearing blue berets.

Epiphanies alter Stone's reality as he learns information about the war that is scarcely reported, such as the French transporting Jews to camps, and the German massacres of French villagers. He reevaluates his life and perceptions, realizing that he misunderstood events he experienced when young. He is horrified at this recognition of his naïveté, arrogance, and ignorance. Climbing the Pyrenees mountain with Annette represents Stone's metaphorical rebirth, as he comes to understand the truth and realize that "Robert Lebeau was Marshall's better self. Annette was his better half." Mirroring his trust for her in previous decades, Stone follows Annette's "blue beret rising and falling in front of him as they climbed into the haze ahead."

Stone's fictional reexamination of his wartime experiences will be relevant to many World War II veterans and civilians in the early twenty-first century. The Honor Flight Network flies aging veterans to visit the National World War II Memorial in Washington, DC. Some veterans travel to European World War II sites, including monuments recognizing resistance efforts to rescue downed aviators. Mason visited the very places she depicted and interacted with witnesses and resistance workers to enhance the authenticity of her narrative. Her historical research enriches sensory descriptions, immersing her readers into scenes of aircrafts in flight. She skillfully uses epistolary techniques to convey information and conceal truths about distant places and events through characters' letters, such as those Stone wrote Loretta during the war.

Critics mostly praised Mason's style in developing characters, settings, dialogue, and plot, particularly her incorporation of details to intensify the story's emotional impact. Effective literary elements include imagery and diction, such as the surname Stone to indicate that protagonist is steady, enduring, and possessing a hardness that enables him to survive. His first name, Marshall, is a homonym for the word martial, emphasizing military identity and the need to exert control. Military and aviation jargon reinforce the realism of scenes that depict Stone's expertise. Although some critics considered Mason's writing predictable and reliant on stereotypes, most reviewers held that the novel celebrated individuals whose wartime contributions were often overshadowed.

Elizabeth D. Schafer

Review Sources

Booklist 107, no. 16 (April 15, 2011): 35.
Kirkus Reviews 79, no. 6 (March 15, 2011): 448.
Library Journal 136, no. 6 (April 1, 2011): 83.
The New York Times Book Review, July 24, 2011, p. 13.
Philadelphia Inquirer, August 21, 2011, p. H12.
Publishers Weekly 258, no. 11 (March 14, 2011): 47.
The Washington Post, June 29, 2011, p. C4.
Washington Times, August 26, 2011, p. C11.

The Girl in the Polka Dot Dress

Author: Beryl Bainbridge (1933–2010)
Publisher: Europa Editions (New York).
  162 pp. $15.00
Type of work: Novel
Time: 1968
Locale: England and the United States, notably Maryland; Washington, DC; upstate New York; Yellowstone National Park; and California

Bainbridge assembles an eccentric cast of characters whose lives intersect with the novel's two protagonists on their westward journey across the United States seeking an enigmatic man whose location, the travelers' final destination, is the site of the assassination of Senator Robert F. Kennedy.

Principal characters:
ROSE, an English woman in her twenties who
    travels to the United States
WASHINGTON HAROLD, a middle-aged American psychologist who transports Rose
    across the United States
DR. FRED WHEELER, a mysterious older man sought by Rose and Harold
JESSE SHAEFER, Harold's university friend and law professor
MIRABELLA, Harold's friend in Wanakena, New York
MRS. WEINER, a theosophist whose vision about the future unnerves Rose
JOHN FURY, California lawyer and horse breeder who employs Sirhan
PHILOPSONA FURY, John's wife
SIRHAN, a stable groom who works for John Fury
WALTER FEDLER, a trained hypnotist

Intrigue and tragedy lurk throughout English author Beryl Bainbridge's posthumously published final novel, *The Girl in the Polka Dot Dress*. Characterizations and plot developments hint at conspiracy, incorporating elements from witness statements following the June 5, 1968, assassination of United States presidential candidate Robert F. Kennedy after his speech celebrating his victory at the California primary. While traveling in the United States in 1968, Bainbridge had heard radio reports describing a woman wearing a polka-dot dress who had allegedly been seen accompanying assassin Sirhan Sirhan at the Ambassador Hotel in Los Angeles, California, where Kennedy was fatally shot. Witnesses saw this mysterious woman leave the crime scene, but she was never seen again. Bainbridge uses this event and the *Los Angeles*

Times article of June 6, 1968, describing the woman as the premise for this gripping and memorable novel.

Anticipation permeates the plot of *The Girl in the Polka Dot Dress*. The story begins with Harold, a narcissistic and affluent middle-aged psychologist, waiting in Baltimore, Maryland, on May 18, 1968, for a young woman named Rose to arrive on a flight from England. Harold has agreed to drive Rose so she can reunite with Dr. Fred Wheeler, an elusive and mysterious man who had aided her when she underwent difficulties. Harold and Rose had met previously in England when he dined at the house of her friends and later walked Rose home, where he recognized Wheeler in a photograph. Prior to that interaction with Rose, Harold had met Wheeler at a reception honoring Robert Kennedy when he was named United States attorney general in 1961. The two men became friends until Harold discovered that Wheeler was having an affair with Harold's wife, Dollie.

Prior to her arrival in the United States, Rose wrote Harold a letter, mentioning that she was bringing a polka-dot dress to wear to her reunion with Wheeler. The whimsical design of her attire is deceptive; people innately trust Rose by her playful clothing style and naively view her as childlike. She comments to Harold, "I can't help thinking that fate has drawn us together." Harold is annoyed by Rose's presence but honors his promise to assist her in locating Wheeler. Although he is helping her, the story also reveals that Harold did not purchase a return plane ticket for Rose, subtly suggesting that she might not require a ticket if she is imprisoned, killed, or vanishes as a result of their trip.

Friction between Rose and Harold intensifies as they prepare for their road trip in Harold's camper, symbolic of his nomadic nature. Harold conceals a gun underneath the driver's seat, which suggests he anticipates something more serious will occur than a simple drive to California. As a passenger, Rose refuses to be passive and comments about places where the pair travels, experiencing culture shock as she sees gun stores and rioters setting fires. Indeed, Rose's journey appears to be more than literal as she finds herself changed by the experience. The passage from the East Coast to the West Coast initiates a shift in her identity from a seemingly innocent, unsophisticated girl to a worldly, seasoned woman capable of detrimentally influencing people she encounters. Gender roles also contribute to Rose's transformation. The misogynistic Harold belittles and chides Rose, attempting to control her so that she is servile. Rose endures his hostilities because she feels indebted to him for helping her reach Wheeler. During the trip, Rose recalls other abuses and hardships she has suffered, hinting that she may be mentally unstable and vulnerable to being manipulated.

As Harold and Rose continue their travels, their movement begins to suggest elements of a chase, with predators seeking to outlast each other to capture prey. They learn more about the whereabouts of Wheeler as they make stops in Washington, DC, and Wanakena, New York. Encountering various acquaintances, the protagonists are drawn into discussions of current events, providing the reader with points of view on the assassination of Martin Luther King Jr. and discussion of political figures including Robert Kennedy and President Lyndon Johnson. These conversations occasionally take on sinister tones as characters advocate for the elimination of politicians with whom they disagree. These themes of vigilantism emerge in Rose's postwar memories as well.

The theme of death is constant in *The Girl in the Polka Dot Dress*. Before departing on the trip, Harold assures that his lawyer will oversee management of his estate in case he dies while traveling. At another point, Rose insists that Harold stop in New York so she can attend a Vietnam soldier's funeral because she is curious to see how Americans conduct that ceremony. Throughout the trip, Rose hears references to assassination threats against Kennedy and witnesses violence and criminal acts involving guns. She survives an armed robbery at a bank where Harold cashes a check. Together, they save a woman from a rapist. A woman's throat is cut outside an inn where the pair stays. Scenes occurring at night intensify dark tones in the text and foreshadow the assassination, which happens after midnight. The image of blood sometimes precedes violence such as when Rose's lip bleeds before Robert Kennedy is assassinated.

(Michael Bailey)

Dame Beryl Bainbridge was a two-time winner of the Whitbread Award and a recipient of the James Tait Black Memorial Prize and the David Cohen British Literature Prize. Five of her novels were short-listed for the Man Booker Prize.

Bainbridge also uses images of flowers to reinforce characterizations. Rose's name, the same as Kennedy's mother, represents a strong figure standing out in a crowd. Rose blossoms during her American adventure, attaining maturity; her beauty lures admirers and their cooperation. The thorns associated with roses also suggest the hazards Rose presents to people. Rose tells Harold that her uncaring father allowed her family's rose garden to perish by denying it fertilizer. Dollie's grave, overgrown with rose bushes, symbolizes Harold's neglect. In England, Harold had embraced the frame containing Wheeler's photograph "as though accepting a bunch of flowers."

Aspects of films Rose watches throughout the narrative are incorporated as literary elements used to depict Rose's journey—especially motifs of crime and deceit, absent friends, and the undercurrent of malice in *The Third Man* (1949). Prior to arriving in Baltimore, Rose had envisioned American homes resembling sets she had seen in movies, and she is therefore surprised at the disheveled condition of the apartment where Harold lives. She wants to visit a Los Angeles nightclub shown in a scene in *Lady Killer* (1933), another overt reference to the thread of violence that runs through the novel. Movies also effectively represent the charade Rose and Harold are performing on their trip, both playing roles in their ulterior motives for undertaking the journey.

As the characters continue westward, stopping in Yellowstone National Park in Wyoming before continuing to California, Bainbridge continues to develop her characters while their personal growth is reflected in the trip itself. Rose's intellectual curiosity is examined as she meets John Fury, a man who claims that he had almost been hit by a bullet Lee Harvey Oswald fired at President John F. Kennedy in Dallas, Texas. Rose also encounters Mrs. Weiner, a theosophist who believes in reincarnation and sees a vision of a man wearing a yellow sweater riding a horse in Rose's future. The issue of mind control is introduced during Rose's visit to Fury's California ranch. Rose notices that Philopsona, Fury's wife, acts erratically; it is later explained that the woman takes hallucinogenic drugs developed during the Korean War to minimize unpleasant memories and thoughts.

It is in the final section of the novel that fiction and nonfiction begin to intersect more plainly. Notions of violence and mind control come to a head as Rose meets Walter Fedler, a man trained in hypnotism who claims that he can hypnotize anyone, including John Fury's stableman Sirhan. Readers familiar with American history will immediately recognize this fictionalized version of Sirhan Sirhan, the real-life assassin of Robert Kennedy. The novel culminates in the characters' arrival at the Ambassador Hotel, with Rose wearing the titular polka dot dress that she carried throughout her journey. On this infamous day, Rose, Harold, and Wheeler meet at last.

Some readers may be disappointed with the unclear conclusion to Bainbridge's unfinished novel, while others may appreciate its ambiguity. Some still might argue that Bainbridge purposefully created an unresolved ending so readers can imagine various possibilities occurring between the fictional and factual characters. Most reviewers perceived Bainbridge's final novel as a convincing work of historical fiction. Despite morbid themes and imagery, many readers will appreciate the book's dry humor and its often comic characters. Bainbridge's deep comprehension of human behavior and motivations are apparent in *The Girl in the Polka Dot Dress*, and it is clear that this novel is representative of her distinctive style. Regardless of their belief in conspiracy theories, readers will be drawn into Bainbridge's darkly funny and thoroughly engrossing final work.

Elizabeth D. Schafer

Review Sources

Booklist 107, no. 22 (August 1, 2011): 20.
Kirkus Reviews 79, no. 16 (August 15, 2011): 1402.
Library Journal 136, no. 13 (August 1, 2011): 80–81.
New Statesman 140, no. 5056 (June 6, 2011): 44.
The New York Times Book Review, September 11, 2011, p. 26.
Publishers Weekly 258, no, 28 (July 11, 2011): 35.
The Washington Post, August 25, 2011 (Web).

G. K. Chesterton

Author: Ian Ker (b. 1942)
Publisher: Oxford University Press (Oxford).
688 pp. $65.00
Type of work: Biography
Time: 1874–1936
Locale: England

A comprehensive look at the life of G. K. Ches-
terton, a leading journalist, essayist, novelist,
and apologist for Roman Catholicism during
the early twentieth century.

Principal personages:
GILBERT KEITH CHESTERTON, journalist, novelist,
    short story writer, essayist
FRANCES BLOGG CHESTERTON, his wife
CECIL CHESTERTON, his younger brother
ADA JONES CHESTERTON, Cecil Chesterton's wife

Ian Ker's *G. K. Chesterton* enters what has recently become the crowded field of
Chesterton studies. While this Chesterton "revival" hardly compares to critics' continued interest in William Shakespeare, Charles Dickens, or Jane Austen, nearly a dozen
new critical studies have been published in the last decade alone, and new editions of
Chesterton's most enduring works have been reissued, several edited by Ker himself.
Most notably, biographers have been busy retelling Chesterton's life story, drawing
from meager records and previous studies to craft new portraits of one of the greatest
thinkers of the early twentieth century. Because of this, Ker's book is likely to be compared to other recent biographies, such as Michael Coren's *Gilbert: The Man Who Was
G. K. Chesterton* (1990) and Joseph Pearce's *Wisdom and Innocence: A Life of G. K.
Chesterton* (1996). Coren sacrifices critical analysis of Chesterton's work in favor of
an examination of his personality, whereas Pearce concentrates almost exclusively
on Chesterton's role as a thinker and prophet. It is likely, too, that Ker's analysis of
Chesterton's early years, when he was forming his philosophy and making his spiritual
journey to Roman Catholicism, may be judged in light of William Oddie's *Chesterton and the Romance of Orthodoxy: The Making of GKC, 1874–1908* (2008), Aidan
Nichols's *G. K. Chesterton: Theologian* (2009), and Kevin Belmonte's *Defiant Joy:
The Remarkable Life and Impact of G. K. Chesterton* (2011). Ker acknowledges a debt
to Oddie, whose careful scholarship earned praise from a number of reviewers, but no
mention is made of Belmonte's or Nichols's books, suggesting that Ker completed his
biography before they were published. What sets Ker's book apart from other biographies of Chesterton is its comprehensiveness. Where others have focused mainly on a
single facet of Chesterton's life—his personality, his literary accomplishments, or his

theology—Ker attempts to cover all aspects of his life and work. Looking at all sides of Chesterton is no easy task.

Born in the later years of Queen Victoria's reign, Gilbert Keith Chesterton lived through World War I and the early years of the great worldwide depression that led to the rise of Adolf Hitler and National Socialism. He married Frances Blogg in 1901 and remained faithful to her until he died. Chesterton began writing as a young man and was prolific throughout his life, contributing his work to newspapers (including a weekly column that he wrote for several decades), composing essays and poetry, and publishing novels and nonfiction books on a variety of topics. At a glance, his many publications provide some sense of his interests; artist G. F. Watts, artist and poet William Blake, politician Herbert Kitchener, reformer William Cobbett, poets Geoffrey Chaucer and Robert Browning, theologian Thomas Aquinas, preacher (and later saint) Francis of Assisi, and novelists Leo Tolstoy and William Makepeace Thackeray all feature in his work. Many of these works reveal as much about Chesterton's ideas—and ideals—as they do about the titular subject. For example, his iconoclastic study of nineteenth-century England is less a survey of the time than an explanation of Chesterton's curious relationship with the ideology of the period. On the other hand, his *Charles Dickens: A Critical Study* (1906) was one of the first extended studies of Dickens and went on to be considered the definitive work on the Victorian novelist for years.

Upon his entry into the London literary scene, Chesterton became a figure to be reckoned with. At one time or another, his associates included historian Hillaire Belloc, novelist Henry James, poet and classicist A. E. Housman (who was his tutor at university), and playwright J. M. Barrie. Also a part of this group were his brother Cecil and Cecil's wife, Ada, a journalist who wrote under the pen name John Keith Prothero to avoid the scandal of her gender being known. Though he argued with his brother over virtually every topic imaginable, Chesterton supported Cecil's enterprise as editor of the *New Witness* and took over the paper when Cecil died during World War I. He and his sister-in-law remained on good terms throughout his lifetime, although she published an unflattering account of Gilbert and Frances after he died. Notable, too, was Chesterton's lifelong association with the Irish playwright and avowed atheist George Bernard Shaw. Chesterton was a young man when they first met, and despite their significant differences in politics and art, their friendship lasted until Chesterton's death.

From his earliest writings, Chesterton presented himself as an optimist and a champion of the common man. He was not a supporter of the liberal idea of progress, and he seemed content with the notion that acceptance of dogma, especially religious dogma, was important for anyone wishing to lead a truly satisfying life. His position put him at odds not only with the fin de siècle writers popular in his youth but also, and especially, with the modernists who captured the literary spotlight during the first three decades of the new century. After Chesterton converted to Roman Catholicism in 1922, his work became an extended defense of his new faith, further alienating many liberal thinkers in England and abroad. At the same time, however, he continued to attract a wide readership for his fiction, especially for novels like *The Napoleon of Notting Hill* (1904) and the Father Brown detective stories. If the intellectual establishment found him difficult to deal with, the common man whom he celebrated so enthusiastically still bought his books and read his newspaper columns, and his lectures in England and America continued to draw large crowds. For nearly three decades, he was, by all accounts, a celebrity.

To treat Chesterton comprehensively requires extensive knowledge of literature, theology, philosophy, and history, and Ian Ker seems to be one of the few scholars qualified to take on this challenge. His 1988 biography of Cardinal John Henry Newman was hailed as a significant achievement in Newman studies, and his subsequent writings on the celebrated Victorian convert to Roman Catholicism won similar praise. The similarities between Newman and Chesterton make the latter an appropriate new focus for Ker, who is convinced that Chesterton is a major figure not only among Catholic authors but among British writers and intellectuals in general. *G. K. Chesterton* is Ker's extended argument in defense of Chesterton's stature.

Unfortunately, Chesterton biographers must contend with a dearth of primary documentation, and Ker is forced to rely on earlier biographies, Chesterton's autobiography, and the few collections of letters and manuscripts that still exist. To his credit, he makes the most of scant materials, constructing a sound chronological account of how Chesterton spent his days. Where he can, Ker provides information about the nature of Chesterton's relationships with family, friends, and professional associates. His main interest, however, is not simply in presenting a record of Chesterton as a writer and celebrity. He also wishes to explore Chesterton's philosophy as it is revealed in the hundreds of essays, books, and newspaper columns he published between 1901 and 1936.

Reverend Ian Ker is on the theology faculty at Oxford University. He is the author or editor of a number of important scholarly studies, including John Henry Newman: A Biography *(1988),* The Catholic Revival in English Literature, 1845–1961 *(2003),* Mere Catholicism *(2006), and the* Cambridge Companion to Newman *(2009).*

Consequently, the major part of *G. K. Chesterton* consists of lengthy summaries of Chesterton's writings, augmented by Ker's analysis. The emphasis is not on the works that made Chesterton famous—the novels, detective stories, and poems—but on those that Ker believes merit attention as major statements of philosophy, theology, and literary criticism. Ker's list of Chesterton's most important books includes *Charles Dickens* (1906), *Orthodoxy* (1908), *The Victorian Age in Literature* (1913), *St. Francis of Assisi* (1923), *The Everlasting Man* (1925), *St. Thomas Aquinas* (1933), and Chesterton's *Autobiography* (1936). Ker provides exceptionally detailed critiques for these, and likewise for *Heretics* (1905), a work he describes as almost great. When he does express his own opinion of Chesterton's works, especially the later ones, he is decidedly pro-Catholic in his assessments of their merit. In fact, he goes out of his way to point out the consistency between many of Chesterton's earlier works, written before he converted but still championing Christianity against the rising tide of atheism, and those he wrote after he was welcomed into the fold by his many Catholic friends. These friends included several priests with whom he and his wife had forged strong bonds even before he was accepted into the Roman Catholic Church. Throughout the book, in the footnotes especially, Ker carries on a running battle with critics who fail to appreciate much of Chesterton's work. While he does not dramatize the point, he hints strongly that the dismissal of Chesterton by some of his contemporaries and those in succeeding generations is the result of misunderstanding or willful blindness, perhaps brought on by a distrust of Chesterton's religious beliefs.

As with most books on controversial figures, one's opinion of Chesterton is likely to color one's judgment of Ker's detailed and carefully documented study. From at least one group of readers, however, Ker will not have to worry about much criticism: members of the various Chesterton Societies in England and America. Chesterton has become a kind of literary saint for some Catholics, and efforts have been launched to have him canonized as a real saint by the Catholic Church. Those not as taken with Chesterton's voluble defense of faith, or with his trenchant antimodernist stance, are likely to find Ker's book less appealing. That divide is already evident in early reactions to *G. K. Chesterton*. For example, the *Catholic Herald* describes the book as a magisterial new biography, while in the *Spectator*, the reviewer laments that it makes Chesterton sound dull. Nevertheless, whatever one makes of Ker's book, one thing is certain: no critic writing on Chesterton in the future will be able to ignore it. For those who find Chesterton a subject of interest, this new biography will provide ample support for his greatness as a writer and thinker. Those who wish to debunk his reputation will have to confront and address the detailed and well-documented case Ker makes for his achievements.

Laurence W. Mazzeno

Review Sources

American Scholar 80, no. 4 (Autumn 2011): 117–20.
Catholic Herald, June 22, 2011 (Web).
Chronicle of Higher Education 58, no. 5 (September 18, 2011): B12–13.
Expository Times 123, no. 1 (October 2011): 47–48.
Kirkus Reviews 79, no. 3 (February 1, 2011): 178.
National Review 63, no. 14 (August 1, 2011): 40–41.
Spectator, April 23, 2011, p. 52.
Times Higher Education, no. 2009 (July 28, 2011): 54–55.
Times Literary Supplement, no. 5645 (June 10, 2011): 3–5.

Grand Pursuit
The Story of Economic Genius

Author: Sylvia Nasar (b. 1947)
Publisher: Simon & Schuster (New York).
576 pp. $35.00
Type of work: Economics, history
Time: The nineteenth and twentieth centuries

Nasar's latest work is a history of economics that discusses how humankind has attempted to understand and control the often-mercurial boom and bust cycles of free-market capitalism.

Principal personages:

CHARLES DICKENS (1812–1870), an English
  novelist and playwright
THOMAS MALTHUS (1766–1834), a British political economist who believed in perpetual
  economic turbulence
KARL MARX (1818–1883), a German theorist
  who prophesied the end of capitalism and
  the rise of communism
ALFRED MARSHALL (1842–1924), a British economist who theorized that productivity
  would translate into increased wages
BEATRICE POTTER WEBB (1858–1943), an early advocate of the welfare state in Great
  Britain
IRVING FISHER (1867–1947), an American economist who recognized the link between
  money supply and economic stability
JOHN KEYNES (1883–1946), a British economist who advocated for deficit spending
  and government activism
JOSEPH SCHUMPETER (1883–1950), an Austro-Hungarian economist credited with the
  concept of creative destruction
FRIEDRICH VON HAYEK (1899–1992), an Austro-Hungarian economist who explored
  the link between money supply and business cycles
PAUL A. SAMUELSON (1915–2009), an American economist who joined the disciplines
  of mathematics and economics

From the collapse of the American housing market to the insolvency of European governments, students of economics might be inclined to think that the early twenty-first century marks a period of unprecedented instability, the causes of which are too complex to understand. However, in spite of lingering malaise, economic stagnation is nothing new in the context of global history, and certainly not in the context of economics. In *Grand Pursuit: The Story of Economic Genius*, author Sylvia Nasar, best known for the award-winning biography *A Beautiful Mind* (1998), traces the evolution of economic theory from the age of Charles Dickens until roughly 1950, detailing how each generation of economists confronted the financial downturns that have plagued global economies since the onset of industrialization.

Dividing her work into three acts titled "Hope," "Fear," and "Confidence," Nasar takes readers on a journey into a subject area that many readers might consider dry. Economists are often perceived as producing research that is devoid of persons and emotions, governed solely by numbers, but *Grand Pursuit* considers many of the great economic theorists in a manner that gives their theories a human face. Nasar does a wonderful job of placing her story in its appropriate historical context. Her vivid descriptions of different time periods and geographic locations, along with the characteristics and idiosyncrasies of her cast of characters, make this a work that transcends the dull label so often affixed to economics. Despite their economic genius, each of Nasar's subjects is presented as a person first and a theorist second, so that they come across as three-dimensional figures possessing both strengths and weaknesses. Readers will relish Nasar's crisp discussion of the factors that shaped Karl Marx's seminal work *Das Kapital* (1867–94), as well as the details of the Marx's personal life. Nasar's characterization of him as a shabby loafer prone to marital infidelity and hypochondria does much to illuminate the personality of perhaps the most well-known of the author's subjects. Many of the figures Nasar covers, such as John Maynard Keynes and Beatrice Potter Webb, receive a similarly in-depth investigation. Others, however, are cursorily mentioned; for instance, Adam Smith, the author of *The Wealth of Nations* (1776), is depicted with broad and often incomplete brush strokes, as is Keynesian economist Milton Friedman. Nasar further muddies the water by introducing figures only to abandon them for many pages. Ordinarily this would not pose much of a problem, but when the list of characters is as extensive as Nasar's, it is often a challenge to keep them all straight.

Nasar begins her story in 1842 with the English writer Charles Dickens, fresh from a whirlwind tour of the United States. While in America, Dickens found the vastness and seemingly limitless resources of the country so impressive that he increasingly took aim at the prevailing theory among English political economists, which anticipated nothing but a perpetual cycle of economic instability coupled with mounting poverty. The foremost proponent of this concept was the Reverend Thomas Malthus, a political economist who theorized that population expansion produced food shortages. When shortfalls occur, fewer children are born, thus thinning the population and restoring the balance between resources and population. Equilibrium is a fleeting thing in Malthus's world, for no sooner do people feel comfortable with their situation than they have more children and bring about the bust cycle, in which job competition prompts wage decreases, food prices soar, and the standard of living plummets. This chain of events continues in perpetuity, or at least that was how Malthus conceptualized it. In a world where industrialization was a new phenomenon, there were few available benchmarks for comparison.

Many logical minds that examined the available evidence arrived at the same interpretation as Malthus. Karl Marx, for one, viewed economics as a zero-sum game,

(John Blais)

Sylvia Nasar is a professor of business journalism at Columbia University's School of Business. She is the author of the award-winning biography A Beautiful Mind *(1998), for which she was a finalist for the Pulitzer Prize. The book inspired the Academy Award–winning film of the same title, directed by Ron Howard in 2001.*

wherein business competition might lead to an increase in production but not to higher wages or standards of living. Under the Marxian model, the world's finite resources go into industrial growth, leaving workers an ever-shrinking piece of the pie. In light of Malthus and Marx, it is not surprising that economics was once dubbed the "dismal science." Indeed, the most esteemed practitioners of political economy—the forerunner of modern economics in the mid-nineteenth century—saw cycles of boom and bust coupled with an ever-growing underbelly of poverty as one of the inevitable consequences of the free-market system. A small but devoted group, typified by individuals such as Dickens, saw the flaw behind this dark vision of economics. Dickens penned his novella *A Christmas Carol* (1843) as a denunciation of the Malthusian notion that suffering was the natural state of man. Before the twentieth century dawned, some began to question the assumptions that made the dismal science so depressing.

Hope came in the pioneering work of Alfred Marshall, who recognized that increased productivity also benefited the working class. Turning Marx's logic on its head, Marshall argued that businesses did not just compete with each other for scarce resources and markets; they also fought over a finite labor pool. In order to attract workers for ever-expanding ventures, businesses increased wages. Growing income meant more consumption and, in turn, more profit. At the beginning of the twentieth century, Beatrice Webb made a similarly optimistic argument, pushing for the formation of a welfare state as a means of offsetting downturns in business cycles. When productivity slackened, Webb observed, unemployment rose and poverty spread. She postulated that if the government intervened in such circumstances and provided varied forms of assistance, stagnant economies would rebound.

Each figure that Nasar highlights contributed work that advanced economics. Marshall saw the link between wages, consumption, and economic growth, while Webb fostered the theory that government assistance in times of difficulty was not a bad thing, as Malthus had contended, but a prerequisite for renewed consumption. The final critical component in the establishment of a new economic approach came from the influential American economist Irving Fisher, who recognized the central role that money supply played in economic stability. According to Fisher, periods of inflation and deflation could be mitigated by sound government regulation of the money supply. Even with the emergence of these disparate theories, it still took several economic calamities for a new approach to emerge, but once it did, it rested on the pioneering work of these economists and thinkers.

World War I devastated the European landscape, leading to social unrest amidst failing businesses and collapsing governments. Many thought that the economic torpor that enveloped world markets foretold the end of the free-market system, and for some, the turmoil vindicated Marx's earlier assertions. Perhaps cycles of economic boom and bust were the inevitable consequences of free-market capitalism after all. Despite fears in the interwar period, however, many still felt optimistic. Fisher, for one, held that episodes of inflation or deflation were entirely manmade and not at all unpredictable, as many had once theorized. Joining Fisher was renowned economist John Maynard Keynes, who shared his belief that seemingly unpredictable markets were actually the byproduct of human actions. Keynes differed from Fisher, however, in his feeling that government intervention, not free enterprise, would ultimately right sputtering economies.

For a book that examines economic calamities and the theories they produced at length, it is rather surprising that *Grand Pursuit* devotes so little attention to the Great Depression, the most significant economic cataclysm of the twentieth century in America. Nasar covers the period, to be sure, but not with the depth and clarity of her dissection of the post–World War I crisis. Following World War II, Nasar makes clear that most of the world's economists recognized the superiority of the free-market system, while also advocating substantive government intervention when the situation warranted in the interest of stabilizing runaway economies. Like previous economic theories, this one would not last forever. Economics is constantly changing to reflect larger social, cultural, and scientific advances. The dismal science may no longer be as dismal, but after the furor caused by the global recession of 2008–9, it is certainly not the sanguine science either.

There is much to commend in Nasar's *Grand Pursuit*, an eloquently written book replete with vibrant character descriptions and memorable recreations of some of the most critical economic dramas of the industrial era. Nasar is at her best when guiding the reader through the byzantine maze of economic theory, and readers will certainly find solace in the fact that the problems plaguing the world's economy in the twenty-first century are not new. It is comforting to think that, given what history has shown, a rebound may be just around the corner. Nasar certainly could have better linked her work to current affairs, just as she could have better covered the slow erosion of popular confidence in economics during the late twentieth century. Still, although economists are bitterly divided over the appropriate solution to existing problems, Nasar wants her readers to take heart in history's lessons that new syntheses and plans for economic prosperity are possible at any time. According to Nasar's historical perspective, slumps are mere blips on the screen, nothing compared to the economic disasters of previous decades. Thankfully, she does not echo Irving Fisher, who, on the eve of the great stock market crash of 1929, famously said that stock prices had reached "a permanently high plateau."

Keith M. Finley

Review Sources

Los Angeles Times, September 11, 2011, p. E10.
New Statesman 140, no. 5078 (November 7, 2011): 48.
The Washington Post, September 18, 2011, p. T4.

The Greater Journey
Americans in Paris

Author: David McCullough (b. 1933)
Publisher: Simon & Schuster (New York).
   576 pp. $37.50
Type of work: History
Time: 1830–1890
Locale: Paris, France

McCullough describes the stories of American students, artists, and politicians who worked, studied, and lived in Paris during the nineteenth century.

Principal personages:

OLIVER WENDELL HOLMES SR. (1809–1894), American physician, poet, and first dean of Harvard Medical School

HENRY BOWDITCH (1808–1892), American physician and specialist on diseases of the chest who was among the first to demonstrate proficiency in the use of stethoscopes

PIERRE CHARLES ALEXANDRE LOUIS (1787–1872), French physician noted for his work on typhoid fever

CHARLES SUMNER (1811–1874), American politician and outspoken opponent of slavery

GEORGE HEALY (1813–1894), American painter noted particularly for his portraits of politicians

MARY CASSATT (1844–1926), American artist considered among the greatest impressionists

JAMES FENIMORE COOPER (1789–1851), American writer noted for his depictions of Native Americans

GEORGE CATLIN (1796–1872), American painter of the West and Native Americans

AUGUSTUS SAINT-GAUDENS (1848–1907), American sculptor noted for the monuments he created of Civil War officers and other notables

ELIHU WASHBURNE (1816–1877), American minister to France during the 1870 siege of Paris

During the nineteenth century, the French capital of Paris was the center of European culture, artistry, and science. The United States, still an emerging economic power, was largely a backwater in these areas. It remained a mark of distinction for families to send their children to Europe for an education, and during the sixty-year period from 1830 to 1890, tens of thousands of Americans made the journey across the Atlantic Ocean to participate in what the continent, and particularly Paris, had to offer. The representative stories provided by author David McCullough in *The Greater Journey* provide the sense of spirit incorporated by some of these men and women, as well as the achievements and changes that resulted when they returned to the United States.

During the 1840s, writer, feminist, and literary critic Margaret Fuller divided the Americans who came to Paris to live into three "species": the "servile" Americans who came to Paris to indulge in fancy clothes, expensive foods, and the chance to mix with the upper classes; the "conceited" Americans, proud of their heritage yet not entirely sure why; and the "thinking" American who came to Paris to participate in its culture and educational opportunities. "Thinking" Americans included artists, sculptors, and architects. One might easily include students of medicine in the latter category. It is this last group, the "thinking" Americans, that McCullough highlights.

The educational opportunities in medicine were particularly attractive to prospective physicians during these years. Medical education in the United States could be considered abysmal by comparison. In the begin-

(William B. McCullough)

David McCullough has authored numerous books about American history. Among his many honors, he has been the recipient of the Presidential Medal of Freedom, two National Book Awards, and the Pulitzer Prize for Truman *(1992)* and John Adams *(2001), as well as more than forty honorary degrees.*

ning of the period McCullough describes, the 1830s, only twenty-one medical schools existed in the United States, and most had only a few faculty members. Mortality from disease, particularly among women, was high. Prospective physicians rarely attended school, preferring to learn the profession by apprenticing with a practicing physician. Even these men (at the time, all physicians were men) were generally poorly trained. Two factors in particular contributed to the situation. Women were loathe to be examined by male physicians and therefore were rarely seen by doctors. In addition, in some states, it was illegal to dissect cadavers, though in the South it was sometimes possible to use the body of a deceased slave. Consequently, cadavers were in short supply; even when available, they were invariably expensive. The result was that few physicians or surgeons had the opportunity to study the internal makeup of the body.

The medical education in the United States was in stark contrast to medical education in Paris. At the École de Médecine, a faculty of twenty-six professors, many the best in Europe, delivered lectures on anatomy, physiology, surgery, pathology, and chemistry, as well as on specialties such as diseases of women and children. There, women did not hesitate at the prospect of being examined by male physicians. Furthermore, cadavers were plentiful and cheap, and human dissection was a common practice available to all students at the school.

McCullough follows the story of several American students as they pursue their medical education. Among these are Henry Bowditch, James Jackson Jr., Jonathan Mason Warren, and Oliver Wendell Holmes Sr., who would someday become father of a Supreme Court jurist. Jackson and Warren were both sons of prominent Boston physicians. McCullough frequently draws on letters and writings from members of the group, so readers are provided first-person insight into not only education in medicine but the outside culture available in the city as well.

Holmes and Bowditch subsequently became deans at Harvard Medical School, instituting many of the practices they learned in their youth. Holmes was also a poet, most noted for penning in 1830 "Old Ironsides," a tribute to the USS *Constitution*, which was made famous in the War of 1812. Holmes's poem is credited with saving the ironclad warship from the scrap heap. Bowditch returned to the United States with more than just his education; he fell in love with an English student living in Paris, Olivia Yardley, who would eventually become his wife.

Jackson and Bowditch were particularly influenced by the exactness demonstrated by French physician Pierre Louis. Unlike many of his contemporaries, Louis was obsessive in his close observations of patients; his methodical use of a new instrument, the stethoscope; and his emphasis on "facts." McCullough uses excerpts from Bowditch's letters in his description of Louis's work. Louis later became the first to identify typhoid fever (also coining the name), work subsequently confirmed by Jackson.

Charles Sumner made his first sojourn to Paris in 1837. Here, McCullough provides the far-reaching implications of seemingly small events and demonstrates how those events produced significant impacts on American history. An imposing presence at more than six feet tall, Sumner initially traveled to Paris simply to increase his general knowledge. He learned French in little over a month in order to better participate in lectures and discussion on a variety of subjects including classical history, geology, philosophy, law, and even medicine. However, it was a subject that he recorded in his diary in January 1838 that had significant repercussions. While attending a lecture at the Sorbonne on the philosophical theory of Heraclitus, one man in a large audience, Sumner looked around and observed that among the participants were a number of black men. Other than their skin color, they seemed to Sumner perfectly in place with the other students.

The significance of Sumner's observation was later obvious; it was the inability to receive any form of education, not their inherent nature, that held down blacks in the United States. In the coming decades, Sumner became one of the most vociferous of abolitionists. He was among the founders of the Free Soil Party, which in its short existence was an advocate for restricting the spread of slavery. In 1851, he was elected by the people of Massachusetts to the United States Senate. With his size and booming voice, coupled with his passion for issues such as abolitionism, he was capable of creating outrage among his opponents. Therefore, it was hardly a surprise when in May 1856, Congressman Preston Brooks from South Carolina took umbrage with some statements Sumner had made and beat him unconscious with his walking cane on the Senate floor.

This incident had broad repercussions. Sumner eventually recovered from the physical trauma; psychologically, he was never the same. Brooks's punishment consisted of paying a hefty fine, but he was considered a hero in the South. In Kansas, an abolitionist named John Brown used the attack as an excuse to murder five innocent men, an event that became known as the Pottawatomie Massacre.

The story of Elihu Washburne is particularly poignant in McCullough's narratives. Washburne had been a lifelong politician, serving sixteen years in Congress prior to his appointment as minister to France by President Ulysses S. Grant. The third of eleven children born to a merchant-farmer living in Maine, Washburn (the "e" was added later) was "hired out" as a boy because the father simply had too many mouths to feed. In a classic American success story, four of the Washburn children eventually served in Congress.

Washburne would serve as a minister in Paris during particularly dark periods in France's history. In July 1870, war was declared between France and Prussia. Quickly defeating the French army, Prussian troops surrounded the capital in September, beginning what became known as the Siege of Paris. Despite pressure to evacuate the city as most Americans had, Washburne chose to remain at his post. McCullough draws heavily on the diary Washburne kept to provide a detailed description of the city during this time. As food became increasingly scarce, lines of a thousand people would form outside shops in the hope that something might be available. McCullough describes how as the people became increasingly desperate, the price of an egg became twice the daily pay of a soldier. In late 1870, the Prussians began a bombardment of the city, which on January 27, 1871, the 131st day of the siege, surrendered. Washburne recorded in his diary, "the most profound quiet reigns. . . ." The death toll in the city was reported to be as high as sixty-six thousand.

McCullough is at his best when describing the culture in Paris and its influence on developing American artists such as Augustus Saint-Gaudens. Saint-Gaudens first arrived in the city in 1867, a nineteen-year-old away from home for the first time. Initially visiting the city to participate in the Éxposition Universelle, the World's Fair highlighting modern culture and unusual items of manufacture and inventions, Saint-Gaudens determined to enroll at the École des Beaux-Arts as a student in sculpture. He had already spent most of his adolescence as an apprentice to cameo makers and had demonstrated an unusual talent in the profession. After a nine-month wait, Saint-Gaudens was admitted to the school. By 1897, when Saint-Gaudens returned to Paris for the last time with his wife and son, he had become one of most renowned American sculptors. Among his most important public works were a statue of Abraham Lincoln in Chicago's Lincoln Park; the Adams Memorial in Rock Creek Park in Washington, DC; the bronze frieze commemorating Colonel Robert Shaw, commanding officer of the African American Fifty-Fourth Massachusetts Regiment in the Civil War; and the monument to General William Tecumseh Sherman near the entrance to New York's Central Park, which he largely completed in Paris.

Saint-Gaudens was merely one of numerous artists and professionals described by McCullough who honed their skills in Paris during the nineteenth century. Painters Mary Cassatt and John Singer Sargent likewise developed their talents while studying under the masters in Paris. Because of her sex, Elizabeth Blackwell was unable to pursue her interests in medicine in the United States and instead studied and received her medical degree in Paris, returning home as the first female physician in the United States. Holmes returned to Paris late in life to revisit the "haunts" from his youth. Much of the city had changed during the ensuing decades. By then, few American students came to Paris to pursue their studies, not because the schools were no longer excellent, but because American physicians studying there had learned how to provide excellent training at home in the United States. This was the true legacy of the city so richly described by the author in *The Greater Journey*.

Richard Adler

Review Sources

Booklist 107, no. 17 (May 1, 2011): 63.
The Economist 399, no. 8736 (June 4, 2011): 94–95.
National Review 63, no. 12 (July 4, 2011): 40–42.
The New Yorker 87, no. 18 (June 27, 2011): 81.
The New York Times Book Review, May 29, 2011, p. 1+.

The Great Night

Author: Chris Adrian (b. 1970)
Publisher: Farrar, Straus and Giroux (New
York). 304 pp. $26.00
Type of work: Novel
Time: 2008
Locale: Buena Vista Park, San Francisco

*William Shakespeare's fantastical romantic
comedy of errors* A Midsummer Night's Dream
*is retold for modern times, as three troubled
mortals find themselves in the thick of the faerie queen Titania's annual bacchanalian festival. Adrian's take on this classic story provides
some dark and profound twists on the original.*

Principal characters:
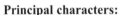
TITANIA, the faerie queen from Shakespeare's
    play
OBERON, Titania's consort, the faerie king
PUCK, Oberon's wily servant who assumes the form of a black Labrador
BOY, a changeling to whom Titania develops a strong maternal attachment
HUFF, a homeless man
MOLLY, a broken-hearted mortal swept into the world of the faeries in San Francis-
    co's Buena Vista Park
RYAN, Molly's former lover
WILL, a broken-hearted mortal seeking to win back his beloved
CAROLINA, Will's former girlfriend
DR. HENRY BLORK, a broken-hearted mortal who has failed to save the life of Boy
BOBBY, Henry's former boyfriend

Chris Adrian's novel *The Great Night* is at once dark and festive. There is both sun-
shine and shadow in his imaginative interweaving of William Shakespeare's play with
contemporary life in San Francisco. Adrian's narrative strategy is to move fluidly
from the mortal world to the magical world, from reality to fantasy, juggling intricate stories about each world with moods that range from elation to melancholy, or
conversely, from despair to joy. The novel begins with Shakespeare's faerie queen
Titania, who has sobered the usual midsummer night's celebration as she mourns the
death of her adoptive changeling human child and her bitter estrangement from King
Oberon. Her consort decamps when the grief-stricken queen coldly informs him that
not only does she not love him anymore, but she had never loved him. Having reconsidered her hasty remarks, Titania now plans to tempt Oberon back by releasing Puck
from his thousand-year enslavement to the faerie king. Here, Adrian creates a far more

frightening and powerful Puck than that of Shakespeare's play. To release the malicious, adversarial Puck is to release his true identity as "The Beast," who will wreak such vengeance and havoc that Oberon will have no choice, Titania assumes, but to return and restore order.

Molly, Henry, and Will—three ordinarily mortals who are each on their way to a party—end up instead as the guests of Titania's besieged faerie court, which lives under the hill in the park. They are each attempting to recover from a broken heart, and although they do not know it, the three are mysteriously connected in other ways. The backstory of each character is carefully developed, from their unhappy childhoods to their current troubled love lives. The most upsetting childhood belongs to Dr. Henry Blork, a pediatric oncologist. Although Henry is reluctant to allow his memories to surface, something terrible happened during certain lost or absent years of his childhood. In the freewheeling, fantastic underground retreat of the faeries, however, Henry allows himself to remember the magical nature of what happened. He comes to believe he was spirited away by Titania's faerie folk, only to be unceremoniously banished at some point later. He found safety (of a sort) in a home of lost and delinquent boys presided over by a pedophile, a setting similar to those found in J. M. Barrie's *Peter Pan* stories and Charles Dickens's novel *Oliver Twist* (1837). This traumatic experience leaves Henry with both a sense of guilt and a conviction that he did not really belong in the "real" world anymore. These missing years also give rise to a neurotic obsession with cleanliness and order, an obsessive-compulsive condition that continues to affect him into adulthood and becomes so exasperating to Bobby, his boyfriend, that he cannot stand it anymore and breaks up with him, leaving Henry utterly bereft.

While keeping company with the faeries, Molly is pulled back to memories of her childhood as a member of an Evangelical Christian family. The family doubles as a singing group and virtuously adopts a series of foster children, one of whom, Peabo, has a disturbing effect on Molly. More so than her actual family, Molly identifies with the mysterious Peabo, and he eventually leads her to realize that her parents' world was one in which she also felt like a transient alien, someone not of this world. After a failed attempt to become a Unitarian minister, Molly finds temporary happiness with a young man named Ryan, who, like Henry, is haunted by a childhood event. Later, when Molly tours the part of the faerie court containing portraits of Titania's changelings, she believes that she sees Ryan's picture among them. Like Henry, Ryan feels he does not belong in the world. He tells Molly that there is another world, a better moon behind the one they see, and that this moon shines on a better world with better people. Eventually, Ryan's unhappiness deepens, until Molly encounters his corpse hanging from a tree, a tragedy that plunges her into a deep depression from which she has yet to recover.

The third mortal's name, Will, echoes that of William Shakespeare, and like the great poet and playwright, Will is an imaginative writer. Will's childhood has been damaged by an alcoholic mother and by the suicide of his brother. He has also lost his girlfriend, Carolina, who leaves him because of his many cavalier infidelities. Both Will and Carolina, who met when she needed his services as an arborist, have lost their brothers to suicide, which may have been their only shared trait. Although the odds

Chris Adrian is the author of Gob's Grief *(2001),* The Children's Hospital *(2006), and* A Better Angel *(2008). He was selected for the New Yorker's 20 Under 40 fiction issue and is a fellow in pediatric hematology-oncology at the University of California, San Francisco.*

are against him, Will, like Titania and Henry, hopes that he can win back his beloved.

The story of Titania's break with Oberon references the stories of Henry and Ryan, but the mortal boy Titania has stolen from the human world most recently has not been discarded. Previously, Titania had adopted changelings and heartlessly abandoned them once she lost interest, but in this instance, she develops profound feelings of mother-love for a changeling known as Boy, an experience which is bittersweet. When Boy is diagnosed with leukemia, the normally glamorous Titania and Oberon must accompany him to a dreary human hospital next to the park, where he will be cared for by Dr. Henry Blork. During this time, Titania and Oberon are subjected to the bleakest of human realities. They are required to disguise themselves as Trudy and Bob Doolittle, owners of an organic orchard, and, bereft of magic, they must rely on the human medical world as it struggles to save their son's life. As their beloved son is forbidden to eat and subjected to arduous treatments, Titania and Oberon are powerless for the first time, standing by helplessly as their child slowly dies in a dreary hospital ward. This loss is something from which Titania will never recover. Like an ordinary mortal, her heart is broken.

Another ordinary mortal experience comes in the form of Titania's relationship with Huff, a homeless man inspired by Shakespeare's clownish Nick Bottom. Like that character, Huff is rehearsing a play, only this play is based not on Greek myth but on *Soylent Green* (1973), a science-fiction movie that warns of a dystopian future in which the human race resorts to cannibalism. Puck's mischievous magic spell bonds Titania to Huff, rendering her helplessly obedient to him. Still powerful in magic, she adds some supernatural artistry to the project.

The dark themes of the *Soylent Green* play recur in the character of Puck. While Titania can do nothing to bring back Boy, she can unleash Puck in all his angry, devilish nature. If he is not stopped, the novel suggests, he will devour the entire world, saving Titania for last as a gesture of gratitude for her granting him freedom. Echoing *Soylent Green*, this dire and cannibalistic possibility is destined to fail once Puck, morphing into a black Labrador, adopts Henry as his counterpart and soul mate. When Titania remembers that Henry was one of the doctors who failed to save her child, the plot takes an unexpected and violent turn in this zany novel, and as a consequence of this turn of events, Puck loses his demonic hound form and shrinks into a sad puppy. Throughout the story, however, Adrian maintains a rich layer of anger and desolation as a counterpoint to the fantastical surface.

While Henry undergoes a metaphysical transformation and develops a transcendent voice and vision, Will and Molly return home together with romance in the air, bringing about a conclusion that moves the novel closer to that of Shakespeare's play. In the end, all the major human characters have come to realize that love is a better magic than that of the faeries. At one reflective point during the marvelous series of sexual and culinary festivals, Molly recognizes that a sense of melancholy loss pervades her sensual delight, so that pleasure and despair mingle together unexpectedly. This is true of *The Great Night* as a whole. A pervasive sense of carnival is evident throughout, but the presence of death and bereavement introduces a tragic element that enriches and complicates the novel. The fantastical aspects are balanced by the aspects of emotional honesty, which ground the novel in the human reality of grief and loss. The blend of heartbreak and happiness that provides Molly a greatness of soul applies to the novel itself, in its mingling of sadness and euphoria. Adrian's empathic, inventive novel proves to be similarly great of soul and a more complex experience than its source of inspiration.

Margaret Boe Birns

Review Sources

Atlanta Journal-Constitution, August 28, 2011, p. 4.
The Boston Globe, April 24, 2011, p. 5.
The Guardian, June 4, 2011, p. 11.
New Statesman 140, no. 5060 (July 4, 2011): 45.
The New York Times Book Review, May 8, 2011, p. 13.
The Observer, June 19, 2011, p. 38.
The Washington Post, May 10, 2011, p. C4.

Great Soul
Mahatma Gandhi and His Struggle with India

Author: Joseph Lelyveld (b. 1937)
Publisher: Alfred A. Knopf (New York). 425 pp.
$28.95; paperback $16.95
Type of work: Biography
Time: 1893–1948
Locale: South Africa and India

*A probing, well-researched biography of one of
the most influential social and political figures
of the twentieth century*

Principal personages:
MOHANDAS KARAMCHAND GANDHI (1869–1948),
  advocate of mass civil disobedience and
  the political and moral leader of the independence movement in India
KASTURBA MAKANJI GANDHI (1869–1944), wife
  of Mohandas Gandhi and partner in his
  fight for social and political justice
HERMANN KALLENBACH (1871–1945), a German-born Jewish architect who was Gandhi's housemate in South Africa for three years
BHIMRAO RAMJI AMBEDKAR (1891–1956), anthropologist, jurist, economist, and
  political leader of the Dalits, who was critical of Gandhi's work on behalf of the
  so-called untouchables

A photograph of Mohandas Gandhi, taken in 1930, shows him bending over to pick up a
piece of salt on Dandi Beach in India as a few of his associates look on. His simple act was
in defiance of a tax on salt imposed by the British raj. What the photograph does not show
is the thousands of Indians who followed him more than 240 miles from Ahmedabad to
Dandi in support of his protest. Gandhi's commitment to satyagraha (civil disobedience)
rooted in ahimsa (translated as "noninjury" from the Sanskrit) prompted Indian poet and
Nobel laureate Rabindranath Tagore to confer upon him the title Mahatma, or "Great
Soul." The Indian honorific amounted to the equivalent of canonization in the West.
Widely revered as a secular saint by Indians and non-Indians alike, Gandhi was willing to
do whatever it took—as long as he could accomplish his purpose peacefully—to achieve
swaraj, or self-rule, for India. His David-and-Goliath battle captured the imagination of
the public and served as a model for future activists involved in similar campaigns, most
notably Martin Luther King Jr., whose advocacy for the use of nonviolent protest was the
cornerstone of his battle for the civil rights of African Americans during the 1960s.

  How did Mohandas Karamchand Gandhi become the Mahatma? In his Pulitzer
Prize–winning *Great Soul*, former *New York Times* executive editor Joseph Lelyveld

probes Gandhi's words and actions, as well as the recollections of those who knew him, to chronicle his transformation. Gandhi has been portrayed in numerous biographies as a compassionate man who advocated for peace and justice, lived unpretentiously in an ashram, ate a vegetarian diet, and spun his own cloth. While Gandhi certainly fit this public profile, Lelyveld searches for the man behind the myth and discovers a complex individual who could be shrewd, manipulative, distant, insensitive, and, at times, outright cruel.

Thus, although respectful of Gandhi's accomplishments, Lelyveld's account is no hagiography, nor is it a complete biography of Gandhi's extraordinary life. Instead, Lelyveld focuses on a period spanning fifty-five years, from 1893, when Gandhi began his career as a young lawyer in South Africa, to his assassination in 1948. Lelyveld is mainly interested in exploring the evolution of Gandhi's inner life and outer persona as he slowly developed into the internationally admired Hindu ascetic and social activist. According to Lelyveld, the Mahatma's self-creation was hardly haphazard. Rather, the author portrays Gandhi as a shrewd politician who carefully crafted and controlled his image, to the point where his recollections in his *Autobiography* sometimes conflict with the public record and the memories of those who knew him.

Lelyveld begins his exploration of Gandhi's transformation with his arrival in South Africa in 1893. Other biographers give little attention to the two decades Gandhi and his family lived in Africa. Lelyveld, however, devotes the first half of his book to showing how the young Indian lawyer's social conscience was forged in the crucible of South African political and social life, where the same prejudice that oppressed blacks also limited the options of other people of color, including Indians. Portraits of Gandhi taken around this time show a nattily attired young man sporting a starched collar, three-piece suit, and tie. Although he dressed in Western clothes, Gandhi frequently wore a turban. When he appeared in court the day after his arrival, the magistrate, apparently offended by the foreign headdress, ordered him to remove it. Gandhi refused and was ejected from the court. While other chroniclers attribute the birth of Gandhi's activism to when he was thrown off a train two weeks later for refusing to give up his first-class seat, Lelyveld claims that the indignity of being forced to remove his turban was the impetus for Gandhi's lifelong quest for social justice.

In subsequent years, Gandhi led several campaigns intended to spotlight the plight of Indians in their adopted country, including protesting the South African government's refusal to allow Indians the right to vote. He was also instrumental in the founding of the Natal Indian Congress in 1894, an organization that became the center of Indian political power in South Africa. His concept of satyagraha developed over a seven-year period, beginning in 1906, when the Transvaal government decreed that Indians must undergo registration. Thousands of Indians followed Gandhi's call to peacefully demonstrate against the government—and followed their leader to prison. In 1914, Gandhi agreed to a compromise with the South African minister of defense, Jan Christian Smuts, which ended the government crackdown on protestors and, according to Lelyveld, was reached with the understanding that Gandhi would then return to India.

Former New York Times executive edi-tor Joseph Lelyveld became interested in Gandhi while working as a correspon-dent in South Africa and India. He is the author of Omaha Blues: A Memory Loop *(2005) and* Move Your Shadow: South Africa, Black and White *(1985), which won the 1986 Pulitzer Prize for General Nonfiction.*

Yet, as Lelyveld points out, the advo-cate of civil rights for Indians was not above prejudice and racism when it came to blacks. Writing in 1908 about his first jail sentence, Gandhi is indignant about being shipped off to a prison intended for "Kaffirs," a deroga-tory term for black South Africans. He notes, "We could understand not being classed with whites, but to be placed on the same level as the Natives seemed too much to put up with." Elsewhere, Lelyveld quotes Gandhi as saying, "If there is one thing the Indian cherishes, it is purity of type. . . . We believe as much in the purity of races as we think they [the whites] do." Although Lelyveld speculates that Gandhi's comments were intended to placate white South Africans, his statements are nonetheless surprising coming from someone who was later lauded as a defender of the downtrodden and oppressed.

Throughout the book, Lelyveld cites instances when Gandhi's actions sometimes conflicted with his deeply held beliefs. When Gandhi returned to India from South Africa in 1915, he studied the issues facing his people and looked for ways to further the case for independence. Paradoxically, he also made political bargains with the Brit-ish raj. During World War I, for example, he agreed to help the British recruit Indians to serve as soldiers in the army, claiming that if Indians ever won their independence, they would have to learn to defend themselves from aggression. His behavior disap-pointed some of his closest followers, who criticized him for his divergence from his commitment to nonviolence.

In his discussion of Gandhi's ever-evolving views concerning untouchability, Le-lyveld uses Gandhi's own words to expose the ambiguities in his thought. Early in his dealings with untouchables, Gandhi said he still believed in some form of the caste system, but he also maintained that for "high and low" to exist was a "sin." Eventually, he claimed that the caste system must be completely abolished before independence from Britain could be achieved. Lelyveld notes that "He'd always maintained that the only reliable guide to his thinking on an issue was the last thing he'd said." As Lelyveld recounts Gandhi's unsuccessful attempts to eliminate the caste system, bring untouchables into mainstream Indian society, and heal the ever-widening breach be-tween Hindus and Muslims, a side of Gandhi often hidden behind the face of the gentle Mahatma emerges—that of a wily, pragmatic politician who knew how to manipulate a situation to achieve his goal.

In addition to satyagraha, Gandhi was a determined practitioner of brahmacha-rya, or celibacy. In his commune in South Africa and later in his ashrams in India, he continually tried to persuade his fellow residents to give up sex, including mar-ried couples. One wonders how his wife, Kasturba, felt about his view that marriage was "positively a hindrance to public and humanitarian work." As he grew older, he became even more insistent that sex between men and women could cause spiritual harm. Yet living a chaste life was not easy for Gandhi, and there is some evidence that he may have sublimated his urges in other ways.

In an explosive chapter titled "Upper House," Lelyveld speculates that Gandhi had a homoerotic relationship with German Jewish architect and bodybuilder Hermann Kallenbach. He quotes from intimate letters that Gandhi sent to Kallenbach, who saved their correspondence. The documents have only recently become available through auction and are new to scholars. Referring to the men as a "couple," Lelyveld notes that it was common knowledge among the close-knit Indian community in South Africa that Gandhi left his wife to live with a man. He quotes from a letter Gandhi sent to Kallenbach when the former was on a trip to London in 1909: "Your portrait (the only one) stands on my mantelpiece in the bedroom. The mantelpiece is opposite to the bed. . . . to show to you and me how completely you have taken possession of my body. This is slavery with a vengeance." Lelyveld offers several quotes that strongly suggest the feelings Gandhi and Kallenbach shared went beyond friendship, although he stops short of saying they physically consummated their relationship. After the publication of *Great Soul,* the people in the province of Gujarat were so incensed over what they perceived to be Lelyveld's innuendos that his book was banned.

To this day, Indians call Gandhi "the father of the nation," but not all revere him. In 1932, Gandhi became more focused on improving the lives of the Dalits, or untouchables. However, his efforts were met with skepticism on the part of the Harijans, or Children of God, as Gandhi called them. They were unhappy with Gandhi because he refused to support their fight to pray in Hindu temples, even though he claimed he was sympathetic to their cause. Their leader, the Columbia University–educated Bhimrao Ramji Ambedkar, openly criticized Gandhi as patronizing and untrustworthy. Gandhi's campaign to end untouchability failed, and although the caste system is now outlawed in India, it is still practiced.

Gandhi's quest to end untouchability was one of the "four pillars" of swaraj. The others were the religious unity between Hindus and Muslims, the practice of nonviolence as a way of life, and the adoption of swadeshi, or self-reliance, by India's rural villagers, who were encouraged by Gandhi to spurn imported goods and sustain themselves through their own handicrafts. None of these goals was achieved during Gandhi's lifetime, and today India remains a nation with a high poverty rate where the enmity between Hindus and Muslims still exists and violence still flares. The only one of Gandhi's objectives that he achieved was the occasion of India's independence in 1947.

Considering the complexities and inconsistencies of Gandhi's character, the title Lelyveld chose for his book, *Great Soul,* may seem somewhat ironic. After all, the Mahatma possessed the same flaws as the rest of us. Yet it is Gandhi's very humanity—his failings, his striving to overcome them, and his compassion and sense of justice—that makes him worthy of the title. Lelyveld does a brilliant job of demythologizing the man who became the Mahatma. However, to put Gandhi's transformation from South African lawyer to Indian activist in context, one should also read Gandhi's *Autobiography* or choose from the myriad of biographies that have been written about him over the past century.

Pegge Bochynski

Review Sources

Atlantic Monthly 308, no. 4 (July/August, 2011): 136–42.
The Christian Science Monitor, March 30, 2011 (Web).
Kirkus Reviews 79, no. 1 (January 1, 2011): 41.
Library Journal 136, no. 1 (January 1, 2011): 104.
The New York Times Book Review, April 10, 2011, p. 6.
Publishers Weekly 258, no. 2 (January 10, 2011): 40.

The Great Stagnation
How America Ate All the Low-Hanging Fruit of
Modern History, Got Sick, and Will (Eventually) Feel Better

Author: Tyler Cowen (b. 1962)
Publisher: Dutton (New York). 128 pp. $12.95
Type of work: Current affairs, economics, history, sociology
Time: Late twentieth and early twenty-first centuries
Locale: United States

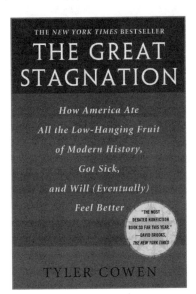

Cowen argues that before the 1970s, the United States benefited from unusually favorable economic conditions, including free land, cheap immigrant labor, and major technological innovations. He contends that all these examples of "low-hanging fruit" have now disappeared, making further rapid economic progress unlikely unless truly major innovations are conceived.

Tyler Cowen's brief volume *The Great Stagnation: How America Ate All the Low-Hanging Fruit of Modern History, Got Sick, and Will (Eventually) Feel Better* began as an electronic book and quickly became widely discussed and debated, leading to its subsequent publication in hardcover format. It clearly lays out its main thesis in its title and subtitle; indeed, the entire book is clearly written and easy to comprehend. Although Cowen is a professional academic and can sling jargon and numbers as well as anyone, in this book he deliberately addresses the broadest audience possible. He argues that for much of the first two centuries of its life as a nation, the United States possessed various unusual economic advantages that have generally disappeared since 1970. These advantages included abundant free land, a huge influx of immigrant labor, the development of revolutionary technologies, and a rapid growth in the number of educated citizens.

Cowen contends that before the 1970s, living standards tended to double rapidly, but that this trend has not continued since then. Even the economic booms of the post-1970 era have produced few jobs, and median family income began to stagnate even before the economic crash of 2008. In fact, for various reasons, economic growth since the 1970s has probably been even less than official statistics suggest. Truly productive innovations have been harder to come by, if only because the major discoveries in most fields tend to be the first ones made. In practically every area of economic life, therefore, the "low-hanging fruit" (a phrase Cowen overuses) has already been picked, and little more is readily available. Even though the United States spends more on research and development than in the past, the most important inventions have already

(Cook's Photo-Art Studio)

Tyler Cowen, a professor of economics at George Mason University, has written and edited numerous books, including Creative Destruction *(2002),* Discover Your Inner Economist *(2007),* Create Your Own Economy *(2009), and* The Age of the Infovore *(2009). He has written for the* New York Times, *the* Wall Street Journal, *the* Washington Post, Slate, *and many other publications, and is cofounder and coauthor of the economics blog* Marginal Revolution.

occurred, and most new developments involve merely modest improvements to already-existing technology. The economy is in some ways more productive than it once was, but job growth has been unimpressive, and major income growth has been limited to a small minority of the population. More productivity has not necessarily resulted in more employment, and in some respects just the opposite has been the case.

Cowen notes that both government spending and spending on government have grown, but gains in productivity have slowed in both the public and the private sectors. Moreover, measuring the productivity of government is extremely difficult, and the methods used may be inaccurate. For example, it is one thing to build a major new highway; it is another to repave that same road. The first act can result in major economic growth, while the second act produces only marginal economic improvement. In fact, Cowen contends, economic statistics are generally becoming less reliable as accurate measures of real economic growth. Government spending has become a larger proportion of overall spending than it was in the past, when the economy was actually growing rapidly. Spending on health care has grown enormously but has resulted in only small improvements in the measurable quality of health; similarly, a dramatic rise in spending on education has not resulted in any dramatic improvement in the quality of education. In other words, in practically every area of the economy, stagnation or even regression seems to have replaced the kind of regular, rapid progress that Americans tended to take for granted in the first two hundred years of the country's history.

Cowen also argues that even the development of computers and the Internet has not had the kind of enormously positive impact on economic growth, especially in terms of job creation, that one might have expected. Computers and the Internet have led to great advancements in personal happiness and satisfaction but not to great increases in employment or income. Cowen notes that companies such as Google, Facebook, eBay, and Twitter employ astonishingly few people. Many proposals to "fix" the economy, such as those of economist and *New York Times* columnist Paul Krugman, hark back to better days and depend on rapid economic growth to be plausible, despite the fact that such rapid economic growth seems to be stalled. Without this kind of growth, these schemes cannot succeed. Meanwhile, some politicians advocate tax cuts without advocating corresponding cuts in spending. Even income redistribution, Cowen says, can be only a quick fix and will not result in any long-term progress.

Some of the most fascinating aspects of Cowen's book involve comparisons and contrasts between American economic history from 1970 to 2010 and the economic history of the country's first two hundred years. He notes, for example, that many economic gains during the industrial period depended on economic assets, such as factories, that were difficult to move out of the country at that time. In the twenty-first century, factories can be moved easily or built elsewhere. Electronic communications, such as the telegraph, radio, and television, initially united Americans, helping people become more productive; however, computers and the Internet have made the United States part of a global economy in which American dominance is decreasing. Big government and big business developed partly as a result of technological progress, but such progress seems to have reached a plateau. For decades, Americans have imagined themselves as richer than they are and have therefore taken on too much financial risk while living primarily on credit. Further indebtedness, whether it is public, private, or both, will ultimately prove unproductive.

Cowen's advice about how to turn around the economic situation of the United States is a bit underwhelming. He notes that the existence of wealthy people in other parts of the world, such as in China and India, may make competitive innovation more likely. He suggests that the Internet may help promote more of a meritocracy and may also promote economic progress in general, even though it has helped generate few actual jobs so far. He predicts that the educational system is likely to become more competitive and thus more productive. He advocates raising the social status of scientists, even though his book makes clear that more money and prestige have been given to scientists during the previous one hundred years than ever before, with returns that seem to have slowed or stagnated. He points to Singapore as an example of a place where scientists are truly valued, although he does not indicate how much scientific innovation takes place there. In general, Cowen's case would be stronger if he had more fully compared and contrasted the economy of the United States with the economies of other developed nations, especially those in Western Europe. Did Europe's economy also grow rapidly because of "low-hanging fruit"? Has Europe's economy slowed recently for the same reasons that the US economy has? Cowen touches on such questions without delving into them in any great detail.

The brevity of *The Great Stagnation* is simultaneously one of its virtues and one of its flaws. He obviously does not want to take the time to make his case in enormous detail, lest he bore the average reader, but various reviewers have suggested that his case would be stronger if he had gone into more detail or if he had anticipated and answered more possible objections to his argument. In particular, one review in the magazine *Reason* cites specific statistics than seem to damage the persuasiveness of Cowen's argument. Also, although the book was widely and legitimately praised as stimulating and thought provoking, various challenges have been raised to Cowen's view of things. Perhaps the most common challenge is that he underplays the likelihood of significant technological innovation, although this is the type of innovation that might well transform the world economy. Cowen, however, points to the Internet as an example of just such an innovation that apparently did not transform things as fully as one might have assumed.

Other critics have suggested that Cowen may be just the latest in a long line of pessimists who have been proved wrong by subsequent events. These critics have also charged that he underestimates the benefits to the US economy of future immigration, that he mistakes a temporary downturn for an extended stagnation, and that he fails to emphasize how deregulation of the economy might unleash strong productive forces. In addition, some critics have complained that Cowen fails to face what they see as the real problem in the contemporary economy, which is the growing divergence between rich and poor and the growing concentration of wealth in the hands of the already wealthy. Cowen anticipates and answers some of these objections, but a slightly longer book might have allowed him to do more justice not only to the claims of his opponents but also to his own.

Robert C. Evans

Review Sources

The American Spectator 44, no. 4 (May 2011): 66–68.
The Economist 398, no. 8723 (March 5, 2011): 84.
Management Today, July/August 2011, p. 25.
The New York Times, February 15, 2011, p. A29.
Policy 27, no. 2 (Winter 2011): 51–52.
Reason 43, no. 1 (May 2011): 62–64.
Regulation 34, no. 2 (Summer 2011): 51–53.

The H.D. Book
The Collected Writings of Robert Duncan

Author: Robert Duncan (1919–1988)
Publisher: University of California (Berkeley and Los Angeles). Illustrated. 696 pp. $49.95.
Editors: Michael Boughn and Victor Coleman
Introduction by Michael Boughn and Victor Coleman
Type of work: Autobiography, essays, literary criticism
Time: Twentieth century
Locale: California, London

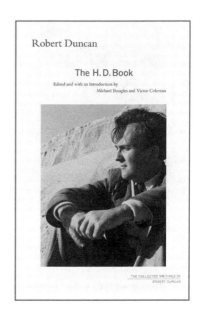

Appearing for the first time in book form, this diverse collection of writings by a well-known poet of the San Francisco Renaissance celebrates his literary hero and friend, the poet and feminist revisionist H.D.

Principal personages:
H.D. (HILDA DOOLITTLE) (1886–1961), American poet, novelist, editor, feminist revisionist
ROBERT DUNCAN (1919–1988), poet of the San Francisco Renaissance and one of the first American men to write openly about being gay
SIGMUND FREUD (1856–1939), Austrian neurologist and founder of psychoanalysis

The H.D. Book by poet Robert Duncan and edited by Michael Boughn and Victor Coleman represents a significant contribution to the study of the roots of modernism. In 1959, Duncan began to compose entries in a daybook that he dedicated to H.D. and her work. The first piece featured in *The H.D. Book* is an anecdotal rendering of his first exposure to her poem "Heat," which was read to him by his high school English teacher—an experience that he claimed had won him over to the beauty of art and the life of the mind.

By 1960, however, many literary taste-makers no longer considered H.D. a serious poet. If she was recognized at all, it was for the poetry she had written thirty-five years earlier as an Imagist. Yet even her Imagist poems were being dropped from key anthologies such as *Modern American and British Poetry*, edited by Karl Shapiro and Richard Wilbur. Writing the daybook became a process by which Duncan hoped to revive critical esteem for her work.

Between 1966 and 1985, Duncan's entries developed into a wider study that he began to publish as separate pieces in what the editors refer to as "little magazines" such as *Caterpillar*, *Tri-Quarterly*, and *Credences*. *The H.D. Book* makes accessible in book form Duncan's passionate personal literary criticism, which for forty years had only been

A poet of the San Francisco Renaissance, Robert Duncan was the author of thirty-five volumes of poetry including The Opening of the Field *(1960),* Roots and Branches *(1964), and* Bending the Bow *(1968). His correspondence with poet Denise Levertov was published posthumously in 2004.*

available as photocopied assemblages. Reproductions of these assemblages have been included in the volume, along with images of handwritten notes, photos of Duncan and H.D. from the early days of their friendship, Duncan's personal reflections of his childhood in California, his dreams of Atlantis, accounts of the Hermetic traditions of his parents, memories of the family mahjong table, and the title page for the aborted Black Sparrow edition of 1971 with acknowledgements to publications such as *Stony Brook* and *Coyote's Journal.* For the editors, the process of assembling such a diverse collection of manuscripts and images into a cohesive volume must have been daunting. They had to collate pieces that Duncan began in different styles or at different times, guess at his meaning where it was unclear, fill in his lacunae, and put it all together, an assemblage of assemblages.

The pieces collected in "Book 1: Beginnings" are Duncan's essays on themes—such as representations of Eros, the self, and conceptions of time and space—that he traced through H.D.'s work. One theme that stands out is H.D.'s "commitment to Hellenistic syncretism," which Duncan found in several of her works, including *The Hedgehog* (1925), *Palimpsest* (1925–26), and *Hedylus* (1927). More layered and less linear than "Book 1," "Book 2: Nights and Days" is formatted more like a daybook and reads like a palimpsest, which H.D. defined in her book *Palimpsest* as "a parchment from which one writing has been erased to make room for another." In the writings collected in "Book 2," Duncan revisited the same themes repeatedly but explored them from different angles. Duncan offered many thought-provoking reflections, including: "The consciousness bent down to a literature lives on its wits in a sulfurous burning. . . . As the other consciousness we see in the light spread out in the heavens. God[']s there; and in the darkness, daemonic stars."

Duncan had the notion that poetry is "What Is" and should not be derived from theory. He also believed that each poet needed to forge a personal methodology, discovering his or her own way into the process of finding emerging forms. Duncan recorded his own remarkable quest for such a poetics, which he refers to as "his soul finding its way" by continually writing, rewriting, and rewriting again, beginning with notes on scraps of paper which he wrote into notebooks, and then typed into a typewriter. Each time, he expanded the text.

Duncan argued that this accretive process of the soul finding its way must happen again and again in an artist's life as "we find our vital sense of this universe must return to this muddle." This occurs because of "the unwrought Eros," and once the work begins, the form of a vital spirit flies up, and takes the form of expression we have come to recognize as art; it is "the artist's block that heightens his awe of the other power in which his material speaks to him."

Perhaps to compensate for being disenchanted with cultural norms of his youth in Bakersfield, California, Duncan explored the occult, including kabbalah, black magic, the Anima Mundi, the *I Ching*, and the Hermetic Order of the Golden Dawn, the ritual cult to which Yeats belonged. Duncan reminisces about his own parents being initiates, "obedient to the directions of the stars in the Zodiac" and recalls color lithographs of Egyptian temples, images upon the table, voices talking, and "the old women looking wisely into the astral light and telling what they saw there." Duncan read the work of Sigmund Freud as part of his studies of the occult. In addition to examining Freud's notion that art is concerned with the remembrance and restoration of the Mother, Duncan asserted that "Poetry itself may even be the Mother of those who have destroyed their mothers."

To make up for what Duncan perceived to be the Judeo-Christian world's dismissal of women, he made central to his work "that range of human experience identified as the feminine," as the editors put it in their introduction. According to them, Duncan saw the feminine as "occulted beneath layers of patriarchal authority, and reflected in the repression of the knowledge of the leading role of women in the creation of modernism." At the time that he began this book, anthologies and university reading lists were predominantly composed of male authors, but Duncan contended that female authors should be included in the literary canon. He related how he found his love for poetry through the agency of H.D. and other women and maintained that both male and female poets were of central importance to his development as a poet.

Duncan claimed that some poems are so prophetic that they can only be realized in the fullness of a poet's life. In Duncan's opinion, "Ion," H.D.'s translation of part of Euripides's play of the same title, was one such poem and its influence could be felt in work she created twenty years later. In his examination of the poem, Duncan explored the layers of interaction between Greek and Egyptian symbolism in her work, as well as her psychoanalysis with Freud. He also pointed to similarities between Freud as a collector of exotic objects and the collections made by Professor Doolittle, her professor father.

Duncan also wrote about the poetic style that H.D. used in her poetry. He described how she constructed suggestive associations with phrases that echoed other phrases and created "a maze of sentences to bind us in its spell, so that we begin to be infected with the sense of other meanings and realms within those presented." Duncan also pointed out H.D.'s technique of circling repetition, in which the reader's resistance is "eroded and transformed."

As significant as H.D. was in Duncan's quest for his own personal poetics, he reflected on many other writers including Walt Whitman, Gertrude Stein, Eugene Field, Elie Faure, Henry Corbin, Helena Blavatsky, Robert Graves, Geza Roheim, Gershom Scholem, Hayyim Vital, Thomas Taylor, Gertrude Williams, John Symonds, Ezra Pound, Charles Olson, James Joyce, John Cocteau, and many others. These references are interspersed for discussion throughout the volume, along with memories of when and how Duncan experienced each writer at various stages of his quest.

And, although H.D. was the focus of his study of the feminine in modernism, Duncan pioneered the study of many other women writers and scholars. For example, he studied the work of Edith Sitwell, Mary Butts, Djuna Barnes, Dorothy Richardson, Mina Loy, and Laura Riding, presenting them as "the hidden inventors of modernism." He also examined *Prolegomena to the Study of Greek Religion* (1903), *Themis* (1912), and other works by classicist Jane Harrison, who had written about the cult of Aphrodite and how it had given way to the cult of the male god Eros. Harrison thus reexamined the archetypal basis of Western Greek myth used in or referenced by many other modernist works.

Duncan additionally explores such diverse topics as the Orphic studies of Robert Eisler; Gnostic studies of G. R. S. Mead; Edward Sapir's reviews of H.D.'s *Collected Works;* various interpretations of Imagism; H.D.'s thoughts on Shakespeare and Jacobean poetry; the image of the seed in H.D.'s work; the essence of poetry in various rites; and, the ritual objects of the Grail romance.

Duncan traced ethnic, historical, and nature imagery as themes of equal importance, interspersing references to Dostoevsky, Joyce, and the involvement of young women with whom he shared poetry. Working in canneries, their dreams and imaginations were taken by the "vision of unreleased powers" as they became involved with Trotskyite politics. Tracing their journeys, Duncan artfully concluded, "The poet, too, is a worker, for the language, even as the field and the factory, belongs to the productive orders and means in which the communal good lies." Indeed, he argued for a rather radical view of poetry that should not be taken to be a profession but seen as part of the daily labor by all towards a common goal.

Batya Weinbaum

Review Sources

The Nation, Feb. 21, 2011 (Web).
The Quarterly Conversation, Sept. 6, 2011 (Web).
Tri-Quarterly, April 4, 2011 (Web).

Heat Wave
The Life and Career of Ethel Waters

Author: Donald Bogle (b. 1945)
Publisher: HarperCollins (New York). 624 pp. $26.99
Type of work: Biography, music, film
Time: 1896–1977
Locale: United States

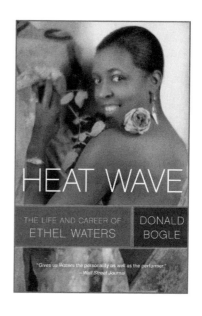

Donald Bogle has written a comprehensive biography of Ethel Waters, the first black woman to sing on radio and perform in a dramatic role on Broadway. Bogle traces her career from early vaudeville and Harlem nightclubs through sixty years as an entertainer on stage, in films, and on television.

Principal personages:

ETHEL WATERS (1896–1977), starting as a teen in Baltimore, she became an internationally known entertainer during her six-decade career

SALLY ANDERSON (1852–1909), Waters's grandmother and mother figure

FLORENZ ZIEGFELD (1867–1932), Broadway producer notable for breaking the color bar for African American dancers and performers

FLETCHER HENDERSON (1897–1952), pianist, bandleader, and recording manager of Black Swan Records

CARL VAN VECHTEN (1880–1964), *New York Times* critic and promoter of African American artists during the Harlem Renaissance

IRVING BERLIN (1888–1989), songwriter who wrote for minstrel shows and hired Waters to perform in a prominent revue

DARRYL ZANUCK (1902–1979), American Hollywood producer, eventually head of Twentieth Century-Fox, who gave Waters breaks and contracts to major films

As with Donald Bogle's previous biography (*Dorothy Dandridge,* 1997), *Heat Wave* is much more than a basic chronology of a performer's life. Bogle delves into the multifaceted career and personal life of Ethel Waters by utilizing comprehensive investigative research to explore her life in the context of the early entertainment industry, its cultural history, and the challenges that African American performers faced during the first half of the twentieth century. Using numerous images, including period documents, as well as material garnered from candid interviews, Bogle channels his historian background to provide a complete and honest look at the life and career of an extremely talented, yet controversial, artist.

Heat Wave opens during the later years of Waters's six-decade career when she is waiting to take the stage in 1950 for the opening night of the Broadway performance of *Member of the Wedding.* There is a sense of nostalgia tinged with nervousness as Bogle imagines Waters reflecting on her career and personal life while she waits off-stage. Through Waters's "reflections," Bogle provides a glimpse into what has come before and what will be expanded on in the book: a long and successful career on stage and in film and television (that for myriad reasons had hit a ten-year dry spell) and a personal life that had been difficult from its inception and was peppered with turmoil and upheaval. There is a great deal at stake in her performance this opening night; Bogle adroitly conveys the excitement mixed with apprehension mixed with a veteran's confidence that Waters could easily have been feeling that evening.

Waters was the product of rape, and her mother, Louise Anderson, was just thirteen years old when she was born. Bogle explains that Louise felt such shame over her daughter's birth that she was emotionally distant, and despite being raised by a compassionate grandmother, Waters always struggled for her mother's love. Waters said of her childhood, "A child growin' up needs laps to cuddle up in . . . that never happened to me. . . . It's a real tragic hurt, wantin' to be wanted so bad." Bogle points out that although Waters constantly yearned for the support of women (perhaps searching to fill the void left by her mother), she was sure to always be in control in relationships with them.

Waters grew up extremely poor in Chester and Philadelphia, Pennsylvania. She moved constantly, was married at thirteen for a brief time, and worked as a chambermaid in a Philadelphia hotel.

On her twenty-first birthday in 1917, Waters performed in an impromptu contest in a Philadelphia nightclub where two vaudeville managers heard her sing and then hired her to perform at the Lincoln Theater in Baltimore, Maryland. Waters soon made a name for herself and went on to travel on the black vaudeville circuit with the singing duo, The Hill Sisters. It wasn't long before Waters's solos were lauded, and she became known to the public as "Sweet Mama Stringbean" for her sensual vocals and tall, slender frame.

During a vaudeville stop in Birmingham, Alabama, Waters was in an accident and was pinned underneath a car. Bogle recounts that whites continued to pass her by, not helping and instead calling racial slurs at her. She was eventually taken to the black wing of a hospital, and when local African Americans heard of the accident, they took up a collection to help. Waters never forgot the kindness of "the people," and for a very long time she did not like or trust whites.

In the early 1920s, Waters went to New York City and began performing in Harlem nightclubs. Bogle spends several pages describing the atmosphere and feel of Harlem as it evolved throughout the decade. Vivid imagery and descriptions are employed to convey the creative impact that Harlem Renaissance artists had on their race and the country as a whole.

Music was also changing. Blues and jazz were becoming popular musical genres with all audiences, and from the start, Waters's voice and singing style stood out. Her music was accessible to both blacks and whites, and even in the loudest of clubs, audiences were known to stop and listen to her sing.

Waters was in control of her music, and while never completely overcome by the emotion of a song, her style let everyone know that she still resonated deeply with the music. Bogle makes it clear that Waters was asserting her independence in her music during the flapper era, when many other women also began to resist convention and exert their independence.

Donald Bogle teaches at New York University's Tisch School of the Arts and at the University of Pennsylvania. He is a cultural critic as well as a bestselling author and biographer. Some of his credits include a study of African Americans in film as well as a biography of Dorothy Dandridge. His work has been adapted for a four-part documentary series for television.

Bogle traces Waters's career, beginning in a small Harlem club called Edmond's Cellar where she drew in white and black audiences who often travelled to Harlem just to hear her sing. The next successful step was a recording contract with African American owned Black Swan Records for whom Waters released two songs and was an immediate commercial success for the company. Bogle provides a brief but complete history of the commercial beginnings for African American singers and recounts the discrimination Waters faced, but never bowed down to, as a dark-skinned African American. By her late twenties, Waters was the highest paid entertainer of the Jazz Age, black or white.

Waters traveled throughout the United States as part of the Black Swan Troubadours, and Bogle provides details of the American cultural and racial atmosphere of the time. In the 1930s, Waters began acting in Broadway productions where she was the first African American to perform in an all-white Broadway show (*As Thousands Cheer*, 1933). After a second appearance in 1935, Waters returned to Broadway in 1939 to perform in *Mamba's Daughters* as the first African American to act in a dramatic role and the first black woman to have her name listed above the title.

During this time, Waters was becoming internationally famous and was adding films to her list of accomplishments. Her first film was a part in *On With the Show* (1929), and she would go on to be cast in the film adaptations of her stage performances in *Cabin in the Sky* (stage, 1940–41; film, 1943) and *The Member of the Wedding* (stage, 1950; film, 1952) for which she won the New York Drama Critics Award in 1950. Her role in the film *Pinky* (1950) would earn her an Academy Award nomination for Best Supporting Actress, the first nomination for an African American since 1939.

Bogle supplements his reporting of Waters's career with insight into her fellow actors, descriptions of parties she attended at private homes, and her connections with other celebrities such as singer Josephine Baker, all the while never wavering from his reporting of the cultural and racial history of the time period as it related to Waters's experiences and career.

For all her talent, Waters is represented as a difficult and often mean-spirited individual. Bogle recounts numerous arguments with fellow performers and actors, the most infamous of which was with co-star Lena Horn during the filming of the all-black musical *Cabin in the Sky* in 1943. After a heated argument between the two women, the movie set was closed for a day, and Bogle reports that the two women never spoke again after that segment was filmed. Bogle learned through firsthand interviews that Waters carried a deep hatred for Horn, and that the set-closing argument probably stemmed from Waters's resentment of Horn and her feeling that the younger, thinner, and lighter-skinned Horn was receiving preferential treatment from the movie directors and producers. Despite Water's reputation and difficult personality, however, Bogle conveys that she was the standard-bearer for future black female performers such as Ella Fitzgerald, Ivie Anderson, and Dinah Washington.

There were other controversies in Waters's life, many of which occurred later in her career. As her career slowed during the 1940s, her bills mounted and she was soon in trouble with the Internal Revenue Service, owing money in back taxes. Additionally, there was a notable change in attitude toward her from the African American community as black leaders and vocal members of the community began to object to the roles she took, which many felt were demeaning to the race. Her portrayal of Granny in the film *Pinky* (1949) is one such role that was criticized by the National Association for the Advancement of Colored People (NAACP), as was Waters's roleas a maid to a white family on the television show *Beulah* (1950–52). Bogle explains that these criticisms served to make Waters more and more conservative in her politics, and she became an anti-communist and a huge supporter of President Richard Nixon.

In 1957, as her career began to slow, Waters began singing and touring with the Billy Graham Crusades. Singing to huge crowds in large arenas, she was able to combine her religious life with her stage life, and she stayed with the Crusades until 1975. During this time she also recorded spirituals, sang in churches, and performed spirituals in nightclubs but did not allow smoking or drinking while she sang. In 1963, Waters was cast as Harriet Tubman's mother in the "Go Down Moses" episode of the television series *The Great Adventure* with Ruby Dee in the role of Tubman. Waters died in 1977 of uterine cancer.

Heat Wave memorializes Waters and brings the woman and performer to life in a way that is comprehensive and free of idealism. Her life and career are examined and explained in the context of the world in which she lived and her place in history. Bogle brings the performer back to life, reviving her career once again for everyone to enjoy.

Batya Weinbaum

Review Sources

Los Angeles Times, February 13, 2011 (Web).
New York Journal of Books, February 8, 2011 (Web).
The Wall Street Journal, February 5, 2011 (Web).
The Washington Post, January 28, 2011 (Web).

Hemingway's Boat
Everything He Loved in Life, and Lost, 1934–1961

Author: Paul Hendrickson
Publisher: Alfred A. Knopf (New York). 507 pp. $30.00
Type of work: Literary biography
Time: 1934–1961, with references to Hemingway's childhood, adolescence, and early literary career
Locale: Key West, Paris, New York City, Africa, Cuba, and Idaho

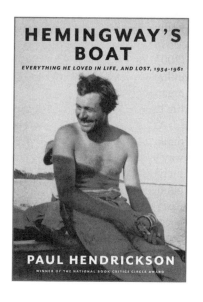

This meticulously researched biography of writer Ernest Hemingway uses his beloved boat, Pilar, *as a conceit to trace his prodigious life and literary career.*

Principal personages:

ERNEST HEMINGWAY (1899–1961), an award-winning American author and journalist

PAULINE HEMINGWAY (1895–1951), Hemingway's second wife and mother of two of his three sons, Patrick and Gregory

GREGORY "GIGI" HEMINGWAY (1931–2001), Hemingway's youngest son, a transvestite physician

PILAR, the thirty-eight-foot motorized fishing boat purchased by Hemingway in 1934

According to biographer Paul Hendrickson, the life of Ernest Hemingway has been examined by "so many scholars and memoirists and respected biographers and hangers-on and pretenders and doctoral students desperate for a dissertation topic" that many readers have lost all sense of the real man. Hendrickson's stated aim for writing this additional contribution to Hemingway scholarship is to unite the words "Hemingway" and "boat" in the same way that "DiMaggio" and "bat" and "Satchmo" and "trumpet" are locked in American minds. Through writing the parallel histories of Hemingway's beloved fishing boat, *Pilar*, and the captain himself, Hendrickson hopes to elicit an understanding that has eluded most other Hemingway biographies. *Hemingway's Boat* is an engrossing and commanding text that successfully combines scholastic research and rich storytelling to shine light on a man and his boat.

The author's interest in Hemingway stretches back to 1980 when he met Ernest Hemingway's younger brother on a flight to Bimini in the Bahamas. During that brief encounter, Leicester Hemingway recounted little-known stories about his famous sibling, most of which turned out to be true. In 1987, Hendrickson, a feature columnist for the Washington Post, interviewed the three Hemingway sons—Jack, Patrick, and Gregory—for a series of articles titled "Papa's Boys." Those interviews revealed memories of their childhood that were warm and good. Hendrickson acknowledges that his idea to write a Hemingway book was germinating as early as 2002 when he was writing his American history book *Sons of Mississippi: A Story of Race and Its Legacy* (2003). Even then, he says, the thought of utilizing Hemingway's famous boat as an organizing framework to tell the story of his life had taken shape.

Paul Hendrickson is a writer for the Washington Post. *His published works include* National Book Critics Circle Award finalist Looking for the Light: The Hidden Life and Art of Marion Post Wolcott *(1992), National Book Award finalist* The Living and the Dead: Robert McNamara and Five Lives of a Lost War *(1997), and National Books Critics Circle Award winner* Sons of Mississippi: A Story of Race and Its Legacy *(2003).*

As Hendrickson blends anecdotes and biographical information to describe Hemingway's life, he also grounds his text in history and the culture of early twentieth-century literature. Hendrickson reminds the reader that the second half of the 1920s saw the publication of some of Hemingway's best work: *In Our Time* (1925), *The Sun Also Rises* (1926), and *A Farewell to Arms* (1929). Despite his literary renown, the author's peers and critics took advantage of opportunities to ridicule the author and his writing, especially in the years leading up to and after his weakest novel, *Across the River and into the Trees* (1950). Some critics suggested his overtly masculine interest in fishing, hunting, and bullfighting masked a sexual insecurity. Hemingway, who called himself Papa, responded to negative reviews and parodies with threats and outrage. Hendrickson references these critiques in many of the thousands of letters Hemingway wrote during his lifetime; some are filled with pride and belligerence, others with tenderness and compassion. A vindication of sorts came in 1953 when *The Old Man and the Sea* won the Pulitzer Prize.

The narrative of *Hemingway's Boat* opens in April 1934 upon Hemingway's return from a big game hunting safari in Africa with his second wife, Pauline. Hendrickson includes a photo of the famous couple relaxing on the rail of the SS *Paris* transatlantic luxury cruise liner in New York City. Authentic newspaper clips reveal the excitement of their dockside arrival as Hendrickson invites the reader to imagine a fictitious newsreel in a darkened movie palace of the 1930s. Hendrickson uses a stream of consciousness writing style—half-based on imagination and half-rooted in historical fact—as a tool to add dimension and color to Hemingway's already larger-than-life story.

What the public did not know about the famous photo on the SS *Paris* was that Hemingway had returned to New York intent on purchasing a thirty-eight-foot cabin cruiser. His boatbuilder of choice was the Wheeler Shipyard in Brooklyn. To pay for its construction, Hemingway used his savings and money he cajoled from *Esquire* editor Arnold Gingrich in return for a series of articles about the safari. Gingrich, hoping to increase his magazine's readership with Hemingway's famous name, complied, and Hemingway commissioned the Wheeler Boatyard to build his beloved boat, *Pilar*.

In *Hemingway's Boat*, the legendary tragedies surrounding Hemingway's family and career are skillfully presented in the context of the man's moods and accomplishments—both on and away from *Pilar*. Episodes of incredible excitement and boating pleasure alternate with well-known retellings of his father's and his brother's suicides.

Hendrickson also includes Pauline's tragic death on an operating table, Gregory's death in a women's jail, and Hemingway's own suicide in 1961. In the twenty-seven years of captaining *Pilar*, Hemingway traveled from Key West to Cuba to Bimini and back in the company of approximately five hundred celebrities, colleagues, family members, and friends. The highs and lows of his lifelong passion for deep-sea fishing and big game hunting correspond to the peaks and valleys of his literary career. Ever the journalist, Hendrickson sticks to the objective truth, including vignettes of the Hemingway's declining editorial judgment, heartless womanizing, rumored homosexuality, hypermasculinity, boorish bad manners, paranoia, and condescending arrogance.

This comprehensive picture of Hemingway also benefits from the inclusion of several previously unpublished personal accounts, as well as the author's own insights, laborious research, and lyrical prose. Information derived from personal interviews with Hemingway's surviving relatives, friends, and colleagues fill entire sections of the book. For example, *Pilar*'s daily fishing logs are introduced through the life story of Arnold Morse Samuelson, an aspiring writer who hitchhiked from Minnesota to Hemingway's door in Key West. By incorporating Samuelson's thoughts and impressions, Hendrickson reveals one of Hemingway's gentler personality traits, depicting the master craftsman who helped struggling writers find their voices. According to Hendrickson, Hemingway not only hired Samuelson to work aboard *Pilar*, but also reviewed Samuelson's articles and suggested publishing venues during their lifelong friendship.

Similarly, the beautifully written and sympathetic portrait of Walter Houk, a surviving friend and confidante from Hemingway's time in Cuba, serves as a counterpoint to the souring relationships the famous man had with the vast majority of his literary colleagues and friends. Houk married Juanita Jensen, Hemingway's personal secretary in Cuba. The wedding reception was held at Hemingway's Cuban home, and the men remained close and devoted until their respective deaths. Alternatively, the angry correspondence between Hemingway and literary giants such Max Perkins, F. Scott Fitzgerald, Ezra Pound, and Gertrude Stein reflect the writer's legendary antagonism or, as Hendrickson suggests, his declining fictional prowess. These stories—and the inclusion of both Hemingway's flaws and his graces—serve to create a well-rounded and honest depiction of the famous author.

The reason for including more obscure accounts is less obvious. Hendrickson tracks down the Wheeler Boatyard heirs in order to record the decline and eventual bankruptcy of the Wheeler Shipyard. Presumably, the detailed trajectory of Wheeler's success and failure is meant to parallel or reinforce the ups and downs of Hemingway's life and career. Hendrickson ends this particular chapter by noting that the death of the Wheeler patriarch occurred only three months before Hemingway's suicide. Other than the purchase of *Pilar* in 1934, however, there appears to be little interaction between Hemingway and the Wheeler Boatyard.

Perhaps the most poignant sections are those pertaining to Hemingway's youngest child, Gregory—known as Gigi as a child—the son purported to be most like Papa. Gregory had a difficult life and went through periods of estrangement from his father;

their relationship was complicated and Hendrickson treats it with obvious care. Gregory died alone in a squalid Miami women's jail cell, after struggling with a lifelong obsession with cross-dressing. Not even a sex change operation could alleviate the guilt and disgust he shared with his hypermasculine father over this practice. Whereas Gregory asserted in his own memoir, *Papa: A Personal Memoir* (1988), that he was the son who most disappointed his father, Hendrickson makes a convincing case that Hemingway provided him much-needed financial, emotional, and medical support. Hemingway's benevolent involvement in his son's troubled life helps provide the "understanding" Hendrickson hopes to achieve with this biography, especially if, as some critics have suggested, Hemingway struggled with his own homosexual tendencies.

While some reviewers have called *Hemingway's Boat* "brilliantly conceived," not all agree. The book is long (five hundred pages, not including a lengthy section of endnotes) and the narrative wanders and is disorganized at times. Hendrickson appears to have anticipated the concern, and the book's prologue alerts readers that some of his storytelling is nonlinear. He likens his book to a journey by boat that is subject to changing currents and winding trajectories, noting that, like life and human history, it does not proceed in a straight line.

Despite these criticisms, *Hemingway's Boat* remains a personal and empathetic look at Ernest Hemingway, the man. Using Hemingway's time on the boat as a means to focus his examination of the author, Hendrickson effectively portrays the large role that *Pilar* played in Hemingway's life and his work. Regardless of whether the book achieves its aim of connecting the words "Hemingway" and "boat" in the minds of readers, the narrative probes the Hemingway myth and creates an endearing and thorough piece of scholarship. Hendrickson concludes that at its "most self-parodistic and Papa-cult worst," the contradictions of Hemingway's work and relationships can be best understood if told in the context of living life.

Cheryl Lawton Malone

Review Sources

The Christian Science Monitor, September 16, 2011 (Web).
The Wall Street Journal, September 24, 2011 (Web).
The Washington Post, September 22, 2011 (Web).

The Hemlock Cup
Socrates, Athens and the Search for the Good Life

Author: Bettany Hughes (b. 1968)
Publisher: Alfred A. Knopf (New York). 528 pp.
$35.00; paperback $17.95
Type of work: Biography, history
Time: 469–399 BCE
Locale: Athens, Greece

This vivid reconstruction of the life of Socrates places the self-styled gadfly within the rich, turbulent context of Athens during the fifth century BCE.

The twenty-first-century author who attempts a biography of Socrates is hobbled by several handicaps. The vast library of commentary already inspired by the Athenian gadfly—the first major figure in Western philosophy—might make one wonder whether there is anything new left to say. Contemporary sources about Socrates are limited to Plato and Xenophon, who were his devoted pupils and featured him favorably in philosophical dialogues, and Aristophanes, who mocked him in his plays. Because of the paucity of hard information about the man, a would-be biographer is forced to rely mainly on speculation and inference. Like Jesus, who did not commit his teachings to writing, Socrates was wary of arresting the flow of thought in written texts, unresponsive words that resist the kind of continuous interrogation that marked his own quest for truth. "And so it is with written words," Socrates complains in Plato's *Phaedrus*; "you might think they spoke as if they had intelligence, but if you question them, wishing to know about their sayings, they always say only one and the same thing." The challenge faced by Bettany Hughes is to do justice to the victim of the most notorious injustice in ancient Athens's legal system.

Helen of Troy led a life that launched a thousand books, but Hughes's first book, *Helen of Troy: Goddess, Princess, Whore* (2005), succeeded more than most in restoring the vitality to a famous but elusive figure of antiquity. Socrates is as much of an enigma, and Hughes, an English historian who has earned acclaim for popularizing the classical world through television, radio, and print, rises to the occasion by emphasizing the theatricality of a participatory democracy in which every male citizen was both actor and spectator. She organizes her second book into eight sections that she calls "acts," creating the effect of an eight-act tragedy that culminates, inexorably, in the death of Socrates.

Hughes begins on a late spring morning in 399 BCE as seventy-year-old Socrates walks through familiar streets on his way to the law courts of the city-state of Athens.

That journey will be completed more than three hundred pages later, after numerous digressions and flashbacks that help to make sense of Socrates's final ordeal. "My ambition is very simple: to re-enter the streets of Athens in real time," Hughes explains. "Not to revisit a Golden Age city, but to look at a real city-state that was forging a great political experiment and riveting a culture; a city that suffered war and plague as well as enjoying great triumphs. . . . To breathe the air Socrates breathed." Hughes evokes the sights, sounds, and odors of the agora, the bustling marketplace in which Socrates, the slovenly, pot-bellied son of a stonemason and a midwife, spent his time cornering fellow Athenians and posing pointed questions about truth, beauty, virtue, and justice. She situates Athens geographically in Attica, surrounded by mountains rich in marble, limestone, clay, and silver but with easy access to the sea. It had recently adopted an innovative political system in which every one of its fifty to sixty thousand adult male citizens was given a voice in public policy. Women were second-class citizens, and slaves—more than one-third of the population—possessed

(Getty Images)

Historian, author, and broadcaster Bettany Hughes has taught at several universities, including Oxford and Cambridge. She is currently a research fellow at King's College, London, and an honorary fellow at Cardiff University. Her first book, Helen of Troy: Goddess, Princess, Whore *(2005), has been translated into ten languages.*

no rights at all. The word *demos-kratia* (literally, people-power) was used for the first time only sixty-four years before the trial of Socrates; by the time they condemned him for allegedly disparaging the gods and corrupting the city's youth, the people of Athens were still adjusting to the novelty of free speech.

Athens is now often thought of as the model for the Greek *polis*, the exemplary city-state, but it was one of about one thousand *poleis* during Socrates's lifetime. More prosperous and self-assured than most of the others, Athens attempted to hold dominion over and exact tribute from many other city-states. Athenians ultimately came to grief over their imperial ambitions. Costly wars with Persia and Sparta demoralized Athens and depleted its treasury and its military forces. In violent civil strife, the city's fragile young democracy was overthrown, restored, and overthrown again. Socrates served loyally and courageously in his city-state's wars, but a growing mood of impatience and intolerance led Athens, once charmed by the cantankerous eccentric, to reject and revile him.

Aside from his final walk to the courts, it is impossible to follow with unquestionable accuracy Socrates's movements during his lifetime. However, Hughes describes her own visits to the sites that he frequented or that played an important part in creating the world in which he lived. Her biography is a "life and times" that is more confident about the times than about the shadowy life. Hughes's travels through the eastern Mediterranean—including Sparta, Melos, Delphi, Samos, and of course Athens—help her conjure up the world in which Socrates moved, but she cannot pinpoint those movements with much precision. Thucydides and other ancient authors provide her with details on battles, festivals, and athletic competitions, but Hughes can only speculate on Socrates's presence. She can, however, be sure that Athens's military and political fortunes, as well as its religious practices, provided the ambience in which Socrates lived out his years. Recent archaeological finds support her contentions. Excavated bone fragments—"eye-sockets are pierced with arrows, shin-bones sliced with axes, teeth smashed back into skulls"—reveal the brutality of the battles the Athenians fought. The marble head of a horse provides evidence of a rich equestrian culture. But Hughes hardly needed to have visited the Sackler Library at Oxford University to examine the newly discovered fragment of Sophocles's play *Epigonoi* in order to know that the Peloponnesian War was a nasty business.

By contrast, a discussion of midwives in ancient Greece, where infant mortality ranged from 10 to 30 percent, might seem a digression, except that it sheds light on the work that Socrates's mother did—the kinds of herbs she probably employed to induce contractions or fumigate the womb, as well as how, at the request of disappointed parents, she exposed unwanted female infants to die. Information about Athenian midwifery also clarifies one of Socrates's most famous metaphors: his claim, according to Plato's *Theaetetus*, that his role, like that of a midwife, is to bring forth wisdom from others. "My art of midwifery is in general like that of midwives," Socrates explains. "The only difference is that my patients are men, not women. My concern is not with the body but with the soul that is in labour. The highest point of my art is to prove by every test whether the offspring of a young man's thought is a false phantom or is something alive and real."

Writing as a historian, not as a philosopher or even a historian of philosophy, Hughes takes her greatest interest in unique historical details, such as the water clock that measured out and allotted time during Socrates's trial, or the mechanical device known as the *kleroterion* that randomly selected five hundred jurors out of the pool of six thousand citizens to determine Socrates's fate. She does not weigh in on the perennially perplexing question of how much the Socrates of the Platonic dialogues is Plato's own concoction. She does, though, emphasize the crucial role Socrates assigned to love, how for him love was integrally connected to virtue, knowledge, and happiness.

As suggested by the title, *The Hemlock Cup* interprets Socrates's life in terms of its conclusion. Hughes in fact observes that had Socrates not become a sacrificial victim of Athens's cultural transition, his reputation might have been diminished and the history of Western thought altered. The book moves relentlessly toward its climax in the trial, in which 280 of the 500 jurors voted to convict Socrates of impiety toward the gods and corruption of the city's youth. While contending that the charges were baseless, Hughes traces the gradual change in Athenian attitudes toward the irrepressible village oddball. In 423 BCE, Socrates himself probably attended a performance of his friend Aristophanes's *The Clouds*, which, by caricaturing him as a "master of twaddle," provided an early sign of disaffection toward him. After years of devastating wars and civil strife, Athenians lost their patience for the kind of questions that Socrates persisted in asking. During the sentencing phase of his trial, Socrates was anything but contrite, scoffing at the court and taunting the jurors with the claim that, rather than condemned, he should be honored as the wisest man in Athens. Of course, for Socrates, wisdom consisted in knowing that one does not know. But, incensed by the defendant's defiance, the jurors thought that they knew exactly what he deserved, voting 340 to160 in favor of death.

Hughes notes that, at twelve drachmas per dose, hemlock was rather expensive, and ordinary prisoners were usually crucified rather than poisoned. But Socrates had influential friends who could help provide the potion, though they also hatched a plot to spirit him away to safety. However, Socrates refused to violate his city's laws, and, rejecting the escape plan, swallowed the lethal substance. Hughes can only speculate about his motives. An ironist to the end, was he trying to flaunt his obedience to a city that had condemned him for disdaining its conventions? Was he seeking to ensure his enduring reputation as a martyr for truth? Was he reaffirming his claim that philosophy is a matter of learning how to die (and live)? Hughes concludes, "Socrates' lifespan marked the beginning and an end of an idea—the idealistic vision of an autonomous, tolerant, democratic Athenian city-state." Her achievement in *The Hemlock Cup* is capturing the material context of that vision and the life of one of history's most extraordinary figures.

Steven G. Kellman

Review Sources

Booklist 107, no. 9/10 (January 15, 2011): 18.
Library Journal 136, no. 1 (January 1, 2011): 100.
Nation 293, no. 13 (September 26, 2011): 33.
The New York Times Book Review, February 20, 2011, p. 12.
Publishers Weekly 257, no. 50 (December 20, 2010): 47.
Times Literary Supplement, no. 5620 (December 17, 2010): 25.
The Wall Street Journal, February 19, 2011, p. C7.
The Washington Post, February 13, 2011, p. B7.
Weekly Standard 16, no. 21 (February 14, 2011): 35–37.
Wilson Quarterly 35, no. 2 (Spring 2011): 109–10.

The Hidden Reality
Parallel Universes and the Deep Laws of the Cosmos

Author: Brian Greene (b. 1963)
Publisher: Alfred A. Knopf (New York). Illustrated. 384 pp. $29.95; paperback $16.95
Type of work: Science

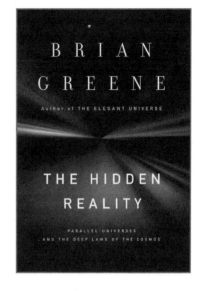

Greene's The Hidden Reality *is an introduction to the theory of the existence of the multiverse, outlining nine variations of the theory and providing the lay reader with the necessary physics history and background to fully understand these concepts.*

Physicist Brian Greene published his first mass-market book, *The Elegant Universe: Superstrings, Hidden Dimensions, and the Quest for the Ultimate Theory*, in 1999. The book, which serves as an introduction to superstring theory, Greene's main field of study, was the basis for a three-part *Nova* special narrated by Greene that originally aired on PBS in 2003. His second book, *The Fabric of the Cosmos: Space, Time, and the Texture of Reality* (2004), investigates the fundamentals of modern physics—space, time, spacetime, and reality—for the nonscientist. Both books quickly became best sellers, and *The Elegant Universe* gained critical acclaim as well, ranking among the finalists for the 2000 Pulitzer Prize for general nonfiction.

The Hidden Reality: Parallel Universes and the Deep Laws of the Cosmos, a recent addition to the current spate of pop-physics books, offers an in-depth introduction to various parallel universe theories and has become a *New York Times* best seller. Written in the same narrative style as Greene's earlier two books, *The Hidden Reality* is filled with simple analogies, metaphors, and anecdotes that help to explain difficult concepts to those with little or no prior knowledge of physics and mathematics. Greene begins each chapter, often the bulk of the chapter, with the necessary history and physics upon which the related theory is based. Readers with a background in physics can easily skip these sections. Greene also includes extensive endnotes that provide more in-depth physics and mathematical details for those interested. Despite using the term "parallel universe" in his subtitle, he instead opts for its synonym "multiverse" throughout the book, although he does not explain the reasoning behind his use of these different terms.

Greene begins with the quilted multiverse theory because, in some ways, it is the simplest to understand. To illustrate the basic premise, Greene uses an analogy of a woman having five hundred dresses and one thousand pairs of shoes and therefore a large but finite number of outfits to represent the finite number of possible particle arrangements. Given enough days, the woman must repeat outfit combinations; similarly, given enough space, universes must repeat as well. Each universe would be contained within its own cosmic horizon, which Greene likens to a patchwork quilt square. In this quilted multiverse, every possible universe option would not only exist but also have exact copies.

Inflationary cosmology, a theory that dates to the 1950s, proposes that the universe rapidly expanded during the early periods after the big bang, thus explaining the measured 2.7 kelvin cosmic background radiation. Greene outlines the eventual accidental discovery of the background radiation and the resulting inflationary theory. To explain the inflationary multiverse, he compares space to a block of swiss cheese in which the holes—universes like ours—are no longer rapidly expanding, while the cheese portions continue to spread, creating more and more holes and increasing the space between them. These holes are known as bubble or pocket universes. Greene explains how and why the various universes would differ, including many quite different from our own. He also details how the quilted multiverse could exist within a bubble multiverse.

In chapter 4, Greene summarizes the history of string theory, the state of the field since his last book, and the direction of future study. The next three multiverse theories he discusses are all based on string theory. The first of these, the brane multiverse, is based on an aspect within string theory known as membranes, or simply "branes," which are mathematical concepts that exist across all eleven dimensions found in string theory. Greene explains that in the "braneworld," we would live within a three-brane, a three-dimensional construct that he compares to a slice of bread. The "extra" dimensions predicted by string theory would exist in other worlds, and these slices would differ from ours in the same way that bubble universes differ. Greene discusses the differences between strings and snippets (open-ended strings with one end secured in a brane), the most important being that while string can travel between branes, snippets cannot. Humans and everything else in our universe, including light, are composed of snippets; we cannot leave our "slice of bread." Therefore, another dimension or braneworld could exist right next to ours without our ever knowing about it. The cyclic multiverse is also based on braneworlds but ones in which these slices routinely interact. Were two braneworlds to collide, everything in them would be destroyed and a new big bang explosion would be ignited. Thus, in this cyclic model, the braneworlds collide, bounce apart in a big bang, attract, collide, and bounce apart again in a never-ending cycle. In chapter 6, Greene details the landscape multiverse theory, an idea that takes into account the large number of possible shapes that string theory's extra dimensions could take. It can also be combined with other multiverse theories, such as the inflationary bubble universes.

Greene then moves on to the quantum multiverse (or "many worlds") theory, which is based on quantum mechanics, the branch of physics that deals with matter and energy's wave-particle duality. The field's creators developed a mathematical formula that predicts probabilities, such as the location of an electron within a closed box. According to the Copenhagen school of thought, when an electron's position is measured, its probable wave (or wave function) collapses, resulting in only one possible outcome.

However, other quantum physicists argue that this is not the case, thus leading to the quantum multiverse concept. To use Greene's example, in the quantum multiverse, the same electron could exist (and be observed) at both Grant's Tomb and Strawberry Fields, but it would exist in each location only in separate, identical universes. The universe would seemingly split, creating universes for each of the possible results. Greene also devotes a large section at the end of the chapter to discussing the ongoing controversy surrounding the "many worlds" idea.

Brian Greene is a professor of physics and mathematics at Columbia University. He has written numerous academic papers on the subject of string theory, as well as the best-selling books The Elegant Universe *(1999) and* The Fabric of the Cosmos *(2004). He is also the cofounder and director of the Columbia University Institute for Strings, Cosmology, and Astroparticle Physics.*

The next multiverse Greene discusses is the one that he finds to be the most bizarre, the holographic multiverse. This theory surmises that our three-dimensional reality is actually a projection taking place on some distant surface. Through a vignette about two roommates (one messy, the other neat), Greene seeks to explain entropy, the amount of disorder in a given system, which then feeds into discussion of black holes, Hawking radiation, and the event horizon. Studying the properties of black holes informs the holographic multiverse theory: such a universe would change with perspective, similar to the difference in views from inside and outside the event horizon of a black hole.

Greene then moves on to a theory highly popularized by science fiction movies such as *The Matrix* (1999) and *The Thirteenth Floor* (1999). According to the simulated multiverse theory, our universe is a creation of either an enormous machine or an alien race or life-form. The concept of a simulated multiverse can raise several existential questions: What is real? What is our consciousness—the voice that we hear in our heads? As Greene shows, there is no way to safely answer these questions and satisfactorily prove that our world is not some sort of fabrication. Scientists have already created very small "universes" using computers, and Greene delves into the possibility of future generations being able to create a self-aware large-scale universe. He goes on to explain the problems with creating a universe in a laboratory, not within a computer. For instance, the experiment would cause a variety of problems if, once created, the universe kept expanding and took over or merged with the original universe.

Lastly, Greene explains the ultimate multiverse, which encompasses all of the others and all of the possible variations of universes, including a universe composed of nothingness. While the other multiverse theories are byproducts of the mathematics behind other theories or of discoveries made while searching for answers to different questions, as Greene relates, the ultimate multiverse was created as a solution. Within the ultimate multiverse, all mathematical equations would explain one possible universe or another, an aspect of the theory that Greene chooses to explore at some length. Interestingly, Greene attributes the origin of this concept to the philosophical rather than the scientific community.

In chapter 7, Greene discusses whether the various multiverse theories can and should be considered science. This is precisely the greatest criticism levied against his work. Many scientists argue that the multiverse theories cannot be considered hard science and are not even valid theories because they cannot be tested or proven using the scientific method. Some critics go so far as to call the multiverse theories science fiction or even theologies. For his part, Greene argues and speculates on ways that some of the theories, such as those involving string, will one day be testable, once the necessary technology has been developed.

The Hidden Reality has received a fair amount of negative critical attention as well as high praise from reviewers who laud its accessibility. Greene's book includes a lot of information already published and, according to some critics, better handled in other books. The unique aspect of *The Hidden Reality* is that it was written by one of the leaders in the field of string theory. Given this, some reviewers criticize Greene for not focusing more on string theory advances and the related multiverses. Readers with a background in physics or science might find the bulk of most chapters to be redundant, comprising material they already know. The endnotes and further reading sections should give the inquisitive reader more than enough in-depth information, though they may prove challenging for those lacking a science background. Some lay readers might find the book a bit cumbersome and wish that Greene had included a glossary or better illustrations. Nevertheless, Greene's humorous, engaging narrative style will ably assist readers in understanding the most complex aspects of each theory.

Jennifer L. Campbell

Review Sources

The Christian Science Monitor, February 11, 2011 (Web).
Chronicle of Higher Education 57, no. 28 (March 18, 2011): B6–7.
New Scientist 209, no. 2798 (February 5, 2011): 30.
The New York Times, January 27, 2011, p. C4.
The Observer, March 19, 2011, p. 43.
Science News 179, no. 9 (April 23, 2011): 34.
Toronto Star, February 4, 2011 (Web).

Horoscopes for the Dead

Author: Billy Collins (b. 1941)
Publisher: Random House (New York).
 128 pp. $24.00
Type of work: Poetry

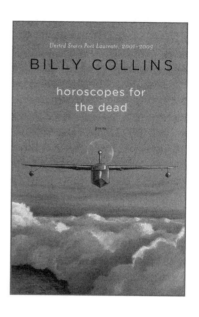

In this engaging and touching collection of poetry, Collins once again mines everyday life for inspiration.

The former poet laureate of the United States, Billy Collins has been at the forefront of American poetry for many years. He has established himself not only as a skilled poet, but also as a very popular poet. Popularity and poetry have not often been linked in contemporary America, poets usually being thought of as outsiders who scribble incomprehensible lines for the praise of fellow poets. Although Collins's first poetry was published during the 1970s, it was not until the 1990s that he gained both critical and public recognition. Beginning with his 1991 collection *Questions About Angels*, the poet began to be appreciated for his "accessible" poetry, work that was identified for its plain talk. Collins gained a following even among readers who up to that point had been adverse to reading poetry; he demonstrated a talent for taking daily American life and presenting it in an artful way. By the end of the 1990s, Collins had earned a reputation as "the most popular poet in America." As with other collections, *Horoscopes for the Dead* shows off the qualities to which his readers have become accustomed.

The everyday events that Collins seems to favor can make for quality verse. With a direct approach and a mischievous sense of humor, the poet disarms the reader's presupposition that a poem has to be difficult to crack open. It has been argued that Collins's poems speak to what was already on the tip of the reader's tongue, so that the poet merely gives voice to what readers knew but did not have the skill to put into words. He makes poetry look like something that everybody could write. In truth, what Collins does is far from easy. In an interview with *Guernica Magazine*, he said that he admires so-called difficult poets like John Ashbery and Jorie Graham, but that "more often than not" he finds difficulty poetry "to be gratuitous and show-offy," as it will most likely scare off a "sensible reader." Collins strongly believes that being clever merely for the sake of it, likewise being incomprehensible just to be incomprehensible, does nothing to advance the poetry as an art form. Over time, Collins has come to the conclusion that clarity in poetry involves taking a real risk. When he decided that writing more clearly was the most appropriate path for him to take, he found himself being more influenced by such poets as Howard Nemerov, Philip Larkin, and

One of the most popular American poets of his generation, Billy Collins is the author of several critically acclaimed collections of poetry. He served as the poet laureate of the United States from 2001 to 2003.

Karl Shapiro. In a real sense, he turned his back on the likes of Wallace Stevens, T. S. Eliot, and Hart Crane, poets who had influenced the younger Collins but whose "involuted" approach to poetry he found no longer served him well.

For Collins, beginning to write a poem can be difficult, but once it is under way, the poem flows to the end. He has mentioned that most of his poems are completed in one sitting, that during the writing process, he will do his best to take on the role of the reader, stopping and reading the lines he has just written as if reading them for the first time. For this process to work, he may only write one or two lines at a time. This approach helps him to get the cadence right; for him, rhythm must add to the progression of the poem. As each line ends, the reader is brought back to the poem's central focus. There is a direct intimacy to his poems. He writes for one reader, not a group or a crowd.

Part of Collins's appeal as a poet has been his use of humor. While some poets wrap themselves up the gloom of the modern times, Collins finds that an appropriate amount of humor or self-deprecation enhances a reader's appreciation of the poem at hand. Allowing the reader to become comfortable with the reading experience has certainly helped to make Collins among the most widely read American poets. He has almost single-handedly demystified poetry for a whole generation of readers. However, for some critics this has led to a trivialization of the genre. While no poet can ever be sure that his work will stand the test of time, there is much to admire about Collins's poetry, and many of those well-worn qualities appear in *Horoscopes for the Dead.*

The collection is divided into four parts, each containing between ten to fourteen poems. Collins opens with "Grave," in which the speaker stands over his parents' grave and has a conversation with each one. The poet begins, "What do you think of my new glasses." There is a "long silence" that descends "on the rows of the dead / and on the fields and the woods beyond." Eventually the speaker lies "down on the ground" and hears his mother say, "They make you look very scholarly." Using his other ear, which is the ear his father likes "to speak into," the speaker hears not a thing. His father remains silent, and it is a silence beyond all other silences. Even the "100 Chinese silences" that the speaker has merely made up out of thin air cannot counter the impact of his father's. Without undo fanfare, Collins has touched on the sensitive nature of a relationship with parents that can carry over even after death. It is a universal theme and it is handled calmly and with a touch of humor. Even with such a morbid subject as death, Collins does not let it get the better of him. As always, the poignancy of his work comes from its understatement.

As a poet who always writes for one reader, Collins does not let his poetry get out of balance. There is a reassuring quality to his work, and he demonstrates a genuine concern for his readers. He has stated that he tries "very assiduously to court the reader and engage him." Some of his methods include introducing familiar settings and situations, without condescending to his audience, and mixing in a healthy portion of mischievous humor. While Collins has been called the "class clown in the schoolhouse of American poetry," the label may do a disservice to what Collins has been able to accomplish. It is true that he is not above poking fun at poetry, or himself, for having too many lofty aspirations. His approach may also go against the grain of so-called serious poets, but Collins's lighter touch is not without its serious commitments. His criticism of poetry in general has involved his suspicion of its intentions.

With *Horoscopes for the Dead*, Collins has kept his realism on the optimistic side. In "Memento Mori," he mentions "It doesn't take much to remind me / what a mayfly I am, / what a soap bubble floating over the children's party." The poet is grateful for everything he has, including "the sweet weeds / and the mouthfuls of colorful wildflowers." He is constantly reminded of his own "mortality." This is all very sobering information, and it keeps his take on the world in check. This is Collins's ninth collection, and he has not lost his playful or positive view on life. One might say that Collins is determined to maintain his childlike wonder for the world around him. He is not swayed by the obvious shortcomings in the world, presenting them in his work with the sense that it is still possible to remain upbeat. In "Good News," Collins describes the trepidation of wondering whether a beloved dog has cancer. The "news came in over the phone" as the poem's speaker works on a recipe to fill the time. After learning that the dog is "not sick, / everything took on a different look / and appeared to be better than it usually is." For this moment, everything is "perfect," and the dog's "brown and white coat / are perfectly designed to be the dog you perfectly are."

Whether Collins has become a prisoner of his own success, unable or unwilling to alter his poetic method, it is apparent that the clarity and comfort that he brings to each collection has served him and his readers well. It can be argued, though, that his presentation of the familiar in ways that welcome the reader into the experience makes for poetry that is touching but not poetry that will be considered great. For now, Collins seems to be the master of his fate, a skilled performer who knows how to best please and inform his audience. According to his publisher, his collections together have sold more than 500,000 copies, an astounding number for a poet. Still, Collins does not set out to compile a best-selling volume of poetry. He writes one poem at a time, and only after a period of time, when he has a large enough batch of good poems, does the idea of a collection enter the picture. For the title poem, Collins took inspiration from the reading of horoscopes and the recent death of a friend. He relished the title for what he calls its "hopeless optimism." Collins begins: "Every morning since you disappeared for good, / I read about you in the daily paper / along with the box scores, the weather, and all the bad news." The speaker takes the time to read the daily horoscope for his dead friend, going so far as to point out what each day has in store for the friend. One day "may not be a wildly romantic time for you," and another day, "I learn that you should not miss / an opportunity to travel and make new friends / though you never cared much about either." Eventually the speaker comes to the conclusion that he would be "better off closing the newspaper," that his friend does not need to change. The friend should remain "lying there in your beautiful blue suit," with "your hands crossed on your chest." In this, as with most of his poems, Collins draws in the reader with events that are comprehensible and welcoming, but as the poem progresses the reader is introduced to new material, a fresh journey. Once again, he makes poetry a touching and instructive enterprise for all concerned.

Jeffry Jensen

Review Sources

Booklist 107, no. 12 (February 15, 2011): 43.
Library Journal 136, no. 1 (January, 2011): 100–101.
Publishers Weekly 257, no. 45 (November 15, 2010): 41.

The Illumination

Author: Kevin Brockmeier (b. 1972)
Publisher: Pantheon Books (New York).
272 pp. $24.95
Type of work: Novel
Time: The present

One Friday night, for no apparent reason, human wounds become visible in the form of radiating light.

Principal characters:
CAROL ANN PAGE, a lonely data analyst whose wounded thumb begins to radiate light
JASON WILLIFORD, a photojournalist who mourns the loss of his wife
PATRICIA WILLIFORD, Jason's wife, killed in a car accident
CHUCK CARTER, an autistic schoolchild who steals Patricia's journal
RYAN SHIFRIN, a religious missionary who experiences a crisis of faith
NINA POGGIONE, a short-story writer who is inspired by Patricia's journal
MORSE PUTNAM STRAWBRIDGE, a homeless book vendor

A fascinating and engaging work of fiction, Kevin Brockmeier's *The Illumination* poses profound questions about love, illness, and longing without once lapsing into melodrama or pretension. The premise is deceptively simple: pain and suffering suddenly become visible in the form of blazing light. Scientists have no explanation for the lights, which vary in intensity depending on the severity of the pain people experience. The novel's ideas come across clearly thanks to the grace and assurance of Brockmeier's writing, which maintains a faith in the power of kindness and generosity. The novel is divided into six separate chapters, each named after a series of seemingly disconnected figures. Emotional and thematic connections emerge as a journal of love letters changes hands from one character to another, revealing a variety of wounds and possibilities for healing.

In the first section, Carol Ann Page, a data analyst for a commercial news service, slices her finger while opening a package from her ex-husband. A doctor's initial diagnosis suggests a minor incision, but suddenly the wound begins to glow with a bright light—the first sign of what soon becomes a global phenomenon. Carol Ann becomes mesmerized by the light, opening her bandages so often that her thumb eventually requires amputation to remove the infection. Recovering from the anesthetic, she meets Patricia Williford, a patient who has been injured in a car accident

Kevin Brockmeier is the author of two previous novels, The Truth about Celia (2003) and The Brief History of the Dead (2006), as well as two collections of stories, Things That Fall from the Sky (2002) and The View from the Seventh Layer (2008). He has also written the children's books City of Names (2002) and Grooves: A Kind of Mystery (2006).

and believes her husband has died. Patricia has kept a journal of love notes from her husband, Jason ("I love the idea of growing old and forgetful together," one note reads), but as she approaches death herself, she gives the journal to Carol Ann, who stows the book with her things and reads from it constantly, imagining the notes speaking directly to her. The doctor, with whom she is about to embark on a date, discovers the journal and warns Carol Ann that the husband is not dead and will try to recover the journal.

Brockmeier devotes the next chapter to Jason Williford, who loses his sense of purpose as he grieves for his wife but gradually resumes his career when he photographs some teenagers whose bodies are covered with lacerations and injuries that blaze with light. One of them, Melissa Wallumrod, invites him to film her snuffing out a cigarette on her wrist, which results in her expulsion from high school and a falling-out with her family. When she moves in with Jason, he begins hanging out with Melissa's friends and eventually participates in their rituals of self-mutilation.

Chuck Carter, an autistic schoolboy, often spies on Jason, his neighbor, and one night he steals the journal, attracted by its shimmering glow. Carter is a despondent loner, harassed at school and berated by his stepfather. He has not spoken in a year and refuses to communicate with anyone except his therapist, via brief notes. After retaliating against a bully, Carter feels so guilty that he gives the journal to a missionary, Ryan Shifrin, who is traveling the globe out of love for his devout, dead sister. He pores over the journal, considering its messages as he narrowly escapes one disaster after another. Lacking any explanation for the pain and disaster he has witnessed, Ryan experiences a religious crisis and abandons the journal in a hotel room.

Nina Poggione, a writer on a book tour, discovers the journal next. As she immerses herself in it, she is reminded of her fiancé, who passed away suddenly. Like many of Brockmeier's characters, Nina lives in a state of isolation and longing, her mouth sores and poor health turning the mere act of speaking into a trial. Nina believes that through the journal she is exchanging notes with her lover and thus experiencing something of what the Willifords shared. However, it is not long before her teenage son gives the journal to Morse Putnam Strawbridge, a homeless man who sells books on the street. While Morse regrets he cannot love the way the Willifords did, he does manage to save a life and offer a selfless kind of love.

Given the sudden and inexplicable nature of the illumination phenomenon, one might be tempted to read the novel through the conventions of science fiction or fantasy; however, it actually comes closer to magical realism. Many of the novel's characters are quick to regard the phenomenon as miraculous, but the doctor treating Carol Ann offers one of the novel's most telling remarks: "Funny how quickly a person can get used to a miracle. Or how quickly a miracle can come to seem commonplace." No one can hide his or her pain, and while many accommodate themselves to the new reality, such as doctors who refine therapies and treatments according to the intensity of the light, others feel like voyeurs invading the privacy of others, gawkers at "the great shared car crash of modern history." For some, like Jason, the illumination provides aesthetic fascination, "an ache inside people that seemed so wonderful sometimes," but for others it represents a reminder of the fundamentally cruel nature of the world. For Chuck, a child who faces abuse every day of his life, "Everything was helpless and needed to be saved from hurt." Even inanimate objects possess feelings; the journal itself "shone with its secret pain." For Ryan, the missionary, the illumination provokes a crisis of faith in a god-abandoned world:

> And there was God, high on His throne, attending to the whole terrible procession of sorrows and traumas, corrosions and illnesses, with a cool, cerebral dispassion. . . . Perhaps the light He had brought to their injuries, or allowed the world to bring, was simply a new kind of ornamentation. The jewelry with which He decorated His lovers. The oil with which He anointed His sons.

In Nina's case, the light only accentuates her sense of loss and pain. One of her fans notes a tendency in her stories to present "characters who have great sectors of what one would ordinarily regard as the common human experience entirely unavailable to them"; as with the illumination, Nina's private pain becomes public artifice. A lab technician who makes a brief appearance near the end of the novel gives the most hopeful and ennobling interpretation of the phenomenon, believing that "the light was effectively immortal, or at least as immortal as the universe itself."

While the meaning of the light varies from character to character, the meaning of the journal remains stable and unambiguous. This arouses many fascinating questions regarding the nature of suffering in contrast to the nature of love, as Brockmeier hints that the latter is more stable than the former. The journal offers a sincere expression of love that links the many disparate characters together, but as beautiful as it is, many readers may not find it so endearing. The novel's message may appear cloying or absurdly sentimental to some, and fairly so; however, the journal itself is actually one of Brockmeier's greatest achievements. Instead of reading as the voice of a professional novelist, the love notes have a ring of authenticity, the sound of a man unafraid to wear his heart on his sleeve. Brockmeier offers lists of notes in each chapter, carefully selected to resonate with each character's story.

Many of the entries are wistful, evocative, and humorous. They celebrate the mundane and ecstatic facets of love: the physical body ("I love the concavities behind your knees, as soft as the skin of a peach"), mundane habits ("I love watching you step so carefully inside your footprints when it snows"), personal quirks ("I love the hard time you have with fractions," "I love your terrible puns), and emotional sincerity ("I love your compassionate heart—your big, sloppy, sentimental heart"). As the homeless vendor Morse Putnam Strawbridge observes, "The diary seemed to broadcast its message straight through the plastic, *I love you, I love you, I love you, I love you,* pulsing like a beacon." In a novel riddled with pain, loss, and loneliness, the beauty of this simple message resonates, and in Brockmeier's hands the message overcomes the risk of mawkish sentimentality and instead comes across as daring and profound. His ability to inspire empathy in his characters and render images in language brings the novel to life.

As straightforward as the message of the journal appears to be, the novel is filled with moments of intriguing ambiguity. The fates of the characters remain largely unknown in the end. The reader is left to wonder if Carol Ann ever has her date with the doctor. Does Jason devolve into a habitual self-mutilator and completely abandon the world he once inhabited? Does Chuck ever find love and understanding? Does Ryan recover his faith? Does Nina succumb to illness and reunite with her fiancé, and are her communications with him merely signs of distress? Does Morse survive his brutal beating at the novel's close? Resolution is clearly not a part of Brockmeier's agenda; instead, one must assume that these stories will play out. Brockmeier draws attention to the common aspects of love and empathy that the journal uncovers in its long journey, suggesting that pain is like a signal that draws people together, enabling the healing process to happen.

David W. Madden

Review Sources

Christian Century 128, no. 9 (May 3, 2011): 53.
Irish Times, April 23, 2011, p. 12.
Library Journal 135, no. 19 (November 15, 2010): 58.
Los Angeles Times, January 23, 2011, p. E9.
The New Yorker 87, no. 4 (September 25, 2011): 73.
The New York Times Book Review, September 25, 2011, p. 15.
The Observer, March 6, 2011, p. 41.
Publishers Weekly 257, no. 42 (October 25, 2010): 26.
Times Literary Supplement, no. 5633 (March 18, 2011): 21.
The Wall Street Journal, January 29, 2011, p. C8.
The Washington Post, March 8, 2011, p. C4.

The Immortalization Commission
Science and the Strange Quest to Cheat Death

Author: John Gray (b. 1948)
Publisher: Farrar, Straus and Giroux (New York). Illustrated. 289 pp. $24.00
Type of work: Biography, ethics, history, philosophy, politics, science, sociology
Time: The late nineteenth and early twentieth centuries
Locale: Great Britain and the Soviet Union

Gray traces the efforts of Victorian and Edwardian scientists to prove that life existed after death, arguing that since Darwinism had undermined traditional religious belief, proof of immortality was sometimes sought by experimental means; he then suggests that Soviet efforts to prove the existence of immortality led to the brutalities and mass murders committed by the Communist regime.

Principal personages:
ARTHUR BALFOUR (1848–1930), a British prime minister and political figure
HENRY SIDGWICK (1838–1900), a philosopher and economist, the first president of the Society for Psychical Research
F. W. H. MYERS (1843–1901), a scholar, poet, and philosopher, a founding member and later president of the Society for Psychical Research
VLADIMIR LENIN (1870–1924), a Marxist revolutionary, the first leader of the Soviet Union
JOSEPH STALIN (1878–1953), a Marxist revolutionary, the second leader of the Soviet Union
H. G. WELLS (1866–1946), an English author and political commentator

John Gray's *The Immortalization Commission: Science and the Strange Quest to Cheat Death* has been widely praised as the latest in a series of skeptical works in which Gray casts a cold eye on utopian fantasies that historical figures have unsuccessfully attempted to realize. In the present volume, he examines two seemingly separate but arguably related phenomena. Gray first discusses efforts made in Victorian and Edwardian Britain to scientifically demonstrate the existence of life after death, then goes on to study attempts made in the Soviet Union to reshape the nature of humanity—attempts that ultimately resulted in mass murder. As many reviewers have noted, the book's two halves seem at times only tenuously linked. The first half presents interesting and often amusing intellectual history, while the second half offers descriptions of appalling arrogance and the misery that almost inevitably resulted. In both sections, Gray focuses as much on personalities as on ideas and behavior, giving the book a heavy biographical emphasis. Throughout the work, but especially in the final chapter, he also reflects on the philosophical and political implications of the impulses he describes.

For many readers, the book's first half will seem the freshest and most intriguing, if only because the stories it tells are not widely known and the personalities are often unfamiliar. In England, the rise of Darwinism led many people to lose faith in traditional religion and traditional beliefs in life after death. Such losses were often very difficult for society to accept, even for Charles Darwin himself, who attended a séance in 1874 designed to explore whether life might still exist beyond the grave. Darwin quickly came to the conclusion that the séance had been a sham, but various other eminent persons, including notable scientific minds, seemed to believe the hypothesis that existence continued in some form after death, or at least were eager to test the possibility. This may explain why the Society for Psychical Research had such luminaries as philosophers and writers Henry Sidgwick, William James, and Henri Bergson as presidents, and also why it attracted the interest of other well-known intellectuals such as Alfred, Lord Tennyson, and John Ruskin, as well as prime ministers W. E. Gladstone and Arthur Balfour. Far from being a collection of obscure cranks, it included many thoughtful scientists who sought honest investigations and exposed a good deal of charlatanism. Many members were keenly interested in knowing whether the human soul might be immortal, often for personal reasons such as the early loss of a loved one. Gray brings many of these now-dead people back to life in his own vivid prose. The book is full of photographs that allow readers to see the people Gray describes and discusses; they are strangely unlabeled, however, and the book also lacks an index.

For many readers, one of the book's most fascinating revelations will be the survival of reams of "scripts," that is, pages of so-called automatic writing believed to have been transmitted to talented transcribers from the other side of the grave. Sometimes these scripts seemed confusing and disappointing to those who received and tried to interpret them; in other cases, however, the scripts tantalizingly suggested that persons actually known to members of the society were indeed communicating from beyond the grave. In fact, some society members even made elaborate arrangements to try to contact their colleagues and loved ones after they died. It is hard not to be touched by the sincerity of all these efforts, although Gray regularly points out the various logical and practical problems inherent in their attempts. In this section of the book, the narrative is clear, the personalities are memorable, and the philosophical reflections are truly thought provoking. Any reader with any genuine curiosity about the prospect of posthumous survival will be intrigued by this section of the volume, especially by Gray's discussions of the various and often highly contradictory ways in which such survival might be imagined. We are so used to thinking of life after death as it has often been conceived in our own culture that we easily forget, or perhaps never even consider, the possibility of numerous other conceptions. However, none of these possibilities is portrayed as very plausible in Gray's estimation, and his reflections on the relations between Darwinism (which he accepts) and posthumous survival (which he does not) are especially interesting.

John Gray, an Oxford-trained emeritus professor at the London School of Economics, is a well-known British intellectual. His many books include False Dawn: The Delusions of Global Capitalism *(1998),* Straw Dogs: Thoughts on Humans and Other Animals *(2003), and* Black Mass: Apocalyptic Religion and the Death of Utopia *(2007). He contributes often to major periodicals and is a frequent commentator in various British media.*

The second half of the book, which deals with the so-called God-builders of the Soviet Union, amounts to a grim revelation of what can happen when human beings try to produce an earthly paradise. Connections between this section of the volume and the section about England are not often apparent. The Soviets engaged in significantly different kinds of activities, with far more gruesome results, than the members of the Society for Psychical Research—so much so, in fact, that it is difficult to believe Gray's claims about the quest for immortality being the main catalyst for Soviet experimentation. In addition to practicing grotesque forms of torture and execution, which are strikingly described by Gray, the Soviets also preserved and displayed Lenin's body for years after he died; in fact, he is still around and still on display, looking better than ever. Some of them hoped that he might one day be revived, even though his brain was quickly sliced up for intensive scientific study. Based on the care with which the Soviets preserved their leader, it seems Gray is right in his assertion that Communism became a form of Soviet religion, with its own set of gods, prophets, priests, infidels, and heretics. Some Soviets, along with Western sympathizers such as H. G. Wells, even hoped that science might one day direct the course of human evolution, producing a superior kind of human being. In the meantime, however, millions met their deaths at the hands of Soviet leaders.

Wells emerges as one of the true villains of this book. Combining extreme arrogance with extreme foolishness, he comes across as a highly intelligent but naive dupe. Another Western advocate of Soviet Communism was *New York Times* correspondent Walter Duranty, who lived in Moscow and lied to his American readers about what was really happening in the Soviet Union. This section of the book discusses the views of a host of other historical figures as well, many of whom Gray represents as cynical and malicious, many of whom eventually became victims of the very society they had championed. Sometimes, in this section of the book, it is difficult to keep the personalities straight, particularly since they are mentioned in connection with an argument that seems vague and only weakly linked to the first half's initial thesis. One reviewer even commented that the second half of the book seems to be the product of free association, and perhaps there is some justice to that claim.

In the book's final chapter, Gray touches on a wide range of topics, including cryonics, global warming, antiaging programs, process theology, argument from design, the possibility of multiverses, and the general relationship between science and religion. Once more there is a hint of free association; numerous reviewers have praised this chapter as philosophically profound and penetrating, while others have suggested that in chapters such as this, Gray has begun to repeat the arguments of his earlier books.

For the most part, however, *The Immortalization Commission* has received very strong reviews. Many of these are from people who clearly agree with his politics, but some have come even from readers who dislike his overall tone of relentless pessimism. Despite its flaws, Gray's book remains a fascinating and thought-provoking philosophical treatise, one that sheds light on the nature of science, faith, and the human condition.

Robert C. Evans

Review Sources

Harper's Magazine 322, no. 1931 (April 2011): 69–71.
Maclean's 124, no. 18 (May 16, 2011): 138.
New Statesman 140, no. 5041 (February 21, 2011): 42–43.
The New York Times Book Review, May 8, 2011, p. 14.
Publishers Weekly 257, no. 49 (December 13, 2010): 44.
The Wall Street Journal, April 6, 2011, p. A17.

In Other Worlds
SF and the Human Imagination

Author: Margaret Atwood (b. 1939)
Publisher: Nan A. Talese (New York). 272 pp.
$24.95
Type of work: Essays, short fiction

This eclectic collection of essays, reviews, and short fiction explores Margaret Atwood's personal connections with the genre of science fiction, as well as science fiction's roots in mythology, utopian fiction, and Victorian literature.

Acclaimed writer Margaret Atwood has long had an ambivalent public relationship with science fiction. Although her novel *The Handmaid's Tale* won the 1987 Arthur C. Clarke Award for best science-fiction novel published in the UK during the previous year and was nominated for the Nebula and Prometheus Awards, Atwood objected to the labeling of her work as science fiction, provoking irritation among science-fiction authors and readers alike, who accused her of wishing to avoid the genre-fiction "ghetto" in order to maintain the respect of the literary fiction community. In a 2009 *Guardian* article, science-fiction and fantasy writer Ursula K. Le Guin asserted that Atwood's dystopian novels *The Handmaid's Tale* (1985), *Oryx and Crake* (2003), and *The Year of the Flood* (2009) all did one of the things science fiction has long done well—"to extrapolate imaginatively from current trends and events to a near-future that's half prediction, half satire"—and went on to suggest that Atwood's idiosyncratic definition of science fiction, one that does not include her dystopian-future novels, "seems designed to protect her novels from being relegated to a genre still shunned by hidebound readers, reviewers and prize-awarders."

In Other Worlds: SF and the Human Imagination reads in part as a rebuttal to Le Guin; as well as being dedicated to her, it begins with an introduction that responds at length to her assertions. It quickly becomes clear that much of the disagreement stems simply from differing definitions, or in Atwood's phrasing, "nomenclatural allegiances, or . . . your system of literary taxonomy." In brief, Atwood's definition of science fiction encompasses what most science-fiction readers would regard as pulp, space opera, or science fantasy—those subgenres with less emphasis on sociology or plausible extrapolation of future technology and more on spaceships and aliens. Her definition of speculative fiction encompasses "hard" science fiction (based on real science) and sociological or anthropological science fiction, the category into which Atwood's dystopias might best fit. Most self-identified science-fiction authors define

(©George Whiteside)

Margaret Atwood has published more than forty books of poetry, fiction, and critical essays and has received numerous awards for her work. She is best known for her novels, including the speculative fiction works The Handmaid's Tale *(1985),* Oryx and Crake *(2003), and* The Year of the Flood *(2009).*

science fiction far more broadly, and many consider speculative fiction to encompass both science fiction and fantasy (and sometimes horror as well).

On the one hand, such genre hairsplitting makes little difference; a good novel is a good novel. But it is true that the literary establishment has long granted more respect and acclaim to literature with fantastic or futuristic elements when it is not labeled as fantasy or science fiction, and that although such books may retread hoary old tropes that make genre readers groan, they seem fresher to an audience unused to genre conventions. And when Atwood asserts that her disinterest in labeling her books as science fiction is for the sake of the science-fiction reader, who will expect aliens and thus be disappointed, it is both a bit condescending and suggestive of a lack of familiarity with the current science-fiction field, which features aliens about as often as fantasy novels feature dragons (which is to say, sometimes). Assuming that science-fiction readers expect aliens in every book and will be disappointed without them is a peculiar assumption, and it is a peculiar way to introduce a book that collects Atwood's musings on the history and cultural significance of science fiction, as well as a number of reviews of various science-fiction works. This preoccupation with the superficial—aliens, spaceships, clothing—threads throughout the book, culminating in a final essay about the covers of *Weird Tales* in the 1930s. Science fiction has great potential as a literature of ideas, which Atwood's own contributions to the genre, acknowledged or not, certainly recognize, so the focus on clothing, particularly as sexual titillation, is an interesting choice.

In Other Worlds is divided into three main sections, followed by a miscellany of appendices. The majority of the material is either reprinted or lectures revised into essay form, with little editing to tie the parts together into a cohesive whole. While the foreword suggests that Atwood's thinking changed somewhat after the debate with Le Guin when they came to understand each other's definitions of science fiction, this new clarity is not reflected much in the remainder of the book, which rambles from memoir to literary criticism, including reviews of Victorian science fiction, nonfiction like environmentalist Bill McKibben's *Enough: Staying Human in an Engineered Age* (2003), and books that are not science fiction by Atwood's own definition, such as George Orwell's *1984* (1949). After the extensive introduction dissecting genre definitions, the remainder of the book seems unable to find a consistent definition to rest upon.

The first section, "In Other Worlds: SF and the Human Imagination," is an edited form of the Richard Ellmann Lectures that Atwood delivered at Emory University in Atlanta, Georgia, in 2010. These reminisce about Atwood's development as a writer and cover a large part of her life, from her earliest forays into science fiction as a child developing worlds of flying space rabbits to her experiences writing her dystopian novels. In between, Atwood went to college and graduate school, where she studied Victorian literature with an emphasis on utopian fiction at a time when anything other than strictly "realistic" fiction was not considered a worthy topic for scholarly criticism. These essays provide insight into Atwood, both as a person and as a writer, as well as an erudite, well-read discussion of a variety of literature that likely influenced later science fiction; the section on utopian and dystopian fiction (where Atwood coins the term "ustopia" to describe the shadow dystopia in every utopia, and the glimmers of utopia in every dystopia) is perhaps the strongest portion of the book. But while these essays, which convey Atwood's dry wit and love of wordplay, likely made riveting lectures, their structure does not translate nearly as well to prose, and the points Atwood makes might have been better presented had the material been reorganized and edited into topical chapters rather than jumping between topics. All the same, this section is the most substantial part of the collection, although many of her points have been made before in science-fiction criticism.

The second section, "Other Deliberations," reprints a number of reviews and essays on science fiction and related topics written by Atwood over the years. Here is where the more confusing aspects of Atwood's genre definitions come into play: the reviews include Orwell's *1984* and Aldous Huxley's *Brave New World* (1932), both dystopian novels that have more in common with Atwood's own novels than with the "squids in space" variety of science fiction that Atwood accurately considers quite different from her own work. The review of McKibben's *Enough*, a cautionary work of nonfiction about the potential future consequences of a society built on unbridled consumerism, also seems out of place by Atwood's definition, as does the essay on H. Rider Haggard's *She* (1887), a book that would seem to fit better into the fantasy category and is not tied back to the development of science fiction in the essay.

While these essays and reviews are often thought-provoking and insightful, again drawing on Atwood's broad knowledge of classic fiction and mythology, they are curiously disconnected from more recent science fiction, save for reviews of Le Guin's *The Birthday of the World and Other Stories* (2002) and Kazuo Ishiguro's *Never Let Me Go* (2005). Here, again, Atwood's biases are strongly in evidence. Her review of *Never Let Me Go*, an alternate-history dystopian novel, is confident and insightful; dystopian (and utopian) fiction is a country in which Atwood feels at home. Her review of Le Guin, on the other hand, after discoursing about genre, does little more than provide summaries of the stories and some brief commentary on common themes. Although Le Guin's work, like Atwood's, fits best into the anthropological or sociological science-fiction tradition, and both deal with superficially similar themes, Le Guin's focus on gender and sexuality is ultimately deeper and more consciously within a feminist framework than Atwood's. The absence of any thoughts on the numerous science-fiction luminaries of more recent years, even mentioned in passing, is surprising; although Atwood prefaces the book with a quotation from Octavia E. Butler, the only discussion of her work is a passing mention that her "quasi-human" alien Oankali are "treated sympathetically," an interpretation of Butler's work that is surprising enough on multiple levels to deserve more discussion.

Like the first section, "Other Deliberations" might have benefited from thematic rearrangement and tightening. Although Atwood notes in the introduction to the section that she edited lightly to remove overlaps and repetitions, the reviews and essays here still have enough repetition to be distracting, as well as repeating themes and commentary from the first section, "In Other Worlds." While there is nothing wrong with simply collecting a group of essays and short stories into a thematic volume of reprints, the lack of coherent focus in the end result can weaken the theme, leaving the reader uncertain as to the actual argument. *In Other Worlds* suffers from this to some degree, as it collects writings that cover a span of time from the 1970s to the 2010s, although primarily from the 1990s and 2000s. During this time, Atwood's opinions naturally evolved, and the juxtapositions create the appearance of contradiction. As well, although Atwood's wide literary and mythological knowledge makes the reviews interesting works of literary criticism, the lack of in-depth references to other works of science fiction leaves the reviewed books curiously adrift, outside of genre in the way Atwood's own books are meant to exist. And yet, books written from within a genre respond to it and are in turn responded to, and to separate them from this interchange of ideas is to ignore important context.

The third section, "Five Tributes," collects some short pieces of science fiction written by Atwood over the years: four short stories and an excerpt from her novel *The Blind Assassin*. For the most part, these pieces fit firmly into the traditional Atwood definition of science fiction, responding to classic science-fiction tropes and themes such as cryogenics, time capsules, postapocalyptic worlds, insectile aliens, and humans as the aliens. These seem to be included to demonstrate Atwood's willingness to write science fiction (apart from her dystopian novels), but are all lightweight pieces—nicely written and well observed, but not particularly surprising or pointed. While they play with science-fiction tropes, they do not twist or subvert them in any unusual way.

In Other Worlds, while not as cohesive or well organized as it might be, still offers insight into the life and mind of a noted author, taking the reader on a ramble though literature, history, and religion. While it does not break much new ground in science-fiction criticism, it does provide an enjoyable introduction to the history of science fiction, or at least a small portion of it. Atwood's style is dry, playful, and peppered with wordplay, sometimes of the painful pun variety, and the essays in particular bring historical insight to science fiction, particularly Atwood's favored "ustopian" subgenre.

Melissa A. Barton

Review Sources

Booklist 108, no. 2 (September 15, 2011): 11–12.
The Christian Science Monitor, October 24, 2011 (Web).
Kirkus Reviews 79, no. 17 (September 1, 2011): 1538.
Library Journal 136, no. 16 (October 1, 2011): 79.
Strange Horizons, October 14, 2011 (Web).
The Telegraph, October 19, 2011 (Web).

In the Garden of Beasts
Love, Terror, and an American Family in Hitler's Berlin

Author: Erik Larson (b. 1954)
Publisher: Crown (New York). 464 pp. $26.00;
paperback $16.00
Type of work: History
Time: 1933–1937
Locale: Primarily Berlin, Chicago, and Washington, DC

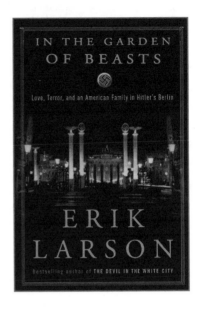

Larson's book is a historical reconstruction of what life was like for the family of William E. Dodd, the American ambassador to Germany from 1933 to 1937, the period in which the newly elected Nazi leader Adolf Hitler was consolidating his grip on Germany.

Principal personages:
WILLIAM E. DODD (1869–1940), US ambassador to Berlin (1933–1937) and former history professor at the University of Chicago
MATTIE DODD (d. 1938), also known as MARTHA JOHNS DODD, Dodd's wife
MARTHA ECCLES DODD (1908–1990), Dodd's daughter
WILLIAM "BILL" E. DODD JR. (1905–1952), Dodd's son
WILLIAM PHILLIPS (1878–1968), US undersecretary of state (1933–1936) and political enemy of Dodd
GEORGE S. MESSERSMITH (1883–1960), US consul general in Berlin (1933–1934)
RUDOLF DIELS (1900–1957), prominent Nazi who briefly served as head of the Gestapo and became one of Martha's lovers
BORIS WINOGRADOV (d.1938), also known as BORIS VINOGRADOV, Russian diplomat posted at the Soviet Embassy in Berlin and another of Martha's lovers

In late 1933, when University of Chicago history professor William E. Dodd arrived in Germany to take on his position as the new US ambassador, the world was still naively looking at Adolf Hitler's new Germany with as much admiration as skepticism. Dodd, a down-to-earth, no-nonsense man who would have preferred to stay home and finish his long overdue historical manuscript, was willing to accept his country's call. He was also initially willing to accept as fact that Nazi Germany was not an extreme government and that their positions were far less inflammatory than their posturing and strong language would suggest. Within the four years of Dodd's residency in Berlin, he and his family came to realize the true, monstrous nature of Nazism. Within *In the Garden of Beasts*, their intellectual and emotional transformation becomes a metaphor for the transformation of the world's opinion of the regime during that time.

Despite being so well known nationally that President Franklin Delano Roosevelt chose him to be the US ambassador, Dodd, a dry, old-fashioned intellectual who had studied in Germany as a young man, was an unusual selection for an ambassadorship. Author Erik Larson spends considerable time describing Dodd's frugality, which seemed to make him the butt of scorn among other US diplomats, men who tended to come from wealthier, more aristocratic families than Dodd had. Not wealthy, unused to servants and the trappings of wealth and lavish parties, Dodd and his family were, as the book's subtitle suggests, simply "an American family."

As much as or perhaps more than, a history of Dodd's tenure as the US ambassador, the book is the story of his daughter, Martha, who was then an attractive, free-spirited young woman in her mid-twenties and quickly became part of the intellectual and social world of Berlin. As described by Larson and scrupulously documented in Martha's letters and other contemporary sources, she was an intimate friend and possibly a lover to a number of important men, most famously writers Thomas Wolfe and Carl Sandburg, who were decades older. In Germany, the list of her lovers/intimate friends included a prince, various writers, Harvard-educated Nazi Ernst "Putzi" Hanfstaengl, and Rudolf Diels, a high-ranking Nazi official who was the first head of the Gestapo, among other things. Martha's most significant lover, and arguably the great love of her life, was Russian embassy diplomat Boris Winogradov, whom she hoped to marry. Through this connection, she may even have been turned into a low-level spy for the Soviets. In an era and a country in which most young women did not openly express their ideas or sexuality, Martha seemed to make a point of flaunting both, as shown by Larson's detailed accounts of her escapades and controversial relationships.

Unlike her father, who did not express or hold positive feelings toward the Nazis, Martha quickly became enamored of the "new Germany" with its robust economy, clean streets, exciting social life, and intellectually stimulating elite. Belying her youth, Martha was already a relatively accomplished journalist by the time the family went to Germany, and she wrote articles describing life in Germany for American-run periodicals. As reports and rumors grew of violence against Jews, foreigners, and anyone who opposed Nazism, Martha continued to maintain the delusion that those extremes were merely isolated incidents. This was evident particularly in one incident in the book, in which she observed a mob mercilessly pursue and taunt a young woman who had supposedly been involved with a Jewish man. Martha was shocked but still maintained that this was merely the mob mentality of a minority. Martha's political beliefs were viewed as dangerous and naive by the US consul general in Berlin at the time, George S. Messersmith, who had had an adversarial position with Dodd nearly from the start. Messersmith was also dismayed by Martha's blatant behavior with men, which he saw as immoral and grossly inappropriate for the daughter of the US ambassador.

According to Larson, Messersmith did little to disguise his contempt for and insubordination toward Dodd, whom he repeatedly belittled in communiqués to Undersecretary of State William Phillips and others, eventually leading to Dodd's removal from his position. Larson devotes considerable space in the book discussing the "pretty good club," a 1930s appellation for what later might be called an "old boy's network." The pretty good club, of which Dodd definitely was not a member, consisted of aristocratic men who were the backbone of the diplomatic corps prior to World War II. Though hardly impoverished, Dodd himself was neither wealthy nor from one of the nation's leading families, a fact that made his supervision of far wealthier underlings within the Berlin embassy particularly difficult. Making matters worse, Dodd continued to stand by his promise that the embassy would run within its allotted budget, including financing his own housing and parties. This approach resulted in sporadic and sparse embassy functions that were ridiculed by those whose personal finances allowed them the opportunity to spend far beyond their government income. The general view of Dodd as penurious and stubborn brought him few friends in American diplomatic crowds, though he seemed quite at ease with his British and French counterparts, among others, in Germany.

(Benjamin Benschneider)

Erik Larson became a staff writer for the Wall Street Journal *and a contributing editor to* Time *magazine before concentrating on long-form historical nonfiction. Like* In the Garden of Beasts, *Larson's books* The Devil in the White City *(2003) and* Thunderstruck *(2006) became international bestsellers, and the former won an Edgar Award for nonfiction crime writing and was a finalist for a National Book Award.*

The most historically informative section of the book is one that details at length the Night of the Long Knives (*Nacht der langen Messer*), the Nazi purge that began on June 30, 1934. For those unfamiliar with the event, Larson offers an hour-by-hour description, naming names, repeating anecdotal accounts, and giving exact locations, so that the reader can understand its speed and horror. Ending just three days later, the event was pivotal in Nazi history and marked the solidification of Hitler's absolute power in Germany. Larson juxtaposes several different experiences from that day, from Martha and Boris's idyllic picnic at the beach to breaking news coming in to American reporters Frederick Birchall of the *New York Times* and Louis Lochner of the Associated Press to the tragic deaths of entire families. Meanwhile, Dodd and the embassy staff remained isolated by a serious lack of information. The result of the violent, remarkably fast, and efficient purge was that even many German officials once considered loyalists were summarily executed for their perceived threats to Hitler. A fascinating section about the first hours of June 30 involves Captain Ernst Röhm, head of the Storm Troopers (*Sturmabteilung*), known as the SA, and once regarded as an unquestioned Hitler loyalist. Röhm was arrested by Hitler himself, who sped to Bad Wiessee and then marched into the Hotel Hanselbauer where Röhm and many of the SA were staying; disbelieving and ironically still loyal, Röhm was executed three days later, one of many leaders branded traitors or morally corrupt as justification for their murders.

Dodd's perception of Germany under Hitler started to change as he became intellectually closer to Franz von Papen, the German vice chancellor, who gave a strongly worded anti-Hitler speech in Marburg not long before the Night of the Long Knives.

After the purge, Dodd was no longer under any gentlemanly delusion that Hitler would become more conciliatory or that the more moderate opposition would be able to have him deposed. He began to make more public criticisms of the regime. While Dodd stayed at his post for more than two years, he spent considerable time on leave in the United States, and his open opposition to Hitler's regime eventually caused him to be recalled by a president and State Department that were far from committed to hostilities with Germany. A major underlying theme of Larson's book is the isolationism and anti-Semitism that ran through the United States during the mid-1930s, particularly among officials such as Phillips.

The final chapters demonstrate the lasting effects the Berlin years had on members of the Dodd family. After Dodd finally left Germany for good, his hope of a long retirement doing scholarly work became short-lived. First, his rather passive wife, Mattie, little more than a shadowy figure in the book, died suddenly in 1938. Faced with deteriorating health and other problems, Dodd died less than two years later, leaving his epic book unfinished. The time in Germany took its toll on the Dodd children as well. Martha, who continued to write extensively, married American millionaire Alfred Stern, but their leftist leanings brought them serious problems in the United States during the McCarthy era. They eventually moved to Prague, where they remained for the rest of their lives. Her brother, Bill, had little success as an adult and was unable to find work with the government because of his own ties to left-wing causes. He died in 1952, at the height of the McCarthy era in the United States.

As in *The Devil in the White City,* Larson's previous work, *In the Garden of Beasts* displays a depth of detail that reflects the painstaking research done for the book. Larson frequently refers to personal papers of the principals, including Martha's own papers, which are housed in the Library of Congress. He also provides excellent footnotes for further research. Several earlier historical works, among them *Resisting Hitler* (2000) by Shareen Blair Brysac and Martha's own memoirs of that time, *Through Embassy Eyes* (1939), dealt with the same period and many of the same people, but Larson's book offers a better narrative. He has a great ability to present dry facts and historical references in an entertaining, and often riveting manner, making the nonfiction book read more like a novel. Those who want mere supposition and anecdotes may find the inclusion of so many dates and facts disconcerting, but for anyone seriously interested in the period, Larson's work present a vivid historical picture of the short time frame he describes.

Patricia King Hanson

Review Sources

Booklist 107, no. 13 (March 1, 2011): 15.
Los Angeles Times, June 20, 2011 (Web).
Maclean's, June 8, 2011 (Web).
The New York Times, June 12, 2011, p. 13.
Publishers Weekly 258, no. 30 (July 25, 2011): 48.

Into the Silence
The Great War, Mallory, and the Conquest of Everest

Author: Wade Davis (b. 1953)
Publisher: Alfred A. Knopf (New York). 672 pp.
$32.50
Type of work: History, biography, travel
Time: 1846–1924
Locale: Tibet, India, Great Britain, and the
western front in Belgium and France

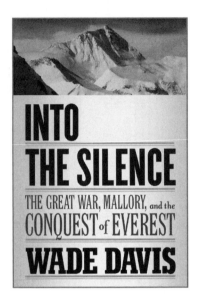

*This meticulously researched account of the
British attempts to climb Mount Everest in the
early 1920s examines the national significance
of the expeditions, the legacies of mountaineer
George Mallory and his fellow climbers, and
the effects of World War I on the men involved.*

Principal personages:
GEORGE MALLORY, a Cambridge-educated
teacher, combat veteran, and acclaimed
mountain climber who participated in the
Everest expeditions of 1921, 1922, and 1924
ANDREW "SANDY" IRVINE, an athletic Oxford student who was Mallory's climbing
partner in June 1924
CHARLES BRUCE, a British general who led the 1922 expedition and initially led the
one in 1924
EDWARD "TEDDY" NORTON, a British army officer who led the 1924 expedition after
Charles Bruce was evacuated
GEORGE FINCH, an Australian chemist and mountain climber who used supplemental
oxygen to set a height record during the 1922 expedition
JOHN NOEL, a filmmaker who documented the 1922 and 1924 expeditions
HOWARD SOMERVELL, a medical doctor who climbed as Norton's partner in 1924
NOEL ODELL, a geologist and experienced mountain climber who believed he saw
Mallory and Irvine on June 8, 1924
CHARLES HOWARD-BURY, an aristocratic Anglo-Irishman who led the Everest expedi-
tion in 1921
OLIVER WHEELER, a Canadian surveyor who used photographic techniques to map
Everest during the 1921 expedition
ARTHUR HINKS, an astronomer and cartographer who dominated the Mount Everest
Committee in London

If a mountain can deserve anything, the world's highest one deserves a book as grand
as *Into the Silence: The Great War, Mallory, and the Conquest of Everest*. After a

dozen years of painstaking research and writing, Wade Davis has produced a detailed account that tells not only of Himalayan mountaineering in the 1920s but also of empire, war, disillusionment, fortitude, and hope. Upon being asked in 1923 why he wanted to climb Everest, the celebrated mountaineer George Mallory famously answered, "Because it's there." Yet, as Davis shows, it was for more than just this reason that Mallory and his companions endured wind, cold, fatigue, and nearly constant danger in order to summit Everest.

Davis opens his book with a dramatic preface in which Mallory and his climbing companion Andrew "Sandy" Irvine leave their camp, located at an elevation of 23,000 feet, on their last—and ultimately doomed—effort to reach Everest's summit. The description of the peak on that morning sets the scene for the rest of the book, introducing the harshness of the Himalayas and some of the men who attempted to survive and triumph there. Davis then moves ahead two days to June 8, 1924, the day Mallory and Irvine were last seen alive as they disappeared into a cloud. In the book's first chapter, he shifts location to the humbler summit of a mountain in the English Lake District, where, on the same day, a group of ladies and gentlemen gathered to dedicate a memorial to those members of the Fell and Rock Climbing Club who died in World War I.

Deviating from strict chronological order so that he can present biography and world history as well as mountain-climbing history, Davis's narrative goes back as far as 1846 to account for the British interest in a mountain for which they then had no name. It was in that year that a British surveying party in colonial India spotted a cluster of faraway mountains and noted the highest among them. After careful but distant scientific observations in 1849, the tedious work of calculating the elevation of the highest summit began, and an Indian mathematician put the figure at 29,002 feet— probably only 28 feet less than the actual mid-nineteenth-century height of a mountain that, through geological processes, still continues to rise.

In the middle of the 1800s, when the height of Everest was being so closely figured, the British Empire was flourishing. Upper- and middle-class Britons were generally optimistic about the future of their nation. The years passed, however, and the Great War began. Nowhere in the book does Davis write more memorably than when he describes the horrors of World War I. It was a war that most of the British on the Everest expeditions of the early 1920s had seen closely, either as officers in combat in the scarred fields of Belgium and France or as surgeons treating the maimed and dying just behind the front lines. Britain and its allies won the war, but at a price; the cost in lives was high and the generation of men who survived was emotionally wounded, as was the nation itself. The memories and lasting effects of war feature heavily in *Into the Silence*, in both the Everest expeditions and the men undertaking them.

Davis posits that the British attempts to climb Everest in 1921, 1922, and 1924 were efforts toward "imperial redemption." Before the war, Britons had seen Americans beat them to the North Pole and Norwegians beat them to the South Pole. Then, during the war, the Germans, the Austrians, and even the Turks had put forth a deadly resistance to British arms. In its aftermath, the nation needed an untarnished victory of British heroism to restore its belief in its own greatness. In a 1920 address to the Royal

Wade Davis, an anthropologist with a doctorate in ethnobotany from Harvard University, is a National Geographic Society explorer-in-residence. He has contributed to numerous periodicals, including Outside *and* National Geographic. *His many books include* The Serpent and the Rainbow *(1985) and* One River: Explorations and Discoveries in the Amazon Rain Forest *(1996).*

Geographic Society, British officer Francis Younghusband noted that although climbing Everest was useless in a mundane sense, it would be good for the human spirit and would serve as a sign of human triumph over the earth. Moreover, some Britons thought, it would be good for British pride. Members of the Alpine Club and the Royal Geographic Society formed the Mount Everest Committee, soon to be dominated by astronomer and cartographer Arthur Hinks, whom Davis describes as an unpleasant man who personally avoided exploring but worked carefully to plan expeditions.

The first expedition, led by the rugged Anglo-Irish aristocrat Charles Howard-Bury, left Darjeeling in May 1921. Its primary purpose was to explore Tibet, observe Everest, and plan the best route up its north face. Only secondarily, if circumstances allowed, was a party to attempt the summit. Eventually, surveyor Oliver Wheeler left the rest of the group and, with porters, spent almost three months photographically surveying the mountain under trying conditions. After rejoining the expedition, he was one of a small party that Mallory led up Everest to more than 23,000 feet before they turned back because of the wind's ominous strength. They were, Davis says, the first ever to place their boots on the mountain.

In 1922, General Charles Bruce replaced Howard-Bury as the leader of the expedition, which featured two innovations. First, the filmmaker John Noel came along to produce a documentary called *Climbing Mount Everest* (1922), which made Mallory a film star. Second, mountaineer and chemist George Finch demonstrated the use of bottles of supplemental oxygen to counter the human body's inability to get adequate oxygen into the bloodstream at extreme elevations. Without the extra oxygen, mountain sickness, also called altitude sickness, would set in. This potentially fatal condition causes sleeplessness and a loss of energy, appetite, and mental sharpness prior to death. Davis points out that Hinks, ignorant of mountain climbing, considered the use of supplemental oxygen to be unsportsmanlike, while even Mallory was suspicious of it at first. Finch's idea eventually won converts when he and Geoffrey Bruce, the general's nephew, used oxygen bottles in their ascent to 27,300 feet, breaking the height record set by Mallory a few days earlier. Death, however, soon came to the 1922 expedition: an avalanche struck a climbing party led by Mallory, killing seven porters, and the British grimly returned to India.

The 1924 expedition was led by General Bruce, who was later replaced by Edward "Teddy" Norton, a veteran of the 1922 expedition. Norton proved himself a superb mountaineer in 1924 when he and Howard Somervell, a medical doctor, both reached the Yellow Band of rock high on Everest's north face. Norton then went even farther, crossing the steep gorge that is now called the Norton Couloir. Despite early successes, however, the 1924 expedition also ended in tragedy, with the events Davis describes in his preface. Mallory and Irvine left their camp on June 6 and climbed toward the summit. Early in the afternoon of June 8, fellow mountaineer Noel Odell thought he saw the two men—tiny black figures in the distance—climbing within striking distance of the summit. But Odell would never know if they reached it. After being glimpsed on the ridge, Mallory and Irvine vanished from sight and never returned to their camp. Without hope that they could still be alive, the remaining members of the expedition left the mountain. When the news of their deaths reached Great Britain, Mallory and Irvine were mourned as fallen heroes.

Seventy-five years later, on the heights of Everest, members of a 1999 search expedition found Mallory's frozen remains. According to Davis, the long-asked question of whether Mallory and Irvine reached the peak remains unanswered. It is most probable that they did not, as Davis learned from the careful comments of the mountaineer who first spotted Mallory's body. Yet, according to the same expert, had snow conditions been just right, Mallory possessed the skill and the fortitude to reach his goal. Davis lauds Mallory's grit and spirit and recognizes his immense contributions to mountaineering and exploration, regardless of whether or not he ultimately reached the summit.

In 1953, Edmund Hillary of New Zealand and Tenzing Norgay of Nepal reached Mallory's goal. Their story, however, is not part of this book. *Into the Silence* is full enough as it is, with maps, a preface, thirteen long chapters, an epilogue, four pages of acknowledgments, forty-five pages of annotated bibliography, and thirty-one pages of index. It is not a book for readers who demand brevity and dislike details, packed as it is with particulars about education, shelter, clothing, food, travel routes, mountain topography, animals, plants, and weather, among many other matters. Beyond the elaborate accounts of the futile expeditions, Davis also delves into questions of British imperialism, international relations, and conflict, writing at length about World War I.

Although its length may seem daunting to some, many readers will enjoy following this meticulous and comprehensive story filled with facts, personal portraits, and the deeds of fallible men who, having known war's horrors, climbed honorably into the silence of death. Whether they are considered acts of heroism or of folly, these expeditions and their roles in history are masterfully described. Davis's work may be imposing in its scope, but for serious readers, it is a fitting tribute to the mountain and the men who sought to conquer it.

Victor Lindsey

Review Sources

Booklist 108, no. 1 (September 1, 2011): 37.
Kirkus Reviews 79, no. 15 (August 1, 2011): 1312–13.
Library Journal 136, no. 15 (September 15, 2011): 86–87.
Publishers Weekly 258, no. 35 (August 29, 2011): 55.

Iphigenia in Forest Hills
Anatomy of a Murder Trial

Author: Janet Malcolm (b. 1934)
Publisher: Yale University Press (New Haven, CT). 168 pp. $25.00
Type of work: Ethics and law
Time: 2009
Locale: New York City

Malcolm's account of a murder trial reveals layer upon layer of complexities and absurdities and seeming contradictions, leading the reader to question the very nature of truth and ambiguity.

Principal personages:
MAZOLTUV "MARINA" BORUKHOVA, a physician charged with arranging her husband's murder
DANIEL MALAKOV, the murdered man, Borukhova's estranged husband
MICHELLE MALAKOV, the daughter of Marina and Daniel
MIKHAIL MALLAYEV, the man charged with carrying out the killing
ROBERT HANOPHY, the presiding judge
BRAD LEVENTHAL, the assistant district attorney and lead prosecutor
STEPHEN SCARING, Borukhova's defense attorney
DAVID SCHNALL, the court-appointed law guardian for Michelle
JANET MALCOLM, the author, a journalist covering the trial for the *New Yorker*

Janet Malcolm's *Iphigenia in Forest Hills: Anatomy of a Murder Trial* offers an account of a trial that took place in New York's Queens Supreme Court in 2009. On October 28, 2007, in the Forest Hills section of Queens County, an orthodontist named Daniel Malakov was shot near a playground in the presence of his four-year-old daughter, Michelle. He died at a nearby hospital soon thereafter. Malakov had walked several blocks from his office to the playground with his daughter to bring her to his estranged wife, Marina Borukhova, for a parental visit.

Married in November 2001, the couple first separated within nine months of their daughter's birth in 2003 and later separated permanently in April 2005. Borukhova claimed that Malakov had abused her physically. In 2005, she submitted to family court the testimony of two witnesses who said they had seen Malakov molesting Michelle. When the allegations were investigated, the witnesses retracted their statements, claiming that they had been threatened and that their false testimonies had been written by Borukhova's sister. The court found their revised accounts credible. In the meantime, the court had appointed David Schnall as law guardian (legal advocate) for Michelle. On October 3, 2007, a court order transferred custody of Michelle from her mother to her father. Borukhova appealed the decision but lost, and on October 23, Michelle was taken from her mother.

Several months after the murder, the police tracked down Mikhail Mallayev to his home in Chamblee, Georgia. Mallayev, who was later positively identified by an eyewitness as the shooter, had left his fingerprints on the bleach bottle he had intended to use as a silencer. Investigators had been alerted by cell phone records showing ninety-one calls between Borukhova and Mallayev, a relative of hers by marriage, in the weeks leading up to Malakov's death. Deposits totaling nearly twenty thousand dollars had been made to Mallayev's accounts, and the source of the money could not be traced. The prosecution maintained that he had been paid by Borukhova to kill her husband.

Janet Malcolm is among the most eminent and controversial journalists of her time. Best known for The Journalist and the Murderer *(1990), a critique of Joe McGinniss's* Fatal Vision *(1983), she is widely cited for her views on journalistic ethics. She has also written books on psychoanalysis, on Sylvia Plath and Ted Hughes, and on Anton Chekhov, among other subjects.*

At first glance, the case seems open and shut, but from the outset, the reader knows that Malcolm does not see it that way. Her subtitle, *Anatomy of a Murder Trial*, alludes to the 1959 film *Anatomy of a Murder*, directed by Otto Preminger, and the best-selling 1958 novel on which the film was based, written by Michigan judge John D. Voelker (under the pseudonym Robert Traver) and inspired by a 1952 trial for which Voelker was the defense attorney. Both the novel and the film invert the familiar trial narrative, in which justice is done and all the seeming contradictions and confusions surrounding the crime are resolved.

The implications of the subtitle are reinforced by the two epigraphs chosen by Malcolm to set the stage for her account of the trial. The first is a statement by Judge Robert Hanophy, who, evidently addressing the author, says, "You seem to think this is extraordinary. It's not. Somebody's life was taken, somebody's arrested, they're indicted, they're tried and they're convicted. That's all this is." The second epigraph, undercutting the first, is a statement from the jury selection: "Everything is ambiguous in life except in court."

Such an emphasis on ambiguity can serve various purposes. One might suppose that Malcolm has written about this trial in order to make the case that, despite what seems to be overwhelming evidence, Borukhova did not in fact order the murder of her husband. However, that is not the approach Malcolm takes. Rather, in the vein of *Anatomy of a Murder*, Malcolm sardonically observes and records a spectacle in which all the participants are flawed and very little makes sense. To illustrate the "malleability of trial evidence," she describes an expert witness for the prosecution, an FBI translator, giving his transcription of a poor-quality recording of a May 2007 telephone conversation between Borukhova and Mallayev in Bukhori (their native tongue) and Russian. Though much of the dialogue is unremarkable, at the very end of the tape, according to the FBI translator, Mallayev asks, "Are you going to make me happy?" to which Borukhova responds, "Yes." The prosecutor made much of this exchange. Then, as Malcolm relates, during the cross-examination, defense attorney Stephen Scaring showed that the translator was rather inept, citing differences between his translation and the translation provided by Borukhova. For example, the FBI translator "had omitted the English words 'Mother's Day' from his text," which, when restored, clarified "a mystifying discussion of a 'crazy house'" as a description of the New York airport on that day. Having established that the FBI expert was less than expert, Scaring then zeroed in on the crucial bit of dialogue, arguing that the FBI translator misheard one key word for another similar word with a very different meaning. On a recording that was so hard to hear, Malcolm says, such a mistake would be easy to make, but "that it so well advanced the narrative of an unsavory association . . . suggests that this was a mishearing by design—unconscious, perhaps, but design nonetheless."

Malcolm makes it clear that this judgment does not apply only to the government, the state, the prosecution, or others seeking to make a case:

> We go through life mishearing and mis-seeing and misunderstanding so that the stories we tell will add up. Trial lawyers push this human tendency to a higher level. They are playing for higher stakes than we are playing for when we tinker with actuality in order to transform the tale told by an idiot into an orderly, self-serving narrative.

That passage, which comes early in the text, is quite a manifesto. At first, it seems generous in its concession that all of us, not just zealous prosecutors and their expert witnesses "go through life mishearing and mis-seeing and misunderstanding." But when Malcolm goes on to frame this perennial human fallibility as a desperate attempt to "transform the tale told by an idiot into an orderly self-serving narrative," the implications are pretty far-reaching. In this light, the trial becomes a stage on which the futile but inextinguishable human desire to impose order on an ultimately meaningless existence appears for our instruction in heightened form. Malcolm is our fearless guide, seeing through the universal deception, telling it like it is. The message, taken to its logical conclusion, would seem to be both nihilistic and self-defeating. If we are all engaged in the same futile exercise, why should we prefer Malcolm's perspective to that of Judge Robert Hanophy, an older man Malcolm describes as possessing "the faux-genial manner that American petty tyrants cultivate"? Loathsome as he appears here—relishing the exercise of his power, no matter how arbitrary—is he not, by Malcolm's own account, simply doing the same thing she is, the same thing we all do?

Malcolm never addresses this question squarely, and for much of the book, the reader may be able to ignore this fact and simply enjoy the ride. Malcolm's narrative voice is beguiling, drawing on a long life of shrewd people-watching but also, oddly enough, suggesting the perspective of a preternaturally gifted child who candidly describes everything she sees, registering her likes and dislikes, her elective affinities and her scorn, with none of the self-censoring that adults have learned. Wherever she looks, Malcolm finds oddities, foolishness, conflicting testimony, worlds within worlds. She delights in an excursus tracing the tangled and uncertain history of the community of Bukharan Jewish émigrés to which both Borukhova and her murdered husband belong and notes the antipathy with which they are regarded by many earlier Russian Jewish immigrants. The Borukhova family we see only at a distance and are left to speculate about, as they did not take Malcolm into their confidence, but we do come to be acquainted with various members of the Malakov family, who invited Malcolm into their homes. Fellow journalists who were covering the trial as well are genially rendered here, though all of them, Malcolm claims, are strongly or moderately persuaded by the prosecution's case and inclined to dislike and distrust Borukhova, whereas Malcolm feels an immediate sympathy for the woman.

Yet Malcolm's narrative is not simply a collection of ambiguities and oddities, with sharp asides on what she regards as the hypocrisies of our legal system—the presumption of innocence, she writes, is "a travesty," and her post-trial conversations with two jurors are devastating, simply by quoting their own reasoning. She does have a case to make, and it centers on the curious figure of David Schnall, the court-appointed law guardian of Borukhova and Malakov's daughter. Perhaps the most disturbing parts of Malcolm's book are those in which she recounts Schnall's role in the case. Schnall represented "the best interests of the child" largely on the basis of his interpretation of interactions between Borukhova, Michelle, and Malakov, rather than seeing the little girl firsthand, a practice that Malcolm tells us is not at all uncommon. Repeated reports detailed Michelle becoming tearful and extremely reluctant to leave her mother when she was supposed to spend time with her father, even though he appeared friendly and caring. These reports are interpreted by Judge Sidney Strauss, whose ruling on the custody dispute was strongly influenced by Schnall, to mean that Michelle should taken from her mother's custody and put in the full custody of her father, who had not even requested it. Malcolm quotes at some length from Judge Strauss's ruling given at the hearing on October 3, 2007, which both Borukhova's and Malakov's representatives had asked to be postponed but Schnall had insisted must take place that day.

Even more bizarre is a telephone conversation between Malcolm and Schnall, in which he breaks away from the subject of the case to reveal to her his supposed deep understanding of what is really going on in the world. Malcolm reproduces some of her notes from Schnall's ravings, which prompted her, she says, to do something she had "never done before as a journalist. I meddled with the story I was reporting." Malcolm called Scaring and faxed him her notes, which Scaring brought before Judge Hanophy with the request to recall Schnall for further questioning to show that he was not a credible witness. The judge quickly dismissed this request.

Hence the concluding sentence of Malcolm's book: "And so," in the custody hearing on October 3, "the curtain rose on the tragedy of Daniel Malakov, Michelle Malakov, and Mazoltuv Borukhova." In the end, as Malcolm would freely admit, she too gives the tangled tale a meaningful shape.

John Wilson

Review Sources

Nation, June 6, 2011 (Web).
The New York Review of Books, April 28, 2011 (Web).
The New York Times Book Review, May 1, 2011, p. 8.
Salon, March 27, 2011 (Web).

A Jane Austen Education
How Six Novels Taught Me about Love, Friendship, and the Things That Really Matter

Author: William Deresiewicz (b. 1964)
Publisher: Penguin (New York). 272 pp.
  $25.95; paperback $15.00
Type of work: Literary biography
Time: 1990–1996
Locale: New York City

Literary critic William Deresiewicz reflects on how he overcame his bias against author Jane Austen and became a more thoughtful and understanding person in the process.

Principal personages:
WILLIAM DERESIEWICZ, a literary critic and
    author who has been influenced by Jane
    Austen's novels
JANE AUSTEN (1775–1817), an English novelist
EMMA WOODHOUSE, the protagonist of Austen's
    novel *Emma*
ELIZABETH BENNET, the protagonist of Austen's novel *Pride and Prejudice*
CATHERINE MORLAND, the protagonist of Austen's novel *Northanger Abbey*
FANNY PRICE, the protagonist of Austen's novel *Mansfield Park*
ANNE ELLIOT, the protagonist of Austen's novel *Persuasion*
ELINOR DASHWOOD, the protagonist of Austen's novel *Sense and Sensibility*

William Deresiewicz is an important figure in contemporary literary criticism of Jane Austen. While working as an English professor at Yale University, he established his reputation as an Austen expert with his book *Jane Austen and the Romantic Poets* (2004). This latest work, *A Jane Austen Education*, solidifies his standing as an engaging and insightful writer, reminding readers why Austen has long been regarded as one of the greatest English novelists and why she remains just as relevant to the modern world as she was in her own time.

    The subtitle of this literary biography—*How Six Novels Taught Me about Love, Friendship, and the Things That Really Matter*—describes the basic premise of the book. Deresiewicz frames each chapter around one of Austen's six early-eighteenth-century novels, combining literary commentary with a memoir describing how reading the novel made him a better person. He reflects on his initial resistance to her work and how his growing appreciation of her oeuvre influenced his life. Over time, her novels help him come to a better understanding of various important aspects of life: maturity, courtesy, responsibility, learning, character, friendship, and love.

William Deresiewicz was an associate professor of English at Yale University until 2008. He is a book critic whose reviews and essays have appeared in the New York Times, *the* New Republic, *the* Nation, *and* American Scholar. *He was nominated for National Magazine Awards in 2008, 2009, and 2011, as well as for the National Book Critics Circle's Nona Balakian Citation for Excellence in Reviewing in 2010 and 2011.*

Prior to his enlightenment, Deresiewicz wants to study modernism and only encounters Austen when required to read *Emma* (1815) for one of his courses. The brash young graduate student feels that she is a dull and narrow author who is irrelevant to modern society, wondering, "Wasn't she the one who wrote those silly romantic fairy tales?" Young Deresiewicz speculates that Austen's novels are stories about common people in country villages, stories that primarily consist of the characters sitting and talking, with "No grand events, no great issues, and, inexplicably for a writer of romance novels, not even any passion."

And then Emma Woodhouse, the title character of Jane Austen's novel *Emma,* comes into his life. Emma lives a very narrow life with her father on the family estate of Hartfield, and her boredom with the quiet society of Highbury occasionally manifests itself as arrogance, nosiness, and insensitivity. In one notable instance, Emma is even cruel in her treatment of gentle and poor Miss Bates, making unnecessary and hurtful remarks towards her. Emma eventually realizes her faults and tries to correct them, and her growing awareness parallels Deresiewicz's as he realizes that "I couldn't deplore Emma's disdain for Miss Bates, or her boredom with the whole commonplace Highbury world, without simultaneously condemning my own."

He realizes that Jane Austen wrote about the minutiae of everyday life because she wanted readers to understand the importance of these details: "By eliminating all the big, noisy events that usually absorb our interest when we read novels—the adventures and affairs, the romances and the crises, even, at times, the plot—Austen was asking us to pay attention to the things we usually miss or don't accord enough esteem, in novels or in life." Deresiewicz not only comes to appreciate Jane Austen's genius as a novelist but also begins to realize that she can provide real lessons for contemporary readers. Austen brings new awareness to the arrogant graduate student: "Everything was interesting, everything was meaningful, every conversation held potential revelations. It was like having my ears turned on for the first time." He realizes that he had to learn "to stop being a defensive, reactive, self-enclosed jerk."

These discoveries about life fostered by reading *Emma* were only the beginning of Deresiewicz's literary relationship with the author. While struggling with his own inner demons about becoming a responsible adult, Deresiewicz "unexpectedly" falls in love with the irrepressible Elizabeth Bennet, the heroine of Jane Austen's novel *Pride and Prejudice* (1813). In this fictional character, he sees a woman who is "Brilliant, witty, full of fun and laughter—the kind of person who makes you feel more alive just being around." As the novel progresses, Elizabeth discovers that although she has many admirable qualities, she is so proud of her own accomplishments that she sometimes ignores the feelings of others. She also trusts her prejudiced judgment much too much. Both of these flaws cause massive upheavals in her life and the lives of her family members. Elizabeth's eventual acknowledgment and correction of her flaws resonates with Deresiewicz, who reveals that "what the novel was really showing me was how to grow up."

As the young graduate student starts to write his dissertation under the guidance of a beloved professor, he reevaluates his role as a teacher of freshman English through his reading of *Northanger Abbey* (1818). Protagonist Catherine Moreland's relationship with Henry Tilney illustrates the complexity of the relationship between teaching and learning. The art of lecturing without being didactic is an important skill, and telling students something rarely results in them learning it. In the novel, Henry's approach to "educating" Catherine is more effective, as he teaches her "by provoking her, taking her by surprise, making her laugh, throwing her off balance, forcing her to figure out what was going on and what it meant—getting her to think, not telling her how." Austen herself encouraged readers to think about her characters and her novels, rather than lecturing to them or explicitly explaining her views. Education, like life, should be a continually surprising and engaging experience.

Deresiewicz also discusses how his struggles with his dissertation and social life were affected by Jane Austen's 1814 novel *Mansfield Park*. He feels an affinity toward its heroine, Fanny Price, and their similar circumstances. Struggling to make friends while living on his own in Brooklyn, Deresiewicz joins a rich prep-school crowd. At first, he is delighted to be invited to their social events, noting that it "was the upper crust, the world of Edith Wharton or F. Scott Fitzgerald updated for the nineties: posh, polished young people who gave off a glow of glamour and sophistication that drew me like a moth . . . I was grateful just to be able to watch." He is mesmerized by the wealth and sophistication of his new acquaintances, only later realizing that, like Fanny Price, he is ultimately just "an outsider, an onlooker." He recognizes that he will never truly belong to this crowd and that, while they may be very impressive on the surface, underneath they are willing to maintain their social status at any cost. Jane Austen's message about wealth in *Mansfield Park* is a powerful one, and Deresiewicz grows to understand that "Being a valuable person—a 'something' rather than a 'nothing'—means having consideration for the people around you. Too much money renders that unnecessary; too little makes it very difficult. Fanny was a heroine, finally, because she was able to put herself aside for other people."

Deresiewicz still has a lot to learn about relationships at this point in his life, and reading *Persuasion* (1818) continues to further his education. In this novel, protagonist Anne Elliot is a single woman, older than Austen's other heroines, who often finds solace in her relationships with friends and family. Drawing parallels between Anne and Austen's life, Deresiewicz realizes that he must continually work at his own friendships in a sustained fashion and that "For adults today, it seemed to me now, community can only be a circle of friends." He also notes that "Putting your friend's welfare before your own: that was Austen's idea of true friendship."

In Austen's final lesson, *Sense and Sensibility* (1811) teaches Deresiewicz about what it is to love someone. He admits to not really enjoying the novel, noting that he finds it depressing and "satiric but not joyful, funny but not comic." His perception of its story changes, however, when he sees the film adaptation directed by Ang Lee and gains a new appreciation for its message about love. In the relationship between heroine Elinor Dashwood and Edward Ferrars, he sees a telling and realistic depiction of love, which he notes "is not about remaining forever young. It's about becoming an adult." Deresiewicz goes on to find love himself, and his relationship is cemented when the woman he is with gives him a copy of *Pride and Prejudice*.

As Deresiewicz moves through the Austen canon, he connects the events and characters to those in his own life. He provides a window into his experiences as a student, a teacher, a reader, and a man, revealing how a series of epiphanies changed his perceptions of life and literature. Readers learn about his confused relationship with his domineering immigrant father, his high school experiences in the Jewish youth movement, his self-imposed isolation as a graduate student, his failed romantic relationships, his desire to find friendship and achieve social status, and, finally, his relationship with the woman who would become his wife.

Readers of *A Jane Austen Education* will appreciate Deresiewicz's documentation of his education and his balance of memoir and literary criticism. It is apparent, however, that his strength is in textual analysis, not self-analysis. At times, the discussion of plot points and their effect on Deresiewicz can be too lengthy and complicated. But the lessons are clear overall, and avid fans of Austen's work will value his fresh takes on the novels. Many readers will also be enchanted by the happy ending, in which, much like the characters he and Austen write about, Deresiewicz has overcome his flaws and misconceptions and found love.

Myra Junyk

Review Sources

The Christian Science Monitor, May 12, 2011 (Web).
Kirkus Reviews, April 15, 2011 (Web).
Library Journal 136, no. 8 (May 1, 2011): 86.
Los Angeles Review of Books, September 5, 2011 (Web).
The New York Times Book Review, June 12, 2011, p. L14.
Salon, May 31, 2011 (Web).

J. D. Salinger
A Life

Author: Kenneth Slawenski (b. 1957)
Publisher: Random House (New York). Illustrated. 450 pp. $27.00
Type of work: Biography
Time: Late nineteenth to early twenty-first century
Locale: United States

Slawenski offers a new biography of J. D. Salinger, the enigmatic and secretive author of such works as The Catcher in the Rye, *who ceased publishing long before he died and went out of his way to protect his personal privacy.*

Principal personages:
J. D. SALINGER (1919–2010), author of *The Catcher in the Rye*, one of the most popular novels in the history of American fiction
CLAIRE DOUGLAS SALINGER (b. 1933), Salinger's wife from 1955 to1966, mother of his daughter and son
WHITT BURNETT (1900–1972), longtime editor of *Story* magazine, an early mentor of Salinger's
JAMIE HAMILTON (1900–1988), English publisher, an early enthusiast and publisher of Salinger's work in the United Kingdom
GUS LOBRANO (1903?–1956), fiction editor of the *New Yorker*, a champion of Salinger's fiction
WILLIAM MAXWELL (1908–2000), editor of the *New Yorker* who took a strong interest in Salinger's fiction
WILLIAM SHAWN (1907–1992), influential editor of the *New Yorker,* who took a personal hand in editing Salinger's fiction

Kenneth Slawenski's new biography of J. D. Salinger, the author of the landmark American novel *The Catcher in the Rye* (1951), is sure to interest anyone who is curious about Salinger's life and works. Of course, one of the most intriguing aspects of his life is that so little is known about it, especially its latter half. From the mid-1960s until his death in 2010, Salinger withdrew almost entirely from the public stage. He lived in a modest home in rural New Hampshire, where he did his best to stay out of sight and out of mind. Evidently, he continued to write, though he never published another creative work. In 2009, Salinger went to enormous legal lengths to prevent the publication of Swedish author Fredrik Colting's unauthorized sequel to *Catcher*, *60 Years Later: Coming through the Rye* (2009). The legal battle with Colting was just one of Salinger's various attempts to maintain an iron-fisted control over his work and reputation. Ironically, the more Salinger sought to keep his life a secret, the more he inspired the almost relentless curiosity of readers for whom *The Catcher in the Rye* was a seminal book of deep personal significance.

Slawenski is clearly one such reader. Although he is certainly willing to discuss Salinger's darker side and touch on some of his complexities, Slawenski's regard for Salinger is almost reverential. On the topic of Salinger's second marriage and his frayed relationships with various associates and mentors, Slawenski's willingness to balance his interest in the subject and his presentation of the facts is particularly evident. For the most part, though, his work displays both the strengths and the weaknesses of a highly committed fan. He is willing to go to great lengths to uncover new information about his subject's life, and indeed, he has turned up information that is extremely valuable; see, for example, his discussion of Salinger's ancestors and family, especially his mother, as well as his presentation of Salinger's harrowing experiences during World War II. Although Slawenski sometimes infers these details from evidence that does not directly mention Salinger by name, there seems to be little reason to doubt most of his conclusions.

Most impressive is the account of Salinger during World War II, in which he is portrayed as a brave, committed soldier and effective battlefield leader. Slawenski is probably correct in arguing that the war had a profound impact on Salinger's psyche. Of course, Salinger was almost entirely silent about this aspect of his life, as he was about so many others, but Slawenski argues persuasively that his wartime experiences— especially his reckoning with his own survival, when so many of his comrades had succumbed to the brutality of the battlefield—served as a crucial turning point in his development as both a person and a writer. Slawenski offers the reader a great deal of research and evidence to support certain views of Salinger's experiences immediately after the war as well. He suggests that Salinger, who was assigned to military intelligence work and stationed near several concentration camps, may have been among the American soldiers who witnessed the horrors of the Holocaust firsthand. Salinger certainly had experience in interrogating former Nazis, as he was a part of the official denazification effort.

Slawenski's thorough approach is on full display as he discusses Salinger's first marriage in Europe, shortly after the war, to a German woman previously known only as "Sylvia." Consulting the passenger manifest of the ship on which Salinger returned to the United States in 1946, Slawenski manages to determine Sylvia's exact name and date of birth as well as a number of other private and professional details, including the title of her university dissertation. He also relates details of her life from after her marriage to Salinger ended (reportedly after a mere eight months), including where she lived, how she occupied her time, and the precise date on which she died. Slawenski adds that many articles about Salinger were discovered among her possessions after she passed away. This is the kind of impressive detail that works most strongly in the book's favor, reassuring readers that the author has gone out of his way to get the facts right and present them responsibly; the reference to the ship's manifest, for instance, is carefully annotated.

Kenneth Slawenski is the founder of the website www.deadcaulfields.com, which is devoted to the life and works of J. D. Salinger. He is a lifelong resident of New Jersey. This is his first book.

It is all the more remarkable, then, that Slawenski makes no mention of certain astonishing claims made in *Dream Catcher* (2000), the controversial memoir of Salinger's daughter, Margaret Salinger. In that book, Margaret asserts that Sylvia was a low-level Nazi, one whom Salinger himself had interrogated prior to their marriage. Margaret draws on the purported memories of close relatives to paint a vivid picture of Sylvia, describing her in great detail. Slawenski presumably has his own reasons for not including this information about Sylvia's appearance. Less understandable, however, is his failure to discuss another of *Dream Catcher*'s claims, namely Margaret's allegation that Salinger once referred to Sylvia's hatred for Jews—a comment that, if true, renders her marriage to Salinger somewhat difficult to understand but may also help explain its ending so quickly (Slawenski attributes this outcome to friction between Sylvia and her domineering mother-in-law). A reader familiar with Margaret's memoir may indeed wonder why does Slawenski not address its startling contentions, or even bring them to the reader's attention.

Slawenski's silence on this particular topic would be less unsettling had he not avoided any discussion, not only of *Dream Catcher*, but also of another sensational and unflattering portrayal of Salinger, Joyce Maynard's memoir *At Home in the World* (1999). During her freshman year at Yale University, Maynard dropped out of school and moved in with Salinger in New Hampshire after the two became romantically involved, despite the age difference of thirty-five years. Slawenski mentions the affair and Maynard's book just briefly before quickly moving on to other matters. Once again, some readers may have found it helpful to know what Slawenski, who obviously admires Salinger, made of Maynard's book, if only to bring her claims into some kind of wider discussion. As his input typically proves insightful, readers would probably have appreciated some input here. Instead, there is almost nothing.

Perhaps Slawenski felt that the story of Salinger's life after he stopped publishing is not especially interesting. However, Salinger's strange withdrawal from public life is, paradoxically, the phase of his life that is most likely to interest many readers. Knowing more about that period might help explain why, exactly, Salinger stopped publishing. Slawenski, with his admirable gift for research, might have been precisely the writer (aside from Salinger himself) to help explain the perplexing twilight of Salinger's final decades. Is this book so circumspect because Slawenski considers it just the first of a multivolume project? Is he hoping that a sequel might even elicit some cooperation from Salinger's heirs? Slawenski's silence on certain crucial subjects only helps fuel these speculations.

In any case, the thinness of the book's final chapters raises many questions regarding what has been intentionally omitted, questions that are, in some ways, as intriguing as Salinger's personal withdrawal. When the next biography of Salinger is written, one hopes its author will try to be as comprehensive as possible, not only examining the memoirs of Margaret Salinger and Joyce Maynard (among others) but also making clearer its relationship to previous Salinger biographies. Those earlier works include Ian Hamilton's *In Search of J. D. Salinger* (1988), a book that became famous when Salinger notoriously took Hamilton to court, as well as the biography that some reviews regard as superior to Slawenski's, Paul Alexander's *Salinger: A Biography* (1999). What readers truly need is a biography of Salinger that is as thorough and painstaking as possible, and although these words certainly describe the early chapters of Slawenski's book, the volume as a whole does not maintain this integrity throughout.

In the meantime, there is much to recommend this book, especially in its coverage of the first half of Salinger's life. Slawenski has read (but apparently cannot quote very extensively from) Salinger's correspondence with various associates, and it is these letters from which much of the early narrative derives. He has also read and carefully considered all of Salinger's fiction, allowing him to draw attention to connections between Salinger's writings and his life. Inevitably, some of his arguments are speculative, but fans of Salinger are especially likely to appreciate the attention he pays to the works. One surprising aspect of the book, in fact, is the revelation of just how many of Salinger's works remain unpublished. Perhaps they have simply disappeared, or perhaps they are lying undiscovered in the files of various periodicals. Of course, the true volume of Salinger's work in the years after his public withdrawal is likely to remain unknown. Various bits of evidence suggest that he never stopped writing, which hints at the possibility that Slawenski's book may indeed someday prove to be the first volume of a much larger and more complicated biographical project.

Robert C. Evans

Review Sources

Booklist 107, no. 7 (December 1, 2010): 72.
Library Journal 136, no. 1 (January 1, 2011): 98.
Library Journal 136, no. 15 (September 15, 2011): 43.
The New York Times Book Review, February 13, 2011, p. 1.
The Telegraph, April 3, 2010, p. 25.
Times Literary Supplement, no. 5588 (May 7, 2010): 30.
USA Today, January 25, 2011, p. D1.
The Wall Street Journal, January 22, 2011, p. C7.
The Washington Post, February 20, 2011, p. B7.
Washington Times, March 11, 2011, p. B6.

Jerusalem
The Biography

Author: Simon Sebag Montefiore (b. 1965)
Publisher: Alfred A. Knopf (New York). Illustrated. 688 pp. $35.00
Type of work: History
Time: 1500 BCE to the present
Locale: Jerusalem, Israel

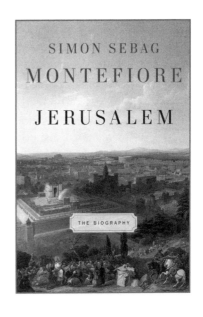

Montefiore presents a detailed narrative history of Jerusalem, studying the continuity of the city in the face of changing empires, dynasties, and religions.

There has been no shortage of published accounts of Jerusalem in the early twenty-first century, as the capital city of Israel continues to fill the pages of international news. Karen Armstrong's much-praised history *Jerusalem: One City, Three Faiths* (1997) has been followed by Eric Cline's *Jerusalem Besieged: From Ancient Canaan to Modern Israel* (2004) and Hershel Shanks's *Jerusalem's Temple Mount: From Solomon to the Golden Dome* (2007), among others. Around the same time that Montefiore's new book *Jerusalem: The Biography* was published in the United Kingdom, James Carroll's *Jerusalem, Jerusalem: How the Ancient City Ignited Our Modern World* (2011) appeared as well.

With this book, Montefiore takes a strikingly different approach from the others. Whereas Armstrong's book is, among other things, a history of religious ideas and practices, and the other two books rely heavily on modern archeological finds, Montefiore's book calls itself a biography rather than a history. This suggests Jerusalem is treated as a person, much as the city is treated in various prophetic utterances throughout the Bible. As a person, "she" has experienced several resurrections (to employ a Judeo-Christian concept) and marriages to three husbands, all of whom still claim her. She has been fought over, ravished, adorned, praised, lamented, and has fallen on times both bad and good. She has been the object of desire and adoration, but also hatred, exclusion, and banishment.

Another biographical aspect of the book concerns Montefiore himself, a somewhat secular Jew. Montefiore's family has had connections with Jerusalem since the mid-nineteenth century, when his Anglo-Italian ancestor, the baronet Sir Moses Montefiore, first journeyed to Jerusalem and devoted himself to the city's well-being. Some of his philanthropic works still stand, including the Mishkenot Sha'ananim, the first Jewish settlement established outside of Jerusalem's walls. Since then, the Montefiore family has kept a toehold in the city, and Montefiore speaks of visiting Jerusalem from the time of his youth. For the first time, he has been able to incorporate family documents into the historical scholarship of Jerusalem. He also includes documents concerning Wasif Jawhariyyeh, a well-known singer and oud player of the early twentieth century, which have never before been put into English.

Montefiore's style, too, is more that of a biographer than an academic historian, and his largely narrative book tends toward the anecdotal. He has a journalist's ear for catchy stories, a good number of which are fairly scatological. He is determinedly secular in his approach, though he still reserves enough sympathy with regard to the religious practices and beliefs of each religion—Judaism, Christianity, Islam—so as not to mock or undermine his subjects' spiritually motivated actions. He does laugh at his subjects' more bizarre manifestations of faith, but on the whole these instances are good natured. He perhaps tends to apply the labels "extreme," "obsessive," and "fanatical" a little too easily, especially to Protestant evangelicals. For the first time in a work of history, Montefiore charts the progress of a phenomenon known as Jerusalem syndrome, a mental condition suffered by some visitors to Jerusalem who come expecting to find an ideal and then cannot cope with the reality, leading to temporary psychosis. Apparently, this condition is regularly treated in Jerusalem mental hospitals.

Although most of the book is narrated chronologically, the opening chapter is set in what was perhaps Jerusalem's darkest hour, its destruction by the Romans in 70 CE. This chapter's graphically detailed descriptions of physical destruction set the tone for the rest of the book; the extreme drama plays out before the reader's eyes, yet with an objectivity that takes into account what transpires on both sides. Montefiore foregrounds the Romanized Jewish historian Josephus, an adviser to the Roman general, as he witnesses his own people being slaughtered and saves the few that he can. In a way, the figure of Josephus is telling of Montefiore himself, a modern Josephus who sees both sides and does what he can to save his own people while advising his Western readers on the larger picture.

However objective this modern Josephus may attempt to be, he clearly has favorites among Jerusalem's former rulers, and these are not necessarily Jews. In his account, early Islamic rulers come across well, especially Muawiya ibn Abi Sufyan ("a much-neglected paragon of how absolute power does not have to corrupt absolutely"), Arab military leader Saladin, and Ottoman sultan Suleiman, who largely rebuilt Jerusalem and welcomed Sephardic Ladino-speaking Jews. Jerusalem's mayors in more recent times also come across well, especially the Husseinis and Teddy Kolleck. According to Montefiore, the main criterion for his approval is a leader's ability to hold the city as an open one, a city available for people of all faiths or no faiths, and to unite disparity under the rule of law in a true civic society.

The book is divided into nine rather unequal sections, a prologue, and an epilogue, and is then followed by over one hundred pages of end material. Within the body of the text are four sets of photographs; the few maps that Montefiore has included, unfortunately, have been tucked away at the back. Although the author has a detailed knowledge of the Jerusalem street atlas, most readers will find his detailed references frustrating, as they cannot be traced out cartographically. Readers seeking further cartographic assistance might consider reading Montefiore's book with Dan Bahat's

(Getty Images)

Simon Sebag Montefiore is the author of the novel Sashenka *(2008) and the nonfiction books* Young Stalin *(2007),* Stalin: The Court of the Red Tsar *(2005), and* Potemkin: Catherine the Great's Imperial Partner *(2005). He is a fellow of the Royal Society of Literature and lives in London.*

Illustrated Atlas of Jerusalem (1990) close at hand.

The first section, "Judaism," is the longest and the least successful of the book. Montefiore traces the history leading up to the fall of Jerusalem, including the ministry of Jesus and the early Christian church within Judaism. A Christian writer would probably have ended the section with the coming of the Romans, thus allowing the earliest days of Christianity a clearer focus. As it is, however, Montefiore downplays Jesus's ministry and influence and gives the early missionary Paul the credit for fashioning Christianity as it emerged. This line of biblical scholarship has been quite fashionable in recent times but is not a mainstream view. What makes this section awkward is Montefiore's reliance on a rather skeptical brand of Old Testament scholarship that certain scholars may consider outmoded. For instance, he writes that David "may have written some of the Psalms," a remark that betrays a degree of skepticism that has little meaning outside the world of Old Testament scholarship. At the same time, Montefiore cheerfully supposes, with no supporting evidence whatsoever, that Zerubbabel may have been assassinated, even though his bias toward the idea is evident in the supposition itself. Surprisingly, Montefiore dismisses the Turin Shroud debate as over and resolved in favor of a medieval provenance, even though a significant amount of counterevidence remains.

Having expressed his skepticism in this particular area, Montefiore gets on with telling his story in a much freer and more energetic style. He has a good working knowledge of archaeology and a tremendous breadth of learning, but certain periods of history are raced over. The Byzantines, for instance, merit only twenty pages, while the Christian Crusades of the eleventh through thirteen centuries enjoy sixty-five pages of good yarns. The eighteenth century gets no more attention than the Byzantines, but the last part, "Zionism," is the second-longest section in the book and the one in which Montefiore most clearly demonstrates his range of knowledge, much of it gathered firsthand. The amount of anecdotal and detailed personal material is fascinating. Figures such as President Chaim Weizmann of Israel, Zionist visionary Theodor Herzl, and eccentric American Bertha Spafford rub shoulders with British general Edmund Allenby, Lieutenant Colonel T. E. Lawrence (more popularly Lawrence of Arabia), the "Families" of the land-owning Muslim grandees, and a cast of many others. This British writer refuses to treat sympathetically the last days of the British Raj, with its disavowal of the Balfour Declaration and its barely concealed anti-Semitism.

One of the things Montefiore does particularly well is trace the recurring patterns of outside involvement and, indeed, domination in Jerusalem's history, "outside" meaning outside the immediate Middle Eastern empire in control at the time. While the immediate empires are fascinating in themselves—the Egyptians, Assyrians, and Babylonians, just to name a few—the powers beyond these regions made significant power plays as well. The Crusades, the Russian attempt to maintain the orthodoxy of the Byzantines, the Napoleonic Wars, and World Wars I and II all involved different Western powers at different junctures in Jerusalem's history. Originally an obscure, out-of-the-way hill fortress, Jerusalem truly became an international city, permanently involved in world politics. Montefiore also traces the changing populace of the city, from its days of fullness, as in the prologue, to its days of Babylonian exile and the later emptiness of the pre-Byzantine era or the mid-nineteenth century. Jewish immigrants, whether Sephardic, Ashkenazic, Yemeni, or Ethiopian, rub shoulders with wealthy pilgrims from Britain or America and the dirt-poor Russian Orthodox, filling the city with strangeness, violence, and exuberance.

Montefiore is fascinated with Jerusalem's continuities and repeating patterns. At first, he is also interested in the "Jerusalem above" concept suggested in the Psalms, but his interest then devolves into the Jerusalem of the future, the millennial city, above all the Jerusalem of the mind and heart. On this subject, his counterpart Armstrong is strongest, so perhaps Montefiore feels ill equipped to pursue it. But in the epilogue, summarizing the last four decades, Montefiore reveals himself again, claiming that he has attempted to show how, historically, "nothing was inevitable, there were always choices." The dilemmas of the early twenty-first century are not more difficult or easy than those of the past. Though he bemoans Palestinian leader Yasser Arafat's lost opportunities to create a two-nation state, Montefiore believes there is still a future for Jerusalem that would involve all its communities—even if they exist only in parallel with one another, as far as this vision might be from the mixed, tolerant community of his youthful memories. With or without God, Montefiore holds that the responsibility of the city's future and salvation lies with humanity.

David Barratt

Review Sources

The Economist 398, no. 8725 (May 17, 2011): 93–94.
The Guardian, January 28, 2011, p. 6.
The New York Times Book Review, October 30, 2011, p. 24.
The Wall Street Journal, October 22, 2011 (Web).

Joan Mitchell
Lady Painter, A Life

Author: Patricia Albers (b. 1949)
Publisher: Alfred A. Knopf (New York).
544 pp. $40.00
Type of work: Biography
Time: 1839–1992
Locale: Chicago, New York, Paris, and Vétheuil, France

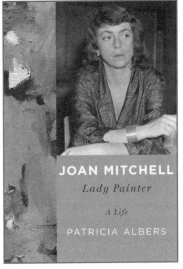

As the first full-scale biography of Joan Mitchell, this well-researched tome builds upon primary sources such as Mitchell's letters and interviews with her family, friends, and peers to provide an intimate and detailed portrayal of the abstract expressionist painter who came of age in the 1950s and 1960s.

Principal personages:
JOAN MITCHELL, an abstract expressionist painter
JAMES HERBERT MITCHELL, her father, a dermatologist
MARION STROBEL MITCHELL, her mother, a poet
SARAH MITCHELL PERRY, her sister
BARNEY ROSSET, her husband of three years, a publisher
JEAN-PAUL RIOPELLE, a Canadian painter and sculptor with whom Mitchell had a
    long-term relationship

In *Joan Mitchell: Lady Painter; A Life*, a detailed account of Joan Mitchell's life and works, author Patricia Albers closely examines Mitchell's personal life, personality, relationships, and paintings. Readers learn about the loves and liaisons of Mitchell's life, as well as those of her parents, grandparents, and great-grandparents. Albers provides ample information about Mitchell's formative years, focusing on her relationship with her father, who badly wanted a son instead of a daughter, as well as her education at a progressive school, her involvement in competitive sports, and the friendships she formed. The biographer also describes Mitchell's decision at the age of twelve to pursue art rather than writing, based on her father's insistence that she choose one area in which to study. Further attention is paid to Mitchell's lackluster years at Smith College, her education at the Art Institute of Chicago, and her eventual move to New York City.

As a young adult, Mitchell immersed herself in the art world of New York City, forming relationships with—and exhibiting alongside—some of the leading painters of the abstract expressionist movement, such as Jackson Pollock, Willem de Kooning, and Hans Hofmann. Like many artists of her day, she spent time in Europe, particularly in France, where she was influenced by the legacy of postimpressionist painters such as Paul Cézanne and Vincent van Gogh. After a short-lived marriage, she returned to France permanently, where she conducted a long-term relationship with the married artist Jean-Paul Riopelle, as well as briefer relationships with other men.

Albers presents an abundance of details about Mitchell's personal relationships and professional life. Mitchell is portrayed as a driven, hard-living woman, determined to succeed. She was involved in intense and tumultuous relationships with multiple artists of the New York school and the avant-garde art world in Europe. She drank hard, partied hard, loved hard, and brawled with both men and women, ultimately dying of lung cancer at the age of sixty-seven. All the elements of a captivating biography are present: wealth, passion, a woman breaking into art circles historically dominated by men, and a bohemian lifestyle peppered with rich and famous friends and acquaintances. Albers's portrayal of the subject is comprehensive, full of deeply researched facts, intense examinations, and input from those who knew Mitchell best. However, reviewers are mixed in their assessment of *Joan Mitchell: Lady Painter; A Life*, with responses to the biography covering a broad spectrum from scathing criticism to high praise.

Patricia Albers is an art critic, curator, and writer. Her biography Shadows, Fire, Snow: The Life of Tina Modotti *(1999) earned a Best Book of 1999 designation by* Library Journal. *She also published the exhibition catalog* Tina Modotti and the Mexican Renaissance *(2000). With a diverse background in art, she has worked as a columnist for* Le Nouveau Photo-Cinema *in Paris, France; director of special programs at the Euphrat Museum of Art at De Anza College in California; and lecturer at the School of Art and Design of San Jose University.*

Albers's biography is significant in that it is the first full-scale biography of Mitchell. It exhaustively covers her personality and personal relationships, revealing many of her more unflattering and negative characteristics, such as her insensitivity, crudeness, and cruelty toward others. It also reveals intimate glimpses of Mitchell's relationships and interactions with well-known artists of the New York school and the Paris art scene. Pleased reviewers note the author's diligent research and the extensive documentation of her sources, visible in more than fifty pages of chapter notes. They praise the book for its coverage of a complex subject, for exposing the artist's dark side, and for its balancing of Mitchell's personality with descriptions of her professional achievements. Giving it high marks, they note it as being of interest to general readers, students, scholars, and museum curators. Others, however, claim that the biography does not do justice to Mitchell, faulting Albers's overwritten descriptions, excessive details, and her sometimes questionable analyses of the artwork. Their disappointment centers on Albers's minute focus and the fact that she leaves out important aspects of what drove Mitchell to endure as a painter. Perhaps they are justified in their response; despite its scale, the biography does fail to give a comprehensive examination of Mitchell's artistic life, instead focusing on her troubled relationships and personality.

While Albers's biography may be of interest to readers who want to understand her complex personality, it may be less appealing to general readers who want an in-depth and balanced portrayal of her life and work. Simply put, the biography contains too much minutiae. Rather than illuminate, the dense and often trivial details tend to detract from the story, making it difficult to discover who Mitchell really is. In some cases, the details stray so far from the subject that it appears as if the author is taking side trips into different topics. These diversions draw attention away from the subject at hand—Mitchell—and focus too much instead on the author and her research. Readers are left with an acute sense of Albers's desire for all of her research data to find its way into the book somewhere, as if she were determined to include every fact she uncovered regardless of whether it has any significant bearing on the topic. For example, the mention of a famous person or location will include a brief portrait or insertion of facts related to that topic. At times, this broad inclusion of background information takes on the tone of an encyclopedia entry. At other times, it results in overly verbose passages, such as when Albers describes Mitchell's new studio in Montparnasse: "Situated in a charming old studio building at 23, rue Campagne-Première, a short street where artist Man Ray, photographer Eugène Atget, writers Louis Aragon and Elsa Triolet, and Rilke himself had once lived and where Godard filmed the ending of *Breathless,* Joan's new place was high ceilinged, light flooded, and appealingly empty." There is no mention of Mitchell interacting with any of these famous residents, nor any acknowledgment that Mitchell either knew or cared that they had once lived on the street.

Just as the mention of a person or location results in a tangential cornucopia of facts, so too do Albers's descriptions of Mitchell's paintings. For example, after describing one painting as "so radiantly and deciduously green," the author quotes from Rainer Maria Rilke's sonnet "Before Summer Rain," beginning with the line "Suddenly, from all the green around you," and analyzes Mitchell's painting as a reflection of her feelings about death, which she believes match those described in Rilke's sonnet. Similarly, some descriptions of events read like embellishments of the facts, or possibly interpretations based on imagination rather than evidence. For example, in describing how, at nine years old, Marion Strobel (Mitchell's mother) discovered her own mother's body after she committed suicide, Albers writes, "Marion would have seen a red fog filter through the bathwater, her mother's hair sway like wild black seaweed, her eyes stare from that white-mask face." Yet Albers provides no supporting information or source in her chapter notes to support that this is what Strobel saw. Nor does she provide any information to verify that Marion's mother committed suicide, though she includes a quote from the *Chicago Daily Tribune* article that claimed she died from pleurisy. In addition, some passages take on a tone one would expect to find in a Harlequin romance novel; Albers describes Mitchell's mother's poetry by saying that "at its finest, her pure and expertly molten language pours into lines as perfect as ingots of Bessemer steel."

Albers draws on primary sources for much of her research, including Mitchell's personal letters and interviews with her former husband, friends, and close associates. While these interviews provide intimate details from those who knew Mitchell well, the views they offer are one-sided and subjective. Too often the biography takes on the tone of a late-night gossip circle in which people recall the most outlandish tales and try to top each other's reminiscences. Much of the emphasis in these stories is on

Mitchell's sex life rather than her art, and while this may please readers who favor scintillating tell-alls, it is just as likely to repel those in search of an objective and balanced overview of Mitchell's life.

While Albers's depiction of Mitchell is at times unflattering, she fawns over her paintings. Yet her descriptions often fail to include a simple communication of what the painting looks like, and her analyses of them may also be suspect. Albers distinguishes her biography by focusing on unique aspects of Mitchell's cognitive abilities—her eidetic, or photographic, memory and her synesthesia, a mixing of senses that caused Mitchell to see music, people, and letters in color—and analyzing her paintings in terms of these abilities, drawing conclusions about how she may have perceived the world and her art. However, although Albers presents quite a bit of information about these topics, they often fail to explain the paintings or the artist. Even scientists are unsure about the role and significance of eidetic memory and synesthesia, so Albers's interpretations do not appear to be supported by scientific consensus.

Despite the great amount of detail, or perhaps because of it, the biography fails to convey what made Mitchell tick and why she is significant. Over the course of its narrative, readers get a sense of what people thought of Mitchell as a person, but perhaps less of a sense of who she was as an artist. Albers provides a vivid accounting of Mitchell's flaws, demons, and debauchery, but in the end, the artist seems to have won out over Mitchell's issues; unlike other abstract expressionist painters of her generation, Mitchell did not self-destruct at a young age but rather painted until her death in 1992.

Barbara C. Lightner

Review Sources

Artnet Magazine, June 21, 2011 (Web).
Kirkus Reviews 79, no. 6 (March 15, 2011): 459.
Library Journal 136, no. 14 (September 1, 2011): 106.
New Republic, August 11, 2011 (Web).
Publishers Weekly 258, no. 12 (March 21, 2011): 63–66.

Joe Dimaggio
The Long Vigil

Author: Jerome Charyn (b. 1937)
Publisher: Yale University Press (New Haven, CT). 192 pp. $24.00
Type of work: History
Time: 1936–1999
Locale: New York City

Jerome Charyn examines Joe DiMaggio, separating "the greatest living ballplayer" from the man haunted by the demons of loneliness and passion.

Principal personages:

JOE DIMAGGIO (1914–1999), a New York Yankee ballplayer who became a baseball icon

MARILYN MONROE (1926–1962), a Hollywood star and sex symbol who was married to DiMaggio

MICKEY MANTLE (1931–1995), a Yankee ballplayer who replaced DiMaggio in the lineup following his retirement in 1951

CASEY STENGEL (1890–1975), the Yankee manager during DiMaggio's last years with the club

DOROTHY ARNOLD DIMAGGIO (1917–1997), the first wife of Joe DiMaggio

BERNARD "TOOTS" SHOR (1903–1977), the owner of a New York City restaurant that was a popular gathering place for celebrities

During the 1920s, New York City was a sports Mecca for baseball fans, due in no small part to the arrival of Babe Ruth. Ruth revolutionized baseball like no single individual before or since. A sportswriter's delight, he gathered crowds wherever he went, whether entering a nightclub or driving down city streets in his coonskin coat. By 1936, however, age and weight had caught up with Ruth, and after one last season in Boston he had retired. It was then that Joe DiMaggio appeared on the New York scene, and the contrast between the two personalities could not have been greater. Where Ruth was outgoing and colorful, DiMaggio was quiet and withdrawn. Ruth loved the limelight, but outside the ballpark DiMaggio spent his time with only a few acquaintances, often sitting at his designated table at Toots Shor's restaurant on Fifty-First Street in Manhattan. Nevertheless, DiMaggio's impact on Yankee baseball cannot be overestimated. He played the cavernous centerfield at Yankee Stadium in a manner matched by few. Until leg injuries impaired him, DiMaggio's hitting matched that of any contemporary. While Charyn's history acknowledges his role as a quiet leader on the field, this is not the book's primary emphasis. With *Joe DiMaggio: The Long Vigil*,

Jerome Charyn is the author of more than fifty novels and other publications. He is the recipient of numerous awards, including two fellowships from the National Endowment for the Arts and a Guggenheim Fellowship. He has taught at several universities, including Stanford, Princeton, and the American University of Paris.

Charyn has attempted to delve into the personality of the man himself, particularly as regards his love affair with Marilyn Monroe.

As Charyn points out, by 1941, his fifth season with the Yankees, DiMaggio was arguably one of the most famous men in America. In 1939, he married showgirl Dorothy Olsen, and when she gave birth to their son, Joe Jr., the baby was celebrated throughout the media. But 1941 was also a turning point in DiMaggio's life. It was clear that America would become involved in World War II, and it was also the year of "the streak," in which DiMaggio hit safely in fifty-six consecutive games, a feat followed by fans everywhere. A song was even written about it. But DiMaggio's personal life was not as serene as the media portrayed. His marriage was failing, due in no small part to mood swings during which he ignored his wife and son. Dorothy went off to Reno, Nevada, contemplating divorce.

As America entered the war, DiMaggio showed no immediate interest in joining the service, but in 1943 he enlisted in the Army Air Corps. His personal reasons were unclear. In *Joe DiMaggio: The Hero's Life* (2000), author Richard Creamer suggests DiMaggio was shamed into enlisting, a possibility that Charyn does not address. Regardless of his motives, DiMaggio had a comparatively easy duty, playing cards with officers and baseball on service teams. During his service, he missed three years with the Yankees and was often, according to Charyn, sullen and morose, more concerned about the money he lost and the entourage he had left behind than doing his duty. It was also during this time that Dorothy divorced him.

Charyn contrasts DiMaggio with his only contemporary rival, Ted Williams, an outfielder with the Boston Red Sox who arrived at the age of twenty and was considered DiMaggio's equal, having batted .406 in 1941. Williams had a dark side as well, but unlike DiMaggio, he lashed out at fans and the Boston media alike. At first reluctant to enter into the draft, Williams's attitude toward the military was very different from DiMaggio's, and he would eventually enlist as a Marine Corps pilot. With the end of the war, Williams missed actual combat, but he enjoyed the camaraderie of the military and broke out of the shell he created around himself.

DiMaggio returned from the service in 1946, and for a time his baseball prowess matched that of his prewar years. However, injuries soon slowed him down and affected his hitting. By the late 1940s, DiMaggio's place in baseball seemed to be sustained by pride alone. In 1949, Casey Stengel was hired as the manager of the Yankees, and though he respected DiMaggio's ability and desire, Stengel felt the deterioration of DiMaggio's play required frequent rests and platooning with other players. Then, in 1951, a new "golden boy" appeared in New York: Mickey Mantle, whom Stengel groomed to replace DiMaggio in the Yankee outfield. DiMaggio never accepted his heir apparent, and Mantle himself blamed DiMaggio's grudge for an incident during the 1951 World Series, when the two players converged on a ball in the outfield and Mantle suffered a severe knee injury that would plague him his entire career.

Well aware that his baseball career was over, DiMaggio retired after the 1951 World Series. Still a young man, he had to decide how to spend the rest of his life and evade the indifference that many former baseball stars faced after retirement. Charyn spends a significant portion of the book delving into the subsequent love/hate relationship that transpired between DiMaggio and Marilyn Monroe. The two allegedly met on a blind date during the spring of 1952. Monroe was a rising star for Twentieth-Century Fox, albeit a sex symbol, a woman literally sleeping her way to the top. DiMaggio of course had his own frequent "dalliances," some while he was still married to Dorothy. But as Charyn notes, DiMaggio's idea of the ideal woman was either a housewife or whore, and he was determined to turn Monroe into a housewife. There is no question that DiMaggio loved Monroe, but the real tragedy of the marriage was that her determination was to become one of Hollywood's biggest stars, an ambition that DiMaggio never understood. A woman whose will exceeded his, Monroe found him too possessive, even boring. He refused to go places with her, fearful that other men would look at her. He preferred to stay home watching movies, especially Westerns, and talked of little beyond baseball.

Two events in particular illustrate DiMaggio's obsession with Monroe and his need to hold a controlling influence over her life. In January 1954, when the couple married, DiMaggio had already planned on a visit to the American troops in Korea, a trip that had been highly successful several years earlier. The decision was made to turn this repeat trip into a honeymoon. What DiMaggio had not expected was the reception Marilyn received from the troops, or her subsequent "vamping about." As Monroe expressed it, "I'll never forget my honeymoon—with the 45th Division." Charyn's second example takes place during the filming of *The Seven-Year Itch* (1955). After the filming of the famous scene in which Monroe stands on a breezy subway grate, a furious DiMaggio returned with his wife to the hotel and proceeded to beat her. She filed for divorce shortly afterwards, after a mere 274 days of marriage.

Monroe certainly had her issues. Charyn briefly describes her problematic childhood and her desire to be taken seriously as an actress. After divorcing DiMaggio, she subsequently married, lost interest in, and divorced the writer Arthur Miller. Monroe descended into a life of pills and alcohol, admitting herself into a psychiatric hospital in 1961. DiMaggio came to her rescue, flying with her to Florida, but again his jealousy would overcome him. His attempts to control her life coincided with numerous affairs and her returning to substance abuse. In August 1962, whether intentionally or by accident, Monroe died of a sedative overdose. DiMaggio never recovered, arranging for fresh roses to be sent to her crypt three times weekly for the next twenty years.

Following Monroe's death in 1962, DiMaggio lived for another thirty-seven years. He was called "the greatest living ballplayer," his reputation exceeding both Willie Mays and Ted Williams, but with time he evolved into a parody of his former self. He had cut himself off from two of his strongest acquaintances (it would be hard to call anyone his friend), Toots Shor and Frank Sinatra, over comments they had made about Monroe. Accumulating a bevy of awards and honorary degrees, DiMaggio was a spokesman for both Mr. Coffee and the Bowery Savings Bank, and a regular at sports shows, where he sold his autograph. Money was never a problem. Morris Engelberg served as his lawyer, sounding board, financial advisor, and "go'fer" starting in the 1980s. DiMaggio's signature on a bat could bring in as much as two thousand dollars, and Engelberg made sure there was no shortage of memorabilia shows. Indeed, Engelberg became almost a surrogate son to DiMaggio, who had long been estranged from Joe Jr. His son had dropped out of Yale, enlisted in the Marines, married, divorced, and had altogether become as aimless in life as his father. When DiMaggio finally caught up with his son, he was told to go away. Instead, it was Engelberg and the coterie of DiMaggio sycophants who remained with him during the last months of his life.

Charyn's book is not that of a typical biography. He provides a psychological study of DiMaggio's life story not so much to explain it as to describe how loneliness and even insecurity played significant roles in his life. There is little attention given to his youth, other than his dropping out of high school after one year and going to work on the docks. Charyn leaves the reader wiser about the man, but perhaps sadder as well. The DiMaggio remembered by fans of the 1940s and 1950s was a baseball icon. Today's audience knows there was more to DiMaggio than that, and Charyn has provided a more realistic peek at the man true complexity.

Richard Adler

Review Sources

Booklist 107, no. 14 (March 15, 2011): 14.
Kirkus Reviews 79, no. 3 (February 1, 2011): 177.
The New York Times Book Review, June 5, 2011, p. 33.

Just One Catch
A Biography of Joseph Heller

Author: Tracy Daugherty (b. 1955)
Publisher: St. Martin's (New York). 560 pp.
$35.00
Type of work: Literary biography
Time: 1923–1999
Locale: New York City and its environs

Just One Catch is the first comprehensive biography of writer Joseph Heller, the author of Catch-22, *one of the most important American novels of the twentieth century.*

Principal personages:

JOSEPH HELLER (1923-1999), a novelist, screenwriter, memoirist, and playwright
SHIRLEY HELD HELLER, his wife of thirty-seven years
GEORGE MANDEL (b. 1920), an artist, writer, and childhood friend of Heller's
IRVING "SPEED" VOGEL (1918-2008), a dedicated friend who collaborated with Heller on one of his two memoirs
FREDERICK KARL (1927-2004), a literary scholar and close colleague of Heller's at Pennsylvania State University
CANDIDA DONADIO, Heller's literary agent
ROBERT GOTTLIEB (b. 1931), the Simon & Schuster editor who published *Catch-22*
VALERIE HUMPHRIES, Heller's nurse and second wife

Joseph Heller wrote one of the landmark novels of the twentieth century. *Catch-22* (1961) not only became an international bestseller but also revolutionized the publishing industry that produced it; the paperback edition of the novel was successful beyond all expectations, and its millions of copies sold brought the novel into the mainstream. *Catch-22* helped to usher in the decade of the 1960s that so changed America, in the process becoming one of the most beloved works of the generation that transformed the country's culture. Tracy Daugherty's *Just One Catch: A Biography of Joseph Heller* is the first complete account of Heller's life and work, and it will undoubtedly become the standard by which readers will judge the writer for some time.

Joseph Heller was born on May 1, 1923, in Brooklyn, and he spent most of his seventy-six years living in and around New York City. His childhood was not a happy one, as his father died when he was five years old and his mother was not particularly warm or affectionate, and Joseph spent much of his youth escaping from home with a gang of friends who made Coney Island their playground. After high school, he held a series of dead-end jobs—as a Western Union messenger in Manhattan, he would absorb pictures of the business world that he would pour into his second novel, *Something Happened* (1974)—until he enlisted in the US Army Air Corps on October 18, 1943, to fight in World War II. Trained as a bombardier and assigned to an airfield on Corsica, Heller flew in B-25s on sixty combat missions in Europe. It was this intense war experience that would become the defining moment of Heller's career and provide him with the foundation of *Catch-22*.

After being released from the Army in 1945, Heller married Shirley Held, a woman he had met at the famous Grossinger's resort hotel in the Catskills. They soon moved to California so that Heller could study at the University of Southern California under the GI Bill. The couple found Los Angeles strange and missed New York, however, so they returned to settle into an apartment on the Upper West Side of Manhattan and Heller completed his college degree at New York University. He continued on to pursue a graduate degree in English from Columbia University before attending Oxford University in England for a year on a Fulbright scholarship. The couple returned to the United States when Heller got a job teaching composition at Pennsylvania State University, then later returned to Manhattan, where he began a series of jobs with a number of magazines, including *Time*, *Look*, and *McCall's*.

Heller had always wanted to be a writer, and he published his first short story soon after the war. By 1948, seven of his stories had been published in such prominent publications as *Esquire* and *Atlantic Monthly*. Heller felt that his fiction often seemed derivative, however, and he really wanted to write a novel. Part of his dilemma was that three iconic novels of World War II had appeared soon after it had ended: Norman Mailer's *The Naked and the Dead* and Irwin Shaw's *The Young Lions* were both published in 1948, and James Jones's *From Here to Eternity* appeared in 1951. It would be another decade before Heller would find his own literary voice and complete *Catch-22*. The first chapter of the novel (originally titled *Catch-18*) appeared in the prestigious *New World Writing* quarterly in 1955 alongside a selection from another work that would soon become a pivotal postwar novel, Jack Kerouac's *On the Road* (1957).

Catch-22 was released in book form in 1961 thanks to Heller's fortuitous acquisition of Candida Donadio as his literary agent and Robert Gottlieb as his editor. Donadio was skilled at finding new, original writers, and she was known for her tenacity in placing their work. Similarly, Robert Gottlieb, who saw the possibilities in Heller's darkly comic novel, was a brilliant young editor at Simon & Schuster who would later become editor-in-chief, then move to a similar position at Knopf before becoming the editor of the *New Yorker* magazine from 1987 to 1992. Fortunately for all three, Gottlieb's firm had recently lost its publishing directors to death and retirement, giving Gottlieb almost free rein to guide Heller's manuscript through production and into bookstores in October 1961.

Catch-22, a darkly humorous allegory about one flyer's struggle to survive the insanity of modern warfare, was unlike any of the realistic-naturalistic World War II novels that had preceded it. The title comes from a conversation between the novel's protagonist, Yossarian, and the base's doctor, Doc Daneeka. Doc Daneeka explains that a man can be grounded from combat by reason of insanity because it would be crazy to fly on his dangerous missions; to be grounded, all he has to do is ask. The catch is that, in asking, he is demonstrating his sanity, and therefore must keep flying missions. "Catch-22" has since become a common everyday term for any illogical situation or circular argument, usually caused by bureaucratic rules. Shortly after its publication and subsequent popularity, *Catch-22* had already started to change American perceptions of war and literature. Jumpy in structure, with scenes recurring in almost nightmarish sequence, the novel also drew on a rich tradition of Yiddish humor. Heller claimed in interviews that *Catch-22*'s black humor, the combination of the comic and the morbid that would become a defining cultural thread of the 1960s, had come from his Coney Island childhood. He also noted that many of the characters and incidents in the novel came directly from his own wartime experience, including the crucial dialogue between the pilot and bombardier and the simple central statement of the dying gunner Snowden ("I'm cold"). *Catch-22* depicts Yossarian as caught up in the madness of war and trapped in the institutional cage of the army—and, ultimately, in modern reality.

Tracy Daugherty is a novelist, essayist, and short-story writer whose work has appeared in such publications as the New Yorker, Vanity Fair, *and the* Georgia Review. *He works as a distinguished professor of English and creative writing at Oregon State University.*

In spite of a vigorous publicity campaign that Gottlieb and Simon & Schuster mounted for the novel, it did not take off immediately in the United States. Its paperback sales, however, were another story. Fueled by word of mouth among young readers—Ken Kesey's novel *One Flew Over the Cuckoo's Nest* (1962), published shortly after *Catch-22*, would have a similar publishing trajectory—the paperback flew off the shelves, and sales reached one million copies in just six weeks. After the success of the novel, Heller worked on screenplays for Hollywood for a few years. In 1968, he staged the antiwar play *We Bombed in New Haven*, and he had teaching stints at Yale University and City College of New York. His second novel, *Something Happened*, was published in 1974 and remained on best-seller lists for twenty-nine weeks. This satire did for American business and capitalism after the Vietnam War what *Catch-22* had done for American institutions and values after World War II. Heller's work following *Something Happened*, however, was never as popular or as critically acclaimed as his earlier work. He wrote five more novels, including *Good as Gold* (1979) and *God Knows* (1984), and a collection of short stories, which earned him huge sums of money but did nothing for his literary reputation. Heller also was responsible for two memoirs—*No Laughing Matter* (1986), which he coauthored with his friend Speed Vogel, and *Now and Then: From Coney Island to Here* (1998)—but both were dismissed by readers as thin and guarded.

His personal life did not work out any better. In December 1981, he was struck by Guillain-Barre syndrome, a rare autoimmune disease that left him paralyzed for almost a year and from which he would struggle to recover delete for the rest of his life. A serious philanderer during his marriage, he divorced his wife of thirty-seven years in a rancorous case in 1984. Heller moved to Long Island and eventually married his live-in nurse, Valerie Humphries, a second marriage that was hardly happier than his first. A difficult man to family and friends, often sarcastic and critical, and a father with few parenting skills who was estranged from his children after his divorce, Heller's personal life paralleled the decline of his writing career. He died from a heart attack on December 12, 1999.

Daugherty's descriptions of Heller's life and work, his analyses of Heller's novels, and his examination of the successes and failures of Heller's career are often insightful. This is more than a literary biography, however, for Daugherty sets out to write a sociological and psychological study as well. He provides background on most of the periods Heller lived through; for example, he describes the cultural tenor of the 1950s and 1960s, when the distinctions between high and low cultures began to break down, allowing the sometimes-slapstick comedy of a novel like *Catch-22* to appear. Daugherty is also good at elucidating the themes that bind Heller's novels together, such as the struggle between fathers and sons, and the figures with whom Heller competed in the New York literary scene who also utilized their Jewish roots and humor in their writing, including authors Saul Bellow and Philip Roth. These analyses are often helpful, but at times the digressions are distracting. When Heller vacations at Grossinger's early in the book for a respite from war and Coney Island, Daugherty stalls the narrative in order to provide a history of the famous resort. Likewise, when the Hellers move into their first Manhattan apartment in the Apthorp Building, the action halts while Daugherty takes readers back in time to the history of the Upper West Side at the end of the nineteenth century.

Daugherty's psychological analyses of Heller's life also seem overblown at times. Heller discovered late in childhood that his older brother and sister were actually his half siblings, born to a woman who had died before Heller's father married his mother, and Daugherty turns this revelation into a major traumatic issue. Heller's life was dramatic enough without reaching to find additional hardships. Daugherty works primarily as a novelist, and his need to set scenes, dramatize characters, and speed up action can be seen in several places throughout the biography, often at the expense of his subject. In the end, however, Heller's own illuminating story shines through. Regardless of its flaws, Daugherty has produced a rich and definitive biography of the legendary American writer. Abounding in context and history, *Just One Catch* is a thorough portrait of a man and the times in which he lived.

David Peck

Review Sources

Booklist 107, no. 19/20 (June 15, 2011): 24.
Kirkus Reviews 79, no. 11 (June 1, 2011): 922–23.
Library Journal 136, no 11 (June 15, 2011): 88–90.
Publishers Weekly 228, no. 20 (May 16, 2011): 65.
The Washington Post, August 18, 2011, p. B6.